theFulton

Special Education

Digest

2nd edition

the Fulton
Special Education
Digest

2nd edition

Selected Resources for Teachers, Parents and Carers

Edited by Ann Worthington
Foreword by Philippa Russell

Routledge
Taylor & Francis Group

LONDON AND NEW YORK

First published 1999 by David Fulton Publishers
Second edition published in 2003

Published 2016 by Routledge
2 Park Square, Milton Park, Abingdon, Oxfordshire OX14 4RN
711 Third Avenue, New York, NY 10017

First issued in hardback 2016

Routledge is an imprint of the Taylor and Francis Group, an informa business

The right of Ann Worthington to be identified as the editor of this work has been
asserted by her in accordance with the Copyright, Designs and Patents Act 1988.

ISBN 13: 978-1-138-15886-3 (hbk)
ISBN 13: 978-1-85346-929-9 (pbk)

Typeset by FiSH Books, London

Contents

Acknowledgements

The editor and publishers would like to thank the following people for their valuable contributions to this book:

Mike Blamires for his extensive material on websites, Alison Closs for providing a much needed Scottish perspective on special needs, Shirley Young of SNIP – Special Needs Information Point – for updating the information for the second edition, Liz Cowne for her informative sections *Introducing Special Educational Needs* and *Links with Other Professionals*, Michael Farrell for his helpful advice on the glossary and Barbara Sakarya and staff at the Turner Library for their useful section on recommended reading, Gillian Goodchild and her colleagues at the Turner Library for updating the information for the second edition.

Thanks also to Maggie Balshaw, Sean Barr, Maggie Bowen, Richard Byers, Stephanie Lorenz, Mary McLean, Leanne Mabberley, Judith Coupe O'Kane, Christina Tilstone and John Worthington for their advice and support in the early stages of the project.

Update Service

The information printed in this book was correct at time of press. Notification of any subsequent changes to postal addresses, telephone/fax numbers or website addresses will be welcome. Please send your amendments to:

Digest Changes
David Fulton Publishers Ltd
The Chiswick Centre
414 Chiswick High Road
London W4 5TF
Tel: 020 8996 3610
Fax: 020 8996 3622

or email: **mail@fultonpublishers.co.uk**

We will be posting the amendments we receive onto our website.
To view this updated information, log onto:

www.fultonpublishers.co.uk

Our website also has details of all our publications, company news, forthcoming titles and links to other websites of interest to parents, teachers and carers.

Foreword

The Government's Programme of Action on Special Educational Needs epitomised the spirit of change and development in meeting special educational needs (SEN) which characterised the last decade of the twentieth century. As the Secretary of State commented in introducing the Programme of Action:

> '...we have set out a vision of excellence for all and a strategy designed to raise the standards of achievement of all children with special needs.'

However, notwithstanding major developments in provision for pupils with SEN, there was continuing concern about disabled pupils' and students' access to education and the exclusion of disability from the Disability Discrimination Act (DDA) 1995. In 1999 the Disability Rights Task Force reported to Government that education should be brought within the DDA and thereby within the Government's longer-term vision of comprehensive and enforceable rights for disabled people. The Disability Rights Commission became operational in 2000 and one of its first major tasks has been the production of the Codes of Practice for the schools and post-16 stages of education under the SEN and Disability Act 2001 (SENDA). SENDA will challenge education providers and LEAs, but it will also offer new opportunities for strategic planning to progressively improve access and inclusion across all education sectors. It will build on the best of current practice but also, hopefully, sensure that disabled pupils (the vast majority of whom will have SEN) do indeed, in the words of the Prime Minister launching 'Valuing People', the new national learning disability strategy: 'gain maximum life chances in order to engage as active citizens in their community'.

In order to achieve its vision, the Government has already highlighted certain key themes, in particular:

- Setting high expectations for all children with SEN or disabilities.

- Better support for parents of children with SEN or disabilities (recognising that children and young people themselves will increasingly become active partners in their own assessments and any subsequent special educational provision).

- Active promotion of inclusion within mainstream settings where possible, but acknowledging that such inclusion will also necessitate developing the role of special schools and specialist services to meet complex needs, often within community settings.

- Shifting the focus in meeting special educational needs from procedures to practical advice and support and, where possible, through earlier identification and intervention.

- Boosting opportunities for the initial and ongoing professional development and competence of teachers and others working in education services.

- Recognising the importance of strategic planning at school and LEA level, in partnership with health and social services, to develop 'whole-school' approaches to access and inclusion and the more effective management of resources.

- Promoting partnership and positive networking in SEN and disability issues at local, regional and national levels.

These are ambitious targets, but ones which the SEN field will be eager to work towards. However, 'visions of excellence', however aspirational, cannot be achieved unless all the key players understand their roles and have access to the expert advice and information which they need to implement the new strategy.

Information, as Winston Churchill once famously said, is strategy and power. *The Fulton Special Education Digest* fills an important information gap in the current literature available on special educational needs. It offers an invaluable, comprehensive and accessible 'jargon free' information resource for parents and carers, schools, LEAs, professionals and voluntary bodies.

The Digest brings together a wide range of essential information – including a concise over-view of current legislation, policy and practice around special educational needs, together with information on over 1000 selected organisations and services which can offer advice and support. The extensive glossary covers both special educational needs and relevant medical conditions and terminology. The addresses and contact telephone number of all LEAs are included, together with the names and addresses of over 1800 special schools in the UK.

Special educational needs can seldom be fully addressed by a single service. The past decade has seen an increasing number of children with very complex disabilities, medical conditions and special educational needs coming into the school system. Improvements in neonatal and medical care will contribute to this trend. Importantly, there are new and positive expectations of children with complex needs and the recognition that their care and education will be a corporate responsibility between mainstream and special schools; child health and social services and of course with parents and carers. The Digest also offers information on the roles and location of a range of relevant professionals in health and social services, and sets out their specific contributions in identifying and meeting special educational needs.

Information resources are changing dramatically, with the increasing use of the Internet and new information technology. But many parents (and professionals) are bewildered by multiple websites. The Digest is the first major information resource to include a specific section on using the Internet; finding relevant websites and making connections with useful networks such as the SENCO Forum.

The Fulton Special Education Digest is particularly timely because it recognises the information needs of an increasingly diverse field of SEN. But it is also timely because it is readable and accessible to parents and professionals; schools and LEAs; teachers and learning support assistants and to the growing range of health and social services professionals; voluntary sector and advice services which are key partners in the Government's programme of action on SEN. Mutual understanding will be essential if that programme is to achieve its key objective of ensuring that all children with special educational needs or disabilities receive a service which offers 'excellence for all'.

Philippa Russell
Director, Council for Disabled Children
November 2002

Section 1

Introducing Special Educational Needs

Introducing Special Educational Needs

Children with special educational needs will always be a focus of attention for parents, teachers and educationalists. Because their needs are different from those of most children, the topic can be an emotive one, never more so if you are a parent who has just discovered that your child is described as having special educational needs. What does this mean? What is involved? Where do you get help? Who do you need to talk to? This introduction answers these questions, and discusses some of the processes that are used everyday in our schools to help such children. The Code of Practice (2001), which is the framework on which all special needs procedures are based, will be explored in detail as will the roles and responsibilities of those involved at the different stages of assessment.

But what do we mean by 'special needs' anyway?

Defining Special Educational Needs

What are Special Educational Needs? The term was introduced in the 1981 Education Act, when it replaced the previous list of disabilities used since the 1944 Education Act. The 1981 Act said:

> A child has a special education need if she or he has a learning difficulty which calls for special educational needs provision to be made. A child has a learning difficulty if he or she has a significantly greater difficulty in learning than the majority of children of the same age, or has a disability which prevents or hinders the child from making use of educational facilities of the kind provided for children of the same age in schools within the area of the Local Education Authority (LEA).

This definition is still in use in more recent Education Acts and government circulars.

The Code of Practice (2001)

The 'Code of Practice' is a Department for Education and Skills (DfES) document which explains how special educational needs should be identified and assessed by schools and LEAs. The Code is a document that schools and LEAs should 'have regard to'. Most of the content is advisory, although some parts are regulations and are therefore legally enforceable. It is, in effect, the framework on which all special needs work is based.

The principles of the Code of Practice are that:

- The needs of all pupils with SEN should be addressed. The Code recognises that there is a continuum of needs and provision which will be made in a wide variety of forms.
- Children with SEN should be offered full access to a broad and balanced and relevant education including an appropriate curriculum for the foundation stage and the National Curriculum.

- The school is responsible for identifying and assessing the majority of pupils and making subsequent SEN provision.
- Parents have a vital role to play in supporting their child's education and the views of the child should be sought and taken into account.

What is a Statement?

A statement is a record of the child's needs, which sets out the targets to aim at in the immediate future. It also sets out the extra provision which the LEA is suggesting as appropriate for the child. This could be extra or specialist teaching, specific programmes to meet individual therapeutic needs or specific teaching and learning strategies which teachers could employ with the child.

During the assessment, advice is gathered from various sources and copies of this are attached to the statement. This advice will be sought from the parents, the school, the educational psychologist and the health service and maybe from other professionals, such as the community paediatrician. The statement is reviewed each year by the school which will suggest any significant changes which need to be made to the LEA. Parents are always invited to attend the annual review meeting and their views are noted.

Only children with very significant needs will require a statement. Most children's needs will be met within the existing resources of their schools.

Roles and Responsibilities

The Code of Practice sets out the various responsibilities for SEN in mainstream schools. The overall responsibilities for these pupils lie with the governors and the head teacher, but every teacher has a responsibility for those pupils with SEN in their classes, and parents, pupils and non-teaching staff all have roles to play. The special educational needs coordinator (SENCO) coordinates the day-to-day policy and practice for SEN at school level.

It is important to remember that everyone has a role to play in a 'whole-school approach' to meeting SEN. All those involved must take notice of the Code of Practice when dealing with pupils with SEN, and must be fully aware of their school's policy on SEN.

A SENCO in a primary school may be a class teacher who takes on this additional responsibility, or it could be the deputy head or the head teacher, or teachers with other additional responsibilities. In secondary schools the SENCO role is more often a full time post, or it may be shared between a team of teachers.

The Code of Practice (2001) defines the role of the SENCO as having responsibility for:

- overseeing the day-to-day operation of the school's SEN policy
- liaising with and advising fellow teachers
- coordinating provision for children with special educational needs

- managing learning support assistants or SEN teams of teachers (secondary schools)
- overseeing the records on all pupils with special educational needs
- liaising with parents of children with special educational needs
- contributing to the in-service training of staff
- liaising with external agencies including the educational psychology service and other support agencies, medical and social services and voluntary bodies.

(Code of Practice (2001) Par 5.32)

The Revised code also says that early years settings should identify a member of staff to be the SENCO. Their role is to:

- ensure liaison with parents and other professionals in respect of children with special educational needs
- advise and support other practitioners in the setting
- ensure that appropriate individual education plans are in place
- ensure that relevant background information about individual children (with SEN) is collected, recorded and updated.

(Code of Practice (2001) Par 4.15)

The Teacher Training Agency (TTA) (1997) has published a set of Standard Competencies for SENCOs. This explains the responsibilities for SEN coordination and sets out the knowledge and skills required to do the job. It is a guide for schools in writing SENCO job descriptions and gives a focus to those seeking SENCO training.

Head Teacher and Governor Responsibility

The statutory duty for SEN remains with the governing body, and is usually vested in the head teacher who is the 'responsible person'. However, there should also be a designated SEN governor to share this responsibility. Schools should also give the name of the person responsible for SEN in their school's SEN policy.

Whole-School Approach

All schools must have a whole-school policy for SEN, and they report on this annually to parents. This report should include a description of 'how resources are allocated to and amongst the pupils with SEN'. Effective schools will manage special educational needs by being clear about the priorities when allocating roles and responsibilities. Effective school policies also depend on good communications between staff members holding these responsibilities. The school moves forward in its development by integrating special needs policies into the school development as a whole, and often what is good practice for SEN is good practice for all.

Local Education Authorities (LEA) Responsibilities

Under the Education Act (1996) LEAs must keep all their arrangements for SEN provision under review, and inform governing bodies of the schools in their area of the review arrangements. The LEA can ask for help from any District Health Authority (DHA) and Social Service Department in carrying out its duties towards children with SEN, and, provided those requests are reasonable, the DHAs and Social Services Departments must comply. LEAs are responsible for all children in their area who are educated at maintained schools, or at independent schools at the expense of the authority, and for those children at non-maintained or independent schools whose needs have been brought to their attention.

LEAs have duties to provide for children aged under 2 with SEN only with the parents' consent. If the parents ask to have their child's needs investigated and assessed, the LEA must do so, although this may not result in a formal statement being made. The District Health Authority must notify parents and the LEA, if in their opinion a child under 5 is likely to have SEN. The Children Act (1989) requires the Authority to identify those children who are in need in their area, but this definition is wider than that of the Education Act and covers children at risk. Health and Social Services Departments should make it clear to schools how contact should be made with their services.

The National Curriculum

All pupils with SEN, whether they have been statemented or not, are entitled to the full National Curriculum, unless an exception is spelled out in the child's SEN statement. National Curriculum assessments and tests, along with other teacher observations, help identify pupils with SEN. The teacher should be alerted by significant discrepancies between a child's attainment in assessments and tests in the core subjects of the National Curriculum, and either the attainment level of the majority of pupils at that age, *or* the performance expected of the child by teachers and parents.

They should also be alerted to specific learning difficulties when there is a significant difference in attainments between one core subject and another.

The National Curriculum was revised in 2000 to allow for more flexibility in teaching, freeing up some time to be spent on the individual needs of pupils who could now work with support or with the help of technological aids, or could work outside the National Curriculum Key Stage of their age group, when necessary. This revision also included an 'Inclusion Statement' which sets out ways schools can adapt curriculum delivery to give opportunities to their diverse populations.

The National Literacy and Numeracy Strategy

In 1998, the government announced the National Literacy and Numeracy Strategies for Primary Schools, in which every school must teach literacy and numeracy through prescribed schemes of work for an hour each day. The National Curriculum regulations were varied to make room for this.

The National Literacy hour began in Autumn 1998; the Numeracy hour, in September 1999. DfEE advice said that pupils with SEN will be expected to take a full part in both the Literacy and Numeracy hours, and some of the time is spent in whole-class teaching, and the rest is spent in group work where differences of pace can be accommodated. Many pupils with difficulties may need extra support to enable them to take part fully. Some schools run parallel sessions for children with different levels of achievement. These are permitted if the school can resource them, but what takes place in the parallel session should be linked to what the rest of the class is doing. For those children with an Individual Education Plan (IEP, explained in detail on p. 8) the plan should make it clear how adult support is to be used during the three parts of the literacy hour and in the numeracy hour.

Identification of those with SEN

The first step in the management of SEN is to decide which children have sufficient need to be placed on the school's SEN register. All children have individual needs, but these are not necessarily related to those learning difficulties or disabilities which are defined by the Code of Practice. To justify a description of SEN a child should have learning difficulties which are causing concern over a period of time, probably to both parents and teachers. The child will not be responding as expected to the curriculum on offer, or cannot cope with the normal classroom environment without additional help.

SENCOs have the responsibility of keeping good records of those with special needs. Once a pupil has been identified, information is gathered and assessment takes place; and this information contributes to a planned piece of teaching aimed at reducing the pupil's learning difficulties. SENCOs have a major role in advising and supporting staff in such planning. The planning of the intervention contributes to an Individual Education Plan (IEP).

Collating Information About the Child

Early Years and Key Stage 1

The assessment of children at the Foundation Stage and Key Stage 1 (3–7 year olds) are largely based on observation, although there are also Standard Assessment Tests (SATs) which form the basis of judgements made at the end of the Key Stage. Teachers at Key Stage 1 have been trained to carry out basic teacher assessments, which means that identifying and planning for the SEN of younger children has become more reliable. Government requirements mean that a 'baseline assessment' must be carried out within a few weeks of a child starting school. This establishes 'where the child is at' in terms of learning, and may act as a screening device to indicate which children have special needs. Children who are identified as having SEN will then need further, more detailed assessment.

It is important to look at the 'whole child' when making further assessments and to remember that young children develop at different rates. A slow start in one area may not indicate a special educational need. The child may just need more time and more experience to develop this area.

Key Stage 2 (7–11 years)

The most common concern of a class teacher at Key Stage 2 is a lack of progress in literacy, resulting in poor progress right across the rest of the curriculum. It is very important that teachers with expertise in helping children with 'problems with print', are consulted and used in planning the Literacy Hour. Careful teaching, which takes account of individual difficulties in acquiring fluency and confidence in reading and writing, will still be needed, and it should be the aim to place only those with exceptional and persistent difficulties with literacy. A few children will require more detailed assessment and teaching, possibly with advice from support services or other agencies.

It is also important not to miss children whose needs may be less obvious, such as quiet children who get overlooked in favour of noisy, attention-seeking ones. There are two ways commonly used to screen pupils in the junior years. One is to use a checklist about observed learning styles, attitudes and behaviours. The other is to use standardised tests of reading, spelling and maths. Teacher-based assessment should also play an important part in identifying effective intervention strategies.

Key Stage 3 (11–14 years)

In secondary schools, form tutors may be the best choice to collate information or alternatively, any subject teacher could inform the SENCO of their concerns. Identification of children with potential SEN cannot reasonably be left to the SENCO alone. Most needs should be met by good curriculum planning and delivery, and progress monitored through good record-keeping.

School Action

A number of pupils, however, fail to make progress, despite their teacher's best efforts. For these children, extra planning is needed in order to 'fine tune' the programme of intervention more precisely. This requires a much more specialised form of planning, which is known as an Individual Education Plan (IEP). This stage is called School Action to show that the responsibility lies with the school to assess and provide for pupils who have additional needs.

The IEP should include information about:

- the short-term targets set for, or by the child
- the teaching strategies to be used
- the provision to be put in place
- when the plan is to be reviewed
- success and/or exit criteria
- outcomes (to be recorded when IEP is reviewed).

The IEP should only record that which is additional to or different from the differentiated curriculum plan which is in place as part of provision for all children. The IEP should focus on 3–4 individual targets chosen from the key areas of communication, literacy, mathematics, behaviour and social skills that match the child's needs. The IEP should be discussed with the child and the parents.

(Code of Practice (2001) Par 5.5)

Information that has been collected by a teacher about their concerns will be used to create the IEP. Information about the pupil's strengths and interests should be noted. It is through these strengths that positive progress will be made. Writing and reviewing IEPs have caused some concerns to schools and to their SENCOs. An IEP is intended to collect information which gives guidance on how best to teach the pupil, and to develop a plan of action, with targets which can be understood and achieved by the pupil and his/her teachers and parents. It must be specific and achievable, but must also be practical to use in ordinary classrooms. Basic information from the IEP must be given to all teachers who teach the pupil. This is on a 'need to know' basis, so that the information is read and used.

Reviewing Individual Education Plans

The purpose of IEPs is to improve the effectiveness of monitoring of SEN pupils through better record-keeping and planning. To ensure this monitoring is regular and informative, every pupil with an IEP must have a regular review of their progress and a revision of their IEP to meet any new needs. This review process is the key to successful SEN management.

It may be much better if colleagues can work together in year groups to do the review; one taking the questioning role and one the answering role. There should be a planned timetable for IEP reviews in every school. Time is always in short supply in schools, so it needs to be specifically set aside for this process. Allocating time for IEP reviews is a role for senior management in the school. It is important that both pupil's/parents' views are noted.

The SENCO will be involved in setting up the review process, acting as consultant to colleagues and helping in decision making for those pupils moving on to School Action Plus.

Pupils with significant needs that affect their progress in one or more aspects of the curriculum and who will require a specialised and supported programme written into their IEP should be clearly identified and the resource implications considered. For these pupils extra advice will be sought.

School Action Plus

Pupils who reach this stage will already have been assessed in great detail. There will have been a working IEP in place for at least two to four terms, and the pupil's learning styles and difficulties will be well known. These pupils will be causing additional concern because they are still not making expected progress, so outside agencies, in particular support services, such as learning support teachers or educational psychologists, will be called in to add their views. These professionals add to the assessment information by carrying out a range of tests or observations, or by working closely with the pupil. Their advice is used to set new targets and strategies.

The purpose of the outsider's assessment is to advise on the IEP for the pupil. More detail about support services will be given in Chapter Two.

The number of pupils at School Action Plus is often limited to the support services available locally, which may vary between LEAs. An IEP could continue to be important for some pupils throughout much of their school life.

Requesting formal multi-professional assessment

For a few pupils whose needs justify further assessment, careful and detailed documentation will be needed about their problems and how these have been met to date. At a School Action Plus review, the views of parents must be sought and the purpose of asking for a formal assessment explained in detail. The possibility that the LEA may not agree to the assessment, or may not issue a statement, must be explained, along with the parents' right of appeal.

The support professionals and agencies who have been involved should contribute to this review, and they will be asked for evidence as part of the multi-professional assessment. Parents can make requests independently, but schools will be required to give evidence about all that has been done for the child to date and which services or agencies have been involved.

Most LEAs have set and published quite stringent criteria for these assessments. LEAs often have standard forms which schools must complete when asking for a formal assessment. These ask schools to show what has been already done at School Action Plus stage, and to explain the child's needs in detail. The Code of Practice clearly says that it is the head teacher's responsibility to decide to ask for a formal assessment, unless a parent has already done so. This decision, however, is usually taken in close cooperation with the SENCO, who will be asked to collect and collate all documentation, IEPs and supporting evidence and either they or the head will write to the LEA making a formal request for an assessment. If the LEA agrees to proceed with the assessment, the school will be asked to write a report about the child, which becomes advice attached to the statement. The parents' views are similarly attached.

Issuing a Statement

If the LEA agrees to the assessment they must carry it out within six months. This may or may not result in a decision by the LEA to give a statement. If the LEA wishes, they can write a 'note in lieu' of a statement, which says the pupil's needs have been discussed, and suggesting strategies to meet them. A draft statement, written using the evidence from all these reports, is sent to the parent who can ask for changes to be made. If the LEA and the parent can't agree to these changes, or if there is a dispute over placement decisions, the parent can then take the matter to the SEN Tribunal. The parent partnerships officer will usually attempt to mediate a mutually satisfactory solution to the parent's request.

Pupils with Statements

Pupils with statements in mainstream schools follow the normal programmes of study, but may have additional programmes provided to meet their needs. Most have either a support assistant or a support teacher for limited periods, to help them learn, and any specific therapy treatments or technical aids are also listed in the statement. IEP planning continues with short-term targets set by the school. Each pupil with a statement has an annual review, to decide whether the statement is still needed and if so, whether it needs to be changed in any way. Changes to the statement are the LEA's responsibility once the report from the annual review is received from the school.

A very few pupils with statements may go to special classes or special schools. They too follow modified programmes of study within the National Curriculum. They may be taught by specialist teachers and have considerable input from therapists who visit some special schools regularly.

Pupils between the ages of 16–19 may continue to have a statement, if they stay at school. If they go to Further Education colleges, their needs will be met by extra funding, but arrangements will need to be made during transition for planning reviews with the individual college.

Monitoring and Inspection

Schools are expected to set their own targets for attainment in literacy and numeracy at primary school, and in GCSE subjects in secondary schools, but this type of overall target setting is not fine-tuned to the needs of individuals. The reviewing of individual needs falls to those who review IEPs and statements on a regular basis, and schools should have ways of making links between the individual target setting and strategies and the overall planning of lessons and schemes of work.

Schools are inspected once every 4–6 years by a team of OFSTED inspectors, and these inspections look at the overall effectiveness of schools, taking into account the particular make-up of the school's population. Inspectors are concerned with the teaching and learning process, but also with the school's efficiency. As far as SEN is concerned, they may look at samples of statements and IEPs, specialised resources and adaptations, and ask whether pupils with SEN have access to the full curriculum, including the National Curriculum and sufficient opportunities to make progress.

The government has issued advice on inclusion giving examples of reasonable steps that schools and LEAs should consider to make the inclusion of a child with a statement of SEN more possible in mainstream schools. In September 2002, The SEN and Disability Act (2001) came into force. Schools will not be able to treat disabled pupils less favourably for a reason relating to their disability. The Disability Rights Code of Practice will explain these new anti-discrimination duties to schools. There will also be advice to LEAs and schools on practical steps to improve their accessibility to a wider range of disabled pupils.

References and Further Reading

DfEE (1998) *The National Literacy Strategy.* London: DfEE.

DfES (2001) *Code of Practice on the identification and assessment of special educational needs.* London: DfES/581.

OFSTED (1997) *The SEN Code of Practice: two years on.* London: HMSO.

SCAA (1997) *Baseline Assessment.* London: SCAA (now QCA).

TTA (1998) *National Standards for Special Educational Needs Coordinators.* London: TTA.

A Short Glossary of Terms

Advice
Reports sent to the LEA as part of the assessment process and attached to the Statement as appendices.

Annual Review
Yearly review of the Statement, targets and provision.

Appendix
The advice from parents and professionals used to draft the Statement and attached to the final document.

Code of Practice
A government document giving advice about assessment and identification of children with special educational needs and including some regulations which are legally binding.

DfES – Department for Education and Skills.

EP – Educational Psychologist.

IEP – Individual Education Plan.

LEA – Local Education Authority. In Northern Ireland, LEAs are called Education and Library Boards (ELBs).

LSC – Learning and Skills Council.

National Curriculum Key Stages
Foundation Stage – Ages 3–5
Stage 1 – Ages 5–7
Stage 2 – Ages 7–11
Stage 3 – Ages 11–14
Stage 4 – Ages 14–16

OFSTED – Office for Standards in Education. A non-ministerial government department for inspection of all schools. Northern Ireland has the Education and Training Inspectorate (ETI) and Wales has the Office of Her Majesty's Chief Inspectors (OHMCI) instead of OFSTED.

Placement
The name of the school given in the Statement.

Provision
Details of the strategies and resources listed on the Statement to implement the targets.

QCA – Qualifications and Curriculum Authority (formerly SCAA). A non-ministerial government department offering advice to the DfES on the content and impact of the National Curriculum. In Wales the equivalent body is ACAC, and in Northern Ireland the CCEA.

Regulation
A legal part of the Code of Practice.

SATs – Standard Assessment Tests, also known as National Curriculum Assessment Tests (NCATs).

SEN – Special Educational Needs.

SENCO – Special Educational Needs Coordinator. (A member of school staff responsible for coordinating SEN within that school. In larger schools there may be a coordinating team.)

Statement
A legal document or record summarising a pupil's special needs and provision.

TTA – Teacher Training Agency. (A non-ministerial government department for establishing and developing standards in teaching.)

Liz Cowne
Responsible Tutor for SENCO training outreach courses at the
Institute of Education (London) and Lecturer/Tutor for MA courses at
Kingston University and the Open University

Introducing Special Educational Needs: What is Different in Scotland?

In a brief postscript to the main chapter it is not possible to do justice to the detail of the concepts and systems relating to special educational needs in Scotland. The new Scottish Parliament brings a greater degree of devolved government to Scotland, but for hundreds of years before that Scotland has had separate systems of education and of justice. The separate legislation and official guidance relating to these systems – both of which are vital in addressing special educational needs – have resulted in some similarities to the systems of England and Wales but also very considerable differences which may increase in the coming years. Currently the legal definition of special educational needs in Scotland is the same, however, this is currently under review. The term 'Additional Support Needs' was the most popular choice as a replacement descriptor during the recent consultation on the Assessment and Recording process. The exact definition of this term is still under debate. A more positive starting point is to note that at least the legal definition of special educational needs is currently the same!

A guide to the resources available on SEN in Scotland follows. The approach taken is to focus on the differences between the Scottish and English systems, as the Welsh and Northern Irish systems have more in common with the English. The following resource lists are grouped under headings indicating the publications which are most useful in explaining the various differences between Scottish and English SEN provision. Page numbers of relevant sections of the publications will be given when appropriate, as well as details of from where the publication can be ordered. A brief note after the publication reference indicates the target audience and, in some cases, the purpose of the publication. This should give some indication of its ease of reading. Some key information agencies are also listed with their contact telephone number.

For information on educational entitlement, the legislative framework and official guidance:

The Education (Scotland) Act 1980 (as amended)
All education authorities will have a copy of the law, as will main public libraries. However it makes for complex and dense reading. Sections 1(1), 1(5), and 14 should be particularly helpful.
£11.65. Available from The Stationery Office. ☎ 0870 606 5566

The Standards in Scotland's Schools etc. Act 2000. Published by the Scottish Executive Education Department (SEED). Of particular interest are sections 1, 2 , 15 and 40.
£7.65. Available from The Stationery Office, 71 Lothian Road, Edinburgh, EH3 9AZ. ☎ 0870 606 5566

Education (Disability Strategies and Pupils' Educational Records) (Scotland) Act 2002, published by SEED.

This Act is currently going through the Scottish Parliament. It is a short, easily read document.

Available from SEED, Pupil Support Division. ☎ 0131 244 7139

www.scotland.gov.uk

A Parents' Guide to Special Educational Needs. Published by Enquire and SEED.

This revised publication is an attractive, comprehensive guide for parents which gives fairly detailed advice about legal rights and responsibilities.

Available from Enquire, in a variety of formats and community languages.

☎ Tel 0131 222 2400

www.childreninscotland.org.uk/enquire.htm

A Parents' Guide to Special Educational Needs. Published by the Scottish Office Education Department (SOED)

Special Educational Needs and Disability Act 2001 – Sections 11–13.

Available from SEED as before.

Scottish Executive consultation on draft guidance and regulation on accessibility strategies.

This is a readable document which outlines the proposed guidance to Local Authorities and Independent and Grant Aided Schools on their new duties under the above Act.

Available from SEED as before.

Guidance on Education of Children Absent from School through Ill-health, Scottish Executive 2001.

This is an extremely accessible document aimed at Local Authorities which uses very effective case studies to illustrate the new duties placed upon them under Section 40 of the Standards in Scotland's School's etc. Act 2000.

Available from SEED, Pupil Support Division. ☎ 0131 244 7139

Circular 4/96, Children and Young Persons with Special Educational Needs : Assessment and Recording. Published by The Scottish Office Education and Industry Department (SOEID)

This is a very detailed document but one which addresses the complexities of record and recording, assessment, complaints and appeals. Any parent or professional who wishes to, or must, explore these matters seriously should refer to this document. It is the nearest equivalent document to the English *Code of Practice*, especially when it is considered with the two other documents, *Effective Provision for Special Educational Needs* and the *Manual of Good Practice*. (See next two sections for details.)

Available from The Scottish Stationery Office. ☎ 0870 606 5566 or Scottish Executive 0131 244 7139

For information on identification, assessment and recording of special educational needs:

Effective Provision for Special Educational Needs. Published by SOEID and Her Majesty's Inspectorate
Although aimed at school and college teachers, this is a readable document which sets out the basic principles on which good practice in special educational provision should be based. It also describes in some detail the staged process of assessment of assessing children to identify their special educational needs.
Free. Available from Her Majesty's Inspectorate. ☎ 0131 244 7106
www.scotland.gov.uk/HMIE

Education (Scotland) Act 1980 (as amended)
As before, but in particular see Section 60.

A Parents' Guide to Special Educational Needs. SEED/Enquire
As before.

Circular 4/96, Children and Young Persons with Special Educational Needs: Assessment and Recording. Published by SOEID
See above.

Assessing our Children's Needs: The Way Forward? Consultation Document, published by SEED 2001
This accessible document is laid out as a set of questions on the issues of identification, assessment and recording of children with SEN and how current policy and practice can be improved.
Available from SEED as before.

Assessing our Children's Needs: The Way Forward? Scottish Executive Response to the Consultation, SEED 2002
Summarises the responses to the above document and details Ministers' outline proposals to carry the recommendations forward.
Available from SEED as before.

The Record of Needs: A Guide for Parents of Children with Special Educational Needs. Published by Enable
This is a fairly detailed booklet for parents. It clearly sets out the processes involved in Assessment and Recording and has a helpful section on how parents can get involved and what they can do if things go wrong.
Available from Enable – Single copies free to parents. Contact Enable for price for multiple copies. ☎ 0141 226 4541

Your Future Needs Assessment. Published by Children in Scotland
Aimed at young people themselves this booklet explains the Future Needs Assessment process in very clear language and sets out young people's legal rights.
Available from Children in Scotland. ☎ 0131 228 8484

Enquire and Children in Scotland Factsheets
Enquire, the National Advice service for SEN in Scotland and Children In Scotland, its host agency, produce double-sided A4 factsheets aimed at parents and professionals on a wide variety of relevant topics.
Available from Enquire as before.
Children in Scotland. ☎ 0131 228 8484
www.childreninscotland.org.uk

For information about roles and responsibilities:

Helping Young People with Additional Support Needs to Make a Successful Transition: Evaluating and Improving Practice. Published by HM Inspectorate of Education
This extremely readable document details examples of good practice being carried out in Scotland with regard to transition of pupils with SEN from school to further education. It would be of use to a wide number of readers, including parents and young people themselves who would find it helpful in informing themselves.

A Manual of Good Practice in Special Educational Needs: Professional Practice in Meeting Special Educational Needs. Published by SOEID
This is another large file which is very much focused on school-based and school co-ordinated provision and services. Partnership with children, parents and other professionals and agencies is emphasised, as is the development of an individually appropriate curriculum. It offers schools – as well as the partners – a framework on which to evaluate the school.
Available from The Scottish Stationery Office. ☎ 0870 606 5566

A Parents' Guide to Special Educational Needs. Published by SEED/Enquire
As before.

Effective Provision for Special Educational Needs Published by SOEID HMIs
As before.

Circular 4/96, Children and Young Persons with Special Educational Needs: Assessment and Recording. Published by SOEID
As before.

For information about placement, policy and special educational provision:

Education (Scotland) Act 1980 (as amended)
As before but see Section 28A in particular.

A Parents' Guide to Special Educational Needs. Published by SEED/Enquire
As before.

Effective Provision for Special Educational Needs. Published by SOEID HMIs.
As before.

Circular 4/96, Children and Young Persons with Special Educational Needs: Assessment and Recording. Published by SOEID
As before.

A Manual of Good Practice in Special Educational Needs: Professional Practice in Meeting Special Educational Needs. Published by SOEID
As before.

For information about the curriculum:

Special Educational Needs within the 5–14 Curriculum: Support for Learning. Published by SCCC
This bulky file is aimed at all teachers working with children in primary school and the first two years of secondary school. It contains both an introductory section about differentiation and how support for learning is organised and put into practice and further separate sections which indicate ways in which the learning of pupils with particular special needs, such as visual impairment for example, may best be supported while including all pupils within the 5–14 curricular framework.
Available for teachers from the Learning and Teaching Scotland. ☎ 08700 100 297
www.ltscotland.com

A Curriculum Framework for Children 3–5. Published by SOEID/SCCC
Although the curriculum framework has still to be finalised, it is inclusive in its planning for children with special educational needs to be educated with their peers while still receiving the specialist services which they require. The document is aimed at teachers and other early years educators, including parents.
Available from Learning and Teaching Scotland – as before

Effective Provision for Special Educational Needs. Published by SOEID/HMI
As before.

A Manual of Good Practice in Special Educational Needs: Professional Practice in Meeting Special Educational Needs. Published by SOEID
As before.

For information about Individual Education Plans (IEPs):

Raising Standards – Setting Targets: Targets for pupils with special educational needs. Published by SOEID HMIs
This teacher-aimed document is part of a wider national drive to improve school effectiveness and pupil performance and indicates ways in which it is expected that pupils with SEN may also participate and benefit from target setting.
Available from Her Majesty's Inspectorate. ☎ 0131 244 7106
www.scotland.gov.uk/HMIE

Success for All. Published by the University of Aberdeen
National Project: Target Setting within IEPs – 'Section 5: Inclusive Education: A framework for auditing effective learning and teaching'.
Available from the University of Aberdeen, Faculty of Education. ☎ 01224 283527
Price £32.50

A Parents' Guide to Special Educational Needs. Published by SEED/Enquire
As before.

Effective Provision for Special Educational Needs. Published by SOEID HMIs
As before.

A Manual of Good Practice in Special Educational Needs: Professional Practice in Meeting Special Educational Needs. Published by SOEID
As before.

For information about priorities in SEN in Scotland:

Special Educational Needs in Scotland: A Discussion Paper. Published by SOEID
Free. Available from The Scottish Stationery Office. ☎ 0870 606 5566

There were two reports in 1999: the Beattie Report about transition to post-school provision for young people with SEN, and the Riddell Report about educational provision for children with severe low incidence disabilities.

Improving our Schools, Special Educational Needs: The Programme of Action, 2000
This well-set-out document describes action being taken by Scottish Ministers to address issues relating to policy and practice in SEN. Refers to both the Riddell and Beattie Reports – See below.
Available from SEED as before.

The Scottish Executive Response to the Report of the Advisory Committee on the Education of Children with Severe Low Incidence Disabilities, 1999. Published by SEED as before.
This document sets out the response of the Scottish Executive to the Advisory Committee report – also known as the Riddell Report as it was chaired by Professor Sheila Riddell – and invites views on measures proposed to meet certain of the report's key recommendations.
Available from SEED as before.

Implementing Inclusiveness Realising Potential – The Beattie Committee Report Summary 1999. Published by the Transitions to Work Division of the Scottish Executive

The Beattie Committee was the Advisory Committee on Post-School Education and Training for Young People with special needs. This document summarises the main conclusions and recommendations from the committee. This and the full document can be obtained from the Scottish Executive, Beattie Action Group, Department of Enterprise and Lifelong Learning. ☎ 0141 248 4774

For information about problems, complaints and appeals:

A Parents' Guide to Special Educational Needs. Published by SOED
As before.

Circular 4/96, Children and Young Persons with Special Educational Needs: Assessment and Recording. Published by SOEID
As before.

Some useful telephone numbers:

Enquire, Edinburgh. ☎ 0131 222 2400 (Helpline)
ENABLE, Glasgow. ☎ 0141 226 4541
Children in Scotland, Edinburgh. ☎ 0131 228 8484
Scottish Autistic Society. ☎ 01259 720044
Down's Syndrome Scotland. ☎ 0131 313 4225
Scottish Child Law Centre, Edinburgh. ☎ 0131 667 6333
Special Needs Information Point. ☎ 0131 536 0583
Independent Special Education Advice. ☎ 0131 454 0082

Alison Closs (**First Edition**)
Senior Lecturer and Researcher in Special Education
Moray House Institute of Education
University of Edinburgh

Shirley Young (**Second Edition**)
Project Manager
Special Needs Information Point (SNIP)
www.snipinfo.org
Tel/Fax: 0131 536 0583

Section 2

Links with Other Professionals

Links with Other Professionals

2

Introduction

This section looks at the range of services provided by LEAs, other external agencies, bodies and groups, which support children with special educational needs, their teachers and parents. Most of these services also offer support to pre-school children and their parents, as well as working with school age children in mainstream and special schools.

The government is committed to an inclusive education system where children will spend as much time as possible in a mainstream school rather than be sent to a special school. When a placement in a mainstream school is not right for a child, they may, if parents wish, attend a special school. The intention is to encourage special schools to become more closely integrated with mainstream schools and the local pattern of provision.

Most children with special educational needs will be able to make progress and take a full part in the mainstream curriculum. Their teachers will often require specialist advice or support to make this happen, which usually comes from the local educational support services, or from within the health service.

Services and Agencies – Who's Who?

One of the key roles for the school's Special Educational Needs Coordinator (SENCO) is that of getting to know, and working with, all the various support services and agencies that are available locally. Added to this, there is a need to be aware of the voluntary organisations which have national networks and local branches or representatives. These organisations provide information on specific disabilities or conditions such as autism or dyspraxia and support parents of children who have these problems. They may be able to put parents in touch with others who have similar difficulties, to form a support network, as well as giving advice to the school. The SENCO or head teacher often plays a co-ordinating role for parents, by putting them in touch with the multi-professional network, or by gathering information from the various agencies who may come into contact with the child and family.

Parents have a key role to play in the education of their child with SEN. They may vary widely in what they can do, from 'key workers' who have for many years co-ordinated information about their child, to parents who are diffident or lack confidence and experience, who need encouragement to share decisions about their children with the school.

The SENCO also has a key role in leading other school staff, and making sure that appropriate in-service training is available. This includes working in partnership with those outside the school. SENCOs also need to be aware of the local special schools and of the links between mainstream and local special schools that have been developed to encourage inclusive practice.

Services Provided by the Local Education Authority

Some services will be found in all areas. Each LEA must have Educational Psychologists, SEN Officers and Education Welfare Officers who work for the LEA.

The Code of Practice explains how the use of external services should be written into the schools SEN Policy (see page 7 for more information on the Code of Practice).

> Maintained schools must publish information that includes the school's arrangements for working in partnership with LEA services, health, social services, the Connexions Service and any relevant local or national voluntary organisation.
>
> All agencies should recognise the need for effective collaboration of services involved with the child and with parents. (10.2 and 10.5 The Code of Practice (2001))

Under the Code of Practice, the LEA must inform schools and parents which education services are available and how these can be accessed and funded.

Educational Psychologists

Educational Psychologists (EPs) and employed by the LEA and work within the Schools' Psychological Service (SPS). The main purpose of the SPS is to advise and assist teachers and schools about the psychological aspects of child development, the nature of developmental and behavioural difficulties which may arise and how these difficulties might be assessed and overcome. EPs are trained and experienced teachers with a psychology degree, and must also have a recognised specialist qualification in educational psychology. EPs can give advice for any pupil, but work most often with those who have reached School Action Plus of the Code of Practice. They must provide written advice to the LEA, when asked, for those pupils undergoing a formal assessment and (see page 10) this advice becomes 'Appendix D' to the statement document.

EPs work with parents and other health professionals for children of pre-school age. They can take referrals directly from parents, but parents are usually put in touch through the LEA, or through the health service.

Education Officer for Statementing

Your LEA will have a section which deals with assessment procedures for statutory assessment of the Code of Practice and the preparation of draft statements. This section is usually headed by an officer who has responsibility for initiating the statutory assessment process, gathering the necessary appendices and then writing and issuing the draft statement, which requires working closely with parents and education and health professionals. This section also receives the head teacher's annual review report.

SEN Inspectors

Most LEAs have an SEN inspector or adviser who is part of the LEA's team. Apart from their general inspection and/or advisory duties, the SEN inspector will usually attend the SEN panel and monitor the LEA's provision for SEN. They are usually responsible for organising in-service training for SENCOs and their schools, often with the help of the Learning Support Services or the School Psychological Service.

SEN Panel

Many LEAs have a panel of officers and teachers or head teachers who meet regularly to help the decision making procedures surrounding formal assessments and the final statement provision. Practice varies however, so in some districts, the Principal Educational Psychologist or the SEN officer may decide which pupils need formal assessment after receiving the paperwork from schools, or whether to issue a statement when the advice is collected and considered. The draft statement is then sent to parents or guardians for comment. The SEN department will deal with the discussions that arise with parents who want changes made to the draft, and if at all possible, the parents' wishes are taken into consideration.

Education Welfare Service (Sometimes called Education Social Workers)

Education Welfare Officers (EWOs) are employed by the LEA to help parents and the LEA meet the statutory obligations in relation to attendance at school. They can play an important role with pupils who also have SEN, in helping maintain contact between home and school and keeping communication going in cases where the child's attendance is sporadic. There are often underlying reasons for poor attendance which relate to learning or behavioural difficulties. A good working partnership between SENCOs and EWOs can be very productive in sorting out some of these difficulties and in easing a pupil back to regular attendance at school.

Services Usually Available Through the LEA

Service for Hearing Impaired (HI) Children

Almost all LEAs have a service for hearing impaired children, which supports pupils of all ages with hearing loss. Contact begins as soon as the child's hearing loss is diagnosed, often in the first year after birth. There is usually a qualified audiologist available to the service, and teachers of deaf children have an additional specialist qualification. Hearing services support pupils and families as well as schools, and give advice and assessment for any pupil identified as having a hearing loss. They work with pupils with or without statements who require regular support about how to use their hearing aids, and about access to the curriculum. Only those pupils known to have a significant hearing loss will be formally assessed, when advice from a qualified teacher of deaf children must be sought by the LEA. This advice is attached as part of the educational advice to the statement.

Services for Visual Impairment (VI)

A teacher with specialist qualifications in visual impairment (VI) works with a wide range of pupils from pre-school to entry to further education. Contact is made as soon as the visual impairment is known, sometimes in the first year after birth. A VI service will work with pupils whether or not they have a SEN statement. If pupils who are known to have significant visual impairment may be formally assessed, advice from a qualified teacher for VI must be sought by the LEA, which is attached as part of an appendix to any statement. Severe visual impairment is a disability that does not occur often, and includes pupils described as partially sighted, with a defect not fully corrected by spectacles, as well as those classified as educationally blind. Such children cannot be taught by normal sighted means and may need Braille and other means of communication which are not dependent on sight. Further information can be obtained from the RNIB.

Behavioural Support Services

Where such services are provided by the LEA, they usually work at school, class and individual pupil levels to help develop strategies for dealing with groups and individuals with behavioural problems. An additional role is to help schools develop good behaviour policies. Some services work directly with any pupil, while others work only with pupils with statements.

The priority for many Behaviour Support Services is to prevent pupils being excluded from school. They also try to re-integrate pupils who have been excluded from school, or who may have attended a Pupil Referral Unit (PRU).

Pupils at risk of exclusion should have a Pastoral Support Programme (PSP) set up jointly by the schools and a multi-agency team and the parents. The aim of the programme is to help the pupil to improve their behaviour. Extra support may be offered by the LEA to the present school or placement at another school may be supported. The other agencies that could be involved are: social services, housing, Connexions and voluntary organisations or the youth service. (Circular 10/99)

Learning Support Services (LSS)

These services differ greatly from authority to authority in the focus of their work. Some work only with statemented pupils, and others will work with pupils identified at School Action Plus as having specific or general learning difficulties. Referral systems also vary, as some services are accessed through the SPS, and others by direct referral from schools. In some LEAs, the service has a contract with each school, but in the majority of cases, assessment and support in planning IEPs is given. Some LSS also manage teams of Learning Support Assistants for those pupils with statements, and there is such a variety of provision that it is important to find out just what your LEA offers.

Advisory Teachers

Low Incidence Disabilities

Many LEAs have advisory teachers who give help to schools about children with specific disabilities. For example, some LEAs may have an advisory teacher for language impaired children. Others may have an advisory teacher for pupils with physical disabilities or severe health problems. There is little consistency between LEAs on what is provided. The SPS will often be the best place to start looking for help for pupils with low incidence disabilities.

Hospital Schools and Home Tuition Service

Hospital schools are special schools, maintained by LEAs, within general or specialist hospitals. Long-stay pupils have a right to education, which in turn requires liaison between hospital teachers and teachers from mainstream schools if continuity is to be effective.

Each local authority should make arrangements for provision of suitable part-time education for those children of compulsory school age, who, for whatever reason, are not receiving education in school. This is usually covered by a home tuition service, which provides teachers who visit the pupil's home for between 5–10 hours a week. The amount of time available for home tuition varies greatly between LEAs, as does its general availability. Children who are ill for long periods may not be on the SEN register, but continuity of education is difficult to ensure, and should be the responsibility of a known and named member of the school's staff, if not the SENCO. This also applies to those receiving home tuition for other reasons. The LEA should have a named EP to work with such services.

Child Health Services

LEA areas often do not exactly overlap with Health Authority boundaries. The availability of health authority services may vary, but there will be a Community Paediatrician and health clinics where health visitors, school nurses and speech and language specialists, and sometimes occupational therapists and physiotherapists, will work. Hospital services also vary, but there will generally be a paediatric service in which physiotherapists, occupational therapists and child psychiatric services can be found. Just how much hospital services work with schools varies enormously, but usually, access to these services is through the child's GP. However, some statemented pupils will require regular direct contact with therapists.

Child and Adolescent Mental Health Services (CAMHS)

Children with mental health problems may receive help from a variety of sources. Some may benefit from referral to CAMHS for specialist assessment or treatment. This organisation can also provide advice, support and consultation to family members, carers and workers from health, social care and education. Referrals to this service are often through the child's general practitioner or through Schools' Psychological Service.

Community Health Services

For the SENCO, the key health worker is often the school nurse. They, together with school doctors, can provide the gateway to therapists and other health workers. If necessary, a special medical can be requested, whether or not the pupil is on the SEN register. It is essential to consult health records; to check that hearing and vision, for example, have been examined. The school health service will have records of all school aged children, but schools may not have direct access to the information as it is confidential.

Pupils on regular medication for conditions such as asthma, diabetes or epilepsy do not have special educational needs as such, but their illness may be the cause of some missed schooling, or their performance may be affected from time to time. Other pupils may have medication which needs to be accessible during school hours, such as asthma inhalers, or medical equipment which needs to be maintained. An obvious example of this is a hearing aid, which would usually be checked by the service for hearing impaired, who work closely with the health authority.

Children with more severe disabilities will have been identified in early childhood by the health authority and the LEA will have been notified. General practitioners however, are less likely to be aware of the Code of Practice, and may need some persuasion to give LEAs and schools information about those with less severe disabilities. The child community health service is the best source of information for schools. They are required to give the advice to LEAs for formal assessments, known as 'Appendix C' in the statement.

Speech and Language/Occupational Therapists

Access to the services varies from place to place. Usually speech and language therapists hold clinics, to which parents would bring their child for an appointment for assessment or treatment. The therapists will visit special schools and units to meet the needs of statemented pupils. There is a move to build stronger partnerships between therapists and schools so that therapies can be built into the curriculum structure where possible, but there are shortages in these services in many districts which makes innovative and preventative practice difficult to achieve.

Social Services

Each Local Authority will have a social service department which has a children's section and usually a section for those with disabilities. In the past it has not been very easy for schools to make contact with social services on anything but a direct referral over individual cases. It has been argued that, within social services, there is a need for a named person at senior management level to have responsibility for liaising with schools.

For children in care, social services officers, or foster carers could usefully be involved in planning the IEPs for pupils. DfEE Circular 13/94 reminds schools of pupils who are being looked after by social services departments. It suggests schools should have a knowledge of the child's life/care plan, a close relationship and liaison with carers and have a designated member of staff for children who are 'looked after'.

Not all such children will have SEN, so they may not be the SENCO's responsibility. Liaison within school between SEN and pastoral care such as form tutors will be important in these cases. Schools need to know how to contact their designated officer from social services, and any referral procedures agreed by the social services department. The SEN policy needs to set out clearly the arrangements for working in partnership with social services and who on the school staff has responsibility for liaison with social services, for collecting and distributing information, and for individual planning which links to children's IEPs. Social services departments have a particular role to play in the transition of pupils with statements at the end of their school career.

Agencies such as Social Services do not always see schools as their clients or as a priority. Social services, in particular, focus on the family, as do Child Guidance services (usually jointly run by health and education). It may be difficult for schools to gain access to these services even for information, although teachers are sometimes invited to case conferences. However, Social Services are required to give advice to the LEAs for pupils known to them who are undergoing a formal assessment. This becomes Appendix E in a statement.

Pre-school Provision for SEN

Pre-school children are usually identified as having some kind of special need either by parents or by medical staff. Many LEAs have a multi-professional team from Education, Health and Social Services which meet regularly. All newly identified cases are discussed briefly and decisions made as to which service will take the key role in working with parents or in starting assessment procedures. LEAs are required to have a pre-school SEN advisory teacher who works closely with Health and Social Services and with the Portage service in coordinating provision, such as nursery placements and planning admissions to schools. It is important that all children with needs which will have educational implications, are identified pre-school and parents are suitably advised and supported.

Portage

The main aim of the Portage service is to enable parents to help teach their own child. It sends workers, trained to deliver a planned approach, to give home-based pre-school education for children with developmental delay, disabilities or any other special educational needs. There is an extensive Portage network in the UK overseen by the National Portage Association.

Other Early Years Provision

Within each borough there now is an Early Years Development and Child Care Partnership which seeks to link all the providers of child care, day care, pre-school and childminders. Places for children identified as having a special educational need are available throughout these settings. These are monitored by both the partnership and OFSTED. Parents can seek advice and support directly from their local partnership through the Children's Information Service in their LEA.

Connexions Service

The Connexions Service has responsibility to work with all young people between the ages of 13–19 in England. It provides guidance and support to young people through their teenage years and into adult life. The Connexions Service is responsible for overseeing the delivery of the Transition Plan for those pupils with statements from Year 9 onwards. The personal advisor must attend the Year 9 annual review and should be invited to all subsequent annual reviews. They help plan Key Stage 4 and post-16 options taking account of the wishes and feelings of the young person concerned. (Par 10.15 and Par 9.57 Code of Practice (2001))

How Do These Services Work?

Once information about what is available locally and how it can be accessed is known, the next step for the SENCOs is to define how these outside agencies and services might be useful to the needs of their SEN pupils.

Contribution to Individual Education Plans (IEP) and Appendices for Statements

Support teachers and educational psychologists can offer general advice to teachers on how to assess children under the Code of Practice and give help with drafting IEPs. In fact, outside support staff are required to contribute to IEP reviews for those on the third stage of the Code of Practice. Both Health and the Education Services will carry out formal assessments after a request from the LEA.

Writing Effective Advice

For schools, the best professional advice is that which helps to contribute to the child's IEP in a practical way. It is not helpful if a report from a professional is full of jargon and results of tests not known to the school.

For pupils with statements, the advice in the appendices will have informed the statement writer, who will have then listed the needs and priority objectives for the school to achieve. When the final statement is received, complete with appendices, the school must then set targets which are reviewed yearly. Support services will continue to play a useful role in helping schools design and implement the programmes described in the provision section of the statement.

Support by Giving Advice on Strategies

The overwhelming demand from teachers, when getting outside advice and support, is for strategies to meet targets which have been set, within the structure of a normal school day and the National Curriculum. Some services may carry out very detailed assessments which still may not support the teacher's work directly, although they may help tease out any factors within the child, e.g. medical reasons for a problem. An understanding of the curriculum and the social context of the classroom and school are also needed, if teachers are to be fully supported in meeting the needs of more complex individuals.

Teachers may need to borrow equipment for a short time to try it out and many will need training about how it should be used. If equipment is given without training in its use, it may just sit in a cupboard. Information Technology, in particular, can help so many pupils with SEN, but knowing which equipment to buy and whether it will fit the pupils' needs is an expert's job. Over time schools will develop this expertise themselves but they need someone to call on to help with complex problems. The SENCO may have to keep track of the extra resources provided or borrowed and be accountable for their effective use.

Access to Services

Some Learning Support Services or SPS may have a range of specialists in their teams. Referrals to the service may initially be through the regular key contact person, but that person will often know someone else who can help in special cases. Educational psychologists usually have good contacts with health and social services and may be the first contact for many referrals. On the other hand, some specialist services, e.g. hearing and visual prefer direct contact. It is up to each service to make the routes for referral clear to schools and parents.

Using a Problem Solving Approach to Work Collaboratively with Teachers and SENCOs

There are a number of puzzling pupils for whom it isn't very clear what is needed. One effective way to help these pupils will be to work with their teachers to enhance their professional and class management skills. If a visiting professional can find time for a joint problem solving session with a group of staff, together they can elicit the information already known and produce questions which then can be followed up in assessment. This will give staff strategies to try themselves, as well as adding focus on the type of further information required.

What Do Parents Need to Know About Services?

Parents need to know which outside services and agencies are available and have the various roles of these services explained, especially if there is more than one agency involved in their child's case. Again, this is best done informally, before the parent has to meet a room full of strangers at an annual review or a case conference. In some cases parents themselves will often be the teacher's best source of information. If, for example the child has been known to the health service since pre-school years, then the parent will know key people from the community health service or the hospitals who have already worked with the child and provided advice.

In very complex cases, the child may be known to up to 30 or so professionals. For very complex disability cases the parent often is effectively the key worker for their child, linking the therapies and advice together into an individual plan. Notes will be kept separately by each service, but it is the parent who has the total picture. Parents need to meet the key workers who work with their child regularly, so that a coherent and manageable programme can be maintained at home as well as at school.

Inclusive Education

All recent legislation and reports have emphasised the goals of inclusive education. This means that all pupils should be able to attend their local mainstream schools, if this is what the parents wish. There are a few children for whom the best provision may still be within a special school or class for some or all of the time, and some parents want special school placements for their child. The views of parents are given full consideration by each LEA for all pupils who have been assessed and are subsequently given a statement of SEN.

Parents of pre-school SEN pupils will often have put their child's name down at the local mainstream school, and in most cases the LEA will support this placement. Occasionally an alternative placement will be suggested where more specialised teaching is available. Parent-partnership officers should be used to resolve any difficulties on placement decisions.

Parent Partnership

The Revised Code of Practice (2001)states that all LEAs must make arrangements for parent partnership services to be set up. Parents must be made aware of this service so they know where to get information and advice. This service may be LEA based or 'bought in' from another provider. The primary role of the parent partnership services is to help parents whose children have been identified as having SEN. These services should be flexible in their approach and consider parents concerns carefully. They should also help parents gain information and give guidance so they are able to reach informed decisions about their child.

The SEN Tribunal

The SEN Tribunal was set up by the Education Act (1993) as a decision-making body to arbitrate between parents and LEAs in disputes related to certain aspects of the statementing process.

It is chaired by a lawyer and has two lay members drawn from education or associated professions. The tribunal has extensive powers. It can require witnesses to attend, or ask for access to records of the child's work. The SENCO may be expected to help to produce this evidence in the form of well kept records, showing both the pupils' progress and the types of intervention and support given by the school. Pupil and parents' views over time will be an important part of this evidence, and class teachers will sometimes be required to produce evidence of curriculum work of the pupil. LEAs must give parents all the information available about their right to appeal, and their time limits to lodge an appeal including a free copy of the parents' leaflet *SEN Tribunals: How to Appeal* (DfEE 1994). LEAs must provide disagreement resolution services. This service can continue to run alongside an appeal to the SEN Tribunal, but parents can access this service at any time during the SEN assessment process. The service offers independent facilities to resolve disagreements, but has no role in the decision-making process.

While an appeal is being conducted, everything should be done to maintain normal professional relationships between the parent and school or support staff. The decision at the tribunal will be binding and the LEA must comply with instructions given by the tribunal. However, if the case is lost, parents have no further appeal to the tribunal, so in the majority of cases, relationships between existing school and parents are likely to have to continue after the hearing is over.

The LEA will hope that by using the parent partnership service conflict and disagreement will be avoided. However, using this service is purely voluntary.

Liz Cowne
Institute of Education
London WC1H 0AL

Education	Health	Social Services
Educational Psychologists	Community Services School Nurse/Doctor Community Paediatrician	Children's Services (sometimes part of generic service)
Educational Welfare Officers		Child Care Officer
Education Officer (statements) or equivalent		
Parent Partnership Officer		
Learning support services	Hospital Paediatrician	Disability Services or part of generic service
Teachers for the: Hearing Impaired Visually Impaired Language Impaired Physically Impaired	Specialist Doctors (Hospitals) Speech and Language Therapist Occupational Therapist Physiotherapist Therapist	
Portage Service for pre-school children	Health Visitors (pre-school)	Day Nurseries
Behaviour Support Services	Child and Adolescent Mental Health Service (CAMHS)	
Pupil Referral Units (PRU)		
Home Tuition Service Hospital Teachers		

Figure 2.1 Showing support services and agencies linked to SEN work. The Early Years Development Childcare Partnership and the Connexions Service work in a multi-disciplinary way in each borough.

Liz Cowne
Responsible Tutor for SENCO training outreach courses at the
Institute of Education (London) and Lecturer/Tutor for MA courses at
Kingston University and the Open University

Section 3

Acronyms and Abbreviations

Acronyms and Abbreviations

3

ADD	Attention Deficit Disorder
ADHD	Attention Deficit Hyperactivity Disorder
ALBSU	Adult Literacy and Basic Skills Unit, now the Basic Skills Agency
BAAT	British Association of Art Therapists
BAC	British Association of Counselling
BATOD	British Assocation of Teachers for the Deaf
BILD	British Institute for Learning Difficulties
BPS	British Psychological Society
BSL	British Sign Language
BMA	British Medical Association
CAB	Citizens Advice Bureau
CAL	Computer Assisted Learning
CB	Challenging Behaviour
CBA	Curriculum-Based Assessment
CHC	Community Health Council
CFF	Common Funding Formula
CMO	Clinical Medical Officer
CP	Cerebral Palsy
CSIE	Centre for Studies on Inclusive Education
CTLD	Community Team for People with Learning Difficulties
DfEE	Department for Education and Employment
DfES	Department for Education and Skills
DHA	District Health Authority
DLA	Disability Living Allowance

DoH	Department of Health
DSI	Dual Sensory Impairment
EBD	Emotional and Behavioural Difficulties
EDY	Education of the Developmentally Young
EP	Educational Psychologist
ERA	Education Reform Act
ESW	Educational Social Worker
EWO	Educational Welfare Officer
FAS	Funding Agency for Schools
FE	Further Education
FEFC	Further Education Funding Council
GEST	Grant for Education Support and Training
GM	Grant Maintained (School)
HA	Health Agency
HAS	Health Advisory Service
HEA	Health Education Authority
HI	Hearing Impaired
IE	Instrumental Enrichment
IEP	Individual Education Plan
INSET	In-Service Education and Training
IQ	Intelligence Quotient
ICT	Information and Communications Technology
IPSEA	Independent Panel for Educational Advice
ITT	Initial Teacher Training
JCPD	Joint Council for Pupils with Disabilities

KS	Key Stage	PGSS	Paget-Gorman Sign System
		PH	Partially Hearing
LEA	Local Education Authority	PHAB	Physically Handicapped and Able Bodied
LCD	Language and Communication Difficulty	PMLD	Profound and Multiple Learning Difficulties
LD	Learning Difficulties		
LMS	Local Management of Schools	PRU	Pupil Referral Unit
		PS	Partially Sighted
LMSS	Local Management of Special Schools	PTR	Pupil-Teacher Ratio
LSA	Learning Support Assistant	QCA	Qualifications and Curriculum Authority
LST	Learning Support Team		
MD	Muscular Dystrophy	SCAA	Schools Curriculum and Assessment Authority, now QCA
ME	Myalgic Encephalomyelitis		
MLD	Moderate Learning Difficulties		
		SEMERC	Special Education Microelectronic Resource Centres
MS	Multiple Sclerosis		
MSD	Multisensory Deprivation		
		SEN	Special Educational Needs
NAI	Non-Accidental Injury	SENCO	Special Educational Needs Coordinator
NASEN	National Association for Special Educational Needs		
		SENIOS	Special Educational Needs in the Ordinary School
NC	National Curriculum		
NCET	National Council for Educational Technology	SENNAC	Special Educational Needs National Advisory Council
NCVO	National Council for Voluntary Organisations	SENTC	Special Educational Needs Training Consortium
NFER	National Foundation for Educational Research	SI	Sensory Impaired
		SIB	Self-Injurious Behaviour
NRA	National Record of Achievement	SLD	Severe Learning Difficulties
		SNA	Special Needs Assistant
NTA	Non-Teaching Assistant, now Learning Support Assistant	SNSA	Special Needs Support Assistant
		SPD	Semantic Pragmatic Disorder
NVQ	National Vocational Qualification	SpLD	Specific Learning Difficulties
OCD	Obsessive Compulsive Disorder	TTA	Teacher Training Agency
OFSTED	Office for Standards in Education	VI	Visually Impaired

Adapted from Farrell, M. (1998) *The Special Education Handbook*, David Fulton Publishers

Section 4

A Glossary of Terms and Medical Conditions

A Glossary of Terms and Medical Conditions

Aarskog Syndrome Features include: Slight to moderate short stature, widely spaced and downward slanting eyes with drooping eyelids, small nose, underdevelopment of upper jawbone, underdeveloped teeth with delayed eruption, short, broad fingers with mild webbing, mildly sunken chest, prominent umbilicus, hernia of groin, undescended testicles, abnormality of the skin of the scrotum, skeletal abnormalities. Males are affected more often and more severely than females. Mild learning difficulty may be present but intellect is unimpaired in most cases. X-linked dominant inheritance.

Abasia Inability to walk as a result of poor coordination.

Abducent Nerve The sixth cranial nerve controlling the rectus muscle, which turns the eye outwards.

Able Children Children who are potentially outstanding in academic, intellectual, creative or artistic ability. Some able children may have difficulties in relating to other children of a similar age. In order to help them reach their full potential, such children require special opportunities to develop their particular skills. Also referred to as gifted children or very able children.

Absence Seizure Onset usually between 4 and 15 years. The child may have a blank or glazed look and be unaware of his or her surroundings. The seizures may last only a few seconds but may occur many times within a twenty-four hour period. The absence state cannot be interrupted by talking, touching etc. and the child is unaware of the seizure once it has passed.

Abstract Thinking The ability to form ideas, theories or imaginary concepts.

Acalculia Difficulty with numbers and mathematical processes. (See Specific Learning Difficulty)

Acataphasia The inability to connect thoughts in an orderly manner.

Achalasia A condition in which the ring-shaped muscle around a natural opening (e.g. the oesophagus) fails to relax.

Acheiria Absence of the hands and feet.

Acidosis A condition in which there is either an abnormal increase of acids or a reduction in the alkali content of the blood.

Acne An eruption of pimples, commonly affecting the face, neck and chest, due to inflammation of the sebaceous glands of the skin.

Acne Rosacea Areas of reddened and coarsened skin on the face, occurring mainly around the nose and cheeks.

Acquired Condition A condition causing physical and/or intellectual damage to the foetus, newborn or older child, which is not inherited from the parents. It is due to an 'external' factor occurring between conception and birth, during or just after birth or during life. An acquired condition may be congenital (i.e. present at birth), but is not hereditary. Damage may result from infection, drugs or poisons in pregnancy, malnutrition or poor health in the mother, injury or lack of oxygen at birth, childhood infections such as meningitis and encephalitis or injury to the child.

(See also Alcohol Effects, Foetal; Cytomegalovirus Infection; Dilatin Syndrome, Foetal; Herpesvirus Infection, Perinatal; Hydantoin Effects, Foetal; Kernicterus; Rubella Effects, Foetal; Syphilis Syndrome, Congenital; Toxoplasmosis, Congenital; Trimethadione Effects, Foetal; Varicella Effects, Foetal; Warfarin Effects, Foetal)

Acrocephalopolysyndactyly, Type 2 (See Carpenter Syndrome)

Acrocephalosyndactyly, Types 1 and 2, Type 3 (See Apert Syndrome; Saethre-Chotzen Syndrome)

Acrocephaly A skull malformation in which the head is tall and somewhat pointed; the result of premature closure of several of the sutures between the bones of the skull. (See also Craniosynostosis; Skull, Bones of the; Sutures of the Skull, Premature Closure of Several)

Acrocyanosis Blueness of the extremities, i.e. the hands, feet, nose and ears.

Acrodysostosis Syndrome Features include: short broad head, low nasal bridge, broad, small and upturned nose, tendency to hold the mouth open, underdeveloped upper jaw, short limbs, progressive deformity of arms, hands and feet, wrinkling of skin on back of hands. Learning difficulty, varying in severity, in the majority of cases. Cause unknown.

Acromegaly An excessive degree of bone growth, especially of the jaw, hands and feet. Associated with overactivity of the pituitary gland.

Acromion The projection on the outer side of the scapula, forming the point of the shoulder.

Adactylia or **Adactyly** Absence of fingers and/or toes.

Adaptive Behaviour The development of skills in social competence, such as self-help (feeding, washing) and communication (speech, writing, reading). Assessment of adaptive behaviour can be made through tests that measure different aspects of social skills, in which the results can be expressed as standard scores or age equivalents. The scales may be completed from information provided by the parents or other person with personal knowledge of the child. For older children with severe learning difficulties, these scales can provide information which relates to developmental aspects of the school curriculum, indicating which skills a child already possesses and which aspects of social competence the curriculum should cover.

Adenofibroma *pl. adenofibromata* A benign tumour composed of fibrous and glandular tissue.

Adenoma *pl. adenomata* A benign tumour composed of glandular tissue.

Adenoma Sebaceum (See Angiofibroma)

Adiposis Abnormal accumulation of fatty tissue.

Adrenoleukodystrophy (ALD) The disease appears in three different forms, categorised by age of onset. In the childhood form (the most common type), the onset is usually between 4 and 8 years, with signs of progressive neurological degeneration; behavioural changes, poor memory, sight defects, weakness of the arms and legs, clumsiness, indistinct speech, spasticity, blindness, quadriplegia. Later, there may be increased skin pigmentation, weakness and weight loss due to decreased function of the adrenal gland. X-linked inheritance in the childhood form.

Advocacy The use of independent professionals or volunteers to speak and act on behalf of people who are unable to represent themselves because of disability. **Self-advocacy:** groups of people with disabilities who come together to establish and obtain their rights. **Lay or citizen advocacy:** the provision of voluntary trained assistants who work on a one-to-one basis with people who have a disability, to enable them to express their needs and/or to ensure that appropriate services are provided. **Legal advocacy:** lawyers who work with people with disabilities, to ensure that they can exercise their rights and, if necessary, to represent them in court.

Afibrinogenaemia A condition in which the blood fails to coagulate as a result of absence of fibrinogen, the clotting agent. May be congenital or acquired.

Age-Appropriate Behaviour The types of behaviour which would be expected in most children of the same age.

Agenesis Partial or total failure of a body part to develop normally.

Agenesis of the Corpus Callosum and **Chorioretinal Abnormality** (See Aicardi Syndrome)

Agenesis of the Corpus Callosum, Partial (See FG Syndrome)

Ageusia Absence of the sense of taste.

Agnathia Partial or total absence of the jaw.

Agnosia Inability to identify objects by using the senses, i.e. through sight, hearing, smell, taste or touch.

Agraphia Inability to express thoughts in writing.

Aicardi Syndrome or **Agenesis of the Corpus Callosum with Chorioretinal Abnormality** Features include: absence of the corpus callosum, infantile spasms and flexion spasms, defects of the choroid and retina, severe learning difficulty. All reported cases have been female. Cause unknown.

Akathisia Restlessness; a tendency to constant movement.

Akinesia Absence or impairment of voluntary movement.

Alalia Partial or total loss of the power of speech.

Albinism A condition in which the eyes, hair and skin are markedly pale and colourless, regardless of family colouring. Due to a congenital absence of skin pigmentation. Nystagmus may occur. Variable modes of inheritance.

Albright Hereditary Osteodystrophy Syndrome or **Pseudohypoparathyroidism** Features, which are variable, include: short stature, obesity, dental defects, short hand and foot bones. In some cases: underdeveloped genital organs, low blood calcium levels, abnormalities of the long bones, seizures. Moderate to severe learning difficulty is common but intellect is unimpaired in some cases. Where present, the hypocalcaemia may diminish of its own accord. X-linked dominant inheritance proposed.

Alcohol Effects, Foetal or **Foetal Alcohol Syndrome** Damage to the developing foetus has occurred in about 30–50% of cases where there has been a high alcohol intake by the mother during pregnancy. Features, which are variable, include: growth deficiency, microcephaly, small eyes with drooping lids, squint, hearing loss, joint abnormalities, tremor, poor coordination, hyperactivity, speech defects. In some cases: heart defects, mild to moderate learning difficulty.

4

Alexander Disease or **Megalencephaly with Hyaline Panneuropathy** Features include: head enlargement within the first year, motor delay, seizures, spasticity, lack of speech development, progressive changes in the white matter of the brain. Life expectancy not exceeding infancy in most cases. In the juvenile-onset form, there may be survival until 8–10 years. The precise metabolic defect is unknown.

Alexia Another name for dyslexia.

Algesia Sensitivity to pain.

Allergen Any substance which, when taken into the body, makes the body oversensitive to it, e.g. pollen, causing hay fever.

Allergy Excessive sensitivity to certain foods, plant products, chemical substances, materials, etc. An allergy may manifest itself in conditions such as hay fever, eczema or nettle rash. Research is being done into allergic reaction as a possible factor in disorders such as hyperactivity, migraine and epilepsy.

Alopecia Loss of hair from the head. It may be in patches (alopecia areata) or complete, temporary or permanent.

Alpha Waves (See Electroencephalography)

Amaurosis Blindness caused by disease of the optic nerve, retina or brain, but without obvious abnormality of the eye.

Amblyopia Dimness of vision.

Ambulatory Able to walk.

Amenorrhoea Failure of the menstrual period to appear at its anticipated time. It may be primary, i.e. never having occurred, or secondary, i.e. having ceased to function as a result of pregnancy or disease.

Amentia Learning difficulty due to lack of normal intellectual development from infancy. Used to differentiate from dementia, which is intellectual impairment as a result of injury or disease occurring later in life.

Ametropia Defective vision.

Amimia Lack or absence of facial expression.

Amnesia Loss of memory.

Amniocentesis or **Amniotic Puncture** The process of obtaining a specimen of the fluid surrounding an unborn baby in the womb, for diagnostic purposes or for detection of abnormality. Usually carried out between the 16th and 18th week of pregnancy. Also performed in later pregnancy to monitor rhesus disease and to test foetal lung maturity.

Amyotrophy Wasting or loss of substance of muscle.

Anaemia A reduction in the number of red blood cells in the blood or in the amount of haemoglobin they carry, resulting in pallor, weakness and giddiness.

Anaesthesia Loss of feeling; absence of sensation.

Anaphylactic Shock A severe reaction to a substance to which an individual is allergic.

Anarthria Inability to speak clearly or to pronounce words.

Anderson-Fabry Disease (See Fabry Syndrome)

Anencephaly A severe abnormality in which there is absence of the brain, resulting in stillbirth or early death. May be accompanied by spina bifida and other defects.

Aneurism A swelling or 'ballooning' in the wall of an artery.

Angelman Syndrome Features include: slow psychomotor development and lax muscle tone in infancy, microcephaly, widely spaced eyes, protruding jaw, stiff jerky movements, tongue protrusion, seizures, prolonged and unprovoked periods of laughter, uncoordinated arm movements, abnormal pattern on electroencephalogram before, during and after the bouts of laughter, severe learning difficulty. A partial deletion of the long arm of chromosome 15 has been found in 50–80% of cases.

Angiectasis Abnormal enlargement of capillaries.

Angiofibroma *pl. angiofibromata* A small benign tumour composed of blood vessels and fibrous tissue. These lesions, which occur around the nose, cheeks and mouth in tuberous sclerosis, are commonly referred to as adenoma sebaceum. But, as the sebaceous glands are not involved, the term angiofibroma is a more appropriate and accurate description. (See also Telangiectatic Fibroma)

Angiokeratoma, Diffuse (See Fabry Syndrome)

Angioma *pl. angiomata* A benign tumour composed of dilated blood vessels.

Anhidrosis Absence or deficiency of sweating.

Aniridia Absence or defect of the iris.

Ankylosis Restriction of movement in a joint due to malformation or to the fusion of bones.

Anodontia Partial or total absence of teeth.

Anoesia Impaired intellect; learning difficulty.

Anophthalmos or **Anophthalmia** Absence of an eye or both eyes.

Anosmia Absence of the sense of smell.

Anteflexion Bending forward of the upper part of an organ or body part.

Anterior Fontanelle The space between the parietal and frontal bones of the skull, which is normally closed by 18 months to 2 years of age. (See Skull, Bones of the; Sutures of the Skull)

Anticonvulsants A range of drugs prescribed to prevent or reduce seizures in epilepsy.

Antiketogenic The term used to describe a food or remedy which prevents or decreases the formation of ketones. (See also Ketone)

Antimongoloid Slant Downward slanting of the outer corner of the eyes, as opposed to the upward slant found in 'mongolism' (former term for Down syndrome).

Antipyretic A substance or treatment used to lower body temperature in fever.

Antisocial Behaviour (See Attention Deficit Disorder; Challenging Behaviour; Emotional and Behavioural Difficulties)

Aortic Murmur (See Murmur)

Apert-Crouzon Disease (See Apert Syndrome)

Apert Syndrome or **Acrocephalosyndactyly, Types 1 and 2** Features include: tall skull with a high and wide forehead due to premature closure of the sutures of the skull (most commonly the coronal and lambdoid), widely spaced and protruding eyes, a flattened appearance to the upper jaw and bridge of nose, pointed tip of nose, prominent chin, high and narrow palate, crowded teeth, symmetrical fusion (of skin alone or both skin and bone) involving the digits of all four limbs. In Type 1, there is fusion of all five digits, in

4

Type 2, the thumb and little fingers are usually free, or only partially fused. Most individuals are of normal intelligence but mild learning difficulty occurs in some cases. Facial cosmetic surgery and repair of syndactyly of the hands is performed during the first few years to improve appearance and dexterity. Type 2 is sometimes referred to as Apert-Crouzon disease or Vogt cephalodactyly. Autosomal dominant inheritance, with most cases representing new mutations. (See also Craniosynostosis: Skull, Bones of the; Sutures of the Skull, Premature Closure of Several)

Apgar Score A method of assessing a baby's condition at birth, in which points are given for colour, heart rate, muscle tone, respiration effort and response to stimulation.

Aphagia Inability to swallow or to eat.

Aphakia Absence of the lens of the eye.

Aphalangia Absence of one or several of the finger and/or toe bones (phalanges).

Aphasia Total or partial loss of the power of speech and/or to understand speech. Often due to disease or injury of the cerebrum.

Aphonia Loss of the voice. Due to disease or injury of the nerves controlling the muscles of speech or infection of the throat and larynx.

Aplasia or **Aplastic** Absence of development; lacking the power to develop. May be applied to an organ, tissue or part.

Aplastic Anaemia A disorder in which the bone marrow fails, partially or completely, to produce red blood cells.

Apnoea Cessation of breathing as a result of a temporary decrease of carbon dioxide or an excessive amount of oxygen in the blood; a breath-holding attack.

Apodia Absence of a foot or feet.

Apraxia 1. Loss of the ability to produce harmonious movements. 2. Abnormal actions, due to a poor understanding of events.

Aqueductal Stenosis or **Stenosis of the Aqueduct of Sylvius** Narrowing of the aqueduct of Sylvius (the canal which connects the third and fourth ventricle of the brain). Due to a variety of causes, including faulty development of the aqueduct, a membranous obstruction, or protrusion of the cerebellum into the upper part of the spinal canal (Arnold Chiari malformation). Commonly associated with hydrocephalus. The disorder arises spontaneously in many cases, but there are two inherited types: X-linked aqueductal stenosis and familial aqueductal stenosis. (See Dandy-Walker Syndrome; Hydrocephalus)

Arachnodactyly Abnormally long, thin and tapering fingers. Literally, 'spider-like fingers'.

Arachnosyndactyly Long, thin and tapering fingers, joined by webbing.

Areflexia Absence of a reflex or reflexes.

Argininosuccinic Aciduria A disorder of amino acid metabolism. Features include: sparse, stubby and fragile hair, seizures, abnormal blood ammonia levels, moderate to severe learning difficulty. Improvement in the condition of the hair and control of ammonia accumulation can be achieved by dietary measures. Autosomal recessive inheritance.

Argyll-Robertson Pupil A condition in which the pupil of the eye does not contract when a light is shone into it, but does contract upon accommodation, i.e. when the patient is asked to look at a far away object, then at something close by.

Arnold Chiari Malformation (See Aqueductal Stenosis)

Arrhythmia Absence of the correct rhythm, e.g. in the heartbeat.

Arthrogryposis Congenital contractures of several joints, either inherited or acquired.

Arthropathy Disease of the joints.

Asemia Inability to communicate by means of speech or signs.

Ash-Leaf Patch (See Hypomelanotic Patch)

Asperger Syndrome Regarded by some as a distinctive condition, Asperger syndrome is viewed by others as the higher-ability aspect of the autistic continuum. Grammatical and complex speech is achieved early but is not used for communication in the normal way. The speech is used oddly, in a monotonous or exaggerated tone. Affected individuals tend to talk at great length on topics which interest them and are apparently indifferent to whether they are listened to or not. Eye contact is avoided and the gaze may wander as they talk. There is thought to be a high level of intelligence in people with Asperger syndrome and a less severe psychological disturbance than in the Kanner form of autism. Because the features are less obvious than those of 'classic' autism, the syndrome may not be diagnosed in early childhood. (See also Autism; Kanner Syndrome; Pervasive Developmental Disorders; Semantic-Pragmatic Disorder)

Asphyxia Neonatorum Impaired breathing in a newly born child.

Aspiration 1. The drawing off of fluid, e.g. from the chest or knee, by suction. 2. A condition in which food is drawn into the windpipe instead of the oesophagus, causing choking.

Aspiration Pneumonia Pneumonia which occurs in patients who are unable to clear the mucous from their air passages by coughing, resulting in the secretions being drawn further down into the lungs.

Assessment Tests These include standardised tests designed to evaluate the rate of normal physical, intellectual and social development in a child, according to his/her age.

Astasia Inability to walk or stand as a result of impaired muscular coordination.

Asthenia Lack of strength, energy or tone.

Asthma A respiratory disorder involving paroxysms of difficult breathing. Attacks may be related to hypersensitivity to foreign substances or associated with emotional upsets. Treatment includes medication and the avoidance of things which in particular cases appear to precipitate attacks, such as the house-dust mite.

Astigmatism An error of refraction in the eye in which the lens and cornea are not truly spherical, so that different rays of light cannot be brought in focus together.

Asynergia A symptom of nervous system disorder in which there is a lack of harmonious and coordinated movement between muscles which have opposite actions, e.g. the extensor and flexor muscles of a joint.

Ataxia A disorder of the nervous system caused by abnormality of, or damage to the cerebellum. It results in the loss of reflexes, the inability to control movements, lack of fine motor control, clumsiness and jerky gait.

Ataxia Telangiectasia Syndrome or **Louis-Bar Syndrome** Features include: onset usually in late infancy or childhood, growth deficiency, telangiectases in the conjunctiva which later spread to other areas of the face, ataxia. Progressive, with

4

life expectancy not usually exceeding late childhood. In some cases: skin changes, eye defects, seizures, intellectual impairment becoming evident as the disease progresses. Autosomal recessive inheritance.

Ataxic Gait (See Gait)

Atelectasis Partial collapse of the lung or lack of expansion of the lung at birth.

Athetosis A form of cerebral palsy in which there are involuntary slow, writhing movements of the limbs and body. Damage to the basal ganglia is one cause of athetosis.

Atonic Seizure A seizure in which there is sudden loss of muscle tone (as opposed to a myoclonic seizure, in which there is abrupt spasm of muscle), falling and loss of consciousness.

Atony Lack of tone or power in a muscle or organ.

Atopic The predisposition to develop a particular condition, e.g. in familial disorders.

Atresia Absence of a natural opening or passage, e.g. of the anus, vagina or oesophagus. Usually a congenital malformation.

Atrophy Wasting, of the body generally or of a part, due to degeneration of the cells. It may be the result of disease, poor nutrition or impaired nerve function.

Atrophy Oculi Congenita (See Norrie Disease)

ATR-X Syndrome An inherited disorder which affects males. Features include: severe learning disability, characteristic facial appearance, absence of speech, feeding problems, sleep disturbance, frequent respiratory infections, genital abnormalities including undescended testicles. There is a degree of anaemia resulting from a mild form of thalassaemia which is similar to, but distinct from, beta-thalassaemia. X-linked inheritance.

Attention Deficit Disorder (ADD) and **Attention Deficit Hyperactivity Disorder (ADHD)** Also termed hyperactivity and hyperkinetic syndrome. Onset usually before the age of seven years, with males affected more than girls. Features include: inability to maintain concentration, impulsive behaviour and constant movement, impaired listening and organisation skills, a tendency to be easily distracted, a lack of inhibition and emotional control. This behaviour often interferes with and inhibits interaction with others. Most children with ADD are of average or above average intelligence but their inability to concentrate along with social and behavioural problems may affect their ability to learn. The cause of ADD is unknown but there is thought to be a genetic predisposition in some families. It has been shown that, in some cases, the symptoms are induced or made worse by sensitivity to certain types of food additives, dyes and artificial flavours. In some cases there may be a genetic factor. Treatment has included dietary approaches, medication, behaviour therapy and biofeedback (monitoring one's own psychological processes).

Aura An unusual feeling experienced by people with epilepsy, just before the onset of a seizure. It may take the form of a sense of cold, a strange smell, a visual manifestation or emotional sensation. It serves as a warning to the individual of the onset of a seizure.

Auricle The projecting part of the outer ear; the pinna. Also used formerly to denote the two upper chambers of the heart (atria).

Autism A non-progressive disorder with onset usually before the age of three.

Features include: language and communication difficulties, extreme reactions to change in routine or environment, reluctance to watch others, avoidance of social contacts, strong attachments to particular objects, obsessive behaviour such as rocking, dangling an object or tapping, the appearance of being completely self-absorbed, unpredictable responses to aural and visual stimulation, delayed acquisition of language with unusual use of language. Hyperactivity and temper tantrums are common if the child's demands are not met. Various causes have been suggested. Research is being carried out into possible physical or biochemical causes. Effective education involves bringing under control inappropriate behaviours, structured programmes on communication and social skills and training to aid the generalisation of skills to a range of settings. (See also Asperger Syndrome; Kanner Syndrome; Pervasive Developmental Disorders; Semantic-Pragmatic Disorder)

Autistic Continuum/Autistic Spectrum The symptoms and characteristics of autism can occur in a wide variety of combinations, from mild to severe. Although autism is defined by a certain set of behaviours, children and adults can exhibit any combination of the behaviours to any degree of severity. Several autism related disorders are grouped under the broad heading 'pervasive developmental disorder' (PDD). The diagnosis of autism is made when a specified number of characteristics are present which are inappropriate for the age of the child. A diagnosis of 'pervasive developmental disorder – not otherwise specified' (PDD–NOS) may be applied when a child shows fewer symptoms than in autism but those symptoms which are present are the same as those exhibited by a child with a diagnosis of autism.

Automatism Actions performed without the conscious will of the individual and without later recollection, sometimes occurring after an epileptic seizure.

Autosomal Dominant Disorder A disorder caused by a dominant mutant (changed) gene located on an autosome. A person with a single copy of the abnormal gene on one chromosome will be affected by the condition, even though they have the normal gene on the partner chromosome. Each child of an affected parent will have a 1 in 2 (50%) chance of inheriting the gene, and of being affected by the disorder. (See also Dominant Inheritance)

Autosomal Recessive Disorder A disorder caused by a 'double dose' of abnormal recessive genes. It occurs when both parents, though healthy themselves, each carry a defective gene for the same disorder. At each conception there is a 1 in 4 (25%) chance that the child will inherit the abnormal gene from both parents (and so will be affected), a 1 in 4 (25%) chance that the child will inherit the normal gene from both parents (and so will be unaffected), and a 1 in 2 (50%) chance that the child will inherit the abnormal gene from one parent and the normal gene from the other (so will be unaffected, but a carrier). (See Recessive Gene)

Babinski Reflex An abnormal reflex response to the stroking of the sole of the foot, found in individuals with nerve damage. The normal reaction is a clenching of the foot with toes downward (plantar reflex). In Babinski reflex the big toe goes up and the toes fan out. The Babinski reflex sometimes occurs in normal infants, but after the age of about two years it is regarded as a sign of neurological disorder.

4

Balanced Translocation or **Reciprocal Translocation** (See Chromosome Abnormality)

Barts Test A pre-natal blood test for the detection of Down syndrome.

Basal Cell Naevus Syndrome or **Gorlin Syndrome** Features include: skin tumours, bulging of forehead, wide nasal bridge, dental cysts, short bones of the hands, spinal curvature, mild to moderate learning difficulty. In some cases: squint and other eye defects, skeletal abnormalities, genital defects. The naevi over the face, upper arms, and trunk may become malignant in adulthood, and surgery may be necessary for their removal. Cause not known but affected individuals are considered to have a genetic disposition to the disease.

Basal Ganglia The nerve cells in the cerebrum which are concerned with co-ordination. Athetoid cerebral palsy may result from damage to the basal ganglia.

Basal Metabolism (See Inborn Error of Metabolism)

Baseline Assessment The assessment of understanding, knowledge, skills and attitudes of children on entry to primary school, which gives a starting point from which a child's progress through Key Stage 1 can be measured. Baseline assessment provides the means to identify each child's learning needs, including those of children with special educational needs. It is also used as an initial assessment to provide a basis on which to judge subsequent progress. Baseline assessment makes an important contribution to value added measures. (See also Value Added)

Basilar Impression An abnormality of the upper spine. Primary; fusion of the first and second vertebrae and the first and second segments of the occipital bone into a single bony mass. Secondary; softening of the cranial bones to the extent that they are no longer capable of supporting the weight of the head.

Batten Disease or **Batten-Spielmeyer-Vogt Disease** A disorder of lipid metabolism. Features include: onset in childhood or adolescence with similar effects to those of Bielschowsky-Jansky disease. Progressive, with a shortened life expectancy. Autosomal recessive inheritance. (See also Bielschowsky-Jansky Disease; Kufs Disease)

Beckwith-Weidemann Syndrome or **Macroglossia, Exomphalos, Giantism Syndrome** Features include: above average weight and length at birth, reddish naevus on forehead and eyelids, prominent eyes, thick skin, accelerated maturation of bone, indentations on the outer ear, breathing problems due to muscular enlargement of the tongue (which usually improves with compensatory growth of the mouth), prominent jaw, umbilical hernia, large kidneys. In some cases: hypoglycaemia in infancy, liver enlargement, overgrowth of a limb or of half the body, tumours of the kidneys and adrenals. Mild to moderate learning difficulty may occur, but intellect is unimpaired in most cases. Ultimate intelligence is largely dependent upon the early recognition and treatment of hypoglycaemia. An abnormality of the short arm of chromosome 11 has been found in some cases.

Behaviour Modification or **Behaviour Therapy** A method of eliminating or reducing inappropriate behaviour and strengthening acceptable behaviour, by means of specially designed teaching procedures.

Behavioural Difficulties (See Emotional and Behavioural Difficulties)

Berger Rhythm The normal rhythmic waves caused by changes in the electrical activity of the brain. Epilepsy produces an abnormal wave pattern.

Bielschowsky-Jansky Disease A disorder of lipid metabolism. Features include: onset in infancy, seizures, ataxia, sight deterioration, learning difficulty. Progressive, with a shortened life expectancy. Autosomal recessive inheritance. (See also Batten Disease; Kufs Disease)

Birth Difficulties (See Perinatal Factors)

Blepharitis Inflammation of the eyelids.

Blepharophimosis Narrowing of the space bordered by the eyelids, due to their poor development.

Blepharoptosis (See Ptosis)

Blepharospasm Loss or impairment of muscular control of the eyelid, resulting in spasm and uncontrolled blinking.

Blissymbols A method of teaching and encouraging communication skills in non-verbal children and adults, using signs and symbols in place of the spoken word. It is made up of symbols, standing for single words, which can be built into phrases or sentences on a board. The individual is taught to indicate by pointing or other physical means.

Bloch-Sulzberger Syndrome (See Incontinentia Pigmenti Syndrome)

Bobath Method A method of therapy, named after a husband and wife team. It was designed to reduce spasticity and restore balance and equilibrium, using physiotherapy and other methods. Parents are instructed in teaching their own children, and advised on correct handling, feeding, play activities etc.

Brachycephaly An abnormally short and broad head. (See Craniosynostosis; Sutures of the Skull)

Brachydactyly or **Brachydactylia** Abnormally short fingers and/or toes.

Bradycardia Abnormally slow heart beat with consequent slow pulse.

Bradykinesia Abnormally slow movements of the body and limbs.

Brain, Centres of the: Occipital region; concerned with the sense of sight. **Temporal region**; concerned with the sense of hearing, taste and smell. **Frontal lobes**; concerned with intellectual function. **Medulla and pons**; concerned with respiration, rate of heart and swallowing. **Inferior frontal gyrus region**; concerned with speech. **Cerebrum**; concerned with intellectual functions and the nervous system.

Brain Damage Damage to the brain as a result of injury or disease. May be congenital or acquired. Causes include; lack of oxygen at birth, trauma before, during or after birth, progressive diseases of the brain, seizure disorders.

Bronchospasm Acute constriction of the bronchial tubes.

Brushfield Spots White dots or speckles in the iris of the eye. A feature of Down syndrome, but also seen frequently in normal individuals.

Bruxism Repetitive grinding of the teeth.

Bulbar Palsy Paralysis of the nerves controlled by the medulla oblongata, which is sometimes referred to as the spinal bulb. These nerves supply the muscles of the mouth, tongue and larynx and their paralysis interferes with swallowing. (See Worster-Drought Syndrome)

Buphthalmos Congenital glaucoma; enlargement of the ball of the eye. Due to failure of the drainage system of the eye and a consequent increase of pressure within it.

4

Cachexia Severe weakness or debility.

Cafe au Lait Spots Flat brown skin patches. A feature of tuberous sclerosis and neurofibromatosis but also found frequently in normal individuals.

Calcaneus (See Talipes)

Camptodactyly or **Camptodactylia** Permanent bending of a finger or fingers. Most common in the 5th, 4th and 3rd fingers in decreasing severity.

Camptomelia Permanent bending of a limb or limbs.

Canavan Disease or **Spongy Degeneration of the Central Nervous System** Features include: apparently normal development for the first few months with head enlargement becoming evident by about 6 months, lack of head control and muscle tone, deterioration of motor activity, optic atrophy, nystagmus, spasticity, feeding difficulties, seizures, degenerative changes of the brain. Life expectancy not usually exceeding five years, though some patients have survived longer. Autosomal recessive inheritance.

Carcinoma A malignant tumour.

Cardiospasm Spasmodic contraction of the sphincter of the cardiac muscle, which surrounds the opening of the oesophagus into the stomach. The contraction causes retention within the oesophagus.

Carpenter Syndrome or **Acrocephalopolysyndactyly, Type 2** Features include: small or elongated skull with a wide forehead due to premature closure of several sutures of the skull, epicanthic folds, small jaw, webbing of digits and/or extra digits, obesity, variable degrees of learning difficulty. In some cases: heart defects, skeletal abnormalities. Autosomal recessive inheritance. (See Craniosynostosis; Skull, Bones of the; Sutures of the Skull, Premature Closure of Several)

Carrier In genetics, a person whose body contains an abnormal gene for a specific disorder without being affected by it. Also used to indicate an individual who carries the micro-organisms of a disease but who has no symptoms.

Cataract Cloudiness or lack of transparency of the lens of the eye.

Cat-Eye Syndrome A small extra chromosome, derived from a number 22 chromosome. Features, which are variable, include: widely spaced eyes, coloboma of iris, choroid and/or retina, small jaw, skin tags on the ears. In some cases: heart defects, kidney defects, anal defects. Moderate to severe learning difficulty is common, but does not occur in every case. (See also Chromosome Abnormality)

Cerebellar Gait (See Gait)

Cerebellar Vermis Agenesis, Familial (See Joubert Syndrome)

Cerebral Giantism (See Sotos Syndrome)

Cerebral Palsy Spastic paralysis. A disorder of the nervous system which results in impaired movement and coordination, varying from mild involvement of a limb to severe incapacity affecting the whole body. Individual education programmes are especially important because of the varied nature of the condition. (See also Ataxia; Athetosis; Spasticity)

Cerebro-Costo-Mandibular Syndrome Features include: growth deficiency, severely underdeveloped jaw, cleft palate, small chest with gaps between the ribs, vertebral anomalies, respiratory difficulty. Moderate to severe learning difficulty occurs in some cases but is not always present. Inheritance pattern not established.

Cerebro-Hepato-Renal Syndrome (See Zellweger Syndrome)

Cerebro-Oculo-Facio-Skeletal Syndrome or **COFS Syndrome** (See Pena-Shokeir Syndrome, Type 2)

Cerebroside Lipidosis (See Gaucher Disease)

Chaining A method of promoting self-help by breaking down a complex skill into its component parts and teaching them in stages. It may be taught in normal sequence, i.e. from beginning to end, or in reverse, i.e. beginning at the last step and working backwards. A task such as putting on and fastening a coat may be broken down into steps this way, each step being learned before progressing to the next.

Challenging Behaviour Socially unacceptable behaviour which inhibits learning to a significant extent and, in its extreme form, may endanger the safety of the individual and that of others. Features include: hyperactivity, refusal to cooperate with others, stereotyped behaviour, eating of inappropriate substances, inappropriate sexual behaviour, screaming and displays of temper, self-injury and injury to others, damage to surroundings. The behaviour should be assessed and measured. Intervention programmes should take account of the learner's needs and abilities. Behavioural or psychotherapeutic approaches may be used and individual planning of specific programmes is necessary. (See also Attention Deficit Disorder)

Charge Association A syndrome of Coloboma, Heart disease, choanal Atresia, Retarded growth, Genital anomalies and Ear anomalies (CHARGE). A combination of malformations seen together more often than could be expected by chance. Features include: growth deficiency, coloboma and other eye defects, heart defects, atresia choanae, ear anomalies/deafness, underdeveloped genital organs in males, mild to severe learning difficulty. In some cases: feeding difficulties, kidney defects. Cause unknown.

Chicken Pox (See Varicella Effects, Foetal)

Chondritis Inflammation of cartilage.

Chondrodysplasia Punctata Syndromes (See Conradi-Hünermann Syndrome; Rhizomelic Chondrodysplasia Punctata Syndrome)

Chondrodystrophy Faulty development of cartilage.

Chondroectodermal Dysplasia (See Ellis van Creveld Syndrome)

Chordee Downward angulation of the penis. May be congenital or acquired. A feature of some multiple abnormality syndromes.

Chorea A disorder of the central nervous system. The symptoms include restlessness and involuntary movement, lack of co-ordination and weakness.

Choreoathetosis A combination of jerking movements and slow writhing movements.

Choreoretinitis Inflammation of the choroid and retina of the eye.

Choroiditis Inflammation of the choroid coat of the eye. It may progress to involve the retina and is then termed chorioretinitis.

Chorionic Villus Sampling A test in which chorion cells (which are situated on the wall of the uterus) are collected from the pregnant mother. These cells share the same origin as the foetal cells and can, therefore, be tested for the presence of certain foetal abnormalities.

Chotzen Syndrome or **Acrocephalosyndactyly, Type 3** (See Saethre-Chotzen Syndrome)

4

Chromosome A rod-shaped structure, present in the nucleus of all body cells except the red blood cells, which carries genetic information. There are normally 46 chromosomes in each cell, arranged in 23 pairs. In humans, both the sperm and the egg (ovum) carry a set of 23 chromosomes. The fertilised ovum, therefore, carries 46. The 46 chromosomes are made up of 44 autosomes and 2 sex chromosomes. Before techniques existed to identify individual chromosomes accurately, they were divided into seven groups for identification purposes: **Group A**, pairs 1–3; **Group B**, pairs 4 and 5; **Group C**, pairs 6–12; **Group D**, pairs 13–15; **Group E**, pairs 16–18; **Group F**, pairs 19 and 20; **Group G**, pairs 21 and 22. The two sex chromosomes make up the remaining pair, giving 46 in all. A normal male has one X and one Y chromosome, therefore males are designated XY. A normal female has two X chromosomes and is designated XX. Each chromosome is shaped roughly like a letter X with its two upper arms shorter than its two lower arms. (See Chromosome Abnormality, Nomenclature)

Chromosome Abnormality A defect in a chromosome or in the arrangement of chromosomes. It may take the form of faulty structure of a chromosome, alteration in the amount of chromosome material or in the position of a chromosome. There may be: 1. Additional material attached to a chromosome (the presence of an extra whole chromosome or part of a chromosome); 2. Absence of a whole chromosome or part of a chromosome; 3. Defective formation of a chromosome; 4. Rearrangement in position between chromosomes or parts of chromosomes. Too much or too little chromosome material interferes with normal body formation and subsequent development. Chromosome abnormalities produce specific physical features. However, there is a wide variation in symptoms between individuals with the same visible chromosome abnormality. Chromosome abnormalities account for a large proportion of children with learning difficulty.

Deletion Absence of a chromosome or part of a chromosome. The absence of a whole autosome is usually lethal but absence of a short arm or long arm, or part of an arm, is fairly common.

Interstitial deletion A situation in which two breaks occur in a chromosome and the intervening material is lost, resulting in an unbalanced amount of chromosome material.

Inversion A chromosome may break in two places and the middle piece re-attach itself after turning upside down. Providing no chromosome material is lost this abnormality should have no effect on an individual. But, he or she may carry the risk of producing eggs or sperm with the incorrect amount of chromosome material. **Pericentric inversion:** An inversion of chromosome material, involving the centromere (the central portion of the chromosome). **Paracentric inversion:** An inversion of chromosome material, not involving the centromere.

Mosaicism A situation in which some cells have the correct number of chromosomes (46) and others have an incorrect number, i.e. too many or too few. For example, in the mosaic form of Down syndrome (trisomy 21) a proportion of the body cells carry 47 chromosomes and the remainder carry the correct number of 46. In a mosaic disorder the extent and severity of features depends upon the proportion of normal cells to abnormal ones and upon which tissues are involved.

Ring formation The two ends of a chromosome may become damaged and curl over so that the ends of the short arm and the long arm almost meet, forming a ring shape.

Tetrasomy The presence of four copies of a chromosome, or part of a chromosome, instead of the normal two.

Translocation A situation in which a chromosome or part of a chromosome is absent from its pair and exchanges position with a chromosome from another pair, or in which two chromosomes are fused together. Balanced (or reciprocal) translocation: The exchange of position between two chromosomes or parts of chromosomes, in which both chromosomes remain intact and no material is lost. The individual is unaffected but any offspring would be at risk of inheriting an unbalanced translocation. Unbalanced translocation: The exchange of position between two chromosomes or parts of chromosomes in which chromosome material is lost. The chromosome count may show the correct number of 46 but closer inspection reveals rearrangement. Robertsonian translocation: A translocation of chromosomes, involving end to end fusion and resulting in a balanced translocation. The individual has 45 chromosomes but, as no significant chromosome material has been lost, is unaffected. Offspring may be affected.

Triploidy The presence of a complete set of extra chromosomes.

Trisomy The addition of a complete extra chromosome, or part of a chromosome to a pair, resulting in three copies of the chromosomal material at that site. Where there is a complete extra chromosome the total chromosome count is 47.

Chromosome Abnormality, Nomenclature Descriptions of particular chromosome formations are written in a shortened form which indicates the total number of chromosomes, the sex of the individual and the number of the abnormal chromosome. The short arm of a chromosome is designated by a letter 'p', the long arm by a letter 'q'. An additional chromosome or portion of a chromosome is designated by a plus sign, the absence of a chromosome or portion of a chromosome by a minus sign, a ring formation by a letter 'r'.

Deletion Example 1. 46, XY 18p-denotes a male (one X and one Y chromosome) with the correct number of chromosomes (46) but with a missing short arm (p) of one number 18 chromosome. Example 2. 45, X0 syndrome denotes a female with absence of one of her X chromosomes.

Ring formation Example. 46, XX 13r denotes a female (two X chromosomes) with the correct total number of chromosomes (46) but with the ends of a number 13 chromosome curved to form a ring.

Trisomy Example 1. 47, XY 21+ denotes a male (one X and one Y chromosome) with a total chromosome count of 47. The extra chromosome is an additional chromosome 21. Example 2. 47, XXY syndrome denotes a male with an additional X chromosome.

Chromosome Abnormality Syndromes Disorders of foetal development due to faulty structure or positioning of a chromosome or chromosomes. Named according to the number of the affected chromosome. Where a particular chromo-

4

somal abnormality has been seen to produce a specific set of features in several individuals more often than would be expected by chance, it is designated as a recognisable syndrome. Many individuals have chromosomal rearrangements which are extremely rare and which have not been observed frequently enough for any specific pattern of features to emerge.

1q+ syndrome Trisomy or partial trisomy of the long arm of chromosome 1. Features include: pointed nose, large and protruding ears, small jaw, long tapering fingers, congenital heart disease, shrinkage or absence of the thymus gland.

3p+ syndrome Trisomy or partial trisomy of the short arm of chromosome 3. Features include: short, broad skull with prominent forehead, widely spaced eyes, epicanthic folds, large mouth, short neck, heart defects. In some cases: cleft palate.

4p+ syndrome Trisomy or partial trisomy of the short arm of chromosome 4. Features include: growth deficiency, microcephaly with prominent forehead, bulbous nose with flat bridge, large tongue, irregular teeth, small pointed lower jaw, enlarged and malformed ears, short neck, flexion of fingers and curving of 5th fingers, undescended testes, spinal curvature, rib abnormality, 'rocker bottom' feet, feeding and breathing problems, learning difficulty.

4p- syndrome or Wolf-Hirschhorn syndrome Deletion or partial deletion of the short arm of chromosome 4. Features include: growth deficiency, asymmetry of skull, microcephaly, lax muscle tone, epicanthic folds, cleft lip and/or palate, downturned corners of the mouth, short upper lip, small jaw, low set ears with skin tag or pit, dimpling on shoulders, elbows and knuckles, abnormal palm creases, club foot, undescended testes and/or hypospadias, heart defects, seizures, recurrent respiratory infections, severe to profound learning difficulty.

5p- syndrome or Cri du Chat syndrome, Lejeune syndrome Deletion or partial deletion of the short arm of chromosome 5. Features include: low birth weight and slow growth, characteristic weak, shrill cry (like the mewing of a cat) in infancy, microcephaly, round face with widely spaced eyes, epicanthic folds, squint, low set and poorly formed ears, facial asymmetry, abnormal palm creases, variable congenital heart defects, severe learning difficulty.

6r syndrome Ring formation of chromosome 6. Features include: microcephaly, small and widely-spaced eyes, low-set ears, flat nasal bridge, mild to severe learning difficulty. In some cases; hydrocephalus, epicanthic folds, high-arched palate, short neck, webbing of fingers and/or toes, clubfoot. The severity of features depends upon the amount of genetic material lost on the short and long arms of the chromosome before it formed a ring.

7q+ syndrome Trisomy or partial trisomy of the long arm of chromosome 7. Features include: low birth weight, widely spaced eyes, small nose, cleft palate, large tongue, large low set ears, spinal curvature, hip dislocation, rib and foot abnormalities, mild to severe learning difficulty.

8+ syndrome, mosaic Trisomy or partial trisomy of chromosome 8, usually mosaic form. Features include: variable growth rate, poor coordination, prominent forehead, deep set and widely spaced eyes, squint, full lips, small jaw, high arched palate, prominent ears, flexing of 2nd–5th fingers, limited elbow movement, deep sole and palm creases, long slim trunk with narrow hips, mild to severe learning difficulty. In some cases: hearing loss. The severity of the features is variable, depending upon the proportion of trisomic cells to normal cells.

9+ syndrome, mosaic Trisomy or partial trisomy of chromosome 9, mosaic form. Features include: growth deficiency, sloping forehead, deep set eyes, prominent bridge of nose with fleshy tip, prominent upper lip covering lower lip, small jaw, low set and malformed ears, joint abnormalities with defective function of hips, knees, feet, elbows and digits, spinal curvature, learning difficulty. In some cases: heart defects, kidney malformations. The severity of the symptoms depends upon the proportion of trisomic cells to normal cells.

9p+ syndrome Trisomy or partial trisomy of the short arm of chromosome 9. Features include: growth deficiency, microcephaly, widely spaced eyes, downward slanting and deep set eyes, prominent nose, downturned corners of the mouth, short fingers and toes, learning difficulty. Spinal curvature may develop in teenage years.

9p- syndrome or 9p monosomy Deletion or partial deletion of the short arm of chromosome 9. Features include: high and pointed skull with flat occiput, prominent and upward slanting eyes, short nose with a flat bridge, small jaw, poorly formed ears, short neck, long middle bones and short end bones of fingers with short nails, foot

defects, heart defects, spinal curvature, widely spaced nipples, hernias, moderate to severe learning difficulty.

10q+ syndrome Trisomy or partial trisomy of the long arm of chromosome 10. Features include: growth deficiency, microcephaly, flat face, high forehead with highly arched eyebrows, small eyes with drooping eyelids, flat nasal bridge, bow-shaped mouth with prominent upper lip, small jaw, cleft palate, malformed ears, webbing of third and fourth toes and other digital anomalies, spinal curvature and rib abnormalities, sunken chest, severe learning difficulty. In some cases: heart defects, kidney defects.

11p+ syndrome Trisomy or partial trisomy of the short arm of chromosome 11. Features include: bulging forehead, squint and other eye defects, downward slanting eyelids, cleft palate, small jaw, lax muscle tone, mild to severe learning difficulty.

11q+ syndrome Trisomy or partial trisomy of the long arm of chromosome 11. Features include: low birth weight, broad flat nose, small jaw with retracted lower lip, heart defects, kidney defects, mild to severe learning difficulty.

11p- syndrome Deletion or partial deletion of the short arm of chromosome 11. Features include: growth deficiency, drooping eyelids and eye defects, prominent lips, small jaw, poorly formed ears, moderate to severe learning difficulty. In some cases: microcephaly, Wilm's tumour.

13+ syndrome or Patau syndrome, D Trisomy syndrome Trisomy of chromosome 13. Features include: severe defects of brain development, microcephaly, seizures and breathing problems in infancy, hearing loss, small eyes,

4

small jaw, cleft lip and/or cleft palate, abnormal and low set ears, forehead haemangiomata, scalp defects, flexing and overlapping of fingers, extra fingers and sometimes toes, skeletal abnormalities, heart defects, hernia, severe learning difficulty. Those with severe effects do not usually survive infancy. Those with the mosaic form tend to have less severe effects and a longer life expectancy.

13p+ syndrome Trisomy or partial trisomy of the short arm of chromosome 13. Features are non-specific and may include: a large nose, underdeveloped jaw, short upper lip and severe learning difficulty.

13q+ syndrome Trisomy or partial trisomy of the long arm of chromosome 13. Features include: haemangiomata of the forehead, short nose, bushy eyebrows with curly lashes, severe learning difficulty. In some cases: abnormal skull shape.

13q- syndrome, 13r syndrome Partial deletion of the long arm, or ring formation of chromosome 13. Features include: growth deficiency, microcephaly, widely spaced eyes, drooping eyelids, small eyes and variety of eye defects, prominent and low set ears, short neck, small or absent thumbs, club foot, skeletal defects, heart defects, mild to severe learning difficulty. The severity and type of abnormalities depends upon the size and location of the missing genetic information. Retinal tumour occurs in about half the cases of 13q- syndrome, but only occasionally in the 13r syndrome.

17p- syndrome or Smith-Magenis syndrome Interstitial deletion of the short arm of chromosome 17. Features include: growth deficiency, short broad skull, underdevelopment of the midface region, protruding lower jaw, hoarse voice, speech delay, hyperactivity, mild to severe learning disability in most cases. In some cases: hearing loss, heart defects. The severity and type of abnormalities depends upon the size and location of the missing genetic information.

18+ syndrome or Edwards syndrome Trisomy of chromosome 18. Features include: growth deficiency, prominent occiput, small jaw and small mouth cavity, low set and poorly formed ears, clenched hand with index finger folded over the third and fifth finger over the fourth, small and widely spaced nipples, bone abnormalities, hernias, mild hairiness of forehead and back, mottling of skin, heart defects, feeding and breathing problems in infancy, severe learning difficulty. Those with all cells affected have severe effects and do not usually survive beyond infancy. Those with the mosaic form can have less severe effects and a longer life expectancy.

18p+ syndrome Trisomy or partial trisomy of the short arm of chromosome 18. Features include: either no specific clinical symptoms with little or no intellectual impairment or similar features to those of the 18+ syndrome (trisomy 18) but in milder form.

18q+ syndrome Trisomy or partial trisomy of the long arm of chromosome 18. Features include: partial characteristics of 18+ syndrome (trisomy 18) including a broad nasal bridge, poorly formed ears, underdeveloped jaw, long fingers, lax muscle tone. The learning difficulty is less severe than in 18+ syndrome, and there is a longer life expectancy. In some cases: seizures. Trisomy for the whole long arm is similar in effect to 18+ syndrome.

18p- syndrome or de Grouchy syndrome Deletion or partial deletion of the short arm of chromosome 18, sometimes as part of a ring formation. Features include: growth deficiency, mild microcephaly, widely spaced eyes with drooping eyelids and epicanthic folds, round face with small jaw, wide mouth with downturned corners, large and prominent ears, sunken chest, mild to severe learning difficulty.

18q- syndrome Deletion or partial deletion of the long arm of chromosome 18, sometimes as part of a ring formation. Features include: growth deficiency, microcephaly, deep set eyes, narrow palate, downturned corners of mouth, long hands with tapering fingers and dimples over knuckles, small genitalia, club foot and/or abnormal toe placement, heart defects, hearing and sight problems, mild to severe learning difficulty.

18r syndrome Ring formation of chromosome 18. Features of both 18p- and 18q- syndromes, including: microcephaly, lax muscle tone, widely spaced eyes, epicanthic folds, low set ears, learning difficulty. In some cases: cleft palate.

20p+ syndrome Trisomy or partial trisomy of the short arm of chromosome 20. Features include: short skull, deep set eyes with upward slant, flat nasal bridge, large and poorly formed ears, abnormal teeth, small tapering fingers with inward curving of fifth fingers, foot positioning defects, spinal curvature, underdeveloped genitalia, heart defects, mild to moderate learning difficulty.

21+ syndrome, Down syndrome or Down's syndrome Trisomy of chromosome 21. Features include: short skull with flat occiput, small nose, epicanthic folds, Brushfield spots, small ears with upper edge folded over, underdeveloped teeth, short hands and fingers with inwardly curving fifth fingers and abnormal palm creases, thickened skin with mottling and dryness, soft and straight hair, underdeveloped genitalia in males, lax muscle tone and double-jointedness, mild to severe learning difficulty. In some cases: squint and other eye defects, respiratory problems, heart defects. Those with the mosaic form tend to have less pronounced features and only mild learning difficulty.

21q- syndrome, 21- syndrome, Ring G or Group G monosomy Deletion or partial deletion of the long arm of chromosome 21, absence of a whole number 21 chromosome or a ring formation. In a few cases, there has been apparent absence of the whole chromosome. This is usually considered to be incompatible with life, so it is possible that there is a chromosome rearrangement or mosaicism in these cases. Features include: microcephaly, downward slanting eyes, large and low set ears, small jaw, arched or cleft palate, genital defects, skeletal defects, club foot, mild to severe learning difficulty. In some cases: cataracts, lax muscle tone. The severity of abnormalities depends upon the size and location of the missing genetic information.

22+ syndrome Trisomy or partial trisomy of chromosome 22. Features include: microcephaly, short nose, squint, large and low set ears, short neck, small jaw, widely spaced nipples, long slim fingers, lax muscle tone, underdeveloped genital organs in males, motor delay and mild to moderate learning difficulty. In some cases: heart defects, cleft lip and/or palate, digestive

4

malformations, lax muscle tone, seizures.

22q- syndrome Deletion or partial deletion of the long arm of chromosome 22. Features include: low set ears, drooping eyelids, epicanthic folds, webbing of 2nd and 3rd toes, inward curving of fifth fingers, lax muscle tone, mild to severe learning difficulty. In some cases: 'spade-like' hands, club feet. The severity of abnormalities depends upon the size and location of the missing genetic information.

Chromosome Abnormality Syndromes, Sex Disorders of foetal development caused by defects in the sex chromosomes, as distinct from the autosomes. (See also Chromosome; Chromosome Abnormality; Chromosome Abnormality, Nomenclature)

X0 syndrome or Turner syndrome Absence of an X chromosome in the female. Features include: either normal facial features or a small, triangular face with drooping eyelids, squint and corneal opacities, broad chest with widely spaced nipples, incomplete secondary sexual characteristics (i.e. breast development, pubic hair growth, menstruation), infertility. In some cases: hearing defects, heart defects, kidney defects. Hormone treatment can be given to promote development of secondary sexual characteristics. Mild learning difficulty may occur, but intelligence is usually within the normal range.

XXX syndrome (or Triple X Syndrome), **XXXX syndrome** Extra X chromosome/s in the female. Females with only one extra X chromosome are of normal appearance, may be of normal intellect or have only mild learning difficulty, and are likely to be fertile. Those with two or more extra X chromosomes have characteristic facial features, normal or irregular menstruation, skeletal abnormalities in some cases, mild to moderate learning difficulty in most cases.

XXXXX syndrome or Penta X Syndrome) Extra X chromosomes in the female. Features include: growth deficiency, upward slanting eyes, short neck, small hands, moderate to severe learning difficulty.

XXY syndrome (or Klinefelter syndrome Extra X chromosome in the male. Features include: long, slim limbs, lack of development of secondary sexual characteristics at puberty, obesity, infertility. Mild to moderate learning difficulty occurs in some cases but most affected males are not intellectually impaired. There may be a tendency to immaturity and behaviour problems. Testosterone therapy at the onset of puberty may result in more masculine development and more stable behaviour. (See also XXXY, XXXXY Syndromes)

XXXY syndrome, XXXXY syndrome Extra X chromosomes in the male. While most individuals with Klinefelter syndrome (XXY syndrome) are of normal intelligence, those with more than one additional X chromosome are likely to have a learning difficulty. Features include: short stature, lax muscle tone, skeletal defects, widely spaced eyes, large and low set ears, protruding jaw, small genitalia and infertility.

XXYY syndrome An extra Y and an extra X chromosome in the male. Features include: abnormal head shape (brachycephaly, microcephaly or dolichocephaly), widely spaced eyes, broad nose, squint, protruding jaw, large ears, joint limitation, short stature. In some cases: spinal curvature. Mild to moderate learning difficulty is common, but intelligence may be within the normal range.

XYY syndrome An extra Y chromosome in the male. Features include: accelerated growth in childhood, relative weakness with poor fine motor control, large teeth, skeletal abnormalities, severe acne in adolescence. In some cases: mild to moderate learning difficulty, behaviour problems.

Chromosomal Abnormality Syndromes (See also Cat-Eye Syndrome; Fragile-X Syndrome; Pallister-Killian Syndrome; Triploidy Syndrome)

Chronic The term used to refer to an illness of long duration, as opposed to acute.

Chronological Age Actual age in years, as opposed to the stage of normal development reached (developmental age).

Citizen Advocacy (See Advocacy)

Claw Foot (See Pes Cavus)

Claw Hand A deformity of the hand in which the wrist and fingers are flexed in a claw-like position.

Cleft Lip A deep ridge in the lip where the tissue has failed to grow together.

Cleft Palate A fissure of the roof of the mouth, due to failure of the plates of the palate to meet in the middle. Often combined with cleft (hare) lip.

Clinodactyly Curving inward of a finger or fingers, most commonly found in the 5th finger.

Clonic Seizure (See also Epilepsy)

Club Foot (See Talipes)

Clumsy Child Syndrome (See Dyspraxia)

Coarctation A condition of stricture or narrowing.

Cockayne Syndrome or **Cockayne Neill Dwarfism** Features include: normal growth and development for the first 2–4 years, with subsequent loss of fat resulting in a thin face with sunken eyes, abnormal pigmentation of the retina and optic atrophy, growth deficiency leading to short stature, stooped posture with limitation of movement in hips, knees and ankles, enlarged liver, scaly dermatitis of areas exposed to sunlight, lack of secondary sexual development, moderate to severe learning difficulty. Progressive. Autosomal recessive inheritance.

Coffin-Lowry Syndrome Features include: coarse facial features with downward slanting and widely spaced eyes, prominent brows, broad nose, large, soft hands with tapering fingers, flat feet, lax ligaments, spinal curvature, muscular weakness. Severe learning difficulty in males. Only a small proportion of affected females have severe learning difficulty, some have mild to moderate learning difficulty and the remainder are intellectually normal. X-linked inheritance.

Coffin-Siris Syndrome Features include: mild to moderate growth deficiency, microcephaly, coarse facial features with full lips, sparse scalp hair with profuse body hair, lax muscle tone and lax joints, underdeveloped or absent fifth finger and toe nails, moderate to severe learning difficulty. Cause not established.

COFS or **Cerebro-Oculo-Facio-Skeletal Syndrome** (See Pena Shokeir Syndrome, Type 3)

Cognition The mental faculty of under-

4

standing, perception and awareness. The characteristic of 'knowing'.

Cognitive Development The development and formation of concepts that follow a fixed pattern, normally emerging within certain stages of development; sensory-motor (0–2 years), pre-conceptual (2–4 years), intuitive (4–7 years), concrete operations (7–11 years), formal operations (11 years onwards). Cognitive development is an important focus of education combined with emotional, physical, moral, cultural and spiritual development.

Cohen Syndrome Features include: smaller than average size of head, high bridge of nose, downward slanting eyes and open mouth, low birth weight, delayed growth, lax muscle tone, long slender fingers and toes with webbing in some cases, deformities of knees, elbows and spine, visual defects, including short sight and squint. In some cases: undescended testicles, delayed puberty, seizures, heart valve defects. Mild to moderate learning difficulties. Autosomal recessive inheritance.

Colic Pain of a spasmodic nature, usually in the abdomen. (See Spasm)

Communication Systems (See Blissymbols, Makaton)

Community Homes Residential communities for people with learning difficulty. Usually based in rural areas, the homes are run as villages where all the residents and staff live and work together. Training is given in agriculture, horticulture, crafts, light industry and social skills.

Complex Partial Seizures or **Temporal Lobe Epilepsy** Seizures arising in the temporal lobe area of the brain, which controls the senses of smell, taste and sound. The patient has an aura which precedes the onset of the main seizure. This may take the form of an odd taste, strange odour or hallucination or there may be emotional sensations such as anger or excitement. There may be automatic, repeated actions. There is confusion and loss of memory after the seizure. (See also Epilepsy)

Conditioning or **Conditioned Reflex** A term used in behaviour modification to denote the training of an individual to respond to a specific stimulus, action or event which he or she is trained to associate with a particular behaviour.

Conduct Behaviour (See Emotional and Behavioural Difficulties)

Conductive Deafness Hearing loss due to impaired conduction of sound waves through the structures of the middle ear.

Congenital Present at birth.

Congenital Abnormality Pertaining to defects which are apparent at birth or soon after. Such defects may be hereditary or acquired. In the acquired form the defect is not inherited but is due to factors which affected the foetus during development.

Congenital Hypothyroidism (See Hypothyroidism, Congenital)

Congenital Suprabulbar Paresis (See Worster-Drought Syndrome)

Conradi-Hünermann Syndrome or **Chondrodysplasia Punctata** Features include: growth deficiency, flat face, asymmetric shortening of limbs, joint contractures, spinal curvature, large skin pores, sparse and coarse hair. Mild to moderate learning difficulty may occur, but is not present in most cases. X-linked dominant inheritance. (See also Rhizomelic Chondrodysplasia Punctata Symdrome)

Consanguinity Blood relationship; marriage between two related people.

Contagious Disease (See Disease)

Convulsion An episode of spasm in which there is alternating contraction and relaxation of muscle, causing irregular movements in a part, or of the whole body. Epilepsy is a common cause of convulsions.

Coordination The movement of the body and its parts harmoniously, in proper relationship to each other and in the correct sequence, under the governing influence of the brain and nervous system.

Cornelia de Lange Syndrome or **de Lange Syndrome** Features include: short, broad skull, bushy eyebrows and curly lashes, small nose, thin lips with down-turned corners, small chin, low pitched and husky voice, short stature, short limbs, small genital organs, lax muscle tone, mottled skin, eye defects, mild to severe learning difficulty. In some cases: cleft palate, absent digits, heart defects. Cause not established.

Coronal Suture The junction of the frontal and parietal bones of the skull, running across the top of the head, from side to side.

Corpus Callosum, Agenesis of Partial or complete absence of the corpus callosum. Features, which are variable, include: microcephaly or macrocephaly, moderate to severe learning difficulty. In some cases: seizures, sight defects, cleft lip and/or palate. (See Aicard Syndrome; FG Syndrome)

Court of Protection Where a person is incapable of managing his/her affairs through mental illness or learning difficulty, those affairs may be put into the hands of a Court of Protection. The Court will manage them while the individual is affected by the disability and/or will appoint a Receiver (usually a relative) to manage the person's affairs.

Coxa Vara A deformity of the hip in which the angle between the neck and the shaft of the thigh bone is decreased, resulting in a shortening and turning outward of the leg.

Cranio-Carpo-Tarsal Dysplasia (See Freeman-Sheldon Syndrome)

Craniofacial Dysostosis (See Crouzon Syndrome)

Craniosynostosis Premature fusion of two or more of the cranial bones. Normally, the bones of the cranium are separate at birth and grow together gradually in the first two years of life. Where two or more bones fuse too early there may be compensatory growth in other areas, resulting in an abnormal head shape. Craniosynostosis may occur as an isolated congenital abnormality or as part of a syndrome of multiple abnormalities. The shape of the skull is determined by variation in the time of fusion, the particular sutures involved and the extent of the fusion. Patients with one closure are almost always of normal intelligence. Individuals who have fusion of several bones are more likely to have varying degrees of learning difficulty. In some cases, early corrective surgery is done to improve appearance and possibly to prevent brain damage. (See also Acrocephaly; Brachycephaly; Dolicho-cephaly; Microcephaly; Oxycephaly: Scaphocephaly; Skull, Bones of the; Sutures of the Skull; Trigonocephaly; Turricephaly)

Craniosynostosis Disorders (See Apert Syndrome; Carpenter Syndrome; Crouzon Syndrome; Saethre-Chotzen Syndrome)

4

Cranium The bony cavity which encloses the brain, as distinguished from the framework of the face.

Cranium Bifidum A condition in which there is a gap between the bones of the skull, due to imperfect fusion. The defect is covered by the scalp, and is usually located on a line drawn down the middle of the skull. Where the defect is large, there may be protrusion of the meninges and sometimes of the substance of the brain. If the protrusion contains only spinal fluid, it is termed a meningocele. If it contains brain tissue, it is termed an encephalocele or meningoencephalocele. In many cases, a meningocele can be surgically removed, leaving the intellect unimpaired. Because of the involvement of neural tissue an encephalocele carries a higher surgical risk, with resulting sight loss, spasticity and skeletal defects in some cases.

Cri du Chat Syndrome or **5p-Syndrome, Lejeune Syndrome** (See Chromosome Abnormality Syndromes)

Crouzon Syndrome or **Craniofacial Dysostosis** Features include: skull with short front to back diameter, widely spaced eyes, underdeveloped nasal bridge and jaw, a normal chin which may appear prominent, high narrow palate, prominent and widely spaced teeth. In some cases: squint, hearing loss. Mild to moderate learning difficulty may occur, but is not present in most cases. Correction of skull deformities can be done in infancy. Autosomal dominant inheritance. (See also Craniosynostosis; Skull, Bones of the; Sutures of the Skull)

Cryptophthalmos Syndrome or **Fraser Syndrome** Cryptophthalmos means 'hidden eye'. Features include: a fold of skin covering one or both eyes, ear deformities, high arched palate, cleft lip and palate, webbing of digits. In some cases: facial abnormalities, genitourinary abnormalities, mild to severe learning difficulty. Autosomal recessive inheritance.

Cryptorchidism Undescended testicles; a condition in which the testicles, instead of descending into the scrotum, remain within the lower abdomen. A feature of a number of multiple abnormality syndromes.

Cued Speech A supportive language approach for people of all ages and all degrees of hearing loss. Compatible with both lip-reading and sign language, cued speech identifies all the sounds of speech by using eight simple hand-shapes on the hand to represent consonant sounds and four positions near the lips to represent vowel sounds.

Cycloplegia Paralysis of the ciliary muscle of the eye, resulting in loss of the power of accommodation.

Cystic Fibrosis Also known as fibrocystic disease of the pancreas, cystic fibrosis is a disorder of the mucus secreting glands of the lungs, pancreas, mouth, sweat glands and gastro intestinal tract. Treatment involves physiotherapy, postural drainage and medication.

Cytomegalovirus Infection An organism causing a common infectious disease, which, when contracted during pregnancy, can cause damage to the unborn infant. Damage does not occur in every case. Some infants have no signs of infection and normal development, some with signs of infection have no effects, some with no immediate signs later show signs of the infection. Features, which are variable, include: microcephaly (either evident at birth or not until later), choreoretinitis, enlargement of the liver, hernias, jaundice, low birth weight. In some cases: hyperactivity, mild to severe spasticity, deafness, mild to severe learning difficulty.

Dandy-Walker Syndrome Hydrocephalus and enlargement of the head due to the presence of cysts in the fourth ventricle of the brain. In some cases the enlarged head is apparent at birth, in others the head is normal at birth with rapid enlargement occurring in the first year. Features include: prominent occiput and brow, slow psychomotor development. In some cases: seizures, lax muscle tone. Early surgical treatment can sometimes result in normal development. Autosomal recessive inheritance. (See also Hydrocephalus)

Deaf/Blind (See Dual Sensory Impairment)

Deep Tendon Reflex The involuntary response of muscle to an external stimulus which results from the state of mild contraction of muscle when at rest, e.g. the jerk of the knee when the tendon of its muscle is tapped. Nervous system disorder may result in loss of reflexes or in an excessive reaction.

Deficiency Disease (See Disease)

Degenerative Disease (See Disease)

De Grouchy Syndrome or **18p- Syndrome** (See Chromosome Abnormality Syndromes)

De Lange Syndrome (See Cornelia De Lange Syndrome)

Deletion of Chromosomes (See Chromosome Abnormality; Chromosome Abnormality, Nomenclature; Chromosome Abnormality Syndromes)

Delta Waves (See Electroencephalography)

Dementia Impairment of the intellect acquired as a result of disease or damage to the brain. Used to contrast with the term amentia, which pertains to learning difficulty arising from a lack of normal intellectual development from birth or infancy.

Demyelinisation Degeneration of the myelin sheath, the fatty covering of nerve fibres.

Dermal Ridges The markings and creases on the palms of the hands, soles of the feet and digits, produced by skin ridges, which form in the foetus between the 13th and 19th weeks. The three basic patterns on the fingertips, palms and soles are termed the arch, the loop and the whorl. The point at which three different ridges meet is termed a triradius. Abnormal patterns may occur in chromosome abnormality disorders, gene mutation or teratogen disorders. While there is an abnormal dermal pattern in many chromosomal abnormalities, no pattern is specific to any one syndrome. (See also Flexion Creases; Ridge Count; Simian Crease)

Dermoid Cyst A cyst which contains skin tissue. May be congenital or acquired.

De Sanctis-Cacchione Syndrome or **Xeroderma Pigmentosa with Learning Disability** Features include: growth deficiency, microcephaly, variable spasticity and seizures, lack of coordination, sensitivity to sunlight, wart-like lesions and other skin eruptions, progressive skin deterioration with predisposition to malignancy, mild to severe learning difficulty. Autosomal recessive inheritance.

Developmental Age The stage of normal development reached by an individual, regardless of his or her chronological age.

Dexterity Manual skill; efficient use of the hands.

Diabetes A disease characterised by excessive passing of urine. Diabetes insipidus is

4

accompanied by great thirst and is treated by medication. Diabetes mellitus is a disturbance of the body's utilisation of glucose. Treatment involves keeping blood glucose and lipid levels within normal limits.

Diagnosis The process of distinguishing one disease from another. Clinical diagnosis; that made from the study of actual symptoms. Differential diagnosis; that made by comparing and contrasting the symptoms with those of other disorders which are similar.

Diaphyseal Dysplasia, Progressive (See Engelmann Disease)

Diastolic Murmur (See Murmur)

Differential Diagnosis (See Diagnosis)

Diffuse Angiokeratoma (See Fabry Syndrome)

Diffuse Cerebral Sclerosis (See Adrenoleukodystrophy)

Dilatin Syndrome, Foetal Features include: growth deficiency, widely spaced eyes, flat nose, cleft lip and/or palate, missing or underdeveloped nails, rib defects, heart defects, learning difficulty. Due to the teratogenic effects on the unborn foetus, of maternal ingestion of the anticonvulsant drug, Phenytoin (Dilatin) in pregnancy.

Diplegia Paralysis of corresponding parts on either side of the body. All four limbs may be affected but it occurs more commonly in the legs than in the arms. (See Little Disease)

Diplopia Double vision.

Disease Any interference with normal health. **Contagious disease**; one which can be transmitted from one person to another by direct contact. **Deficiency disease**; one which is due to a lack of vitamins or other substance essential to health. **Degenerative disease**; one in which there is deterioration of tissues. **Functional disease**; one which intereferes with the function of an organ without structural change occurring in that organ. **Infective disease**; one which is due to a specific organism and can be transmitted to others. **Malignant disease**; one in which there are severe symptoms with progressive deterioration and which is likely to be fatal. **Metabolic disease**; one in which there is faulty digestion, absorption or assimilation of food or impaired cell function. **Organic disease**; one which produces structural change in an organ and is of a physical rather than a psychological nature. **Secondary disease**; one which results from another (primary) disease.

DNA The abbreviation for deoxyribonucleic acid; the essential 'building blocks' for all genetic material.

Dolichocephaly Long-headed; a skull which is abnormally long in its front to back dimension. (See also Craniosynostosis; Skull, Bones of the; Sutures of the Skull)

Doman Delacato A method of treatment developed in the USA. It is based on intensive sensory stimulation, with the aim of enabling healthy brain cells in brain injured children to take over from the damaged ones.

Dominant Inheritance (See Autosomal Dominant Disorder)

Donohue Syndrome or **Leprechaunism Syndrome** Features include: growth deficiency with emaciated appearance, broad nose with flaring nostrils, eyes which appear large, receding chin, thick lips, large low set ears, sparse subcutaneous fat, loose wrinkled skin, hands and feet large in proportion to the limbs, clinodactyly, genital defects, hernias, slow psychomotor development, feeding problems. Life expectancy not usually exceeding infancy. May be due to cellular resistance to insulin. Autosomal recessive inheritance.

Down Syndrome or **Down's Syndrome** or **Trisomy 21 Syndrome (21+)** The most common chromosomal disorder associated with learning disability. The characteristic features found in individuals with Down syndrome were first described by John Langdon Down in 1866. In 1959, Professor Lejeune proved that Down syndrome is a genetic condition caused by an extra number 21 chromosome. There are three types of Down syndrome: 95% of affected individuals have the type known as standard trisomy 21 (Type 1) in which there is a whole extra chromosome 21 in every cell. There is no known reason why it occurs. Approximately 1 in 100 have the translocation type (Type 2) in which affected individuals inherit the condition from their mother or father because of a translocation: part or all of chromosome 21 is translocated to another chromosome, usually number 14. Mosaic trisomy 21 (Type 3) is also rare. This occurs when faulty cell division results in some cells having 46 chromosomes and some having 47. The percentage of cells carrying 47 chromosomes instead of 46 varies from person to person. (See also Chromosome Abnormality; Chromosome Abnormality Syndromes)

D. Trisomy or **13+ Syndrome, Patau Syndrome** (See Chromosome Abnormality Syndromes)

Dual Sensory Impairment A combination of impairment of sight and hearing. In some cases the sensory impairment is combined with physical disability and/or learning disability. In educating children with dual sensory impairment, it is important to make an early rigorous assessment, to support and educate parents and to give specialised provision and teaching.

Dubowitz Syndrome Features include: growth deficiency, high pitched and hoarse cry, mild microcephaly, small face with small jaw, widely spaced eyes with underdeveloped or drooping lids, sparse hair on scalp and outer edges of eyebrows, eczema-like skin disorder, mild learning difficulty. Autosomal recessive inheritance.

Duchenne Muscular Dystrophy Features include: onset between 1 and 6 years, manifesting as clumsiness, falling, unusual gait, Gower sign, enlarged thigh muscles with progressive weakness and wasting, tightness of heel tendons, weakness of joints, respiratory problems, learning difficulty in about one third of cases. The disease occurs only in boys. X-linked inheritance.

Ductless Gland A gland without a duct. The term is applied to any one of certain glands whose secretion is absorbed directly into the bloodstream, which conveys it to different parts of the body. Several of the endocrine glands are of this type.

Ductus Arteriosus The passage which connects the pulmonary artery and the aorta in the foetus. This normally closes at birth, ceases to function, and is converted into a fibrous cord. **Patent ductus arteriosus:** One of the most common congenital heart defects, in which the ductus arteriosus fails to close at birth. Responds well to surgical correction.

Duration Recording A term used in behaviour modification to denote a measurement of the length of time an individual is occupied in a particular task or activity.

Dwarfism Short stature; arrested growth.

4

It may be proportionate or disproportionate.

Dysarthria Speech impairment or difficulty with the pronunciation of words. Due to disease of the muscles or nerves concerned with the mechanisms of speech or disorder of the central nervous system.

Dysautonomia, Familial (See Riley-Day Syndrome)

Dyscalculia Difficulty with mathematics generally but particularly with arithmetical operations. (See Specific Learning Difficulty)

Dysgenesis Impaired or faulty development.

Dysgraphia Difficulty with writing.

Dyslalia The use of infantile forms of speech to an abnormally late age.

Dyslexia Difficulty in the interpretation of written language in a person who has no visual impairment, hearing impairment or intellectual impairment. Confusion of letters may lead to difficulties in other areas, such as arithmetic, but spelling is not necessarily impaired. Affected children may be unable to distinguish right from left. Reading is slow and hesitant and the child may substitute words for those they are unable to read. The child may show frustration, aggression and difficulty with forming social relationships with his/her peers. Intellectual ability and sensory perception are usually unaffected. (See Specific Learning Diffculty)

Dysmorphia Faulty development; an abnormality.

Dysostosis Faulty or defective formation of bone.

Dysphagia Difficulty in swallowing.

Dysphasia Difficulty in speaking clearly, not amounting to total loss of speech.

Dysphonia Difficulty in controlling voice production.

Dysplasia Faulty or abnormal development of a body part.

Dyspnoea Difficulty in breathing.

Dyspraxia A disorder in which there is impaired or immature development of movement skills, understanding of language and thought processes. Motor skills, such as catching, throwing and construction may be difficult and the child may be regarded as 'clumsy'. He or she may find it difficult to understand sensory information and to relate it to actions and to plan and organise their thoughts. The cause is thought to be an immaturity of brain function rather than damage to the brain. Also known as 'Clumsy child' syndrome, minimal brain dysfunction or perceptuo-motor dysfunction.

Dyssynergia Jerky, disconnected movement.

Dystaxia Difficulty with the control of movement.

Dystonia Impaired or abnormal muscular tension, resulting in involuntary spasmodic movements and loss of function. It may be generalised or restricted to one part of the body.

Dystrophia or **Dystrophy** A term meaning defective or faulty nutrition. Generally applied to some developmental change in the muscles, occurring independently of the nervous system, resulting in degeneration and loss of function.

Dystrophia Myotonica (See Myotonic Dystrophy)

Echolalia Meaningless repetition by an individual of words spoken to him or her.

Echopraxia Repetition by an individual of actions observed by him or her.

Eclampsia The general term for epilepsy of sudden onset. Often used to refer to convulsions associated with high blood pressure in pregnancy.

Ectasia or **Ectasis** Abnormal stretching or dilation.

Ecthyma A skin disorder in which there is an eruption of pimples with a hardened base. The result of inflammation.

Ectopia Lentis Displacement of the lens of the eye.

Ectrodactyly or **Ectrodactylia** Congenital absence of the middle digit/s of the hands or feet.

Ectromelia Congenital shortening or absence of a limb or limbs.

Ectropion Contraction of the skin of the eyelid (usually the lower), causing the lid to be turned inside out.

Eczema A superficial disorder of the skin, resulting in small blisters. These burst and leave a red raw surface, which dries, cracks and itches. May be caused by local irritation or allergy.

Edema (See Oedema)

Edwards Syndrome or **18+ Syndrome** (See Chromosome Abnormality Syndromes)

EEG (See Electroencephalography)

Elective or **Selective Mutism** A rare disorder, slightly more frequent in females than in males, in which a child chooses not to speak in a social setting, though comprehension and verbal ability are usually intact. Affected children may talk normally at home but refuse to speak at school. However, in some cases, speech is withheld in all social environments. Some children may resort to the use of gesture or words of one syllable. Temper tantrums and negative behaviour may affect the child's progress in school and his or her social life. The condition may persist for a period of weeks or months but in a small number of cases it has been found to continue for several years. The condition may be caused by trauma (such as hospitalisation) at an early age, language or speech disorder or learning difficulty. Elective mutism may be present before the age of 5 years but may not become apparent until the child starts school.

Electroencephalogram or **EEG** (See Electroencephalography)

Electroencephalography A system of recording the rhythmic waves of electric energy discharged by the nerve cells in the brain. Normal waves (alpha waves) occur with a frequency between 8–12 per second, abnormal waves (delta waves) with a frequency of 7 per second, or less. Abnormal waves occur in cases of brain tumour and in epilepsy. The tracing produced is termed an electroencephalogram. (See also Epilepsy; Hypsarrhythmia)

Electro-Oculography (See Electroretinogram)

Electroretinogram The method of recording movements of the eye, usually to assess the functioning of the retina. Formerly called electro-oculography.

Ellis van Creveld Syndrome or **Chondroectodermal Dysplasia** Features include: short stature, short limbs, small chest, extra fingers, small or absent nails, thin sparse hair, underdevelopment or absence of teeth with either premature or delayed eruption. In some cases: extra toes, heart defects, breathing problems. Mild to moderate learning difficulty may occur but

4

intelligence is usually within the normal range. Autosomal recessive inheritance.

Emotional and Behavioural Difficulties
A range of difficulties including anxiety, phobia, obsessive/compulsive behaviour, withdrawal, depression, hypochondria (neurotic behaviour), disruption, aggression, lack of cooperation, inattentiveness, delinquency (antisocial behaviour), bizarre thoughts and behaviour, lack of contact with reality, disorderliness of thought and action (psychotic behaviour). Some children with emotional and behavioural difficulties may be particularly vulnerable or disruptive in school and will require educational provision geared to their particular needs.

> **Educational implications** Psychotherapy, behaviour therapy or counselling may be built into the school's provision as necessary. Children with emotional and behavioural difficulties benefit from various forms of therapy including play therapy, music therapy, drama therapy, art therapy and so on. Also, they may benefit from certain aspects of the curriculum which allow the release and expression of emotions, such as art, drama and dance. However, insecure children may be drawn to the more predictable and secure aspects of provision such as mathematics and science.

> **Medical implications** Certain medical conditions may, unless action is taken, adversely affect a child's academic attainment and may lead to emotional and behavioural difficulties. The conditions may restrict the child's ability to take part in the school curriculum. The effects of medication may make education more difficult. Children with conditions such as cystic fibrosis may have periods in hospital and may develop emotional and behavioural

difficulties because of restrictions imposed by the condition or because of the nature of the treatment required. Care should be taken that the child is not excluded from any curriculum activity because of anxiety about the child's care or treatment.

Emprosthotonus A muscular spasm in which the body arches forward. (See Opisthotonus)

Encephalitis Inflammation of the substance of the brain. A frequent cause of learning difficulty or impairment of intellectual function. Usually caused by a viral infection and may be a complication of one of the common infectious diseases, e.g. measles.

Encephalocele Protrusion of a portion of the brain through the bones of the skull. (See Cranium Bifidum)

Encephaloma *pl. encephalomata* Tumour of the brain.

Encephalomyelitis Inflammation of the brain and spinal cord.

Encephalomyelopathy Disease of the brain and spinal cord.

Encephalopathy Acute or chronic disturbance of brain function.

Encephalopathy, Infantile Subacute (See Leigh Disease)

Enchondroma *pl. enchondromata* A tumour composed of cartilaginous tissue, within the shaft of a bone.

Encopresis Involuntary excretion of faeces, i.e. the waste matter content of the bowel.

Endocarditis Inflammation of the lining of the heart.

Engelmann Disease or **Diaphyseal Dysplasia, Progressive** Features, which are variable, include: progressive thickening of bone, small face with prominent eyes and forehead, flat nasal bridge, leg pains, weak muscles, delay in sexual maturation. In some cases: curvature of the spine, long thin arms, small hands and feet, full rounded lower legs, sight defects, hearing loss, knock knee. Mild learning difficulty may occur, but intelligence is unimpaired in most cases. Autosomal dominant inheritance.

Enophthalmos Abnormal withdrawal of the eye into its socket.

Entropion Turning inward of the margin of the eyelid, so that the lashes rub against the ball of the eye.

Enuresis Involuntary passing of urine.

Enzyme, Deficient Activity of Where there is defective activity or absence of an enzyme or enzymes, the breaking down of substances in the body is interfered with. This results in the accumulation and/or deficiency of essential substances, which may result in physical disorder and, in some cases, varying degrees of intellectual impairment. (See also Inborn Error of Metabolism)

Epicanthic Fold or **Epicanthal Fold** A small vertical fold of skin on the inner angle of the eye (canthus) from the upper eyelid to the beginning of the nose. Usually secondary to a low nasal bridge. A characteristic of a number of disorders, including Down syndrome, but also found frequently in normal individuals.

Epicanthus An alternative term for epicanthic fold.

Epilepsy A sudden discharge of energy from the brain, resulting in convulsions and mild to severe changes in the level of consciousness. **Grand mal**; a major attack in which there is loss of consciousness and convulsions. **Infantile spasm**; brief episodes of muscle spasm. **Petit mal**; a fleeting and momentary absence of awareness, without convulsions, occurring singly or in sequence. **Salaam spasm**; an attack in which the patient suddenly falls forward with arms stiff and outstretched. In educating children with epilepsy, the teacher should be aware of drowsiness and inattention and repeat missed material as necessary. Care is needed with risky physical activities. (See also Absence Seizure; Atonic Seizure; Aura; Complex Partial Seizure; Electroencephalography; Hypsarrythmia; Infantile Spasm; Jacksonian Epilepsy; Landau-Kleffner Syndrome; Lennox-Gastaut Syndrome; Myoclonic Seizure; Pyknolepsy; Status Epilepticus; Tonic Seizure; West Syndrome)

Epiloia (See Tuberous Scleroris)

Epiphora Watering of the eye or an overflow of tears due to obstruction of the tear duct.

Epiphysitis Inflammation at the end of a long bone, just outside a joint.

Epispadias An abnormal opening on the upper side of the penis.

Epithelioma *pl. epitheliomata* A malignant tumour arising in the epithelium.

Equinovarus (See Talipes)

Equinus (See Talipes)

Esotropia Convergent squint.

Exanthematous The term used to refer to a disease which is accompanied by a skin eruption.

Exomphalos Umbilical hernia; a membrane-covered protrusion of the abdominal organs through the umbilicus.

Exophthalmic Goitre A disorder in which there is enlargement of the thyroid gland, resulting in protrusion of the eyes

4

and swelling in the front of the neck. Usually caused by deficiency of iodine in the diet or overactivity of thyroid function.

Exostosis *pl. exostoses* A bony outgrowth from the surface of a bone, usually at the junction of the extremity with the shaft. Occasionally inherited.

Expressive Language Communication by gesture, spoken word, signing etc.

Extensor Reflex Involuntary straightening (extension) of a part when tapped or stroked, e.g. the straightening of the leg when the tendon of the knee is tapped.

Extinction A term used in behaviour modification for the holding back of a reward so that a particular behaviour decreases in frequency or a learned response is eliminated.

Fabry Syndrome or **Anderson-Fabry Disease, Diffuse Angiokeratoma** A disorder of lipid metabolism. Features, which are variable, include: onset in childhood or adulthood, corneal opacities, burning pain in the hands and feet, clusters of small dark lesions around the knees, hips and genital area, progressive kidney disorder. In some cases: seizures, attacks of fever, blood and blood vessel disorders, partial paralysis, loss of previously acquired skills due to cerebral complications.

Facies The expression or appearance of the face, often an indication of the presence of a general disorder or abnormality, or of disease in other parts of the body.

Fading A term used in behaviour modification for the gradual removal of cues, prompts or rewards during teaching sessions, so that the desired behaviour begins to be produced without prompting.

Familial The term used to describe a disease or disability which affects several members of the same family.

Familial Cerebellar Vermis Agenesis (See Joubert Syndrome)

Familial Dysautonomia (See Riley-Day Syndrome)

Familial Neurovisceral Lipidosis (See Gangliosidosis, Generalised)

Fanconi Anaemia or **Fanconi Pancytopenia Syndrome** Features include: small stature, microcephaly, underdeveloped or absent thumb, pallor, respiratory infections and bleeding under the skin, brownish colouring of the skin, small penis and testes and sometimes undescended testes in males. In some cases: eye defects, hearing defects, heart defects, skeletal defects, learning difficulty. Formerly life expectancy was limited to 2 years after the onset of the pancytopenia, but treatment is now available which can prolong life. Autosomal recessive inheritance.

Farber Lipogranulomatosis A disorder of lipid metabolism. Features include: onset in the first months of life with swelling of the joints of the hands and later of the knees, wrists and ankles, hoarse cry, nodules under the skin, enlargement of lymph nodes, degeneration of brain cells. Intellectual deterioration in most cases. Progressive, with life expectancy not exceeding infancy in severe cases.

Fatty Degeneration Abnormal changes in the body cells due to the appearance in them of fat droplets. May be a result of defective nerve or blood supply.

Febrile Convulsion A seizure induced by fever.

F G Syndrome or **Opitz-Kaveggia Syndrome** Features include: short stature, disproportionately large head, upward sweep of frontal hair, small underdeveloped ears, broad big toes, joint contractures, lax muscle tone, imperforate anus, heart defects, seizures, partial absence of the corpus callosum, moderate to severe learning difficulty. All reported cases have been males but some female carriers may have certain physical characteristics related to FG syndrome. X-linked inheritance.

Fibrillary Tremor (See Tremor)

Fibrillation Quivering, twitching contraction of muscle fibres, acting singly or in isolated groups instead of together.

Fibrosis Formation of fibrous or scar tissue in place of normal tissue.

Fibrous Dysplasia An uncommon disease in which areas of bone are replaced by fibrous tissue, rendering the bone fragile and easily fractured. May involve only one bone or several.

Fine Motor Skills (See Motor Skills)

Fistula An abnormal channel connecting the cavity of one organ with another, or of a cavity and the surface of the body, where none should exist.

Fit A convulsion or seizure. (See Epilepsy)

Flat Foot (See Pes Planus)

Flexion Creases Creases upon the palm of the hand, sole of the foot and digits. There are usually three flexion creases on the palm, two on each finger and one on each thumb. These creases denote the attachment of the skin to the structures beneath. (See also Dermal Ridges; Ridge Count; Simian Crease)

Flexion Spasm Muscular spasm in a limb or part, causing it to bend.

Floating Harbor Syndrome Named after an American hospital where the syndrome was first observed. Features include: growth delay becoming apparent in infancy, bone age delay giving the impression of a relatively large head while limbs remain in proportion, distinctive facial features developing in infancy, broad nose, wide mouth with thin lips, deep set eyes,

abnormally long eyelashes and small triangular shaped face, dental abnormalities, delayed language development. In some cases: inward curving of the fifth finger, clubbing of fingers, excessive hair growth. Mild learning difficulty is present in some cases. Cause not known.

Focal Epilepsy (See Jacksonian Epilepsy)

Focal Dermal Hypoplasia (See Goltz Syndrome)

Foetal Alcohol Effects or **Foetal Alcohol Syndrome** (See Alcohol Effects, Foetal)

Foetal Dilatin Syndrome (See Dilatin Syndrome, Foetal)

Foetal Hydantoin Effects or **Foetal Hydantoin Syndrome** (See Hydantoin Effects, Foetal)

Foetal Rubella Effects (See Rubella Effects, Foetal)

Foetal Trimethadione Effects or **Foetal Trimethadione Syndrome** (See Trimethadione Effects, Foetal)

Foetal Varicella Effects (See Varicella Effects, Foetal)

Foetal Warfarin Effects or **Foetal Warfarin Syndrome** (See Warfarin Effects, Foetal)

Fontanelle (See Skull, Bones of the; Sutures of the Skull)

Formes Fruste The term used to describe a disorder when it occurs in a form in which the features are not typical of that disorder.

Fragile-X Syndrome or **Martin-Bell Syndrome, Renpenning Syndrome** Features include: increased growth in childhood, large head with elongated face, prominent jaw, long ears, lax muscle tone, hyperextensible joints, poor coordination, hyperactivity, mild to severe learning

4

difficulty and speech problems in males. In some cases; enlarged testicles, mitral heart valve defect, seizures. Carrier females may be unaffected but some may have mild speech and learning difficulty. Due to the breaking off of the bottom tip of an X chromosome, making it appear fragile. (See also Chromosome Abnormality)

Franceschetti-Klein-Syndrome (See Treacher-Collins Syndrome)

Fraser Syndrome (See Cryptophthalmos Syndrome)

Freeman-Sheldon Syndrome or **Cranio-Carpo-Tarsal Dysplasia** Features include: expressionless face with small, tightly pursed mouth, deep set eyes, squint, drooping eyelids, small nose with broad bridge, dimpling on chin, high palate, small tongue, tendency to nasal speech, flexion of fingers, club foot, hernia, undescended testicles. Mild learning difficulty may be present, but intelligence is usually within the normal range. In some cases: small stature, curvature of spine. Autosomal dominant inheritance in most cases but autosomal recessive inheritance has been found in some families.

Frequency Recording A term used in behaviour modification to describe the recording of the number of times a particular behaviour occurs within a specific time.

Frolich Syndrome A disorder in children caused by disturbed pituitary function, results in sluggishness, obesity and delayed sexual development. A feature of Laurence-Moon-Bardet-Beidl syndrome.

Frontal Bone The bone of the forehead which protects the frontal lobes of the brain.

Frontonasal Dysplasia Sequence (See Median Cleft Face Syndrome)

Fucosidosis A disorder of carbohydrate metabolism. Features include: normal development for several months followed by neurological deterioration, broad nose, thick lips with enlarged tongue and salivary glands, thick skin with abundant sweating, spinal curvature, spasticity, loss of previously acquired skills due to cerebral complications. Autosomal recessive inheritance.

Functional Disease (See Disease)

Fusion Defects of the Skull (See Craniosynostosis; Cranium Bifidum; Skull, Bones of the; Sutures of the Skull, Premature Closure of Several)

Gait The manner of walking. **Ataxic gait**; a clumsy and jerky walk with uncoordinated movement. **Spastic gait**; a stiff, spasmodic walk in which the foot is raised high and placed down heavily.

Galactosaemia A disorder of carbohydrate metabolism. Diagnosis and dietary treatment from birth results in improvement of physical effects and normal or near normal growth and development. In untreated cases, features include: weight loss, jaundice, anaemia, enlargement of liver, cataracts, weakness, lax muscle tone, loss of skills due to neurological deterioration. Autosomal recessive inheritance.

Gamma Globulin An antibody, carried in the blood, which provides immunity against certain infectious diseases, e.g. measles. Formerly, it was given to pregnant mothers who were exposed to or developed rubella (German measles). Inoculation of teenage girls as a preventative measure against rubella is now the preferred approach. Also used in the prevention of Rhesus incompatibility. (See Rhesus Factor)

Gangliosidosis, Generalised (GM1) or **Familial Neurovisceral Lipidosis** A disorder of lipid metabolism. In the infantile type, features include: growth deficiency, lax muscle tone, feeding problems, coarse facial features, liver enlargement, progressive bone changes, joint limitation, flexion contractures of elbows, fingers and hands. In some cases: mild intellectual and motor impairment, a red spot in the eye. Progressive. Autosomal recessive inheritance.

Gangliosidosis (GM2) (See Tay Sachs Disease)

Gaucher Disease or **Cerebroside Lipidosis** A disorder of lipid metabolism. Features include: **Non-cerebral, juvenile type (Type 1)**: onset in childhood, adolescence or adulthood, with enlargement of spleen, bruising and fractures. **Cerebral, infantile type (Type 2)**: neurological deterioration noticed in the first months, backward positioning of the head, facial weakness, squint, feeding difficulties, lax muscle tone, enlargement of liver and spleen producing an enlarged abdomen, degeneration of the nervous system, severe intellectual impairment. Life expectancy limited to infancy in most cases. **Subacute neuronopathic type (Type 3)**: A rare form of the disease in which the symptoms and signs are similar to those of Type 2 but milder and later in onset. Autosomal recessive inheritance.

Genes Units of hereditary material which are arranged along the length of chromosomes. Genes determine foetal development, characteristics, growth and function.

Genetic Counselling Information and support provided by a specialist doctor and his or her team, to parents who may be at risk of producing a child with a disability. Parents are advised to seek genetic counselling if there is a known disorder in the family or if they have already had a child

with a disability and there is a possibility that subsequent children will also be affected.

Genotype The genetic composition of an individual.

Genu Valgum A deformity of the lower limbs in which the legs turn away from each other when they are straightened, with the result that the knees knock together.

Genu Varum Bow leg.

German Measles (See Rubella; Rubella Effects, Foetal)

Giantism Abnormal and excessive growth of the body.

Giantism, Cerebral (See Sotos Syndrome)

Gibbus Humped back.

Gifted Children (See Able Children)

Glaucoma An abnormal increase of pressure within the eyeball, which may progress and lead to blindness. It is due to a building up of fluid in the eye as a result of blockage of the drainage duct, or to an excessive amount of fluid.

Glioma *pl. gliomata* A tumour of the brain or spinal cord, composed of neuroglia, the connective tissue which supports the nerve cells and nerve fibres.

Globoid Cell Leukodystrophy or **Krabbe Disease** A disorder of lipid metabolism. Features include: normal development for several months with onset of irritability and spasm at 4–6 months, development of an abnormal posture in which the arms are rigidly bent and the legs held stiff and straight, attacks of high fever and sweating, excessive salivation, deterioration of voluntary movements, optic atrophy, seizures. Progressive, with life expectancy not usually exceeding 5 years. Autosomal recessive inheritance.

4

Glossitis Inflammation of the tongue.

Glycogen Storage Disease, Type 2 or **Pompe Disease** A disorder of carbohydrate metabolism. Features include: **Infantile form**: onset at birth or within a few months, feeding difficulties, lack of or loss of motor skills, enlarged and protruding tongue, firm and enlarged muscles lacking in tone, muscular weakness, facial paralysis, enlargement of heart and liver. Progressive, with life expectancy not exceeding infancy in most cases. **Childhood form**: onset of symptoms in late infancy or early childhood, slower rate of progression than in the infantile form, muscular weakness, minimal cardiac involvement, variable organ involvement. Survival into the teens in most cases. Autosomal recessive inheritance.

Goitre (See Exophthalmic Goitre)

Goldenhar Syndrome or **Hemifacial Microsomia** Features, which are variable, include: underdevelopment of one side of the face involving the cheek bone, jaw and ear, skin tags in front of the ear, vertebral abnormalities. In some cases: hearing loss, lesions on the eye and other eye defects, limb abnormalities, heart defects, lung defects. Mild learning difficulty may occur but intellect is unimpaired in most cases. Usually sporadic.

Goltz Syndrome or **Focal Dermal Hypoplasia** Features include: areas of thin skin with a fatty layer bulging through, altered pigmentation of the skin with nodules around the lips and anus, irregular and underdeveloped teeth, eye defects, poorly formed nails, webbing of fingers and/or toes, eye abnormalities. In some cases: deafness, mild to moderate learning difficulty. X-linked dominant inheritance proposed.

Gonadal Dysgenesis Impaired development of the gonads, which are the male or female sex glands, i.e. ovaries or testes.

Gonadotrophins The hormones which stimulate the function of the gonads (the ovaries and testes). They control the secretion of testosterone and the production of sperm in the male and the secretion of oestrogen and progesterone and the production of ova in the female.

Gorlin Syndrome (See Basal Cell Naevus Syndrome)

Gower Sign A procedure in which an individual raises themselves from the floor by putting their hands onto their knees to keep the legs extended, then pushes the trunk upward by 'walking' the hands up the thighs. A feature of some muscular disorders, including Duchenne muscular dystrophy.

Grand Mal A convulsive epileptic attack of the more severe type. (See also Epilepsy)

Griffiths Scales A series of scales designed to assess the level of normal development in movement, social behaviour, sight, hand-eye coordination and speech in infants and young children.

Gross Motor Skills (See Motor Skills)

Group G Monosomy and Ring G (See Chromosome Abnormality Syndromes)

Growth Hormone A hormone produced by the pituitary gland. Deficiency of the hormone causes retarded growth, an excessive production results in increased growth.

Guthrie Test A biological method of detecting phenylketonuria in a sample of blood. Used for the mass screening of infants for early detection of the disorder.

Gynaecomastia Abnormal increase in size of the male breast. Sometimes a feature of Klinefelter syndrome.

Haemophilia A hereditary disease characterised by a tendency to excessive bleeding even after slight injuries. Recurrent bleeding to the joints can lead to physical disability. Treatment of bleeding is through the intravenous administration of an antihaemophiliac factor (Factor 8). At school, the child would avoid heavy physical contact sports but would be able to participate in sports such as running or swimming.

Hallermann-Streiff Syndrome or **Oculomandibulodyscephaly with Hypotrichosis Syndrome** Features include: short stature, short broad skull, beaked tip of nose in infants and long thin nose in older individuals, severely underdeveloped lower jaw producing a small chin, eye defects, including squint and nystagmus, sparse hair of scalp, eyebrows and eyelashes, thin and tense skin on face and scalp, low set ears, malformed/underdeveloped/absent teeth, hyperextensible joints, small penis and undescended testicles in males, feeding and breathing problems. Intellect is usually unimpaired but moderate to severe learning difficulty occurs in some cases. Autosomal dominant inheritance proposed.

Hallucination A disorder of perception which causes an individual to see, hear or sense something which has no actual existence.

Hallux Valgus Bending of the big toe towards the other toes, to an abnormal degree.

Hallux Varus Bending of the big toe outwards, towards the other foot.

Hamartoma *pl. hamartomata* A developmental defect resulting in an abnormal mixture of tissues, often with a tumour-like excess of one or more tissues.

Hand-Eye Coordination The ability to coordinate movement of the hands according to a specific visual task, e.g. the threading of a needle.

Hare Lip A notch of the upper lip; cleft lip. Often associated with cleft palate.

Hartnup Disease A disorder of amino acid metabolism. Features, which are variable, include: onset in childhood with the appearance of an inflamed rash on the face, hands and feet on exposure to sunlight, later healing to leave areas of brown discolouration. In some cases: ataxia, eye defects, tremor, mild to moderate learning difficulty. Nicotinamide therapy may improve the symptoms and in some cases the disorder improves without treatment. Autosomal recessive inheritance.

Hearing Impairment Complete or partial loss of the sense of hearing, which may be caused by damage to the inner ear and/or auditory nerves, often affecting the hearing of higher frequencies more than that of lower frequencies (sensori-neural hearing loss) or as a result of middle ear infection, malformations of the inner ear or obstruction of the middle ear impairing the transmission of sound into the middle ear system and affecting all levels of sound frequency (conductive hearing loss). If a pupil with hearing impairment is taught in a mainstream school, support will be necessary from specialist teachers and audiologists. The appropriate form of communication should be used, i.e. speech, sign language or both.

Hemianopia Loss of half the usual field of vision.

Hemiatrophy Wasting of half of the body or half a part of the body (e.g. the face) resulting in one side being smaller than the other. May be due to faulty development or a result of nervous system disorder.

Hemifacial Microsomia (See Goldenhar Syndrome)

Hemihypertrophy Overdevelopment or overgrowth of one side of the body or a part of the body, so that one side is larger the other.

Hemimegalencephaly A rare brain malformation in which an entire cerebral hemisphere is enlarged. Features include: seizures in infancy, delay in psychomotor development, mild to severe learning difficulties. In some cases there is also enlargement of one side of the face and skin disorders. Formerly, the condition often resulted in death in infancy but recent advances in treatment have improved the rate of survival.

Hemiparesis Weakness of muscle on one side of the body, resulting in partial loss of function.

Hemiplegia Paralysis of one side of the body.

Hepatolenticular Degeneration, Progressive (See Wilson Disease)

Hereditary Characteristics, Hereditary Disorders Those characteristics or disorders which are genetically transmitted by parents to their offspring.

Heredity Transmission of characteristics from parents to their offspring; the genetic make-up of an individual.

Hernia Protrusion of an organ or part into or through the wall of the cavity in which it is situated.

Herpes Simplex or **Cold Sore** An acute infectious disease producing small blisters around the mouth and sometimes the genital organs. The virus may remain in the body and be activated from time to time. In some cases herpes virus in the mother can produce generalised infection in a developing foetus.

Herpesvirus Infection, Perinatal Damage to the developing foetus due to herpes simplex virus infection in the mother. The infection may be transmitted to the child via the placenta, via the mother's infected genital organs or during birth. Features, which are variable, include: microcephaly or hydrocephalus, low birth weight, eye infections, skin lesions, motor and learning difficulty. In some cases there are no physical signs of infection. In affected infants the symptoms vary from mild to severe, depending on the extent of neurological damage by the virus. Those with infection outside of the nervous system usually have no effects. (See also Herpes Simplex)

Herpes Zoster or **Shingles** A disease producing inflammation of the skin, caused by the same virus as that which is responsible for chicken pox. It is a different virus from that responsible for herpes simplex.

Heterozygote A carrier of a recessive genetic disorder.

Heterozygous The term used in genetics to describe a pair of genes in which one is mutant (changed) and the other is normal.

Hiatus Hernia Protrusion of a portion of the stomach through the opening in the diaphragm by which the oesophagus passes into the abdomen.

Holoprosencephaly Sequence A group of congenital defects in which there is severe malformation, variable in its effects, but which may amount to absence of the nose, profound eye abnormalities, sometimes involving fusion of both eyes, midline cleft lip and severe abnormalities of the fore-brain. Life expectancy limited in severe cases. Common in Trisomy 13 syndrome.

Holotelencephaly A term occasionally used for holoprosencephaly. (see Holoprosencephaly Sequence)

Homocystinuria A disorder of amino acid metabolism. Features include: flushing of the face on exertion or in hot weather, partial dislocation of the lens, short sight, narrow high palate and crowded teeth, fine and fair hair, long limbs, long slender digits, vascular defects. In some cases: seizures, hemiplegia, mild to severe learning difficulty. Autosomal recessive inheritance.

Homozygous The term used in genetics to describe a pair of genes which are both the same, e.g. where both are mutant (changed).

Horseshoe Kidney A common congenital defect of kidney formation, resulting from a partial fusion of the two kidneys, forming a 'horseshoe' shape. It is more common in males. Kidney function may be normal, but in some cases there are kidney function abnormalities.

Hunter Disease or **Hunter Syndrome, Mucopolysaccharidosis 2, MPS 2** (See Mucopolysaccharidoses; Mucopolysaccharidosis 2)

Hurler-Scheie Genetic Compound or **Mucopolysaccharidosis 1 H-S, MPS 1 H-S** (See Mucopolysaccharidoses; Mucopolysaccharidosis 1 H-S)

Hurler Disease or **Hurler Syndrome, Mucopolysaccharidosis 1 H, MPS 1 H** (See Mucopolysaccharidoses; Mucopolysaccharidosis 1 H)

Hyaline Cells Transparent white blood cells.

Hydantoin Effects, Foetal or **Foetal Hydantoin Syndrome** Damage to the developing foetus, thought to be due to the taking of certain anticonvulsants, or combinations of anticonvulsants and barbiturates by the mother during pregnancy, as a treatment for epilepsy. Damage does not occur in every case. Features, which are variable, include: growth deficiency, widely spaced eyes, short nose, cleft lip and palate, coarse and abundant hair, squint, short neck, rib defects, widely spaced nipples, hernias, abnormal palm crease, abnormalities of finger bones with short or underdeveloped nails. In some cases: abnormal skull shape, heart defects, kidney defects, digestive system defects, genital defects, mild to moderate learning difficulty.

Hydranencephaly or **Hydrencephaly** A severe defect of the brain in which the cerebral hemispheres are completely or almost completely absent. In their place there is a thin sac of fluid, covered by the meninges. Affected children may have no obvious physical signs at birth, but head enlargement develops within several weeks. Features include: lack of development, swallowing difficulty, eye defects, seizures. Life expectancy is limited to infancy in most cases.

Hydrocephalus Faulty distribution of cerebrospinal fluid, usually resulting in a large head because of fluid accumulation. The pressure on the brain causes intellectual impairment unless treatment is given by the insertion of a valve to drain off the fluid. In arrested cases intelligence may be unimpaired or only mildly impaired. Hydrocephalus occurs as a feature in a number of multiple abnormality disorders. Sometimes referred to, incorrectly, as water on the brain. Causes include: birth defects, haemorrhage, viral infection,

4

meningitis or genetic factors. (See also Aqueductal Stenosis; Dandy-Walker Syndrome; Spitz-Holter Valve)

Hydronephrosis A chronic condition in which the kidney becomes distended with urine due to obstruction or narrowing of the urethra or as a result of malformation.

Hydrotherapy Treatment involving the internal or external use of water.

Hyoid Bone The U-shaped bone situated at the base of the tongue.

Hyperactivity Excessive activity, usually in children. Features include restlessness, sleeplessness, inability to concentrate or to direct activities. Some cases of hyperactivity can be alleviated by dietary adjustment. (See Attention Deficit Disorder; Challenging Behaviour)

Hyperaemia An excessive amount of blood in a part, resulting in congestion.

Hyperalgia Excessive sensitivity to pain.

Hyperasthenia Severe weakness.

Hypercalcaemia Syndrome, Idiopathic Infantile (See Williams Syndrome)

Hyperglycaemia An excessive amount of sugar in the blood.

Hyperhidrosis or **Hyperhydrosis** Excessive sweating.

Hyperinsulinaemia An excessive amount of insulin in the blood.

Hyperkeratosis Excessively thick and 'horny' skin.

Hyperkinesis Overactivity; excessive movement.

Hyperkinetic Syndrome (See Attention Deficit Disorder)

Hyperlexia An exceptional ability to use words at a very early age; far above what would be expected at the chronological age and/or an intense fascination with numbers or letters. This may be combined with difficulty in understanding and using verbal language, reciprocal interaction with others or with a significant nonverbal learning disability.

Hypermetropia or **Hyperopia** Longsightedness.

Hyperphagia Abnormally excessive appetite; overeating.

Hyperpigmentation An excessive amount of colour in a part. Usually applied to darkened areas on the skin.

Hyperpituitarism Overactivity of the pituitary gland, which may cause acromegaly ('giantism').

Hyperplasia Overdevelopment; excessive formation of tissue due to overproduction of its cells.

Hyperpyrexia Excessively high body temperature; fever.

Hypertelorism Increased distance between two structures or organs. Usually applied to abnormal wideness between the eyes.

Hypertension Abnormally high tension or pressure, particularly applied to blood vessels (high blood pressure).

Hyperthermia Abnormally high body temperature.

Hyperthyroidism Excessive activity of the thyroid gland producing restlessness, sweating, raised body temperature and increased pulse and respiration rate.

Hypertonia An increased degree of tone or tension, usually applied to muscle.

Hypertrichosis or **Hypertrichiasis** Excessive growth of hair on the head or body.

Hypertrophy Overgrowth or thickening of a part or an organ, produced by the increase of its tissues.

Hyperuricaemia, Infantile (See Lesch-Nyhan Syndrome)

Hyperventilation Abnormally rapid and deep breathing; 'overbreathing'.

Hypochromatic Patch (See Hypomelanotic Patch)

Hypochromic Lack of pigmentation or colouring.

Hypodontia Deficiency in number or formation of the teeth.

Hypoglycaemia A decrease in the amount of sugar in the blood.

Hypoglycaemia, Neonatal (See Beckwith-Weidemann Syndrome)

Hypogonadism Deficient production of the hormones secreted by the ovaries and testes.

Hypohidrosis or **Hypohydrosis** Deficiency of sweat production.

Hypomelanosis Lack of skin colour due to a deficiency of melanin.

Hypomelanotic Patch An area of depigmented skin.

Hypomelanosis of Ito Syndrome or **Incontinentia Pigmentosa Achromians** Features include: large skull, squint, pale or white streaks or patches on the skin, limbs and/or trunk as a result of decreased pigmentation, seizures, variable degree of learning difficulty. In some cases: spinal curvature as a result of asymmetrical leg length. Cause not established.

Hypopigmentation A decreased amount of colour in a part, e.g. the eyes.

Hypopituitarism Lack of pituitary function.

Hypoplasia or **Hypoplastic** Underdevelopment of a part or organ.

Hypospadias A malformation in which the opening of the urethra is situated on the under surface of the penis.

Hypotelorism Decreased distance between two structures, usually applied to abnormal closeness of the eyes.

Hypotension Low blood pressure.

Hypothermia Abnormally low body temperature.

Hypothyroidism, Congenital A disorder with a variety of causes, including defective thyroid gland development, thyroid hormone deficiency, medication in pregnancy, hereditary syndromes. Early diagnosis and treatment can prevent or lessen the symptoms. In untreated cases the features include: short stature, lax muscle tone, short neck, dry and scaly skin with a yellowish colour, coarse and brittle hair, puffy eyelids, flat nasal bridge, thick and broad tongue, hoarse voice, slow heart rate, delayed sexual development, mild learning difficulty.

Hypotonia or **Hypotonicity** Lack of muscle tone; 'floppiness'.

Hypotrichosis Sparseness or lack of hair.

Hypsarrythmia A type of infantile spasm, characterised by a high voltage wave pattern on an electroencephalogram. (See also Epilepsy)

I-Cell Disease or Mucolipidosis, Type 2 (See Leroy I-Cell Syndrome)

Ichthyosis A disorder of the skin, resulting in the formation of dry scales on a rough, cracked surface. Can be inherited in several ways.

Idiopathic The term used to describe a disorder of unknown cause.

IEP (See Individual Education Plan)

4

Imperforate Lack of a normal opening in a body organ, e.g. the anus.

Impetigo A contagious inflammation of the skin, producing pustules which dry up and leave scabs.

Inborn Error of Metabolism or **Metabolic Disease** An inherited disorder caused by a relative deficiency or absence of a single enzyme, resulting in imperfect cell function or defective digestion and absorption of nutrients. This leads to accumulation of substances which would normally be broken down and/or deficiency of other substances essential to health, with consequent damage to tissues and organs. In some disorders there is rapid deterioration and severe effects, in others there is a more gradual onset, less severe effects with slow or minimal progression. The effects of metabolic disorder may be purely physical or may involve both physical and intellectual deterioration. The age at which symptoms of metabolic disorder become apparent varies from soon after birth to several months or years after birth. Certain metabolic diseases can be inherited. There have been many advances in the early recognition, treatment and prenatal detection of some types of metabolic disorder. While no treatment is yet available for some types, others can be reversed or improved, providing they are diagnosed early enough. There are several disorders which are thought to be metabolic in origin, but in which the basic enzyme defect has not yet been defined. (See also Enzyme, Deficient Activity of)

Incidence The proportion of individuals affected by a disorder, compared to the unaffected population.

Inclusive Education A movement which aims to encourage schools to change their structure, grouping of pupils and support services in order to meet the needs of all their pupils, including those with special educational needs.

Incompatible Behaviour A term used in behaviour modification to denote a behaviour which opposes or is inconsistent with another.

Incontinentia Pigmenti Syndrome or **Bloch-Sulzberger Syndrome** Features include: development of skin lesions within the first year, beginning as blisters and progressing to areas of thickened skin and finally to streaks of grey or brown pigmentation. The pigmentation fades over subsequent years, leaving normal or slightly atrophied areas. In some cases the disorder is accompanied by other features, including: abnormal teeth and nails, bone abnormalities, eye defects, hair loss, spasticity, seizures, moderate to severe learning difficulty. Cause not established. In familial cases, X-linked dominant inheritance.

Incontinentia Pigmentosa Achromians (See Hypomelanosis of Ito Syndrome)

Incoordination Inability to produce harmonious movements as a result of disorder of the brain, sensory nerves, motor system or muscles.

Individual Education Plan (IEP) A plan which decribes targets set for an individual child and the plans made by the school to ensure that those targets are achieved.

Infantile Neuroaxonal Dystrophy or **Seitelberger Disease** A progressive disease of the nervous system, characterised by swellings in the nerves of the spinal cord and brain stem. Development is normal until around the end of the first year, then there is progressive spasticity, loss of reflexes and deterioration of visual, motor and intellectual function. Life expectancy not usually exceeding 10 years. Autosomal recessive inheritance.

Infantile Spasm A form of epilepsy, occurring in infants, in which there are brief episodes of muscle spasm. Onset is usually around 6 months. The seizures may disappear by 2 years. The spasms may be successfully controlled with the administration of adrenocorticotrophic hormone (ACTH). (See also Epilepsy; Hypsarrhythmia; Lennox-Gastaut Syndrome; West Syndrome)

Infantilism, Sexual Incomplete or imperfect sexual development in puberty, resulting in lack of adult sexual features.

Infective Disease (See Disease)

Iniencephaly A severe abnormality in which part of the substance of the brain protrudes through the fissures of the skull.

Instrumental Conditioning A term used in behaviour modification to denote learning by means of trial and error, in which the gaining of a reward or the avoiding of a punishment is dependent upon producing the appropriate behaviour.

Integration A movement to see that schools provide additional arrangements, within the normal school structure, to provide for pupils with special educational needs.

Intention Tremor (See Tremor)

Interstitial Deletion (See Chromosome Abnormality)

Inversion of Chromosomes (See Chromosome Abnormality)

IQ Abbreviation for Intelligence Quotient, the score achieved in a specially designed intelligence test. The average or 'normal' IQ is placed at 100. Scores inform judgements of levels of learning difficulty. (See also Learning Difficulty)

Iridectomy Removal of the iris. Partial iridectomy is often used to treat cataracts in children.

Jacksonian Epilepsy or **Focal Epilepsy** Seizures in which jerking spasms occur in one part of the body, sometimes spreading quickly to other areas, usually without loss of consciousness. The seizures occur in the part related to the irritated area of the brain and are due to a lesion in the cerebral cortex. (See also Epilepsy)

Jaundice Yellowness of the skin and tissues, best seen in the eyes by natural light. Due to an excess of bile pigment in the tissues.

Jaw-Winking Sign A condition in which the third and fifth cranial nerves are abnormally connected. One of the functions of the third nerve is the opening of the eyelid. As one of its functions, the fifth nerve controls the jaw muscles. In this disorder, the eyelid droops (ptosis) and opens when the jaw is moved. If the ptosis is severe or persistent, an operation to lift the eyelid may be necessary. A feature of some multiple abnormality syndromes.

Joubert Syndrome or **Familial Cerebellar Vermis Agenesis** Features include: nystagmus, ataxia, alternating hyperpnoea (rapid breathing) and apnoea (cessation of breathing), lax muscle tone, learning difficulty. Due to failure of development of the vermis (a small structure within the cerebellum). Cause not established.

Kabuki Syndrome Features include: short stature, unusual facial features, skeletal abnormalities, unusual skin ridges on fingers, toes, palms and soles, abnormally long opening between upper and lower eyelids, broad depressed tip of nose, outward turning of one third of lower eyelid, high arched eyebrows, cleft and/or high-arched palate, dental abnormalities, inward curving of fifth fingers and hip joint, spinal curvature. Learning difficulty from mild to severe. Cause unknown.

4

Kanner Syndrome The term sometimes used to refer to the classic type of autism. Speech is delayed or never attained and there are severe psychological, behavioural and social problems. (See also Asperger Syndrome; Autism)

Keratitis Inflammation of the cornea.

Keratoconus Conical cornea; a lesion which produces a basin-shaped depression in the posterior surface of the cornea.

Keratosis A disorder of the skin, characterised by overgrowth of its outer surface. It arises on exposure to sunlight and takes the form of dry scales with redness of the surrounding skin.

Kernicterus or **Nuclear Jaundice** Damage to the brain due to severe neonatal jaundice, commonly caused by Rhesus incompatibility. The neurological symptoms may appear soon after birth, with lethargy and lax muscle tone. In untreated cases there is impaired motor development and athetoid posturing. In some cases: hearing loss, mild to severe learning difficulty. Rhesus incompatibility can now be detected and treated by exchange transfusion immediately after birth and its recurrence in subsequent pregnancies can be prevented by the administration of gamma globulin to the mother shortly after the birth of the affected child.

Kernig Sign A sign found in cases of meningitis in which the individual is unable to straighten the knee when the hip is flexed at a right angle to the body, or finds it extremely painful. A healthy person's hip can be flexed at a right angle with the body when the knee is straight.

Ketogenic Diet A diet containing excessive amounts of fat and resulting in the excretion of acetone and other ketone bodies in the urine. Sometimes used in the treatment of epilepsy and chronic infections of the urinary tract.

Ketone An acetone substance, produced in the body from imperfect metabolism of fats.

Kinaesthetic Sensation The sensory impulses of muscles and joints which indicate to the brain their position and state of contraction, so that the brain is able to maintain smooth motion and correct posture.

Kinky Hair Syndrome (See Menkes Syndrome)

Klinefelter Syndrome or **XXY Syndrome** (See Chromosome Abnormality Syndromes, Sex)

Klippel-Feil Sequence Features include: fusion of the cervical vertebrae or reduction in the number of vertebrae, restricting neck movement. In some cases: webbing of the neck, torticollis, facial asymmetry, deafness, heart defects, spinal curvature. The sequence may occur as part of a multiple abnormality disorder with learning difficulty as one of the features.

Klippel-Trenaunay-Weber Syndrome Features, which are variable, include: overgrowth of one or both limbs evident at birth or developing in infancy, haemangiomata on any area, but most commonly on the lower trunk, buttocks, abdomen and legs, occurring usually on one side of the body, but occasionally involving both sides. In some cases: swelling of the affected limb/s, skin ulceration, joint discomfort, skeletal abnormalities, abdominal bleeding due to abnormal blood vessels. Cause unknown.

Knock Knee (See Genu Valgum)

Koilonychia Hollow and depressed nails, producing a 'spoon' shape. Sometimes associated with chronic anaemia.

Krabbe Disease (See Globoid Cell Leukodystrophy)

Kufs Disease or **Batten Disease, Adult Form** A disorder of lipid metabolism in which the features are similar to those of Batten disease. Normal development in childhood, with onset of symptoms in adulthood, leading to ocular changes and intellectual deterioration. Autosomal recessive inheritance and autosomal dominant inheritance have been reported. (See also Batten Disease; Bielschowsky-Jansky Disease)

Kyphoscoliosis A combination of kyphosis and scoliosis, in which there is curvature of the spine in both an outward and sideways direction.

Kyphosis Outward curvature of the spine; 'hump back'.

Lambdoid Suture The suture between the parietal bones and the occipital bone of the skull.

Landau-Kleffner Syndrome Features include: language disturbance and epilepsy. The epilepsy may be relatively mild. At onset there is difficulty with the understanding of speech, followed by increasing difficulty with spoken language, sometimes amounting to loss of speech. There may be varying degrees of behavioural problems. Eventual outcome varies but in many reported cases there has been significant improvement in, or complete recovery of language skills over a period of months or years. Cause not established. (See also Epilepsy)

Langer-Giedion Syndrome (Trichorhinophalangeal Syndrome Type 2) Features include: mild microcephaly, mild growth deficiency, large protruding ears, heavy brows, elongated philtrum, thin upper lip, sparse scalp hair, lax muscle tone, bone abnormalities (exostoses and tendency to fractures), looseness of skin in infancy which improves with age, hearing loss, speech delay, mild to moderate learning difficulty. Defects of the long arm of chromosome 8 have been reported.

Laurence-Moon-Bardet-Beidl Syndrome Features, which are variable, include: widely spaced eyes, nystagmus, retinal defects and night blindness, digital anomalies including extra digit/s and/or webbing of digits, obesity, short stature, underdeveloped genital organs. Mild to moderate learning difficulty is common. In some cases: hearing defects, kidney defects. Autosomal recessive inheritance.

Lay Advocacy (See Advocacy)

Learning Difficulty In assessing learning difficulty, many factors (medical, social, environmental etc.) are taken into account. In many cases the cause of learning difficulty is unknown but among the known causes are: chromosomal defects, maternal infection, metabolic disease, birth trauma, accident or infection in infancy or childhood and inherited disorders. There is wide variation in severity and the terms 'mild', 'moderate', 'severe' and 'profound' may be used to indicate the degree of learning difficulty in an individual. (See also Acalculia; Dyscalculia; Dyslexia; IQ; Moderate Learning Difficulties; Profound Learning Difficulties; Severe Learning Difficulties; Specific Learning Difficulties)

Leber Congenital Amaurosis Features include: nystagmus, impaired vision, optic atrophy, pigmentary changes in retina. In some cases: cataract, microphthalmia, lax muscle tone, Mild to moderate learning difficulty. Leber amaurosis may occur as one feature of a multiple abnormality disorder. Autosomal recessive inheritance in most cases.

4

Legal Advocacy (See Advocacy)

Leigh Disease or **Infantile Subacute Encephalopathy** A metabolic disease, characterised by lesions of the brain, spinal cord and optic nerve. Features include: onset between the ages of 3 months and 2 years, low body weight, poor sucking ability, loss of head control, seizures, ataxia, irritability, physical and progressive neurological deterioration. Limited life expectancy.

Lejeune Syndrome or **5p- Syndrome, Cri du Chat Syndrome** (See Chromosome Abnormality Syndromes)

Lennox-Gastaut Syndrome Features include: a mixed seizure pattern, consisting of petit mal seizures, grand mal seizures and myoclonic seizures, which are difficult to control. Onset is usually in early childhood and may be preceded by West syndrome. Intellectual deterioration, behaviour problems and autistic features may be present. (See also Epilepsy)

Leprechaunism (See Donohue Syndrome)

Leroy I-Cell Syndrome or **Mucolipidosis, Type 2** A disorder of lipid metabolism. Features include: low birth weight with severe growth deficiency, high narrow forehead, puffy eyelids, low nasal bridge, marked overgrowth of gum, joint limitation, thick and tight skin from infancy, mild liver enlargement, progression of physical features up to about 2 years, learning difficulty. Autosomal recessive inheritance.

Lesch-Nyhan Syndrome or **Infantile Hyperuricaemia** A disorder of uric acid metabolism. Features include: spasticity, below average weight and height, involuntary movements and tremor, athetosis, self-mutilation, moderate to severe learning difficulty. The disorder occurs only in males. Progressive, with life expectancy not usually exceeding puberty. X-linked inheritance.

Leucoderma Abnormal white patches on the skin as a result of congenital absence of pigmentation.

Linear Sebaceous Naevus Sequence or **Naevus Sebaceous of Jadassohn** Features include: skin lesions present at birth, yellow/orange papules in a patch or linear streak in the middle of the forehead. In some cases: eye anomalies, seizures. Moderate to severe learning difficulty is common. There may be large, pigmented naevi on the neck, trunk, back and extremities, but these naevi are also found frequently in otherwise normal individuals. Cause not established.

Lipodystrophy Syndrome Faulty metabolism of fat resulting in partial or complete absence of adipose tissue. Total lipodystrophy; Features include: absence of fatty tissue under the skin, enlarged tongue, enlarged liver and spleen, large hands and feet. Learning difficulty may occur but intellect is usually unimpaired. Autosomal recessive inheritance in the congenital type. Partial lipodystrophy. Features include: onset from infancy to the fourth decade, absence of facial fat and variable loss of fatty tissue from the arms, body and hips. Central nervous system dysfunction occurs in some cases. May be congenital or acquired.

Lipomucopolysaccharidosis or **Mucolipidosis Type 1** (See Sialidosis)

Lissencephaly or **Miller-Dieker Syndrome** Features include: microcephaly, small nose, small jaw, wrinkling of central forehead and upper lip (especially when crying), lax muscle tone, seizures, failure to thrive and frequent infections, heart defects, incomplete development of the convolutions on the brain's surface, producing variable reduction in their depth, severe learning difficulty. Life expectancy not usually exceeding infancy. Autosomal recessive inheritance.

Little disease Spastic diplegia. A congenital muscular rigidity in which the legs are stiff and tend to cross. If walking is achieved there is a 'scissoring' gait.

Lobe A major division in an organ, e.g. the lobes of the liver, lungs or brain.

Long Arm of Chromosome, Deletion of (See Chromosome; Chromosome Abnormality; Chromosome Abnormality Syndromes)

Lordosis A deformity of the spine in which there is an abnormal forward curve, usually of the lumbar spine, i.e. the normal curve is exaggerated.

Louis-Bar Syndrome (See Ataxia Telangiectasia Syndrome)

Lowe Syndrome or **Oculo-Cerebro-Renal Syndrome** A disorder of amino acid metabolism. It is progressive, though deterioration can be slowed by treatment with vitamin D. Features include: cataracts and other eye defects, lax muscle tone, bone disorders, kidney damage, learning difficulty. X-linked recessive inheritance.

Lymphoedema Swelling of a part or organ as a result of fluid accumulation. Caused by obstruction of the lymph drainage glands.

Macrocephaly An abnormally large head.

Macroglossia An abnormally large tongue.

Macroglossia, Exomphalos, Giantism Syndrome (See Beckwith-Weidemann Syndrome)

Macrogyria Abnormally deep or wide folds (gyri) on the surface of the brain.

Macro-orchidism Large testicles.

Macrosomia A large body.

Macrostomia An abnormally large opening between the lips, due to a cleftlike extension of the corners of the mouth.

Malar Pertaining to the cheek or cheekbones.

Malar Bones The cheekbones.

Malignant Disease (See Disease)

Makaton A form of sign language, originally developed for use with people with hearing loss, now widely used as an aid to communication for non-verbalising children and adults.

Malocclusion Poor closure of the mouth because of faulty alignment of the teeth.

Mandible The lower jaw bone.

Mandibulo-Facial Dysostosis (See Treacher-Collins Syndrome)

Mannosidosis A disorder of carbohydrate metabolism. Features include: prominent forehead, enlarged tongue, lens opacity, lax muscle tone, spinal curvature, restlessness and vomiting, slow development. Progressive. Autosomal recessive inheritance.

Maple Syrup Urine Disease A disorder of amino acid metabolism. In untreated cases, features include: feeding and breathing difficulties, characteristic smell in the urine, brain damage, convulsions and paralysis. Early detection and treatment with a special diet can prevent brain damage. Autosomal recessive inheritance.

Marasmus Progressive wasting of the tissues, especially in young children.

Marinesco-Sjogren Syndrome Features include: mild to moderate growth deficiency, cerebellar ataxia, muscular weak-

4

ness and/or lax muscle tone, eye defects, moderate to severe learning difficulty. A degenerative disorder affecting the cortical areas of the cerebellum. Autosomal recessive inheritance.

Maroteaux-Lamy Disease or Maroteaux-Lamy Syndrome, Mucopolysaccharidosis 6, MPS 6 (See Mucopolysaccharidoses, Mucopolysaccharidosis 6)

Maroteaux-Lamy Pyknodysostosis Syndrome Features include: small stature, bone abnormality with a tendency to fractures, prominence of frontal and occipital bones, prominent nose, narrow palate, irregular or absent teeth with dental decay, poorly developed finger bones, flat nails, spinal curvature. Mild learning difficulty may occur but intellect is unimpaired in most cases. Cause not established.

Marshall-Smith Syndrome Features include: accelerated growth in length without weight increase, failure to thrive, long skull with a prominent forehead, prominent eyes, upturned nose, bluish whites of the eyes, broadness of proximal and middle bone of fingers, accelerated maturation of bone, recurrent respiratory infections in infancy, motor delay and learning difficulty. Life expectancy not usually exceeding 2 years. Cause unknown.

Martin-Bell Syndrome (See Fragile X Syndrome)

Maxilla The upper jaw bone.

Meckel-Gruber Syndrome Features include: growth deficiency, microcephaly with encephalocele, underdeveloped eyes and ears, cleft palate, abnormalities of digits, club foot, incomplete brain development. In some cases: limb defects, heart and lung defects, kidney defects. Because of the severity of the abnormalities, affected infants usually do not survive early infancy. Autosomal recessive inheritance.

Median Cleft Face Syndrome or Frontonasal Dysplasia Sequence Features, which are variable, include: widely spaced eyes, a midline cleft varying from a notched tip of the nose to involvement of the whole mid-facial area from forehead to lip, V-shape hairline. In some cases: squint, cleft eyelid, hearing loss. Occasionally, mild to severe learning difficulty is present but intellect is unimpaired in most cases. Autosomal recessive inheritance.

Megalencephaly or **Megaloencephaly** An abnormally large head. Sometimes associated with hydrocephalus.

Megalencephaly with Hyaline Panneuropathy (See Alexander Disease)

Mendelian Inheritance or **Mendelism** The ways in which characteristics or diseases, determined by single genes, are transmitted through families. First described in plants by Gregor Mendel in the 19th century.

Meningitis Inflammation of the meninges, the membranes which surround the brain and spinal cord. The meninges has three layers; the dura mater, the arachnoid mater and the pia mater.

Meningocele A protrusion of the meninges through a defect in the skull, producing a sac filled with cerebrospinal fluid. Because there is no involvement of brain tissue a meningocele may often be treated surgically, leaving the intellect unimpaired. (See also Encephalocele; Meningomyelocele)

Meningoencephalitis Inflammation of both the brain and the meninges.

Meningomyelocele A protrusion of the meninges and a portion of the spinal cord or nerve roots through a defect in the vertebral column (spina bifida). The defect most commonly occurs in the lumbar region, less commonly in the thoracic and sacral areas. Head enlargement due to hydrocephalus may be apparent at birth or may become evident later. Those without hydrocephalus may have normal intelligence, those with hydrocephalus may have mild to moderate learning difficulty. Early surgery can reduce the possibility of paralysis in some cases. Meningomyelocele may occur as part of a syndrome, recognisable by the presence of other associated malformations. (See Encephalocele; Meningocele; Spina Bifida)

Menkes Syndrome or **Menkes Kinky Hair Syndrome** A disorder in which there is defective absorption of copper. Features include: full cheeks, lack of expression, normal hair at birth which later becomes light, sparse and stubby with twisting and partial breakage, dry and thick skin, bone disorders with tendency to fractures, lax muscle tone, irritability, feeding difficulty. Progressive, with life expectancy not usually exceeding 3 years. X-linked recessive inheritance.

Metabolic Disease (See Disease; Enzyme, Deficient Activity of; Inborn Error of Metabolism)

Metachromatic Leukodystrophy or **Sulfatide Lipidosis** A disorder of lipid metabolism. Features include: normal development until after the first year with no obvious physical symptoms, difficulty in standing often occurring as a first sign, lax muscle tone in the legs, lack of arm co-ordination, intellectual deterioration. Limitation of life expectancy in many cases, but individuals with late onset may survive into the teens. Autosomal recessive inheritance.

Metatarsus Adductus Turning inward of the feet; 'pigeon-toes'.

Metatarsus Varus A deformity characterised by the bending of one foot towards the other foot.

Metopic Suture The suture joining the frontal bones, running from the top of the forehead to the centre of the head.

Microcephaly An abnormally small cranium, sometimes with a face of normal size. The result of premature closure of the sutures of the skull. In general, the smaller the head, the greater the degree of learning disability but microcephaly is not always accompanied by intellectual impairment. Microcephaly can exist without any additional abnormalities (microcephaly vera or true microcephaly) or it can be one feature of a multiple abnormality syndrome. Causes include: maternal infections (e.g. rubella, cytomegalovirus), head injury, lack of oxygen at birth, meningitis, chromosome abnormality, inherited multiple abnormality syndromes. (See also Craniosynostosis)

Microcephaly Vera or **True Microcephaly** The term is used to denote microcephaly in which there is no demonstrable cause and where there are no accompanying congenital abnormalities. The abnormally small skull may be apparent at birth or may become evident after a few months. The face is of normal size, the forehead is long, narrow and markedly receding, and the cranium is abnormally small. Spasticity and mild to severe learning difficulty are common.

Microdontia Abnormally small teeth.

Micrognathia An abnormally small jaw.

Micropenis An abnormally small penis.

Micropthalmia Abnormal smallness of one or both eyes.

4

Microstomia A decrease in width of the opening to the mouth.

Miller-Dieker Syndrome (See Lissencephaly)

Minimal Brain Dysfunction (See Dyspraxia)

Mitral Murmur (See Murmur)

Mitral Stenosis A disorder in which the opening between the left atrium and the left ventricle is narrowed, resulting in malfunction of the mitral valve.

Modelling Learning by means of demonstration and imitation.

Moderate Learning Difficulties Individuals with moderate learning difficulties (MLD) may have difficulties acquiring basic literacy and numeracy skills. They may have speech and language difficulties, poorly developed personal and social skills and emotional and behavioural difficulties. Schools should formulate, monitor and regularly evaluate individual education plans, including literacy and/or numeracy support programmes. The subjects of a broad and balanced curriculum are covered at a slower pace and with an emphasis on practical learning through doing. (See also Learning Difficulty)

Moebius Sequence, Moebius Syndrome Features include: expressionless facial features due to paralysis of the nerves of the face (commonly the 6th and 7th but sometimes involving other facial nerves), limitation of tongue movement, small jaw, feeding difficulties, speech defects. In some cases: drooping eyelids, protruding ears, small jaw, club foot. Mild to moderate learning difficulty in about 10% of cases. The Moebius sequence may occur as part of a multiple abnormality disorder (Moebius syndrome) in association with reduction of limbs, webbing of digits and

rib defects. Usually sporadic though the syndrome is considered to be inherited as an autosomal dominant trait.

Monoplegia Paralysis of a single limb or body part.

Monosomy Absence of a whole chromosome or arm of a chromosome.

Monosomy, Group G or 21q- Syndrome, 21- Syndrome (See Chromosome Abnormality Syndromes)

Morquio Disease or Morquio Syndrome, Mucopolysaccharidosis 4, MPS 4 (See Mucopolysaccharidoses; Mucopolysaccharidosis 4)

Mosaic Form of Chromosome Abnormality (See Chromosome Abnormality; Chromosome Abnormality Syndromes)

Mosaicism (See Chromosome Abnormality)

Motor Development Achievement of coordinated and purposeful movement.

Motor Impairment A loss of or decrease in control of movement which may interfere with larger movements of the body, such as standing, walking and sitting (gross motor skills) and/or those which require smaller movements, such as grasping, reaching out, touching (fine motor skills). Impaired motor development may, in some instances, be treated by physiotherapy. In some cases, it is related to learning difficulties in that the neurological impairment which causes the motor impairment may also cause learning difficulties. An intensive approach to treating motor impairments is conductive education in which two or more specially trained staff work with a small group of children throughout the day in a residential setting.

Motor Skills Gross motor skills; those which concern large movements of the whole body, e.g. standing, walking or sitting. **Fine motor skills;** those which require the use of hands and arms, e.g. grasping, reaching out, touching.

Motor System The system controlling bodily movement, as opposed to the sensory system.

Mucolipidosis, Type 1 (See Sialidosis)

Mucolipidosis, Type 2 (See Leroy I-Cell Disease)

Mucolipidosis, Type 3 (See Pseudo-Hurler Polydystrophy)

Mucopolysaccharidoses A group of disorders caused by defective activity or absence of one or more enzymes required for the breakdown of complex sugars within the body. This results in progressive accumulation of these complex molecules in bone and other connective tissue, and in some cases in the liver, spleen and brain. The accumulation gives rise to the clinical features of the disorders. There are several types, with varying clinical manifestations, some of which are associated with varying degrees of learning difficulty.

Mucopolysacchiridosis 1 H, (MPS 1 H) or Hurler Disease Features include: slowing down of growth beginning in the first year and leading to short stature, macrocephaly with prominent forehead, coarsening of facial features, full lips, flared nostrils, low nasal bridge, rhinitis and noisy respiration, hearing loss, cloudy corneas of the eye, enlarged gums and tongue, joint limitation, spinal curvature, enlarged liver and spleen, hernia. Affected children are usually of pleasant and placid disposition. The disorder is progressive, and life expectancy is usually limited to about ten years. Autosomal recessive inheritance.

Mucopolysaccharidosis 1 H-S, (MPS 1 H-S) or Hurler-Scheie Genetic Compound Features are intermediate between those of the Hurler and Scheie diseases, and include: gradual development of signs and symptoms during the first few years, with initial growth acceleration giving way to growth deficiency, large skull, low nasal bridge, prominent lips, corneal clouding, thickened skin, joint limitation. Very gradual progression towards mild to moderate disabilities, with no intellectual impairment or only mild learning difficulty. Autosomal recessive inheritance.

Mucopolysaccharidosis 1 S, (MPS 1 S) or Scheie Disease Features include: broad mouth with full lips and often rather square jaw, corneal clouding, some joint limitation, broad and short hands and feet, heart valve defect, hernias. Little, if any, impairment of intelligence. Autosomal recessive inheritance.

Mucopolysaccharidosis 2, (MPS 2) or Hunter Disease Two forms, mild and severe. **Severe;** onset from infancy with deterioration of physical development, macrocephaly, coarsening of facial features, broadening of bones and stiffening of joints, enlarged liver and spleen, hernias, rhinitis, deafness, learning difficulty in some cases. **Mild;** onset in infancy or early childhood, with features similar to the juvenile type, but with more gradual onset and progression and usually normal intellectual development. In the severe type, life expectancy does not usually exceed the teenage years but the mild type is compatible with adult life. There are two important differences between Hunter disease and Hurler disease; 1. Corneal clouding does not occur in Hunter disease but is present in Hurler disease. 2. Hunter disease occurs only in males, whereas Hurler syndrome affects both males and females. Nerve deafness presents a more severe problem in Hunter disease than in Hurler disease. X-linked inheritance.

Mucopolysaccharidosis 3, (MPS 3) or Sanfillipo Disease Four types, A, B, C and D, with the same clinical features. Features include: onset in early childhood when the child appears big and strong, with slowing down of growth occurring in late childhood, well after the onset of neurological problems. In some cases: liver and spleen enlargement, mild coarsening of facial features, tendency to upper respiratory infections which may lead to hearing loss, hyperactivity, intellectual regression. In most cases life expectancy does not exceed the teens or early twenties but some affected individuals survive into adulthood. Autosomal recessive inheritance.

Mucopolysaccharidosis 4, (MPS 4) or Morquio Disease Features include: onset between 1 and 3 years, severe shortness of stature, slight corneal clouding, severe vertebral abnormalities leading to spinal curvature, other bone and joint abnormalities. In some cases: unusual facial features with 'dish-like' shape, heart valve defects, enlargement or liver, hernia. Learning difficulty occurs very occasionally, but is not present in most cases. Autosomal recessive inheritance.

Mucopolysaccharidosis Now classified as MPS 1S, since both are caused by defect of the same enzyme.

Mucopolysaccharidosis 6, (MPS 6) or Maroteaux-Lamy Disease Two forms, mild and severe. Features are similar to those of Hurler disease, but with a slower progression and little, if any, intellectual impairment. **Mild type;** may be very mild with corneal clouding, claw hands and a degree of deafness with normal facial features and no other abnormalities. In other cases there may be short stature, hip abnormalities, heart defects. **Severe type;**

skeletal abnormalities, corneal clouding. In some cases: hydrocephalus. Life expectancy not usually exceeding the teens in very severe cases. Cases of intermediate severity have been observed. Autosomal recessive inheritance.

Multifactorial Inheritance (See Polygenic Inheritance)

Multiple Abnormality Syndrome, Congenital A disorder in which there are defects of various parts of the body occurring together. There may be considerable variation in the number, extent and severity of features between individuals with the same specific disorder. A multiple abnormality disorder may be congenital or acquired. (See also Syndrome)

Murmur An uneven rustling sound heard over the heart and various blood vessels in certain disorders of the heart. **Aortic murmur;** indicative of aortic valve disorder. **Diastolic murmur;** heard after the second heart sound. **Mitral murmur;** indicative of mitral valve incompetence. **Systolic murmur;** heard during systole, i.e. contraction of the heart muscle.

Muscular Dystrophy, Duchenne Type (See Duchenne Muscular Dystrophy)

Mutant Gene An altered or changed gene.

Mutation A change in a gene which occurs by chance.

Mutism (See Elective Mutism)

Myasthenia Muscular weakness.

Myelitis Inflammation of the spinal cord or bone marrow resulting from injury, disease or fever, or from inflammation extending from the membrane of the cord.

Myeloma *pl. myelomata* A tumour of bone marrow cells.

Myoclonic Seizure A type of epilepsy which takes the form of brief, involuntary and forceful contractions of the muscles, without loss of consciousness. Often a result of brain disease such as meningitis or encephalitis. (See also Epilepsy)

Myoclonia or **Myoclonus** Brief, involuntary spasms of muscle.

Myoma *pl. myomata* A tumour composed of muscle tissue.

Myopathy A condition in which weakness and wasting occurs in muscles, without apparent disorder of the nervous system.

Myopia Short-sightedness.

Myositis Inflammation of muscle.

Myotonia Delay in the relaxation of muscle after voluntary contraction.

Myotonic Dystrophy or **Dystrophia Myotonica** Onset is usually in adult life, but babies born of affected women may have a severe congenital form of the disease. In the infantile form, features may include: respiratory and feeding difficulties, muscular weakness and wasting, eye defects, heart defects, club foot, learning difficulty. Autosomal dominant inheritance.

Myxoedema A disorder caused by inadequacy of thyroid secretion, resulting in slowness, lethargy, coldness and puffiness of tissues.

Myxoma *pl. myxomata* A tumour composed of mucous tissue.

Naevus *pl. naevi* An area of excessive colour upon the skin, consisting of dilated blood vessels (haemangioma) or pigmented cells (melanoma or mole).

Naevus Flammeus A flat, reddish-purple area on the skin. It usually occurs on the face, but may be present elsewhere on the body; a 'port wine stain'.

Naevus Sebaceous of Jadassohn (See Linear Sebaceous Naevus Sequence)

Naevus Sebaceum Slightly raised, firm yellow plaques, usually occurring on the face or scalp. Formed by a collection of sebaceous glands.

Nanism A general term for dwarfism.

Nebula Cloudiness of the cornea, resulting in hazy vision.

Negative Reinforcement (See Reinforcement, Negative)

Neoplasm Literally, 'new formation'; a term for a diseased new growth or tumour.

Nephritis Inflammation of the kidneys.

Nervous System The nervous system consists of cells and fibres. The fibres are long processes extending from the nerve cells. The brain and spinal cord are often referred to as the central nervous system. The nerves which lead from the brain and spinal cord to the outlying parts of the body make up the peripheral nervous system; those which carry impulses to and from blood vessels, glands and organ make up the autonomic nervous system. (See also Sympathetic Nervous System)

Neural Tube Defect Defective development of the brain and spinal cord.

Neuroaxonal Dystrophy, Infantile (See Infantile Neuroaxonal Dystrophy)

Neurocutaneous Disease A disease which affects both the nervous system and the skin, which share a common origin in the embryo.

Neurocutaneous Melanosis Sequence Features include: the presence at birth of dark thickened naevi over the abdomen, trunk and thighs, seizures and developmental deterioration in early infancy. Life expectancy limited to infancy in most cases. Sporadic, cause unknown.

4

Neurofibroma *pl. neurofibromata* A tumour composed of nerve and fibrous tissue.

Neurofibromatosis or **Von Recklinghausen Disease** Features, which are variable, include: cafe au lait patches, neurofibromata of the skin, sometimes of the bones, and occasionally of the brain. Mild learning difficulty may occur, but intellect is unimpaired in most cases. Autosomal dominant inheritance with many cases representing new mutations.

Neuroma *pl. neuromata* A tumour upon a nerve or in nerve tissue.

Neuropathy Disease or disorder of the nervous system.

Neurotic Behaviour (See Emotional and Behavioural Difficulties)

Neurovisceral Lipidosis, Familial (See Gangliosidosis, Generalised)

Niemann-Pick Disease or **Sphingomyelin Lipidosis** A disorder of lipid metabolism. Several types. **Type A (acute infantile)** Features include: onset during the first year, listlessness and lax muscle tone, sight deterioration, feeding problems, motor delay and loss of or failure to acquire normal skills. Life expectancy usually not exceeding infancy. **Type B** Features include: onset between 2 and 6 years with spleen enlargement and later liver enlargement, normal intelligence, slower progression than in Type A, with potential survival into adulthood. Autosomal recessive inheritance.

Nocturia Excessive passing of urine during the night.

Node A rounded lump or protuberance.

Nodule A small swelling or protuberance.

Non-Disjunction The failure of a pair of chromosomes to separate, resulting in an unequal number of 'daughter' cells.

Non-Specific The term used to describe a disorder which has no established identity or cause, and consists merely of a group of symptoms. The opposite of specific.

Non-Verbal Communication Communication by means of signs, symbols or gestures. (See Blissymbols; Makaton)

Noonan Syndrome A disorder in which many of the features resemble those of Turner (X0) syndrome, but which occurs in both males and females (Turner syndrome occurs only in females) and the chromosome pattern is normal. Features include: short stature, widely spaced eyes, drooping eyelids, dental anomalies, webbing of the neck or short broad neck, clinodactyly, spinal curvature and other skeletal anomalies, heart defects, underdeveloped genital organs, mild to moderate learning difficulty, usually with good social performance. Primarily autosomal dominant inheritance.

Normalisation The concept of care which is based on the principle that people with learning difficulty should be provided with the same quality of education, leisure and living conditions as the rest of the population.

Norm-Referenced Assessment A form of assessment which compares a child's performance with what an average child of the same age would be expected to do.

Norrie Disease or **Atrophy Oculi Congenita** Features, which are variable, include: eye opacities evident at birth or soon after, with little or no vision. Mild to profound learning difficulty (or intellectual deterioration after initial normal development) is present in about 50% of individuals. In some cases: short stature, neurosensory hearing loss. X-linked inheritance.

Nuclear Jaundice (See Kernicterus)

Nystagmus Involuntary flickering movements of the eyeball, from side to side, up and down, or in a circular movement.

Occipital Bone or **Occiput** The bone at the lower hinder part of the head, where it merges with the neck.

Occupational Therapy The provision of interesting and congenial work, within the limitation of a patient's physical and mental condition, to aid recovery. An occupational therapist will advise on the use of equipment, toys, art, music or craft to improve the dexterity and alertness of children with physical disability or learning difficulty.

Oculo-Cerebro-Renal Syndrome (See Lowe Syndrome)

Oculomandibulodyscephaly with Hypotrichosis Syndrome (See Hallermann-Streiff Syndrome)

Ocular-Motor Skills The coordination of eye and hand to perform tasks.

Oedema Swelling due to an accumulation of fluid in the tissues.

OFD Syndrome (See Oral-Facial-Digital Syndrome)

Oligodactyly Fewer than the normal number of fingers and/or toes.

Oligophrenia Impairment of intellect, congenital or acquired.

Omphalitis Inflammation of the umbilicus or navel.

Omphalocele Umbilical hernia. Another name for exomphalos.

Ophthalmia Inflammation of the eye, especially of the conjunctiva.

Ophthalmitis Inflammation of the eyeball.

Ophthalmoplegia Paralysis of the muscles of one or both eyes.

Opisthotonic Posture (See Opisthotonus)

Opisthotonus A spasm in which the muscles of the neck and back are extremely rigid, causing the back to be arched and the head thrown backward. Sometimes a feature of meningitis.

Opitz Syndrome Initially considered to represent two different disorders; Opitz G syndrome and Opitz BBB syndrome. Research suggests that the two syndromes are a single disorder, with wide variations in type and severity of features. Features, which are variable, include: widely spaced eyes, weak, hoarse cry in infancy, swallowing difficulty, small jaw, genital abnormalities in males, urinary tract abnormalities, mild learning difficulty. In some cases; cleft lip and/or palate, squint, downward slanting eyes, cranial asymmetry, heart defects. Autosomal dominant inheritance.

Opitz-Kaveggia Syndrome (See FG Syndrome)

Optic Atrophy Wasting of the eye or of the optic nerve, where it joins the retina.

Oral-Facial-Digital Syndrome or **OFD Syndrome** Characterised by neurological disturbances, facial abnormalities, shortened limbs and deformities of the hands and feet. Divided into four types, characterised by specific features. **Type 1:** a partial cleft of mid upper lip, tongue and gum, webbing between gum and cheek, broad nasal bridge, short and thin tip of nose, prominent brow, absence of teeth (especially the lower incisors), deep grooves across the palate, additional fingers and/or toes on one side of body and joined by webbing, shortness and/or curving of digits, coarse and sparse scalp hair. **Type 2:** similar to Type 1 but the additional and

4

webbed digits occur on both sides of the body. **Type 3**: extra teeth, 'jaw-winking' signs. **Type 4**: shortened limbs, pyschomotor delay, abnormalities of jaw, tongue and teeth, ocular abnormalities. Autosomal recessive inheritance in Types 1, 2 and 3, X-linked inheritance in Type 4.

Organic Disease (See Disease)

Osteitis Inflammation of a bone or bones.

Osteochondritis Inflammation of both bone and cartilage.

Osteopathy The method of treatment which employs the manipulation of bones and other parts, in order to restore them to efficient function.

Osteopetrosis, Infantile or **Albers-Schönberg Syndrome** A metabolic disorder which results in overproduction of bone. Features include: enlarged head with prominent brow, optic atrophy, progressive increase in bone density, anaemia, dental defects, liver and spleen enlargement. In some cases brain damage may result in varying degrees of learning difficulty. Blood transfusion is used as a treatment for the anaemia. Life expectancy is usually limited, but bone marrow transplantation has resulted in improvement in some cases. Autosomal recessive inheritance. There is a milder form which may not be recognised until adolescence or early adulthood. This type is generally considerd to be dominantly inherited but an autosomal recessive form has been described.

Osteoporosis A disorder in which the bones are excessively porous due to deficiency of calcium salts. May be due to hormone or protein deficiency.

Ostomy An artificial opening in the abdominal region for the discharge of faeces or urine.

Otitis Inflammation of the ear. **Otitis media**: inflammation of the middle ear.

Oto-Palato-Digital Syndrome or **Taybi Syndrome** Features include: small stature, prominent and thick frontal bone and occipital bones, underdeveloped facial bones with small nose and mouth, hearing loss, defects of the teeth, cleft soft palate, speech defects, small trunk, limitation of elbow movement, short finger and thumb bones and short nails, mild to moderate learning difficulty. X-linked inheritance.

Oxycephaly A deformity of the skull in which the top is pointed and the forehead abnormally high. Due to premature closure of the coronal suture and sometimes other sutures of the skull. (See also Craniosynostosis; Sutures of the Skull, Premature Closure of Several)

Ozena An offensive discharge from the nose as a result of ulceration or inflammation of its mucous membrane lining.

Pachygyria Thickening in the surface of the brain resulting in poor definition of the convolutions (gyri). Pachygyria results in variable 'smoothing out' of the brain's surface, which normally consists of deep folds.

Pachymeningitis Inflammation and thickening of the dura mater of the brain and spinal cord.

Pachysomia Excessive thickening of soft parts of the body.

Paget-Gorman System A system of signing, used to promote communication with children who have little or no speech.

Pallister-Killian Syndrome or **Tetrasomy 12p** Tetrasomy of the short arm of chromosome 12. Features include: growth deficiency, lax muscle tone, hearing loss, seizures, areas of decreased skin pigmentation, sparse scalp hair with unusual distribution, mild to severe delay in psychomotor development. All reported cases have been sporadic. (See also Chromosome Abnormality)

Palmar Crease (See Dermal Ridges; Ridge Count; Simian Crease)

Palsy An alternative term for Paralysis.

Palsy, Bulbar (See Bulbar Palsy)

Pancytopenia Syndrome, Fanconi (See Fanconi Anaemia Syndrome)

Panneuropathy The term used to describe a disorder affecting the whole of the nervous system.

Papilla *pl. papillae* A small natural projection or elevation on skin or mucous membrane.

Papilloma *pl. papillomata* A tumour composed of papillae, growing from the skin or mucous membrane.

Paracentric Inversion (See Chromosome Abnormality)

Paralysis Loss of muscular power and sensation due to interference with the nerve supply to a part.

Paraphasia Incorrect usage of words or order of words as a result of disorder in the speech region of the brain.

Paraplegia Paralysis of the legs and lower trunk, usually including paralysis of the bladder and rectum.

Paresis Weakening or slight paralysis of a part with reduced function, as opposed to complete paralysis in which there is total loss of function.

Parietal Bones The bones which form the sides of the skull and part of its roof.

Paroxysm A sudden attack of a disease or symptom.

Patau Syndrome or 13+ Syndrome (See Chromosome Abnormality Syndromes)

Patent Ductus Arteriosus (See Ductus Arteriosus)

Pathognomonic Specially characteristic signs or symptoms of a disease, on the presence of which diagnosis depends.

Pathological Demand Avoidance Syndrome A pervasive developmental disorder which has some genetic links with autism. However, there are some basic differences in the features of the two conditions and the way they are managed. Affected children show a passive early history which may mask the degree of abnormality. Language may be delayed and while not disordered in itself, the content may be odd. Individuals with the syndrome resist and avoid the ordinary demands of life, using skilful strategies which are socially manipulative (distracting adults, using excuses, appearing to become physically incapacitated, withdrawal into fantasy, bombarding the adult with words to drown out demands, screaming, kicking, hitting out). There is a surface sociability, apparent lack of social identity or pride, a tendency to be comfortable in role play and pretending, obsessional behaviour, clumsiness and physical awkwardness.

Pectus Carinatum Protruding chest.

Pectus Excavatum Sunken chest; an indentation of the lower part of the breast bone, producing round shoulders and a hollow, thin and underdeveloped chest.

Pena-Shokeir Syndrome, Type 1 Features include: growth deficiency, prominent and widely spaced eyes, small mouth and jaw, flexing of limbs and digits, lack of lung development, profound brain abnormalities. Because of the severity of the

4

defects, life expectancy is limited to early infancy. Autosomal recessive inheritance.

Pena-Shokeir Syndrome, Type 2 or **Cerebro-Oculo-Facio-Skeletal Syndrome, COFS Syndrome** Features include: failure to thrive with lack of growth and no weight increase, microcephaly, upper lip overlapping the lower, deep set eyes, flexing of fingers/elbows/knees, abundant hair, spinal curvature, widely spaced nipples, decrease in the white matter of the brain. Life expectancy not usually exceeding 5 years. Autosomal recessive inheritance.

Penta X Syndrome or **XXXXX Syndrome** (See Chromosomal Abnormality Syndromes, Sex)

Perception The ability to understand and interpret impressions by means of the senses, e.g. sight, hearing, touch, smell and taste.

Perceptual Disorder Difficulty in interpreting sensory information; inability to recognise what is seen, despite normal vision, inability to interpret sounds or to understand the meaning of spoken words, despite normal hearing, difficulty with recognising objects by touch, confusion of left and right, problems with reading and writing. Special diagnostic tests are used to measure eye-motor coordination, figure ground perception, form constancy, position in space and spatial relationships. Training programmes aiming to compensate for perceptual disorders seek to improve visual perception and perceptuo-motor skills, assuming that if these are improved, then learning difficulties will be eased.

Perceptual Skills The ability to make sense of shapes and patterns.

Perceptuo-Motor Dysfunction (See Dyspraxia)

Pericardium The smooth membrane surrounding the heart.

Pericentric Inversion (See Chromosome Abnormality)

Perinatal Factors Events which occur in the process of birth or soon after birth (from birth to four weeks) may cause conditions which lead to special educational needs. These events include birth asphyxia resulting in anoxia or hypoxia and mechanical injury to the brain. (See also Brain Damage)

Peripatetic Teacher A teacher, employed to work with children at home or in hospital when they are unable to attend school.

Peripheral Nervous System (See Nervous System)

Periventricular Leukomalacia (PVIL) An injury to part of the brain near the ventricles, resulting in lack of oxygen. Usually occurs in premature infants.

Pertussis Whooping cough.

Pervasive Developmental Disorders A group of uncommon disorders in which social skills are deficient and the development of verbal and non-verbal communication is impaired. Affected individuals are unable to take part in activities which require a degree of imagination and there is delayed development of intellect, language skills and motor skills. The condition varies in degree from individual to individual. Autism is the most well-known pervasive developmental disorder. (See also Asperger Syndrome; Autism; Kanner Syndrome)

Pes Cavus A deformity of the foot, in which the arch is abnormally high, the foot is shortened and the heel and toes turn downward; 'claw foot'.

Pes Equinovarus (See Talipes)

Pes Planus Flat foot. A deformity of the foot in which the arch is flattened, so that the inner edge of the foot touches the ground.

Petit Mal (See Epilepsy; Pyknolepsy)

Phakoma Patches of grey/white colouring in the retina. Sometimes a feature of tuberous sclerosis.

Phenocopy A syndrome or disease which is indistinguishable from another with a different cause.

Phenotype The total of all the characteristics of an individual which can be observed; anatomical, physiological, biochemical and psychological. Also used to describe the external physical appearance of an individual.

Phenylketonuria A disorder of amino acid metabolism. If untreated, there is accumulation of phenylalanine and resulting brain damage. The disorder is tested for routinely in infancy, and treatment results in normal development and life expectancy. Attempts are being made to prevent damage to the foetus in pregnant women who have treated phenylketonuria, by control of their intake of phenylalanine. In untreated infants, the features include: fair hair and pale blue eyes due to lack of pigmentation (regardless of family colouring), learning difficulty. Autosomal recessive inheritance.

Phocomelia A severe reduction in size or absence of the top part of a limb, with the result that the extremity of the limb (hand or foot) is situated abnormally close to the trunk.

Photophobia Inability to tolerate light.

Photosensitivity Sensitivity to light.

Phthisis Progressive wasting and enfeeblement. Originally used to describe severe tuberculosis.

Physical Disability Disabilities limiting mobility, due to congenital defects, accident, injury or disease. Including children with physical disabilities in mainstream school may involve adapting buildings, the use of mobility aids such as wheel-chairs and adaptive equipment.

Physiotherapy The method of treatment which employs physical and natural measures, such as light, heat, water etc. Therapists are trained to assess motor abilities and to carry out treatment to promote better movement and bodily strength. They will also advise on aids and appliances.

Pica An eating disorder, manifesting in the eating of inedible or unnatural substances, or a craving for them.

Pierre Robin Syndrome (See Robin Sequence)

Plantar Reflex (See Babinski Reflex)

Pleiotropic The term used to denote a single gene causing many abnormalities.

Plica The term used to denote a folded structure in the body.

Pneumonia Inflammation of the lungs. (See also Aspiration Pneumonia)

Poikilocyte An abnormally shaped blood corpuscle found in some types of anaemia.

Poikiloderma Congenitale Syndrome (See Rothmund-Thomson Syndrome)

Polydactyly One or more extra fingers or toes.

Polygenic Inheritance or **Multifactorial Inheritance** The type of inheritance involved in many common single malformations, e.g. neural tube defects, some congenital heart defects and some cases of cleft lip and palate. Many genes

4

are thought to be involved in the formation of these parts of the body and in some families there is a genetic predisposition for these conditions to occur. However, it is also thought that environmental factors have some part to play in the production of an abnormality. This type of inheritance is sometimes referred to as multifactorial.

Polyneuropathy A disorder involving many nerves or much of the nervous system.

Polysyndactyly One or more extra fingers or toes, joined by webbing.

Polyuria The passing of excessive quantities of urine.

Pompe Disease (See Glycogen Storage Disease, Type 2)

Porencephaly A disorder in which cyst-like spaces or cavities occur in or upon the brain as a result of faulty development or haemorrhage at birth.

Port Wine Stain A form of naevus, in the form of deep red or purple colouration of the skin.

Portage A teaching package developed in the USA to enable parents of young children with special educational needs to work with them at home. A team, usually comprising of a teacher, a health visitor and a family service worker, guides the parents through various stages of development and advises on the teaching approach. It covers six areas; infant stimulation, socialisation, language, self-help skills, cognitive development and motor development.

Positive Reinforcement (See Reinforcement, Postive)

Prader-Willi Syndrome or **Prader-Willi-Labhart Syndrome** Features, which are variable, include: growth deficiency, lax muscle tone, small hands and feet, squint, thick skin, underdevelopment of genital organs, speech and walking delay, excessive appetite becoming apparent in early childhood, moderate to severe learning difficulty. There may be some behaviour problems associated with the demand for food. Diabetes may be a late complication. A deletion in the long arm of chromosome 15 has been found in over half of reported cases.

Predisposition Susceptibility to a specific disease or disorder.

Premature Closure of Sutures (See Sutures of the Skull, Premature Closure of Several)

Prevalence The extent to which a disorder occurs within a given population.

Primary Reinforcement (See Reinforcement)

Proband An individual who forms the starting point for the study of family genetics.

Process A outgrowth or protuberance.

Profound and **Multiple Learning Difficulties (PMLD)** The existence in one individual of physical and sensory impairments resulting in an inability to function beyond the earliest level of development. Pupils with PMLD may have physical and sensory impairments, challenging behaviour and communication difficulties. A multi-professional approach is necessary with teachers, therapists and others working closely together. Among the principles which should guide the curriculum are that it should involve planning based on the pupil's needs, interests, aptitudes and achievements. It should be broad and balanced and provide progression and continuity. Pupils should have access to programmes of study which enable them to make progress and which show achievement. (See also Learning Difficulty)

Progeria Premature ageing.

Prognathia or **Prognathism** Projection of the jaw.

Prognathous Having a projecting jaw.

Progressive Disorder A disorder in which there is deterioration. The progression may be slow or rapid.

Progressive Hepatolenticular Degeneration (See Wilson Disease)

Prompt A term used in behaviour modification to denote a physical or verbal cue designed to produce a specific response or behaviour in an individual.

Pronation The downward turning of the palm of the hand.

Prosthesis The fitting of an artificial part or parts to the body, or any artificial cosmetic, social or environmental device which makes up for a deficiency.

Pseudo-Hurler Polydystrophy or **Mucolipidosis, Type 3** Features include: onset between 1 and 4 years, growth deficiency, mild coarsening of facial features, mild corneal opacities, stiffness of joints, heart valve defects, mild to moderate deterioration of the central nervous system, mild learning difficulty. The features are similar to those of Hurler syndrome and Leroy 1-cell disease, but are of a milder nature. Autosomal recessive inheritance.

Pseudohypoparathyroidism (See Albright Hereditary Osteodystrophy Syndrome)

Psychomotor Development The development of bodily movement skills, speech and learning.

Psychomotor Impairment Impairment of motor activity, speech and learning.

Psychotic Behaviour (See Emotional and Behavioural Difficulties)

Pterygium Webbing; a piece of extra tissue between two structures where none should exist, i.e. in the front of the elbow or back of the knee. Also applied to a portion of opaque tissue which may form over the cornea.

Pterygium Colli Webbing of the neck.

Ptosis Drooping of an organ. Commonly applied to drooping of the upper eyelids.

Purpura Purple spots and patches caused by the leakage of blood into the tissues under the skin.

Pus Thick yellowish fluid found in abscesses, ulcers and discharging surfaces. It is the result of inflammation due to bacterial infection and is composed mainly of dead white blood cells.

Pustule A small pimple containing pus.

Pyknolepsy Slight and almost continuous fits in which there is sudden and temporary loss of consciousness, but no convulsions. (See also Epilepsy)

Pyloric Stenosis Narrowing of the opening from the lower part of the stomach into the duodenum. May be congenital or acquired.

Pyrexia A rise in body temperature; fever.

Quadriparesis Weakness of all four limbs.

Quadriplegia Paralysis of all four limbs.

Rate Recording A term used in behaviour modification to denote the recording of the number of times a behaviour has occurred.

4

Receptive Aphasia Impairment of the understanding of language.

Recessive Gene A gene which is the weaker of a pair and whose characteristic is only expressed if paired with another recessive gene for the same characteristic. (See also Autosomal Recessive Disorder)

Recessive Inheritance (See Autosomal Recessive Disorder)

Reciprocal Translocation (See Chromosome Abnormality)

Reflex Arc The system of sensory and motor neurones which carry out a reflex action.

Reinforcement, Negative A term used in behaviour modification to denote the withdrawal of something a person dislikes, or of a punishment, so that the individual learns that he can remove it by appropriate behaviour.

Reinforcement, Positive A term used in behaviour modification to denote the provision of something a person likes, or a reward, to encourage appropriate behaviour.

Reinforcement, Primary A term used in behaviour modification to denote a reinforcement which is not specially created, but is rewarding in itself, such as food or a show of affection.

Relapse Recurrence of a disease or symptoms after a degree of recovery.

Remission Lessening or disappearance of the symptoms of a disease for a time.

Remittent Subsiding at intervals.

Renpenning Syndrome (See Fragile-X Syndrome)

Respite Care The provision of services which provide breaks for parents of children with special needs. Care may be given in the child's home, in the home of a respite foster family or in residential establishments. Respite care is provided by social services departments, voluntary organisations or by support groups run by parents.

Retinitis Pigmentosa A degenerative disorder which affects the retina of the eye. It can be inherited in several ways as an isolated disease and sometimes occurs as one feature of a multiple abnormality disorder.

Retrolental Fibroplasia An acquired condition in premature infants, in which there is too much oxygen in the blood, resulting in partial or total blindness.

Rett Syndrome Features include: apparently normal development for the first few months, then psychomotor deterioration, absent or defective speech, lack of facial expression, seizures, characteristic walk, persistent and bizarre movements of the hands, raised ammonia levels, loss of previously acquired skills, resulting in severe learning difficulty. Slowly progressive with continued deterioration. All reported cases have been female. X-linked dominant inheritance.

Reward An alternative term for reinforcement in behaviour modification.

Reye Syndrome Features include: initial normal development with onset varying from infancy to adolescence, vomiting, changes in consciousness sometimes amounting to coma, raised blood ammonia levels, fatty changes in the liver and other organs. In some cases: ammonia intoxication resulting in brain damage and intellectual and physical deterioration. Diagnosis can only be made with certainty by carrying out liver biopsy during the acute stage of the illness. The cause is not established, but onset has been observed after viral infection, suggesting that there may be an abnormal response or abnormal sensitivity to relatively common viral infections or toxins.

Rheumatoid Disorders A disorder characterised by inflammation, degeneration and derangement of connective tissues in particular those of the joints. It is associated with pain, stiffness and restrictions of movement.

Rhinitis Inflammation of the mucous membrane in the nose resulting in thick mucous discharge, i.e. catarrh.

Rhizomelic Chondrodysplasia Punctata Syndrome Features include: slow growth, small skull, flat face with low nasal bridge, cataracts, shortening of the upper arm and thigh bones, multiple joint contractures, irregularity of vertebrae, poor development of the pelvis. In some cases: spasticity, mild to severe learning difficulty. Autosomal recessive inheritance. (See also Conradi-Hünermann Syndrome)

Rickets A childhood disorder in which there is softening of the bones due to deficiency of vitamin D and calcium in the diet. If untreated, deformity may result.

Ridge Count The number of ridges on the soles of the feet and the palms of the hands. In certain conditions, notably chromosome disorders, palms and soles can show unusual patterns and prints. Diagnosis of specific conditions is sometimes aided by observing these patterns. (See also Dermal Ridges; Flexion Creases)

Rigor A sudden attack of shivering and sweating due to a sudden rise in body temperature.

Riley-Day Syndrome or **Familial Dysautonomia Types 1 & 2** Features include: swallowing difficulty, vomiting, breath-holding attacks in infancy, blotchy skin, excessive sweating, decreased sensitiv-ity to pain, lack of tear production, taste deficiency, bouts of fever, frequent urination, poor coordination, spinal curvature in mid to late childhood, progressive neurological deterioration. In Type 2 seizures and mild to severe learning difficulty occur in some individuals. Type 1; Autosomal dominant inheritance. Type 2; Autosomal recessive inheritance.

Ring 18 Abnormality or **18r Syndrome** (See Chromosome Abnormality Syndromes)

Ring D Abnormality or **13r Syndrome** (See Chromosome Abnormality Syndromes)

Ring Formation of Chromosome (See Chromosome Abnormality)

Roberts Syndrome Features include: small, short and broad skull, profound growth deficiency, protruding eyes, cleft lip and/or palate, small jaw, eye defects, severe shortening of limbs with absence of digits and/or webbing of digits, severe learning difficulty. In some cases: kidney defects, heart defects. Short life expectancy in most cases. Autosomal recessive inheritance.

Robertsonian Translocation (See Chromosome Abnormality)

Robin Sequence, Pierre Robin Syndrome Faulty development of the lower jaw in foetal life which causes the tongue to be pushed up, preventing closure of the palate. Feeding difficulties and respiratory distress are common but tend to improve with age. The prognosis is very good for children in whom the Robin sequence is the only abnormality, providing there is early attention to feeding and breathing difficulties and corrective surgery where required. The Robin sequence can also occur as one of the features in a multiple abnormality syndrome (Pierre Robin syndrome) in which there may be eye and skeletal defects and varying degrees of learning difficulty. Cause not established.

Rocker-Bottom Feet An abnormality of the feet in which the soles curve outwards, rather than inward, giving them a 'rocker' appearance.

Romberg Sign Inability to stand upright without swaying when the eyes are closed. A result of disorder of the nervous system.

Rothmund Thomson Syndrome or **Poikiloderma Congenitale** Features, which are variable include: small stature, scattered red or pink colouring of cheeks, later replaced by net-like patterns which spread to the ears and extremities, then to the rest of the body, sparse and short hair, thick skin, cataracts. In some cases: deficiencies or absence of teeth, skeletal anomalies. Mild learning difficulty occurs in some cases, but intellect is unimpaired in most cases. Autosomal recessive inheritance.

Rubella German measles. When contracted by a woman in early pregnancy, rubella may result in defects of the brain, ears and eyes in the foetus. Inoculation of teenage girls is used to prevent rubella in future pregnancies.

Rubella Effects, Foetal or **Rubella Syndrome** Multiple defects affecting the foetus as a result of the mother having had rubella in early pregnancy. Damage occurs in about 50% of cases. Features, which are variable, include: eye defects, hearing loss, enlarged liver and spleen, hernias, low birth weight, heart defects, mild to severe learning difficulty. The risk of abnormality in the foetus is higher in mothers infected during early pregnancy.

Rubeola An alternative name for measles.

Rubenstein-Taybi Syndrome Features include: characteristic facial features with microcephaly, widely spaced eyes, squint, drooping eyelids, pointed nose, obstructed nasal passages, high narrow palate, low set and malformed ears, short stature, lax muscle tone, stiff gait, wide and flat digits with broad thumbs, mild to severe learning difficulty. In some cases: clinodactyly, overlapping of digits, duplication of thumb, seizures, heart defects, kidney defects. Usually sporadic.

Saethre-Chotzen Syndrome or **Acrocephalosyndactyly, Type 3** Features, which are variable, include: short and broad skull, facial asymmetry, widely spaced eyes with drooping eyelids, prominent nose and protruding jaw, soft tissue webbing of the areas of the fingers closest to the palm, usually only involving two or three digits. In some cases: small stature, hearing defects, squint, kidney defects, heart defects. Mild to moderate learning difficulty may occur but intellect is unimpaired in most cases. The syndactyly requires surgery only for cosmetic reasons. Autosomal dominant inheritance proposed. (See Craniosynostosis; Skull, Bones of the; Sutures of the Skull)

Saggital Suture The junction of the parietal bones of the skull, running from the middle to the back of the top of the head.

Salaam Spasm A feature of some types of epilepsy in which the patient suddenly falls forward with arms out, as though in a form of greeting. (See also Epilepsy)

Salivation Excessive flow of saliva; 'dribbling'.

Sanfillipo Disease or **Sanfillipo Syndrome, Mucopolysaccharidosis 3, MPS 3** (See Mucopolysaccharidoses; Mucopolysaccharidosis 3)

Sarcoma *pl. sarcomata* A malignant tumour composed of connective tissue cells.

Satiation A term used in behaviour modification to denote a situation in which a reward has lost its effectiveness because it has been used for too long a time.

Scaphocephaly A long narrow head shape caused by premature closure of the saggital suture. (See also Craniosynostosis; Skull, Bones of the; Sutures of the Skull)

Scheie Disease or **Scheie Syndrome, Mucopolysaccharidosis 1 S, MPS 1 S** (See Mucopolysaccharidoses; Mucopolysaccharidosis 1 S)

Schizencephaly An abnormality of brain development in which it is cleft from the surface to the deep structures. These clefts usually follow the lines of the fissures which divide the lobes. The affected part is usually underdeveloped.

School Phobia/School Refusal School phobia is a term which may be applied to a child who develops a strong resistance to leaving home because of internal emotional conflicts or distress, not necessarily connected with school. When a child shows a rational and conscious resistance to going to school, the term 'school refusal' is more appropriate.

Scissor-Leg Deformity (See Little Disease)

Scleroderma A disease in which the skin becomes hardened, resulting in a stiffening of the joints, wasting of muscle and limitation of movement.

Sclerosis A condition in which organs become hardened and lose their function as a result of overproduction of connective and fibrous tissue.

Scoliosis Curvature of the spine, most commonly applied to a lateral curve (i.e. to one side).

Seborrhoea A disorder of the sebaceous glands in which there is an excessive secretion of sebum, resulting in oily scaling upon the skin.

Seckel Syndrome Features include: severe short stature, microcephaly, small facial features, prominent nose, widely spaced eyes, low set and malformed ears, curvature of fingers, feeding difficulties, poor weight gain, moderate to severe learning difficulty. In some cases: hip, knee, ankle or foot deformities. Autosomal recessive inheritance.

Secondary Disease, Secondary Disorder (See Disease)

Seitelberger Disease (See Infantile Neuroaxonal Dystrophy)

Selective Mutism (See Elective Mutism)

Self-Advocacy (See Advocacy)

Self-Injurious Behaviour Repeated behaviour which causes physical harm, such as self-biting, head-banging, gouging of the eyes and pulling out of hair. People with severe learning difficulties and those with certain types of mental illness can exhibit this type of behaviour. Self-injurious behaviour is a feature of Lesch-Nyhan syndrome, an inherited metabolic disorder. Other possible causes include self-stimulation as a result of insufficient external stimulation, attention seeking and avoidance of unwanted situations. Treatment may include behaviour modification techniques. Where the potential for injury is sufficiently serious, aversion therapy may be considered.

Seizure Threshold The tolerance level of the brain for electrical activity. If that level is exceeded, a seizure results.

4

Semantic-Pragmatic Disorder An inability to use speech appropriately and difficulty in understanding the meaning of the spoken word. Features include; delayed language development, problems with understanding questions, mixing up 'I' and 'you', repeating phrases out of context and difficulty in following conversations. This condition was originally thought to be distinct from autism but many people with autism also have semantic pragmatic disorder and most children diagnosed with semantic-pragmatic disorder also have some mild autistic features. It has been proposed that semantic-pragmatic disorder should be included in the autistic continuum and that children with semantic-pragmatic disorder might be more accurately described as high-functioning autistic. Asperger syndrome is considered by some to be a distinct syndrome while others regard it as synonymous with the higher levels of functioning of individuals on the autistic spectrum. Children with semantic-pragmatic difficulties are usually late in talking whereas children with Asperger syndrome are usually able to form sentences before the age of three. There are also differences in the results of verbal and performance IQ tests between children with Asperger syndrome and those with semantic-pragmatic disorder. Studies suggest that there may be a single underlying cognitive impairment which produces both semantic-pragmatic disorder and autistic features. (See also Asperger Syndrome; Autism)

Sensory Training A teaching method in which there is stimulation of all the senses, to promote the maximum responsiveness.

Sepsis Infection of the body by pus-forming bacteria.

Sequelae The effects or symptoms liable to result from a specific disease, e.g. a chest infection following measles.

Severe Learning Difficulties (SLD) Severe learning difficulties are caused by many factors. These include: chromosome abnormalities, genetic disorders, prenatal factors (infections, chemicals e.g. alcohol, or malnutrition in the mother), perinatal factors (birth injury or lack of oxygen), postnatal factors and acquired factors (infections e.g. meningitis, malnutrition, toxic effects e.g. lead, or brain damage due to head injury). The curriculum for pupils with SLD should be broad and balanced and underpinned by the National Curriculum. It has a developmental dimension, aiming to develop knowledge, skills and attitudes which will assist the pupil in later life to be as autonomous as possible and to live in the community as appropriate. (See also Learning Difficulty)

Sex Chromosome Abnormality Syndromes (See Chromosome Abnormality Syndromes, Sex)

Sex Chromosomes (See Chromosome)

Shagreen Patch An area of skin, raised and thickened and sometimes pinkish in colour. A feature of tuberous sclerosis.

Short Arm Deletion of Chromosomes (See Chromosome; Chromosome Abnormality; Chromosome Abnormality Syndromes)

Sialidosis or Mucolipidosis, Type 1 Formerly termed lipomucopolysaccharidosis. A metabolic disorder, characterised by features similar to those of Hurler syndrome, but of a milder nature. Features include: short trunk with relatively long limbs, cherry-red spot in the eye, impaired hearing, lax muscle tone, tremor and jerky movements. Slowly progressive, with moderate learning difficulty. Autosomal recessive inheritance.

Simian Crease or **Simian Line** An abnormal palm crease found in about 5% of the normal population, but also found commonly in Down syndrome and other chromosomal disorders. 1. The two outer creases on the palm fuse and form a single line (simian line or transverse palmar crease). 2. The two outer creases are not fused but a third small crease is present (transitional simian crease). (See also Dermal Ridges; Flexion Creases; Ridge Count)

Simple Partial Seizure Onset usually between 4 and 12 years. The child may experience an aura, a feeling of discomfort or dread and there may be increased pulse rate and flushing of face. Consciousness is not lost. A Jacksonian or focal motor seizure is one type.

Sjogren-Larsson Syndrome Features include: short stature, scaly and thickened skin in most areas except the face, brittle and sparse hair, spasticity, speech defects, moderate to severe learning difficulty. Autosomal recessive inheritance.

Skeleton The system of bone and cartilage which forms and protects the internal structures and organs of the body. **Axial skeleton**; consists of the skull, the vertebral column, the ribs and the breast-bone. **Appendicular skeleton**; consists of the bones of the four limbs.

Skull, Bones of the The skull is composed of 22 bones. The face has 14 bones, the cranium 8 bones. The cranial bones are joined and locked together by sutures (similar to a seam). At birth, these sutures are not developed, so areas of the skull are left unjoined. These areas are the 'soft spots' or fontanelles. The bones grow outwards until, by about 2 years old, they are fused together. The last of the fontanelles to close (the anterior fontanelle) is the 'soft spot' on the top of the head. In certain disorders, the skull bones fuse prematurely, causing an abnormal head shape. (See Craniosynostosis; Frontal Bone; Malar Bone; Mandible; Maxilla; Occipital Bone; Parietal Bone; Sphenoid Bone; Sutures of the Skull; Temporal Bone)

Smith-Lemli-Opitz Syndrome Features include: microcephaly, low birth weight, characteristic facial appearance with an upturned nose, underdeveloped chin and drooping eyelids, feeding difficulties and lax muscle tone in infancy, below average height and weight, abnormality of the genital organs in males, mild to severe learning difficulty. In some cases: extra and/or webbed and/or short digits, club foot, dislocation of hips, spasticity, heart defects. Autosomal recessive inheritance.

Smith-Magenis Syndrome or **Chromosome 17p Deletion** (See Chromosome Abnormality Syndromes)

Sotos Syndrome or **Cerebral Giantism** Features include: large head with prominent forehead, long face, above normal weight and height at birth and in childhood, feeding problems, receding hairline, widely spaced eyes, drooping eyelids, large and protruding ears, disproportionately large hands and feet, general clumsiness and awkward gait. Adults may be normal in height or excessively tall. Mild learning difficulty is common, but intellect may be unimpaired. Autosomal dominant inheritance has been documented but most cases are sporadic.

Spasm An involuntary and sometimes painful contraction of muscle, or of the muscular wall of a hollow organ. Spasms of the whole body are referred to as convulsions, painful spasms of muscles or

4

limbs as cramp, those in the stomach and abdomen as colic. **Clonic spasm;** twitching or rapid alternating contraction and relaxation of muscle. **Tonic spasm;** a firm strong contraction with rigidity of muscle.

Spasmodic In the nature of spasm; sudden contraction of muscle followed by relaxation.

Spastic Diplegia (See Little Disease)

Spastic Gait (See Gait)

Spasticity A tendency to spasm, with rigidity of muscle. Commonly associated with disorder of the nervous system, such as cerebral palsy, in which there is interference with the control of muscle tension. (See also Cerebral Palsy; Ataxia; Athetosis)

Special Care Unit A unit within a special school or centre for children and adults who have severe or profound learning difficulty, often combined with severe physical disability, or who have very severe behaviour problems. A unit usually has a high staff to pupil ratio, so that the children or adults may receive the constant attention they require.

Specially Resourced Schools Mainstream schools that have special facilities and specially trained staff to provide for children with special educational needs.

Specific Disorder A disorder which has a definite cause and identity, as opposed to one which is not named and consists merely of a group of symptoms (non-specific).

Specific Learning Difficulty (SpLD) A particular difficulty in one area of learning in a child who performs satisfactorily in other areas. Types of specific learning difficulty include acalculia, dyscalculia and dyslexia. The areas of difficulty should be identified, educational programmes should be provided to address them, and the programmes should be monitored to assess their effectiveness and modified as necessary. Multi-sensory teaching methods may be used. If difficulties relate to poor listening skills and a poor memory for auditory sequences, the teacher may check understanding by asking the pupil to repeat instructions. If pupils have difficulties relating to classroom organisation, the teacher should make sure that the pupil knows where resources are kept and can retrieve them. A variety of forms of presentation can help such as pictorial aids and artefacts as well as the spoken word. (See also Acalculia; Dyscalculia; Dyslexia; Learning Difficulty)

Speech and Language Difficulties Language is used to refer to aspects of grammar while speech refers to the physical utterances a person makes. Language difficulty may occur without speech difficulty and vice versa but speech and language difficulties often occur together. Because of the detrimental implications for learning and communication, speech and language therapy is essential for children who have speech and language problems. Therapy is important as part of an overall strategy involving classroom related work. In the classroom, pupils with receptive difficulties may be helped by the teacher simplifying or repeating instructions. The social dimension in language is encouraged in the classroom as teachers seek to extend the pupil's language in different curriculum areas.

Speech and Language Therapy Assessment and treatment of speech and language difficulties, such as problems of voice production, articulation and language. Therapists are usually employed by the local authority and work in schools and health clinics. They will advise parents on the treatment of speech and language difficulties and methods of helping their children at home.

Sphenoid Bone The wedge-shaped bone which forms part of the base of the skull and houses the pituitary gland.

Sphingomyelin Lipidosis (See Niemann-Pick Disease)

Spina Bifida A defect in the development of the spinal column, and in some cases the spinal cord. It results in a gap in the vertebrae, so that the spinal cord is protected only by the skin. Membranes surrounding the cord bulge out and produce a swelling in the small of the back. Sometimes associated with hydrocephalus. (See also Meningomyelocele)

Spitz-Holter Valve A valve used for the treatment of hydrocephalus. It is inserted into a catheter and placed into the ventricle of the brain, so enabling the accumulated cerebrospinal fluid to drain away.

Spongy Degeneration of the Central Nervous System (See Canavan Disease)

Spontaneous Fracture A fracture which results from minimal pressure or from a normal amount of movement. A complication of diseased bone.

Squamous Scaly.

Squamosal Suture The joining point between the parietal bones and the temporal bones of the skull, on either side of the head.

Squint (See Strabismus)

Status Epilepticus A state of continuous epileptic seizures. The temperature rises to a high level and may further damage the brain if the seizures are not interrupted. The condition requires immediate admission to hospital. (See also Epilepsy)

Stenosis Unnatural narrowing of a passage or opening in the body. Commonly used to refer to narrowing in the openings of the heart in which the valves are situated, e.g. mitral stenosis.

Stenosis of the Aqueduct of Sylvius (See Aqueductal Stenosis)

Stertorous A snoring sound in breathing.

Sthenic Abnormally strong and active. Used to describe conditions in which there is abnormal increase in the action of an organ, e.g. the heart, as a result of disease.

Stigma *pl. stigmata* A spot or mark which is especially characteristic of a condition, disorder or defect.

Stomatitis Inflammation of the mucous membrane of the mouth, simple or with ulceration.

Strabismus Squint; a turning of either eye from its normal direction. **Convergent squint**; the eye is turned inward towards the nose. **Divergent squint**; the eye is turned outwards.

Stricture Narrowing of a natural passage or channel of the body, such as the oesophagus, bowel or urethra.

Stridor A harsh crowing sound heard during breathing, produced by narrowing of the larynx.

Stroma The tissue which forms the covering and framework of an organ, as opposed to its functioning tissue (parenchyma).

Structured Programme A teaching programme specially designed to help a child who has a particular educational difficulty.

Sturge-Weber Syndrome Features include: a 'port wine stain' on half the face and sometimes half the body, eye defects (choroidal angioma, glaucoma), seizures, paresis. In some cases: port wine stain on both sides of body, absence of port wine stain, disproportionate size of the two

4

halves of the body. Mild to severe learning difficulty occurs in some cases. Cause not established.

Sulfatide Lipidosis (See Metachromatic Leukodystrophy)

Supination Turning upwards, e.g. applied to the turning of the forearm and hand so that the palm faces upwards.

Suprabulbar Palsy (See Bulbar Palsy)

Suprabulbar Paresis, Congenital (See Worster-Drought Syndrome)

Sutures of the Skull The lines of junction between the bones of the skull. The bones, which are separate of birth, grow together gradually during the first two years of life. In some disorders the sutures close too early, resulting in skull deformity. (See Craniosynostosis; Coronal Suture; Lambdoid Suture; Metopic Suture; Saggital Suture; Skull, Bones of the; Squamosal Suture)

Sutures of the Skull, Premature Closure of Several If all the sutures of the skull are prematurely fused, the head remains small, the forehead is high and narrow, and the head is pointed towards the crown. Untreated patients may have symptoms of intracranial pressure and may be intellectually impaired but in many cases early corrective surgery results in normal intelligence. (See Craniosynostosis; Skull, Bones of the)

Sympathetic Nervous System The part of the autonomic nervous system which sends out nerve fibres to the involuntary muscles, e.g. those of the heart and intestines. (See also Nervous System)

Syndactyly Partial or complete fusion of two or more fingers or toes. The fusion may be of skin alone or composed of both skin and bone. Popularly known as 'webbed' fingers or toes. A feature of a number of multiple abnormality disorders.

Syndrome The term applied to a group of symptoms or features, occurring together regularly enough to constitute a disorder to which a particular name is given. In recognising a specific multiple abnormality syndrome, several factors are taken into account: 1. A minor abnormality occurring on its own is not indicative of a syndrome; 2. A specific abnormality can occur in several different syndromes; 3. It is not necessary for every associated abnormality to be present in every affected individual; 4. The number and severity of features may vary between individuals with the same syndrome.

Syphilis A venereal disease. A mother affected by syphilis during pregnancy may pass the infection on to her unborn child, with resulting damage. The presence of syphilis in a pregnant mother can be detected and treatment given to prevent damage to the foetus. In untreated cases there may be intellectual and physical abnormalities, varying from mild to severe.

Syphilis Syndrome, Congenital Damage to the developing foetus as a result of transmission of syphilis infection from the mother after the fourth month of pregnancy. In untreated cases features include: premature birth, protruding abdomen, withered skin, nasal discharge, copper coloured or red lesions around the genitals and back of thighs, bone abnormalities, irregular pupils of the eyes, dental defects, learning difficulty. In some cases: deafness, seizures. The effects of syphilis infection in infants can be cured or improved by early diagnosis and treatment with penicillin.

Systemic Pertaining to a whole system, the whole body or group of organs, as distinct from a separate part, e.g. the circulatory system or digestive system.

Systolic Murmur (See Murmur)

Tachycardia Abnormally rapid action of the heart and a resulting increase in pulse rate.

Tachypnoea Abnormally rapid breathing.

Talipes Club foot. There are several types, named according to the direction of the deformity. **Talipes calcaneus**; the toes are bent up so that the person walks on the heels. **Talipes equinus**; the heel is bent up so that the person walks on the toes. **Talipes valgus**; the ankle bends inward so that the sole of the foot bends outwards and the person walks on the inside of the foot. **Talipes varus**; the ankle bends outward so that the sole of the foot turns inward and the person walks on the outside of the foot. These deformities may occur in combination, e.g. talipes equino-varus or talipes calcaneo-varus. Talipes may be congenital or acquired.

Target Behaviour A term used in behaviour modification to denote the aspect of an individual's behaviour which is to be changed by training.

Targets or **Teaching Objectives** The skills that a school aims to achieve with an individual child, in a specified period of time.

Taybi Syndrome (See Oto-Palatal-Digital Syndrome)

Tay Sachs Disease or **Gangliosidosis (GM2)** A disorder of lipid metabolism. Features include: apparently normal development for several months then deterioration of motor development, progressive loss of vision from 9–12 months, rigidity, spasticity, seizures, hyperactive reflexes,

intellectual deterioration. Progressive, with life expectancy not usually exceeding 5 years. There is a juvenile type with later onset and longer life expectancy and an adult type with less severe effects. Autosomal recessive inheritance.

Telangiectasis A web-like or radiating pattern of abnormally dilated blood capillaries occurring, mostly on the face, in certain disorders of circulation.

Telangiectatic Fibroma *pl. telangiectatic fibromata* A tumour formed from fibrous tissue and blood vessels, radiating in a web-like pattern. Present around the nose and cheek areas in cases of tuberous sclerosis. (See also Angiofibroma)

Telangioma A tumour composed of dilated capillaries.

Telecanthus Abnormal placement of the inner canthus (the angle made by the junction of the upper and lower lids which forms the corners of the eyes), producing the effect of widely spaced eyes.

Temporal Bone The bones, one at each side of the skull, which contain the organs of hearing, taste and smell.

Temporal Lobe Epilepsy (See Complex Partial Seizures)

Teratogen A substance or combination of substances (e.g. a drug) which is potentially capable of producing defects in an unborn child, when a pregnant woman consumes or is exposed to it.

Teratogenesis The production of physical defects in the foetus.

Teratogen Syndromes (See Alcohol Effects, Foetal; Dilatin Syndrome, Foetal; Hydantoin Effects, Foetal; Trimethadione Effects, Foetal; Warfarin Effects, Foetal)

Tetralogy of Fallot A relatively common congenital heart disorder, consisting of

4

four main features: narrowing of the pulmonary valve, defect in the partition separating the two ventricles, overriding of both ventricles by the aorta, marked overgrowth of the right ventricle.

Tetraplegia Paralysis of all four limbs.

Tetrasomy (See Chromosome Abnormality)

Tetrasomy 12p (See Pallister-Killian Syndrome)

Thrombocytopenia A disease in which there is a marked reduction in the number of platelets (thrombocytes) in the blood.

Tic A twitch or series of twitches due to involuntary contraction of the muscles. Occurs commonly in the muscles of the face.

Time Out A method used in behaviour modification in which an individual is temporarily deprived of the reward of attention, approval or company, to reduce an inappropriate behaviour.

Tissue Masses of cells or fibres of various types which form all the structures in the body.

Todd's Paralysis A temporary period of paralysis, following certain types of epileptic seizure.

Tonic Seizure A form of epilepsy in which there are tonic spasms. (See also Epilepsy)

Tonic Spasm Firm, strong and prolonged muscular contraction, producing rigidity of muscle. There may be rigidity of the whole body at the beginning of an epileptic seizure, which then gives way to a series of convulsive movements (clonic spasms).

Tonic/Clonic Seizure A seizure in which there is alternating contraction and relaxation of muscle.

Torsion Twisting. It may occur in the narrow neck of a tumour or organ, causing constriction of the blood vessels and other structures.

Torticollis Contraction of one or more of the muscles of the neck, resulting in abnormal position of the head. It may occur on one side only, pulling the head into a sideways position; 'wry neck'.

Toxoid or **Anatoxin** A toxin which has been treated to reduce or remove its poisonous properties, but retains its power to stimulate the production of an antibody in the blood, e.g. diphtheria toxoid.

Toxoplasmosis, Congenital Damage to the developing foetus due to a parasite which may be acquired by the mother during pregnancy. In some cases, the foetus is aborted or stillborn. In those who survive, the features include: microcephaly or hydrocephaly, choreoretinitis, cataracts, enlargement of liver and spleen, jaundice, pallor, deafness. In some cases: glaucoma, seizures, mild to severe learning difficulty.

Tracheostomy An opening made into the trachea for the insertion of a tube. Used to provide an airway when normal breathing is impaired.

Transitional Simian Crease (See Simian Crease)

Translocation of Chromosomes (See Chromosome Abnormality)

Transverse Palmar Crease (See Simian Crease)

Treacher-Collins Syndrome or **Mandibulofacial Dysostosis, Franceschetti-Klein Syndrome** Features include: underdevelopment of the ears, cheek bones and chin, downward turning eyes and mouth, high palate and crowded teeth. In some cases: malformed ears, deafness. Mild learning difficulty may occur but intellect is unimpaired in most cases. Where learning difficulty is present, it may be as a result of hearing loss. Autosomal dominant inheritance.

Tremor A very fine trembling or jerking spasm. It may be seen in any projecting part, such as the hands, or in muscles. **Coarse tremor;** one which interferes with activities such as the ability to drink without spilling. **Fine tremor;** one in which there is trembling of the tongue or hands when held out. **Intention tremor;** one which occurs on attempting a specific movement. **Very fine tremor;** one which is visible in the muscles of the face or limbs (fibrillary tremor).

Trichiasis Irritation of the eyeball due to friction from abnormal positioning of the eyelashes.

Trichorhinophalangeal Syndrome Type 2 (See Langer-Giedion Syndrome)

Trichorrhoea The falling out of hair.

Trichosis An abnormal growth of hair.

Trigeminal Nerves The fifth pair of cranial nerves, each of which is divided into three main branches; the mandibular nerve, the maxillary nerve and the ophthalmic nerve.

Trigonocephaly A deformity of the skull in which there are deep indentations in the bones at each side of the forehead, resulting from premature closure of the metopic suture. (See also Craniosynostosis; Skull, Bones of the; Sutures of the Skull)

Trimethadione Effects, Foetal or **Foetal Trimethadione Syndrome** Damage to the developing foetus as a result of the administration of tremethadione or paramethadione to the mother during pregnancy. Damage does not occur in every case. Features, which are variable, include: growth deficiency, short skull, short upturned nose with broad, low bridge, prominent forehead, eyebrows almost meeting in the middle with a striking upslant to their outer edge, squint, drooping eyelids, epicanthic folds, cleft lip and/or palate, small jaw, poorly developed external ears, heart defects, genital abnormalities, speech disorders, mild to severe learning difficulty.

Triple X Syndrome or **XXX Syndrome** (See Chromosomal Abnormality Syndromes, Sex)

Triploidy (See Chromosome Abnormality)

Triploidy Syndrome Due to a complete extra set of chromosomes. Features include: low birth weight, lax muscle tone, webbing of digits, heart defects, learning difficulty. (See also Chromosome Abnormality)

Trisomy of Chromosomes (See Chromosome Abnormality; Chromosome Abnormality Syndromes)

Tubercle A small swelling or rounded prominence on a bone.

Tuberculous Meningitis Inflammation of the substance of the brain. When diagnosis is made early, treatment results in recovery. In untreated cases, there is usually resulting brain damage.

Tuberous Sclerosis or **Epiloia** A neurocutaneous disorder. Features, which are variable, include: multiple nodules on the nose, cheeks and upper lip areas of the face and under the nails, white, oval-shaped areas and cafe au lait spots. In some cases: seizures, calcified lesions of the brain, bone lesions, kidney tumours. Severe learning difficulty occurs in about 50% of affected individuals but intellect is unimpaired in

4

many cases. Autosomal dominant inheritance proposed.

Tumour A swelling, due to diseased growth of tissue. It may be benign, malignant or inflammatory.

Turner Syndrome or **X0 Syndrome** (See Chromosome Abnormality Syndromes, Sex)

Turricephaly A dome-shaped head caused by premature closure of the sutures between the frontal, parietal and occipital bones of the skull. (See also Craniosynostosis; Skull, Bones of the; Sutures of the Skull)

Unbalanced Translocation (See Chromosome Abnormality)

Ulcer An abrasion of the skin or mucous membrane. Caused by injury, infection, pressure or nerve damage.

Uncinate Fit A hallucination of smell or taste as a consequence of tumour on the part of the brain which is concerned with smell and taste, or as a manifestation of epilepsy.

Valgus Turning outward, e.g. talipes valgus, in which there is outward turning of the foot.

Value Added The enhancement of effectiveness of schools in adding value to their provision for all children, including those with special educational needs, by monitoring progress as distinct from pupil attainment only. This involves assessing prior attainment (input) and subsequent attainment (output), looking at the socioeconomic situation of pupils, gender differences, involvement of parents and the school's self-evaluation and improvement. If, when all of these factors have been considered, there is greater progress than expected, this reflects the value added by the school. (See also Baseline Assessment)

Varicella An alternative term for chicken pox.

Varicella Effects, Foetal Damage to the foetus as a result of the mother being infected by varicella (chicken pox) in the first 8–19 weeks of pregnancy. Features include: growth deficiency, choreoretinitis, underdevelopment of a limb and/or severely reduced digits, scars on the skin, seizures, learning difficulty.

Varus Turning inward, e.g. talipes varus, in which there is inward turning of the foot.

Verruca The Latin term for a wart. (See also Wart)

Verrucous Wart-like or covered with warts. (See also Wart)

Very Able Children (See Able Children)

Virilism Development of masculine characteristics in a female.

Visual Acuity Clarity and acuteness of vision.

Visual Impairment Impairment of the sense of sight, from minor visual loss to total absence of sight, including defects of visual acuity (clarity and acuteness of vision), limitations of the field of vision, defective colour vision. Causes include malformation of the cornea, the lens or globe of the eye, hereditary diseases of the eye, maternal rubella (German measles in pregnancy). For teaching purposes, an assessment of functional vision is made and this and other information is used to design a suitable education programme. Provision may include special teaching materials, low vision aids and equipment and ensuring suitable levels of illumination for work.

Von Recklinghausen Disease (See Neurofibromatosis)

Warfarin Effects, Foetal or **Foetal Warfarin Syndrome** Damage to the developing foetus as a result of treatment of the mother with an anticoagulant preparation (e.g. warfarin) during the early months of pregnancy. Damage does not occur in every case. Features, which are variable, include: lack of development of the nose with depressed tip, shortened fingers with underdeveloped nails. In some cases: skeletal defects, heart defects. Those who are severely affected may not survive infancy. Some who survive have severe learning difficulty but about a third of the known cases have had no effects apart from malformation of the nose.

Warnock Report The report concerning special education, produced by the Warnock committee in 1978. The proposals included a recommendation that children with special needs should be integrated into the ordinary school system, and that all children, however severe their disability, should be educated as fully as possible from as early an age as possible.

Wart A small overgrowth of papillae upon the skin as a result of viral infection. (See also Verruca)

Water on the Brain A term sometimes incorrectly used to denote hydrocephalus. The fluid accumulated in hydrocephalus is not water, but cerebrospinal fluid. (See Hydrocephalus)

Weaver Syndrome A disorder characterised by accelerated maturation of bone and physical growth. Features include: overgrowth of prenatal onset or soon after birth, low-pitched, hoarse cry, flattened back of head, broad forehead, large ears, small jaw, widely spaced and downward slanting eyes, thin hair, loose skin, flexion of fingers/toes, broad thumbs. In some cases: inward curving toes, club foot and other abnormalities of bones of foot, limited elbow and knee extension, progressive spasticity of limbs, increased muscle tone, psychomotor delay. Most cases have been sporadic but autosomal dominant inheritance has been proposed.

Webbed Fingers, Webbed Toes (See Syndactyly)

Wechsler Intelligence Scale for Children (WISC) A range of tests to measure overall intelligence or verbal and non-verbal (performance) skills separately.

Wechsler Pre-school and **Primary Scale of Intelligence (WPPSI)** A range of tests designed to measure intelligence in young children.

West Syndrome Infantile spasms with onset usually between 3 and 6 months of age. The seizures take the form of very rapid convulsions with head-nodding and/or flexion of the whole body. These spasms are characterised by hypsarrythmia (a specific pattern on an electroencephalogram). Development may be interrupted and skills may be lost with the onset of the spasms. The administration of adrenocorticotropic hormone is often effective in stopping the spasms. Causes include brain developmental defects, birth injury, anoxia, metabolic defects, meningitis, brain tumours. X-linked inheritance has been suggested in some cases. (See also Hypsarrythmia; Infantile Spasms)

Whooping Cough or **Pertussis** An infectious disease of the mucous membrane lining the air passages which manifests in recurring attacks of convulsive coughing, followed by a peculiar loud drawing in of the breath. Occasionally, the violence of the cough may rupture a blood

4

vessel in the brain, causing brain damage.

Whooping Cough Vaccination Inoculation of infants with treated vaccine as a preventative measure against whooping cough. In a few cases, vaccination has resulted in convulsions and brain damage, so great care is now taken to ensure that any history of allergy, epilepsy etc., is considered before a baby is vaccinated.

Williams Syndrome or **Hypercalcaemia Syndrome, Idiopathic Infantile** Features, which are variable, include: mild growth deficiency, failure to thrive in infancy, microcephaly, hoarse voice, characteristic 'elfin' facial features with epicanthic folds, short and upturned nose with flattened bridge, widely-spaced eyes, low set ears with pointed tip, small chin, full cheeks, prominent lips, partial absence of teeth, aortic stenosis and other heart valve defects, fretfulness and feeding difficulties in infancy, with a friendly outgoing personality usually developing later. Mild learning difficulty is common but is not always present. In infancy, there may be increased calcification in the long bones and internal organs, which may remain for a number of months but disappears of its own accord in due course. The features of the condition vary from mild to severe. Cause not established but some individuals have been found to have chromosome deletions.

Wilm's Tumour Congenital malignant tumour of the kidneys.

Wilson Disease or **Progressive Hepatolenticular Degeneration** A disorder of copper metabolism. In untreated cases, features include: progressive tremor, rigidity, abnormal colouring of the cornea, jaundice, anaemia, bruising, liver degeneration, accumulation of copper deposits in several organs of the body. Initial development may be normal, and deterioration of motor and intellectual abilities may not be noticed until the school years, or even later. If the disorder is diagnosed early, treatment can be given which will improve the neurological symptoms. Autosomal recessive inheritance.

WISC (See Wechsler Intelligence Scale for Children)

Wolf-Hirschhorn Syndrome or **4p-Syndrome** (See Chromosome Abnormality Syndromes)

Worster-Drought Syndrome or **Congenital Suprabulbar Paresis** A disorder of the bulbar muscles, resulting in weakness of the muscles of the lips, tongue and soft palate. In more severe cases, the laryngeal and pharyngeal muscles may also be involved including the tongue, resulting in difficulty moving the tongue, problems with articulation, mild motor problems, early problems with poor sucking and swallowing ability, and continuous salivation. Most affected children are of normal intelligence but mild learning difficulty occurs in some cases. In a few cases, small changes in the temporal lobes of the brain have been found.

Word Blindness A term sometimes use to denote dyslexia.

Wormian Bones or **Supernumerary Bones** Additional bones of varying sizes sometimes occurring in the sutures between the bones of the skull.

WPPSI (See Wechsler Pre-school and Primary Scale of Intelligence)

Xanthoma or **Xanthelasma** Flat areas of yellow pigmentation on the skin, occurring commonly on the eyelids. Due to abnormal deposits of lipids.

Xeroderma A skin condition, producing

redness, dryness and the copious formation of scales.

Xeroderma Pigmentosa Syndrome
Features, which are variable, include: sensitivity to light, excessive tear production, skin lesions resembling freckles appearing on exposed parts of the body in infancy, childhood or adulthood. These lesions fuse and form larger areas on exposure to sunlight and growths which develop from the pigmented spots later undergo malignant changes. In some cases: small stature, telangiectases, angiomata, dental defects, hearing defects, spasticity, ataxia, delayed sexual development. Neurological dysfunction and varying degrees of learning difficulty may occur in some affected individuals. Autosomal recessive inheritance.

Xeroderma Pigmentosa with Learning Difficulty (See De Sanctis-Cacchione Syndrome)

Xerophthalmia A thickened and dry condition of the cornea, which appears as greyish spots and obscures vision. A sign of vitamin A deficiency.

Xerosis Abnormal dryness, especially of the eyes.

Xerostomia Abnormal dryness of the mouth, as a result of a lack of saliva.

X-Linked Inheritance Inheritance in which the genes responsible for a characteristic or abnormality are carried on an X chromosome. A female who carries an abnormal recessive gene is a carrier, but unaffected, since the partner gene on her other X chromosome is normal. At each conception there are four possibilities: 1. The father will donate a normal X chromosome and the mother her normal X, resulting in a normal daughter. 2. The father will donate a normal X and the mother her X containing the recessive gene, resulting in a normal daughter who is a carrier. 3. The father will donate a Y chromosome and the mother her normal X, resulting in a normal son. 4. The father will donate a Y and the mother her X containing the abnormal gene, resulting in a son who will be affected, since he will have no normal partner gene to compensate for the X-linked recessive gene from his mother. If a male with an X-linked disorder reproduces, there are two possibilities: 1. He will pass on his Y chromosome, and his male offspring will be normal. 2. He will pass on his X chromosome with the defective gene, and his female offspring will be carriers.

X and Y Chromosome Syndromes (See Chromosome Abnormality Syndromes, Sex)

X0 Syndrome or **Turner Syndrome** (See Chromosome Abnormality Syndromes, Sex)

XXX Syndrome or **Triple X Syndrome** (See Chromosome Abnormality Syndromes, Sex)

XXXX Syndrome (See Chromosome Abnormality Syndromes, Sex)

XXXXX Syndrome or **Penta X Syndrome** (See Chromosome Abnormality Syndromes, Sex)

XXXY Syndrome (See Chromosome Abnormality Syndromes, Sex)

XXXXY Syndrome (See Chromosome Abnormality Syndromes, Sex)

XXY Syndrome or **Klinefelter Syndrome** (See Chromosome Abnormality Syndromes, Sex)

XXYY Syndrome (See Chromosome Abnormality Syndromes, Sex)

4

XYY Syndrome (See Chromosome Abnormality Syndromes, Sex)

Zellweger Syndrome or **Cerebro-Hepato-Renal Syndrome** Features include: growth deficiency, flat occiput and flat face with a high forehead, Brushfield spots, feeding and breathing difficulties, lax muscle tone, seizures, defects of early brain development, liver enlargement, kidney cysts, heart defects, joint contractures, club foot, raised blood iron levels, developmental delay. In some cases: sight defects, genital defects, bone abnormalities. Progressive, with a life expectancy usually not exceeding early infancy. Autosomal recessive inheritance.

Zygodactyly Webbing of two fingers, usually the third and fourth, sometimes accompanied by a similar webbing of the toes.

Section 5

Useful Addresses: Organisations, Charities and Services

Useful Addresses: Organisations, Charities and Services

Contents

Organisations

18–30 PLUS
7-11 Armstrong Road, London W3 7JL
☎ 020 8743 1110 Textphone 020 8742 9151
0845 0744 600 'lo call' voice and text
🖹 020 8742 9043
Support, information and leisure activities for young people with hearing impairment.

Abdominal Exstrophies
(Contact GEEPS)

Abdominal Migraine
(See CVS Association)

Abortion
(See Women's Health)

Abuse of People with Disabilities
(See Beyond Words; Voice UK; Sexuality and Relationships Section)

Accidents
(See Child Accident Prevention Trust)

Achondroplasia
(See Bone Dysplasia Group; Restricted Growth Association)

Acne Support Group
P.O. Box 9, Newquay, Cornwall TR9 6WG
☎ 0870 870 2263
website: www.stopspots.org
Support: self-help: contacts: information: newsletter. Caters for acne vulgaris and rosacea.

Acromegaly
(See Pituitary Foundation)

ACT (Aid for Children with Tracheostomies)
72 Oakridge, Thornhill, Cardiff CF14 9BQ
☎ & 🖹 029 2075 5932
email: actuk@aol.com
website: members.aol.com/actuk/ACT
Support: contacts: information: newsletter. Leaflet 'A Guide for Schools'

ACT (Association for Children with Life-Threatening or Terminal Conditions and their families)
Orchard House, Orchard Lane, Bristol BS1 5DT
☎ 0117 922 1556 – information line
🖹 0117 930 4707 – admin
ACT (Association for Children with Life-threatening or Terminal conditions and their families) aims to provide information on support services available for families whose children have life-threatening or terminal conditions, regardless of the particular diseases involved. It is involved in consultation and contact between service providers and campaigners to encourage the development of children's palliative care services.

Action 19 Plus
c/o Campaigns Dept, Scope, 6–10 Market Road, London N7 9PW
☎ 020 7619 7244 🖹 020 7619 7380
A consortium of voluntary organisations, individuals and parent groups concerned with the provision of services for disabled people over the age of 19. Publishes 'Guide to Getting What You Want From Your Local Authority At 19 Plus' – guide costs £5 to disabled people, parents, carers and advocates otherwise £10. Free quarterly newsletter.

Action for Sick Children
c/o National Children's Bureau, 8 Wakley Street, London EC1V 7QE
☎ 020 7843 6444
website: www.actionforsickchildren.org.uk
Brings together parents and professionals to encourage the highest standard of care for children in hospital and at home. Local branches, publications, practical help and support for families.

Action for Sick Children, Scotland
15 Smith's Place, Edinburgh EH6 8NT
☎ 0131 553 6553

Adams-Oliver Syndrome Support Group
11 Berry Place, Fairwater, Cardiff CF5 3LQ
☎ 029 2056 1388
Support: contacts: information

ADD Information Services
P.O. Box 340, Edgware, Middlesex HA8 9HL
☎ 020 8905 2013 🖹 020 8386 6466
email: addiss@compuserve.com
website: www.addiss.co.uk
National organisation providing information and support to parents, teachers and healthcare

professionals. Catalogue of books and videos on ADHD and related difficulties and list of the 150+ support groups around the UK.

ADD/ADHD Family Support Group UK
Mrs G Mead, 1a High Street, Dilton Marsh, Westbury, Wilts BA13 4DL
☎ 01373 826045 📠 01373 825158
For parents of children diagnosed as having attention deficit disorder or attention deficit hyperactivity disorder and parents and professionals seeking diagnosis. Support: contacts: information

Addison's Disease Self-Help Group
Mrs D Kenward, 21 George Road, Guildford, Surrey GU1 4NP
☎ & 📠 01483 830673
email: deana@adshg.freeserve.co.uk
Support: contacts: information: newsletter

ADDnet UK
10 Troughton Road, Charlton, London W7 7QH
☎ & 📠 020 8305 1023
website: www.btinternet.com/~black.ice/addnet/
Network for AD/HD support groups.

ADHD National Alliance
209-211 City Road, London EC1V 1JN
☎ 020 7608 8760
0808 808 3555 – Mon-Fri 10-4pm
📠 020 7608 8701
email: jim@cafamily.org.uk

Adipogenital/Retinitis Pigmentosa/Polydactyly Syndrome
(See LMBB Society; Retinitis Pigmentosa Society)

Adoption (Post-Adoption Centre)
Post-Adoption Centre, 5 Torriano Mews, Torriano Avenue, Kentish Town, London NW5 2RZ
☎ 020 7284 0555
Advice line: 0870 777 2197 (Mon, Tues, Weds, Fri 10am-1pm, Thurs 5:30-7pm) 📠 0870 777 2167
website: www.postadoptioncentre.org.uk
Provides contacts, information, publications, support and a newsletter for anyone involved with adoption; adoptive parents, adopted children or adults and relatives.

Adoption and Fostering
(See also Barnardo's; Catholic Children's Crusade of Rescue; Catholic Child Welfare Council; NCH; Parents for Children; Thomas Coram Foundation)

Adoption and Fostering, British Associaton for
Skyline House, 200 Union Street, London SE1 0LX
☎ 020 7593 2000 📠 020 7593 2001

email: mail@baaf.org.uk
website: www.baaf.org.uk
The leading UK wide membership organisation for those concerned with adoption, fostering and childcare.

Adoption Service, Independent
Jane Tilton, 121-123 Camberwell Road, London SE5 0HB
☎ 020 7703 1088 📠 020 7277 1688

Adoption UK
Manor Farm, Appletree Road, Chipping Warden, Banbury, Oxon OX17 1LH
☎ 01295 660121
0870 7700 450 📠 01295 660123
email: admin@adoptionuk.org.uk
Support, information and encouragement to prospective adoptees and established adoptive families. Bi-monthly magazine (membership £25 per annum), publications.

Adrenal Hyperplasia, Congenital
(See CAH Group)

Adrenoleukodystrophy (ALD) Family Support Trust
30-32 Morley House, 320 Regent Street, London W1R 5AB
☎ 020 7631 3336 📠 020 7631 3337
email: info@aldfst.org.uk
Support, information and fundraising for research into adrenoleukodystrophy (Schilders disease, sudanophilic leukodystrophy)

Advocacy Partners
6 Lind Road, Sutton, Surrey SM1 4PJ
☎ 020 8643 7111 📠 020 8643 7199
Supports and promotes advocacy relationships for people with learning disabilities, older people and those with sensory or physical disabilities. Branches in several areas (See also One-To-One; People First)

AFASIC (Association for All Speech and Language Impaired Children)
AFASIC, 2nd Floor, 50-52 Great Sutton Street, London EC1V 0DJ
☎ (admin) 020 7490 9410
Helpline 0845 355 5577 📠 020 7251 2834
email: info@afasic.org.uk
website: www.afasic.org.uk
For parents of children or young people who are affected by disorders of speech and language but do not have any other disabilities. Schools, educational and speech therapy advice, local groups, research into good practice, support, information, publications. Do not cater for young adults with acquired dysphasia. (See also Communication Skills)

Agammaglobulinaemia X-Linked
(Contact Primary Immunodeficiency Association)

Agorophobia
(See National Phobics Society)

Agyria
(Contact Lissencephaly Contact Group)

Aicardi Syndrome
(See CORPAL)

AIDS Helpline, National
85-89 Duke Street, Liverpool L1 5AP
0800 567123
Information and advice, free leaflets about prevention of AIDS and other sexually transmitted infections, testing procedures etc. Ethnic languages service.

AIDS/HIV in Children
(See AIDS Helpline, National; Body Positive; Positive Options; Terrence Higgins Trust)

AIS Support Group (UK)
P.O. Box 269, Banbury, Oxon OX15 6YT
☎ 01295 670140
email: orchids@talk21.com
website: www.medhelp.org/www.ais
Support and contacts for parents of children with androgen insensitivity and incomplete androgen insensitivity, including androgen resistance syndrome, XY feminising testes syndrome, Gilbert-Dreyfus syndrome, Goldberg-Maxwell syndrome, gonadal dysgenesis (Swyers syndrome), Lubs syndrome, Mayer-Rokitansky-Kuster-Hauser syndrome, Morris's syndrome, Mullerian dysgenesis, pseudo-hermaphrodite syndrome, Reifenstein syndrome, testicular feminisation, 5 alpha-reductase deficiency, leydig cell hyperplasia.

Alagille Syndrome
(Contact Liver Disease Foundation, Children's)

Albinism Fellowship
P.O. Box 77, Burnley, Lancs BB11 5GN
Helpline 01282 771900 (Tues and Fri, 2-3pm)
email: albinism@bughunter.co.uk
website: www.albinism.org.uk
Support: contacts: information: newsletter. Advice and support for people with albinism, their families and interested professionals.

Alcohol Effects, Foetal
(See Foetal Alcohol Syndrome Trust)

Allergic Disorders, Association for
Mrs C Barker, 24 Chiltern Road, Ramsbottom, Bury, Lancs BL0 9LF
☎ 01706 828256
Support: contacts: information

Allergy
(See also Anaphylaxis Campaign; Environmental Therapy, Society for; Pesticide Exposure, Action On)

Allergy and Environmental Therapy, British Institute for
Ffyonnonwen, Llangwryryfon, Aberystwyth SY23 4EY
☎ 01974 241 376 🖷 01974 241795
email: allergy@onetel.net
website: www.allergy.org.uk www.hayfever.cc
Researches allergy treatments, offers training for therapists and maintains a register of qualified therapists.

Allergy Association, Food and Chemical
Mrs E Rothera, 27 Ferringham Lane, Ferring, Worthing, West Sussex BN12 5NB
Support: information. Booklet 'Understanding Allergies' £2.00 plus A5 size stamped addressed envelope. (See also Environmental Therapy, Society for Letter answering service only).

Allergy UK
Deepdene House, 30 Bellegrove Road, Welling, Kent DA16 3PY
☎ 020 8303 8525
Helpline 020 8303 8583 (Mon-Fri 9am-9pm, w/e 10am-1pm) 🖷 020 8303 8792
website: www.allergyuk.org

Allergy, Action Against
P.O. Box 278, Twickenham, Middlesex TW1 4QQ
☎ 020 8892 2711
email: AAA@actionagainstallergy.freeserve.co.uk
website: www.rowantree.co.uk/info/allergy
Support: information: newsletter: publications

Allergy, National Society for Research into
Mrs E Rose, P.O. Box 45, Hinckley, Leicester LE10 1JY
☎ 01455 250715 or 01455 291294
email: n.s.r.a.allergy@virgin.net
Support: information: newsletter

Allergy-Induced Autism
(See Autism, Allergy-induced)

Alopecia Society, The Children's
P.O. Box 2505, 3 Upperton Road, Eastbourne, East Sussex BN21 1AA
☎ 01323 412723
email: hair@mistral.co.uk
website: www.gic.co.uk/alopecia/
Part of Alopecia Action. Support and information for children affected by hair loss. (See also Hairline International)

5

Alpha 1-Antitrypsin Deficiency
Alpha 1 Support, 5a Kennersdene, Tynemouth
NE30 2NB
☎ 01606 44943
email: ian.k.rowan@onyxnet.co.uk
website: www.alpha1.org
Support, information and advice to patients, families and doctors.

Alpha Thalassaemia and Learning Disability on the X Chromosome
(See ATR-X Support Group)

Alstrom Syndrome UK
Mrs K Parkinson, 49 Southfield Avenue, Paignton,
Devon TQ3 1LH
☎ & 🖹 01803 524238
email: info@alstrom.org.uk
website: www.alstrom.org.uk
Support: contacts: information: newsletter

Alternating Hemiplegia Support Group
Mrs G Bailey, 80 London Road, Datchet, Slough,
Berks SL3 9LQ
☎ 01753 546268
Support: contacts

Alternative Therapies
The Henry Spink Foundation, 4th Floor, 170
Tottenham Court Road, London W1T 7HA
☎ 020 7388 9843 🖹 020 7387 0342
email: info@henryspink.org
website: www.henryspink.org

Amyoplasia Congenita
(Contact Arthrogryposis Group)

Amyotrophic Lateral Sclerosis
(Contact Motor Neurone Disease Association)

Anaemia, Congenital Aplastic
(See Aplastic Anaemia Support Group UK)

Anaphylaxis Campaign, The
P.O. Box 275, Farnborough, Hants GU14 6SX
☎ 01252 542029 🖹 01252 377140
website: www.anaphylaxis.org.uk/
Information on severe allergic reaction, support, newsletter, promotion of awareness of anaphylaxis in the food industry, medical profession, government bodies and the general public.

Andersen Syndrome
(Contact Glycogen Storage Diseases, Association for)

Anderson-Fabry Disease
(Contact Fabry's Disease Support Group)

Androgen Insensitivity/Resistance Syndrome
(See AIS Support Group (UK))

Anencephaly Support Group
Debra Lindesay, 29 Hawkwood Close, Malvern,
Worcs WR14 1QU
☎ 01684 573974
Provides support and information to anyone who has had a pregnancy affected by anencephaly (incomplete development of the brain). Please enclose SAE.

Angelman Syndrome Support Group
Mrs S Woolven, 15 Place Crescent, Waterlooville,
Portsmouth, Hants PO7 5UR
☎ 023 9226 4224 🖹 023 9224 1977
Support: contacts: information (See also Assert)

Aniridia Support Network
Mrs Yvonne Booth, 55 Penrith Gardens,
Thornbury, Plymouth, Devon PL6 8UX
☎ & 🖹 01752 789258
email: ybooth8709@aol.com
Support, contacts, information for parents of children with aniridia (absence of the iris of the eye).

Ankylosing Spondylitis Society, National
P.O. Box 179, Mayfield TN20 6ZL
☎ 01435 873527 🖹 01435 873027
email: nass@nass.co.uk
website: www.nass.co.uk
Support: self help: contacts: literature: newsletter

Anophthalmia
(See MACS)

Anorchidism Support Group (ASG)
P.O. Box 3025, Harold Hill, Romford, Essex RM3
8GX
☎ 01708 372597 🖹 01708 372597
email: asg.uk@virgin.net
website: www.community.nj.com/cc/
anorchidismsupportgroup or
www.freespace.virgin.net/asg.uk
Support, contacts and information for parents of boys affected by anorchidism–congenital absence of the testes (testicles), vanishing testes syndrome, anorchia, testicular regression syndrome, undescended testes.

Anorexia
(See Careline: Eating Disorders Association)

Anoxic Seizures, Reflex
(See STARS)

Anthony Nolan Bone Marrow Trust
The Royal Free Hospital, Pond Street, Hampstead,
London NW3 2QG

Donor recruitment hotline number 0990 111533
email: kay@anthonynolan.com
website: www.anthonynolan.com/

Anti-Bullying Campaign
185 Tower Bridge Road, London SE1 2UF
☎ 020 7378 1446 🖷 020 7378 8374
email: Anti-Bullying@compuserve.com
website: ourworld.compuserve.com/homepages/
Anti-Bullying
*Offers support and help to schoolchildren who are being
bullied. Information, publications.*

ANTS (Ann's Neurological Trust Society)
c/o Syringomyelia Service, Queen Elizabeth's
Hospital, Edgbaston, Birmingham B15 2TH
☎ 0121 697 8254 🖷 0121 697 8246
email: anne.lane@university-b.wrmids.nhs.uk
website: www.ants.org.uk
*Support, contacts and information for people affected
by syringomyelia and/or Arnold Chiari malformation.*

Apert Syndrome
(See Headlines)

Aplastic Anaemia Support Group
Mrs B Dettmar, 16 Sidney Road, Borstal, Rochester,
Kent ME1 3HF
☎ & 🖷 01634 844062
*Support, contacts and information for parents of
children with acquired aplastic anaemia.*

Apnoea, Neonatal
(Contact BLISS)

ARC (Antenatal Results and Choices)
73-75 Charlotte Street, London W1P 1LB
☎ & 🖷 020 7631 0280
Helpline 020 7631 0285
email: arcsatfa@aol.com
*Information and support to parents through antenatal
testing and when a serious abnormality is diagnosed in
their unborn baby.*

ARISE – The Scoliosis Research Trust
The Graham Hill Building, Royal National
Orthopaedic Hospital Trust, Brockley Hill,
Stanmore, Middlesex HA7 4LP
☎ & 🖷 020 8954 8939
Contacts: information: newsletter

Arm and Hand Deficiencies
(See Lady Hoare Trust; Reach)

Arnold Chiari Malformation
(See ANTS)

Aromatherapy and Massage In Profound & Multiple Disability
(See Mencap PIMD Section)

Arthritis Association, Children's Chronic (CCAA)
Caroline Cox, Ground Floor Office, Amber Gate,
City Walls Road, Worcester, Worcs WR1 2AH
☎ 01905 745595
website: www.ccaa.org.uk
*Support, contacts and information for parents of
children affected by juvenile arthritis.*

Arthritis Care
18 Stephenson Way, London NW1 2HD
☎ 020 7380 6500
Helpline 0800 8800 4050 🖷 020 7380 6505
email: agreenwood@compuserve.com
website: www.arthritiscare.org.uk
*Arthritis care is the only national voluntary
organisation working with and for all people with
arthritis. It aims to promote their health, well-being
and independence through services, support, self-help,
information and influence. It has 580 branches and
groups, and 66,000 committed supporters.*

Arthritis in Children and Young People
(See Lady Hoare Trust)

Arthritis Research Campaign
P.O. Box 177, Chesterfield, Derbyshire S41 7TD
☎ 01246 558033 🖷 01246 558007
email: info@arc.org.uk
website: www.arc.org.uk/
*Many regional and local branches: advice:
information: research*

Arthrogryposis Group, The (TAG)
Beak Cottage, Dunley, Stourport on Severn, Glos
DY13 0TZ
☎ & 🖷 01747 822655
email: info@tagonline.org.uk
website: www.tagonline.org.uk
Support: self help: contacts: information: newsletter

Arthro-Ophthalmopathy, Hereditary Progressive
(Contact Stickler Syndrome Support Group)

Artificial Feeding
(See Half-PINNT; PINNT)

ASBAH (Association for Spina Bifida & Hydrocephalus)
42 Park Road, Peterborough, Cambs PE1 2UQ
☎ 01733 555988 🖷 01733 555985
email: postmaster@asbah.org

5

website: www.asbah.org
Information, support and publications for people with hydrocephalus and/or spina bifida and other neural tube defects. Advice on education and further education, information, publications, area and specialist advisers. (See Spina Bifida Association, Scottish)

Asperger Syndrome
(See Autistic Society, National; Autism Independent UK; OAASIS)

Aspergillosis
(Contact Lung Foundation, British)

Assert (Angelman Syndrome Support, Education & Research Trust)
P.O. Box 505, Sittingbourne, Kent ME10 1NE
☎ & 🖹 01268 415940 (families)
☎ & 🖹 01795 429061 (professionals)
email: assert@angelmanuk.org
website: www.angelmanuk.org
Support: contacts: information: newsletter: telephone Helpline: meetings. (See also Angelman Syndrome Support Group)

Asthma Campaign, National
Providence House, Providence Place, London N1 0NT
☎ 020 7226 2260
Helpline 0845 701 0203 (Mon-Fri., 9am-7pm) 🖹 020 7704 0740
website: www.asthma.org.uk
Information: advice: publications: research. (See also Lung Foundation, British)

Ataxia UK
Winchester House, Kennington Park, Cranmer Road, London SW9 6EJ
☎ 020 7582 1444
Helpline 020 7820 3900 🖹 020 7582 9444
email: office@ataxia.org.uk
website: www.ataxia.org.uk
Support: contacts: information: publications: newsletter: fund-raising for research. for people affected by Friedrich's ataxia, cerebellar ataxia and all inherited ataxias.

Ataxia-Telangiectasia (AT) Society
Mrs Maureen Poupard, c/o IACR, Rothampstead, Harpenden, Herts AL5 2JQ
☎ 01582 760733 🖹 01582 760162
email: ATCharity@aol.com
website: www.atsociety.org.uk
Support: contacts: information: newsletter. National Ataxia-Telangiectasia clinic, research into the condition.

Ataxic Cerebral Palsy
(See Capability Scotland; Scope)

Atherosclerosis, Familial
(See Heart UK)

Athetoid Cerebral Palsy
(See Capability Scotland; Scope)

ATR-X Support Group
Mrs D Walker, 82 The Crescent, Northwich, Cheshire CW9 8AD
☎ 01606 44943
Support: self-help: contacts. for parents of children who have Alpha-thalassaemia with learning disability on the X chromosome.

Attention Deficit Disorder & Attention Deficit / Hyperactivity Disorder
(See ADD Information Service; ADDnet; ADHD National Alliance: ADD/ADHD Family Support Group; Hyperactive Children's Support Group)

Auriculovertebral Syndrome
(Contact Goldenhar Syndrome Support Group)

Autism
(See also OAASIS)

Autism Independent UK
199-203 Blandford Avenue, Kettering, Northants NN16 9AT
☎ 01536 523274 🖹 01536 523274
email: autism@autismuk.com
website: www.autismuk.com
Lobbies for increased autism awareness to enhance the quality of life of the individual and families. Organises training and education programmes for parents and professionals. Provides a diagnostic and assessment centre for visiting consultants. Provides an Information and Resource centre, including access to legal advice. Operates a Help-line for parents and professionals. Maintains a website that provides access to new research and other issues. Provides low-cost holiday facilities for families with autistic children. Produces a yearly report for parents and professionals.

Autism, Allergy-Induced
Meryll Nee, 210 Pineapple Road, Stritchley, Birmingham B30 2TY
☎ & 🖹 0121 444 6450
email: aia@kessick.demon.co.uk
website: www.kessick.co.uk/aia
Information and advice for parents of children who have autism which is caused by or exacerbated by allergy.

Autistic Children, Scottish Society for
Hilton House, Alloa Business Park, Whins Road, Alloa FK10 3SA
☎ 01259 720044 🖹 01259 720051

email: ssac@autism-in-scotland.org.uk
website: www.autism-in-scotland.org.uk
Contacts: support: information: support: newsletter

Autistic Research Organisation, The International
49 Orchard Avenue, Shirley, Croydon, Surrey CR0 7NE
☎ 020 8777 0095 🗎 020 8776 2362
email: iaro@autismresearchww.freeserve.co.uk
website: www.charitynet.org
Information: newsletter: research projects

Autistic Society, The National
393 City Road, London EC1V 1NG
☎ 020 7833 2299
Information Centre 0870 600 8585 (Mon-Fri 10am-4pm) Professionals – 020 7903 3599
🗎 020 7833 9666
email: nas@nas.org.uk website: www.nas.org.uk
Advice, information and support through regional groups, newsletter. Runs six specialist schools for pupils with autistic spectrum disorders. Many publications on all aspects of autism, including Asperger syndrome.

Autistic Society, The National (Scotland)
111 Union Street, Glasgow, Strathclyde G1 3TA
☎ 0141 221 8090 🗎 0141 221 8118
email: nas.scot.dev.fund@dial.pipex.com

Autistic Society Wales, The National
Suite C1, William Knox House, Brittanic Way, Llandarcy, Neath, W. Glamorgan SA10 6EL
☎ 01792 815915 🗎 01792 815911
email: wales@nas.org.uk

Back Care
16 Elmtree Road, Teddington, Middlesex TW11 8ST
☎ 020 8977 5474 🗎 020 8943 5318
email: info@backcare.org.uk
website: www.backpain.org.uk
Self-help groups, research and publications.

Bardet-Beidl Syndrome
(Contact LMMB Society)

Barnardo's
Tanners Lane, Barkingside, Ilford, Essex IG6 1QG
☎ 020 8550 8822 🗎 020 8551 6870
Many services in all areas of the UK; schools for children with emotional and behavioural difficulties; support for children with special needs in mainstream schools; support in transition to adulthood; family support; fostering and adoption; community groups; working for children's health and safety. Regional/national offices in Belfast, Halesowen, Newcastle-upon-Tyne, Liverpool, Edinburgh, Cardiff and Leeds.

Barnardo's AIDS/HIV Project
(See Positive Options)

Barnardo's Cymru
11-15 Columbus Walk, Brigantine Place, Atlantic Wharf, Cardiff CF10 4BZ
☎ 029 2049 3387 🗎 029 2048 9802

Barnardo's Cystic Fibrosis Projects
Barnardo's runs several regional projects for children with cystic fibrosis, in Birmingham, Newcastle-upon-Tyne, Nottingham and Leeds. Contact the Ilford office for addresses of existing services.

Barnardo's Northern Ireland
542-544 Upper Newtownards Road, Belfast BT4 3HE
☎ 01232 672366 🗎 01232 672399

Barnardo's Scotland
235 Corstophine Road, Edinburgh EH12 7AR
☎ 0131 334 9893 🗎 0131 316 4008

Barnardo's South West England
Unit 19, Eastern Business Centre, Felix Road, Easton, Bristol, BS5 0HE
☎ 0117 941 5841 🗎 0117 941 5841

Basal Cell Naevus Syndrome
(Contact Gorlin Syndrome Support Group)

Batten Disease Family Association
c/o Heather House, Heather Drive, Tadley RG26 4QR
☎ 01636 708028 🗎 01484 660386
email: BDFA@hotmail.com
website: www.bdfauk.fresserve.co.uk
Support: contacts: information: conferences

BBC Disability Programmes Unit
Room G504, BBC White City, 201 Wood Lane, London W12 7TS
☎ & Minicom 020 8752 4993 🗎 020 8752 4542
email: dpu@bbc.co.uk

Beckwith-Wiedemann Support Group
Mr R Baker, The Drum & Monkey, Hazelbury Bryan, Sturminster Newton, Dorset DT10 2EE
☎ 01258 817573 (evenings) or 07889 211000 (day)
🗎 01202 205325
email: rbaker5165@aol.com
Support: contacts: information: newsletter: publications

BEES Support Group
Karen Brummell, 8 Burnbray Avenue, Burnage, Manchester M19 1DA
email: k@brummell.freeserve.co.uk
Support, contacts and information for parents of

5

children with exstrophy of the bladder, epispadias and ectopia vesicae. (See Incontinent and Stoma Children, Charity for)

Befriending Network

Nicholas Albery, 20 Heber Road, London NW2 6AA

☎ 020 8208 2853

Trained volunteers who visit people who have terminal or life-threatening illness, and their carers, to offer practical and emotional support in the home. (See Advocacy Partners; Carers UK; Carers, Princess Royal Trust for; Crossroads Caring for Carers; Community Service Volunteers; Face To Face)

Behavioural Difficulties

(See Challenging Behaviour Foundation; Emotional and Behavioural Difficulties, Association of Workers for Children with)

Bell's Palsy

(Contact Let's Face It Support Network)

Ben Hardwick Fund

12 Nassau Road, Barnes, London SW13 9QE

☎ 020 8741 8499

Financial assistance for parents of children affected by primary liver disease, for costs incurred as a result of their illness, such as travel and in-hospital expenses.

Bereavement

(See also Child Death; Careline; Child Bereavement Trust; Compassionate Friends; Cruse; Laura Centre; SANDS; Sudden Death Support Association)

Bereavement Counselling Service, Jewish

P.O. Box 6748, London N3 3BX

☎ & 📠 020 8349 0839

Covers North West London and Redbridge. Limited service in SW London.

Bereavement, Counselling People with Learning Disabilities

(See Beyond Words)

Bereavement, Twin/s

(See TAMBA)

Beyond Words

The BMJ Bookshop, DBMA House, London WC1H 9JR

☎ 020 7383 6244 📠 020 7245 1231 (Royal College of Psychiatry)

website: www.BMSBookshop.co.uk

A series of books for people with learning disabilities, published by St George's Hospital Medical school and the Royal College of Psychiatry. The series is intended to assist in the counselling of people with learning disabilities. Titles include; 'Going to Court' (for those

who may need to attend court as a witness), 'You're Nicked' (for those who have been accused of a crime and are facing police procedures), 'In The Dock' (for those who have been charged or have to appear as a defendant in a court). Details of all further titles on request. (See also Mencap Legal Department)

Biliary Hypoplasia/Atresia

(Contact Liver Disease Foundation, Children's)

Birth Defects Foundation

BDF Centre, Hemlock Way, Cannock, Staffs WS11 2GF

☎ 08700 707020 📠 01543 468999

email: enquiries@birthdefects.co.uk

website: www.birthdefects.co.uk

Offers support and information to families affected by any form of birth defect. Funds medical research.

Birthmark Support Group

P.O. Box 3932, Weymouth, Dorset DT4 9YG

email: info@birthmarksupportgroup.org.uk

website: www.birthmarksupportgroup.org.uk

Information, support and advice for anyone affected by a birthmark. Produce newsletters, medical information packs and offer contact with others in similar situations.

Bladder Exstrophy

(See BEES; Incontinent and Stoma Children, The Charity for)

Blepharospasm

(Contact Dystonia Society)

Blind Children's Society, The National

Bradbury House, Market Street, Highbridge, Somerset TA9 3BW

☎ 01278 764764 📠 01278 764790

email: enquiries@nbcs.org.uk

website: www.nbcs.org.uk

Blind People, Action for

14-16 Verney Road, London SE16 3DZ

☎ 020 7635 4800 📠 020 7635 4900

email: info@afbp.org

website: www.afbp.org

Information, publications, employment and training, sheltered workshops and homeworkers scheme for visually impaired people.

Blind, Henshaws Society for the

John Derby House, 88-92 Talbot Road, Old Trafford, Manchester M16 0GS

☎ 0161 872 1234 📠 0161 848 9889

email: info@hsbp.co.uk

Information, support, courses, leisure activities, holidays, residential care, community outreach services. Covers northern England and north Wales. Runs several schools and further educational facilities in the North West and Merseyside.

Blind, National Federation of the, (UK)
Sir John Wilson House, 215 Kirkgate, Wakefield, West Yorks WF1 1JG
☎ 01924 291313 📠 01924 200244
email: nfbuk@nfbuk.org
website: www.nfbuk.org
Support for people with visual impairment

Blind, Royal National Institute for the
(See RNIB)

Blind, Wales Council for the
3rd Floor, Shand House, 20 Newport Road, Cardiff CF2 1DB
☎ 01222 473954 📠 01222 455710
Awareness training, transcription into Braille, tape, large print, disk and CD-ROM, advice on computer equipment, sports and recreation.

Blindness
(See also Look; Vision Aid)

BLISS – The Premature Baby Charity
68 South Lambeth Road, London SW8 1RL
☎ 0870 7700 337
Helpline   0500   618140   (10.30am-4.30pm, Mon-Fri) 📠 0870 7700 338
email: information@bliss.org.uk
website: www.bliss.org.uk
Support for parents of premature and sick newborn babies needing special care; funding for neonatal equipment, nurse training and research, campaigning.

Bobath Centre
(See Education Section)

Body Dysmorphic Disorder (BDD)
(See National Phobics Society)

Body Positive
14 Greek Street, Soho, London W1V 5LE
☎ 020 7287 8010 Helpline 0800 616200
📠 020 7287 8020
email: bp@bodypositive.demon.co.uk
website: www.bbpositive.co.uk
Support, advice, information and publications for anyone affected by, or living with, HIV infection or AIDS.

Bone Dysplasia Group
c/o Child Growth Foundation, 2 Mayfield Avenue, Chiswick, London W4 1PW
☎ 020 8994 7625 📠 020 8995 9075
Support and contacts for parents of children affected by abnormalities of bone development which result in increased or decreased stature.

Bone Marrow Donation
(See Anthony Nolan Bone Marrow Trust)

Bowel Defects & Abnormalities
(See GEEPS; Gut Motility Disorders Support Network; Incontinent and Stoma Children, The Charity for)

Brachial Plexus Paralysis
(Contact Erb's Palsy Support Group)

Brain & Spine Foundation, British
7 Winchester House, Kennington Park, Cranmer Road, London SW9 6EJ
☎ 0207 793 5900
0808 808 1000 📠 020 7793 5939
The Brain and Spine Foundation aims to maximise the quality of life for people with neurological disorders and to reduce neurological disability by providing a national focus for research, education and information.

Brain Dysfunction, Minimal
(Contact Dyspraxia Foundation)

Brain Injured Children, British Institute for
(See Education Section)

Brain Injured Children's Rehabilitation Centres
(See Child Brain Injury Trust; Rescue)

Brain Tumour Action
124 Crewe Road South, Edinburgh EH4 2NK
☎ 0131 315 7299
0131 466 3116
email: lorraine@braintumouraction.org.uk
website: www.braintumouraction.org.uk
Support for children and adults affected by brain tumour, their families and carers throughout the UK.

Brain Tumour Foundation
P.O. Box 162, New Malden, Surrey KT3 4WH
☎ & 📠 020 8336 2020
email: btf.uk@virgin.net
Support, advice, information and publications for people affected by benign or malignant brain tumours as well as families and health professionals.

Brain Tumour Society, UK
Jane Stephens, BAC House, Bonehurst Road, Horley, Surrey RH6 8QG
☎ 01293 781479
01293 781479 📠 01293 826266
email (admin): info@braintumour.org
website: www.braintumour.org
A charity working with other charities throughout the UK. Support: contacts: information: newsletter: publications

5

Brain, Congenital Absence of
(See Anencephaly Support Group)

Brainwave Centre for Rehabilitation and Development
(See Education Section)

Breath-Holding Attacks, Chronic/Severe
(Contact STARS)

Breughel Syndrome
(See Dystonia Society)

Brissaud Syndrome Type 2
(Contact Tourette Syndrome Association UK)

British Heart Foundation
14 Fitzhardinge Street, London W1H 6DH
☎ 020 7935 0185
0870 608 65 66 🖹 020 7486 5820
email: internet@bhf.org.uk
website: www.bhf.org.uk
The major organisation for people with heart disease. Publications, information, support groups.

Brittle Bone Society
30 Guthrie Street, Dundee DD1 5BS
☎ 01382 204446/7
Helpline 08000 282459 🖹 01382 206771
email: bbs@brittlebone.org
website: www.brittlebone.org
Support: contacts: information: newsletter: publications for children with osteogenesis imperfecta (brittle bone disease) and their families.

Broad Thumb/Great Toe Syndrome
(Contact Rubinstein-Taybi Syndrome Support Group)

Broadcasting Support Services
Union House, Shepherd Bush Green, London W12 8AU
☎ 020 8735 5000 🖹 020 8735 5099
Provision of information, fact sheets, leaflets etc. on programmes broadcast on all broadcasting media. Information service on addresses of organisations, support groups.

Bronchiectasis
(Contact Lung Foundation, British)

Bronchitis, Chronic
(Contact Lung Foundation, British)

Brothers and Sisters of People with Learning Difficulty
(See SIBS; SIBS Encounter)

Bruton's Disease
(Contact Primary Immunodeficiency Association)

Bulbar Palsy/Pseudobulbar Palsy
(See Worster-Drought Syndrome Support Group)

Bulimia
(See Careline; Eating Disorders Association)

Bullous Ichthyosis Erythroderma
(See Ichthyosis Support Group)

Bully Alert UK
Rosalie Everatt, 33 Kingsdown Park, Tankerton, Kent CT5 2DT
☎ & 🖹 01227 277933

Bullying
(See also Anti-Bullying Campaign; Bully Alert UK; Careline; Childline; Kidscape)

Burn Association, British
Secretariat, Burn Centre, Acute Block, Wythenshawe Hospital, Southmoor Road, Manchester M23 9LT
☎ & 🖹 0161 291 6323
email: bba@smuht.nwest.nhs.uk

CAH Group
Miss M Cull, 17 Newton Road, Lichfield, Staffs WS13 7EF
☎ 01543 252961
email: webmaster@cah.org.uk
website: www.cah.org.uk
Support: contacts: information. For parents of children affected by congenital adrenal hyperplasia. Affiliated to CLIMB.

Calve-Perthes Disease
(Contact Perthes Association)

Cancer
(See also Christian Lewis Children's Cancer Care; Leukaemia CARE Society; Elimination of Leukaemia Fund; Leukaemia Research Fund; Sue Ryder Care)

Cancer and Leukaemia in Childhood (CLIC)
CLIC, Abbey Wood, Bristol BS34 7JU
☎ 0117 311 2600 🖹 0117 311 2649
email: clic@clic-charity.demon.co.uk
website: www.click.uk.com
Support, information, homes, domiciliary care nurse for children with cancer or leukaemia and their families.

Cancer Care for Children, Sargent
Griffin House, 161 Hammersmith Road, London W6 8SG
☎ 020 8752 2800 🖹 020 8752 2806
email: care@sargent.org.uk

Counselling, support and information for young people up to the age of 21 affected by cancer or leukaemia. Social workers, financial grants, holiday homes in Scotland and Northern Ireland.

Cancer Care Society
11 The Cornmarket, Romsey, Hants S051 8GB
☎ 01794 830300 📠 01794 518133
email: info@cancercaresoc.demon.co.uk
website: www.cancercaresoc.demon.co.uk
Support, one-to-one and group counselling, reflexology, aromatherapy, support groups

Cancer Help Centre, Bristol
Grove House, Cornwallis Grove, Clifton, Bristol BS8 4PG
Helpline 0117 980 9500 📠 0117 923 9184
Contacts, information, support, newsletter, publications, self-help training, professional training courses, speakers on holistic and complimentary medicine.

Cancer Information Centre, Tenovus
Tenovus, College Buildings, Courtenay Road, Splott, Cardiff CF1 1SA
☎ 01222 497700 Freephone
Helpline 0800 526527 📠 01222 489919
Support: contacts: information: publications: counselling: trained nurses: medical social work

Cancer Society, Irish
5 Northumberland Road, Dublin 4, Ireland
☎ (353) 1 2310500
1800 200 700 – weekdays 9-5 📠 (353) 1 2310555
email: info@irishcancer.ie
website: www.cancer.ie

Cancer, New Approaches to
St Peter's Hospital, Guildford Road, Chertsey, Surrey KT16 0PZ
☎ 0800 389 2662
email: help@anac.org.uk
website: www.anac.org.uk
Holistic and self-help methods of coping with cancer.

CancerBACUP
3 Bath Place, Rivington Street, London EC2A 3JR
☎ 020 7696 9003
Helpline 0808 800 1234 📠 020 7696 9002
email: info@cancerbacup.org
website: www.cancerbacup.org.uk
Advice, counselling, support and information for people with cancer, their relatives and friends. Regional and local branches, publications.

Cancerlink
Macmillan Cancer Fund, 89 Albert Embankment, London SE1 7UQ

☎ 020 7840 7840
Helpline 0808 808 2020 Textphone Helpline 0808 800 0121 📠 020 7840 4886
email: cancerlink@cancerlink.org.uk
website: www.cancerlink.org
Support: contacts: information: newsletter: publications. Training and consultancy for self-help and support groups

Candida Society, National
P.O. Box 151, Orpington, Kent BR5 1UJ
☎ 01689 813039
email: info@candida-society.org.uk
website: www.candida-society.org.uk
Information for sufferers and professionals (See also Cystitis and Candida Advice Service)

Candidiasis, Chronic Mucocutaneous
(Contact Primary Immunodeficiency Association)

Cardiomyopathy Association
40 The Metro Centre, Tolpits Lane, Watford, Herts WD1 9SB
☎ 01923 249977
Helpline 0800 018 1024 📠 01923 249987
email: cmaassoc@aol.com
website: www.cardiomyopathy.org
Support for people affected by hypertrophic cardiomyopathy or dilated cardiomyopathy.

Care and Befriending Schemes
(See Advocacy Partners; Befriending Network; Carers UK; Carers, Princess Royal Trust; Caring Matters Now; Community Service Volunteers; Crossroads Caring for Carers)

Careline
Cardinal Heenan Centre, 326 High Road, Ilford, Essex IG1 1QP
☎ 020 8514 5444
Helpline 020 8514 1177 (Mon-Fri 10am-4pm & 7pm-10pm)
website: www.carelineuk.org
Confidential counselling service for children, young people and adults, on any issue which causes stress, including family problems, eating disorders, bullying, child abuse, bereavement, disability, depression, anxiety and phobia. Referrals to appropriate support agencies.

Carers UK
20-25 Glasshouse Yard, London EC1A 4JT
☎ 020 7490 8818 Advice line 0808 808 7777 (10am-12pm, 2pm-4pm) 📠 020 7490 8824
email: internet@ukcarers.org
website: www.carersonline.org.uk
Umbrella organisation for carers' groups. Offers information, contacts, advice and support to anyone

5

caring for an elderly, sick or disabled person at home. Will put enquirers in touch with a local carers' group. (See Befriending Network; Caring Matters Now; Carers, Princess Royal Trust; for Community Service Volunteers)

Carers, Princess Royal Trust for
142 Minories, London EC3N 1LB
☎ 020 7480 7788 ▤ 020 7481 4729
email: info@carers.org
website: www.carers.org
A national network of carers

Caring Matters Now
Bridge Chapel Centre, Heath Road, Garston, Liverpool L19 4XR
☎ 0151 281 9716 ▤ 0151 281 9717
Contact Jodi and Val Unsworth
website: www.caringmattersnow.co.uk

Carpenter Syndrome
(Contact Headlines)

Catalepsy/Cataplexy
(Contact Narcolepsy Association UK)

Cataract in Children
Cat's Eyes, c/o Contact a Family, 209-211 City Road, London EC1V 1JN
☎ 020 7608 8700 ▤ 020 7608 8701
email: kirsty@majolly.freeserve.co.uk
website: www.cats-eyes.freeserve.co.uk
Support: contacts: information

Catholic Child Welfare Council
St Joseph's, Watford Way, Hendon, London NW4 4TY
☎ & ▤ 020 8203 6323
email: ccwc@compuserve.com
Adoption, fostering and a variety of services supporting children and families in all areas of the UK.

Catholic Children's Crusade of Rescue
73 Charles Square, London W10 6EJ
☎ 020 8969 5305 ▤ 020 8960 1464
email: info@cathchild.org.uk
website: www.cathchild.org.uk
Adoption and fostering, welfare, child and adolescent psychotherapy, counselling.

CDLS Foundation UK
Mr A Peaford, Tall Trees, 106 Lodge Lane, Grays, Essex RM16 2UL
☎ 01375 376439 ▤ 01375 376439
email: info@cdls.org.uk
website: www.cdls.org.uk
Support: self-help: contacts: information: newsletter. For parents of children affected by Cornelia de Lange syndrome

Central Hypoventilation Syndrome, Congenital
(See Ondine's Support Group)

Central Nervous System, Tumours of
(See Brain and Spine Foundation; Brain Tumour Foundation; Brain Tumour Organisations)

Cerebellar Ataxia/Atrophy/Degeneration
(Contact Ataxia UK)

Cerebra (Foundation for the Brain Injured Child)
Gill Gleeson, Parent Network Manager, 13 Guildhall Square, Carmarthen SA31 1PR
☎ 01267 244203 – voice 01267 244220 – minicom 0800 3281159 ▤ 01267 244213
email: info@cerebra.org.uk
website: www.cerebra.org.uk
Supports research in hospitals and universities into brain dysfunction and development of effective therapies. PARNET, the parent network, provides information and links for families, a newsletter and a postal lending library. All PARNET services are free.

Cerebral Giantism
(Contact Sotos Syndrome Support Group)

Cerebral Palsy
(See Capability Scotland; Scope)

Cerebroside Lipidosis
(Contact Gaucher's Association)

CGD Research Trust & Support Group
Manor Farm, Wimborne St Giles, Wimborne, Dorset BH21 5NL
☎ & ▤ 01725 517977
email: rosemarie.cgdrt@dial.pipex.com
website: www.cgd.org.uk
Contacts: information: newsletter. Fundraising for research and to raise awareness. Support for children suffering from chronic granulomatous disease and their families. Funds the employment of a CGD Clinical Nurse Specialist. Holds annual Family Days and Medical Conferences.

Challenging Behaviour Foundation
Viviene Cooper, 32 Tywdall Lane, Gillingham, Kent ME8 6HX
☎ & ▤ 01634 302207
email: vivcooper@thecbf.freeserve.co.uk
website: www.thecbf.org.uk
Contacts, information, publications on dealing with challenging behaviours, newsletter. (See also Emotional and Behavioural Difficulties, Association of Workers for Children with)

Changing Faces
1 and 2 Junction Mews, Paddington, London
W2 1PN
☎ 020 7706 4232 📠 020 7706 4234
email: info@changingfaces.co.uk
website: www.timewarp.demon.co.uk/cfaces
*Support, advice, counselling, publications and
activities for people who have a facial disfigurement
due to accident, disease etc. (See Disfigurement
Guidance Centre; Let's Face It Support Network; Skin
Camouflage, British Association for)*

Charcot-Marie-Tooth Disease
(Contact CMT UK)

CHARGE Association Family Support Group
82 Gwendoline Avenue, Upton Park, London
E13 0RD
☎ 020 8552 6961
email: levey@cs.com
website: www.sense.org.uk/sensory-impairment/
charge.html
*Support: information: contacts: newsletter: publications:
meetings*

Chediak-Higashi Syndrome
(Contact Primary Immunodeficiency Association)

Chemical Allergy
(See Allergy Organisations)

Chemicals, Environmental
(See Pesticide Exposure, Action on)

Cheshire Foundation
(See Leonard Cheshire)

Chest, Heart & Stroke Association
(See Stroke Association, The)

Chest, Heart & Stroke, Scotland
65 North Castle Street, Edinburgh EH2 3LT
☎ 0131 225 6963 Advice line 0345 720720
(Mon-Fri 9.30am-12.30pm & 1.30am-4pm)
📠 0131 220 6313
email: chss@dial.pipex.com
Support: information: publications: newsletter

Child Abuse
(See Careline; Childline; Sexuality and Relationships
Section; Kidscape; NSPCC; Voice UK)

Child Accident Prevention Trust (CAPT)
4th Floor, Clerk's Court, 18-20 Farringdon Lane,
London EC1R 3AU
☎ 020 7608 3828 📠 020 7608 3674
email: safe@capt.org.uk
website: www.capt.org.uk
*A UK-wide organisation that aims to reduce the
number and severity of childhood accidents in Great
Britain and Northern Ireland. Publications available.*

Child Bereavement Trust
Aston House, High Street, West Wycombe, Bucks
HP14 3AG
☎ 01494 446648 📠 01494 440057
Information and Support Line 0800 357 1000
email: enquiries@childbereavement.org.uk
website: www.childbereavement.org.uk
*A national charity which provides training and support
for professionals to enable them to meet the needs of
grieving families. Resources and information for
bereaved families and professionals. Booklet, training
programme and resource list available on request and on
website. The Trust is not an individual counselling
service.*

Child Brain Injury Trust (CBIT), The
7 King Edward Court, King Edward St.,
Nottingham NG1 1EW
☎ 0115 941 0006
email: info@cbituk.org
*Information, support, research. Caters for parents of
children with traumatic brain injury or acquired brain
injury. (See also Headway)*

Child Death
(See Bereavement Organisations; Careline;
Compassionate Friends; Cot Death Trust, Scottish;
Laura Centre; SANDS)

Child Death Helpline Department
Great Ormond Street Hospital, London WC1N 3JH
☎ 020 7813 8551
Helpline 0800 282 986 (Mon-Sun 7pm-10pm,
Mon, Wed & Fri 10am-1pm) 📠 020 7813 8516
email: contact@childdeathhelpline.org
website: www.childdeathhelpline.org.uk

Child Development and Rehabilitation Centres
(See Education Section)

Child Growth Foundation
2 Mayfield Avenue, Chiswick, London W4 1PW
☎ 020 8995 0257 📠 020 8995 9075
email: cgflondon@aol.com
website: www.cgf.org.uk
*Contacts, information and support for anyone with a
growth disorder and for parents of affected children.
The Foundation covers conditions causing excessive
growth as well as those causing restricted growth. Acts
as an umbrella group for several support groups for
specific conditions. (See also Restricted Growth
Association)*

5

Child Protection Helpline
(See Careline; Childline; NSPCC)

Child Psychotherapy Trust
Star House, 104-108 Grafton Road, London NW5 4BD
☎ 020 7284 1355 🖷 020 7284 2755
email: cpt@globalnet.co.uk
website: www.childpsychotherapy.org.uk
Information for parents, carers and professionals working with children who have emotional and/or behavioural problems.

Childbirth Trust, National
Alexandra House, Oldham Terrace, Acton, London W3 6NH
☎ 0870 7703236 🖷 020 8992 5929
website: www.nct-online.org
Information, publications and advice on all aspects of pregnancy and childbirth.

Childcare/Nannies for Special Needs
(See Daycare Trust; Snap Child Care Agency)

Childhood Nephrotic Support
Sandra Warhurst, 7 Bonnymead, Cotgrave, Nottingham NG12 3HQ
☎ 0115 989 2975
Support: contacts: information: newsletter: publications. (See Nephrotic Syndrome Support Group)

Childline
Studd Street, London N1 0QW
☎ 020 7239 1000
Helpline and free telephone line for children needing support 0800 1111 🖷 020 7239 1001
Freepost 1111, London N1 0BR
email: info@childline.org.uk
website: www.childline.org.uk
Childline is the UK's FREE helpline for children and young people in trouble or danger. It provides a confidential phone counselling service for any child with any problem, 24 hours a day, every day. It listens, comforts and protects. Trained counsellors provide support and advice and refer childern in danger to appropriate helping agencies. Childline also brings to public attention issues affecting children's welfare and rights.

Children in Hospital
(See Action for Sick Children)

Children in Scotland
(See Enquire)

Children's Bureau, National
8 Wakley Street, London EC1V 7QE
☎ 020 7843 6000 🖷 020 7278 9512
email: membership@ncb.org.uk
website: www.ncb.org.uk
An inter-disciplinary service, concerned with the needs of children at home and in school. Extensive library and information service on all issues relating to children, including drug education, sex education, play, parenting education. Research and consultancy, conferences.

Children's Hospices
(See Education Section)

Children's Society, The
Edward Rudolf House, Margery Street, London WC1X OJL
☎ 020 7837 4299 🖷 020 7837 0211
email: information@childsoc.org.uk
website: www.the-childrens-society.org.uk
Residential care: fostering: adoption. (See also under Adoption; Fostering)

Chiropractic Patients Association
8 Centre One, Lysander Way, Old Sarum Park, Salisbury, Wilts SP4 6BU
☎ 01722 415027 🖷 01722 415028
email: cpa@dial.pipex.com
A patients' organisation, providing an information helpline, furthering the acceptance of chiropractic treatment and supporting research and education.

Cholesterol, Inherited High Levels
(See Heart UK)

Chondroectodermal Dysplasia
(Contact Ellis-van Creveld Foundation)

Chorea, Chronic Degenerative
(Contact Huntingdon's Disease Association)

Christian Fellowship
(See Leisure Section)

Christian Lewis Children's Cancer Care
Child Care Centre, 62 Walter Road, Swansea, W. Glamorgan SA1 4PT
☎ 01792 480500 🖷 01792 480700
email: enquiries@childens-cancer-care.org.uk
website: www.childrens-cancer-care.org.uk
Family Care Services – via a dedicated telephone line providing a confidential 'listening ear' for anyone who is or has ever been affected by childhood cancer. Bereavement support, befriending, self-help, parents' support groups, compassionate care grants. Play therapy. Crisis breaks via four mobile home sites in Wales. Disneyland Paris and Disney World Florida Holiday Programmes and comprehensive travel insurance cover. An opportunity to stay at Donna's Dream House in Blackpool subject to certain criteria.

Christmas Disease
(Contact Haemophilia Society)

Chromosome 13 Trisomy (Patau Syndrome)
(Contact SOFT UK)

Chromosome 18 Trisomy (Edwards Syndrome)
(Contact SOFT UK)

Chromosome 21 Trisomy
(Contact Down's Syndrome Association)

Chromosome 22q 11 Group
The 22q11 Group, P.O. Box 48, Altrincham WA14 5FB
☎ 07020 911 400
email: 22q11@melcom.cix.co.uk
website: www.cix.co.uk/~melcom/22q11
Support, contacts and information for parents of children affected by velo-cardio-facial syndrome (Shprintzen syndrome) and/or Di George syndrome, which are due to a deletion of a specific site on the long arm of chromosome 22 (22q 11 deletion).

Chromosome Disorders, Rare
(See Unique)

Chromosome Five, Short Arm Deletion
(Contact Cri Du Chat Syndrome Support Group)

Chromosome Four, Short Arm Deletion
(Contact Wolf-Hirschhorn Syndrome Support Group)

Chronic and Long-Term Medical Conditions
(See Long-Term Medical Conditions Alliance)

Chronic Fatigue Syndrome
(See ME Organisations)

Chronic Granulomatous Disease
(See CGD Support Group and Research Trust)

Chronic Mucocutaneous Candidiasis
(Contact Primary Immunodeficiency Association)

Chronic Obstructive Airways Disease
(Contact Lung Foundation, British)

Church Action On Disability (CHAD)
50 Scrutton Street, London EC2A 4XQ
☎ 0207 452 2085
A national organisation, addressing attitudes in the churches to all forms of disability. Aims to encourage development in church communities, so that disabled people can take a realistic part in the spiritual and social life of the church. Regular newsletter and events.

Churg-Strauss Syndrome
(See Guillain-Barre Syndrome Support Group; Stuart Strange Trust and Arthritis Care)

Ciliary Dyskinesia, Primary
(Contact PCD Family Support Group)

CJD Support Group
Birchwood, Heath Top, Ashley Heath, Market Drayton, Shropshire TF9 4QR
☎ & 🖹 01630 673993
Helpline 01630 673973
email: cjdnet@alzheimers.org.uk
website: www.cjdsupport.net
Information and support for people affected by all strains of Creutzfeldt-Jacob disease, their families and carers.

CLAPA (Cleft Lip and Palate Association)
235-237 Finchley Road, London NW3 6LS
☎ 020 7431 0033 🖹 020 7431 8881
email: info@clapa.com
website: www.clapa.com
Advice, information and support for parents of children with cleft lip and/or palate, with advice on treatments and surgical procedures, feeding etc. Newsletter and publications. Branches in most parts of the UK, many of them centred around hospitals which undertake cleft palate repair.

Cleft Lip/Palate
(See CLAPA)

Climb
Climb Building, 176 Nantwich Road, Crewe CW2 6BG
☎ 0870 7700 325 🖹 0870 7700 327
email: info@climb.org.uk
website: www.climb.org
Formerly Research Trust for Metabolic Disease in Children. Advice, information, support and contacts for parents of children with inherited metabolic disorders (i.e. those due to defective enzyme activity). Raises funds for research into detection and treatment. Newsletter, information, conferences. List of disorders catered for on request.

Cloacal Exstrophy
(Contact Bees Support Group; Incontinent and Stoma Children, The Charity for)

Cloverleaf Syndrome
(Contact Headlines)

5

Club Foot
(Contact Steps)

'Clumsy Child' Syndrome
(Contact Dyspraxia Foundation)

CMD Support
Mrs M West, 21 Morrison Drive, Pitcorthie, Dunfermline, Fife KY11 8DJ
☎ 01383 736084
email: cmd@globalnet.co.uk
Support, contacts and information for parents of children affected by congenital muscular dystrophy.

CMT United Kingdom
P.O. Box 5089, Christchurch BH23 2WJ
☎ 0870 7744314
email: secretary@cmt.org.uk
website: www.cmt.org.uk
Caters for Charcot-Marie-Tooth disease (peroneal muscular atrophy or hereditary motor and sensory neuropathy. Support: self help: literature: newsletter: publications.

CMV (Congenital) Association
(See Congenital CMV Association)

COA Support Group
Mrs R Evans, 20 Sheridan Road, Whipton, Exeter, Devon EX4 8EY
☎ 01392 460618 (after 6pm)
Support, contacts and information for parents of children with congenital oculomotor apraxia (Cogan syndrome)

Coeliac UK
P.O. Box 220, High Wycombe, Bucks HP11 2HY
☎ 01494 437278
0870 444 8804 – National Rate Number
Mon-Fri 10-4 🖷 01494 474349
email: admin@coeliac.co.uk
website: www.coeliac.co.uk
Support: contacts: publications. Caters for coeliac disease and dermatitis herpetiformis. Also has professional, associate and corporate grades of membership.

Coffin-Lowry Syndrome Support Group
Mrs L Nolan, 25 Ashling Gardens, Denmead, Waterlooville, Hants PO7 6PR
☎ 01705 610226 (after 6pm)
Support: contacts: information

Coffin-Siris Support Network
225 Shear Brow, Blackburn, Lancs. BB1 8DU
☎ 01254 727101
website: www.coffin-siris.org.uk
Support: contacts: information

Cogan Syndrome
(See COA Support Group)

Cohen Syndrome Support Group
45 Compton Way, Middleton Junction, Middleton, Manchester M24 2BU
☎ 0161 653 0867
email: cohensyndrome@hotmail.com
Support: contacts: information: newsletter

Colitis and Crohn's Disease, National Association for
4 Beaumont House, Sutton Road, St Albans, Herts AL1 5HH
☎ 01727 830038 Information 0845 130 2233
🖷 01727 862550
email: nacc@nacc.org.uk
website: www.nacc.org.uk
(See Crohn's in Childhood Research Association)

College of Health Waiting List Helpline
St Margaret's House, 21 Old Ford Road, London E2 9PL
☎ 020 8983 11133 🖷 020 8983 1553
National Waiting List Helpline 020 8983 1553
email: info@tcom.demon.co.uk
website: www.collegeofhealth.org.uk
Provides information on shorter hospital waiting lists and self-help groups.

Coloboma Contact Group
Peter Attenborough, 10 Mugdrum Place, Newburgh, Cupar, Fife KY14 6DD
☎ & 🖷 01337 840754
Affiliated to MACS

Colostomy Association, British
15 Station Road, Reading, Berks RG1 1LG
☎ & Helpline 0800 328 4257 🖷 0118 956 9095
email: sue@bcass.org.uk
website: www.bcass.org.uk
Support: information: publications

Colostomy in Children
(Contact Incontinent and Stoma Children, The Charity for)

Combined Immune Deficiency Disease
(Contact Primary Immunodeficiency Association)

Communication Skills, Absence or Loss of
(See AFASIC; ICAN; Nuffield Hearing and Speech Centre; Speakability)

Community Hygiene Concern
Hospital for Tropical Diseases, 4 St Pancras Way, London NW1 0PE
☎ 020 7387 1990

Helpline 020 8341 7167160 🖺 020 8292 7208
website: www.chc.org
Provides information and advice on dealing with head lice and toxocara. Supplies 'Bug-Buster Kit' a safe, non-pesticidal method of getting rid of head lice. Teacher pack and other materials for school and health professionals (See Alopecia Society, Children's)

Community Service Volunteers
237 Pentonville Road, London N1 9NJ
☎ 020 7278 6601 🖺 020 7837 9621
email: volunteer@csv.org.uk / bwilliams@csv.org.uk
Offers people aged 16+ the opportunity to make a difference by volunteering full or part-time in social care or community environments. CSV voluteers do not need any previous experience, specialist skills or minimum qualifications to become involved. Volunteers live away from home and receive free accomodation and food plus an allowance. A CSV local community part-time scheme is available for vulnerable people, e.g. with special needs, includind support and supervision.

Compassionate Friends, The
53 North Street, Bedminster, Bristol BS3 1EN
☎ 0117 966 5202
Helpline 0117 953 9639 🖺 0117 914 4368
email: info@tcf.org.uk
website: www.tcf.org.uk
A nationwide organisation offering support and friendship to parents whose children have died. Contact points in many areas. (See also under Bereavement)

Compulsion Disorders
(See Careline; Obsessive Action)

Conductive Education
(See Education Section)

Cone Dysfunction
(Contact Nystagmus Network)

Congenital CMV Association
Keri Dudley, 128 Northfields Lane, Brixham, Devon TQ5 8RH
☎ 01803 856496
Support: contacts: information: newsletter. For parents of children affected by cytomegalovirus infection during the mother's pregnancy.

Congenital Hypotonia Support Group
Natasha Brown, Flat 1, Frognal Court, 158 Finchley Road, London NW3 5HL
email: tash@lacobrown.freeserve.co.uk
website: www.freespace.virgin.net/bch.hypotonia or www.hypotonia.co.uk
Support: contacts: information

Congenital Neutropenia
(Contact Primary Immunodeficiency Association)

Constipation, Chronic
(See Digestive Disorders Foundation)

Contact a Family
209-211 City Road, London EC1V 1JN
☎ 020 7608 8700 🖺 020 7608 8701
email: info@cafamily.org.uk
website: www.cafamily.org.uk
A national charity supporting families who care for a child with any type of special need or disability. Advice on setting up support groups, quarterly journal, publications, network of local support groups for parents of children with any type of special needs. Regional and project offices in all areas of the UK.

Contact a Family, Northern Ireland
Bridge Community Centre, 50 Railway Street, Lisburn BT28 1XP
☎ & 🖺 028 9262 7552
0808 808 3555
email: nireland@cafamily.org.uk
website: www.cafamily.org.uk

Contact a Family, Scotland
Norton Park, 57 Albion Road, Edinburgh EH7 5QY
☎ 0131 475 2608
0808 808 3555 – for carers and parents, subscribes to 'language line' 🖺 0131 475 2609
email: scotland@cafamily.org.uk
website: www.cafamily.org.uk

Contact a Family, Wales
Tridents Court, East Moors Road, Cardiff CF24 5TD
☎ 029 2044 9569 🖺 029 2047 0851
email: wales@cafamily.org.uk

Cooley's Anaemia
(Contact Thalassaemia Society, UK)

Coprolalia/Generalised Tic Syndrome
(Contact Tourette Syndrome UK Association)

Cori Syndrome
(Contact Glycogen Storage Diseases Association)

Cornelia De Lange Syndrome
(See CDLS Foundation UK)

CORPAL
240 Malden Way, New Malden KT3 5QU
☎ 020 8404 6620
email: corpal@blueyonder.co.uk
website: www.corpal.org.uk
Support, contacts and information for parents of

5

children affected by agenesis of the corpus callosum and Aicardi syndrome.

Costello Syndrome Support Group, International

Colin Stone, 90 Parkfield Road North, New Moston, Manchester M40 3RQ
☎ 0161 682 2479
email: c.stone8@ntlworld.com
website: www.costellokids.co.uk/
www.costellokids.org.uk
Conference, information, contacts, medical information and research.

Cot Death

(See Bereavement Organisations; Careline; Child Death Helpline; Compassionate Friends; Foundation for the Study of Infant Deaths; Laura Centre; Sands; Sudden Death Support Network)

Cot Death Society

Maple House, Units 6 and 8, Padgate Business Park, Warrington WA1 4JN
☎ 01925 850086 ▤ 01925 851943
website: www.cotdeathsociety.org.uk
Provides monitors, on referral, to parents of babies considered to be at risk from cot death.

Cot Death Trust, The Scottish

Royal Hospital for Sick Children, Yorkhill, Glasgow G3 8SJ
☎ 0141 357 3946 (9am-5pm, Mon-Fri)
▤ 0141 334 1376
email: h.brooke@clinmed.gla.ac.uk

Counselling & Psychotherapy, British Association for

1 Regent Place, Rugby, Warks CV21 2PJ
☎ 0870 443 5252
email: bac@bac.co.uk
Information on training in counselling. Produces a lists of local counsellors. (Enclose SAE)

Cranial Osteopathic Association

478 Barker Street, Enfield, Middlesex EN1 3QS
☎ 020 8367 5561 ▤ 020 8202 6686
Will provide information on the application of cranial osteopathy and a list of practising therapists. The therapists listed cater for a wide range of conditions, including damage resulting from birth trauma, conditions related to head injury, and migraine, tinnitus etc. Conferences, training courses.

Craniofacial Abnormalities

(See Headlines)

Craniosacral Therapists, International Register of

9 St George Mews, Primrose Hill, London NW1 8XE
☎ 020 7483 0120

Creutzfeldt-Jacob Disease

(See CJD Support Group)

Cri du Chat Syndrome Support Group

Mrs A Stokes, 7 Penny Lane, Barwell, Leicestershire LE9 8HJ
☎ 01455 841680 ▤ 01455 842054
email: cdssg@yahoo.co.uk
website: www.cridchat.u-net.com
Support: contacts: information: newsletter: publications: annual get-together for parents of children with Cri du Chat syndrome (chromosome 5p deletion).

Crime: Accusation of People with Learning Disability

(See Beyond Words)

Crohn's in Childhood Research Association (CICRA)

Parkgate House, 356 West Barnes Lane, Motspur Park, Surrey KT3 6NB
☎ 020 8949 6209 ▤ 020 8942 2044
email: support@cicra.org
website: www.cicra.org
Support: contacts: information. (See Colitis and Crohn's Disease, National Association for)

Crossroads Caring for Carers

10 Regent Place, Rugby CV21 2PN
☎ 01788 573653 ▤ 01788 565498
email: communications@ukonline.co.uk
website: www.crossroads.org.uk
Provides practical support for carers, caring for people of any age or disability. A carer support worker undertakes agreed caring tasks and this service gives carers 'time to be themselves'.

Crossroads Scotland

24 George Square, Glasgow G2 1EG
☎ 0141 226 3793
email: enquiries@crossroads-scot.k-web.co.uk
Offers support and practical help for anyone in Scotland, responsible for the care of a disabled, sick or elderly person at home.

Crouzon Syndrome

(See Headlines)

Cruse Bereavement Care

Cruse House, 126 Sheen Road, Richmond, Surrey TW9 1UR
☎ 020 89399530

0870 1671677 🖷 020 8940 7638
email: info@crusebereavementcare.org.uk
website: www.crusebereavementcare.org.uk
Offers help to bereaved people, in any way and whatever their age. Contact and support through 200 groups in the UK. Newsletter, training for professionals.

Cry-Sis
BM Cry-sis, London WC1N 3XX
Helpline 020 7404 5011
website: www.www-our-space.co.uk/serene.htm
Support and advice for parents of babies and young children who are excessively demanding or cry excessively.

Cued Speech, National Centre for
(See under AFASIC)

Cushing Care
Mrs V Howarth, Meadows, Woodplumpton Village, Preston, Lancs PR4 0LJ
☎ & 🖷 01172 690680
Support: contacts: information. Please send SAE for details. (See also Pituitary Foundation)

Cushing's Treatment and Help, Association for
ACTH, Ivanhoe, 54 Powney Road, Maidenhead, Berks SL6 6EQ
☎ 01628 670389 🖷 01628 615403
email: cushingsacth@btinternet.com
website: www.cushingsacth.co.uk
Information and support for people affected by any form of Cushing syndrome or disease. Newsletter, support by medical panel, nationwide association with members. (See also Pituitary Foundation)

Cutis Hyperelasticum
(Contact Ehlers-Danlos Syndrome Support Group)

CVS Association
Mrs N Kipping, 5 St Anthony's Avenue, Lilliput, Dorset BH14 8JQ
☎ 01202 709194
email: cvsa@avnet.co.uk
website: www.nacvs.org.uk/cvsdir/index.shtm
Support: contacts: information: annual meeting. For parents of children affected by cyclical vomiting and abdominal migraine in childhood.

Cyclical Neutropenia
(Contact Primary Immunodeficiency Association)

Cyclical Vomiting Syndrome
(See CVS Association)

Cystic Encephalomalacia
(Contact Porencephaly Contact Group)

Cystic Fibrosis Trust
11 London Road, Bromley, Kent BR1 1BY
☎ 020 8464 7211
0845 859 1000 🖷 020 8313 0472
email: enquiries@cftrust.org.uk
website: www.cftrust.org.uk
Support: information: newsletter. (See also Barnardo's Cystic Fibrosis Projects)

Cystic Hygroma Support Group
Woodhill House, Cuckfield Lane, Warninglid, Haywards Heath, West Sussex RH17 5SN
☎ 01444 461155
Support: contacts: information: newsletter. Caters for parents of children affected by lymphangioma and cystic hygroma, with or without haemangioma.

Cystitis & Candida Information Service
Mrs A Kilmartin, Flat 9, 6-9 Bridgewater Square, London EC2Y 8AG
☎ & 🖷 020 7256 2993
email: angela.kilmartin@dial.pip.com
website: www.angela.kilmartin.dial.pipex.com
Support: information: publications. (See also Interstitial Cystitis Support Group)

Cytomegalovirus, Congenital (CMV)
(See Congenital CMV Association)

DAF Syndrome
(See Niemann-Pick Disease Group)

Dancing Eye Syndrome Support Trust
Mrs J Stanton-Roberts, 78 Quantock Road, Worthing, West Sussex BN13 2HQ
☎ & 🖷 01903 532383
email: support@dancingeyes.org.uk
website: www.dancingeyes.org.uk
Support: contacts: information. Dancing Eye syndrome is also known as opsoclonus myoclonus or Kinsbourne syndrome.

Dandy-Walker Network
Mrs J McKeown, 19 Ennismore Road, Liverpool L13 2AR
☎ 0151 281 1341
Support: contacts: information: newsletter: publications

Daycare Trust
21 St George's Road, London SE1 6ES
☎ 020 7840 3350 🖷 020 7840 3355
email: info@daycaretrust.org.uk
website: www.daycaretrust.org.uk
Advice and information for parents about childcare,

5

research into childcare provision, publishes 'Check out Childcare'. (See SNAP Childcare Agency)

De Lange Syndrome
(Contact CDLS Foundation UK)

Deaf Association, The British
1-3 Worship Street, London EC2A 2AB
☎ 020 7588 3520 Text 020 7588 3529
0870 770 3300 (tel) and 0800 6522 965 (text)
▤ 020 7588 3527
video phone 020 7496 9539
email: helpline@bda.org.uk
website: www.britishdeafassociation.org.uk
The British Deaf Association (BDA) is the largest national organisation run by deaf people for deaf people. They represent the UK's deaf community, a community united by shared experiences, history and, above all, by a common language: British Sign Language (BSL). The headquarters are in London but they have offices in Edinburgh, Cardiff, Belfast and Warrington.

Deaf Children's Society, National (NDCS)
15 Dufferin Street, London EC1Y 8UR
☎ 020 7490 8656
Helpline 020 7250 0123 (Mon-Fri 10am-5pm, up to 7pm Tues) ▤ 020 7251 5020
email: ndcs@ndcs.org.uk
website: www.ndcs.org.uk
Wide range of services; advice, advocacy, schools, colleges, educational advice, technology and communication advice, leisure facilities, holiday facilities, publications, conferences.

Deaf People, Royal National Institute for the
(See RNID)

Deaf, Wales Council for the
Glenview House, Courthouse Street, Pontypridd CF37 1JY
☎ 01443 485687 & 01443 485686
Minicom 01443 485686 ▤ 01443 408555
Information on all services and activities for people in Wales who have hearing loss.

Deaf/Blind and Rubella Association
(See Sense)

Deafblind UK
100 Bridge Street, Peterborough, Cambs PE14 1DY
☎ & Minicom 01733 358100
Helpline 0800 132320 ▤ 01733 358356
email: info@deafblind.org.uk
website: www.deafblind.org.uk
Brings together deafblind people. Visiting service, community care, activities, holidays, living accommodation, information and advice.

Deafblind Scotland
21 Alexander Avenue, Lenzie, Glasgow G66 5BG
☎ & Minicom 0141 777 6111
Helpline (24hours) 0800 132 320 ▤ 0141 775 3311
email: info@deafblindscotland.org.uk

Deafened People, National Association of (NADP)
P.O. Box 50, Amersham, Bucks HP6 6XB
☎ 01494 723613 ▤ 01494 431932
email: enquiries@nadp.org.uk
website: www.nadp.org.uk
Advice and support to those who have lost all or part of their hearing. Helpline, information and publications, quarterly magazine, network of local groups.

Deafness
(See Hearing Voices Network, National; Hearing Concern)

deafPLUS
Prospect Hall, 12 College Walk, Bristol Road, Selly Oak, Birmingham B29 6LE
☎ 0121 415 2080 ▤ 0121 415 2081
Personal support, working with the individual. Information Services – what you need, when and where you need it. Training Programme – by and for deaf people.

DEBRA
DEBRA House, 13 Wellington Business Park, Duke's Ride, Crowthorne, Berks RG45 6LS
☎ 01344 771961 ▤ 01344 762661
email: debra.uk@btinternet.com
website: www.debra.org.uk
Support: contacts: information: newsletter: healthcare team. For parents of children affected by epidermolysis bullosa.

Delayed Myelin Matters
Elaine Bennett, 4 Ross House, Ross Road, Twickenham TW2 6JP
☎ 020 8894 1969
Support, contacts and information for parents of children affected by delayed myelinisation.

Deletion of Chromosomes
(See Cri du Chat Syndrome Support Group; Wolf-Hirschhorn Syndrome Support Group; Unique)

Dental Amalgams
(See PAMA)

Dental Anxiety and Phobia Association
43 Harley Street, London W1G 9RP
☎ 020 7580 0011
website: www.healthyteeth.com

Dental Care in Profound and Multiple Disability
(See Mencap PIMD Project)

Dental Health Foundation, British
Sharon Broom, Smile House, 2 East Union Street, Rugby, Warks CV22 6AJ
☎ 0870 770 4000
0870 333 1188 ▤ 0870 770 4010
email: mail@dentalhealth.org.uk
website: www.dentalhealth.org.uk
Advice and information on dental care and treatment.

Dentistry for the Handicapped, British Society of
Sue Greening, 62 Brandreth Road, Penylan, Cardiff CF2 5LD
☎ 01633 838356
Advice sheets and booklets. Register of dental practitioners with a special interest in treating people with a disability. Home visits possible in some cases.

Depression in People with Learning Disability
(See Beyond Words)

Dermatitis Herpetiformis
(Contact Coeliac Society)

Dermatological Disorders
(See Skinship)

Dermatomyositis
(See Myositis Support Group)

Di George Syndrome
(Contact Chromosome 22q11 Group)

Diabetes Foundation, Juvenile
25 Gosfield Street, London W1P 8EB
☎ 020 7436 3112 ▤ 020 7436 3039
Support and information for young people with diabetes

Diabetes Insipidus
(Contact Pituitary Foundation; Climb)

Diabetes UK
10 Park Way, London NW1 7AA
☎ 020 7424 1000 ▤ 020 7424 1001
email: info@diabetes.org.uk
website: www.diabetes.org.uk
National organisation for people who have diabetes mellitus. Information, advice, holiday facilities

Diabetes, Insulin-Dependent
(See Insulin-Dependent Diabetes Trust)

Dial UK (Disablement Information & Advice Line)
Park Lodge, St Catherine's Hospital, Tickhill Road, Balby, Doncaster, Yorks DN4 8QN

☎ 01302 310123 Minicom 01302 310123
▤ 01302 310404
email: dialuk@aol.com
website: http://members.aol.com/dialuk
Local centres in all areas of the UK, offering information on all aspects of disability. (See ADAIP)

Diamond-Blackfan Anaemia Support Group
17 Isis Avenue, Bicester, Oxon OX6 8GR
☎ 01869 369836
email: jayson.whitaker@tesco.net
website: www.diamondblackfan.org.uk
Support: contacts: information

Diaphragmatic Hernia Support Network
(See Patches)

Diaphyseal Aclasis
(See Hereditary Multiple Exostoses Support Group)

Diarrhoea, Chronic
(See Digestive Disorders Foundation)

Diastrophic Dysplasia/Dwarfism
(Contact Child Growth Foundation; Restricted Growth Association)

Different Strokes
9 Canon Harnett Court, Wolverton Mill, Milton Keynes, Herts MK12 5NF
☎ 0845 1307172 ▤ 01908 313501
email: info@differentstrokes.co.uk
website: www.differentstrokes.co.uk
Support for young people who have suffered a stroke, nationwide exercise classes, contacts, information, newsletter.

Digestive Disorders Foundation
P.O. Box 251, Edgware, Middlesex HA8 6HG
website: www.digestivedisorders.org.uk
Produces information leaflets on a range of digestive disorders (diarrhoea, constipation etc.).

Disabilities, Parents with
(See Disability, Pregnancy and Parenthood International; Parentability)

Disability and Rehabilitation, Royal Association for
(See RADAR)

Disability Action (N. Ireland)
2 Annadale Avenue, Belfast BT7 3JH

5

☎ 01232 491011 🖹 01232 491627
Information on all aspects of living with a disability.

Disability Advice and Welfare Network
64-66 Bickerstaffe Street, St Helens, Lancs WA10 1DS
☎ Freephone 0800 073 0171 🖹 01744 451215
website: www.abilityonline.org.uk/disability-advice-and welfare-ne.htm
Information on all aspects of disability.

Disability Federation of Ireland
Fumbally Court, Fumbally Lane, Dublin 8, Ireland
☎ 3531 4547978 🖹 3531 4547981
email: info@disability-federation.ie
website: www.disability-federation.ie
The national support organisation and advocate for volutary organisations in Ireland, covering all areas of disability. DFI has ongoing involvement with over 200 organisations and groups throughout Ireland, and holds as a core value the right of people with disabilities, and their families, to fully exercise citizenship.

Disability Wales
Llys Ifor, Crescent Road, Caerphilly CF83 1XL
☎ 01222 887325 🖹 01222 888702
email: info@dwac.demon.co.uk
Information on all aspects of disability; access, aids and equipment, benefits, education and employment, holidays, housing, leisure, etc.

Disability, Pregnancy & Parenthood International (DPPI)
National Centre for Disabled Parents, Unit F9, 89-93 Fonthill Road, London N4 3JH
☎ 020 7263 3088 – admin 🖹 020 7263 6399
info service – text (0800 018 9949)
voice – (0800 018 4730)
email: info@dppi.org.uk
website: www.dppi.org.uk
Promotes the networking of information and experience on all aspects of pregnancy and parenthood. Information service aimed at disabled people who are already parents or are considering parenthood, and professionals working with disabled parents. Quarterly international newsletter. (See also Disabled Parents Network)

Disabled Children, Council for
National Children's Bureau, 8 Wakley Street, London EC1V 7QE
☎ 020 7843 1900 🖹 020 7843 6313
email: cdc@ncb.org.uk
website: www.ncb.org.uk/cdc.htm
Promotes collaborative work and partnerships between various agencies, parents and children and provides a national forum for the discussion, development and dissemination of a wide range of policy and practice issues relating to service provision. Support for children and young people with disabilities and special educational needs.

Disabled Parents Network
P.O. Box 5876, Towcester, London NN1 7ZN
☎ 020 7263 3088 – admin
Helpline 0870 241 0450
email: information@disabledparentsnetwork.org.uk
website: www.disabledparentsnetwork.org.uk
Support, information and advice for parents with a disability. (See Disability, Pregnancy and Parenthood International)

Disabled Persons Transport Advisory Committee (DPTAC)
DPTAC Secretariat, Zone 1/14 Great Minster House, 76 Marsham Street, London SW1P 4DR
☎ 020 7944 8011 🖹 020 7944 6998
email: dptac@dft.gsi.gov.uk
website: www.dptac.gov.uk
DPTAC is the statutory advisor to the Government on the transport needs of disabled people. It also advises on issues in relation to the built environment and access for disabled people.

Disablement Information & Advice Line
(See Dial UK)

Disfigurement Guidance Centre (DGC)
P.O. Box 7, Cupar, Fife KY15 4PF
☎ 01337 870281 🖹 01337 870310
website: www.dgc.org.uk or
www.skinlaserdirectory.org.uk
Support, information and advice for people with any type of disfigurement. Advice on treatments, clinics for medically referred patients. Produces a directory of Skin Laser Clinics (free to GPs, £5.00 to others).

Disfigurement, Facial
(See Birthmark Support Group; Changing Faces; Disfigurement Guidance Centre; Let's Face It Support Network; Skin Camouflage, British Association for)

Dislocation of Hip, Congenital
(Contact Steps)

Down's Heart Group
Mrs P Green, 17 Cantilupe Close, Eaton Bray, Dunstable, Beds LU6 2EA
☎ 01525 220379 🖹 01525 221553
email: downs_heart_group@msn.com
website: www.downs-heart.downsnet.org
Support group for parents of children who have Down's

syndrome, plus a heart defect. Newsletter, information, video for parents.

Down's Syndrome Association
155 Mitcham Road, London SW17 9PG
☎ 020 8682 4001 📠 020 8682 4012
email: info@downs-syndrome.org.uk
website: www.downs-syndrome.org.uk
Local parent groups in all areas of the UK. Wide range of publications on all aspects of Down's syndrome, assessments, educational advice.

Down's Syndrome Scotland
158-160 Balgreen Road, Edinburgh EH11 3AU
☎ 0131 313 4225 📠 0131 313 4285
email: info@dsscotland.org.uk
website: www.dsscotland.org.uk
Information; publications; educational advice; ageing; and Down's Syndrome.

Dreams Come True Charity
York House, Knockhundred Row, Midhurst, W. Sussex GU29 9DQ
☎ 01730 815000 📠 01730 813141
website: www.dctc.org.uk
A nationwide charity whose aim is to lift the spirits of seriously and terminally ill children (aged 2-21) by enabling them to fulfil their most treasured dreams, which can be as varied as a child's imagination. Examples: holidays, equipment, meeting personalities etc. (see Starlight Children's Foundation; Make a Wish Foundation UK) (provide funding for the child and one carer).

Drug Education
(See Children's Bureau, National)

DSFA
Lydia Parbury, FCO, OAB Room 1/95, London SW1A 2PA
☎ 020 7008 0282
email: lydia.parbury@fco.gov.uk
Support, contacts and information for parents working in the British Diplomatic Services who have children with special needs, especially for families moving from country to country. Advice on residential homes and schools in the UK and abroad.

Duchenne Family Support Group
37a Highbury New Park, Islington, London N5 2EN
☎ 0870 241 1857
Helpline 0870 606 1604
email: dfsg@duchenne.demon.co.uk
website: www.dfsg.org.uk
Support: contacts: information: newsletter

'Dwarfism'
(Contact Restricted Growth Association; Child Growth Foundation)

Dysautonomia Society of Great Britain
P.O. Box 17679, London NW4 1WS
☎ 020 8958 8760 📠 020 8357 0038
Support, contacts, information. Fund-raising to send patients to America for assessment and campaign to raise awareness of the disorder.

Dyskeratosis Congenita Society
Dr I Dokal, Dept of Haematology, Imperial College School of Medicine, Hammersmith Hospital, Du Cane Road, London W12 0NN
☎ 020 8383 1956
Support: contacts: information

Dyslexia Association, British
98 London Road, Reading, Berks RG1 5AU
☎ 0118 966 8271 📠 0118 935 1927
email: info@dyslexiahelp-bda.demon.co.uk
website: www.bda-dyslexia.org.uk
Support: contacts: information: publications: newsletter

Dyslexia Centre, Helen Arkell
Frensham, Farnham, Surrey GU10 3BW
☎ 01252 792400 📠 01252 795669
website: www.arkellcentre.org.uk
Information: support: publications: assessments: specialist tuition: conferences: courses: services for schools: consultations: bursaries.

Dyslexia in Scotland
Stirling Business Centre, Wellgreen, Stirling FK8 2DZ
☎ & Helpline 01786 446650 📠 01786 471235
email: info@dyslexia-in-scotland.org

Dyslexia Institute
133 Gresham Road, Staines, Middlesex TW18 2AJ
☎ 01784 463851 📠 01784 460747
email: info@dyslexia-inst.org.uk
website: www.dyslexia-inst.org.uk
Assessment, teaching and teacher training, teaching resources, information and advice service for people of all ages who have dyslexia.

Dysmennorhoea
(See PMS Help; Premenstrual Syndrome, National Association for; Premenstrual Society, The; Women's Health)

Dysphasic Adults, Action for
1 Royal Street, London SE1 7LL
☎ 020 7261 9572 📠 020 7928 9542
For adults who have speech and communication difficulties due to stroke, accident, illness etc. (See Aids and Equipment Section; Education Section)

5

Dyspraxia Foundation
8 West Alley, Hitchin, Herts SG5 1EG
☎ 01462 455016
Helpline: 01462 454986 ▤ 01462 455052
email: dyspraxiafoundation@hotmail.com
website: www.dyspraxiafoundation.org.uk
Support, contacts, information, publications and newsletter for parents of children diagnosed as having dyspraxia (minimal brain dysfunction/clumsy child syndrome). (See also Nuffield; Hearing and Speech Centre; OAASIS)

Dystonia Society, The & Young Dystonia
46-47 Britton Street, London EC1M 5UJ
☎ 020 7490 5671 ▤ 020 7490 5672
website: www.dystonia.org.uk
Self-help group for sufferers from chronic involuntary muscle spasm, i.e.; generalised dystonia, blepharospasm, spasmodic torticollis, writer's cramp, dystonia muscular deformans, oromandibular dystonia, laryngeal dystonia, Meige's disease. Also runs a group for young people with dystonia.

Dystonic Lipidosis, Juvenile
(See Niemann-Pick Disease Group)

Dystrophic Epidermolysis Bullosa
(See DEBRA)

Ear, Atresia of
(Contact Treacher-Collins Syndrome Family Support Group)

Eating Disorders Association
First Floor, Wensum House, 103 Prince of Wales Road, Norwich, Norfolk NR1 1DW
☎ 0870 770 3256
Helpline: 0845 634 1414 (weekdays 8:30am-8:30pm) ▤ 01603 664915
email: info@edauk.com
website: www.edauk.com
A UK wide charity (formed in 1989 by the amalgamation of three established eating disorders charities) providing information, help and support for people affected by eating disorders and, in particular, anorexia and bulimia nervosa.

Echo: Parent To Parent Befriending Service
(See Mencap in Wales)

E-Coli Infection
(Contact HUSH)

Ectodermal Dysplasia Society
108 Charlton Lane, Cheltenham, Glos GL53 9EA
☎ 01242 261332
email: ed.support@virgin.net

website: www.ectodermaldysplasia.org.uk
Support: contacts: information

Ectopia Vesicae
(Contact BEES; Incontinent and Stoma Children, The Charity for)

Eczema Society, National
Hill House, Highgate Hill, London N9 5NA
☎ 020 7281 3553
0870 241 3604 ▤ 020 7281 6395
website: www.eczema.org
Support: information: quarterly journal: publications. Booklet for teachers regarding eczema in schools.

Edwards Syndrome (Trisomy 18)
(Contact SOFT UK)

Ehlers-Danlos Syndrome Support Group
Ashley Greene, P.O. Box 335, Farnham, Surrey GU10 1XJ
☎ 01252 690940 ▤ 01252 404573
email: director@ehlers-danlos.org
website: www.ehlers-danlos.org
Support: contacts: information: publications: national conferences

Elected Termination for Foetal Abnormality
(See ARC)

Elective Mutism
(See Selective Mutism Information and Research Association)

Elimination of Leukaemia Fund (ELF)
Marcia Murrell, Administrator, 291 Kirkdale, Sydenham, London SE26 4QD
☎ 020 8778 5353 ▤ 020 8778 7117
email: elffund@ukonline.org
website: www.leukaemia-elf.org.uk
Raises funds to advance the treatment and cure of leukaemia and related blood cancers. Information, publications, help with fund-raising.

Ellis-Van Creveld Foundation
Mrs Y Sutton, Farthingale Farm, Hackmans Lane, Purleigh, Chelmsford, Essex CM3 6RW
☎ 01621 828914 (evenings)
Support: contacts: newsletter

EMG Syndrome
(Contact Beckwith-Weidemann Support Group)

Emotional and Behavioural Difficulties, Association of Workers for Children with (AWCEBD)
Mrs Alan Rimmer, Charlton Court, East Sutton, Maidstone, Kent ME17 3DQ

☎ 01622 834104 🖷 01622 844220
email: awcebd@mistral.co.uk
website: www.awcebd.co.uk
Support: contacts: information: conferences

Emphysema
(Contact Lung Foundation, British)

Enable
6th Floor, 7 Buchanan Street, Glasgow G1 3HL
☎ 0141 226 4541 (Mon-Thurs 1.30pm–4.45pm &
Fri 1.30–4 pm) 🖷 0141 204 4398
email: info@enable.org.uk or enable@enable.org.uk
website: www.enable.org.uk
*The major organisation catering for people with
learning disabilities in Scotland. Support, contacts,
information, publications, local branches, supported
living, out of school projects.*

Encephalitis Support Group
Mrs E Dowell, 44a Market Place, Malton, N. Yorks
YO17 7LW
☎ & 🖷 01653 699599
email: info@esg.org.uk
website: www.esg.org.uk
*Support: contacts: information: newsletter. Information
and education pack.*

Encephalofacial Angiomatosis
(Contact Sturge-Weber Syndrome Foundation UK)

Encephalomyelitis Myalgia
(See ME)

Encephalomyelitis, Acute Disseminated
(See Encephalitis Support Group)

Endochondromatosis
(Contact Ollier Disease Self-Help Group)

Enquire
Children in Scotland, 5 Shandwick Place,
Edinburgh EH2 4RG
☎ 0131 228 8484
0131 222 2400 🖷 0131 228 9852
Typetalk – 0800 959 598
email: enquire.SENinfo@childreninscotland.org.uk
*The National Information and Advice Service for
special educational needs in Scotland.*

Enteral Nutrition Therapy
(See Half PINNT; PINNT)

Enuresis (Incontinence)
(See Aids and Equipment Section)

Environment-Related Allergy
(See Allergy Organisations)

Eosinophilic Granuloma
(Contact Histiocytosis Family Support Association
UK)

Epidermolysis Bullosa
(See DEBRA)

Epilepsy Action (British Epilepsy Association)
Gate Way Drive, Yeadon, Leeds, West Yorks LS19
7XY
☎ 0113 210 8800
Helpline 0808 800 5050 (Mon-Thurs 9am-4.30pm
Fri. 9am-4pm) 🖷 0113 242 8804
email: epilepsy@bea.org.uk
website: www.epilepsy.org.uk
*Local and regional branches, support, information,
publications, assessment, training, employment etc.*

Epilepsy Action Scotland
48 Govan Road, Glasgow G51 1JL
☎ 0141 427 4911
Helpline 0141 427 5225 🖷 0141 419 1709
email: enquiries@epilepsyscotland.org.uk
website: www.epilepsyscotland.org.uk
*Support: contacts; information; newsletter:
publications: fund-raising: day services: field work staff;
training; helpline; website, branches and support
groups; lobbying and campaigning.*

Epilepsy Bereaved
P.O. Box 112, Wantage DO, Oxon OX12 8XT
☎ & 🖷 01235 772850 Support Line for parents
01235 772852
website: www.bodley.ox.ac.uk/external/epilepsy
*Self-help group for families and friends of people with
epilepsy who have died suddenly. Mutual support,
information and research into sudden unexpected
death in epilepsy (SUDE). Send SAE for information.*

Epilepsy, David Lewis Centre for
Mill Lane, Warford, Nr Alderley Edge, Cheshire
SK9 7UD
☎ 01565 640000 🖷 01565 872829
website: www.davidlewis.org.uk
*Assessment: treatment: education and further
education: care: rehabilitation*

Epilepsy, Generalised Flexion
(See West Syndrome Support Group)

Epilepsy, National Society for
Chesham Lane, Chalfont St Peter, Bucks SL9 ORJ
☎ 01494 601300
Helpline 01494 601400 (Mon-Fri 10am-4pm)
🖷 01494 871927

5

website: www.epilepsynse.org.uk
Support: contacts: information: newsletter membership scheme: publications: research: medical assessment: training

Epiphyseal Dysplasia, Multiple (MED)
(See Bone Dysplasia Group; Perthes Association; Restricted Growth Association)

Epispadias
(Contact BEES Support Group)

Erb's Palsy Support Group
Mrs K Hillyer, 60 Anchorway Road, Coventry CV3 6JJ
☎ 024 7641 3293 🖷 024 7641 9857
email: erbspalsygroup@supanet.com
Support: contacts: information; newsletter: annual family day

Erythromelalgia
(Contact Raynaud's and Scleroderma Association)

Exomphalos
(Contact GEEPS; Incontinent and Stoma Children, the Charity for)

Exomphalos/Macroglossia/Giantism Syndrome
(Contact Beckwith-Wiedemann Support Group)

Exploring Parenthood
Latimer Education Centre, 194 Freston Road, London W10 6TT
☎ 020 8960 1678
The sharing of parent-skills, mutual support, workshops etc. Includes adoptive parents and parents of children with special needs.

Exstrophy of the Bladder
(See BEES; Incontinent and Stoma Children, The Charity for)

Eye Care for People with Learning Disabilities
(Contact RNIB)

Eye Conditions, Specific
(See Specific Eye Conditions)

Eyecare Trust, The
P.O. Box 131
Market Rasen, Lincs LN8 5TS
☎ 01673 857847 🖷 01673 857696
email: eis@btinternet.com
website: www.eye-care.org.uk
Information and publications on all aspects of eye care.

FA UK
Ann Dudarenko, 82 Park Hills Road, Bury, Lancs BL9 9AP
☎ 0161 797 4114
website: www.fanconi-anaemia.co.uk
Support, contacts and information for families affected by Fanconi anaemia.

Fabry's Disease Support Group
Mrs S Hill, 10 Broadmeadow Road, Wyke Regis, Weymouth, Dorset DT4 9BS
☎ & 🖷 01305 774443
email: fabry@wdi.co.uk
Support: contacts: information

Face to Face
Alistair Bailey, Face to Face Scheme, 16 Colchester Vale, Forest Row, East Sussex RH18 5HJ
☎ 01342 824723
Schemes being set up in all areas of the country, to offer parents of children newly diagnosed as having a disability the support of a more experienced parent, who is trained and available to give support.

Facial Disfigurement
(See Birthmark Support Group; Changing Faces, Disfigurement Guidance Centre; Let's Face It Support Network; Skin Camouflage, British Association for)

Facioauriculovertebral Syndrome
(Contact Goldenhar Syndrome Family Support Group)

Facioscapulohumeral Muscular Dystrophy
(See FSH Muscular Dystrophy Support Group)

Fainting Attacks, Chronic
(See STARS)

Familial Dysautonomia
(See Dysautonomia Society of Great Britain)

Familial Gout
(See PUMPA)

Familial Haemorrhagic Telangiectasia
(See Telangiectasia Self-Help Group)

Familial Hypercholesterolaemia
(Contact Heart UK)

Familial Hyperlipidaemia
(Contact Heart UK)

Familial Spastic Paraplegia
(See FSP Group)

Families Need Fathers
134 Curtain Road, London EC2A 3AR
☎ & 🖷 020 7613 5060
website: fnf.org.uk/
Help and advice in co-parenting, information on access to children, joint custody arrangements etc. (See Gingerbread; One Parent Families, National Council for)

Family Therapy, Institute of
24-32 Stephenson Way, London NW1 2HX
☎ 020 7391 9150 🖷 020 7391 9169
website: www.instituteoffamilytherapy.org.uk
A comprehensive service for families and couples facing a wide range of family problems.

Family Welfare Association
501-505 Kingsland Road, Dalston, London E8 4AU
☎ 020 7254 6251 🖷 020 7249 5443
email: head.office@fwa.org.uk
website: www.fwa.org.net
Casework service to offer support and advice to families of children with special needs. Financial help for families in need.

Fanconi Anaemia
(See FA UK)

Fathering
(See Families Need Fathers)

Fatigue Syndrome
(See ME Organisations)

Feminising Testes Syndrome
(See AIS Support Group UK)

Fibrosing Alveolitis
(Contact Lung Foundation, British)

Flexion Epilepsy, Generalised
(Contact West Syndrome Support Group)

Floating Harbor Syndrome Contact Group
Mrs S Sinclair, 27 Hatfield Road, Dagenham, Essex RM9 6JR
☎ 020 8517 6842
Support: contacts: information: newsletter

Foetal Abnormality, Elected Termination for
(See ARC)

Foetal Alcohol Syndrome Trust
P.O. Box 30, Walton, Liverpool L9 8HU
☎ & 🖷 0151 284 2900
email: margaret@fastrust.freeserve.co.uk

Information on the effects of foetal alcohol syndrome, support by telephone and letter, contact between families, raising public awareness of effects of excessive drinking during pregnancy.

Foetal Anti-Convulsant Syndrome Association, National
Linda Hamilton, Newton of Brux, Glenkindie, Alford, Aberdeenshire AB33 8RX
☎ & 🖷 01975 571340
email: facsline@aol.com
website: www.facsline.org
Support, contacts and information for parents of children damaged by anti-convulsant drugs prescribed in pregnancy (foetal valproate, phenytoin and carbamezapine syndromes).

Folks
3 Stone Buildings (Ground Floor), Lincoln's Inn, London WC2A 3XL
☎ 0870 847 0707 🖷 01302 752662
email: 101361.250@compuserve.com
website: www.bobjanet.demon.co.uk
Support, contacts and information for parents of children with Landau-Kleffner syndrome.

Foresight
Mrs B Barnes, 28 The Paddock, Godalming, Surrey GU7 1XD
☎ 01483 427839 🖷 01483 427668
Works to promote optimal health and nutritional status in prospective parents PRIOR to conception, to aid research into identification and removal of potential health hazards to foetal development. Hair analysis and full programmes for preconceptual health. Books, booklets, video, poster, etc. available. Send SAE with stamp for further information.

Fostering Network, The
87 Blackfriars Road, London SE1 8HA
☎ 020 7620 6400
020 7620 2100 – Mon, Tues, Thurs & Fri 12.30-4pm 🖷 020 7620 6401
Info Line 020 7261 1884 – Wed – Fri 12-3pm
email: info@fostering.net
website: www.fostering.net
Deals with all foster care issues and aims to improve services for young people in foster care. Information: publications: training: helpline consultancy.

Foundation for the Study of Infant Deaths
Artillery House, 11-19 Artillery Row, London SW1P 1RT
☎ 020 7222 8001
Helpline 020 7233 2090 🖷 020 7222 8002

5

email: fsid@sids.org.uk
website: www.sids.org.uk/fsid/
Support, befriending and information for families, funding for research into causes and prevention of cot death.

Fragile-X Society, The
Mrs L Walker, 53 Winchelsea Lane, Hastings, East Sussex TN35 4LG
☎ 01424 813147
email: lesleywalker@fragilex.k-web.co.uk
website: www.fragilex.org.uk
Support: contacts: information: newsletter: publications: twice-yearly conferences.

Franceschetti-Klein Syndrome
(Contact Treacher-Collins Syndrome Family Support Group)

Friedrich's Ataxia
(Contact Ataxia UK)

FSH Muscular Dystrophy Support Group
8 Caldecote Gardens, Bushey Heath, Herts WD23 4GP
☎ 020 8950 7500 🗎 020 8950 7300
email: fshgroup@hotmail.com
website: www.fsh-group.org
Aims to improve the quality of life for all those with FSH and those who care for them. Offers support and encouragement to families and individuals who have FSH.

FSP Group
Mrs S Langton, 111 Queens Road, Leicester LE2 3FL
☎ 0116 270 0450
Helpline 01702 218184
email: fspgroup@aol.com
website: www.fspgroup.org
Support, contacts and information for anyone affected by familial spastic paraplegia (Struempell-Lorraine syndrome)

Fucosidosis
(Contact MPS Society)

Galactosaemia Support Group
Mrs S Bevington, 31 Cotysmore Road, Sutton Coldfield, West Midlands B75 6BJ
☎ 0121 378 5143
email: sue@gsg1.freeserve.co.uk
website: http://gsgnews.tripod.com
Support: contacts: information: newsletter

Gastro-Oesophageal Reflux
(Contact Gut Motility Disorders Support Network; TOFS)

Gastroschisis
(Contact GEEPS; Incontinent and Stoma Children, The Charity for)

Gastrostomy Tube Feeding
(Contact Half PINNT; PINNT; TOFS)

Gaucher's Association
Mrs S Lewis, 25 West Cottages, London NW6 1RJ
☎ 020 7433 1121 🗎 020 7431 5883
email: support@gaucherassociation.org.uk
website: www.gaucher.org.uk
Support: self-help: contacts: information: newsletter: meetings: conference

GEEPS
Ms T Evans, 104 Riversdale Road, Romford, Essex RM5 2NS
☎ 01708 738134
Support: contacts: information: newsletter. For parents of children affected by gastroschisis and exomphalos.

Generalised Tic Syndrome
(See Tourette Syndrome Association UK)

Genetic Interest Group
Unit 4D, Leroy House, 436 Essex Road, London N1 3QP
☎ 020 7704 3141
email: mail@gig.org.uk
website: www.gig.org.uk
A forum and umbrella group for voluntary organisations catering for genetic disorders. Newsletter. Produces a list of genetics clinics and specialist services.

German Measles in Pregnancy, Damage due to
(Contact Sense)

GHD Support Group
c/o Child Growth Foundation, 2 Mayfield Avenue, Chiswick, London W4 1PW
☎ 020 8995 0257 / 020 8994 7625
🗎 020 8995 9075
Caters for growth hormone deficiency disorders, including pituitary hormone deficiency (hypopituitarism/panhypopituitarism). Support: self-help: contacts: literature: newsletter.

Giant Cell Arteritis
(See Stuart Strange Trust and Arthritis Care)

Giantism, Exomphalos & Macroglossia Syndrome
(Contact Beckwith-Weidemann Support Group)

Gilbert-Dreyfus Syndrome
(See AIS Support Group UK)

Gilles De La Tourette Syndrome
(See Tourette Syndrome UK Association)

Gingerbread
7 Sovereign Court, Sovereign Close, London E1W 3HW
☎ 020 7488 9300 🖷 020 7488 9333
email: office@gingerbread.org.uk
website: www.gingerbread.org.uk
Information, support and activities for one-parent families and their children. (See Families Need Fathers; One Parent Families, National Council for)

Glanzmann's Thromboasthenia Contact Group
Mrs M Buxton, 28 Duke Road, Newton, Hyde, Cheshire SK14 4JB
☎ 0161 368 0219
Support: contacts: information: publications.

Glaucoma Association, International
108c, Warner Road, London SE5 9HQ
☎ 020 7737 3265 🖷 020 7346 5929
email: iga@kcl.ac.uk
website: www.iga.org.uk
(See also Tadpoles)

Glomerulonephritis
(Contact Kidney Patient Association, British)

Gluten Sensitivity
(Contact Coeliac UK)

Glycogen Storage Diseases, Association for (UK)
Mrs A Phillips, 9 Lindop Road, Hale, Cheshire WA15 9DZ
☎ 0161 980 7303 🖷 0161 226 3813
email: president@agsd.org.uk
website: www.agsd.org.uk
Support: contacts: information: newsletter: publications

Goldberg-Maxwell Syndrome
(See AIS Support Group UK)

Goldenhar Syndrome Family Support Group
Ms N Woodgate, 9 Hartley Court Gardens, Cranbrook, Kent TN17 3QY
☎ 01580 714042
Support: contacts: information: newsletter; family meetings

Gorlin Syndrome Support Group
Mr J Costello, 11 Blackberry Way, Penwortham, Preston, Lancs PR1 9LQ
☎ 01772 517624

email: gorlin-group@blueyonder.co.uk
website: www.gorlin-group.pwp.blueyonder.co.uk
Support: contacts: information

Gout, Familial/Juvenile
(See PUMPA)

Grandparents' Association
Moot House, The Stow, Harlow, Essex CM20 3AG
☎ 01279 444964 🖷 01279 428040
email: info@grandparents-federation.org.uk
Advice and information for grandparents who have no contact with their grandchildren and those whose grandchildren are in care, or any areas of concern to grandparents.

Granulomatous Diseases, Chronic
(Contact CGD Support Group/Research Trust)

Greig Syndrome
(Contact Headlines)

Group B Strep Support
Jane Plumb, P.O. Box 203, Haywards Heath, Sussex RH16 1GF
☎ 01444 416176 🖷 0870 161 5540
email: info@gbss.org.uk
website: www.gbss.org.uk
Support, contacts and information for parents of children damaged by the Group B streptococcus virus.

Growth Accelerated
(Contact Child Growth Foundation)

Growth Hormone Deficiency
(See GHD Support Group)

Growth, Restricted/Delayed
(See Restricted Growth Association; Child Growth Foundation)

Guillain-Barre Syndrome Support Group
LCC Offices, Eastgate, Sleaford, Lincs NG34 7EB
☎ & 🖷 01529 304615
Helpline 0800 374803
email: admin@gbs.org.uk
website: www.gbs.org.uk
Support: contacts: information: newsletter

Gut Motility Disorders Support Network
Mrs L Prior, Westcott Farm, Oakford, Tiverton, Devon EX16 9EZ
☎ 01398 351173 (mornings)
email: help@gmdnet.org.uk
Support and information for parents of children affected by disorders caused by abnormal motility of the bowel, including congenital neuropathies and myopathies of the bowel, Hirschsprung disease, hollow

5

visceral myopathy, gastro-oesophageal reflux. Caters mainly for children but will help adults affected by gut motility disorders.

Haemochromatosis Society
Ms J Fernau, Hollybush House, Hadley Green Road, Barnet, Herts EN5 5PR
☎ & 🖷 020 8449 1363
email: ghsoc@compuserve.com
website: www.ghsoc.org
Support: self-help: contacts: information: newsletter

Haemolytic Uremia
(See HUSH)

Haemophagocytic Lymphohistiocytosis
(See Histiocytosis Family Support Association UK)

Haemophilia Society, The
3rd Floor, Chesterfield House, 385 Euston Road, London NW1 3AU
☎ 020 7380 0600
Helpline 0800 018 6068 🖷 020 7387 8220
email: info@haemophilia.org.uk
website: www.haemophilia.org.uk
Support: contacts: information: newsletter

Haemorrhagic Telangiectasia, Hereditary
(See Telangiectasia Self-Help Group)

Hair Loss
(See Alopecia Society, Children's; Hairline International)

Hairline International
Lyons Court, 1668 High Street, Knowle, West Midlands B93 0LY
☎ 01564 775281 🖷 01564 782270
website: www.hairlineinternational.com

Half PINNT
3 St Martins Close, Harpenden, Herts AL5 5JG
☎ 01582 765238
email: PINNT@dial.pipex.com
Support, advice and information for parents of children who are fed artificially by intravenous methods, gastrostomy, jejunostomy or naso-gastric tube. Run in conjunction with PINNT.

Hand & Arm Deficencies
(See Lady Hoare Trust; Reach)

Hand-Schuller-Christian Syndrome
(Contact Histiocytosis Family Support Association UK)

Harlequin Ichthyosis
(See Ichthyosis Support Group)

Hayfever
(See Allergy organisations)

Head Injury in Children
(See Child Brain Injury Trust)

Head Injury Re-Education (HIRE)
(See HIRE)
email: hire.office@virgin.net
website: www.headinjuryreeducation.org

Head Injury Rehabilitation Service
The Children's Trust, Tadworth Court, Tadworth, Surrey KT20 5RU
☎ 01737 357171 🖷 01737 375637
In-patient rehabilitation service for children with acquired head injury.

Head Injury Trust for Scotland (HITS)
Anderson Chambers, Market Street, Galashiels, Scotland
☎ & 🖷 01896 751818
or HITS Head Office, P.O. Box 3740, 161-181 Whitefield Road, Govan, Glasgow G51 2XY
☎ 0141 425 1000 🖷 0141 425 1100
The Galasheils office provides community-based rehabilitation for children and adults with head injury. For support, advice and information contact HITS Head Office.

Headlice
(See Community Hygiene Concern; Alopecia Society, Children's)

Headlines (Craniofacial Support Group)
Mr Steve Moody, 44 Helmsdale Road, Leamington Spa, Warks CV32 7DW
☎ 01926 334629
email: stevemoody@headlines.org.uk
website: http://headlines.org.uk
Caters for craniosynostosis/craniostenosis disorders, such as saggital synostosis and conditions in which craniosynostosis is a feature, e.g.: Apert, Carpenter, Cloverleaf, Crouzon, Pfeiffer and Saethre-Chotzen syndromes. Support: contacts: information: family days and meetings.

Headway (National Head Injuries Association)
Headway, 4 King Edward Court, King Edward Street, Nottingham NG1 1EW
☎ 0115 924 0800 🖷 0115 958 4446
email: headway-national@demon.co.uk
website: www.headway.org.uk
Support, information, newsletter, publications for people (generally adults) affected by head injury as a result of accident and for those who have suffered loss of

skills, memory impairment etc. due to brain damage after illness, such as encephalitis. (See also Child Brain Injury Trust, The)

Health Education Authority

Trevelyan House, 30 Great Peter Street, London SW1P 2HW

☎ 020 7222 5300 🖹 020 7413 8900

website: www.hea.org.uk

Britain's leading provider of health promotion. Information database of resources available via their website. Publication 'Health Related Resources for People with Learning Disabilities'.

Health Information Service, National

Freephone 0800 665544 (10am-5pm, Mon-Fri)

Information on NHS services, treatment waiting times, information about common illnesses and treatments, complaints about NHS services and local NHS Charter standards

Health Protection Libraries (Scotland)

Health Education Board, The Priory, Canaan Lane, Edinburgh EH10 4SG

☎ 0131 536 5595 or 0645 125442

Minicom 0131 536 5593 🖹 0131 536 5502

Information service on all health and disability topics.

Hearing Concern

7-11 Armstrong Road, London W3 7JL

☎ 020 8743 1110 Minicom 020 8742 9151

0845 0744 600 🖹 020 8742 9043

email: info@hearingconcern.org.uk

website: www.hearingconcern.org.uk

Self-help groups, throughout the country, for adults with hearing loss. Aims to provide education through their hearing scheme and training for in-home support, encourages lip reading and clear speech and campaigns for hearing aid research and development. Helpdesk offering advice and support. Membership organisation. Publications and events.

Hearing Impairment in Young Adults

(See 18–30 plus)

Hearing Voices Network, National

c/o Creative Support, 35 Dale Street, Manchester M1 2HF

☎ & 🖹 0161 228 3896 (10.30-3.30 Mon, Tues, Wed & Fri)

Allows people to explore their voice-hearing experiences in a secure and confidential way. Self-help groups for sufferers and professionals.

Heart Disease

(See Left Heart Matters)

Heart Disease, Familial

(See Family Heart Association)

Heart Disorders

Association for Children with, 26 Elizabeth Drive, Helmshore, Rossendale, Lancs BB4 4JB

☎ & 🖹 01706 213632

website: www.achd.org.uk

Support: contacts: information: newsletter: publications

Heart Disorders Plus Down's Syndrome

(See Down's Heart Group)

Heart Disorders, Association for Children with (Scotland)

7 Parkview, North Downside Road, Aberdeen AB23 8DF

☎ 01224 702963

Support: contacts: information: newsletter: publications

Heart Federation, Children's

52 Kennington Oval, London SE11 5SW

☎ 020 7820 8517

Helpline 0808 808 5000 (Mon-Fri 9.30am-9. 30pm)

🖹 020 7735 8718

email: chf@dircon.co.uk

website: www.childrens-heart-fed.org.uk

Information sheets can be downloaded (copyright waived)

Contacts: information: support: newsletter: annual conference; publications: referrals to local and specialist groups

Heart Transplant

(Contact Cardiomyopathy Association)

Heart UK

7 North Road, Maidenhead, Berks SL6 1PE

☎ 01628 628638 🖹 01628 628698

email: fh@familyheart.org

website: www.familyheart.org

Support: self-help: contacts: information: newsletter: training for health care professionals. Caters for people affected by familial (inherited) atherosclerosis, hyperlipidaemia, hypercholesterolaemia and coronary heart problems related to high cholesterol. Formerly Family Heart Association.

Heartbeat (Northern Ireland)

9 Turloughs Hill, Annalong Newry, Belfast BT34 4XD

☎ 028 4376 8786

email: mckibben@btinternet.com

5

Help for Health Trust
Highcroft, Romsey Road, Winchester, Hants SO22
5DH
☎ 01962 849100
Helpline 0800 665544 (9am-5pm, Mon-Fri)
🖹 01962 849079
email: admin@hfht.demon.co.uk
website: www.hfht.demon.co.uk
Free confidential health information service, providing
information about diagnosed medical conditions and
treatments, local and national self-help groups, local
NHS services, personal health care and patients' rights.

Hemifacial Microsomia
(Contact Goldenhar Syndrome Family Support
Group)

HemiHelp
2nd Floor, Bedford House, 215 Balham High Road,
London SW17 7BQ
☎ 020 8767 0210
Helpline 020 8672 3179 (Mon-Fri 10am-1pm)
🖹 020 8767 0319
email: support@hemihelp.org.uk
website: www.hemihelp.org.uk
Support: self-help: contacts: information: newsletter.
For parents of children affected by hemiplegia.

Hemimegalencephaly
(Contact HME Contact Group)

Hemiplegia
(See HemiHelp)

Hemiplegia, Alternating
(See Alternating Hemiplegia Support Group)

Henoch-Schonlein Purpura
(See Stuart Strange Trust and Arthritis Care)

**Hereditary Multiple Exostoses Support
Group**
P.O. Box 395, Headington DO, Oxford OX3 9WF
☎ 01438 861 866
email: hmesg@ox1.co.uk
website: www.ox1.co.uk/hmesg/
Support, contacts and information for people affected
by hereditary multiple exostoses (diaphyseal aclasis).

Herpes Viruses Association
41 North Road, London N7 9DP
☎ Minicom 0207 607 9661
020 76099061
website: www.herpes.org.uk
Support and advice for people suffering from herpes
virus infections, e.g. herpes simplex, herpes zoster
(shingles), post-herpetic neuralgia. Send SAE for details.

Hips, Congenital Dislocated
(Contact Steps)

Hirschsprung Disease
(Contact Gut Motility Disorders Support Network;
Incontinent and Stoma Children, The Charity for)

**Histiocytosis Family Support Association
UK**
Roselidden House, Rowes Lane, Wendron, Helston,
Cornwall TR13 0PT
☎ 01326 569219
email: ajes954836@aol.com
Support: contacts: information

HITS (UK) Family Support Network
Mrs Sandra Field, 33 Fernworthy Close, Torquay,
Devon TQ2 7JQ
☎ 01803 401018
email: tgrant@hitsuk.freeserve.co.uk or
tgrant@uk.ey.com
website: www.e-fervour.com/hits
Support by phone, letter, three newsletters per year,
family days, internet chat room and e-mail. For more
information please contact Terri Grant or Sandra
Field. For parents of children affected by Hypomelatosis
of it.

HIV & AIDS
(See AIDS Helpline; Body Positive; Positive
Options; Terrence Higgins Trust)

HME Contact Group
Mr & Mrs D Kerr, 3 Linn Drive, Netherlee,
Glasgow G44 3PT
☎ 0141 633 2617
email: hmecontactgroup@tinyworld.co.uk
website: www.cv.quik.com.au/hmegroup/Scot01
Support, contacts, information and annual family
meeting for parents of children affected by
hemimegalencephaly.

Hodgkins Disease
(See Lymphoma Association)

Hollow Visceral Myopathy
(See Gut Motility Disorders Support Network)

Holt-Oram Syndrome Support Group
Mr A Sigsworth, 21 Forth Road, Redcar, Cleveland
TS10 1PN
☎ & 🖹 01642 501283
email: asiggy@ntlworld.com
Support: contacts: information

Home Start UK
2 Salisbury Road, Leicester LE5 6HL

☎ 0116 233 9955 🖹 0116 233 0232
A voluntary organisation which offers support, friendship and practical help at home to parents of children under 5 years, with the aim of preventing crisis and family breakdown. There are currently 200 Home Start schemes in the UK. (See Parentline *Plus)*

Hormone Deficiency, Growth/Pituitary
(See GHD Support Group; Restricted Growth Association)

Horner Syndrome with Paralysis of the Arm
(Contact Erb's Palsy Support Group)

Hospices
(See Education and Residential Care Section)

Hospital Waiting List Helpline
(See College of Health)

Hunter Syndrome
(Contact MPS Society)

Huntington's Disease Association
108 Battersea High Street, London SW11 3HP
☎ 020 7223 7000 🖹 020 7223 9489
email: info@hda.org.uk
website: www.hda.org.uk
Support: advice: information: genetic counselling: regional care advisory service.

Huntington's Disease Association, Northern Ireland
Department of Medical Genetics, Floor A, Belfast City Hospital Trust, 51 Lisburn Road, Belfast B79 7AB
☎ 028 9026 3555 🖹 028 9023 6911

Hurler Syndrome
(Contact MPS Society)

HUSH (UK E-Coli Support Group)
P.O. Box 159, Hayes, Middlesex UB4 8XE
☎ 0800 731 4679
Support, information and advice for parents of children affected by one of the haemolytic uraemia group of disorders, including the type caused by E-Coli infection

Hydranencephaly Support Group, International
Mrs Agnes Marshall, 15 Mount Terrace, Lochans, Stranraer, Wigtownshire, Scotland DG1 9AR
☎ 01776 820482
email: agnes@marshall6250.fsnet.co.uk
website: http://onward.to/hydranencephaly
Support, contacts and information for parents of children affected by hydranencephaly.

Hydrocephalus Network
ASBAH, 42 Park Road, Peterborough, Cambs PE1 2UQ
☎ 01733 555988 🖹 01733 555985
email: postmaster@asbah.org
website: www.asbah.org
Support: contacts: information

Hyper Ige Syndrome
(Contact Primary Immunodeficiency Association)

Hyperactive Children's Support Group (HCSG)
71 Whyke Lane, Chichester, West Sussex PO19 7PD
☎ 01243 551313 🖹 01243 552019
email: hacsg@hacsg.org.uk
website: www.hacsg,org.uk
Uses nutritional and dietary therapies to help children with hyperactivity, attention deficit disorder (ADD) and attention deficit hyperactivity disorder (ADHD). For a FREE Introductory pack send a SAE.

Hyperactivity/Attention Deficit Disorder
(See ADD Information Service; ADDnet; ADD/ADHD Family Support Group; ADHD National Alliance)

Hypercalcaemia, Infantile
(Contact Williams Syndrome Foundation)

Hypercholesterolaemia, Familial
(See Heart UK)

Hyperekplexia (Hyperexplexia) Support Group
Stephanie Samson, 216 Westcott Crescent, Hanwell, London W7 1NU
☎ 020 8578 0456
Support, contacts and information for parents of children affected by hyperexplexia, also known as startle disease or 'stiff baby' syndrome. The condition is sometimes termed hyperekplexia.

Hyperlipidaemia, Familial
(Contact Heart UK)

Hypermobility Syndrome Association
HMSA, 15 Oakdene, Alton GU34 2AJ
website: www.hypermobility.org
Support, information and contacts for people affected by hypermobility syndrome.

Hyperpyrexia, Malignant
(See Malignant Hyperthermia Association)

Hyperreflexia
(See Hyperexplexia Support Group)

5

Hypersensitive Arteritis
(See Stuart Strange Trust and Arthritis Care)

Hyperthermia, Malignant
(See Malignant Hyperthermia Association)

Hypertriglyceridaemia
(Contact Heart UK)

Hypertrophic Cardiomyopathy
(Contact Cardiomyopathy Association)

Hypochondroplasia
(Contact Restricted Growth Association)

Hypogammaglobulinaemia
(Contact Primary Immunodeficiency Association)

Hypoglycaemia (Neonatal), Visceromegaly & Hypohydrotic Ectodermal Dysplasia
(See Ectodermal Dysplasia Society)

Hypohydrotic Ectodermal Dysplasia
(Contact Ectodermal Dysplasia Society)

Hypomelanosis of Ito Support Group
(See HITS (UK) Family Support Group)

Hypophosphataemia, X-Linked
(See XLH Network)

Hypophosphataemic Rickets, Dominant
(See XLH Network)

Hypopituitarism
(Contact GHD Support Group)

Hypoplastic Left Heart Syndrome
(See Left Heart Matters)

Hypospadias Support Group
Jane Clarke, 10 Aveley Close, Paddington, Warrington, Cheshire WA13 3UD
☎ 01925 496510
website: www.hypospadias.co.uk
Support, contacts and information for parents of boys affected by hypospadias.

Hypothyroidism
(Contact Thyroid Foundation, British)

Hypotonia, Benign Congenital
(See Congenital Hypotonia Support Group)

Hypoventilation, Congenital Central
(See Ondine's Support Group)

Hypsarrythmia
(Contact West Syndrome Support Group)

IBS Network
Ms P Nunn, Northern General Hospital, Sheffield, Yorks S5 7AU
☎ 0114 261 1531(answerphone)
Helpline 01543 492192 (Mon – Fri 6-8pm)
email: p.j.nunn@sheffield.ac.uk
website: www.ibsnetwork.org.uk
The IBS Network is a self-help organisation for people with irritable bowel syndrome offering information, support and advice. Quarterly Journal, 'Gut Reaction', covers a wide variety of topics relating to IBS. Facts sheets available. Members receive a can't wait/ membership card. Research. Media List. Reveiwing Scheme. Befrienders and Penfriends. Telephone contacts. Helpline. Local self-help groups. E-mail discussion groups. Campaigns. For further details please send a SAE and £1 coin to address given or visit website www.ibsnetwork.org.uk. Enquiries from Health professionals and the media welcome.

ICAN (Invalid Children's Aid Nationwide)
4 Dyer's Buildings, Holborn, London EC1N 2QP
☎ 0870 010 4066 ▧ 0870 010 4067
email: info@ican.org.uk
website: www.ican.org.uk
Advice, support and information for parents of children with speech and communication problems.

I-Cell Disease
(Contact MPS Society)

Ichthyosis Support Group
Shelly Batt, Secretary, 2 Copnor, Woolton Hill, Nr Newbury, Berkshire RG20 9XH
☎ 01635 253829 ▧ 01635 255560
email: shelly@batt27.freeserve.co.uk
website: www.ichthyosis.co.uk
Support: contacts: information. Caters for ichthyosis vulgaris, X-linked ichthyosis, non-bullous icthyosiform erythroderma, lamellar ichthyosis, bullous ichthyosis erythroderma and Harlequin ichthyosis, Netherton Syndrome.

Idiopathic Thrombocytopenia Purpura
(See ITP Support Association)

Ileostomy and Internal Pouch Support Group
Peverill House, 1-5 Mill Road, Ballyclare, Co Antrim BT39 9DR
☎ 0800 0184724 ▧ 028 9332 4606
email: ia@ileostomypouch.demon.co.uk
website: www.ileostomypouch.demon.co.uk
Support: contacts: support: newsletter: publications

Ileostomy In Children
(Contact Incontinent and Stoma Children, the Charity for))

Immotile Cilia
(Contact PCD Family Support Group)

Immune Deficiency Disorders, Primary
(See Primary Immunodeficiency Association)

Immunisation
(See Informed Parent; Jabs; Vaccine-Damaged Children, Association of Parents of; Victims of Vaccination Support Group)

Imperforate Anus
(Contact Incontinent and Stoma Children)

Incontinence Advice Services
(See Aids and Equipment Section)

Incontinent and Stoma Children, Charity for (NASPCS)
Mr J Malcolm, 51 Anderson Drive, Valley View Park, Darvel, Ayrshire KA17 0DE
☎ 01560 322024
Support and contacts for parents of children with imperforate anus and associated defects. Now covers any condition resulting in incontinence problems, whether or not requiring a stoma (colostomy, ileostomy, urostomy etc). Caters for: imperforate anus, Hirschsprung's disease, ectopia vesicae VATER syndrome, prune belly syndrome, gastroschisis, cloacal exstrophy, intestinal neuronal dysplasia.

Incontinentia Pigmentosa
(Contact Ectodermal Dysplasia Society)

Infant Death/Cot Death
(See Bereavement Organisations; Child Death Helpline; Compassionate Friends; Cot Death Trust, Scottish; Foundation for The Study of Infant Deaths; Laura Centre; SANDS: Sudden Death Support Association)

Infantile Hypercalcaemia
(See Williams Syndrome Foundation)

Inflammatory Bowel Disease
(See Crohn's in Childhood Research Association; Colitis and Crohn's Disease, National Association for)

Information Service on Disability
West Midlands Rehabilitation Centre, 91 Oak Tree Lane, Selly Oak, Birmingham B29 6JA
☎ 0121 627 1627
Helpline 0121 414 1495 🖷 0121 627 8210
Information on all aspects of disability

Informed Parent, The
P.O. Box 870, Harrow, Middlesex HA3 7UW
☎ & 🖷 020 8861 1022
website: www.informedparent.co.uk

Aims to promote awareness and understanding about immunisation and vaccination in order to preserve the freedom of an informed choice, to support parents regardless of the decisions they make and to inform parents of the alternatives to vaccination. Please send SAE. Annual subscription for TIP quarterly newsletter. (See Jabs; Vaccine-Damaged Children, Association for; Victims of Vaccination Support Group).

Insulin-Dependent Diabetes Trust
P.O. Box 294, Northampton NN1 4XS
☎ 01604 622837 🖷 01604 622838
email: enquiries@iddinternational.org
website: www.iddinternational.org
Contacts: support: information: publications: newsletter. Advice to patients and parents of children with diabetes who suffer adverse effects from genetically produced 'human' insulin and who may be better suited to natural insulins.

Internal Pouch
(See Ileostomy and Internal Pouch Support Group)

Interstitial Cystitis Support Group
Mr A Walker, 76 High Street, Stony Stratford, Bucks MK11 1AH
☎ & 🖷 01908 569169
email: info@interstitial cystitis.co.uk
website: www.interstitialcystitis.co.uk
Provides support and information through a network of more than thirty local groups.

Intestinal Abnormalities/Defects
(See GEEPS; Gut Motility Disorders Support Network; Incontinent and Stoma Children, The Charity for)

Intestinal Neuronal Dysplasia
(Contact Incontinent and Stoma Children, the Charity for; Gut Motility Disorders Support Group)

Intestinal Pseudo-Obstruction
(Contact Gut Motility Disorders Support Network)

Intravenous Feeding
(See Half PINNT; PINNT)

Iris of the Eye, Absence of
(See Aniridia Support Network)

Irritable Bowel Syndrome
(See IBS Network)

5

ITP Support Association
Mrs S Watson, Synehurst, Kimbolton Road, Bolnhurst, Beds MK44 2EW
☎ & 🖹 0870 7770 559
website: http://itpsupport.org.uk
Support, contacts, information and advice on referrals for sufferers from idiopathic thrombocytopenia purpura. Send A5 SAE for information pack with 2 x 1st class stamps.

Ivemark Syndrome Association
Mrs I Gladki, 6 Ashbourne Crescent, Taunton, Somerset TA1 2RB
☎ 01823 257430
email: ingi@ingrid-gladki.freeserve.co.uk
Support: contacts: information

Jabs
Mrs J Fletcher, 1 Gawsworth Road, Golborne, Warrington WA3 3RF
☎ 01942 713565 🖹 01942 201323
email: jabs@argonet.co.uk
website: www.jabs.org.uk
Support, contacts, information and newsletter for parents of children who have neurological or physical problems relating to vaccine damage. (See Informed Parent; Vaccine-Damaged Children, Association for; Victims of Vaccination Support Group))

Jejunostomy Feeding
(See Half PINNT; PINNT)

Jennifer Trust for Spinal Muscular Atrophy
Elta House, Birmingham Road, Stratford-upon-Avon, Warks CV37 0AQ
☎ 01789 267520
Helpline (families only) 0800 975 3100
🖹 01789 268371
email: jennifer@jtsma.demon.co.uk
website: www.jtsma.demon.co.uk
Caters for children affected by spinal muscular atrophy, including Werdnig-Hoffman, Kugelberg-Welander and intermediate types. Support: contacts: information: newsletter

Jervill-Lange-Nielson Syndrome
(See Long QT Family Support Group)

Jewish Bereavement Counselling Service
(See Bereavement Counselling Service, Jewish)

Jewish Blind and Disabled
Care and Campaign Office, 164 East End Road, Finchley, London N2 0RR
☎ 020 8883 1000 🖹 020 8444 6729

email: info@jblind.cix.co.uk
website: www.cix.co.uk/~jblind

Jewish Care
Jewish Care, Stuart Young House, 221 Golders Green Road, London NW11 9DQ
☎ 020 8458 3282 🖹 020 8455 7185
Offers a very wide range of services; information, schools, holidays, domiciliary care, befriending, social work, etc. Specialist services for partially sighted, blind or physically disabled people.

Job's Syndrome
(Contact Primary Immunodeficiency Association)

Juvenile/Familial Gout
(See PUMPA)

Kabuki Syndrome Support Group
168 Newshaw Lane, Hadfield, Glossop, Derbyshire SK13 2AY
☎ 01457 860110
Support, contacts and information for parents of children with Kabuki Syndrome.

Kartagener Syndrome
(Contact PCD Family Support Group)

Kawasaki Support Group
Mrs S Davidson, 13 Norwood Grove, Potters Green, Coventry CV2 2FR
☎ 024 7661 2178
Support: contacts: information: newsletter: publications. Kawasaki syndrome is also known as mucocutaneous lymph node syndrome.

Keratoconus Self-Help
P.O. Box 26251, London W3 9WQ
☎ 020 8993 4759
website: www.keratoconus-group.org.uk
Support and information

Kidney Federation, National
6 Stanley Street, Worksop, Notts S81 7HX
☎ 01909 487795
Helpline 0845 601 0209 🖹 01909 481723
email: nkt@kidney.org.uk
website: www.kidney.org.uk
Regional groups: information and advice: publications: newsletter

Kidney Patient Association, British
BKPA, Bordon, Hants GU35 9JZ
☎ 01420 472021/2 🖹 01420 475831
website: www.bkpa.1to1.org
Support: contacts: information: publications: financial aid: holiday dialysis service

Kidney Research Fund, National
King's Chambers, Priestgate, Peterborough PE1 1FG
☎ 01733 704650
Helpline 0845 300 1499 🖷 01733 704 660
email: helpline@nkrf.org.uk
website: www.nkrf.org.uk
Advice: information: publications: funding for research

Kids – Working with Children with Special Needs
6 Aztec Row, Berners Road, London N1 0PW
☎ 020 7359 3635 🖷 020 7359 8238
website: www.kids-online.org.uk
Help and support for parents/carers of children with physical and learning difficulties.

Kidscape
2 Grosvenor Gardens, London SW1W 0DH
☎ 020 7730 3300 🖷 020 7730 7081
website: www.kidscape.org.uk/kidscape
Provides information and advice for children on dealing with bullying, getting lost, approaches by strangers etc. Telephone counselling for parents, training for schools. (See Careline; Child Accident Prevention Trust; Childline)

Kinsbourne Syndrome
(See Dancing Eye Syndrome Support Trust)

Klinefelter Syndrome Association
Mrs S Cook, 56 Little Yeldham Road, Little Yeldham, Halstead, Essex CO9 4QT
☎ 01787 237460 (after 5pm)
website: www.ksa-uk.co.uk
Support and information for parents and carers of boys affected by Klinefelter syndrome. Also caters for those with adult sons who are in the care of their family because of learning difficulty or other special needs.

Klippel-Trenaunay Syndrome Support Group
Carol Wilson, 9 Newland Avenue, Cudworth, Barnsley, Yorks S72 8UZ
☎ 01226 780085
email: zoo02038@zoo.co.uk
Support: contacts: information. Caters for Klippel-Trenaunay syndrome and Klippel-Trenaunay-Weber syndrome.

Klippel-Trenaunay-Weber Syndrome
(See Klippel-Trenaunay Support Group)

Klumpke's Paralysis
(Contact Erb's Palsy Support Group)

Kohler's Disease
(Contact Perthes Association)

Kugelberg-Welander Syndrome
(See Jennifer Trust for Spinal Muscular Atrophy)

Lady Hoare Trust
1st Floor, 89 Albert Embankment, London SE1 7TP
☎ 020 7820 9989 🖷 020 7582 8251
email: info@lhtchildren.org.uk
Support and practical help for parents of children affected by any type of juvenile arthritis and those with muscle or limb deficiency. Employs a network of qualified fieldworkers, social workers, helps with equipment etc.

Lambert-Eaton Myasthenia Syndrome
(Contact Myasthenia Gravis Association)

Landau-Kleffner Syndrome
(See Folks)

Landouzy-Dejerine Syndrome
(Contact FSH Muscular Dystrophy Support Group)

Landry's Syndrome
(Contact Guillain-Barre Syndrome Support Group)

Langerhans Cell Histiocytosis
(Contact Histiocytosis Support Group UK)

Language Disorders
(See AFASIC; Nuffield; and Speech Centre ICAN; Speakability)

Larsen's Syndrome Support Group
Mrs K Scotland, Arlin Bridge, Moles Hill, Oxshott, Surrey KT22 0QB
☎ 01372 842243
Support: contacts: information.

Laryngeal Dystonia
(Contact Dystonia Society, The)

Laser Treatment for Skin Conditions
(See Disfigurement Guidance Centre)

Laura Centre, The
4 Tower Street, Leicester, Leics LE1 6WS
☎ 0116 254 4341 🖷 0116 254 5981
Counselling service and befriending network, therapeutic groups, information and consultation for anyone who has experienced the death of a child, or any child affected by death.

Laurence-Moon-Bardet-Beidl Syndrome
(See LMBB Society)

Learning Disabilities
(See Advocacy Partners; Enable; Mencap; Mental Health Foundation; One to One; People First; Prospects for People with Learning Disabilities; PAMIS; Values Into Action)

5

Learning Disabilities, British Institute of (BILD)
Campion House, Green Street, Kidderminster, Worcs DY10 1JL
☎ 01562 723010
website: www.bild.org.uk
BILD is a national charity, committed to improving the quality of life of people with learning disabilities. They do this by advancing education, research and practice and by better ways of working with and for children and adults with learning disabilities. They provide education, training, information, publications, journals, membership services, research and consultancy.

Leber Congenital Amaurosis Group (Plan)
Cheryl Marley, Windrush, Vernon Avenue, Harcourt Hill, Oxford OX2 9AU
☎ 01865 726319 ▤ 01865 726320
email: cheryl@hcm.vnn.vn
website: www.freeyellow.com/members4/leberslink/index.html
Information and support for parents of children affected by Leber congenital amaurosis (a different condition from Leber optic neuropathy)

Left Heart Matters
24 Calthorpe Road, Edgbaston, Birmingham B15 1RP
☎ 0121 455 8982 ▤ 0121 455 8983
website: www.lhm.org.uk
Information, contacts and support for parents of children affected by hypoplastic left heart syndrome.

Leg and Foot Defects
(Contact Steps)

Legg-Calve-Perthes Syndrome
(Contact Perthes Association)

Leigh Encephalopathy/Leigh Disease
(Contact Climb)

Lejeune Syndrome
(Contact Cri du Chat Syndrome Support Group)

Lennox-Gastaut Syndrome Support Group
Andrew Gibson, 9 South View, Burrough-on-the-Hill, Melton Mowbray, Leics LE14 2JJ
☎ 01664 454305
email: GIBBO1@lennox-gastaut.freeserve.co.uk
Support: contacts: information

Leonard Cheshire
Central Office, 30 Millbank, London SW1P 4QD
☎ 020 7802 8200 ▤ 020 7802 8250
email: info@london.leonard-cheshire.org.uk
website: www.leonard-cheshire.org.uk

Runs a wide range of services for disabled people around the UK.

Leroy (I-Cell) Disease
(Contact MPS Society)

Lesch-Nyhan Syndrome
(See PUMPA)

Let's Face It Support Network
Christine Piff, 14 Fallowfield, Yately, Hampshire GU46 6LW
☎ 01252 879630 ▤ 01252 872633
email: chrisletsfaceit@aol.com/
julialetsfaceit@aol.com
website: www.letsfaceit.force9.co.uk
Support network linking adults and children who have a facial difference as a result of congenital defect, accident, scarring, birthmarks, disease or surgery. Publications.

Letterer-Siwe Disease
(Contact Histiocytosis Family Support Association UK)

Leukaemia
(See Elimination of Leukaemia Fund)

Leukaemia CARE Society
2 Shrubbery Avenue, Worcester, Worcs WR1 1QH
☎ 01905 330003
Helpline 0800 169 6680 ▤ 01905 330090
email: info@leukaemiacare.org.uk
website: www.leukaemiacare.org.uk
24 hour CARE line: regional CARE Teams: support groups: information and booklets: financial assistance: holiday programme.

Leukaemia in Childhood
(See Cancer and Leukaemia in Childhood)

Leukaemia Research Fund
43 Great Ormond Street, London WC1N 3JJ
☎ 020 7405 0101 ▤ 020 7242 1488
email: info@lrf.org.uk
website: www.lrf.org.uk
Research, publications on all forms of leukaemia.

Leukodystrophies
(Contact Climb)

Libraries for Special Needs
(See Education Section; Leisure Section)

Life-Threatening Illness in Children
(See ACT; React)

Limb Deficiency
(See Lady Hoare Trust; Reach; Steps)

Limb/Scalp Defects, Adams-Oliver Type
(See Adams-Oliver Syndrome Support Group)

Limbless Children
(See Peggy and Friends)

Linear Scleroderma
(See Raynaud's and Scleroderma Association)

Linear Sebaceous Naevus Syndrome
(Contact HME Contact Group)

Lissencephaly Contact Group
Nayyer Ahmed, Cedar Wood, Lea Lane, Cookley,
Kidderminster, Worcs DY10 3RH
☎ 01562 851429
website: www.lissencephaly.org.uk
Contacts: information: newsletter: publications. Also caters for neuronal migration disorders, such as pachygyria, polymicrogyria, Miller-Dieker syndrome, Walker-Warburg syndrome.

Liver Disease Foundation, Children's
36 Great Charles Street, Queensway, Birmingham
B3 3JY
☎ 0121 212 3839 📠 0121 212 4300
email: info@childliverdisease.org
website: www.childliverdisease.org
Support: contacts: information: newsletter (See Ben Hardwick Fund)

Liver Trust, British
Ransomes Europark, Ipswich, Suffolk IP13 9QG
☎ 01473 276326 – admin 📠 01473 276327
email: info@britishlivertrust.org.uk
website: www.britishlivertrust.org.uk
Information, newsletter, publications. Caters for all aspects of liver disease.

LMBB Society
1 Blackthorn Avenue, Southborough, Tunbridge
Wells, Kent TN4 9YA
☎ 01892 682680
email: julie.sales@lmbbs.org.uk
website: www.lmbbs.org.uk
Support: contacts: information: newsletter. Publications 'Introducing LMBBS', 'The LMBBS Child at School' and 'LMBBS-more than meets the eye' (a comprehensive medical account of the syndrome).

Long QT Family Support Group
P.O. Box 146, Crawley, Sussex RH10 7YQ
☎ 01293 888584
email: lqts_family_supp@hotmail.com or
support@longqt.org.uk
Support and information for people affected by Long QT syndrome, which results in abnormal heart rhythm.

Long-Term Medical Conditions Alliance (LMCA)
Unit 212, 16 Baldwins Gardens, London EC1N 7RJ
☎ 020 7813 3637 📠 020 7813 3640
email: alliance@lmca.demon.co.uk
website: www.lmca.org.uk
An umbrella body whose members are national voluntary organisations concerned to meet the needs of people with long-term illness. Campaigns for change and provides support to its members.

Look
c/o Queen Alexandra College, 49 Court Oak Road,
Birmingham B17 9TG
☎ 0121 428 5038 📠 0121 427 9800
email: office@look-uk.org
website: www.look-uk.org
Look provides information, support and help to families of visually impaired children. Family Support Officers work directly with families offering emotional support and advice regarding education, benefits and eye conditions. Look links parents in orders to share experiences and to support each other as individuals or as part of local parents group. The Youth Project promotes independence amongst young visually impaired people.

Lowe Syndrome Support Group (UK)
Mrs J Oliver, 29 Gleneagles Drive, Penwortham,
Preston, Lancs PR1 0JT
☎ 01772 745070
email: info@lowesyndrome.org
website: www.lowesyndrome.org
Support: contacts: information: newsletter

Lower Limbs, Abnormalities of
(Contact Steps)

Lub's Syndrome
(See AIS Support Group UK)

Lung Foundation, British
78 Hatton Garden, London EC1 8JR
☎ 020 7831 5831 📠 020 7831 5832
email: blf@britishlungfoundation.com
website: www.lunguk.org
Information: newsletter: publications: fund-raising for research. Several regional branches and local groups. Caters for all types of lung disease, including asthma, aspergillosis, bronchial asthma, bronchiectasis, chronic bronchitis, emphysema, pulmonary fibrosis, fibrosing alveolitis, occupational lung diseases, sarcoidosis.

Lupus Erythmatosus, Systemic
(See Lupus UK; Arthritis Care; Raynaud's and
Scleroderma Association)

5

Lupus UK

St James House, Eastern Road, Romford, Essex
RM1 3NH
☎ 01708 731251 ▤ 01708 731252
*Support: contacts: information: newsletter. (See
Arthritis Care; Raynaud's and Scleroderma Association)*

Lymphangioma

(See Cystic Hygroma Support Group)

Lymphoedema Support Network

St Luke's Crypt, Sydney Street, London SW3 6NH
☎ 020 7351 0990
Helpline 020 7351 4480 ▤ 020 7349 9809
email: adminlsn@lymphoedema.freeserve.co.uk
website: www.lymphoedema.org/lsn
*The LSN is a national charity that provides
information and support to people with lymphoedema.
It runs a telephone helpline, produces a quarterly
newsletter and a wide range of fact sheets, and
maintains an up-to-date website. It works to raise
awareness of lymphoedema and campaigns for better
national standards of care.*

Lymphoma Association

P.O. Box 386, Ayelsbury, Bucks HP20 2GA
☎ 01296 619400
0808 808 5555 (Mon – Fri 9 – 5) ▤ 01296 619414
website: www.lymphoma.org.uk
*Support: contacts: information: newsletter:
publications. Caters for Hodgkin's disease and non-
Hodgkin's lymphoma.*

Macmillan Cancer Relief

89 Albert Embankment, London SE1 7UQ
☎ 020 7840 7840 ▤ 020 7840 7841
email: cancerline@macmillan.org.uk
website: www.macmillan.org.uk
*Macmillan Cancer Relief raises funds for specialist
Macmillan Nurses and Doctors who deliver the best in
cancer care. Build vitally needed treatment centres, give
financial help to those who need it most, and provide a
range of cancer information both locally and
nationally.*

Macroglossia, Exomphalos, Giantism Syndrome

(Contact Beckwith-Weidemann Support Group)

MACS (Micro and Anophthalmia Children's Society)

Mrs M Bourne, 1 Skyrmans Fee, Kirby Cross,
Frinton-on-Sea, Essex CO13 0RN
☎ 0870 600 6227 ▤ 01255 850 696
email: enquiries@macs.org.uk
website: www.macs.org.uk

*Support: contacts: information. For parents of children
affected by anophthalmia, microphthalmia and
coloboma. (See Coloboma Contact Group)*

Macular Disease Society

P.O. Box 16, Denbigh LL16 5ZA
Helpline 0800 328 2849
website: www.maculardisease.org
*Support, contacts, information, newsletter and
publications for people affected by macular
degeneration or macular dystrophy.*

Makaton Vocabulary

(See Education Section)

Make a Wish Foundation UK

Suite B, Rossmore House, 26-42 Park Street,
Camberley, Surrey GU15 3PL
☎ 01276 24127 ▤ 01276 683727
*Organises special treats for children with serious or
terminal illness. (See Dreams Come True Charity;
Starlight Children's Foundation)*

Male Pseudo-Hermaphroditism

(See AIS Support Group UK)

Male Pseudo-Hermaphroditism

(See AIS Support Group UK)

Malignant Hyperthermia Association, British

11 Gorse Close, Newthorpe, Nottingham NG16 2BZ
☎ 01159 691169 ext 45293 (daytime) or 01773
717901 (evening)
email: bmha-helpline@lineone.net
website: www.bmha.co.uk
Also known as Malignant hyperpyrexia
Support: contacts: information.

Mandibulodysostosis

(Contact Treacher-Collins Syndrome Family
Support Group)

Manic Depression Fellowship

21 St Georges Road, London SE1 6ES
☎ 020 7793 2600 ▤ 020 7793 2693
website: www.mdf.org.uk
*Support and advice for sufferers from manic depression,
their families and carers.*

Mannosidosis

(Contact MPS Society)

Marfan Association UK

Rochester House, 5 Aldershot Road, Fleet, Hants
GU51 3NG
☎ 01252 810472 ▤ 01252 810473

email: marfan@tinyonline.co.uk
website: www.marfan.org.uk
Support: contacts: information: newsletter. Also caters for disorders which overlap with Marfan syndrome.

Marie Curie Cancer Care
89 Albert Embankment, London SE1 7TP
☎ 020 7599 7777 ▤ 020 7599 7270
email: info@mariecurie.org.uk
website: www.mariecurie.org.uk
Residential care and nursing: support: home nursing: research

Maroteaux-Lamy Syndrome
(See MPS Society)

Match (Mothers Apart From Their Children)
BM Problems, London WC1N 3XX
website: www.match1979.co.uk
Support and self-help group for mothers who live apart from their children, for whatever reason.

Mayer-Rokhapsky-Kuster-Hauser Syndrome
(See AIS Support Group UK)

McCardle Disease
(Contact Glycogen Storage Diseases Association)

McCune-Albright Syndrome
(Contact Ollier Disease Self-Help Group)

ME (Myalgic Encephalopathy) Association, The
4 Top Angel, Buckingham Industrial Park, Buckingham MK18 1TH
Helpline 08707 443011 (Mon, Tues & Thurs 2-4pm, Wed & Fri 10-12noon) ▤ 01280 821602
email: enquiries@meassociation.org.uk
website: www.meassociation.org.uk
Support: information: newsletter. For people affected by myalgic encephalopathy and chronic fatigue syndrome. (See Tymes Trust)

ME and Chronic Fatigue Centre, National
Harold Wood Hospital, Gubbins Lane, Harold Wood, Romford, Essex RM3 0BE
☎ 01708 370850 ▤ 01708 378032
email: nmecent@aol.com
website: www.nmec.org.uk
Offers support, advice and therapy for patients suffering from chronic fatigue syndrome or ME. Consultant clinics for patients referred by their GP. (See Tymes Trust)

ME, Action for
P.O. Box 1302, Wells, Somerset BA5 1YE
☎ 01749 670799 ▤ 01749 672561

email: admin@afme.org.uk
website: www.afme.org.uk
Support: contacts: information: newsletter. For people affected by myalgic encephalomyelitis or chronic fatigue syndrome. (See Tymes Trust)

ME, Association of Young People with
AYME, P.O. Box 605, Milton Keynes MK2 2XD
☎ 01908 373300 ▤ 01908 274136
email: info@ayme.org.uk
website: www.ayme.org.uk
Information and support for young people affected by ME, magazine, information for schools. (See Tymes Trust)

MED (Multiple Epiphyseal Dysplasia)
(Contact Perthes Association)

Medical Accidents, Victims of
(See Finance Section)

Meige's Disease
(Contact Dystonia Society)

Melanocytic Naevus, Congenital
(See Birthmark Support Group)

Melnick Needles Syndrome
(See MNS Support Group)

Mencap
115-123 Golden Lane, London EC1Y 0RT
☎ 020 7454 0454 ▤ 020 7608 3254
email: information@mencap.org.uk
website: www.mencap.org.uk
The major organisation for parents of children and adults with learning disabilities (formerly termed mental handicap). Over 400 affiliated branches in the United Kingdom. Family support services, educational advice, schools, colleges, respite care facilities, holiday homes, employment and training centres, housing, research, clubs and leisure facilities, information service, quarterly magazine. (See Enable; Learning Disabilities, British Institute of)

Mencap in Wales
31 Lambourne Crescent, Cardiff Business Park, Parc Ty Glas, Llanishen, Cardiff CF4 5GG
☎ 01222 747588 ▤ 01222 747550
Support, information, local groups. Runs ECHO, parent to parent befriending service.

Mencap PIMD Section
Optimum House, Clippers Quay, Salford Quays, Manchester M5 2XP
☎ 0161 888 1200 ext 206 ▤ 0161 888 1211
Information and advice for parents, carers and professionals involved in the care of people who have

5

profound intellectual and multiple disabilities. Runs seminars and workshops for parents and carers, teaching play techniques, art, music and movement, aromatherapy, massage, beauty therapy, sensory therapy. Runs summer playschemes. Publishes resource packs on communication and feeding, dental care and healthy eating, physical management, challenging behaviour, leisure and benefits and allowances. (See PAMIS)

Meniere's Disease Society
98 Maybury Road, Woking, Surrey GU21 5HX
☎ 01483 740597 Minicom 01483 771207
🖷 01483 755411
email: info@menieres.org.uk
website: www.menieres.org.uk
Support: information: magazine

Meningitis Research Foundation
Unit 9, Thornbury Office Park, Midland Way, Thornbury, Bristol BS35 2BS
☎ 01454 281811
Helpline 0808 800 3344 🖷 01454 281094
email: info@meningitis.org.uk
website: www.meningitis.org
Support and befriending: contacts: information: publications: fund-raising for research. Caters for children and adults affected by meningitis and septicaemia and their families.

Meningitis Trust
Fern House, Bath Road, Stroud, Gloucester, Glos GL5 3TJ
☎ 01453 768000
0845 6000 800 🖷 01453 768001
email: info@meningitis-trust.org
website: www.meningitis-trust.org
Support: contacts: information: newsletter

Mental Health Foundation, The
7th Floor, 73 Victoria Street, London SW1H 0HW
☎ 020 7802 0300 🖷 020 7802 0301
email: mhf@mhf.org.uk
website: www.mentalhealth.org.uk
Information for patients, families and professionals. Provides grants for community or research projects which will enhance the lives of people with mental illness or learning disability. Surveys, publications.

Mental Health of Children and Adolescents
(See YoungMinds)

Mentally Handicapped of Ireland, National Association for
NAMHI, 5 Fitzwilliam Place, Dublin 2, Ireland
☎ 00 353 1676 6035

Mercury Amalgams
(See PAMA)

Metabolic Diseases in Children
(See Climb)

Microcephaly Support Group
Mrs J Smith, 'Kymbec', 22 Auctioneers Court, Auctioneers Way, Northampton NN1 1EY
☎ 01604 603743
website: www.ayles.demon.co.uk/microcep.htm
Support: self-help: contacts: newsletter

Microphthalmia
(Contact MACS)

Microscopic Arteritis
(See Stuart Strange Trust and Arthritis Care)

Migraine Action Association
Unit 6, Oakley Hay Lodge Business Park, Great Folds Road, Great Oakley, Northants NN18 9AS
☎ 01536 461 333 🖷 01536 461 444
email: info@migraine.org.uk
website: www.migraine.org.uk
Support: information: newsletter: research

Migraine Trust
45 Great Ormond Street, London WC1N 3HZ
020 7831 4818 – Mon-Fri 9am-5pm
🖷 020 7831 5174
email: info@migrainetrust.org
website: www.migraintrust.org
Information and publications, branches and self-help group

Miller-Dieker Syndrome
(Contact Lissencephaly Contact Group)

Mind (National Association for Mental Health)
Granta House, 15-19 Broadway, London E15 4BQ
☎ 020 8519 2122 🖷 020 8522 1725
website: www.mind.org.uk
Support for people with mental illness, through local groups. Information, campaigning body. Branches in all areas of the UK. (See YoungMinds)

Minimal Brain Dysfunction
(Contact Dyspraxia Foundation)

Miscarriage Association
c/o Clayton Hospital, Northgate, Wakefield, W. Yorks WF1 3JS
☎ 01924 200799 🖷 01924 298834
website: www.miscarriageassociation.org.uk
Support and information for on the subject of pregnancy loss.(See also Pregnancy Advisory Service; Women's Health)

Mitochondrial Cytopathies
(Contact Climb)

MNS Support Group
Gill Carter, 4 Kinver Lane, Bexhill-on-Sea, E. Sussex TN40 2ST
☎ 01424 217790
Support, contacts and information for parents of children affected by Melnick-Needles syndrome.

Moebius Syndrome Support Group
41 Westley Avenue, Whitley Bay NE25 8DF
☎ & 🖷 0191 253 2090
email: moebiusuk@aol.com
Support: contacts: information: newsletter. Fundraising for research, conference every two years.

Monosomy X Syndrome
(Contact Turner Syndrome Support Society)

Morphoea
(Contact Raynaud's and Scleroderma Association)

Morquio Syndrome
(See MPS Society)

Morris's Syndrome
(See AIS Support Group UK)

Mothers Apart From Their Children
(See Match)

Motor and Sensory Neuropathy, Hereditary
(Contact CMT UK)

Motor Learning Difficulty
(Contact Dyspraxia Foundation)

Motor Neurone Disease Association
P.O. Box 246, Northampton NN1 2PR
☎ 01604 250505
Helpline 08457 626262 (Mon-Fri 9am-10.30pm, Sat & Sun 10am-6pm) 🖷 01604 624726
email: enquiries@mndassociation.org
website: www.mndassociation.org
Support: counselling: information: newsletter: equipment loan: limited financial assistance: local support groups: research

Motor Neurone Disease Association, Scottish
76 Firhill Road, Glasgow G20 7BA
☎ 0141 945 1077 🖷 0141 945 2578
email: info@scotmnd.sol.co.uk
website: www.scotmnd.org.uk

MOVE (Movement Opportunities In Education)
(See Education Section)

MPS Society (The Society for Mucopolysaccharide Diseases)
46 Woodside Road, Amersham, Bucks HP6 6AJ
☎ 01494 434156 🖷 01494 434252
email: mps@mpssociety.co.uk
website: www.mpssociety.co.uk
For parents with children affected by mucopolysaccharide diseases, which include Hurler syndrome, Hunter syndrome, Sanfillipo syndrome, Morquio syndrome, Maroteaux-Lamy syndrome, Scheie syndrome and Sly syndrome. Also caters for the lipidoses. Support: contacts: information: newsletter.

MPS Society, Northern Office
168 Hesketh Lane, Tarleton, Lancs PR4 6AT
☎ 01772 815516 🖷 01772 814821
email: 1060.3374@compuserve.com

Mucocutaneous Candidiasis
(Contact Primary Immunodeficiency Association)

Mucocutaneous Lymph Node Syndrome
(Contact Kawasaki Support Group)

Mucopolysaccharide Diseases
(See MPS Society)

Mullerian Duct Dysgenesis
(See AIS Support Group UK)

Multiple and Profound Disability
(See Mencap PIMD Section; PAMIS)

Multiple Births Support Groups
(See TAMBA)

Multiple Epiphyseal Dysplasia (MED)
(Contact Perthes Association)

Multiple Exostosis, Hereditary
(See Hereditary Multiple Exostosis Support Group)

Multiple Sclerosis Action Group
Action MS, Knockbracken Healthcare Park, Saintfield Road, Belfast BT8 8BH
☎ 028 907 907 07
0800 028 88 33 – 7pm-11pm (every evening)
🖷 028 9040 2010
email: info@actionms.co.uk
website: www.actionms.co.uk
Support: contacts: information: quarterly magazine: publications: advocacy and medi-care holidays

Multiple Sclerosis Resource Centre
7 Peartree Business Centre, Peartree Road, Stanway, Colchester, Essex CO3 0JN
☎ 01206 505444
Helpline 0800 783 0518 🖷 01206 505449

5

email: themsrc@yahoo.com
website: www.msrc.co.uk
Network of groups and list of therapy groups. Supporting anyone affected by MS. Bi-monthly magazine. 24 hr Telephone Consultancy (020 8422 2144)

Multiple Sclerosis Society, The
MS National Centre, 372 Edgware Road, London NW2 6ND
☎ 020 8438 0700
Helpline 0808 800 8000 (Mon-Fri 9am-9pm) 📠 020 8438 0701
email: info@mssociety.org.uk
website: www.mssociety.org.uk
Support: information: local groups

Multiple Sclerosis Society, The (Scotland)
2a North Charlotte Street, Edinburgh EH2 4HR
☎ 0131 225 3600
Support: information: publications

Multiple Sclerosis Therapy Centres, Federation of
Bradbury House, 155 Barker Lane, Bedford MK41 9RX
☎ 01234 325781 📠 01234 365242
website: www.ms-selfhelp.org
Provides information and produces a comprehensive list of MS therapy centres in the UK.

Muscular Dystrophy Campaign
7-11 Prescott Place, London SW4 6BS
☎ 020 7720 8055 📠 020 7498 0670
email: info@muscular-dystrophy.org
website: www.muscular-dystrophy.org
Local groups, information, advice, literature, medical research. Caters for a wide range of muscular disorders, in addition to muscular dystrophy.

Myalgic Encephalomyelitis
(See ME Organisations; Tymes Trust)

Myasthenia Gravis Association
Chester Park, Alfreton Road, Derby DE21 4AS
☎ 01332 290219
Helpline 0800 919922 📠 01332 293641
website: www.mgauk.org
Support: contacts: information: newsletter

Myelin Development, Delayed
(See Delayed Myelin Matters)

Myelitis, Transverse
(Contact Spinal Injuries Association)

Myopathies
(Contact Muscular Dystrophy Campaign)

Myositis Support Group
Mr L Oakley, 146 Newtown Road, Woolston, Southampton, Hants SO2 9HR
☎ 023 8044 9708 📠 023 8039 6402
email: enquiry@myositis.org.uk
website: www.myositis.org.uk
Support, contacts and information for people affected by dermatomyositis and polymyositis.

Myotonia Congenita
(Contact Myotonic Dystrophy Support Group)

Myotonic Dystrophy Support Group
Mrs M A Bowler, 35a Carlton Hill, Carlton, Notts NG4 1GZ
☎ 0115 987 0080 📠 0115 987 6462
email: mdsg@tesco.net
website: www.mdsguk.org
Support: contacts: information: newsletter

Naevoid Basal Cell Carcinoma
(Contact Gorlin Syndrome Support group)

Nail-Patella Syndrome Support Group
Mrs Joanne Holland, 21 Robinswood Drive, Castle Grange, Noddle Hill Way, Hull HU7 4ZD
☎ 01482 878722
email: joanne-holland@lineone.net
Support: contacts: information

Nannies/Childminders for Children with Special Needs
(See Daycare Trust; Snap Childcare Agency)

Narcolepsy Association UK
First Floor, Craven House, 121 Kingsway, London WC2B 6PA
☎ 020 7721 8904 📠 020 8395 5505
email: info@narcolepsy.org.uk
website: www.narcolepsy.org.uk
Support and advice for people with narcolepsy (uncontrollable sleeping) and catalepsy/cataplexy.

Naso-Gastric Tube Feeding
(See Half PINNT; PINNT)

NASPCS
(See Incontinent and Stoma Children, Charity for)

National Cancer Alliance
P.O. Box 579, Oxford OX4 1LB
☎ 0870 770 2648 📠 0870 770 2649
email: nationalcanceralliance@btinternet.com
website: www.nationalcanceralliance.co.uk
Information, publications, newsletter. Aims to voice the concerns and views and represent the interests of cancer patients and their carers and advocate on their behalf.

National Phobics Society

Zion CRC, 339 Stretford Road, Hulme, Manchester M15 4ZY

☎ 0161 227 9898 ▤ 0161 227 9862

email: natphob.soc@good.co.uk

website: www.phobics-society.org.uk

Contacts: information: publications: support: newsletter: therapy tapes: clinical hypnotherapy: counselling: self-help groups. Caters for all types of anxiety disorder, including panic attacks, obsessive compulsive disorder (OCD), agoraphobia, body dysmorphic disorder (BDD), social phobia, school phobia and cognitive behavioural disorder.

NCH (National Children's Homes)

85 Highbury Park, London N5 1UD

☎ 020 7226 2033 ▤ 020 7226 2537

email: webmaster@nch.org.uk

website: www.nch.org.uk

Family support: homes: holidays: fostering and adoption. Over 400 projects nationwide: 4 Special Schools: special units: early years provision.

Neonatal Death

(See Bereavement Services; Compassionate Friends; Cot Death Trust, Scottish; Foundation for the Study of Infant Deaths; Laura Centre; SANDS; Sudden Death Support Association)

Nephrotic Syndrome Support Group

Mr D Crisp, 13 Greenway, Bishops Lydeard, Somerset TA4 3BY

☎ 01823 432892 ▤ 01823 432800

Contacts: information: support (See Childhood Nephrotic Support)

Neuroblastoma Society, The

Michael Webb, 1 New Street, Wells, Somerset BA5 2LA

☎ 01749 676604

email: nsoc@ukonline.co.uk

website: http://web.ukonline.co.uk/nsoc

Support: contacts: information: newsletter: fund-raising for research

Neurofibromatosis Association

82 London Road, Kingston-upon-Thames, Surrey KT2 6PX

☎ 020 8547 1636 ▤ 020 8974 5601

email: nfa@zetnet.co.uk

website: www.nfa-uk.org.uk

Support: contacts: information: newsletter: publications. Neurofibromatosis is also known as von Recklinghausen disease.

Neuronal Dysplasia, Intestinal

(See Gut Motility Disorders Support Network; Incontinent and Stoma Children, The Charity for)

Neuronal Migration Disorders

(Contact Lissencephaly Contact Group)

Neuropathies, Hereditary Sensory and Motor

(Contact CMT UK)

Neuropathy Trust, The (for peripheral neuropathy)

P.O. Box 26, Nantwich, Cheshire CW5 5FP

email: info@neuropathy-trust.org

website: www.neuropathy-trust.org

Neutropenia (Congenital), Pancreatic Insufficiency and Growth Failure

(Contact Shwachman-Diamond Syndrome Support)

Neutropenia, Congenital

(Contact Primary Immunodeficiency Association)

Neville's Disease

(See Niemann-Pick Disease Group)

NHS Direct

National Health Service Information Line

☎ 0845 4647

NHS Ombudsman

(also listed in Finance section under Health Service ombudsman)

Will investigate complaints about clinical decisions made by doctors and other health professionals, private hospitals or nursing homes. Patients must first have had their complaints examined by the new NHS procedure. The Ombudsman will only investigate complaints only if they cannot be sorted out at local level. Information leaflet available from health authorities, libraries and Citizen's Advice Bureaux.

Niemann-Pick Disease Group (UK)

Mrs Susan Green, Kingslaw House, East Brae, East Wemyss, Kirkcaldy, Fife KY1 4RS

☎ & ▤ 01592 580672

email: niemann-pick@zetnet.co.uk

website: www.nnpdf.org/npdg-uk

Caters for parents of children with Niemann-Pick disease, Types A, B and C, Neville's disease, Sphingomyelin lipidosis, DAF syndrome, Juvenile dystonic lipidosis. Support: contacts: information: newsletter: publications: family conferences (See also Climb)

Nineteen-Plus Adults with Disabilities

(See Action 19 Plus)

5

Non-Bullous Erythroderma
(See Ichthyosis Support Group)

Non-Hodgkins Lymphoma
(See Lymphoma Association)

Noonan Syndrome Society
Mrs Sheila Brown OBE, Birth Defects Foundation, BDF Centre, Hemlock Way, Cannock, Staffs WS11 2GF
☎ 01543 468 888 (admin.)
08700 707 020 🖷 01543 468999
The Noonan Syndrome Society no longer exists as a separate group. The Birth Defects Foundation can provide information and contacts for families in which there is a member with Noonan syndrome.

NSPCC (National Society for the Prevention of Cruelty to Children)
42 Curtain Road, London EC2A 3NH
☎ 020 7825 2500 (reception/switchboard)
Child Protection Helpline 0808 800 5000
🖷 020 7825 2525
email: infounit@nspcc.org.uk
website: www.nspcc.org.uk/

Nuffield Hearing and Speech Centre
Royal National Throat, Nose and Ear Hospital, Grays Inn Road, London WC1X 8DN
☎ 020 7915 1300 ext 4269 🖷 020 7915 1666
direct – 020 7915 1569
Deals with the diagnosis of all hearing problems, balance problems, speech and language difficulties, particularly dyspraxia, phonological or central processing problems. Also has an interest in specific learning disabilities, such as dyslexia.

Nystagmus Network
108c Harlesden Road, St Alban's, Herts AL1 4JZ
☎ 01727 851 818
Helpline 01392 272573
email: NystagmusN@aol.com
website: www.nystagmusnet.org
Support: contacts: information: newsletter

OAASIS
Brock House, Grigg Lane, Brockenhurst, Hants S042 7RE
09068 633201 🖷 01590 622687
email: oaasis@lesleygroup.co.uk
Educational and general advice on attention deficit/hyperactivity disorder, Asperger syndrome, autism, dyspraxia, Tourette syndrome. Newsletter, publications. Occasional training day for parents.

Obsessive Action
Aberdeen Centre, 22-26 Highbury Grove, London

N5 2EA
☎ 020 7226 4000
Support and information for people affected by compulsions, phobias and obsessive behaviour. (See Careline: Phobics Society, National)

Obsessive-Compulsive Disorder (OCD)
(See National Phobics Society)

Obstructive Airways Disease, Chronic
(Contact Lung Foundation, British)

Ocular Motor Apraxia, Congenital
(See COA Support Group)

Oesophageal Atresia
(Contact TOFS)

OHDO Syndrome Family Network
Pat Seville, 36 Borrowdale Avenue, Gatley, Cheadle, Cheshire SK8 4QF
☎ 0161 428 8583
email: patricia@seville44.fsnet.co.uk
website: www.seville44.fsnet.co.uk
Support: contacts: information

Ollier Disease Self-Help Group
Andrew Harter, Tithings New Barn, Swalcliffe, Banbury, Oxon OX15 5DR
☎ 01295 788001 🖷 01295 788002
email: andrewh@harter.co.uk
For parents of children with Ollier's disease (endochondromatosis). Also caters for McCune Albright syndrome (polyostotic fibrous dysplasia) and some other skeletal dysplasias.

Ondine's Support Group
Mrs L Middleton, 24 Larners Road, Toftwood, Dereham, Norfolk NR19 1LE
☎ 01362 696509
email: cchssupp@hotmail.com
Support, contacts and information for parents of children affected by congenital central hypoventilation syndrome (originally called 'Ondine's Curse'), in which there is a failure of automatic control of breathing during sleep.

One Parent Families, National Council for
255 Kentish Town Road, London NW5 2LX
☎ 020 7267 1361
0800 018 5026 🖷 020 7482 4851
(See Families Need Fathers; Gingerbread)

One Parent Families, Scotland
13 Gayfield Square, Edinburgh EH1 3NX
☎ 0800 018 5026 🖷 0131 557 7899
email: info@opfs.org.uk
website: www.opfs.org.uk

One-To-One International
Chris Root, P.O. Box 311, Bolton, Lancs BL6 5FL
☎ 01204 692121
Befriending scheme of volunteers working with people with learning difficulties, in long stay hospitals or living in the community. Encourages community participation in sports, games and other activities. Support: self-help: information

Opsoclonus Myoclonus
(See Dancing Eye Syndrome Support Trust)

Organ Donor Society, British
BODY, Balsham, Cambridge CB1 6DL
☎ & 📄 01223 893636 (prior call requested for 📄)
email: body@argonet.co.uk
website: www.argonet.co.uk/body
Emotional support and information for families involved in organ donation and transplantation, educational roadshow for schools and colleges, information packs.

Organ Transplantation
(See Transplant Support Network)

Organic Acidaemias
(Contact Climb)

Oromandibular Dystonia
(Contact Dystonia Society)

Osgood-Schlatter Disease
(Contact Perthes Association)

Osler-Weber-Rendu Disease
(Contact Telangiectasia Self-Help Group)

Osteochondromatosis, Multiple
(See Hereditary Multiple Exostosis Support Group)

Osteogenesis Imperfecta
(See Brittle Bone Society)

Osteopathic Council, General
Osteopathy House, 176 Tower Bridge Road, London SE1 3LU
☎ 020 7357 6655 📄 020 7357 0011
email: info@osteopathy.org.uk
website: www.osteopathy.org.uk
Publishes fact sheets and lists of osteopaths in all areas of the UK.

Osteopetrosis Trust (OST)
Mrs M Wright, 10 Cumberland Avenue, Fixby, Huddersfield HD2 2JJ
☎ 01484 545974
email: magken@mwright86.fsnet.co.uk
website: www.ost.org.uk
Support: contacts: information

Osteoporosis, Juvenile
National Osteoporosis Society, Manor Farm, Skinners Hill, Bath BA2 0PJ
☎ 01761 471771
Helpline: 01761 472721 📄 01761 471104
email: info@nos.org.uk
website: www.nos.org.uk
Information and advice.

Otto Syndrome
(Contact Arthrogryposis Group)

Overuse Injury
(See RSI Association)

Pachygyria
(See Lissencephaly Contact Group)

Pain Concern
P.O. Box 13256, Haddington EH41 4YD
☎ 01620 822572 (Mon-Fri 9-5)
01620 822572 (Friday evening 6.30-7.30pm)
📄 01620 829138
email: painconcern@btinternet.com
website: www.painconcern.org.uk
Information and support, listening ear helpline, free pain management leaflets, Quarterly magazine 'Pain Matters'.

Pain Relief Foundation
Clinical Sciences Centre, University Hospital Aintree, Lower Lane, Fazakerley, Liverpool L9 7AL
☎ 0151 529 5820 📄 0151 529 5821
email: pri@liv.ac.uk
website: www.painrelieffoundation.org.uk
Research into causes, methods of improved treatment for, and seeking cures for, chronic pain of all types. Contacts: information: support: newsletter: publications

Pain Society, The
9 Bedford Square, London WC1B 3RE
☎ 020 7636 2750 📄 020 7323 2015
email: painsoc@compuserve.com
website: www.ncl.ac.uk/~nrh/painsoc
Information, advice and lists of pain management clinics for people coping with chronic pain.

Palate, Cleft
(See CLAPA)

Pallid Syncope
(See STARS)

PAMA (Patients Against Mercury Amalgams)
6-9 Bridgewater Square, London EC2Y 8AG
24hr Infoline – 020 7256 2994

5

email: angela.kilmartin@dial.pip.com
website: www.angela.kilmartin.dial.pipex.com
Information on mercury poisoning.

PAMIS (Profound and Multiple Impairment Service)

White Top Research Unit, Frankland Building, The University, Dundee DD1 4HN
☎ 01382 345154 🖷 01382 227464
A UK-wide organisation concerned with the needs of people with profound learning disabilities, sometimes combined with physical or sensory impairments. Information, training and workshops for parents and professionals

Pancreatic Insufficiency (Congenital), Neutropenia and Growth Failure

(Contact Shwachman-Diamond Syndrome Support)

Pancreatitis Supporters Network

Mr J Armour, P.O. Box 8938, Birmingham B13 9FW
☎ & 🖷 0121 449 0667
email: psn@pancreatitis.org.uk
website: www.pancreatitis.org.uk
Support: self-help: contacts: information. Loan of X-Pan 2000 machines to members. Benefits advice, set of booklets and information pack, Pancreatic Pen Pals (Internet), Discussion Board (internet) where to get specialists.

Panhypopituitarism

(Contact GHD Support Group)

Panic Attacks

(See Careline; National Phobics Society; Obsessive Action)

Paraplegia, Familial Spastic

(See FSP Group)

Parasites/Parasytic Disease

(Contact Community Hygiene Concern)

Parent Network

Room 2, Winchester House, 11 Cranmer Road, London SW9 6EJ
☎ 020 7735 1214 🖷 020 7735 4692
email: info@parentnetwork.demon.co.uk
A national organisation with branches in thirty local areas to support parents and help them to improve their relationship with their children, courses for professionals.

Parent Partnership Network, National

Council for Disabled Children, 8 Wakely Street, London EC1V 7QE
☎ 020 7843 6058 🖷 020 7278 9512
Aims to promote parent partnership services based in both the LEA and voluntary sector. The network provides direct support and advice to parents and advice to parent partnership coordinators working with parents of children with special educational needs. Also provides a newsletter and information exchanges on specific aspects of parent partnership work.

Parent Partnership Services, National Association of

Mr D Reid, c/o Parent Partnership Service, Hampshire County Council Education, The Castle, Winchester, Hants SO23 8UG
☎ 01962 845870 🖷 01962 846219
email: davereid@hants.gov.uk
Aims to facilitate communication between parents, schools, statutory and voluntary organisations and to influence policy and practice at local and national level.

Parentability

c/o The National Childbirth Trust, Alexandra House, Oldham Terrace, London W3 6NH
☎ 020 8992 2616 🖷 020 8992 5929
Network of parents who have disabilities. Supports disabled parents through pregnancy, childbirth and parenthood. Contacts, professional links, equipment helpline, fact sheets.

Parenteral Nutrition Therapy

(See Half PINNT; PINNT)

Parenting Education

(See Children's Bureau, National)

Parentline Plus

Unit 520, Highgate Studios, 53-57 Highgate Road, London NW5 1TL
☎ 020 7284 5500
Helpline 0808 800 2222
website: www.parentlineplus.org.uk
A family support service providing a national helpline for any parent or carer of a child or children who is experiencing any kind of difficulty. (See Home Start UK; Kidscape)

Parents' Aid

Hare Street Family Centre, Harberts Road, Harlow, Essex CM19 4EU
☎ 01279 452166
Support and advice for parents of children in local authority care or on an at risk register. Information and advice.

Parents at Work

45 Beech Street, London EC2Y 8AD
☎ 020 7628 3565
Helpline 020 7588 0802 (Wed-Fri)
🖷 020 7628 3591
email: info@parentsatwork.org.uk
website: www.parentsatwork.org.uk/

Support for parents who work or wish to work who are also caring for children with special needs. Newsletter publications.

Parents for Children
41 Southgate Road, London N1 3JP
☎ 020 7359 7530 🖷 020 7226 7840
Adoption and fostering agency, specialising in finding homes for children who are considered 'hard to place' because of special needs.

Parents of Perthes Support Group
Sheila Trever, 6 Ash Close, Sproatley, Hull HU11 4XE
☎ 01482 814721 (before 7pm – answer machine at other times)
email: sheila@audi44.freeserve.co.uk
website: www.audi44.freeserve.co.uk
Advice, support, information and referrals to mainstream service providers, newsletters, national members days out, pen pal scheme.

Parents under Stress
(See Careline; Home Start UK; Parentline Plus)

Parents with Disabilities
(See Disability, Pregnancy and Parenthood International; Disabled Parents Network; Parentability)

Partially Sighted Society, The
P.O. Box 322, Doncaster DN1 2XA
☎ 01302 323132
Support: contacts: information: newsletter: low vision assessments for magnifying aids: brochure of daily living aids

Patau Syndrome (Trisomy 13)
(Contact SOFT UK)

Patches (Diaphragmatic Hernia Support Network)
16 Hillson Drive, Fareham, Hants PO15 6EX
☎ 01329 841436
Support: contacts: newsletter

Pathological Demand Avoidance Syndrome
(See PDA Contact Group)

Patients Association, The
P.O. Box 935, Harrow, Middlesex HA1 3YJ
☎ 020 8423 9111 (admin)
Helpline 020 8423 8999 (10am-4pm, Mon-Fri)
🖷 020 8423 9119
An advice service and collective voice for patients and health professionals. Provides information on patients' rights, complaints procedures and access to the health service.

Patients Forum
c/o CLARU, 11 John Street, London WC1N 2EB
☎ 020 7831 6799 🖷 020 7831 8810
email: info@thepatientsforum.org.uk
website: www.thepatientsforum.or.uk
A federation of national and regional organisations working towards improved healthcare for patients, their families and carers.

PCD Family Support Group
Mrs M O'Donnell, 16 Graham Road, Mitcham, Surrey CR4 2HA
☎ 020 8646 3770
email: odonnellfam@btinternet
website: http://freespace.virgin.net/andy.gorton/index.htm
Support: contacts: information: newsletter. Caters for primary ciliary dyskinesia, immotile cilia and Kartagener syndrome. Free video for affected members.

PDA Contact Group
Jan Seaborne, 24 Daybrook Road, London SW19 3DH
☎ 020 8715 6179
email: jan@pdacontact.org.uk
website: www.pdacontact.org.uk
Support, contacts and information for professionals and parents of children diagnosed with pathological demand avoidance syndrome, a pervasive developmental disorder related to Autism and Asperger Syndrome. Annual Conference; newsletter for all members. Egroup facility for parent members.

Peggy and Friends
Mrs Mandy Giddings, The Hollies, Penn Common, Bramshaw, Lyndhurst, Hants SO43 7JN
☎ 01794 399811
website: www.peggyandfriends.org
Support and advice for parents and carers of children who have lost a limb or limbs, information on artificial limbs, aids and equipment.

Pelizaeus-Merzbacher Support Group
c/o Contact a Family, 209-211 City Road, London EC1V 1JN
☎ 020 7608 8700 🖷 020 7608 8701
email: info@cafamily.org.uk
website: www.cafamily.org.uk
(See also Climb)

Pelvic Inflammatory Disease
(Contact Women's Health)

People First
3rd Floor, Kentish Town Road, London SW8 1RL
☎ 020 7485 6660

5

An organisation, run by and for people with learning difficulties, promoting independence and self-advocacy. Information available on receipt of a SAE. (See also Advocacy Partners)

Perceptuomotor Dysfunction
(Contact Dyspraxia Foundation)

Period Pain
(See PMS Help; Premenstrual Syndrome, National Association for; Premenstrual Society, The; Women's Health)

Peroneal Muscular Atrophy
(Contact CMT UK)

Personal Safety for Children
(See Child Accident Prevention Trust; Kidscape)

Perthes Association
15 Recreation Road, Guildford, Surrey GU1 1HE
☎ 01483 306637 📠 01483 503213
email: admin@perthes.org.uk
website: www.perthes.org.uk
Support: contacts: information: newsletter. Caters for Perthe's disease, multiple epiphyseal dysplasia (MED), Osgood-Schlatter disease, Severs disease, Kohlers disease, Scheurmann disease. (See Parents of Perthes Support Group)

Pesticide Exposure, Action On (PEX)
Eurolink Centre, 49 Effra Road, London SW2 1BZ
☎ 020 7274 8895 📠 020 7274 9084
email: pesttrust@gn.apc.org
website: www.pan-uk.org
Offers support to anyone who is suffering from the effects of pesticide poisoning, however caused. Counselling, information, collation of information, newsletter. (See Allergy Association, Food and Chemical; Allergy Environmental Therapy, British Institute for)

Peto Institute Therapy
(See Education Section)

Pfeiffer Syndrome
(Contact Headlines)

Phenylketonuria, National Society for (PKU Society)
P.O. Box 26642, London N14 4ZF
☎ 020 8364 3010
Helpline 0845 603 9136 📠 0870 122 1864
email: info@nspku.org
website: www.nspku.org
Support: contacts: information: newsletter (See Climb)

Phobia
(See National Phobics Society; Obsessive Action)

Phonological Processing Problems
(See Nuffield Hearing and Speech Centre)

Pierre-Robin Support Group UK
P.O. Box 27913, London SE7 7WL
☎ & 📠 020 8858 6274
website: www.pierrerobinuk.org
Support: self-help: contacts: information. Caters for parents of children with Pierre-Robin sequence and Pierre-Robin syndrome.

PINNT
P.O. Box 3126, Christchurch, Dorset BH23 2XS
☎ & 📠 01202 481625
email: PINNT@dial.pipex.com
website: www.PINNT.com
Support and advice for adult patients on intravenous or naso-gastric nutrition therapy. (See Half PINNT)

Pituitary Foundation, The
P.O. Box 1944, Bristol BS99 2UB
☎ 0870 770 8699 📠 0870 770 8699
email: helpline@pitpat.demon.co.uk
website: www.pituitary.org.uk
Information and support for patients and carers affected by pituitary disorders. Caters for Cushing disease, diabetes insipidus, prolactinoma and acromegaly. Publications.

Pituitary Hormone Deficiency
(See GHD Support Group)

PIXIE (Pseudoxanthoma Elasticum Support Group)
Mrs E Lax, 15 Mead Close, Marlow, Bucks SL7 1HR
☎ & 📠 01628 476687
email: pxeurope@aol.com
website: www.pxe.org.uk
Support: contacts: information: newsletter

Play
(See Children's Bureau, National; Leisure Section)

PMS Help
P. O. Box 83, Hereford HR4 8QY
Postal service, offering help and support for women with pre-menstrual syndrome, post-natal depression and the menopause; booklets, books and videos available to purchase. Able to give talks, workshops or lectures to interested persons, both professional and lay groups.

Poland Syndrome
(Contact Reach)

Polio Fellowship, British

Unit A, Eagle Office Centre, The Runway, South Ruislip, Middlesex HA4 6SE
☎ 020 8842 0555
Helpline 0800 0180586 ▤ 020 8842 0555
email: info@britishpolio.org
For people affected by poliomyelitis. Offers social, cultural and recreational facilities, financial and welfare advice, residential and holiday accommodation, publications and journal.

Polyarteritis Nodosa

(See Stuart Strange Trust and Arthritis Care)

Polychondritis, Relapsing

(See Relapsing Polychondritis Support Group)

Polycystic Kidney Disease

(Contact Kidney Patient Association)

Polymicrogyria

(Contact Lissencephaly Contact Group)

Polymyositis

(See Myositis Support Group)

Polyneuritis, Acute Idiopathic

(Contact Guillain-Barre Syndrome Support Group)

Polyneuropathy

(Contact Guillain-Barre Syndrome Support Group)

Pompe Disease

(Contact Glycogen Storage Diseases, Association for UK)

Porencephaly Contact Group

Fairwinds, 10 Cherrytree Lane, Seaview, Isle of Wight PO34 5JF
☎ 01983 612262
email: l.s.w@btinternet.com
Support: contacts

Porphyria Charitable Trust

David Wharrie and Co, Woodside House, Ashton, Chester CH3 8AE
☎ 01829 751544
Advice and information for sufferers, raises funds for medical research. (See also Climb)

Portage Service

(See Education Section)

Positive Options

Barnardo's, William Morris Hall, 6 Somers Road, Walthamstow, London E17 6RX
☎ 020 8520 6625 ▤ 020 8520 3307
Support, information and advice on HIV/AIDS-related topics, with special emphasis on affected children. Volunteer services to families and young people living with HIV or AIDS.

Post-Herpetic Neuralgia

(See Herpes Viruses Association)

Post-Viral Syndrome

(Contact ME and Chronic Fatigue Associations)

Potter Syndrome Support Group

Mrs S Bonsall, 46 Borfa Green, Welshpool, Powys SY21 7QF
☎ 01938 553755
Support: contacts: information

Practical Guide for Disabled People

Department of Health Publications Centre, P.O. Box 410, Wetherby, Yorks LS23 7LN
A free 168-page book (HB6), published by the Department of Health. Information on; Social Services, National Health Service, Voluntary Organisations, Independent Living, Money Matters, Housing and Home, Equipment and Aids, Work, Education and Training, Getting Around, Holidays and Leisure, Personal and Sexual Relationships. Also contains sections on specific disabilities; deafness or hearing impairment, blindness or partial sight, physical disability, communication disability, mental illness, learning disability, children with disability and carers. Also available on audio cassette (HB6A) and Braille (HB6B).

Prader-Willi Syndrome Association (UK)

125A London Road, Derby DE1 2QQ
☎ 01332 365676 ▤ 01332 360401
email: info@pwsa-uk.demon.co.uk
website: www.pwsa.co.uk
Support: contacts: information: newsletter: talks about the syndrome

Precocious Puberty

(Contact Premature Sexual Maturation Support Group)

Preconceptual Advice

(See Foresight)

Pregnancy and Disability

(See Disabled Parents Network; Parentability)

Pregnancy Advisory Service, British

Austy Manor, Wootton Wawen, Solihull, West Midlands B95 6BX
☎ 01564 793225
Helpline 0845 730 4030 ▤ 01564 794935
email: info@bpas.org
website: www.bpas.org
Offers information and treatment for unplanned

5

pregnancy including pregnancy testing, crisis pregnancy counselling, emergency contraception, a choice of surgical and medical abortion, post abortion counselling, sterilisation, vasectomy and vasectomy reversal.

Premature Babies
(See BLISS; Wellbeing; Childbirth Trust, National)

Premature Sexual Maturation Support Group
PSM Support Group, c/o Child Growth Foundation, 2 Mayfield Avenue, Chiswick, London W4 1PW
☎ 020 8995 0257 / 020 8994 7625
🖹 020 8995 9075

Premenstrual Society (PREMSOC)
P. O. Box 429, Addlestone, Surrey KT15 1DZ
☎ 01932 872560
Information and support, educational courses, workshops and training. Assists in the setting-up of local self-help groups. Please send SAE for routine enquiries. (See PMS Help)

Premenstrual Syndrome, National Association for (NAPS)
Christopher Ryan, 41 Old Road, East Peckham, Kent TN12 5AP
☎ 0870 777 2178 / 0870 777 2177
email: naps@pms.org.uk
website: www.pms.org.uk
Contacts: information: support: newsletter: publications: research database for medical practitioners.

Pressure Sores
(See Wound Care Society)

Primary Ciliary Dyskinesia
(See PCD Family Support Group)

Primary Immunodeficiency Association, The
Alliance House, 12 Caxton Street, London SW1H 0QS
☎ 020 7976 7640
Helpline 0845 603 9158 (Mon-Thurs, 7pm-10pm)
🖹 020 7976 7641
email: pimmune@dial.pipex.com
website: www.pia.org.uk
Support: self-help: contacts: information. Fund-raising for research, regional meetings, benefits and welfare advice. Caters for over 80 primary immunodeficiencies (genetic disorders of the immune system).

Profound Intellectual and Multiple Disabilities
(See PAMIS; Mencap PIMD Section)

Progressive Supranuclear Palsy
(See PSP Association)

Prolactinoma
(Contact Pituitary Foundation)

Prospects for People with Learning Disabilities
Maureen Wise, P.O. Box 351, Reading, Berks RG1 7AL
☎ 0118 9508781 🖹 0118 9391683
email: info@prospects.org.uk
Support and day opportunities for adults with learning disabilities.

Proteus Network UK
31 Baswich Lane, Weeping Cross, Stafford, Staffs ST17 0BH
☎ 01785 254953
email: jharr88251@aol.com & info@proteus-uk.org
website: www.proteus-uk.org
Support: contacts: information: publications: newsletter

Prune-Belly Syndrome
(Contact Incontinent and Stoma Children, Charity for)

Pseudoachondroplasia
(See Restricted Growth Association; Child Growth Foundation)

Pseudohurler Polydystrophy
(Contact MPS Society)

Pseudoxanthoma Elasticum
(See PIXIE)

Psoriasis Association, The
7 Milton Street, Northampton NN2 7JG
☎ 01604 711129 🖹 01604 792894
email: mail@psoriasis.demon.co.uk
Contacts: support: information: newsletter; publications: conferences and meetings. Caters for psoriasis and psoriatic arthritis.

Psoriatic Arthropathy Alliance
P.O. Box 111, St Albans, Herts AL2 3JQ
☎ & 🖹 01923 672837
email: info@paalliance.org.uk
website: www.paalliance.org.uk
Support: contacts: information: publications: conference

PSP Association, The
The Old Rectory, Wappenham, Towcester, Northants NN12 8SQ
☎ 01327 860299 🖹 01327 861007
email: psp.eur@virgin.net
website: www.pspeur.org
Support and information for people affected by progressive supranuclear palsy, Steele-Richardson Olszewski syndrome. Telephone counselling service, local support groups, promotion of research.

Pulmonary Fibrosis
(Contact Lung Foundation, British)

Pulmonary Hypertension Association UK
P.O. Box 2760, Lewes, Sussex BN8 4WA
☎ 07010 715074 / 0800 389 8156
website: www.pha-uk.com

PUMPA (Purine Metabolic Patients Association)
71 Newcomen Street, London SE1 1YT
☎ & 🖹 020 7378 6079
email: info@pumpa.co.uk
website: www.pumpa.co.uk
Support, contacts and information for parents of children affected by the purine and pyrimidine metabolic disorders (including familial/juvenile gout and Lesch-Nyhan syndrome).

Purine and Pyrimidine Metabolic Disorders
(See PUMPA)

Pyrimidine Disorders
(See PUMPA)

RADAR (Royal Association for Disability and Rehabilitation)
12 City Forum, 250 City Road, London EC1V 8AF
☎ 020 7250 3222 🖹 020 7250 0212
website: www.radar.org.uk
Provides regularly updated holiday guides on holidays in the UK, sport and activity holidays. Publications: Holidays in Britain and Ireland 2003; also online version of holiday guide

Rare Chromosome Syndromes
(See Unique)

Raynaud's and Scleroderma Association
112 Crewe Road, Alsager, Cheshire ST7 2JA
☎ 01270 872776
Helpline 0800 917 2494 🖹 01270 883556
email: webmaster@raynauds.demon.co.uk
website: www.raynauds.demon.co.uk
Contacts: information: newsletter. Caters for Raynaud's disease, scleroderma, systemic lupus erythmatosus, erythromelalgia, Sjogren's syndrome.

Reach
P.O. Box 54, Helston TR13 8WD
☎ 0845 1306225 🖹 01872 262098
email: reach@reach.org.uk
website: www.reach.org.uk
Support, contacts, information and advice for parents of children with any type of arm or hand deficiency.

Support: self help: contacts: newsletter (See Lady Hoare Trust)

React
St Luke's House, 270 Sandycombe Road, Kew, Richmond, Surrey TW9 3NP
☎ 020 8940 2575 🖹 020 8940 2050
email: react@reactcharity.org
website: react-kew.demon.co.uk/
Research, financial help for equipment not available on the NHS, education and practical help for children and young people with potentially terminal illness, responding to their needs and those of their families. (See ACT)

Reflex Anoxic Seizures
(See STARS)

Reflex Sympathetic Dystrophy
(See RSDS Support Group)

Rehabilitation
(See RADAR)

Reifenstein Syndrome
(See AIS Support Group UK)

Relapsing Polychondritis Support Group
Anne Colman, 21 Staneway, Leam Lane, Gateshead NE10 8LR
☎ 0191 469 2342
email: colmananne@hotmail.com
website: www.groups.yahoo.com/relapsingpolychondritisuk
Online support group
Support: self-help: contacts: information: newsletter

Relationship Problems
(See Sexuality and Relationships Section)

Rendu-Osler-Weber Syndrome
(Contact Telangiectasia Self-Help Group)

Repetitive Strain Injury
(See RSI Association)

Research Trust for Metabolic Diseases in Children
(See Climb)

Re-SOLVE
30a High Street, Stone, Staffs ST15 8AW
☎ 01785 817885
Helpline: 0808 800 2345 🖹 01785 813205
Information and advice of detecting and dealing with solvent abuse. (See Solvent Abuse Resource Group)

5

Respiratory Diseases
(Contact Lung Foundation, British)

Respiratory Distress Syndrome in Newborn
(Contact BLISS)

Respite Care Services
(See Education and Residential Care Section)

Restricted Growth Association
P.O. Box 4744, Dorchester DT2 9FA
☎ 01308 898445
email: rga1@talk21.com
website: www.rgaonline.org.uk
Caters for all forms of restricted growth, including achondroplasia, hypochondroplasia, pseudoachondroplasia, epiphyseal dysplasia, growth hormone deficiency etc. Support: self help: contacts: literature: newsletter (See also Child Growth Foundation)

Retinitis Pigmentosa Society, British
P.O. Box 350, Buckingham, Bucks MK18 5EL
☎ 01280 860363
Helpline 01280 860363 🖹 01280 860515
email: lynda@brps.demon.co.uk
website: www.brps.demon.co.uk
Support: contacts: information: newsletter

Retinoblastoma Society, The
St Bartholomew's Hospital, West Smithfield, London EC1A 7BE
☎ 020 7600 3309 (admin and helpline)
020 7600 3309 🖹 020 7600 8579
email: rbinfo@rbsociety.org.uk
website: www.rbsociety.org.uk
Support: contacts: information

Rett Syndrome Association, Scotland
Mrs I Allan, 15 Tanzieknowe Drive, Cambuslang, Glasgow G72 8RG
☎ 0141 641 7662

Rett Syndrome Association, UK
RSAUK, 113 Friern Barnet Road, London N11 3EU
☎ 020 8361 5161 (local) 0870 770 3266 (national)
🖹 020 8368 6123 (local) 0870 770 3265 (national)
email: info@rettsyndrome.org.uk
website: www.rettsyndrome.org.uk
Support: contacts: information: magazine: publications

Reye's Syndrome Foundation
Mrs G Denney, 15 Nicholas Gardens, Pyrford, Woking, Surrey GU22 8SD
☎ 01932 346843
Contacts: information: newsletter

Rheumatism
(See Arthritis Organisations)

Riley-Day Syndrome
(See Dysautonomia Society)

RNIB (Royal National Institute for the Blind)
105 Judd Street, London WC1H 9NE
☎ 020 7388 1266
Helpline 0845 766 9999 🖹 020 7388 2034
email: helpline @rnib.org.uk
website: www.rnib.org.uk
Services in all areas of the UK; schools and educational advisory services, colleges, courses, employment, holiday services, leisure and sport services, publications, aids and equipment. Many local branches, providing their own facilities or resource centres. Details from London office.

RNIB Scotland
Dunedin House, 25 Ravelston Terrace, Edinburgh EH4 3TP
☎ 0131 311 8500 🖹 0131 311 8529

RNIB Sensory Support Service
Northern Ireland, 16 Bishop Street, Londonderry BT48 6PW
☎ 028 71374619 or minicom 028 71377323
🖹 028 71374810
Support: contacts: information: newsletter: publications

RNIB, Northern Ireland
40 Linenhall Street, Belfast BT2 8BG
☎ 01232 329373 🖹 01232 439118
email: Mmcilwrath@rnib.org.uk
Support: contacts: information: newsletter: publications

RNID (Royal National Institute for Deaf People)
19-23 Featherstone Street, London EC1Y 8SL
voice – 0808 808 0123 or text – 0808 808 9000 both freephone 🖹 helpline 020 7296 8199
website: www. rnid.org.uk
RNID campaigns, researches and provides information to help raise deaf awareness and improve the lives of deaf and hard of hearing people in the UK. RNID also has a range of equipment and products for deaf and hard of hearing people.

Robin Anomalad/Sequence
(See Pierre-Robin Support Group)

Romano-Ward Syndrome
(See Long QT Family Support Group)

Rosacea
(Contact Acne Support Group)

RSDS Support Group
White Horses, 9 South Cliff, Bexhill-on-Sea, E. Sussex TN39 4EJ
☎ 01424 730336
Support, contacts and information for people affected by reflex sympathetic dystrophy (Sudek's atrophy).

RSI Association
380-384 Harrow Road, London W9 2HU
☎ 020 7266 2000
Helpline 0800 018 5012 – Mon, Wed & Fri 11-5
website: www.demon.co.uk/rsi/rsia
Information and support for people affected by repetitive strain injury, also known as work-related upper limb disorder (WRULD) or overuse injury.

Rubella Damage, Congenital (Sight/Hearing Loss)
(Contact Sense)

Rubinstein-Taybi Syndrome Support Group
Rosemary A Robertson, Appledore Cottage, Dilwyn, Herefordshire HR4 8EU
☎ 01568 720350
website: www.rts-support.co.uk
Support: contacts: information: newsletter

Russell-Silver Syndrome
(See Silver-Russell Syndrome Support Group)

Sacral Agenesis Contact Group
Mrs H Gillard, 15 Elizabeth Gardens, Dibden Purlieu, Southampton, Hants SO4 5NF
☎ 023 8084 2662
Support: contacts: information

Saethre-Chotzen Syndrome Support Group
Mrs L Nixon, 17 Grindleton Road, Blackburn, Lancs BB2 6NZ
☎ 01254 52703
Support: contacts: information (See Headlines)

Safety Training for Children
(See Child Accident Prevention Trust; Kidscape)

Saggital Synostosis
(Contact Headlines)

Salaam Seizures
(Contact West Syndrome Support Group)

SANDS (Stillbirth and Neonatal Death Society)
28 Portland Place, London W1N 4DE
☎ 020 7436 7940
Helpline 020 7436 5881 ▤ 020 7436 3715
email: support@uk-sands.org
website: www.uk-sands.org
Offers support to parents who have lost a baby soon after birth or within the first months. Newsletter: contacts: information

Sane and Saneline
1st Floor, Cityside House, 40 Adler Street, London E1 1EE
☎ 020 7375 1002 (admin)
Helpline 0845 767 8000 (12 noon-2am, every day)
▤ 020 7375 2162
email: info@sane.org.uk
website: www.sane.org.uk
Support, contacts, newsletter, publications, advice and information for people affected by mental health problems (including schizophrenia) and their families. Research, fund-raising, campaigning for better services.

Sanfillipo Syndrome
(See MPS Society)

Sarcoidisis Association, UK
Mrs A Cooke, 19 Ashurst Close, Blackbrook, St Helens, Lancs WA11 9DN
☎ 01744 28020
Support: information: advice (See Lung Foundation, British)

SATFA
(Now ARC)

Scheie Disease
(See MPS Society)

Scheurmann Disease
(Contact Perthes Association)

Schilder's Disease
(Contact Adrenoleukodystrophy Family Support Trust)

Schizophrenia Association of Great Britain, The
Bryn Hyfred, The Crescent, Bangor, Gwynedd LL57 2AG
☎ & ▤ 01248 354048
email: info@saqb.co.uk
website: www.saqb.co.uk
Information: support: publications: newsletter: research (See Sane and Saneline)

Schizophrenia Fellowship, National (NSF)
28 Castle Street, Kingston-upon-Thames, Surrey KT1 1SS

☎ 020 8547 3937 Advice service 020 8974 6814 (Mon-Fri, 10am-3pm) 🖻 020 8547 3862
email: nsf@nsf.org.uk
website: www.nsf.org.uk
Offers carers' support, help and advisory services, housing, day care, employment prospects, newsletter, publications. (See Sane and Saneline)

School Phobia
(See National Phobics Society)

Scleroderma
(See Raynaud's and Scleroderma Association)

Scoliosis Association, UK
2 Ivebury Court, 325 Latimer Road, London W10 6RA
☎ & 🖻 020 8964 5343
Helpline 020 8964 1166 (Mon-Fri, 10am-3pm)
email: info@sauk.org.uk
website: www.sauk.org.uk
Support: contacts: information: newsletter: regional meetings

Scope
6-10 Market Road, London N7 9PN
☎ 020 7619 7100
Cerebral palsy Helpline 0808 800 3333 (weekdays, 9am-9pm, weekends, 2pm-6pm)
email: cphelpline@scope.org.uk
website: www.scope.org.uk
Wide range of services for children and adults affected by cerebral palsy, and their families. Research, schools, colleges, training and employment, holiday, leisure and sport facilities, support and information, publications. Six regional offices and 200 affiliated groups. Information, support and advice. (See Capability Scotland)

Scope (Wales)
Scope Cwmpas Cymru, Brunel House, Ynys Bridge Court, Gwaelod-y-Garth, Cardiff CF4 8SS
☎ 01222 813913 🖻 01222 813866

Scope Family Services, Advisory and Assessment Centre
16 Fitzroy Square, London W1P 5HQ
☎ 020 7387 9571 🖻 020 7383 3205
Wide range of services including advice on aids and equipment, personal and family counselling, educational advice and assessments, leisure and sport facilities, holidays, publications.

Scottish Huntington's Association
Thistle House, 61 Main Road, Elderslie, Johnstone PA5 9BA
☎ 01505 322245 🖻 01505 382980

email: sha-admin@hdscotland.org
website: www.hdscotland.org

Seasonal Affective Disorder Association (SAD)
SAD, P.O. Box 989, Steyning BN44 3HG
☎ 01903 814942 🖻 01903 879939
Advice, support and information for people affected by SAD (a type of winter depression caused by biochemical imbalance due to lack of sunlight). Please send SAE for details.

SED Tarda
(Contact Perthes Association; Restricted Growth Association)

Selective Mutism Information and Research Association
Mrs L Whittington, SMIRA, 13 Humberside Drive, Leicester LE5 0RE
☎ 0116 212 7411
Support: contacts: information: newsletter. Special education contact and support for teachers.

Self-Advocacy for People with Learning Difficulties
(See Advocacy Partners; One to One International; People First)

Self-Help Groups, Setting Up
(See Contact a Family)

Semantic Pragmatic Disorder
(Contact Autism Organisations)

Sense (The National Deaf/Blind and Rubella Association)
11-13 Clifton Terrace, Finsbury Park, London N4 3SR
☎ 020 7272 7774 🖻 020 7272 6012
email: enquiries@sense.org.uk
website: www.sense.org.uk
Sense is the national voluntary organisation supporting and campaigning for people who are deafblind or have associated disabilities, their families, their carers, and professionals who work with them. People of all ages and with widely varying conditions use Sense's specialist services. Founded as a parents self-help group in 1955, Sense is now the leading national organisation working with deafblind people.

Sense, Wales
Sense Cymru, Shand House, 20 Newport Road, Cardiff CF2 1YB
☎ & 🖻 01222 457641
Minicom 01222 499644
Support: contacts: information: newsletter

Sense, Northern Ireland
Family Centre, Manor House, 51 Mallusk Road, Newtownabbey, Belfast BT36 4RU
☎ 028 9083 3430 🖷 028 9084 4232
email: senseni@sensewest.org.uk
Support: contacts: information: newsletter

Sense, Scotland
5th Floor, 45 Finneston Place, Glasgow G3 8JU
☎ 0141 564 2444 Minicom 0141 564 2442
🖷 0141 564 2443
email: info@sensescotland.org.uk
Support services for families with children who have complex support needs because of deafblindness or sensory impairment, learning disability, physical disability or healthcare needs.

Sensory and Motor Neuropathy, Hereditary
(See CMT UK)

Septicaemia
(Contact Meningitis Research Foundation)

Severs Disease
(Contact Perthes Association; Parents at Perthes Support)

Sexual Problems
(See Children's Bureau, National; Sexuality and Relationship Section)

Shingles Support Society
41 North Road, London N7 9DP
☎ 020 7609 9061
website: www.herpes.org.uk/shingles
Self-help information and drug treatment for shingles pain (PHN). Send SAE and small donation for 19 page pack which includes 6 pages for the GP written by consultant neurologist.

Short Stature
(See Child Growth Foundation; Restricted Growth Association)

Shprintzen Syndrome (Velo-Cardio-Facial Syndrome)
(See Chromosome 22q 11 Group)

Shwachman-Diamond Syndrome Support
5 Lincoln Road, Washingborough, Lincoln LN4 1EQ
☎ & 🖷 01522 792039
0800 781 2122
email: info@shwachman-diamond support.org
website: www.shwachmandiamondsupport.org
Support: medical advisory board: website: information: contacts

Sialic Acid Storage Disease
(Contact MPS Society)

Sialidosis
(Contact MPS Society)

SIBS
c/o Mencap, 115-123 Golden Lane, London EC21Y 0RT
☎ 020 7454 0454 🖷 020 7608 3254
Support, contacts and newsletter for anyone whose brother or sister has a learning difficulty.

SIBS Encounter
website: www.sibspace.org
A site set up to enable brothers and sisters of a person with special need to exchange information and support.

Sicca Syndrome
(see Sjogren's Syndrome Association, British)

Sickle Cell and Thalassaemia Centre
Beverley Smalling, 457 Queensbridge Road, Hackney E8 3TS
☎ 020 7853 6700 🖷 020 7853 6709

Sickle Cell Society
54 Station Road, London NW10 4UA
☎ 020 8961 7795 🖷 020 8961 8346
email: sicklecellsoc@btinternet.com
website: www.sicklecellsociety.org
Support: contacts: information: newsletter

Sight Impairment
(See Blind, Henshaw's Society for the; Look; Partially Sighted Society; RNIB; Vision Aid)

Signed Speech
(See Education Section)

Silver-Russell Syndrome Support Group
c/o Child Growth Foundation, 2 Mayfield Avenue, Chiswick, London W4 1PW
☎ 020 8995 0257 / 020 8994 7625
🖷 020 8995 9075
Support: contacts: information

Single Parents
(See One Parent Families)

Sitting-In/Care Services
(See Befriending Network; Carers UK; Carers, Princess Royal Trust for; Caring Matters Now; Community Service Volunteers; Crossroads Caring for Carers)

Sjogren Syndrome Association, British
Unit 1 Manor Workshops, Nailsea Wall Lane, West End, Nailsea, Bristol BS48 2DD
☎ 01275 854215

5

email: bssassociation@compuserve.com
website: ourworld.compuserve.com/homepages/
bssassociation
Support: self-help: information (See Raynaud's and Scleroderma Association)

Skin Camouflage
(See Changing Faces; Disfigurement Guidance Centre; Let's Face It Support Network; Skin Camouflage, British Association for)

Skin Camouflage, The British Association for (BASC)
P.O. Box 202, c/o Resources for Business, South Park Road, Macclesfield, Cheshire SK11 6FP
website: www.skin-camouflage.net
Offers advice and assistance to people affected by facial or bodily disfigurement or scarring.

Skin Diseases
(See Skinship UK)

Skinship UK
Mr A Medicks, Plascow Cottage, Kirkgunzeon, Dumfries DG2 8JT
☎ 01387 760567
Aims to increase awareness of the effects of skin diseases, to provide information on all types of skin disorder and to enable sufferers to exchange mutual support and share experiences.

Sleeping, Involuntary
(See Narcolepsy Association UK)

Smith-Magenis Syndrome Foundation
42 Blackmore Road, Malvern, Worcs WR14 1QT
☎ 01684 566606
Support: self-help: contacts.

Snap Childcare Agency
Snap Childcare Ltd, 91-93 Great Eastern Street, Shoreditch, London EC2A 3HZ
☎ 020 7729 2200
email: snapchildcare@aol.com
website: www.snapchildcare.co.uk
Recruitment agency providing nannies and childcare workers for children who have special needs. (See Daycare Trust) Nationwide service, home/office visits available, carers for 12 year old +, carers for elderly.

SOFT UK
48 Froggatts Ride, Walmley, Sutton Coldfield, W. Midlands B76 2TQ
☎ 0121 351 3122 – 24 hr Helpline
Professional contact – 01730 261258
▤ 0121 681 1318
email: enquiries@soft.org.uk
website: www.soft.org.uk

Support: contacts: information: newsletter: annual conference: feeding equipment: videos: prenatal and bereavement befrienders. For parents of children affected by Edwards syndrome (Trisomy 18) and Patau syndrome (Trisomy 13).

Solvent Abuse Resource Group
68 Darwen Street, Blackburn, Lancs BB1 6BE
☎ 01254 677493 ▤ 01254 677503
email: sarg@airtime.co.uk
Information on solvent abuse. (See Re-SOLVE)

SOS
c/o CancerBACUP, 3 Bath Place, Rivington Street, London EC2A 3DR
☎ 020 7696 9003
Helpline 0808 800 1234 ▤ 020 7696 9002
website: www.cancerbacup.org.uk
Advice, information and support for men/boys affected by testicular cancer.
(See CancerBACUP)

Sotos Syndrome Support Group
c/o Child Growth Foundation, 2 Mayfield Avenue, Chiswick, London W4 1PW
☎ 020 8995 0257 / 020 8994 7625
▤ 020 8995 9075
Support: contacts: information: newsletter

Spasmodic Torticollis
(Contact Dystonia Society)

Spastic Paraplegia, Familial
(Contact FSP Group)

Speakability
1 Royal Street, London SE1 7LL
☎ 020 7261 9572
Helpline 0808 8089752 ▤ 020 7928 9542
email: info@speakability.org.uk
website: www.speakability.org
Information and advice on speech and language problems.

Special Care Units, Babies/Children in
(See Action for Sick Children; BLISS)

Special Wishes, Treats etc.
(See Finance Section)

Specific Eye Conditions (SPECS)
P.O.Box 118, Westerham TN16 3WR
☎ 01959 570 142
email: jo.moore@eyeconditions.org.uk
website: www.eyeconditions.org.uk
Information about specific eye conditions on their website, working with support groups catering for visual disorders, promoting new groups, meetings, publications.

Speech and Language Therapists, Royal College of
2 White Hart Yard, London SE1 1NX
☎ 020 7378 1200 🖷 020 7403 7254
email: postmaster@rcslt.org
website: www.rcslt.org
Information on communication, speech and language disorders, swallowing/feeding difficulties, speech and language services. Leaflets and guidance on finding independent speech and language therapists.

Speech Disorders
(See AFASIC; Dysphasic Adults, Action; ICAN; Nuffield Hearing and Speech Centre; Speakability)

Sphingomyelin Lipidosis
(See Niemann-Pick Disease Group)

Spina Bifida and Hydrocephalus, Association for
(See ASBAH)

Spina Bifida Association, Scottish
190 Queensferry Road, Edinburgh EH4 2BW
☎ 0131 332 0743 🖷 0131 343 3651
email: mail@ssba.org.uk
Support: contacts: information: newsletter: publications: advocacy: holidays

Spinal Curvature
(See Scoliosis Association UK)

Spinal Injuries Association
76 St James's Lane, Muswell Hill, London N10 3DF
☎ 020 8444 2121
Freephone Helpline 0800 980 0501 (9.30am-4.30pm) 🖷 020 8444 3761
email: sia@spinal.co.uk
website: www.spinal.co.uk
The Spinal Injuries Association is the leading national charity for spinal cord injured people and all those concerned with their well-being. Established in 1974, with HRH The Princess Royal as its Patron, SIA offers information, advice and on-going support to spinal cord injured people on all aspects of living with their disability. SIA's services include a Helpline providing information and advice, a Peer Support scheme to assist those undergoing treatment in Spinal Injuries Centres and a range of expert publications, including a bi-monthly magazine, addressing a wide spectrum of issues of interest and concern to spinal cord injured people. Membership to SIA is open to all.

Spinal Injuries Scotland
Festival Business Centre, 150 Brand Street, Glasgow G51 1DH
☎ 0141 314 0056

Counselling Helpline 0141 314 0057
email: info@sisonline.org
website: www.sisonline.org
Information: support: newsletter: sports division: unit visits: legal advice: welfare benefits service.

Spinal Muscular Atrophy
(See Jennifer Trust for Spinal Muscular Atrophy)

Spinal Tumours
(See Brain and Spine Foundation, British)

Spinocerebellar Degeneration
(Contact Ataxia UK)

Spondylitis, Juvenile
(Contact Arthritis Care; Lady Hoare Trust)

Spondylo-Epiphyseal Dysplasia Tarda
(Contact Perthes Association; Restricted Growth Association)

Stammering Association, The British
15 Old Ford Road, London E2 9PJ
☎ 020 8983 1003 Parents' helpline 0845 603 2001
email: mail@stammering.org
website: www.stammering.org
Support: self-help groups: information: newsletter

Stammering Children, Michael Palin Centre for
Finsbury Health Centre, Pine Street, London EC1R 0LP
☎ 020 7530 4238 🖷 020 7833 3842
website: www.stammeringcentre.org
Assessment, information and advice for parents of children who stammer.

Starlight Children's Foundation
MacMillan House, Paddington Station, London W2 1HD
☎ 020 7262 2881 🖷 020 7402 7403
email: info@starlight.org.uk
website: www.starlight.org.uk
Aims to grant wishes to children (4-18 years) who are chronically, critically or terminally ill. Will arrange meetings with famous people, organise special trips or experiences, or provide items which will bring happiness to the child in his or her own environment. (See Dreams Come True Charity; Make A Wish Foundation)

STARS (Syncope Trust and Reflex Anoxic Seizures)
P.O. Box 175, Stratford-upon-Avon, Warks CV37 8YD
☎ & 🖷 01789 450564
0800 028 6362

email: trudie@stars.org.uk
website: www.stars.org.uk
Support, self-help, information, and videos: regional meetings for parents of children affected by reflex anoxic seizures (pallid infantile seizures/white breathholding seizures). Also caters for syncope and severe breathholding not associated with reflex anoxic seizures or epilepsy.

Startle Disease
(See Hyperekplexia Support Group)

Stationery Office, The
The Publications Centre, 51 Nine Elms Road, London SW8 5DR
☎ 020 7873 0011 (enquiries)
020 7873 9090 (orders) 🖷 020 7873 8200
email: npg.marketing @theso.co.uk
website: www.national-publishing.co.uk
A wide range of publications on health matters (mental health, nutrition, primary health care etc.) many published on behalf of government and official bodies. Catalogues available on request.

Steele-Richardson Olszewski Syndrome
(See PSP Association)

Stepfamily Association, National
Chapel House, 18 Hatton Place, London EC1N 8RU
☎ 020 7209 2460
Helpline and Stepfamily Telephone Counselling Service 01702 559900 🖷 020 7209 2461
email: tnsa@ukonline.co.uk
website: www.webcreations.co.uk/stepfamily
Information, publications, training for professionals working with families.

Steps
Mrs S Banton, Lymm Court, 11 Eagle Brow, Lymm, Cheshire WA13 0LP
☎ 0871 7170044
email: info@steps-charity.org.uk
website: www.steps-charity.org.uk
Support: contacts: information: newsletter. Caters for disorders or deficiencies of the lower limbs, e.g. talipes (club foot), congenital dislocated hip and related conditions.

Stickler Syndrome Support Group
P.O. Box 371, Walton-on-Thames, Surrey KT12 2YS
☎ & 🖷 01932 267635
email: info@stickler.org.uk
website: www.stickler.org
Support: contacts: information: publication on the syndrome

'Stiff Baby' Syndrome
(See Hyperekplexia Support Group)

Stillbirth and Neonatal Death Society
(See SANDS)

Stills Disease
(Contact Arthritis Care; Lady Hoare Trust)

Stoma
(See Incontinent and Stoma Children, The Charity for)

Stroke Association, The
Stroke House, Whitecross Street, London EC1Y 8JJ
☎ 020 7566 0300 (Mon-Fri, 10am-5pm)
0845 3033100 Mon-Fri 9-5pm 🖷 020 7490 2686
email: stroke@stroke.org.uk
website: www.stroke.org.uk
Support: contacts: information: local groups. (See Brain and Spine Foundation, British; Chest, Heart and Stroke, Scotland; Different Strokes)

Struempell-Lorraine Syndrome
(Contact FSP Group)

Stuart Strange Trust and Arthritis Care
Mrs L Strange, 19 Dovedale, Stevenage, Herts SG2 9EP
☎ 01438 360565
Support, contacts and information. Caters for Wegener's granulomatosis, microscopic arteritis, hypersensitivity vasculitis, giant cell arteritis, Churg-Strauss vasculitis, polyarteritis nodosa, Henoch-Schonlein purpura, Takayasu's arteritis.

Sturge-Weber Syndrome Foundation UK
Burleigh, 348 Pinhoe Road, Exeter, Devon EX4 8AF
☎ & 🖷 01392 464675
email: support@sturge-weber.org.uk
website: www.sturgeweber.org.uk
Support: contacts: information: newsletter: annual Family Weekend Conference

Sudanophilic Leukodystrophy
(See Adrenoleukodystrophy Family Support Trust)

Sudden Death Support Association
Sarah Firth, Dolphin House, Part Lane, Swallowfield, Reading, Berks RG7 1TB
☎ 0118 9889797
For relatives and friends who have experienced a sudden death.

Sudden Infant Death Syndrome
(See Compassionate Friends; Cot Death Trust, Scottish; Foundation for the Study of Infant Deaths; Laura Centre; SANDS; Sudden Death Support Association)

SUDE (Sudden Unexpected Death in Epilepsy)
(See Epilepsy Bereaved)

Sudek's Atrophy
(Contact RSDS Support Group)

Sue Ryder Care
1st Floor, King's House, King's Street, Sudbury, Suffolk CO10 2ED
☎ 01787 280252
Residential homes for people with a disability or chronic illness. Counselling, respite care, bereavement counselling.

Sulphatase Deficiency, Multiple
(Contact MPS Society)

Support Groups, Setting Up
(See Contact A Family)

Supra-Bulbar Palsy
(See Worster-Drought Syndrome Support Group)

Supranuclear Palsy, Progressive
(See PSP Association)

SWAN (Syndromes Without a Name)
Mrs E Swingwood, 16 Achilles Close, Great Wyrley, Nr Walsall, W. Midlands WS6 6JW
☎ & 🖷 01922 701234
email: undiagnosed@clara.co.uk
website: www.undiagnosed.clara.net
Support, contacts and information for parents of children with learning disability, physical disability or multiple disability, for whom no specific diagnosis has been made.

Swyers Syndrome
(See AIS Support Group UK)

Syncope
(See STARS)

Syringomyelia
(See ANTS)

Systemic Sclerosis
(Contact Raynaud's and Scleroderma Association)

Tadpoles
65 Bushbarns, West Cheshunt EN7 6ED
☎ 01992 627490 (daytime only)
Support, contacts and information for parents of children with glaucoma. (See Glaucoma Association, International)

Tak Tent Cancer Suport (Scotland)
Tak Tent Office, Flat 5, 30 Shelley Court, Gartnavel Complex, Glasgow G12 9YN

☎ 0141 211 0122 🖷 0141 2110010
email: tak.tent@care4free.net
website: www.taktent.org.uk
Will provide information on self-help groups in Scotland, including a project for 16-25 year olds. Information, support, newsletter and counselling for anyone affected by cancer.

Takayasu's Arteritis
(See Stuart Strange Trust and Arthritis Care)

Talipes
(Contact Steps)

TAMBA
2 The Willows, Gardner Road, Guildford, Surrey GU1 4PG
☎ 0870 770 3303
Helpline 01732 868 8000 (Mon-Fri, 7pm-11pm, Weekends, 10am-11pm)
🖷 0870 121 4001 / 0151 348 0765
email: enquiries@tamba.org.uk
website: www.tamba.org.uk
Support, information and newsletter for parents of twins, triplets etc. Incorporates several specialist support groups, such as a special needs group, bereavement group etc.

TAR Syndrome Support Group
Little Wings, Whatfield Road, Elmsett, Ipswich, Suffolk IP7 6LS
☎ 01473 657535 (8-9pm)
Support and contacts for parents of children with thrombocytopenia/absent radius syndrome (TAR syndrome).

Tay Sachs Foundation
Mrs J Clare, Lady Sarah Cohen House, Asher Loftus Way, Colney Hatch Lane, London N11 3ND
☎ 020 8920 4144 🖷 020 8920 4419
email: info@jcare.org
Information, screening, fundraising for research. (See also Climb)

Telangiectasia Self-Help Group
Mrs D Lawson, 39 Sunny Croft, Downley, High Wycombe, Bucks HP13 5UQ
☎ 01494 528047
email: info@telangiectasia.co.uk
website: www.telangiectasia.co.uk
Support: self-help: contacts: newsletter

Terminal Conditions in Children
(See ACT; React)

Termination for Foetal Abnormality
(See ARC)

5

Terrence Higgins Trust, The
52-54 Grays Inn Road, London WC1X 8JU
☎ 020 7831 0330
email: info@tht.org.uk
website: www.tht.org.uk
Support and information for people affected by HIV and AIDS and their families.

Testicles/Testes, Congenital Absence of
(See Anorchidism Support Group)

Testicular Cancer
(See SOS)

Testicular Regression/Feminisation Syndrome
(See Anorchidism Support Group)

Thalassaemia Society, UK
19 The Broadway, Southgate Circus, London N14 6PH
☎ 020 8882 0011 ▤ 020 8882 8618
email: office@ukts.org.uk
website: www.ukts.org
Support: contacts: information: newsletter: funding for research (See Sickle Cell and Thalassaemia Centre)

Thomas Coram Foundation for Children
40 Brunswick Square, London WC1N 1AZ
☎ 020 7278 2424 ▤ 020 7837 8084
Offers a wide range of services for children and young people; day care, special needs adoption and fostering, welfare services.

Thomsen's Myotonia, Congenital
(Contact Myotonic Dystrophy Support Group)

Thromboasthenia
(See TAR Syndrome Support Group)

Thrombocytopenia Purpura, Idiopathic
(See ITP Support Association)

Thyroid Eye Disease (TED) Association
'Solstice', Sea Road, Winchelsea Beach, Sussex TN36 4LH
☎ 01797 222338
email: tedassn@eclipse.co.uk
Information, advice and support for people affected by thyroid eye disease. Will provide patients with information and names of hospitals which have an awareness of TED.

Thyroid Foundation, British
P.O. Box 97, Clifford, Wetherby, W. Yorks LS23 6XD
Paediatric (enquiries about children only) contact:
28 Richmond Place, Bath BA1 5PZ
Support and information for people affected by thyroid disorders. Further information on receipt of large SAE.

Tinnitus
Helpline, RNID, 19-23 Featherstone Street, London EZ1Y 8SL
☎ 020 7296 8000
Helpline 0808 808 6666 (voice)
0808 808 0007 (text) ▤ 020 7296 8066
email: tinnitushelpline@btinternet.com
website: www.rnid.org.uk

Tinnitus Association, The British
Ground Floor, Unit 5, Acorn Business Park, Woodseats Close, Sheffield S8 0TB
☎ 0114 2509933
Helpline 0800 018 0527 ▤ 0114 2587059
email: info@tinnitus.org.uk
website: www.tinnitus.org.uk
A self-help organisation for people affected by tinnitus. Quarterly journal, self-help groups throughout the UK, fund-raising for research.

TOFS
St Georges Centre, 91 Victoria Road, Netherfield, Notts NG4 2NN
☎ 0115 961 3092 ▤ 0115 961 3097
email: info@tofs.org.uk
website: www.tofs.org.uk
Information, support and contacts for parents of children with tracheo-oesophageal fistula and/or oesophageal atresia and associated swallowing problems, e.g. gastro-oesophageal reflux, tube feeding etc. Also caters for VATER Association and VACTERL Association.

Tourette Syndrome (UK) Association
P.O. Box 26149, Dunfermline, Fife KY12 9WT
☎ & ▤ 0845 4 581 252 (24 hr voicemail)
email: enquiries@tsa.org.uk
website: www.tsa.org.uk – with a doctor online to answer general questions
Contacts: information: newsletter: bulletins: meetings.

Toxic Shock Syndrome Information Service
P.O. Box 450, Godalming, Surrey GU7 1GR
☎ & ▤ 01483 418561
website: www.tssis.com
Information on recognising, preventing and treating toxic shock syndrome.

Toxocara
(See Community Hygiene Concern)

Tracheo-Oesophageal Fistula
(See TOFS)

Tracheostomy, Aid for Children with
(See ACT)

Transplant Support Network, The
Room 8, Temple Row Centre, 23 Temple Row, Keighley, W. Yorks BD21 2AH
☎ & ▤ 01535 692323
Helpline 01535 210101
email: phatton@tsnet.demon.co.uk
website: www.transplantsupportnetwork.org.uk
Information, advice and support before, during and after organ transplantation.

Transverse Myelitis
(Contact Guillain-Barre Syndrome Support Group)

Treacher-Collins Syndrome Family Support Group
Mrs S Moore, 114 Vincent Road, Thorpe Hamlet, Norwich, Norfolk NR1 4HH
☎ & ▤ 01603 433736
email: neil@treachercollins.net
website: www.treachercollins.net
Support: contacts: information: newsletter

Treats for Sick and Disabled Children
(See Dreams Come True Charity, Make a Wish Foundation, Starlight Children's Foundation)

Tremor Foundation, International
Mrs K Walsh, DSC, Harold Wood Hospital, Gubbins Lane, Romford, Essex RM3 0BE
☎ 01708 370850 ▤ 01708 378032
email: nmec@aol.com

Triple X Syndrome Support Group
Helen Clements, 32 Francemary Road, Brockley, London SE4 1JS
☎ 020 8690 9445
email: helenclements@hotmail.com
website: www.triple-X.org
Support, publications, contacts and information for parents of girls with Triple X syndrome (47XXX syndrome)

Trisomy 13/Trisomy 18
(Contact SOFT UK)

Trisomy 21
(See Down's Syndrome Association; Down's Heart Group)

Tube-Feeding
(Contact TOFS; Half-PINNT; PINNT)

Tuberculosis
(Contact Lung Foundation, British)

Tuberous Sclerosis Association
P.O. Box 9644, Bromsgrove, Worcs B61 0FP
☎ 01527 871898 ▤ 01527 579452
email: support@tuberous-sclerosis.org
website: www.tuberous-sclerosis.org
National organisation, with regional groups. Support: information: contacts: newsletter: conferences: meetings

Tumours of Brain/Spine
(See Brain and Spine Foundation; Brain Tumour Foundation; Brain Tumour Societies)

Turner Syndrome Support Society (UK)
12 Irving Quadrant, Hardgate, Clydebank G81 6A2
☎ 01389 380385 ▤ 01389 380384
email: Turner.syndrome@tss.org.uk
website: www.tss.org.uk/
Support, contacts and information for parents and for women affected by Turner syndrome (X0 syndrome)

Twins Bereavement Group
(See TAMBA)

Twins with Special Needs
(See TAMBA)

Tymes Trust
P.O. Box 4347, Stock, Ingatestone CM4 9TE
☎ 01245 401080 ▤ 01245 401080
email: jane@youngactiononline.com
website: www.youngactiononline.com
Support, advice and information for young people (under 26 years) affected by myalgic encephalomyelitis (ME), specialist education advice for teachers of children with ME/Chronic Fatique Syndrome, from professionals in the medical and educational fields.

Ulcerative Colitis
(See Colitis and Crohn's Disease, National Association for; Crohn's in Childhood Research Association)

Undescended Testes
(See Anorchidism Support Group)

Undiagnosed Children Support Group
(See SWAN)

Unique
P.O. Box 2189, Caterham, Surrey CR3 5GN
☎ 01883 330766 ▤ 01883 330766
email: info@rarechromo.org
website: www.rarechromo.org
Contacts, information and self-help group for parents of children with disabilities and special needs caused by rare chromosomal abnormalities. Newsletter. The Little Yellow Book – a guide to rare chromosome disorders. 24 hour answerphone.

5

Urostomy Association
Buckland, Beaumont Park, Danbury, Essex CM3 4DE
☎ 01245 224294 📠 01245 227569
email: ua@centraloffice.fsnet.co.uk

Urostomy in Children
(See Incontinent and Stoma Children, The Charity for)

Usher Resources
Marylin Kilsby, Usher Services, Sense, 11-13 Clifton Terrace, London N4 3SR
☎ 020 7272 7774 📠 020 7272 3862
email: enquiries@sense.org.uk

Vaccine-Damaged Children, Association of Parents of
78 Campden Road, Shipston-on-Stour CV36 4AP
☎ 01608 661595 📠 01608 663432
Information for parents of children affected by vaccination Send SAE for details. (See Informed Parent; Jabs; Victims of Vaccination Support Group)

VACTERL Association
(See TOFS)

Values into Action
Oxford House, Derbyshire Street, London E2 6HG
☎ 020 7729 5436 📠 020 7729 7797
email: general@viauk.org
website: www.viauk.org
Campaigns for the integration of people with learning difficulties into all aspects of society and aims to improve their quality of life. Publishes books and research reports. Quarterly newsletter for all members.

Vanishing Testes Syndrome
(See Anorchidism Support Group)

Vasculitis
(See Stuart Strange Trust and Arthritis Care)

VATER Association
(See TOFS)

Velo-Cardio-Facial Syndrome (Shprintzen Syndrome)
(See Chromosome 22q11 Group)

Ventilator-Assisted Breathing in Babies
(Contact BLISS)

Vesico-Intestinal Fissure
(Contact GEEPS)

VHL Contact Group
Ms B Stone, 22 Knightstone Close, Kingsbury Episcopi, Martock, Somerset TA12 6BZ
Support: contacts: information. For people affected by von Hippel-Lindau syndrome.

Victims of Medical Accidents
(See Finance and Legal Section)

Victims of Vaccination Support Group
Ms O Price, 27 Malcolm Grove, Rednal, Birmingham B45 9BS
☎ 0121 243 7759 📠 0121 628 1321

Viral Fatigue Syndrome
(Contact ME Organisations)

Vision Aid
106 Junction Road, Bolton, Lancs BL3 4NE
☎ 01204 64265 📠 01204 855937
email: visionaid@charity.vfree.com
An organisation providing help, advice and support to visually impaired children, and their families throughout the UK. Their purpose is to turn initial fears into hope, giving families encouragement and support as they cope with the difficult diagnosis of blindness in their child.

Vitiligo Society
125 Kennington Road, London SE11 6SF
☎ 020 7840 0855
Helpline 0800 018 2631 📠 020 7840 0866
email: all@vitiligosociety.org.uk
website: www.vitiligosociety.org.uk
Support: contacts: information: newsletter: publications

Voice UK
The College Business Centre, Uttoxeter New Road, Derby DE22 3WZ
☎ 01332 519872 📠 01332 521392
email: claranet-voiceuk@clara.net
website: www.voiceuk.claranet
Support and information for adults and children with learning disability who have been abused, their families and carers. Telephone support and information line. National network of parent contact points. Publications. (See Sexuality and Relationships Section)

Voices, Hearing
(See Hearing Voices Network)

Voluntary Organisations, National Council for (NCVO)
Regent's Wharf, 8 All Saints' Street, London N1 9RL
☎ 020 7713 6161 📠 020 7713 6300
email: ncvo@ncvo-vol.org.uk

Von Gierke Disease
(Contact Glycogen Storage Diseases Association)

Von Hippel-Lindau Syndrome
(See VHL Contact Group)

Von Recklinghausen's Disease
(See Neurofibromatosis Association)

Von Willebrand Disease
(Contact Haemophilia Society, The)

Waardenburg Syndrome
(Contact Deaf Children's Society, National)

Waiting List Helpline
(See College of Health)

Walker-Warburg Syndrome
(Contact Lissencephaly Contact Group)

Weaver Syndrome
(Contact Sotos Syndrome Support Group)

Wegener's Granulomatosis
(Contact Stuart Strange Trust and Arthritis Care)

Wellbeing
27 Sussex Place, Regents Park, London NW1 4SP
☎ 020 7722 6400 🖷 020 7724 7725
email: wellbeing@rcog.org.uk
website: www.wellbeing.org.uk
The fundraising and research arm of the Royal College of Obstetritians and Gynaecologists. Funds scientific and medical research throughout the UK into woman's cancers, pregnancy and birth, and quality of life issues such as endometriosis and PCOS.

Werdnig-Hoffman Syndrome
(See Jennifer Trust for Spinal Muscular Atrophy)

West Syndrome Support Group
Mrs E Samuel, 8 Waddon Close, Croydon, Surrey CR0 4JT
☎ 020 8680 8449
Contacts, support and information for parents of children affected by West syndrome (salaam seizures, hypsarrhythmia, jack-knife seizures, infantile spasms with developmental delay).
White Breath-Holding Seizures
(See STARS)

Williams Syndrome Foundation Ltd
161 High Street, Tonbridge, Kent TN9 1BX
☎ 01732 365152 🖷 01732 360178
email: john.nelson-wsfoundation@btinternet.com
website: www.williams-syndrome.org.uk
Support: contacts: information: newsletter: events. Caters for children or adults with a diagnosis of Williams syndrome or congenital infantile hypercalcaemia.

Winchester Syndrome
(Contact MPS Society)

Wiskott-Aldrich Syndrome
(Contact Primary Immunodeficiency Association)

Wolf-Hirschhorn Syndrome Support Group
Mr E Bulmer, 1 Hawthorn Villas, Holmes Chapel, Cheshire CW4 7AR
☎ & 🖷 01634 264816
email: tbulmer147@hotmail.com
website: www.whs.webk.co.uk
Support: contacts: information: newsletter. For parents of children with Wolf-Hirschhorn Syndrome (4p deletion syndrome).

Women's Health
52 Featherstone Street, London EC1Y 8RT
☎ Health Enquiry Line 020 7251 6580
0845 125 5254 🖷 020 250 4152
minicom – 0107 490 5489
email: health@womenshealthlondon.org.uk
website: www.womenshealthlondon.org.uk
Information and support on gynaecological and sexual health issues, including abortion, fibroids, heavy bleeding, HRT, hysterectomy, menopause, pelvic inflammatory disease and premenstrual syndrome. Quaterly newsletter, information leaflets on specific woman's health issues, and series of booklets for women with learning difficulties (currently available: thrush, hysterectomy, problem periods).

Working Parents of Children with Special Needs
(See Parents at Work)

Work-Related Upper Limb Disorder (WRULD)
(See RSI Association)

Worster-Drought Syndrome Support Group
212 Ashcroft Road, Ipswich, Suffolk IP1 6AF
☎ 01473 240761
email: national.contact@wdssg.org.uk
website: www.wdssg.org.uk
Support: contacts: information: newsletter: publications

Wound Care Society
P.O. Box 170, Hartford, Huntingdon, Cambs PE29 1PL
email: woundcare.society@btinternet.com
website: www.wound.care.society.org
Advice on dealing with any type of wound: leg ulcers, pressure sores etc.

5

Xeroderma Pigmentosum Support Group

XP Support Group, 2 Strawberry Close, Prestwood, Great Missenden HP16 0SG

☎ 01494 890981 ▤ 01494 864439

email: info@xpsupport.org.uk

website: www.xpsupportgroup.org.uk

XLH Network

Elpha Green Cottage, Sparty Lea, Allendale, Hexham, Northumberland NE47 9UT

☎ 01434 685047 ▤ 01434 685179

email: info@xlhnetwork.org

website: www.xlhnetwork.org

Support for people affected by x-linked hypophosphataemia and autosomal dominant hypophosphatemic rickets, via their Internet website, by letter and telephone to those who are not online, contacts, information.

X-Linked Hypophosphataemia

(See XLH Network)

X0 Syndrome

(Contact Turner Syndrome Society)

XXX Syndrome

(See Triple X Syndrome Support Group)

XXY Syndrome

(Contact Klinefelter Syndrome Association)

XY Gonadal Dysgenesis

(See AIS Support Group UK)

YoungMinds

2nd Floor, 102-108 Clerkenwell Road, London EC1M 5SA

☎ 020 7336 8445

Parents Information Service 0800 018 2138 (Mon & Fri, 10am-1pm, Tues, Wed & Thurs, 1pm-4pm)

▤ 020 7336 8446

email: enquiries@youngminds.org.uk

website: www.youngminds.org.uk

YoungMinds is the national charity commited to improving the mental health of all children. Services include the Parents' Information Service, a free, confidential telephone helpline offering information and advice to any adult with concerns about the mental health of a child. YoungMinds also offers training and consultancy, information leaflets and booklets for young people and publishes YoungMinds magazine.

Education

ACE Centre Advisory Trust
92 Windmill Road, Headington, Oxford OX3 7DR
☎ 01865 759800 🖷 01865 759810
email: info@ace-centre.org.uk
website: www.ace-centre.org.uk
An independent charity which assesses young people in education with spoken or written communication difficulties and advises on approaches to improving their communication skills using the latest methods. Information on signing systems.

Acorn Educational Ltd
32 Queen Eleanor Road, Geddington, Kettering, Northants NN14 1AY
☎ 01536 400212 🖷 01536 400962
email: acorn-education@compu~lynx.co.uk
website: www.acorneducational.co.uk
Suppliers of educational resources for pre-school and special needs, aids to child development. Catalogue on request.

Advance Housing and Support Ltd
2 Witan Way, Witney, Oxon OX28 6FH
☎ 01993 772885 🖷 01993 700258
Supported housing for people with learning disabilities or mental illness.

Advisory Centre for Education (ACE)
Unit 1C, Aberdeen Studios, 22-24 Highbury Grove, London N5 2DQ
☎ 020 7354 8318
0808 8005793 🖷 020 7354 9069
exclusion line: 020 77049822
email: ace.ed@easynet.co.uk
website: www.ace-ed.org.uk
Educational advice, information and support for parents of children aged 5-16 in maintained schools, including those with special educational needs. Publications: 'Special Education Handbook', 'Going to the SEN Tribunal', 'Special Educational Needs; sources of help'. Regular journal, often containing articles or supplements on special education. Many informative publications. Advice on assessment and statementing

Advisory Unit, The: Computers in Education
126 Great North Road, Hatfield, Herts AL9 5JZ
☎ 01707 266714 🖷 01707 273684
email: sales@advisory-unit.org.uk
website: www.advisory-unit.org.uk/

An independent organisation offering IT services and educational services to schools. Advice to teachers on using computers effectively.

Beyond Words
The BMJ Bookshop, Burton Street, London WC1H 9JR
☎ 020 7383 6244 / 6638 🖷 020 7245 1231 (Royal College of Psychiatry)
or Book sales, Royal College of Psychiatry, 17 Belgrave Square, London SW1X 8PG
A series of books for people with learning disabilities, published by St George's Hospital Medical School and the Royal College of Psychiatry. The series is intended to assist in the counselling of people with learning disabilities. Titles include; 'Going to Court' (for those who may need to attend court as a witness), 'You're Nicked' (for those who have been accused of a crime and are facing police procedures), 'In The Dock' (for those who have been charged or have to appear as a defendant in a court). Details of all further titles on request. (See also Mencap Legal Department)

Blissymbols Communication UK
92 Windmill Road, Headington, Oxford OX3 7DR
☎ 01608 676455
email: nelms@ace-centre.org.uk
Blissymbols uses nine basic shapes to represent 2,500 vocabulary items. Send SAE for details.

Bobath Centre, The
250 East End Road, Finchley, London N2 8AU
☎ 020 8444 3355 🖷 020 8444 3399
email: info@bobath.co.uk
website: www.bobath.org.uk
Assessment and therapy for children with cerebral palsy. Consultation and advice service for parents. Also runs centres in Wales and Scotland.

Books for Children with Special Needs
(See Clearvision Project; National Library for the Blind; Reach)

Boston-Higashi School Parents' Association (BHSPA)
71 Heath Park Road, Romford, Essex RM2 5UL
Boston-Higashi schools cater for children and young adults with autism. Information pack available on receipt of 9x4 SAE plus £1.00 stamps to cover postage.

5

Botton Village
Danby, Whitby, N. Yorks Y021 2NJ
☎ 01287 660871 📠 01287 660888
email: botton@camphill.org.uk
website: web.ukonline.co.uk/members/
botton.village/
A home for over 160 adults with learning disabilities, living in extended families run by houseparents. Run by Camphill Communities.

Brain Injury in Children
(See also Useful addresses: Organisations)

Brain Injured Children, British Institute for
Knowle Hall, Knowle, Bridgwater, Somerset TA7 8PJ
☎ 01278 684060 📠 01278 685573
email: info@bibic.org.uk
website: www.bibic.org.uk
BIBIC is a registered charity founded in 1972. It exists to maximise the potential of children with conditions affecting their sensory, social, communication, motor and learning abilities. Children have an interdisciplinary assessment and depending on their needs they are given an individual theraoy plan that may involve physical, sensory, nutrition, reflexes, social and communication activities. Families and carers are taught how to carry out the activities, how often to do them and why they are important to their child's development.

Brain Injury Rehabilitation and Development, Centre for
5 Lower Brook Street, Ipswich, Suffolk IP4 1AG
☎ 01473 219505 📠 01473 219707
A non-residential treatment charity working with brain-injured children and adults and those who have dyspraxia, dysphasia, hyperactivity etc.

Brainwave Centre for Rehabilitation and Development
Huntworth Gate, Bridgwater, Somerset TA6 6LQ
☎ 01278 429089 📠 01278 429622
email: brainwavetherapy@hotmail.com
website: www.brainwave.org.uk
Private centre, offering therapy for children with brain damage, brain injury or stroke. (See Child Development Centre; Tadworth Court Rehabilitation Service)

Bridget's Trust, The
Tennis Court Road, Cambridge CB2 1QF
☎ 01223 354 312 📠 01223 461324
email: bridgets-admin@lists.cam.ac.uk
website: www.bridgets.org.uk

Provides grants; support and 24-hour care and accommodation for physically disabled students studying in Cambridge.

British Sign Language Training
(See CACDP)

CACDP (Council for the Advancement of Communication with Deaf People)
Durham University Science Park, Block 4, Stockton Road, Durham DH1 3UZ
☎ 0191 383 1155 📠 0191 383 7914
email: durham@cacdp.demon.co.uk
website: www.cacdp.demon.co.uk
Promotes communication between deaf and hearing people, offers training and recognised examinations in British Sign Language and other forms of communication used by deaf people. Produces Directory of Sign Language Interpreters, Directory of Lipspeakers, Directory of Interpreters for Deaf/Blind People, Directory of Speech to Text Interpreters.

Camphill Communities
19 South Road, Stourbridge, West Midlands DY8 3YA
☎ 01384 441505 📠 01384 372122
email: info@camphill.org.uk
website: www.camphill.org.uk
Villages, run on community lines, for adolescents and adults with learning difficulty. The emphasis is on interdependence. Based on Rudolf Steiner philosophy. Communities in Hertfordshire, Yorkshire, Gloucestershire, W. Midlands, Scotland, Ireland and Wales.

Capability Scotland
ASCS, 11 Ellersly Road, Edinburgh EH12 6HY
☎ 0131 313 5510 📠 0131 346 1681
email: ascs@capability-scotland.org.uk
Provides education services and schools, accommodation, therapy, day and employment centres, social services, advice and information for children and adults with disabilities.

CARE (Cottage and Rural Enterprise Ltd)
9 Weir Road, Kibworth, Leicester LE8 0LQ
☎ 0116 279 3225 📠 0116 279 6384
email: carecentral@freeuk.com
website: www.care-ltd.co.uk
A national charity that responds to the changing needs of people with learning disabilities. It offers a range of residential accomodation, group and independent living options, a choice of meaningful daytime workshop activities, accredited training and supported employment opportunities.

Carematch (Residential Care Computer Service)
(See Disability Care Register)
286 Camden Road, London N7 0BJ
☎ 0171 609 9966
A computerised database offering physically disabled people information about suitable residential care, counselling and advice about alternatives. Fee £20.00 for outside London.

Caresearch
(See Residential Care, The Association for)

Caring and Sharing Trust
Cotton's Farmhouse, Whiston Road, Cogenhoe, Northants NN7 1NL
☎ 01604 891487 🖨 01604 890405
Day Care Centre for people with learning disabilities using drama, music and art therapies as a form of therapy.

Caspari Foundation for Educational Therapy and Therapeutic Teaching, The
Caspari House, 1 Noel Road, Islington, London N1 8HQ
☎ 020 7704 1977 🖨 020 7704 783
email: administrator@casparihouse.fsnet.co.uk
website: www.caspari.org.uk
Formerly FAETT (Forum for the Advancement of Educational Therapy and Therapeutic Teaching. Advice for parents and teachers on the emotional factors in learning and failure to learn. Provides contacts, information, publications, journals and runs regular training events

Centre for Studies on Inclusive Education
(See CSIE)

Cerebral Palsy
(See Bobath Centre; Scope; Scottish Centre for Children with Motor Impairments)

Cheshire Foundation Housing Association
The Coach House, Gresham Road, Staines, Middlesex TW18 2AE
☎ 01784 490910 🖨 01784 490510
email: info@cfha.demon.co.uk
Supplies housing for people with physical disabilities, learning disabilities or who are recovering from a mental illness, with care and support.

Child Development, St Briavels Centre for
St Briavels, Dixton Road, Monmouth, Gwent NP25 3PR
☎ 01600 713822 🖨 01600 715663
email: info@stbriavels.org
website: www.stbriavels.org

Private centre which offers assessment of children with any kind of learning disability and/or physical disability and provides a home treatment programme. Parents are taught how to carry out the therapy at home.(See Brainwave Centre for Rehabilitation and Development; Brain Injured Children, British Institute for; Tadworth Court Rehabilitation Service)

Children's Hospice Association, Scotland (CHAS)
18 Hanover Street, Edinburgh EH2 2EN
☎ 0131 226 4933 🖨 0131 220 1626
website: www.chas.org.uk
Rachel House in Kinross offers respite and terminal care, both in the hospice and at home, for children with life-threatening and life-shortening conditions and provides care and support for the whole family.

Children's Hospices, Association of
Kings House, 14 Orchard Street, Bristol BS1 5EH
☎ 0117 905 5082 🖨 0117 905 3340
email: info@childhospice.org.uk
website: www.childhospice.org.uk
An umbrella group, bringing together children's hospice services in the UK. There are now hospices operating in most areas of the UK. Details and addresses of all current hospice services is available from the Association. Links to all member hospices are listed on the Association's website. (See Zoe's Place Baby Hospice)

Children's Residential Care Unit
National Children's Bureau, 8 Wakley Street, London EC1V 7QE
☎ 020 7843 6090 🖨 020 7278 9512
email: membership@ncb.org.uk
website: www.ncb.org.uk
Specialist information service on residential care for children.

Children's Society, The
Edward Rudolf House, Margery Street, London WC1X 0JL
☎ 020 7841 4436 🖨 020 7841 4500
email: info@childrenssociety.org.uk
website: www.the-childrens-society.org.uk/
Residential facilities, fostering, adoption.

Clearvision Project
Linden Lodge School, 61 Princes Way, London SW19 6JB
☎ 020 8789 9575
website: www.clearvisionproject.org
Nationwide postal lending library of children's books for braille and print readers to share. Free service to families, fees charged to schools, libraries etc.

5

Communication in Education, Aids to
(See ACE Centre Advisory Trust)

Computers/Computer Software/Technology
(See Aids and Equipment Section)

Computers in Education
(See Advisory Unit: Computers in Education)

Conductive Education
(See Peto Andras Institute; Scottish Centre for Children with Motor Impairments)

Conductive Education, The Foundation for
Cannon Hill House, Russell Road, Moseley, Birmingham B13 8RD
☎ 0121 449 1569 🖷 0121 449 1611
email: foundation@conductive-education.org.uk
website: www.conductive-education.org.uk
The Foundation for Conductive Education is a national charity established in 1986 to develop and advance the science and skill of Conductive Education in the UK. The National Institute of Conductive Education was created by the Foundation in 1995 to provide a centre of excellence for the development of this approach. The National Institute of Conductive Education provides direct services to children and adults with motor disabilities; cerebral palsy, multiple sclerosis, Parkinson's disease, children with dyspraxia and those who have suffered strokes and head injuries. Through a system of positive teaching, learning support, Conductive Education maximises their control over bodily movement in ways that are relevant to daily living. The National Institute also undertakes research and offers a comprehensive range of professionally orientated, skills-based training courses at all levels. Covers UK and overseas.

Cope Directory of Post-16 Residential Education and Training
Lifetime Careers Publishing, 7 Ascot Road, White Horse Business Park, Trowbridge, Wilts BA14 0XA
☎ 01225 716023 🖷 01225 716025
email: sales@lifetimecareers.wiltshire.co.uk
website: www.lifetime-publishing.co.uk
Produces 'Compendium of Post-16 Residential Education and Training for Young People with Special Needs'. Price £24.95 plus postage and packing.

Craighalbert Centre
(See Scottish Centre for Children with Motor Impairments)

Crypt Foundation, The
(Now Living Options)

CSIE (Centre for Studies on Inclusive Education)
1 Redland Close, Elm Lane, Redland, Bristol BS6 6UE
☎ 0117 923 8450 🖷 0117 923 8460
website: inclusion.uwe.ac.uk/csie/csiehome.htm
Research, studies, publications on the integration of children with special needs into ordinary schools. Advice on assessment, statementing, appeals. (See Network 81; Parents for Inclusion)

Cued Speech Association UK
Corner House, Bay View, Stoke Fleming, Dartmouth, Devon TQ6 0QX
☎ 01803 770944 🖷 01803 770946
email: info@cuedspeech.co.uk
website: www.cuedspeech.co.uk
Cued Speech is a simple sound-based system which uses eight handshapes in four positions near the mouth to clarify the lip patterns of normal speech as to make spoken language clear to deaf and hearing-impaired people.

Deaf People, Council for the Advancement of Communication with
(See CACDP)

Department for Education and Skills
Sanctuary Buildings, Great Smith Street, London SW1P 3BT
☎ 0870 000 2288 (general enquiries)
🖷 01928 794248
email: info@dfes.gov.uk
www.dfes.gov.uk

Department for Education and Skills Publications Centre
☎ 0845 602 2260
Publishes 'Special Educational Needs – a Guide for Parents' and 'Code of Practice on the Identification and Assessment of Special Educational Needs'.

Diplomatic Service Families and Special Needs
(See DSFA, Useful addresses: Organisations)

Directory of Social Change (DSC)
24 Stephenson Way, London NW1 2DP
☎ 020 7391 4800 🖷 020 7931 4808
email: info@dsc.org.uk
website: www.dsc.org.uk
Publishes directories and guides, including; 'Guide to Grants for Individuals in Need', the 'Educational Grants Directory' and the 'Schools funding Guide'. See website for more information on these and other titles.

Disability Care Register

Care Choices Ltd, Valley Court, Croydon, Nr Royston, Herts SG8 0HF

☎ 01223 207770 / 0800 3892077

0800 3892077 📠 01223 207108

email: careselect@carechoices.co.uk

Care Choices Ltd is a leading publisher of care information in the UK. The Disability Care Register (DCR) is a comprehensive database of residential, nursing and day registered accommodation for adults with disabilities. The DCR is a FREE service and will provide a short list of suitable care providers within 24 hours, free of charge and without obligation. (See also Carematch, Residential Care, Computer Service)

Disability, Northern Ireland Council on

Disability Action, 2 Annadale Avenue, Belfast BT7 3JH

☎ 028 9029 7880 📠 028 9049 1627

email: hq@disabilityaction.org

website: www.disabilityaction.org

Information on all aspects of disability, including employment, training and housing.

Duke of Edinburgh's Award Scheme

Gulliver House, Madeira Walk, Windsor, Berks SL4 1EU

☎ 01753 727400

email: info@theaward.org

website: www.theaward.org

Education of Sick Children

(See National Association for the Education of Sick Children)

Education Otherwise

P.O. Box 7420, London N9 9SG

0870 7300074

email: enquiries@education-otherwise.org

website: www.education-otherwise.org

A national charity providing information and support for home educating families. Run entirely by volunteers with specialist help available in many areas including the withdrawal of children with special educational needs from school, into home education. Advice and support for children suffering from school phobia and their families. Contact list, newsletter, local groups and publications also available.

Educational Grants

(See Directory of Social Change; Higher Education Funding Council, Scotland; Family Welfare Association; Learning and Skills Council; Snowdon Award Scheme; Open University; Skill; Wentwood Education Trust)

Educational Software/Technology

(See Aids and Equipment Section)

Educational Therapy and Therapeutic Teaching, Forum for the Advancement of

(See Caspari Foundation)

Electronic Equipment and Aids

(See Aids and Equipment Section)

Elizabeth Fitzroy Support

Steve Jenkin, Caxton House, Lower Street, Haslemere, Surrey GU27 2PE

☎ 01428 656766 📠 01428 643262

Support for people with profound learning disabilities and any associated physical disabilities. Day services for students and non-residents who may have lesser learning disabilities.

Employment for People with Disabilities

(See Shaw Trust; Mencap Pathway Employment Service; Remploy; Queen Elizabeth's Foundation for Disabled People; Lifetime Careers Publishing; RADAR)

Employment Opportunities for People with Disabilities

123 Minories, London EC3N 1NT

☎ 020 7481 2727 📠 020 7481 9797

email: eopps.ho@care4free.net

website: www.opportunities.org.uk

Advice to people with disabilities on; preparing a CV, interview guidance and preparation, assistance with job applications, advice on related skills and ongoing support. Help and advice offered to employers who require information for their recruitment needs. (See Mencap Pathway Employment Service; Shaw Trust)

ENHAM Village Centre

Enham Place, Enham Alamein, Andover, Hants SP11 6JS

☎ 01264 345800 📠 01264 333638

email: learning@enham.co.uk

website: www.enham.org.uk

Provides vocational assessment training, rehabilitation housing care for people with disabilities.

Epilepsy in Young People

(See National Centre for Young People with Epilepsy)

Epilepsy Association, British (Epilepsy Action)

Gate Way Drive, Yeadon, Leeds LS19 7XY

☎ 0113 210 8800

Helpline 0808 800 5050 (Mon-Thurs 9am-4.30pm, Fri 9am-4pm) 📠 0113 242 8804

email: epilepsy@bea.org.uk

website: www.epilepsy.org.uk

5

Local and regional branches, support, information, publications, assessment, training, employment etc.

Family Based Respite Care, National Association for
(See Shared Care Network)

Family Investment Limited
Parkview, Derringstone Hill, Barham, Nr Canterbury, Kent CT4 6QB
Helps families to come together to invest in a group home, so that their relatives can be provided with a place in that home, when necessary.

Family Welfare Association Educational Grants Advisory Service
501-505 Kingsland Road, London E8 4AU
☎ 020 7254 6251 ▤ 020 7249 5443
Advice on non-statutory sources of funding. Publishes 'Money for Study'.

Forum for the Advancement of Educational Therapy and Therapeutic Teaching (FAETT)
(Now The Caspari Foundation)

Fostering and Adoption Organisations
(See Organisations Section)

Funding for Education
(See Educational Grants)

Further Education for Special Needs
(See Cope Directory of Post-16 Residential Education and Training)

Further Education Funding Council
(Now Learning and Skills Council)

Gabbitas Educational Consultants
Carrington House, 126-130 Regent Street, London W1R 6EE
☎ 020 7734 0161 ▤ 020 7437 1764
email: admin@gabbitas.co.uk
website: www.gabbitas.co.uk
Advisory service for parents and students on all aspects of education, including special needs provision. Private service, so fees are charged. Further information and details of charges on request. (See Schools for Special Needs, Gabbitas Guide to)

Gifted Children, National Association for (NACE)
Elder House, Milton Keynes, Bucks MK9 1LR
☎ 01908 673677 ▤ 01908 673679
email: nagc@rmplc.co.uk
website: www.nagc.org
Support and advice for parents, teachers and other professionals concerned with the development of gifted children. Telephone helpline, counselling service.

Head Injury
(See Useful addresses: Organisations)

Hearing and Speech Centre, Nuffield
Royal National Throat, Nose and Ear Hospital, Grays Inn Road, London WC1X 8DA
☎ 020 7915 1300
Deals with the diagnosis of all hearing problems, balance problems, speech and language difficulties, particularly dyspraxia, phonological or central processing problems. Also has an interest in specific learning disabilities, such as dyslexia.

Hereward College
Bramston Crescent, Tile Hill Lane, Coventry CV4 9SW
☎ 01247 646 1231 ▤ 01203 694305
email: enquiries@hereward.ac.uk
A national integrated college where residential and day students with physical and sensory disabilities together with non-disabled students, have access to equal opportunities, regardless of disability. In addition to a wide range of academic courses, the college provides physiotherapy, speech therapy, conductive education and a 24-hour medical and enabling service.

Hesley Group, The
The Coach House, Hesley Hall, Tickhill, Doncaster DN11 9HH
☎ 01302 866906 ▤ 01302 865473
email: enquiries@hesleygroup.co.uk
website: www.hesleygroup.co.uk
Runs seven residential schools and three residential colleges in the UK for children and young adults who have emotional, behavioural or complex learning difficulties, challenging behaviour, autism and Asperger syndrome. Also funds an information and advice service for parents, OAASIS.

Higher Education Funding Council, Scotland
Donaldson House, 97 Haymarket Terrace, Edinburgh EH12 5HD
☎ 0131 313 6500 ▤ 0131 313 6501
email: info@shefc.ac.uk

Home Farm Trust
Merchants House, Wapping Road, Bristol BS1 4RW
☎ 0117 927 3746 ▤ 0117 922 5938
email: marketing@hft.org.uk
website: www.hft.org.uk
Homes, care and individual service for people with learning disabilities. Residential and day services, carer support service. Emphasis on independence and freedom of choice for residents.

Home Teaching
(See Education Otherwise)

Horticultural Therapy
(See Leisure Section)

Hospices, Children's
(See Children's Hospices Association: Zoe's Place Baby Hospice)

ICAC (Initiative on Communication Aids for Children)
(See Aids and Equipment Section)

ICAN (Invalid Children's Aid Nationwide)
4 Dyers Buildings, Holborn, London EC1N 2QP
☎ 0870 010 4066 📠 0870 010 4067
email: info@ican.org.uk
website: www.ican.org.uk
Schools for children with speech and communication problems in Nottingham, Surrey and Sussex. Advisory and support services.

Inclusive Education
(See CSIE)

Independent Panel for Special Education Advice
(See IPSEA)

Information Technology
(See Aids and Equipment Section)

Integration in Education
(See CSIE; Network 81; Parents for Inclusion)

Interpreters for Deaf and Deaf/Blind People, Directory of
(See CACDP)

IPSEA (Independent Panel for Education Advice)
6 Carlow Mews, Woodbridge, Suffolk IP12 1EA
☎ 01394 382814
Advice Line 0800 018 4016
website: www.ipsea.org.uk
Independent advice and support for parents whose children have special educational needs. Free service.

Language of Sign Used as an Educational Resource
(See LASER)

L'Arche Ltd
10 Briggate, Silsden, Keighley, W. Yorks BD20 9JT
☎ 01535 656186 📠 01535 656426
email: info@larche.org.uk
website: www.larche.org.uk

Runs residential communities for adults who have learning disabilities.

LASER (Language of Sign Used as an Educational Resource)
8 Church Lane, Kimpton, Hitchin, Herts SG4 8RP
☎ 01438 832676 Minicom 01438 832676
📠 01438 833699
email: laser@adept@nildram.co.uk
Promotes the use of British Sign Language/English in the education of deaf children. Workshops for parents, teachers and researchers into bilingualism. Information on request.

Learning and Skills Council
Cheylesmore House, Quinton Road, Coventry, Warks CV1 2WT
☎ 0845 019 4170 📠 024 7682 3695
email: info@lsc.gov.uk
website: www.lsc.gov.uk

Learning Difficulties Helpline
Rathbone C.I., 4th Floor, Churchgate House, 56 Oxford Street, Manchester M1 6EU
☎ 0161 236 5358 📠 0161 236 4539
email: ldh@rathbone-ci.co.uk
website: www.rathbone-ci.co.uk
Advice on special educational needs, assessment, statementing, appeals for parents and carers. Provides information on various difficulties and the school-based stages.

Learning Through Landscapes
3rd Floor, Southside Offices, The Law Courts, Winchester, Hants SO23 9DL
☎ 01962 846258 📠 01962 896099
email: schoolgrounds-uk@ltl.org.uk
website: www.ltl.org.uk
A national charity dedicated to helping schools improve their grounds for the benefit of their children, providing a learning resource and influencing pupils' attitudes and behaviour. Information and advice on all aspects of school grounds, training events and conferences, research into good practice, publications, videos

Legal Advice for Tribunals/Exclusion Disputes
(See Finance, Benefits, Legal Advice Section)

Leonard Cheshire
Central Office, 30 Millbank, London SW1P 4QD
☎ 020 78028200 📠 020 78028250
email: info@london.leonard-cheshire.org.uk
website: www.leonard-cheshire.org.uk
Residential and nursing homes, care at home services. Entry to residential homes limited to 18-65 years, care at home provided to any age.

5

Letterbox Library
71-73 Allen Road, Stoke Newington, London N16 8RY
☎ 020 7503 4801 🖷 020 7503 4800
email: info@letterboxlibrary.com
website: www.letterboxlibrary.com
Publishes books to help children deal with loss, bullying, a new baby or death in the family and books which show positive images of children with disabilities and children from different cultures. Details of titles on request.

Library Association, The
7 Ridgemount Street, London WC1E 7AE
☎ 020 2550 0561 🖷 020 7255 0501
email: info@la-hq.org.uk
website: www.la-hq.org.uk
Information and guides to large print publications, reading aids, talking books, tape services.

Library for the Blind
(See National Library for the Blind)

Lifetime Careers Publishing
Biblios PDS Ltd, Star Road, Partridge Green, West Sussex RH13 8LD
☎ 01403 710851 🖷 01403 711143
Publishes careers resources for young people with special needs, including 'I Can' – a resource to help students learn new skills and how they relate to the world of work and 'If I Were' – a practical introduction to jobs with few or no qualifications. Details of other publications on request.

Linkage Community Trust Specialist Residential FE College
Toynton Hall, Toynton All Saints, Spilsby, Lincs PE23 5AE
☎ 01790 752499 🖷 01790 754058
A Linkage Special Residential College. Residential further education courses for people with learning disabilities, including students with also have sight or hearing impairment, epilepsy, or mobility problems. Age of intake 16 years to mid 20's.

Lipspeakers, Directory of
(See CACDP)

Listening Books
12 Lant Street, London SE1 1QH
☎ 020 7407 9417 🖷 020 7403 1377
email: info@listening-books.org.uk
website: www.listening-books.org.uk
Audio book service for people who have difficulty with reading, whether through a physical disability or injury, sight problems or learning difficulty, including

dyslexia. Based on a lending library system; tapes are sent out and returned by post and postage is free. Subscription fee charged.

Living Options
Kimbridge House, Kimbridge Road, East Wittering, Chichester, Sussex PO20 8PE
☎ 01243 671865 🖷 01243 671865
Formerly The Crypt Foundation. Runs small group homes for people with physical disabilities, aged 18-30 years.

Lodge Trust
The Lodge, Main Street, Market Overton, Oakham, Leics LE15 7PL
☎ 01572 767234 🖷 01572 767503
website: www.lodgetrust.org.uk
Residential home and work training for adults with learning disabilities based on Christian principles.

MacIntyre Care
602 South Seventh Street, Milton Keynes, Bucks MK9 2JA
☎ 01908 230100 🖷 01908 695643
email: admin@macintyre-care.org.uk
website: www.macintyre-care.org
Two residential schools, providing 24-hour, 52 weeks a year education and support for children with complex learning disabilities.

Makaton Vocabulary Development Project
31 Firwood Drive, Camberley, Surrey GU15 3QD
☎ 01276 61390 🖷 01276 681368
email: mvdp@makaton.org
website: www.makaton.org
Information, training in the use of Makaton sign language with non-communicating children.

Martha Trust Hereford Ltd
Hampton Green, Old Eign Hill, Hereford HR1 1UB
☎ 01432 279314 🖷 01432 271585
email: disabled@martha-trust-hereford.org.uk
website: www.martha-trust-hereford.org.uk
Lifelong and respite care for children with physical disabilities plus learning disabilities and are non-ambulant. Therapy facilities for children with lesser disabilities.

Mencap Access Project (Employment)
Mencap National Centre, 123 Golden Lane, London EC1Y 0RT
☎ 020 7454 0454 🖷 020 7608 3254
email: help@mencap.org.uk
website: www.mencap.org.uk
Aims to provide people with learning disabilities with the opportunity to undertake employment, accredited training and community activities.

Mencap Homes Foundation
An organisation which aims to provide appropriate housing for people with learning disabilities. Contact Mencap for details.

Mencap Pathway Employment Service
Mencap National Centre, 123 Golden Lane, London EC1Y 0RT
☎ 020 7454 0454 🖷 020 7608 3254
email: help@mencap.org.uk
website: www.mencap.org.uk
Aims to place people with learning difficulty into jobs in industry, commerce, local government etc. The employer is reimbursed with the employee's wages during an initial training and settling in period. A fellow worker, carefully chosen, is designated to keep an eye on the trainee. Scheme operating in several areas. Details on request.

Mencap PIMD Section
Beverley Dawkins, National Officer (PIMD), Mencap National Centre, 123 Golden Lane, London EC1Y 0RT
☎ 020 7454 0454 🖷 020 7696 6930
email: beverley.dawkins@mencap.org.uk
website: www.mencap.org.uk
Information and advice for parents, carers and professionals involved in the care of people who have profound intellectual and multiple disabilities. Runs seminars and workshops for parents and carers, teaching play techniques, art, music and movement, aromatherapy, massage, beauty therapy, sensory therapy. Runs summer playschemes. Publishes resource packs on communication and feeding, dental care and healthy eating, physical management, challenging behaviour, leisure and benefits and allowances. (See PAMIS)

Montessori Centre, London
18 Balderton Street, London W1K 6TG
☎ 020 7493 0165 🖷 020 7629 7808
email: information@montessori.ac.uk
website: www.montessori.ac.uk
Courses in special needs education for teachers, health care workers and parents.

MOVE (Movement Opportunities in Education)
MOVE International (Europe), Centre for Educational Development, University of Wolverhampton, Gorwy Road, Walsall, W. Midlands WS1 3BD
☎ 01922 323066 🖷 01922 322858
email: move-europe@compuserve.com
website: www.wlv.ac.uk/sed/move/

The MOVE programme aims to provide mobility for people who have difficulty with sitting, standing and walking for use in schools, centres and at home. Runs training courses for teachers, conferences, newsletter.

Music Therapy
(See Leisure Section)

National Association for the Education of Sick Children
Regus House, Herald Way, Pegasus Business Park, Castle Donington DE74 2TZ
☎ 01332 638 586 🖷 01332 638206
email: naescl@aol.com
website: www.sickchildren.org.uk

National Centre for Young People with Epilepsy (formerly St Piers)
St Piers Lane, Lingfield, Surrey RH7 6PW
☎ 01342 832243 🖷 01342 834639
website: www.ncype.org.uk
NCYPE is the main provider of specialised services for young people with epilepsy. NCYPE admits students who do not have epilepsy but would benefit from the services offered. The centre offers St Piers school, St Piers Further Education College, residential accommodation, 24 hour medical centre, assessment service and resource centre.

National Children's Homes
(See NCH)

National Extension College
The Michael Young Centre, Purbeck Road, Cambridge CB2 2HN
☎ 01223 450200 🖷 01223 400399
email: info@nec.ac.uk
website: www.nec.ac.uk
Courses for home study. Grants, pre-enrolment guidance, tutor and post-enrolment support for people with disabilities, over the age of 16.

National Library for the Blind
Far Cromwell Road, Bredbury, Stockport, Cheshire SK6 2SG
☎ 0161 355 2000
0161 355 2000 🖷 0161 355 2098
minicom – 0161 355 2043
email: enquiries@nlbuk.org
website: www.nlbuk.org
NLB provides a wide range of information services for visually impaired people. Services include Braille and Moon lending library service and electronic library and information services. NLB also works to promote access for visually impaired people to 'mainstream' library and information services.

5

National Specialist Colleges (NATSPEC)
110 Vicarage Street, Langley, Old Bury B68 8JS
☎ & 🖷 0121 544 9003
email: h4tchriswberry@supanet.com
website: www.natspec.org.uk
Aims to promote opportunities for high quality further education in residential and day settings, for students with learning difficulties or disabilities. Produces a Directory of National Specialist Colleges.

NCH (National Children's Homes)
85 Highbury Park, London N5 1UD
☎ 020 7704 7000 🖷 020 7226 2537
website: www.nch.org.uk
Residential schools for children who have a physical disability and/or learning difficulty. Details on request.

Network 81
1-7 Woodfield Terrace, Stanstead, Essex CM24 8AJ
Advice Line 0870 770 3306 (10am-2pm Mon-Fri)
🖷 0870 770 3263
Advice and information on the integration of children with special needs into ordinary schools. (See CSIE; Parents for Inclusion)

Norwood Ravenswood
Broadway House, 80-82 The Broadway, Stanmore, Middlesex HA7 4HB
☎ 020 8954 4555 🖷 020 8420 6800
email: norwoodravenswood@nwrw.org
website: www.nwrw.org
Long term and short term residential facilities for people with learning disabilities in Berkshire and London. Community welfare service, youth services, training and hospital visiting schemes.

OAASIS
Brock House, Grigg Lane, Brockenhurst, Hants SO42 7RE
Helpline: 09068 633201
email: oaasis@hesleygroup.co.uk
website: www.oaasis.co.uk
Educational advice and publications on attention deficit/hyperactivity disorder, Asperger syndrome, autism, dyspraxia, Tourette syndrome. Part of The Hesley Group.

Open College of the Arts
Unit 1B, Redbrook Business Park, Wilthorpe Road, Barnsley, S. Yorks S75 1JN
☎ 01226 730495 🖷 01226 730838
email: open.arts@ukonline.co.uk
website: www.oca-uk.com
Wide range of arts courses for home study. Guide to courses on request.

Open University, The
P.O. Box 724, Milton Keynes MK7 6ZS
☎ 01908 274066 🖷 01908 653744
email: general-enquiries@open.ac.uk
website: www.open.ac.uk
Provides many facilities for students with disabilities, including special study resources, interpreters and local-based teaching staff.

Outdoor Education Centres/Courses
(See Holidays, Travel, Mobility Section)

Outdoor Learning, Institute of
12 St Andrew's Churchyard, Penrith, Cumbria CA11 7YE
☎ 01768 891065 🖷 01768 891914
email: institute@outdoor-learning.org
website: www.outdoor-learning.org
Support, develops and promotes the achievement of learning through purposeful and planned outdoor experiences. Information, publications, including 'Outdoor Education and Special Educational Needs'.

Paget-Gorman Society
2 Downland Bungalows, Dowland Lane, Smallfield, Horley, Surrey RH6 9SD
☎ 0134 284 2308
email: PruP@compuserve.com
website: www.pgss.org
A specifically generated language with topic based signs.

PAMIS (Profound and Multiple Impairment Service)
White Top Research Unit, Frankland Building, The University, Dundee DD1 4HN
☎ 01382 345154 🖷 01382 227464
email: pamis@dundee.ac.uk
website: www.pamis.gov.uk
A UK-wide organisation concerned with the needs of people with profound learning disabilities, sometimes combined with physical disabilities or sensory impairment. Information, training for parents and professionals. (See Mencap PIMD Section)

Papworth Trust
Papworth Everard, Cambridge CB3 8RG
☎ 01480 830341 🖷 01480 830781
email: info@papworth.org.uk
website: www.papworth.org.uk
Assessment, residential care, employment, training, support housing for people with physical disabilities.

Parents for Inclusion
Unit 2, Ground Floor, 70 South Lambeth Road, London SW8 1RL
Helpline 020 7582 5008 (Mon, Tues, Wed 10am-12pm, 1-3pm)

☎ 020 7735 7735 (admin) 🖷 020 7735 3828
email: info@parentsforinclusion.org
website: www.parentsforinclusion.org
Information and advice on assessment and statementing procedures and any issue relevant to special educational needs. (See CSIE; Network 81)

Pathway Employment Service
(See Mencap Pathway Employment Service)

Pengwern College of Further Education
Rhuddlan, Near Rhyl, Denbighshire LL18 5UH
☎ 01745 590281 🖷 01745 591736
email: jeff@halljw.demon.co.uk
website: lineone.net/~lufton.manor/pengwern
One of three residential and day further education colleges run by Mencap. For details of other establishments, contact Mencap. (Organisations Section)

Peto Andras Institute
c/o Scope, 6 Market Road, London N7 9PW
☎ 020 7619 7100
Helpline 0808 800 3333 (weekdays 9am-9pm, weekends 2pm-6pm) 🖷 020 7619 7399
email: cphelpline@scope.org.uk
website: www.scope.org.uk
Offers assessments by trained conductors to children with cerebral palsy, aged 6 months to 14 years. Wide range of services.

Playgroups
(See Pre-School Learning Alliance)

Portage Association, National
P.O. Box 3075, Yeovil, Somerset BA21 3FB
☎ & 🖷 01935 71641
email: npa@portageuk.freeserve.co.uk
website: www.portage.org.uk
Will provide details of local schemes on request. Portage provides teams of advisers who work with parents of children with disabilities, of pre-school age, in their own home.

Post-16 Residential Education and Training
(See Cope Directory)

Pre-school Learning Alliance
69 Kings Cross Road, London WC1X 9LL
☎ 020 7833 0991 🖷 020 837 4942
email: pla@pre-school.org.uk
website: www.pre-school.org.uk
An educational charity, providing education and care to children under five, including those with special educational needs. Training workshops and courses on special educational needs.

Profound Intellectual and Multiple Disabilities
(See Mencap PIMD Section; PAMIS)

Queen Elizabeth's Foundation for Disabled People
Leatherhead Court, Leatherhead, Surrey KT22 0BN
☎ 01372 841100 🖷 01372 844657
email: tony.richins@qefd.org
website: www.qefd.org
Training College for people with disabilities to achieve employment. Publishes 'Directory of Opportunities for School-Leavers with Disabilities'. Details on request.

RADAR (Royal Association for Disability and Rehabilitation)
12 City Forum, 250 City Road, London EC1V 8AF
☎ 020 7250 3222 🖷 020 7250 0212
email: radar@radar.org.uk
website: www.radar.org.uk
Advice on education, training, rehabilitation, employment. Publications and directories on all aspects of living with a disability.

Rathbone Training
4th Floor, Churchgate House, 56 Oxford Street, Manchester M1 6LU
☎ 0161 238 6327
0800 917 6790 / (Asian) – 0800 085 4528
🖷 0161 238 6356
email: advice@rathbonetraining.co.uk
website: www.rathbonetraining.co.uk
Free, impartial and confidential advice and information to parents/carers of children with special educational needs, helping them to gain for their children education appropriate to their potential.

Ravenswood Foundation
(Now Norwood Ravenswood)

Reach Resource Centre (National Advisory Centre for Children with Reading Difficulties)
California Country Park, Nine Mile Ride, Finchampstead, Herts RG40 4HT
☎ 0118 973 7575
email: webmaster@reach-reading.demon.co.uk
website: www.reach-reading.demon.co.uk
A national resource centre for children with reading difficulties. Reference library and advisory service for anyone who cares for or educates a child whose disability affects his or her ability to read books. Holds over 5000 children's books and 1000 reference books, computer software, audio-visual material etc. Enquiries can be made by letter, telephone or personal visit. Families welcome.

5

Remploy Ltd

415 Edgware Road, Cricklewood, London NW2 6LR

☎ 020 8235 0500 🖹 020 8235 0576

website: www.remploy.co.uk

Sheltered workshops in many areas, for people with any kind of disability. Developing joint employment models for training and integrating disabled people into the labour market.

Rescare

Rayner House, 23 Higher Hillgate, Stockport, Cheshire SK1 3ER

☎ 0161 474 7323 🖹 0161 480 3668

email: office@rescare.org.uk

website: www.rescare.org.uk

An organisation run by families which works for the relief and welfare of people with learning disabilities in all types of residential care, including the family home.

Residential Care, The Association for (ARC)

ARC House, Marsden Street, Chesterfield, Derbyshire S40 1JY

☎ 01246 555043/44 🖹 01246 555045

An umbrella agency which brings together those who provide residential and day services for people with a learning disability. Runs a Caresearch service to provide information on vacancies in residential accommodation for children and adults with special needs (search fee charged). See Carematch (Residential Care Computer Service)

Residential Care, The Association for (Scotland)

ARC Scotland, Eric Liddell Centre, 15 Morningside Road, Edinburgh EH10 4DP

☎ 0131 446 0880 🖹 0131 446 3340

email: arc.scotland@arcuk.org.uk

website: www.arcuk.org.uk

Respite Care

(See Shared Care Network)

RNIB Customer Services

P.O. Box 173, Peterborough, Cambs PE2 6WS

☎ 0845 702 3153 🖹 01733 371555

email: cservices@rnib.org.uk

website: www.rnib.org.uk

Information resource centre and suppliers of publications, aids and equipment, games, library services, tape and publishing services for visually impaired people.

RNIB Education and Employment Service

105 Judd St, London WC1H 9NE

☎ 020 7388 1266 🖹 020 7388 2034

Helpline: 0845 766 9999

email: helpline@rnib.org.uk

website: www.rnib.org.uk

Services in all areas of the UK; pre-16 and post-16 services, schools and educational advisory services, colleges, courses, employment.

RNIB Housing Service

Christine Petch, Garrow House, 190 Kensal Road, North Kensington, London W10 5BT

☎ 020 8960 3426 🖹 020 8960 3593

email: housing@rnib.org.uk

website: www.rnib.org.uk

Information and advice on housing for people with visual impairment.

RNIB Student Support Service

P. O. Box 40, Loughborough, Leics LE11 3DG

☎ 01509 211995 🖹 01509 232013

website: www.rnib.org.uk

RNIB Talking Book Service

Falcon Park, Neasden Lane, London NW10 1TB

☎ 020 8438 9000 / 0845 762 6843

🖹 020 8438 9001

email: fpswitchboard@rnib.org.uk

website: www.rnib.org.uk

Royal National College for The Blind (RNC)

College Road, Hereford HR1 1EB

☎ 01432 265725 🖹 01432 376 628

email: info@rncb.ac.uk

website: www.rncb.ac.uk

A large residential college preparing visually impaired students for a wide range of nationally recognised qualifications.

School Phobia

(See Education Otherwise; Organisations Section)

School-Leavers With Disabilities, Directory of Opportunities

(See Queen Elizabeth's Foundation for Disabled People)

Schools for Special Needs, Gabbitas Guide to

Kogan Page, 120 Pentonville Road, London N1 9JN

☎ 020 7278 6433 🖹 020 7278 4612

A directory of schools and further education establishments catering for special needs. (See Gabbitas Educational Consultants; Special Schools in Britain Directory)

Schools Health Education Unit

Renslade House, Bonhay Road, Exeter, Devon EX4 3AY

☎ 01392 667272 📠 01392 667269

email: sheu@sheu.org.uk

website: www.ex.ac.uk/sheu/sheu.html

A research unit offering surveys, research and evaluation services to all those concerned with the health and social development of young people. Publications relevant to all school ages.

Scope Educational and Assessment Services

6 Market Road, London N7 9PW

☎ 020 7619 7100

Helpline 0808 800 3333 (weekdays 9am-9pm, weekends 2pm-6pm) 📠 020 7619 7399

email: cphelpline@scope.org.uk

website: www.scope.org.uk

Range of services for parents of children with cerebral palsy, including educational advice, family counselling. 'Schools and Colleges Pack' available. Scope is responsible for a number of schools and colleges: Beaumont College of Further Education – Lancaster, Beech Tree School – Preston, Craig-y-Parc School – Cardiff, Hawksworth Hall School – Leeds, Ingfield Manor School – Billinghurst (Conductive Education approach), Meldreth Manor School – Cambridge, Rutland House School – Nottingham (Conductive Education approach), Trengweath School – Plymouth. Full details on request.

Scope Employment Service

Sterling House, 10B Harding Way, St Ives, Cambridgeshire PE17 4WR

☎ 01480 309615 📠 01480 309636

email: frances.parker@scope.org.uk

website: www.scope.org.uk

Scottish Centre for Children with Motor Impairments, The

Craighalbert Centre, 1 Craighalbert Way, Cumbernauld, Scotland G68 0LS

☎ 01236 456100 📠 01236 736889

email: sccmi@craighalbert.co.uk

website: www.craighalbert.org.uk

Conductive education within national guidelines of education in Scotland, on a full-time or part-time basis, for children with cerebral palsy or similar motor disorders, aged 0-7 years.

Scottish Sensory Centre

Moray House, University of Edinburgh, Holyrood Road, Edinburgh EH8 8AQ

☎ 0131 651 6078 📠 0131 558 6502

email: viscotland@ed.ac.uk

website: www.ssc.mhie.ac.uk

Promotes and supports new developments and effective practices in the education of children and young people with sensory impairments, i.e. visual, hearing and deafblindness.

Shared Care Network

Units 63-66, Easton Business Centre, Felix Road, Bristol BS5 0HE

☎ 0117 941 5361 📠 0117 941 5362

email: shared-care@bristol.ac.uk

website: www.sharedcarenetwork.org.uk

An umbrella group for family-based short-term care services for children with disabilities, linking them up with families or carers willing to provide occasional care. Directory of services in England, Wales and Northern Ireland.

Shaw Trust

Shaw House, Epsom Square, White Horse Business Park, Trowbridge, Wilts BA14 0XJ

☎ 01225 716300 📠 01225 716334

email: stir@shaw-trust.org.uk

website: www.shaw-trust.org.uk

Training and job-finding service for people with disabilities. (See Employment Opportunities for People with Disabilities; Mencap Pathway Employment Service)

Sick Children, Education of

(See National Association for the Education of Sick Children)

Sign Language Interpreters, Directory of

(See CACDP)

Signalong

Communication Language Centre, North Pondside, Historic Dockyard, Chatham, Kent ME4 4TY

☎ 01634 819915

email: mkennard@signalong.org.uk

website: www.signalong.org.uk

Child orientated system containing signs for a wide variety of toys and child centred activities. Over 9000 signs available. BSL signs are used with supporting CD and picture/symbol material.

Signed Speech

(See Blisssymbols Communication UK; CACDP; Cued Speech Association; LASER; Paget-Gorman Society; Makaton Vocabulary Development Project; Signalong)

Skill (National Bureau for Students with Disabilities)

Chapter House, 18-20 Crucifix Lane, London SE1 3JW

☎ 020 7450 0620
Information service 0800 328 5050
▤ 020 7450 0650
email: skill@skill.org.uk
website: www.skill.org.uk
Information and publications on post-16 education, training and employment for disabled people, details of obtaining grants for study.

Snowdon Award Scheme
City Business Centre, 6 Brighton Road, Horsham, W. Sussex RH13 5BB
☎ 01403 211252 ▤ 01403 271553
email: info@snowdonawardsscheme.org.uk
website: www.snowdonawardscheme.org.uk
The Snowdon Award Scheme provides grants of up to £2,000 to physically disabled students for disability-related costs of further education, higher education or training within the UK, which are not covered by statutory sources. Examples include costs of computers, notetakers, interpreters, wheelchairs, travel and accommodation. Preferred age 17-25 but mature students are considered, funds permitting.

Sons of Divine Providence, The
13 Lower Teddington Road, Kingston upon Thames, Surrey KT1 4EU
☎ 020 8977 5130 ▤ 020 8977 0105
email: betty@orione.fsnet.co.uk
website: www.sonsofdivenprovidence.org
Residential care for adults with learning disabilities and people who are elderly. Horticultural training centre for people with learning disabilities.

Spadework Ltd
Riding Lane, Hildenborough, Tonbridge, Kent TN11 9LP
☎ 01732 870002
Provides training opportunities for adults with learning disabilities, to prepare them for an independent life within the community.

Special Education Advice, Independent Panel for
(See IPSEA)

Special Education National Information Line
(See Learning Difficulties Helpline)

Special Educational Needs Information Service
The Turner Library Whitefield School and Centre, Macdonald Road, Walthamstow, London E17 4AZ
☎ 020 8531 8703 ext 150 ▤ 020 8527 0907
email: lib@whitefield.org.uk
website: whitefield.org.uk
Information and advice on all aspects of special educational needs.

Special Educational Needs, National Association for (NASEN)
NASEN House, 4-5 Amber Business Village, Amber Close, Amington, Tamworth, Staffs B77 4RP
☎ 01827 311500 ▤ 01827 313005
email: welcome @nasen.org.uk
website: www.nasen.org.uk
Body of teachers and other professionals concerned with the education and welfare of children with special needs. Information, publications.

Special Needs Adviser FCO
Jennifer Steeples, Foreign & Commowealth Office (Oslo), King Charles Street, London SW1A 2AH
☎ 00/47/22 50 9119
email: jsteeples@msn,com
Offers information on schools and residential homes in the UK and abroad, particular for parents moving from country to country. All aspects of special needs advice, especially from a parent's perspective.

Special Schools in Britain Directory
Network Publishing Ltd, Sugarbrook Court, Aston Road, Bromsgrove, Worcs B60 3EX
☎ 01527 834411 ▤ 01527 578548
Directory of schools catering for special needs. (See Schools for Special Needs, Gabbitas Guide To)

Specialist Colleges
(See National Specialist Colleges)

Speech to Text Interpreters, Directory of
(See CACDP)

Speech, Language and Hearing Centre, The
1-5 St Christopher Place, Chalton Street, London NW1 1JF
☎ 020 7383 3834 ▤ 020 7383 3099
email: info@speech-lang.org.uk
website: www.speech-lang.org.uk
(See also Hearing and Speech Centre, Nuffield)

Speechmark Publishing Ltd
Telford Road, Bicester, Oxon OX26 4LQ
☎ 01869 244644 ▤ 01869 320040
email: info@speechmark.net
website: www.speechmark.net
Speechmark Publishing (formerly known as Winslow Publishing) produces practical books, resources and colourcards for practitioners and students in the areas of; speech and language therapy, special needs

education, rehabilitation, occupational therapy, elderly care, psychology, mental health and social care. Catalogue on request.

St Piers
(See National Centre for Young People with Epilepsy)

Stationery Office, The
HMSO, St Clements House, 2-16 Colgate, Norwich, Norfolk NR3 1BQ
☎ 0870 600 5522 🖶 0870 600 5533
email: customer.services @theso.co.uk
website: www.the-stationery-office.co.uk
A wide range of publications on educational issues; National Curriculum, Ofsted reports, teachers and training, school management and electronic publications. Catalogue on request.

Student Grants and Loans for Higher Education; A Brief Guide
Department for Education and Skills,
☎ 020 7510 0150
website: www.dfes.gov.uk

Students with Disabilities
(See Open University; Skill)

Students with Disabilities, National Bureau for
(See Skill)

Tadworth Court Rehabilitation Service
The Children's Trust, Tadworth Court, Tadworth, Surrey KT20 5RU
☎ 01737 365085 🖶 01737 365084
website: www.thechildrenstrust.org.uk
In-patient rehabilitation service for children with acquired head injury.

Tadworth Court Respite Care
Tadworth Court Children's Hospital, Tadworth, Surrey KT20 5RU
☎ 01737 357171 🖶 01737 375637
Short-term care for children with learning difficulty, physical disability and multiple disabilities aged 0-16 years.

Teaching at Home
(See Education Otherwise)

Treloar Disability and Assessment Centre
Holybourne, Alton, Hants GU34 4EN
☎ 01420 547403 🖶 01420 547434

United Response
113 Upper Richmond Road, Putney, London SW15 2LT
☎ 020 8246 5200 🖶 020 8780 9538
email: info@united-response.co.uk
website: www.united-response.co.uk
Runs several homes, in Yorkshire, Derbyshire, Wiltshire, Kent, Lancashire, Suffolk, Sussex and London, for people with learning disabilities, over the age of 16 years.

Weelsby Hall FE College
Weelsby Hall Further Education College, Weelsby Road, Grimsby, Lincs DN32 9RU
☎ & 🖶 01472 361334
Run by Linkage Trust

Wentwood Education Trust
32 Monk Street, Abergavenny, Gwent NP7 5NW
☎ 01873 852432 🖶 01873 857589

Winged Fellowship Trust
Angel House, 20-32 Pentonville Road, London N1 9XD
☎ 020 7833 2594 🖶 020 7278 0370
email: admin@wft.org.uk
website: www.wft.org.uk
Provides supported holidays for disabled children and adults.

YAMSEN (Yorkshire Association for Music & Special Education Needs)
(Formerly YHAMSE)
The West Park Centre, Spen Lane, Leeds LS16 5BE
email: Diane.Paterson2@btopenworld.com
website: www.yamsen.org.uk

Zoe's Place Baby Hospice
Life Health Centre, Yew Tree Lane, West Derby, Liverpool L12 9HH
☎ 0151 228 0353 🖶 0151 252 2280
website: www.digiserve.com/hauraki/zoe
Hospice for babies and toddlers up to the age of three years.

5

Sexuality and Relationships

Abuse

(See Beyond Words; Respond; Voice UK)

Albany Trust

The Art of Health and Yoga, 280 Balham High Road, London SW17 8AL

☎ 020 8767 1827

Counselling and psychotherapy for people needing help with personal relationships, identity problems or psychosexual problems.

Beyond Words

The BMJ Bookshop, Burton Street, London WC1H 9JR

☎ 020 7383 6244 / 6638 ▤ 020 7245 1231 (Royal College of Psychiatry)

or Book Sales, Royal College of Psychiatry, 17 Belgrave Square, London SW1X 8PG

A series of books for people with learning disabilities, published by St George's Hospital Medical School and the Royal College of Psychiatry. The series is intended to assist in the counselling of people with learning disabilities. Titles include; 'Going to Court' (for those who may need to attend court as a witness), 'You're Nicked' (for those who have been accused of a crime and are facing police procedures), 'In The Dock' (for those who have been charged or have to appear as a defendant in a court). Details of all further titles on request. (See also Mencap Legal Department)

BILD (Learning Disability, British Institute of)

Campion House, Green Street, Kidderminster, Worcs DY10 1JL

☎ 01562 723 010

website: www.bild.org.uk

Regular courses and conferences throughout the year, and in various parts of the country, on all aspects of learning disability. These include courses for teachers, counsellors, therapists etc. on sex education, sexual counselling and related topics. Also publishes a list of reading material on sex and personal relationships for people with a disability. Details on request.

Brook

Studio 421, Highgate Studios, 53-79 Highgate Road, London NW5 1TL

☎ 020 7284 6040

Helpline 0800 0185023 ▤ 020 7264 6050

email: info@brookcentres.org.uk

website: www.brook.org.uk

Contraceptive and counselling service for people under 25 years old. Information packs and publications, provides free confidential sexual health advice.

Careline

Cardinal Heenan Centre, 326 High Road, Ilford, Essex IG1 1QP

☎ 020 8514 5444

Helpline/Counselling 020 8514 1177/020 8478 7943

A confidential counselling and listening service for children, young people and adults suffering relationship problems, sexual abuse, grief or emotional trauma.

Cerebral Palsy

(See Scope)

Disabled Children, Council for

National Children's Bureau, 8 Wakley Street, London EC1V 7QE

☎ 020 7843 6000 ▤ 020 7278 9512

email: membership@ncb.org.uk

website: www.ncb.org.uk

Publications on sex education and disability.

Discern

Chadburn House, Weighbridge Road, Littleworth, Mansfield, Notts NG18 1AH

☎ & ▤ 01623 623732

email: info@discerncounselling.org.uk

website: www.discerncounselling.org.uk

Counselling for people with physical or learning disabilities who have queries regarding sexuality, relationships and emotional issues. Training for carers, partners of disabled people in emotional matters.

Family Planning Association

2-12 Pentonville Road, London N1 9FP

Helpline and Information Service 020 7837 5432 (9am-7pm, Mon-Fri) ▤ 020 7837 3042

website: www.fpa.org.uk

Provides information on all aspects of sex, contraception and family planning, including advice for people with disabilities. Runs courses for teachers, social workers, counsellors etc.

Gender Trust, The

P.O. Box 3192, Brighton BN1 3WR
Information line 07000 790347
email: gentrust@mistral.co.uk
website: www.home.freeuk.com/gentrust/home/htm
Assessment counselling, legal and medical advice for people with gender identity disorders and their families. Resource centre for professionals. Not a membership organisation or self-help group.

Learning Disabilities, Counselling on Sex and Personal Relationships

(See Beyond Words; Mencap; Discern)

Mencap

115-123 Golden Lane, London EC1Y 0TJ
☎ 020 7454 0454 🖨 020 7608 3254
email: information@mencap.org.uk
website: www.mencap.org.uk
Advice and information service. Several publications on sex education and sexual needs in people with learning difficulties. (See Beyond Words; Discern)

Respond

3rd Floor, 24-32 Stephenson Way, London NW1 2HD
☎ 020 7383 0700
0808 8080700 🖨 020 7387 1222
email: helpline@respond.org.uk
website: www.respond.org.uk
Provides psychotherapy, risk/investigative assessments and counselling for people with learning disabilities who have been sexually abused or who have experienced trauma. Deals with both victims and perpetrators of sexual and other abuse. Free telephone helpline. Group work, training and consultancy. Information for professionals, parents and carers. (See Beyond Words; Voice UK)

Scope

6 Market Road, London N7 9PW
☎ 020 7619 7100
Cerebral palsy helpline 0800 800 3333
🖨 020 7619 7399
email: cphelpline@scope.org.uk
website: www.scope.org.uk
Wide range of publications on various aspects of sex education and relationships for people with cerebral palsy. Counselling.

Sex Education Forum

National Children's Bureau, 8 Wakley Street, London EC1V 7QE
☎ 020 7843 6056 🖨 020 7843 6053
email: sexedforum@ncb.org.uk
website: www.ncb.org.uk/sef
A nationwide group which promotes effective sex education.

SPOD (The Association to Aid the Sexual and Personal Relationships of People with a Disability)

286 Camden Road, London N7 0BJ
☎ 020 7607 8851 🖨 020 7700 0236
email: spoduk@aol.com
website: www.spod-uk.org
The major national organisation offering advice, support and information on sexual and personal relationships for people with any kind of disability. They provide a centre for the collection of information, an advisory service for disabled people, therapists, carers etc. and run training courses for workers. Produces a series of advisory leaflets.

Voice UK

The College Business Centre, Uttoxeter Road, Derby DE22 3WZ
☎ 01332 202555 🖨 01332 295888
email: voice:clara.net
website: www.voiceuk.clara.net
Support and information for adults and children with learning disability who have been abused, their families and carers. Telephone support and information line. National network of parent contact points. Publications.

Women's Health (Resource and Information Centre)

52 Featherstone Street, London EC1Y 8RT
Helpline 07092 228194 🖨 0207 608 0928
email: editor@womens-health.co.uk
website: www.womens-health.co.uk
Information and advice, publications on all aspects of women's health and specific disorders affecting women, including contraception, premenstrual syndrome, sterilisation, abortion, sexually transmitted disease.

5

Aids and Equipment

There are several organisations that publish extensive lists or catalogues of aids and equipment, with addresses of manufacturers and suppliers. Some have a continuous information service, issuing lists of aids with new items added, and updating previous lists. These are sent at regular intervals on subscription.

Abilitynet
P.O. 94, Warwick CV34 5WS
☎ Freephone helpline 0800 269545
▤ 01926 407425
email: enquiries@abilitynet.co.uk
website: www.abilitynet.co.uk
Works with individuals, professionals and employers to provide information on computer technology for people with disabilities. Assessments free. Introductory sessions for disabled people and their carers. Factsheet available on keyboard and mouse alternatives to screen readers for severe visual impairment.

Aidis Trust, The
Mr P Ross, 1 Albany Park, Cabot Lane, Poole, Dorset BH17 7BX
☎ 01202 695244 ▤ 01202 695322
email: info@aidis.org
website: www.aidis.org
Provides computer communications equipment for people of all ages who have severe physical disabilities: equipment to enable people to write, voice output communications, aids. Assessment undertaken when required.

Anything Left-Handed
18 Avenue Road, Belmont, Surrey SM2 6JD
☎ 020 8770 3722
020 8722 4878 ▤ 020 8715 1220
email: enquiries@anythingleft-handed.co.uk
website: www.anythingleft-handed.co.uk
Produces a wide range of articles designed specifically for left-handed people with discounts for schools. Also run the Left-Handers Club which provides help and advice for parents and teachers including free Handwriting Factsheet, and Teacher Training Video on helping left-handed children. Free membership on the www.anythingleft-handed website.

BECTA (British Educational Communications and Technology Agency)
Millburn Hill Road, The Science Park, Coventry, Warks CV4 7JJ
☎ 024 7641 6994 ▤ 024 7641 1418
email: becta@becta.org.uk
website: www.becta.org.uk
Supports the Department of Education and Skill's objective to drive up standards and will be developing the use of information technology in education and identifying the role of IT opportunities for special educational needs.

Blind, Royal National Society for the
(See RNIB Customer Services)

British Computer Society Disability Group, the (BCDDG)
Dr Geoff Busby MBE FBCS Ceng, c/o Marconi Plc, West Hanningfield Road, Great Baddow, Chelmsford, Essex CM2 8HN
☎ 01245 242950 ▤ 01245 242924
email: disability.grp@bcs.co.uk
website: www.bcs.org/disability or www.abilitymagazine.co.uk

British Red Cross Society
9 Grosvenor Crescent, London SW1X 7EJ
☎ 020 7235 5454 ▤ 020 7245 6315
email: information@redcross.org.uk
website: www.redcross.org.uk
Loan of medical equipment such as wheelchairs bed rests, commodes, etc. on short term basis. Medical loan centres in several areas of the UK.

British Telecom Age & Disability Team
Burne House (PP 905), Bell Street, London NW1 5BZ
☎ 0800 800150 Minicom 0800 243123
▤ 020 7724 8232
email: disability@bt.com
website: www.bt.com/world/community
Advice and help on telecommunications and services for people with special needs; amplified phones, priority fault repair, equipment to facilitate the use of the telephone. Talks and presentation to clubs, charities and professionals, loan of equipment to resource centres and professionals for demonstration purposes, workshops with schools.

Chailey Heritage Clinical Services
Donna Cowan, Rehabilitation Engineering Services, Beggars Wood Road, North Chailey,

Lewes, East Sussex BN8 4JN
☎ 01825 722112 🖷 01825 724729
An NHS service working alongside a non-maintained special school providing services to pupils with severe or complex physical disability and to outpatients nationwide. Clinical assessment, prescription, assistive technology for most activities of daily living, especially postural management.

Clothing & Fashion
(See Disabled Living; Solemates)

Communication for the Disabled, Foundation for
(Now Abilitynet)

Computer Access Equipment for Special Needs
Keytools Ltd, P.O. Box 700, Southampton, Hants SO17 1LQ
☎ 023 8058 4314 🖷 023 8055 6902
email: info@keytools.com
website: www.keytools.com
Catalogue on request.

Computer Association of the Blind, British
BCM, P.O. Box 950, London WC1N 3XX
☎ 0845 660 6234 🖷 01245 478317
email: info@bcab.org.uk
website: www.bcab.org.uk
(See also Electronic Aids for the Blind; RNIB Customer Services)

Computers for Special Needs
Neil Sleight, Top Class Computers, 14 Gordon Close, Old Marston, Oxford OX3 0RG
☎ 01865 241081
email: nsleight@aol.com
Advice, support and equipment to help children or adults with special needs to access and benefit from computers. Visiting service to access needs follow-up support as required. (See also Aidis Trust)

Computers for the Disabled
41 New Waverley Road, Noak Bridge, Basildon, Essex SS15 4BJ
☎ 01268 284834 🖷 01268 479028
email: bigpaulh@blueyonder.co.uk
website: www.cftd.co.uk
The only UK Registered Charity that supplies PCs and Multimedia Internet-ready systems to the disabled free from any profit or cash rewards.

Continence Foundation, The
307 Hatton Square, 16 Baldwins Gardens, London EC1N 7RJ
☎ 020 7404 6875 (admin)

Helpline 0845 345 0165 (9:30-1:00 Mon-Fri)
🖷 020 7404 6876
email: continence.foundation@dial.pipex.com
website: www.continence-foundation.org.uk
Information and advice on incontinence aids. (See also Incontinence Advisory Service)

Deaf Children's Society Technology Information Centre
15 Dufferin Street, London EC1Y 8UR
Helpline 020 7250 0123 🖷 020 7251 5020
email: technology@ndcs.org.uk
website: www.ndcs.org.uk
(See also under RNID)

Demand (Design & Manufacture for Disability)
The Old Chapel, Mallard Road, Abbots Langley, Herts WD5 0GQ
☎ 01923 681800 🖷 01923 682400
email: info@demand.org.uk
website: www.demand.org.uk
An organisation which designs and manufactures one-off items of furniture and equipment for children and adults with disabilities where no other solution is available. (See also Medical Engineering Research Unit; Remap GB)

Dialability Information & Equipment Centre
Rivermead Centre, Abingdon Road, Oxford OX1 4XD
☎ 01865 791818
email: helpline@dialability.org.uk
website: www.dialability.org.uk
Countrywide advice line.

Disability Action (Northern Ireland)
2 Annadale Avenue, Belfast BT7 3JH
☎ 028 9029 7880 Textphone 028 9064 5779 🖷 028 9049 1627
email: hq@disabilityaction.org
Information and advice on all aspects of disability.

Disability Equipment Register
4 Chatterton Road, Yate, Bristol BS37 4BJ
☎ 01454 318818 🖷 01454 883870
email: disabreg@dial.pipex.com
website: www.disabreg.dial.pipex.com
A nationwide service for disabled people, their families and carers, to enable them to buy and sell used equipment on a one-to-one direct basis via the monthly magazine which is sent to all subscribers.

5

Disability Wales

Wernddu Court, Caerphilly Business Park, Van Road, Caerphilly CF83 3ED

☎ 029 2088 7325 ▤ 029 2088 8702

email: info@dwac.demon.co.uk

website: www.disabilitywales.org

Information on all aspects of disability; access, aids and equipment, benefits, education and employment, holidays, housing, leisure, etc.

Disabled Living

Redbank House, 4 St Chad's Street, Cheetham, Manchester M8 8QA

☎ 0161 214 5959 ▤ 0161 835 3591

email: info@disabledliving.co.uk

website: www.disabledliving.co.uk

Information and advice on all aspects of living with a disability. Incorporates The Style Centre: an organisation of disabled people and the clothing and fashion industries working to ensure that a national network of clothing services is available to meet the needs of those with special clothing needs and those of disabled people.

Disabled Living Centres Council

Redbank House, 4 St Chad's Street, Cheetham, Manchester M8 8QA

☎ 0161 834 1044 Textphone 0161 839 0885 ▤ 0161 839 0802

email: dlcc@dlcc.org.uk

website: www.dlcc.org.uk

Disabled Living Centres provide a permanent display of equipment and provide an information and advice service on aids and equipment for people with disabilities. The Disabled Living Council is the coordinating body for these centres. A list of Disabled Living Centres in all areas of the country is available on their website or available from the address above. (See end of this section for list of Disabled Living Centres)

Disabled Living Foundation

380-384 Harrow Road, London W9 2HU

☎ 020 7289 6111 Minicom 0870 603 9176 (10am-4pm, Mon-Fri)

Helpline 0870 603 9177 ▤ 020 7266 2922

email: advice@dlf.org.uk

website: www.dlf.org.uk

The major advice and information service specialising in the practical aspects of living with a disability. They maintain an Aids Centre, where aids of all kinds can be seen and demonstrated and produce regularly updated information sheets and publications. Individuals or organisations who wish to receive regularly updated information about equipment, can do so on subscription to the DLF Hamilton Index. This contains 23 individual sections and is published in four parts. Each part is in a separate ring binder containing five or six sections. One part of the index is updated every four months, giving a sixteen-month update cycle. Each section gives details of the most generally available equipment, including brief descriptions of the items, names and addresses of manufacturers and/or major suppliers, other relevant publications, other information sources and – where appropriate – notes on supply. Sections can be purchased separately. Fact sheet on raising funds for equipment. Subjects covered are as follows: Transport: Eating and Drinking Equipment: Beds and Bed Accessories: Chairs and Chair Accessories: Children's Equipment (General): Powered Wheelchairs: Scooters and Buggies: Manual Wheelchairs: Equipment for positioning, Standing and Walking: Pressure Relief: Notes on Incontinence: Personal Toilet: Personal Care: Telephones, Alarms and Intercoms: Children's Equipment (Mobility and Support): Household and Environmental Fittings: Clothing: Hoists, Lifts and Lifting Equipment: Leisure Activities: Footwear: Communication: Children's Equipment (Development and Play): Office Furniture and Equipment.

Easylink Electronics

Factory 7, Grange Road, Geddington, Northants NN14 1AL

☎ 01536 744788 ▤ 01536 744988

email: enquiries@easylink.uk.co.uk

website: www.easylinkuk.co.uk

Suppliers of communication equipment for people with special needs including epilepsy seizure monitors, visual telephone call indicators and call systems.

Educational Software Catalogue

REM, Great Western House, Langport, Somerset TA10 9YU

☎ 01458 254700 ▤ 01458 254701

email: info@r-e-m.co.uk

website: www.rem.co.uk

Free 84-page special needs and basic skills catalogue that caters for a wide range of age and ability including input devices such as switches, touch screens, keyboards.

Electronic Aids for the Blind

Suite 4b, 71-75 High Street, Chislehurst, Kent BR7 5AG

☎ 020 8295 3636 ▤ 020 8295 3737

email: admin@eabnet.org.uk

website: www.eabnet.org.uk

Provides specialist or suitably adapted electronic aids for partially sighted and blind children and adults in cases where no statutory or personal resources exist to meet the cost. (See also RNIB Customer Services; Computer Association of the Blind)

Enuresis Resource & Information Centre

ERIC, 34 Old School House, Britannia Road, Kingswood, Bristol BS15 8DB

☎ 0117 960 3060 ▤ 0117 960 0401

email: info@eric.org.uk

website: www.enuresis.org.uk

Epilepsy Seizure Monitors

(See Easylink Electronics)

Equipment Exchange Services

(See Disability Equipment Register)

Family Fund Trust, The

P.O. Box 50, York YO1 9ZX

☎ 01904 621115 Textphone 01904 658085

textphone 01904 652625

email: info@familyfundtrust.org.uk

website: www.familyfundtrust.org.uk

Grants may be given to help with the cost of equipment such as a washing machine to families in which there is a severely disabled child under the age of 16. Applications should be made in writing, giving the child's full name and date of birth, brief details of the child's disability and kind of help requested.

Granada Television Centre

Quay Street, Manchester M60 9EA

☎ 0161 827 2719 ▤ 0161 827 2966

email: sis@granadamedia.com

website: www.granada-learning.com

Provision of educational software, training and advice on the use of information technology and access devices.

Hearing Dogs for Deaf People

The Grange, Wycombe Road, Saunderton, Princes Risborough, Bucks HP27 9NS

☎ 01844 348100 (voice & Minicom)

▤ 01844 348101

email: info@hearing-dogs.co.uk

website: www.hearing.dogs.co.uk

Identification Wear for Medical Conditions

(See Medic-Alert Foundation; SOS Talisman)

Incontinence Advisory Service

Disabled Living Foundation, 380-384 Harrow Road, London W9 2HU

Helpline 0870 603 9177 ☎ 020 7289 6111

▤ 020 7266 2922

email: advice@dlf.org.uk

website: www.dlf.org.uk

(See also Continence Foundation)

Keep Able

Customer Services, Sterling Park, Pedmore Road, Brierley, West Midlands DY5 1TB

☎ 08705 202122 (to request a catalogue)

▤ 01384 480802

website: www.keepable.co.uk

Retailer of specialist goods for elderly and disabled people. Several stores in the UK. Home assessments available for larger items.

Medical Engineering Research Unit (MERU)

8 Damson Way, Orchard Hill, Queen Mary's Avenue, Carshalton, Surrey SM5 4NR

☎ 020 8770 8284 ▤ 020 8770 8286

email: johnw@meru.org.uk

website: www.meru.org.uk

Undertakes projects for individual children with problems or requirements which cannot be satisfied by commercially available equipment, aids or toys. Also, its Interface Centre Service gives disabled children control, through innovative solutions. (See also Demand; Remap GB)

Medic-Alert Foundation

12 Bridge Wharf, 156 Caledonian Road, London N1 9UU

☎ 020 7833 3034 ▤ 020 7278 0647

email: info@medicalert.co.uk

website: www.medicalert.org

Produces a range of items (bracelets etc.) which carry a medical or health message.

National Council for Educational Technology

(See BECTA)

QED Ltd

1 Prince Alfred Street, Gosport, Hants PO12 1QH

☎ 0870 787 8850 ▤ 0870 787 8860

email: sales@QEDLtd.com

website: www.qedltd.com

Manufacturers of innovative products for people with special needs.

RADAR (Royal Association for Disability & Rehabilitation)

12 City Forum, 250 City Road, London EC1V 8AF

☎ 020 7250 3222 Minicom 020 7250 4119

▤ 020 7250 0212

email: radar@radar.org.uk

website: www.radar.org.uk

Advises on all aspects of disabled living. Many publications on all topics including aids and equipment. A fund is available for a small number of grants for electronic aids or equipment.

5

Raising Funds for Equipment
(Contact Disabled Living Foundation)

Rehabilitation Engineering Movement Advisory Panels
(See Remap GB)

Remap GB
Hazeldene, Ightham, Sevenoaks, Kent TN15 9AD
☎ 0845 130 0456 📠 0845 130 0789
email: info@remap.org.uk
website: www.remap.org.uk
Design, manufacture and supply of technical equipment to people with disabilities. Where no commercial equipment is suitable, modification of equipment to suit individual needs. Run by professional engineers, no fee charged to disabled people. Over 100 Remap panels in the UK. (See also Medical Engineering Research Unit; Demand)

Remploy Orthitics Ltd
Manor Mill Lane, Millshaw, Leeds LS11 8DF
☎ 01132 726970 📠 01132 726971
email: direct.sales@remploy.co.uk
website: www.remploy.co.uk
Range of products including active user chairs, indoor and outdoor powered wheelchairs, stroke rehabilitation systems, orthopaedic appliances, ready-to-wear footwear and soft products.

Rifton Equipment
Robertsbridge, East Sussex TN32 5DR
☎ 0800 387457 📠 0800 387531
email: sales@communityplaythings.com
website: www.communityplaythings.com
Produces a catalogue of aids and equipment for children and adults with disabilities. Catalogue on request.

RNIB Customer Services
P.O. Box 173, Peterborough, Cambs PE2 6WS
☎ 01345 023153 Minicom 0345 585691
📠 01733 371555
email: cservices@rnib.org.uk
website: www.rnib.org.uk
Information resource centre and suppliers of publications, aids and equipment, games, library services, tape and publishing services for visually impaired people. (See also Electronic Aids for the Blind; Computer Association of the Blind)

RNID
RNID, 19-23 Featherstone Street, London EC1Y 8SL
Freephone 0808 808 0123
Text Freephone 0808 808 9000 📠 020 7296 8199
email: information@rnid.org.uk
website: www.rnid.org.uk
Equipment and products for deaf and hard of hearing people. (See also Deaf Children's Society)

RNID Sound Advantage
1 Metro Centre, Peterborough PE2 7UH
☎ 01733 232607 Textphone 01733 238020
📠 01733 361161
website: rnid.org.uk
Provision of listening, alerting and telecommunication equipment to deaf and hard of hearing people, together with induction loops for professional application.

Scope
6 Market Road, London N7 9PW
☎ 020 7619 7100
Cerebral palsy Helpline 0808 800 3333
Minicom 0800 626216 📠 020 7619 7331
website: www.scope.org.uk
Information on aids and equipment for people with cerebral palsy.

Sequal Trust, The
3 Ploughman's Corner, Wharf Road, Ellesmere, Shropshire ST12 0EJ
☎ 01691 624222 📠 01691 624222
email: solutions@rnid.org.uk
website: www.the-sequal-trust.org.uk
Assists severely physically disabled people by providing special electrical and electronic equipment.

Smith & Nephew Ltd
Heron House, 15 Adam Street, London WC2N 6LA
☎ 020 7401 7646 📠 020 7930 3353
email: cphelpline@scope.org.uk
website: www.smith-nephew.com
Manufacturer and supplier of disability aids and equipment.

Solemates
46 Gordon Road, Chingford, London E4 6BU
☎ 020 8524 2423
email: sequal@freenet.co.uk
website: www.solemates.com

SOS Talisman
21 Grays Court, Ley Street, Ilford, Essex
☎ 020 8554 5579 📠 020 8554 1090
website: www.sos-talisman.com
Produces a range of items (bracelets etc.) which carry a medical or health message. (See also Medic-Alert Foundation)

Special Needs Research Unit (SNRU)
University of Northumbria & Newcastle, 1 Coach Lane, Coach Lane Campus, Newcastle upon Tyne

NE7 7TW
☎ 0191 227 4211 📄 0191 266 4061
website: www.snru.unn.demon.co.uk
Produces a register of aids, manufacturers, software etc.

Telephones for People with Special Needs
(See British Telecom Age & Disability Team)

Toys
(See Leisure Section)

Wales Council for the Disabled
(See Disability Wales)

Ways and Means & Nottingham Rehabilitation
Ludlow Hill Road, West Bridgford, Nottingham NG2 6HD
☎ 01159 45200
email: info@nrs-uk.co.uk
website: www.nrs-uk.co.uk/htm/ways&means
Catalogue of aids and equipment.

Wheelchair Provision
(See Mobility Trust, in Useful organisations: Holidays, Travel, Mobility)

5

Disabled Living Centres in the UK

Aylesbury
Independent Living Exhibition, Brookside Centre, Station Way, Aylesbury, Bucks HP20 2SQ
☎ 01296 398616 🗎 01296 435 110
email: ile-aylesbury@hotmail.com

Beckenham
Beckenham Independent Living Centre, Lewis House, 30 Beckenham Road, Beckenham, Kent BR3 4LS
☎ 020 8663 3345 🗎 020 8663 1442
email: bath.bromley@virgin.net

Belfast
Disabled Living Centre, Regional Disablement Services, Musgrave Park Hospital, Stockman's Lane, Belfast BT97JB
☎ 028 9066 9501 🗎 028 90663008

Birmingham
Birmingham Centre for Independent Living, St Mark's Street, Springhill, Birmingham B1 2HU
☎ 0121 200 2262 🗎 0121 200 2250

Boston
Disabled Living Centre, British Red Cross, Scott House, 35 Skirbeck Road, Boston PE21 6DG
☎ 01205 367 597

Bristol
Disabled Living Centre (West of England), Gill Avenue, Fishponds, Bristol BS162QQ
☎ 0117 965 3651 🗎 0117 965 3652
email: info@bristoldlc.org
website: www.dlcbristol.org

Caerphilly
Centre for Help and Advice for the Disabled, Ty Clyd Bungalow, Helo Fargoed, Bargoed, Caerphilly CF81 8PP
☎ 01443 822 262 🗎 01443 822 286

Castleford
Highfield House Disability Centre, Love Lane, Castleford, West Yorks WF10 5RT
☎ 01977 724 012 🗎 01977 727 095

*Crewe
Independent Living Centre, Leighton Hospital, Middlewich Road, Crewe, Cheshire CW1 4QJ

☎ 01270 612343 🗎 01606 79260
*This centre is presently closed – it is hoped that it will re-opn in April 2003. Telephone and advice service available on 01625 661740. Alternatively contact Northwich or Macclesfield offices.

Dewsbury
Social Services Information Point, Walsh Building, Town Hall Way, Dewsbury, West Yorks WF12 8EQ
☎ 01924 325070 🗎 01924 325 077

Doncaster
South Yorkshire Centre for Inclusive Living, Heavens Walk, Doncaster DN4 5HZ
☎ 01302 769219 🗎 01302 327778
email: information@sycil.org.uk
website: www.sycil.org.uk

Dundee
The Ability Centre, The Mackinnon Centre, 491 Brook Street, Broughty Ferry, Dundee DD5 2DZ
☎ 01382 436 860 🗎 01382 436 858
email: Ability.Centre@dundeecity.gov.uk

Dunstable
The Disability Resource Centre, Poynters House, Poynters Road, Dunstable, Beds LU5 4TP
☎ 01582 470900 🗎 01582 470 959
email: drcbeds@cwcom.net
website: www.drcbeds.co.uk

Eastbourne
East Sussex Disability Association, 1 Faraday Close, Hampden Park, Eastbourne BN22 9BH
☎ 01323 514 500 🗎 01323 514 501
email: info@esda.org.uk
website: www.esda.org.uk

Edinburgh
Lothian Disabled Living Centre, Astley Ainslie Hospital, Grange Loan, Edinburgh EH9 2HL
☎ 0131 537 9190
email: lothiandlc@genie.co.uk

Elgin
Moray Resource Centre, Maisondieu Road, Elgin, Morayshire IV3O 1RX
☎ 01343 551339 🗎 01343 542 014
email: info.dlc@comm.moray.gov.uk

Exeter
Independent Living Centre, St Loye's Foundation,

Topsham Road, Exeter EX2 6EP
☎ 01392 286239 🖹 01392 286 239

Grangemouth
Dundas Resource Centre, Oxgang Road, Grangemouth, Stirlingshire FK3 9EF
☎ 01324 504311 🖹 01324 504312

Halton
Halton Independent Living Centre, Colliers Lane, Runcorn, Cheshire WA7 1HB
☎ 01928 563340 🖹 01928 582 950
email: hrussell@hillingdon.gov.uk

Hillingdon
Hillingdon Independent Resource Centre, Royal Lane, Hillingdon, Middlesex UB8 3QX
☎ 01895 233691 🖹 01895 813 843

Leeds
The William Merritt Disabled Living Centre, St Mary's Hospital, Green Hill Road, Armley, Leeds LS12 3QE
☎ 0113 305 5332 🖹 0113 231 9291
email: williammerrittdlc@cwcom.net

Leicester
Leicestershire Disabled Living Centre, Red Cross Medical Aid Department, 76 Clarendon Park Road, Leicester LE2 3AD
☎ 0116 270 0515 🖹 0116 244 8625

Liverpool
Liverpool Disabled Living Centre, 101-103 Kempston Street, Liverpool L3 8HE
☎ 0151 298 2055 🖹 0151 298 2952

London
The Disabled Living Foundation, 380-394 Harrow Road, London W9 2HU
☎ 020 7289 6111 🖹 020 7266 2922
email: advice@dlf.org.uk
website: www.dlf.org.uk

Lowestoft
Waveney Centre for Independent Living, 161 Rotterdam Road, Lowestoft, Suffolk NR32 2EZ
☎ 01502 405 454 🖹 01502 405 454
email: WCIL@socserv.suffolkcc.gov.uk

Macclesfield
Disabled Living Centre, Gawsworth Building, Macclesfield General Hospital, Victoria Road, Macclesfield SK10 3BL
☎ 01625 661740 🖹 01625 661 245

Manchester
Disabled Living, Redbank House, 4 Chad's Street, Manchester M8 8QA
☎ 0161 214 5959 🖹 0161 835 3591
email: info@disabledliving.co.uk
website: www.disabledliving.co.uk

Milton Keynes
Centre for Intergrated Living, 330 Saxon Gate West, Central Milton Keynes, Bucks MK9 2ES
☎ 01908 231 344 🖹 01908 231 335
email: maggie@mkcil.aol.com

Newcastle
Disability North, The Dene Centre, Castles Farm Road, Newcastle upon Tyne NE3 1PH
☎ 0191 284 0480 🖹 0191 213 0910
email: reception@disabilitynorth.org.uk
website: www.disabilitynorth.org.uk

Newton Aycliffe
Pioneering Care Partners, Cobblers Hall, Off Burn Lane, Newton Aycliffe, Co. Durham DL5 4SF
☎ 01325 321234 🖹 01325 301129
email: liz@pcp.uk.net

Northwich
Independent Living Centre, Victoria Infirmary, Winnington Hill, Northwich, Cheshire CW8 1AW
☎ 01606 79260 🖹 01606 79260

Nottingham
Disabilities Living Centre, Lenton Business Centre, Lenton Boulevard, Nottingham NG7 2BY
☎ 0115 942 0391 🖹 0115 978 8113
email: enquiries@dlcnotts.co.uk
website: www.dlcnotts.co.uk

Oxford
Dialability (Oxfordshire) Ltd, Rivermead Centre, Abingdon Road, Oxford OX1 4XD
☎ 01865 791818 🖹 01865 798723
email: manager@dialability.org.uk
website: www.dialability.org.uk

Paisley
Disability Centre for Independent Living, Mile End Centre, 30 Seedhill Road, Paisley, Renfrewshire PA1 1SA
☎ 0141 847 4959 🖹 0141 847 7267

Papworth
Cambridgeshire Disability Resouce Centre, Lower Pendrill Court, Papworth Everard, Cambridgeshire CB3 9UY
☎ 01480 830 495 🖹 01480 830 495

Semington
Independent Living Centre, St George's Road, Semington, Wilts BA14 6JQ
☎ 01380 871007 🖹 01380 871113

5

Shrewsbury
Shropshire Disability Resource Centre, Lancaster Road, Harlescott, Shrewsbury SY1 3NJ
☎ 01743 444 599 ▤ 01743 461 349
email: Jhall@shropshiredisability.org

Southampton
Southampton Aid and Equipment Centre, Royal Hants South Hospital, Brintons Terrace, Southampton SO14 0YG
☎ 023 8082 5288 ▤ 023 8082 5254
(For further information, contact Disabled Living Centres Council)

Stamford
Disabled Living Centre, 33 Ryhall Road, Stamford, Lincs PE9 1UF
☎ 01780 480 599 ▤ 01780 480 603
email: brcdlc@ukonline.co.uk

Stockport
Independant Living Centre, St Thomas' Hospital, Shaw Heath, Stockport, Cheshire SK3 8BL
☎ 0161 419 4476 ▤ 0161 419 4480

Swindon
Options Plus, The Independent Living Centre, Marshgate, Stratton Road, Swindon SN1 2PN
☎ 01793 643966
email: info@optionsplus.co.uk
website: www.optionsplus.co.uk

Truro
Cornwall Mobility Centre, Tehidy House, Royal Cornwall Hospital, Truro, Cornwall TR1 3LJ
☎ 01872 254 920 ▤ 01872 254 921

Walsall
Disabled Living Centre, The Shrubbery, The Crescent, Walsall WS1 2DE
☎ 01922 821 120 ▤ 01922 643 603

Warrington
Warrington Centre for Independent Living, Beaufort Street, Off Old Liverpool Road, Warrington, Cheshire WA5 1BA
☎ 01925 638 867 ▤ 01925 241 852
email: cil-wdis@tiscali.co.uk
website: www.wdis.org.uk

Welwyn Garden City
Hertfordshire Action on Disability, The Woodside Centre, The Commons, Welwyn Garden City, Herts ALT 4DD
☎ 01707 324 581 ▤ 01707 371 297
email: info@hadnet.co.uk
website: www.hadnet.co.uk

Wolverhampton
Neville Garratt Centre for Independent Living, Wolverhampton Social Services, Bell Street, Wolverhampton WV1 3PR
☎ 01902 533 666 ▤ 01902 553 677

Leisure

Most large organisations for specific disabilities will provide information on the leisure and sport services appropriate to their members' needs. Contact the relevant organisation; Scope, Mencap, RNIB, RNID etc. Addresses below or in the Organisations section. For information on specific activities such as play, sport etc, contact the appropriate national coordinating body, e.g. Play Matters, sports organisations, etc. Some organisations listed in the Holidays, Travel and Mobility section provide residential courses or holidays offering arts and sport activities.

Abilitynet
(See Aids and Equipment Section)

Access/Accessible Environments
(See Holidays, Travel, Mobility Section)

Action for Leisure
c/o Warwickshire College, Moreton Morrell Centre, Moreton Morrell, Warks CV35 9BL
☎ 01926 650195 ▤ 01925 650104

Adventure Education
(See Outdoor Learning and Adventure, Institute for)

Adventure Playgrounds
(See Kidsactive)

Anglers, National Federation of
Halliday House, Egginton Junction, Derbyshire DE65 6GU
☎ 01283 734735 ▤ 01283 734799
website: www.fire.org.uk/nfa
Provides opportunities for disabled anglers, regional officers for the disabled, booklet on teaching angling to people with disabilities.

Angling Link
9 Yew Tree Road, Delves, Walsall, West Midlands WS5 4NQ
☎ 01922 860912 ▤ 01922 860912
email: alink@globalnet.co.uk
website: www.bvp.net/alink
An organisation formed by disabled anglers for disabled anglers and their carers. Special section for children and young people.

Archery Society, The Grand National
Lilleshall National Sports Centre, Newport, Shropshire TF10 9AT
☎ 01952 677888 ▤ 01952 606019
email: enquiries@gnas.org
website: www.gnas.org
Over 1,000 archery clubs in all areas of the UK including 65 specifically for people with disabilities.

Art for Physically Disabled People, The Society for
(See Conquest Art)

Arts
(See Kingfisher Barn in Holidays Section)

Arts Council of England
14 Great Peter Street, London SW1P 3NQ
☎ 020 7333 0100
020 7973 6517 (Mon – Fri 2pm – 5pm)
▤ 020 7973 6590
email: enquiries@artscouncil.org.uk
website: www.artscouncil.org.uk

Arts Council, Scottish
12 Manor Place, Edinburgh EH3 7DD
☎ 0131 226 6051 ▤ 0131 225 9833
email: administrator@scottisharts.org.uk
website: www.sac.org.uk

Arts Disability Wales
Chapter Arts Centre, Market Road, Canton, Cardiff CF5 1QE
☎ 02920 377885 ▤ 02920 395211
email: arts.disability@enablis.co.uk
Information and training for disabled people and arts organisations.

Arts Funding
(See Directory of Social Change)

Ballet for Special Needs
(See Theatre Dance Association, British)

Basketball
(See Wheelchair Basketball Association)

Big Print Ltd
P.O. Box 308, Warrington, Cheshire WA1 1JE
☎ 01925 242222 Freephone 0800 124007
▤ 01925 418656
email: tbuckley@big-print.co.uk

5

website: www.big-print.co.uk

Large print national weekly newspaper designed for people who have difficulty with reading standard type. Available by subscription. Free sample copy on request.

Blind, National Library for the

Far Cromwell Road, Bredbury, Stockport, Cheshire SK6 2SG

☎ 0161 355 2000 🖹 0161 355 2098

email: enquiries@nlbuk.org

website: www.nlbuk.org

Library of Braille and Moon volumes including children's books and music. Free post and free lending service, information and advice service. (See also Calibre; RNIB Talking Book Service)

Boccia Federation, British

Dean Thomas, 11 Churchill Park, Colwick, Nottingham NG4 2HF

☎ 0115 987 2002 🖹 0115 940 2984

Courses and demonstrations of boccia for people with cerebral palsy.

Books for Children with Special Needs

(see Calibre; Listening Books; Reach Resource Centre; RNIB Talking Book Service)

Braille Press, Scottish

Mr J H Adams, Craigmillar Park, Edinburgh EH16 5NB

☎ 0131 662 4445 🖹 0131 662 1968

email: scot.braille@dial.pipex.com

website: www.scottish-braille-press.org

Printers and publishers of Braille and producers of audio, large print, material on disk and tactile diagrams for people with visual impairment.

Calibre

New Road, Weston Turville, Aylesbury, Bucks HP22 5XQ

☎ 01296 432339 🖹 01296 392599

email: diana.clark@calibre.org.uk

website: www.calibre.org.uk

Free postal library of unabridged recorded books for visually impaired and print disabled people.

Canoe Union, British

John Dudderidge House, Adbolton Lane, West Bridgford, Notts NG2 5AS

☎ 0115 982 1100 🖹 0115 982 1797

email: info@bcu.org.uk

website: www.bcu.org.uk

Governing body for canoeing clubs and organisations in the UK. Training, courses, awards, advice for people with disabilities to participate in canoeing.

Catholic Handicapped Fellowship, National

Mr J Mair, 15 Woodlands Park Drive, Blaydon, Tyne and Wear NE21 5PQ

☎ 0191 414 3221

Clubs, outings, parties, religious instruction for children and young adults with physical or learning disabilities.

Causeway PROSPECTS

P.O. Box 351, Reading, Berks RG1 7AL

☎ 0118 950 8781 🖹 0118 939 1683

email: causeway@prospects.org.uk

Causeway PROSPECTS produces resource materials and gives support to help churches start special groups for people with learning disabilities which provide simplified bible study and worship. Care homes, run on Christian principles, in several areas of the country.

Challengers

Disability Challenge, Stoke Park, Guildford, Surrey GU1 1TU

☎ 01483 579390 🖹 01483 302947

email: dchallenge@clara.net

An activity centre available to anyone in Surrey, Sussex, Hampshire and outer London Boroughs and other areas within driving distance. Wide range of indoor and outdoor facilities including soft play area and multi-sensory room specially adapted or designed for children with special needs. Caters for families, special schools, hospitals, children's homes and organisations. Facilities for parents and toddlers. Siblings are encouraged to participate.

Children's Play Council

8 Wakley Street, London EC1V 7QE

☎ 020 7843 6016 or 6094 🖹 020 7278 9512

Christian Fellowship

(See Causeway PROSPECTS; Disabled Christians Fellowship)

City Farms and Community Gardens, National Federation of

The Green House, Hereford Street, Bedminster, Bristol BS3 4NA

☎ 0117 923 1800 🖹 0117 923 1900

email: admin@farmgarden.org.uk

website: www.farmgarden.org.uk

Can provide contacts to 65 City Farms and almost 1200 Community Gardens throughout the UK, some of which offer opportunities for people with special needs. Teaching resource information.

Communication for the Disabled, Foundation for

(See Abilitynet in Aids and Equipment Section)

Computers/Computer Software for Special Needs
(See Aids and Equipment Section)

Conquest Art
Conquest Art Centre, Cox Lane Day Centre, Cox Lane, West Ewell, Surrey KT19 9PL
☎ 020 8397 6157 📠 020 8397 6157
Runs art classes for people with physical disabilities. Magazine and exhibitions.

Creative Drama
(See Sesame Institute UK)

Cycling
(See Tandem Club)

Dance
(See Theatre Dance Association, British)

Deaf Sports Council, British
7a Bridge Street, Otley, W. Yorks LS21 1BQ
☎ 01943 850214 Minicom 01943 850828
Promotes amateur games and sports for deaf people in Great Britain and Northern Ireland.

Directory of Social Change
24 Stephenson Way, London NW1 2DP
☎ 020 7209 5151 📠 020 7209 5049
email: info@dsc.org.uk
website: www.dsc.org.uk
Publishes 'The Sports Funding Guide', 'The Arts Funding Guide' and 'Youth Funding Guide'.

Disability Arts Forum, The National
Mea House, Ellison Place, Newcastle upon Tyne NE1 8XS
☎ 0191 261 1628 Minicom 0191 261 2237
📠 0191 222 0573
email: ndaf@ndaf.org
Promotes and develops arts with disabled people locally, regionally and nationally. Supports the development of Disability Arts Forums and maintains a network through which disability arts organisations can assist each other, promotes arts events in all parts of the UK.

Disability Sport England
The Dolphin Centre, Horsemarket, Darlington DL1 5RP
☎ 01325 369554 📠 01325 485874
email: patbennett@darlingtondse.freeserve.co.uk
website: www.disabilitysport.org.uk
Aims to make healthy lifestyle and participation in sport a reality for disabled children and adults and to make sport accessible for everyone. Advice, information and details of local centres on request.

Disability, Northern Ireland Council on
Disability Action, 2 Annadale Avenue, Belfast BT7 3JH
☎ 028 9049 1011 Qwerty Text phone 028 9064 5779 📠 028 9049 1627
Information on all aspects of disability including sports and leisure.

Disabled Christians Fellowship, The
Miss J Edwards, Global House, Ashley Avenue, Epsom KT18 5AD
☎ 01372 737046 📠 0117 983 0388
email: jenny@throughtheroof.org
website: www.throughtheroof.org
Links members up by correspondence and tapes, and holidays in England and Cyprus. (See also Causeway PROSPECTS)

Down's Syndrome Theatre Company
(See Kaleidoscope Theatre)

Drama
(See Graeae Theatre Company; Sesame Institute UK)

Drama for the Blind, Advisory Service for Drama, Recreation and Lifestyles Department
RNIB, 105 Judd Street, London WC1H 9NE
☎ 020 7388 1266 📠 020 7388 2034
email: cservices@rnib.org.uk
website: www.rnib.org.uk

Draughts Association, English
Mr I Caws, 54 Mayfield Road, Ryde, Isle of Wight PO33 3PR
☎ 01983 565484
Postal draughts for people with disabilities or who are confined to their home. Quarterly journal issued free to members.

Duke of Edinburgh Award Scheme
Gulliver House, Madeira Walk, Windsor, Berks SL4 1EU
☎ 01753 810753 📠 01753 810666
email: info@theaward.org
website: www.theaward.org
Publishes a book describing the ways in which disabled people can participate in the Duke of Edinburgh award schemes.

Educational Software
(See Aids and Equipment)

English Heritage Education
Freepost 22 (WD214), London W1E 5EZ
☎ 020 7973 3442 📠 020 7973 3443

5

email: education@English-heritage.org.uk
website: www.English-heritage.org.uk
Publishes a guide for people with disabilities.

Extend
22 Maltings Drive, Wheathampstead, Herts AL4 8QL
☎ 01582 832760 📠 01582 832760
email: admin@extend.org.uk
website: www.extend.org.uk
Recreational movement to music for people over 60 years and people of any age who have disabilities. Please send SAE for information.

Family Fund Trust, The
P.O. Box 50, York YO1 9ZX
☎ 01904 621115 📠 01904 652625
textphone 01904 658805
email: info@familytrustfund.org.uk
website: www.familytrustfund.org.uk
Grants may be given to help with the cost of leisure activities to families in which there is a severely disabled child under the age of 16. Applications should be made in writing, giving the child's full name and date of birth, brief details of the child's disability and kind of help requested.

Fishing
(See Anglers, National Federation of; Angling Link)

Funding for Arts, Guide to
(See Directory of Social Change)

Funding for Sports, Guide to
(See Directory of Social Change)

Gardening and Horticulture
(See Gardening for Disabled Trust; THRIVE)

Gardening for Disabled Trust
Hayes Farmhouse, Peasmarsh, East Sussex TN31 6XR
📠 01580 852130
email: info@gardeninginthe weald.co.uk
website: www.gardening in the weald.co.uk
Gives advice and information to individuals who need garden adaptations or special tools in order to maintain their own gardens. Helps organisations to provide an environment in which their clients or residents can take an active and physical part in gardening. Provides small grants to people all over the UK so that they may continue to garden despite age, disability or illness. (See also THRIVE)

Gateway Clubs, National Federation of
Mencap, 115-123 Golden Lane, London EC1Y OTJ
☎ 020 7454 0454 📠 020 7696 5540
email: information@mencap.org.uk

website: www.mencap.org.uk
Runs clubs in all areas for people with learning difficulties aged 13-14 plus, with clubs for younger children in some areas. These clubs provide opportunities for participation in all types of sport, art and music activities.

Golf
(See Handigolf Foundation)

Graeae Theatre Company
Hampstead Town Hall Centre, 213 Haverstock Hill, London NW3 4QP
☎ 020 7681 4755 📠 020 7681 4756
email: info@graeae.org
website: www.graeae.org
A professional theatre company of disabled people which tours nationally and internationally.

Girlguiding UK
17-19 Buckingham Palace Road, London SW1W 0PT
☎ 020 7834 6242 📠 020 828 8312
email: chq@girlguiding.org.uk
website: www.girlguiding.org.uk
Girlguiding welcomes girls and young women with disabilities. Large print and braille copies of girls handbooks are available from the above address.

Gymnastics
(See Special Gymnastics Association)

Handbell Ringing
(See Mayola Music Ltd)

Handigolf Foundation, The
Stone Cottage, Launton Road, Stratton Audley, Bicester, Oxon OX6 9BW
☎ 01908 655102 📠 01908 653858
website: www.handigolf.org
Aims to make golf available to people with physical disabilities, integrated with able-bodied players.

Horticultural Society, The Royal
P.O. Box 313, London SW1P 2PE
☎ 020 7821 3000 📠 020 7828 2304
website: www.rhs.org.uk
Produces a bibliography of publications on horticulture for people with a disability. (See also Gardening for Disabled Trust; THRIVE)

Hospital Play Staff, National Association for
Judy Walker, 21 Rosefield Road, Staines, Middlesex TW18 4NB
email: hospitalplay@msn.com
website: www.nahps.org.uk

Promotes play for children and teenagers in hospital, supports staff who lead play programmes. Fact sheets and pamphlets on all aspects of special needs and environment of children in hospital, professional journal, advice on training and standards.

Kaleidoscope Theatre
Kemberton Hall, Kemberton, Shropshire TF11 9LH
☎ 01952 588766
An integrated theatre company, some of whose members happen to have Down's Syndrome, which performs original plays and runs occasional workshops.

Kids Club Network
Bellerive House, 3 Muirfield Crescent, London E14 9SZ
National development agency for out-of-school care. Offers practical help and support to those wishing to start a club, information line for parents, playworkers and schools.

Kidsactive (formerly HAPA)
Pryor's Bank, Bishop's Park, London SW6 3LA
☎ 020 7736 4443 ▤ 020 7731 4426
website: www.kidsactive.org.uk
Runs six adventure playgrounds for disabled children in the London area. Offers a national information service to promote all aspects of play and disability, especially the development of inclusive services. Magazine, publications and resources on play.

Learning Disability, UK Sports Association
(See Sports Association for People with Learning Disability, UK)

Leisure, Art, Music and Movement for People with Profound and Multiple Disabilities
(See Mencap PIMD in Organisations Section)

Letterbox Library
71-73 Allen Road, Stoke Newington, London N16 8RY
☎ 020 7503 4801 ▤ 020 7503 4800
email: info@letterboxlibrary.com
website: www.letterboxlibrary.com
Books which show positive images of children with disabilities and children from different cultures. Details of titles on request.

Leybourne Grange Riding Centre
Jo Fletcher, Birling Road, Leybourne, West Malling, Kent ME20 7RT
☎ 01732 872844
Riding lessons for children and adults with disabilities.

Libraries for Children with Special Needs
(See Calibre; Listening Books; Reach Resource Centre; RNIB Talking Book Service)

Listening Books
12 Lant Street, London SE1 1QH
☎ 020 7407 9417 ▤ 020 7403 1377
email: info@listening-books.org.uk
website: www.listening-books.org.uk
Listening Books provides a postal audio-book library service to anyone who suffers from an illness or disability which makes it impossible or difficult to hold a book, turn its pages, or read it in the usual way.

Mayola Music Ltd
205 High Street, Clapham Village, Beds MK41 6AJ
☎ 01234 262474 ▤ 01234 262475
email: music@mayola.com
Supplies handbells, handchimes and music including advice on ringing relevant to all disabilities.

Mencap Gateway Clubs
(See Gateway Clubs, National Federation of)

Mime for Deaf Children
(See Deaf Children's Society, National in Organisations Section)

Mini-Olympics Ltd
Mr J Thomas MBE, 23 Mansfields, Writtle, Chelmsford, Essex CM1 3NH
☎ 01245 420041 ▤ 01245 420041
Regional and national sporting events for people with learning disability.

Modern Dance (Special Needs)
(See Theatre Dance Association, British)

Movement to Music, Exercise
(See Extend; Sesame Institute UK)

Museums for Sight Impaired People
Discovering Museums; A guide to museums in the UK for blind and partially sighted people. Available from RNIB Leisure Services.

Music for the Disabled
Frederick A Gallacher, 13 Willow Road, Fancombe, Godalming, Surrey GU2 6RP
☎ 01483 427400
email: fred.weylec@ukgateway.net
(See also Wingfield Trust)

Music in Hospitals, Council for
74 Queen's Road, Horsham, Surrey KT12 5LW
☎ 01932 252809 ▤ 01932 252966
email: info@music-inhospitals.org.uk
Provides live concerts throughout the UK in hospitals,

5

hospices, nursing homes and schools for children with special needs. Musicians are chosen not only for their high musicianship but also for their communication skills.

Music Therapy, British Society for
25 Rosslyn Avenue, East Barnet, Herts EN4 8DH
☎ 020 8368 8879 🖷 020 8368 8879
email: denize@bsmt.demon.co.uk
website: www.bsmt.org
Promotes the use of music therapy in the treatment and education of children and adults with a disability. Can offer assessments and referrals and advise on professional training. Runs courses, an annual conference and has a list of publications available on request. (See also Nordoff-Robbins Music Therapy Centre)

National Trust, The
Mark Dyer, Access for All Adviser, 36 Queen Anne's Gate, London SW1H 9AS
☎ 020 7447 6742
0870 458 4000 🖷 020 8466 6824
email: enquiries@thenationaltrust.org.uk
website: www.nationaltrust.org.uk
The National Trust welcomes all visitors to its properties and publishes a free annual booklet containing details of access to those properties which may be particularly enjoyed by disabled visitors. This is available in standard and large print and on tape from: The National Trust Membership Department, PO Box 39, Bromley, Kent BR1 3XL. The property guidebooks are available in Braille and large print at properties. The necessary companion of a disabled visitor is given free admission on request.

Nordoff-Robbins Music Therapy Centre
Ms P Etkin, Director, 2 Lissenden Gardens, London NW5 1PP
☎ 020 7267 4496 🖷 020 7267 4369
email: admin@nordoff-robbins.org.uk
website: www.nordoff-robbins.org.uk
Resource centre for the research, study and application of music therapy, especially for people with disabilities. (See also Music Therapy)

Orchestras, Youth
(See Youth Orchestras)

Outdoor Learning and Adventure, Institute for
12, St Andrew's Churchyard, Penrith, Cumbria CA11 7YE
☎ 01768 861065 🖷 01768 891914
email: institute@outdoor-learning.org
website: www.outdoor-learning.org

Supports, develops and promotes the achievement of learning through purposeful and planned outdoor experiences. Information, publications including 'Outdoor Education and Special Educational Needs' and 'The Outdoor Source Book' – directory of outdoor providers including specialists in disabilities.

Outward Bound Trust
207 Waterloo Road, London SE1 8XD
☎ 0870 513 4227 🖷 017684 86983
email: enquiries@outwardbound-uk.org
website: www.outwardbound-uk.org
Several centres providing a wide range of activities for people with any type of disability.

Paralympic Association, British
Impact House, Room 514, 2 Edridge Road, Croydon, Surrey CR9 1PJ
☎ 020 8681 9655 🖷 020 8681 9650
email: info@paralympics.org.uk
website: www.paralympics.org.uk
Coordinates and funds the entry of Great Britain's team to the winter and summer paralympic games. Caters for amputees, visually impaired people, wheelchair users, people with learning disability and those with cerebal palsy.

PHAB Ltd
Summit House, 50 Wandle Road, Croydon, Surrey CR0 1DF
☎ 020 8667 9443 🖷 020 8681 1399
email: info@phabengland.org.uk
website: www.phabengland.org.uk
Runs local groups in all areas of the UK for physically disabled and able-bodied people, offering a wide range of activities including sport, drama, music, art etc. Addresses of PHAB Northern Ireland and PHAB Wales on request or on website.

Play and Leisure Advice
(See Kidsactive; Toy and Leisure Libraries, National Association of)

Play Information Centre, National
359-361 Euston Road, London NW1 3AL
☎ 020 7383 5455 🖷 020 7387 3152
199 Knightsbridge, London SW7 1DE
☎ 020 7584 6464 🖷 020 7584 0248
email: npfanpic@aol.com
Information and publications on playgroup safety and other play topics.

Play Matters
(See Toy and Leisure Libraries, National Association of)

Play, National Centre for
Edinburgh University, Cramond Campus, Edinburgh EH4 6JD
☎ 0131 312 8088 🖹 0131 312 8088

Playing Fields Association, National
Stanley House, St Chad's Place, London WC1X 9HH
☎ 020 7833 5360 🖹 020 7833 5365
email: npfa@npfa.co.uk
website: www.npfa.co.uk

Pre-School Learning Alliance
69 Kings Cross Road, London WC1X 9LL
☎ 020 7833 0991
Helpline 020 7837 5513 🖹 020 7837 4942
email: pla@pre-school.org.uk
website: www.pre-school.org.uk

Puppet Centre Trust
BAC, Lavender Hill, London SW11 5TN
☎ 020 7228 5335 🖹 020 7228 8863
email: PCT@puppetcentre.demon.co.uk
website: www.puppetcentre.com
A resource centre devoted to puppetry and animation with information available to the general public and educational establishments. Does not cater specifically for special needs.

Ramblers Association
2nd Floor, Camelford House, 87-90 Albert Embankment, London SE1 7TW
☎ 020 7339 8500 🖹 020 7339 8501
email: ramblers@london.ramblers.org.uk
website: www.ramblers.org.uk
Currently encouraging members to include people with special needs in their walks programmes. If the association is contacted by anyone with special needs, they will try to link them up with a local group which can include them.

Reach Resource Centre
California Country Park, Nine Mile Ride, Finchampstead, Berks RG30 4HT
☎ 0118 973 7575
Helpline 0845 604 0414 🖹 0118 973 7105
email: reach@reach-reading.demon.co.uk
website: www.reach-reading.demon.co.uk
A national resource for children with reading difficulties. Reference library and advisory service for anyone who cares for or educates a child whose disability affects his or her ability to read books. Holds over 5,000 children's books and 1,000 reference books, computer software and audio-visual material. Enquiries can be made by letter, telephone or personal visit. (See also Books for Children with Special Needs in Education Section)

Riding for the Disabled Association
Lavinia Norfolk House, Avenue R, Stoneleigh Park CV8 2LY
☎ 024 7669 6510 🖹 024 7669 6532
website: www.riding-for-disabled.org.uk
Aims to provide disabled people of all ages with the opportunity to ride and/or to carriage drive to benefit their health and well being. Currently over 600 groups in the UK.

Rifton Equipment Community Products (UK) Ltd
Rifton/Community Playthings, Robertsbridge, East Sussex TN32 5DR
☎ 0800 387457 🖹 0800 387531
Catalogue of equipment for children with special needs.

RNIB Customer Services
P.O. Box 173, Peterborough, Cambs PE2 6WS
☎ 0845 702 3153 🖹 01733 371555
email: cservice@rnib.org.uk
website: www.rnib.org.uk
Suppliers of books, equipment etc. for people with visual impairment.

RNIB Talking Book Service
RNIB Falcon Park, Neasden Lane, London NW10 1TB
☎ 020 8438 8000 🖹 020 8438 9001
email: wembsc@rnib.org.uk
website: www.rnib.org.uk
(See also Books for Children with Special Needs in Education Section)

Rompa Ltd
Goytside Road, Chesterfield, Derbyshire S40 2PH
☎ 01246 211777 🖹 01246 221802
email: sales@rompa.co.uk
website: www.rompa.co.uk
Suppliers of play, leisure, therapy and sport equipment for people of all ages who have learning disabilities or physical disabilities.

RYA Sailability
RYA House, Romsey Road, Eastleigh, Hants SO50 9YA
☎ 01489 788766 🖹 01703 620545
email: smyths@ryasailablity.org.uk
website: www.rya.org.uk/sailabil
The national organising charity for disabled sailing providing events, training, technology support, group support and competition. Over 40 local clubs.

Scope Leisure Resource Centre
17 Clews Road, Oakenshaw, Redditch, Worcs B98 7ST

5

☎ 01527 404808 📠 01527 404808
website: www.scope.org.uk
Information on sport, leisure and arts facilities. Primarily for people with cerebral palsy but the service is also available to people with any form of disability. Equipment, video and book library.

Scope Recreational Services
11 Churchill Park, Colwick, Notts NG4 2HF
☎ 0115 987 2002 📠 0115 940 2984
website: www.scope.org.uk
Information on sports for people with cerebral palsy.

Scout Association, The
Programme and Development Dept, Gilwell Park, Bury Road, Chingford, London E4 7QW
☎ 020 8524 5246 📠 020 8498 5329
email: ukgilscout@aol.com
website: www.scoutbase.org.uk/
Many local groups will offer membership to boys who have a disability.

Scrabble Club, Postal
33 Amberley Road, Leyton, London E10 7ER
☎ 01702 204722
Scrabble by correspondence for people with mobility problems. Operates over the whole of the UK.

Sesame Institute UK
27 Blackfriars Road, Christ Church, London SE1 8NY
☎ 020 7633 9690 📠 020 7633 9690
email: sesameinstituteuk@ btinternet.com
website: www.btinternet.com/~sesameuk
Promotes a way of working with people who have mental health problems using drama and movement. Postgraduate training and short courses.

Shape
LVSRC, 356 Holloway Road, London N7 6PA
☎ 020 7619 6160
Minicom – 020 7619 6161 📠 020 7619 6162
email: info@shapearts.org.uk
Opens up access to the arts, enabling greater participation by disabled people and older people. Runs arts workshops, projects and events, certificate and diploma arts management courses, short training courses and placements for disabled people. National Deaf Arts Programme and Ticket Scheme with reduced price tickets and volunteer drivers for disabled people.

Ski Association, British Disabled
Stevenstone, Roe Down's Road, Medstead, Alton, Hants GU34 5LG
☎ 01420 562142

Special Gymnastics Association
Wingate Centre, Wrenbury Hall Drive, Wrenbury, Nantwich, Cheshire CW5 8ES
☎ 01270 780456 📠 01270 780456
email: gym@wingate-sga.org.uk
website: wingate-sga.org.uk
Information on gymnastics for children and adults with disabilities. Special converted accommodation in Cheshire. Activity holidays for groups or organisations. Four day residential sport and leisure holidays, offering gymnastics, arts, crafts.

Sport Association for the Disabled, British (BSAD)
(See Disability Sport England)

Sports Association for People with Learning Disability, UK
Unit 9, Milner Way, Ossett, West Yorks WF5 9JN
☎ 01924 267555 📠 01924 267666
email: info@sapld.co.uk
website: www.esapld.co.uk
Coordinating body of sports associations catering for people with learning disabilities.

Sports Centres for Disabled People
RADAR Information Dept, 12 City Forum, 250 City Road, London EC1V 8AF
☎ 020 7250 3222 📠 020 7250 0212
email: radar@radar.org.uk
website: www.radar.org.uk
Publishes a guide 'Sports Centres for Disabled People' which lists facilities in England and Wales.

Sports Funding, Guide to
(See Directory of Social Change)

Sportscotland
Caledonia House, South Gyle, Edinburgh EH12 9DQ
☎ 0131 317 7200 📠 0131 317 7202
website: www.sportscotland.org.uk
Coordinating sports in Scotland. National agency dedicated to promoting sporting opportunities for all Scots.

Swimming Clubs for the Disabled, National Association of
Rosemary O'Leary, The Willows, Mayles Lane, Wickham, Hants PO17 5ND
☎ 01329 833689
Coordinating body of swimming clubs for people with disabilities.

Swimming Therapy, Halliwick Association of
Eric Dilley, c/o ADKC Centre, Whitstable House,

Silchester Road, London W10 6SB
☎ 020 8968 7609 📄 020 8968 7609
website: www.halliwick.org
Provides opportunities for recreational and competitive swimming for disabled people of any age, using specialised teaching techniques. Around 150 clubs in Britain. Books, videos and courses for amateurs and professionals.

Talking Newspapers Association of the UK
National Recording Centre, 10 Browning Road, Heathfield, E. Sussex TN21 8DB
☎ 01435 866102 📄 01435 865422
email: info@tnauk.org.uk
website: www.tnauk.org.uk
Provides taped readings of Sunday newspapers, radio and television journals, etc. for a small subscription fee. Provides material in audio and electronic formats.

Tandem Club, The
Mr P Hallowell, Hon Sec, 25 Hendred Way, Abingdon, Oxon OX14 2AN
☎ 01235 525161 📄 01235 445706
email: pjhallowell@rl.ac.uk
website: www.tandem-club.org.uk
Helps people with visual or physical disability to enjoy cycling.

Tap Dancing, Special Needs
(See Theatre Dance Association, British)

Television for Bedridden People
(See Wireless for the Bedridden)

Theatre
(See Graeae Theatre Company; Kaleidoscope Theatre; Shape)

Theatre Dance Association, British
Kim Rochelle, IAC, Garden Street, Leicester LE1 3UA
☎ 01543 416762 📄 0116 251 4781
email: info@btda.org.uk
website: www.btda.org.uk
Encourages participation in all forms of dance by people with special needs.

THRIVE (Horticultural Therapy)
The Geoffrey Udall Centre, Beech Hill, Reading, Berks RG7 2AT
☎ 0118 988 5688 📄 0118 988 5677
email: info@thrive.org.uk
website: www.thrive.org.uk
Advice and publications, consultancy, training and therapeutic day services for gardeners with a disability

and for organisations using horticulture and gardening for education, therapy, rehabilitation and training. Range of leaflets and books on gardening for children with special needs. (See also Gardening for Disabled Trust; Horticultural Society)

Toy and Leisure Libraries, National Association of
68 Churchway, London NW1 1LT
☎ 020 7387 9592 📄 020 7383 2714
email: admin@natll.ukf.net
website: www.natll.org.uk
Produces a complete list of toys suitable for children with special needs, toy manufacturers and designers, and a list of the many Toy Libraries operating all over the UK. Many Toy Libraries also incorporate an information service and parent support groups. Leisure libraries for adults with special needs. Support and befriending for parents and carers. They are unable to supply information to students due to lack of resources. Incorporates Play Matters. (See also Play Information Centre, National)

Water Sports Centre, National
Adbolton Lane, Holme Pierrepont, Nottingham NG12 2LU
☎ 0115 982 1212
email: holme.pierrepont@leisureconnochon.co.uk
website: www.nationalsportscentres.co.uk

Water-Ski Association, British Disabled
The Tony Edge National Centre, Heron Lake, Hythe End, Wraysbury, Middlesex TW19 6HW
☎ 01784 483664 📄 01784 482747
email: heron.lake@ukonline.co.uk
website: www.bdwsa.org.uk

Wheelchair Basketball Association
104 London Road, Chatteris, Cambs PE16 6SF
☎ 01354 695560 📄 01354 695752
email: sspilkawba@aol.com
website: www.gbwba.org,uk
Details on request.

Wheelchair Sports Foundation
Guttman Road Sports Centre, Stoke Mandeville, Bucks HP21 9PP
☎ 01296 395995 📄 01296 424171
email: enquiries@britishwheelchairsports.org.uk
website: www.wheelbase.org/research/paad/wheelpower/
Creates opportunities for people in wheelchairs to participate in and enjoy sport at all levels and ages.

5

Wireless for the Bedridden

159a High Street, Hornchurch, Essex RM11 3YB
☎ 01708 621101
0800 0182137 ▤ 01708 620816
Provides radio and television sets to people who are housebound or disabled who cannot afford to rent or hire a set for themselves. Application form on request.

Wireless for the Blind Fund, British

Gabriel House, 34 New Road, Chatham, Kent ME4 4QR
☎ 01634 832501 ▤ 01634 817485
email: info@blind.org
website: www.blind.org.uk/CD
Supplies radios and radio/cassette players for people registered as visually impaired and who are in need.

Word Share Magazine

John Wilkinson, 8 Bodmin Moor Close, North Hykenham, Lincs LN6 9BB
☎ 01522 694421
email: johnwilkinson@breathemail.net
A journal written by people with disabilities or past retirement age. Welcomes items of creative writing.

Write Away

1 Thorpe Close, London W10 5XL
☎ 020 8964 4225 ▤ 020 8964 3532
email: members@writeaway.org
Penfriend scheme for people with special needs and disabilities. Opportunities to communicate with pen and paper, audio and braille.

YMCA Day Camps

Warlies Park House, Horseshoe Hill, Waltham Abbey, Essex EN9 3SL
☎ 01992 652272 ▤ 01992 652273
email: day-camp@ymca.org.uk
Easter and Summer holiday activity schemes for 5-16 year olds in Kent, Middlesex and Essex.

YMCA England

640 Forest Road, Walthamstow, London E17 3BR
☎ 020 8520 5599 ▤ 020 8509 3190
email: press@england.ymca.org.uk
website: www.ymca.org.uk
Recreational activities, sports, through local centres.

Yoga, The British Wheel of

25 Jermyn Street, Sleaford, Lincs NG34 7RV
☎ 01529 306851 ▤ 01529 303233
email: office@bwy.org.uk
website: www.members.aol.com/wheelyoga/
The governing body of yoga in the UK. Yoga is adapted by individual teachers to cater for people affected by a range of conditions, on either an individual or group basis. Details of local contacts on request.

Youth Band Association, British

193 Leeds Road, Heckmondwike, W. Yorks WF16 9DR
☎ 01924 407222
email: secretary@byba.org.uk
website: www.byba.org.uk

Youth Clubs for People with Learning Disability

(See Gateway Clubs, National Federation of)

Youth Orchestras, National Association of

Ainslie House, 11 St Colme Street, Edinburgh EH3 6AG
☎ 0131 539 1087 ▤ 0131 539 1069
email: admin@nayo.org.uk
website: www.nayo.org.uk
Produces a list of individual youth orchestras, a magazine and information on concerts. Access to disabled people at NAYO's annual Festival of British Youth Orchestras in Glasgow and Edinburgh. Free admission for children.

Youth, UK

2nd Floor, Kirby House, 20-24 Kirby Street, London EC1N 8TS
☎ 020 7242 4045 ▤ 020 7242 4125
email: info@ukyouth.org
website: www.ukyouth.org
Promotes opportunities for young people to develop skills and interests and provides activities such as art, drama and dance, health education, environmental action, community work and international exchanges, in clubs and projects all over the UK.

Finance, Benefits, Legal Advice

Adaptations for Disability

Department of The Environment, Food and Rural Affairs (DEFRA), Defra Helpline, 3-8 Whitehall Place, London SW1A 2HU

☎ 08459 335577 ▤ 020 7270 8419

website: www.defra.gov.uk/

Publishes 'Need Help with Repairs or Adaptations to your Home?'. Disabled Facilities Grants leaflet 96HC202B

Benefit Enquiry Line

Victoria House, 9th Floor, Ormskirk Road, Preston, Lancs PR1 2QP

☎ 0800 88 22 00 Textphone users 0800 24 33 55

▤ 01772 238953

Benefits Information Guides

☎ 0800 882200 Textphone users 0800 243355

Information on all UK benefits, qualifying conditions and amounts payable. Leaflet GL23; Social Security Benefits Rates. Leaflet MG1; A Guide to Benefits, Pensions and Tax Credits. Leaflet HB5; A Guide to Non-contributory Benefits for Disabled people and their Carers. Leaflet ONE SD4; Caring for Someone?. Leaflet ONE SD3; Long-term Ill or Disabled? Leaflet HB6; A Practical Guide for Disabled People. Leaflet HC11; Are you Entitled to Help with Health Costs? Available from Benefits Enquiry Line or from social security offices.

Beyond Words Series

The BMJ Bookshop, Burton Street, London WC1H 9JR

☎ 020 383 6244/6638

▤ 020 7245 1231 (Royal College of Psychiatry) or Book sales, Royal College of Psychiatry, 17 Belgrave Square, London SW1X 8PG

A series of books for people with learning disabilities, published by St George's Hospital Medical School and the Royal College of Psychiatry. The series is intended to assist in the counselling of people with learning disabilities. Titles include; 'Going to Court' (for those who may need to attend court as a witness), 'You're Nicked' (for those who have been accused of a crime and are facing police procedures), 'In The Dock' (for those who have been charged or have to appear as a defendant in a court). Details of all further titles on request. (See also Mencap Legal Department)

Child Poverty Action Group

94 White Lion Street, London N1 9PF

☎ 020 7837 7979 ▤ 020 7837 6414

email: staff@cpag.demon.co.uk

website: www.cpag.org.uk

Information and advisory service on welfare rights, benefits and financial matters. Publications on benefits, rights and aspects of poverty.

Child Support Agency (HQ)

Child Support Literature Line, Room BP6201, DWP Longbenton, Newcastle-upon-Tyne NE98 1YX

Advice Line 08457 133133 (8am-8pm, Mon-Fri, 8.30am-5pm, Sat)

email: csa-nel@dwp.gsi.gov.uk

website: www.dss.gov.uk/csa/

DSS leaflet CSA2001; For Parents who Live Apart.

Children's Legal Centre

Education Advocacy Unit, University of Essex, Wivenhoe Park, Colchester, Essex CO4 3SQ

☎ 01206 874807

Advice Line 01206 873820 (10-12am, 2-4.30pm, Mon-Fri) ▤ 01206 874026

website: www2.essex.ac.uk/clc

Legal advice by telephone, free legal representation at SEN tribunals in SE England, representation of children in exclusion disputes.

Children's Rights Alliance

94 White Lion Street, London N1 9PF

☎ 020 7278 8222 ▤ 020 7278 9552

website: www.londoncsights.org.uk

Please note they are unable to offer personal advice.

Citizen's Advice Bureaux

Local CABs will provide advice, information and practical help on benefits and legal issues.

Crime, Accusation of, in People with Learning Disability

(See Beyond Words Series; Mencap Legal Department)

Department for Work and Pensions (was Department of Social Security)

Disability Unit, Level 6, Adelphi Building, 1-11 John Adam Street, London WC2N 6HT

☎ 020 7712 2171 (9am-5pm, Mon-Fri)

▤ 020 7712 2386

website: www.dss.gov.uk/asd

5

Department of Health (DoH) Publications Unit

P.O. Box 410, Wetherby, W. Yorks LS23 7LN
Literature line 0800 555777
website: www.doh.gov.uk/pub/docs/doh/
cmo99_01.pdf
Very wide range of leaflets and booklets on all aspects of health.

DIAL UK (Disablement Information and Advice Line)

Park Lodge, St Catherine's Hospital, Tickhill Road, Balby, Doncaster, Yorks DN4 8QN
☎ 01302 310123 Minicom 01302 310123
🖹 01302 310404
website: www.dialuk.org.uk
Local centres in all areas of the UK, offering information on all aspects of disability.

Directory of Social Change (DSC)

24 Stephenson Way, London N4 3EG
☎ 020 7209 4422 🖹 020 7209 4130
website: www.dsc.org.uk
Publishes directories and guides, including; 'Guide to Grants for Individuals in Need'. Prices and details of other guides on request.

Disability Alliance

Michele Holland, Administrative Assistant, Universal House, 88-94 Wentworth Street, London E1 7SA
☎ 020 7247 8776 (also minicom)
020 7247 8776 (also minicom) 🖹 020 7247 8765
email: office.da@dial.pipex.com
website: www.disabilityalliance.org
Disability Alliance is commited to breaking the link between poverty and disability by providing information to disabled people about their entitlements and campaigning for improvements to the social security system and for increases in disability benefits so that they better reflect the real costs of disability.

Disability and Carer's Directorate

Government Buildings, Warbreck House, Warbreck Hill, Blackpool, Lancs FY2 0YE
☎ 0845 7123456 🖹 01253 331266

Disability Law Service

Room 241, 29th Floor, 49-51 Bedford Row, London WC1R 4LR
☎ & Minicom & Advice Line 020 7831 8031
(10.30am-1pm, 2pm-4.30pm, Mon-Fri)
🖹 020 7831 5582
website: www.mkurrein.co.uk/work/disablaw.htm
Free, confidential legal advice to people with disabilities, their families, carers and enablers, including discrimination, housing and community care, welfare, benefits and consumer issues.

Disability Living Allowance (DLA) Unit

Government Buildings, Warbreck House, Warbreck Hill, Blackpool FY2 0YE
Customer Care Helpline 0845 7123456
Minicom 0845 224433 🖹 01253 331266
A tax-free social security benefit for children or adults who need help with getting around, help with personal care or help with both of these. Leaflet DS706 – Disability Living Allowance for Children under 16. Leaflet DS704 Disability Living Allowance (over 16) from local social security offices or call the Benefits Enquiry Line (0800 882200) for more information.

Disabled Facilities Grants

DETR Free Literature, P.O. Box 236, West Yorks LS23 7NB
☎ 0870 122 6236 Textphone 0870 120 7405
🖹 0870 122 6237
Leaflet explaining the Disabled Facilities Grant

Disablement Income Group (DIG)

P.O. Box 5743, Finchingfield, Essex CM7 4PW
☎ 01371 811621 🖹 01372 811633
Will offer personal guidance on any financial problem relating to disabled people and their families. Publishes a wide range of explanatory leaflets and booklets, including 'Social Security Benefits'; a series of booklets explaining the main benefits.

Family Credit Unit

Family Credit Union, Government Buildings, Cop Lane, Penwortham, Preston, Lancs PR4 0BR
Helpline 08456 095000
A weekly tax-free benefit for working people bringing up children, where one parent is working more than 16 hours per week.

Family Fund Trust, The

P.O. Box 50, York YO1 9ZX
☎ 01904 621115 🖹 01904 652625
textphone 01904 658085
email: info@familytrustfund.org.uk
website: www.familyfundtrust.org.uk
The purpose of the Family Fund Trust is to ease the stress on families who care for very severely disabled children under 16 by providing grants and information relevant to the care of the child. The Trust is an independent organisation registered as a charity and funded by government administrations of England, Northern Ireland, Scotland and Wales. Grants given include washing machines, holidays, leisure activities, driving lessons, bedding, clothing and other items, related to the care of the child. Further

details of the Trust's disability and financial guidelines are available from the Information Officer, The Family Trust, PO Box 50, York YO1 9ZX. Families should apply in writing, giving the child's full name and date of birth, brief details of the child's disability and kind of help requested.

Family Investment for the Handicapped
51 Old Dover Road, Canterbury, Kent CT1 3DE
☎ 01227 456963
Helps families to come together to invest in a group home, so that their relatives can be provided with a place in that home, when necessary.

Family Rights Group
The Print House, 18 Ashwin Street, London E8 3DL
☎ 020 7923 2628
Advice Line 0800 731 1696 (1.30pm-3.00pm, Mon-Fri) 🖳 020 7923 2683
website: www.frg.org.uk
Advice for families involved in child protection procedures or with children in residential accommodation or in care.

Family Service Units
207 Old Marylebone Road, London NW1 5QP
☎ 020 7402 5175 🖳 020 7724 1829
website: www.fsu.org.uk
Counselling, advocacy, welfare and legal advice for families.

Family Welfare Association
501-505 Kingsland Road, Dalston, London E8 4AU
☎ 020 7254 6251 🖳 020 7249 5443
Some grants for families in need. Branches in most cities.

Free Milk for Disabled Children
Disability Benefits Unit, Room C122A, Lobby D, Warbreck House, Warbreck Hill, Blackpool FY2 0YE
☎ 0845 7123456
Customer Care Helpline 0845 7123456
Minicom 0345 224433 🖳 01253 331266
website: www.dss.gov.uk/lifeevent/benefits/free_milk.htm
Tokens for seven pints of milk per week for parents of children between 5 and 16 years who are so disabled, mentally or physically, that they cannot attend school. Recipients do not need to be in receipt of any social security benefits to qualify. Form RW20 from the Disability Benefits Unit or social security offices.

Funderfinder
65 Raglan Road, Leeds, W. Yorks LS2 9DZ
☎ 0113 243 3008 🖳 0113 243 2966
email: info@funderfinder.org.uk
website: www.funderfinder.org.uk

Produces a software package called 'People In Need' (PIN) which helps individuals to identify charitable trusts that may give them a grant. Funderfinder does not undertake searches but will tell enquirers where they can access PIN locally.

Funding for Education
(See Educational Grants in Education Section)

Grants for Individuals and Organisation, Guides to
(See Directory of Social Change)

Health Costs Benefits
Leaflet HC11; Are You Entitled to Help with Health Costs?. From social security offices or the Benefits Agency.

Health Service Ombudsman
Millbank Tower, Millbank, London SW1P 4QP
☎ 0845 015 4033 🖳 020 7217 4160
textphone 020 7217 4066
email: offsc.Enquiries@ombudsman.gsi.gov.uk
website: www.ombudsman.org.uk
Will investigate complaints about clinical decisions made about doctors and other health professionals, only if care funded by the NHS. Patients must first have their complaints examined by current NHS procedures. The Ombudsman will only investigate complaints if they cannot be sorted out at local level. Information leaflet available from health authorities, libraries and Citizens Advice Bureaux. NB Complaints cannot be made by e-mail but general enquiries by e-mail are welcomed.

House of Commons Public Information Office
House of Commons, London SW1A 2DG
☎ 020 7219 4272 🖳 020 7219 5839
website: www.parliament.uk/commons

House of Lords Public Information Office
House of Lords, London SW1A 0PW
☎ 020 7219 3107 (Mon-Thurs 10am – 4pm, Fri 10am – 2pm when house is sitting)
email: hlinfo@parliament.uk
website: www.publications.parliament.uk/pa/ld

Independent Living Fund
P.O. Box 183, Nottingham, Notts NG8 3RD
☎ 0115 942 8191/8192
0115 942 8223 🖳 0115 929 3156
website: www.ilf.org.uk
A fund, set up by the government, to provide discretionary grants for severely disabled people (over 16 years) to give them the opportunity of living

independently at home instead of in residential care, by helping to pay towards the cost of their personal and/or domestic care. In order to be eligible certain criteria all need to be fulfilled by potential applicants.

Invalid Care Allowance Unit

Palatine House, Lancaster Road, Preston, Lancs PR1 1HB

☎ 01253 856123 Textphone 01772 899 489

🖳 01772 899354

email: ICA-customer-service@dulp.gsi.gov.uk

A weekly cash benefit paid to people who spend at least 35 hours a week caring for someone, over the age of 16, who is severely disabled, and who is receiving DLA at the middle or highest rate.

Invalids at Home

Bamford Cottage, South Hill Avenue, Harrow, Middlesex HA1 3PA

☎ 020 8864 3818

Small grants for people who are severely disabled and are living at home. All applications must be made by a social worker, occupational therapist or similarly professional person.

Law Society Children Panel, The

Ipsley Court, Redditch, Worcs B98 0TD

☎ 01527 504433 🖳 01527 510213

website: www.lawsociety.org.uk

Holds a list of solicitors offering legal advice on a variety of issues, especially those affecting children.

Legal Aid

(Contact Local Citizen's Advice Bureau)

Legal Services Commission (Community Legal Service and Criminal Defence Service)

85 Grays Inn Road, London WC1X 8TX

☎ 020 7759 0000

website: www.legalservices.gov.uk

Life-Threatening Illness and Disability in Children

(See React)

Medical Accidents, Action for Victims of

44 High Street, Croydon, Surrey CR0 1YB

☎ 020 8686 8333 🖳 020 8667 9065

website: www.avma.org.uk

Advice, information for people who feel that something has gone wrong with their treatment. Details on request.

Mencap Legal Department

Information and advice on welfare, legal rights, making of wills etc. as applied to people with learning disability. Contact Mencap Head Office. (See also Beyond Words Series)

Mencap Trusteeship Scheme

123 Golden Lane, London EC1Y 0RT

☎ 020 7454 0454 🖳 020 7696 5540

website: www.mencap.org.uk

A service for parents of children and adults with learning difficulties, which provides for a specially appointed visitor to keep in close contact with the child (or adult), and watch over his or her interests, after the death of the parents. It provides personal care and interest, acknowledgement of Christmas, and birthdays etc. and help with sorting out any problems concerning the individual. Arrangements are made in which the parents can either take out a simple form of insurance or leave a lump sum in a Trust Fund in their will. Explanatory booklet available.

National Consumer Council

20 Grosvenor Gardens, London SW1 0DH

☎ 020 7730 3469 🖳 020 7730 0191

website: www.ncc.org.uk

Advice on health, welfare and legal matters.

RADAR

12 City Forum, 250 City Road, London EC1V 8AF

☎ 020 7250 3222 🖳 020 7250 0212

website: www.radar.org.uk

Information and publications on financial and legal matters relating to people with disabilities.

React

St Luke's House, 270 Sandycombe Road, Kew, Richmond, Surrey TW9 3NP

☎ 020 8940 2575 🖳 020 8940 2050

website: react-kew.demon.co.uk/

Makes grants for special aids or equipment for children who have a life-threatening illness or disability.

RNIB Customer Services

P.O. Box 173, Peterborough, Cambs PE2 6WS

☎ 01345 023153 🖳 01733 37 1555

website: www.rnib.org.uk

Guides to benefits and legal matters for people with visual impairment.

Special Wishes, Treats

(See Organisations Section)

Trusteeship Visitors Scheme (Learning Disability)

(See Mencap Trusteeship Scheme)

Vaccine Damage Payments Unit

Palatine House, Lancaster Road, Preston, Lancs PR1 1HB

☎ 01772 899944 🖳 01772 899873

website: www.dup.gov.uk/lifeevent/benefits/vaccine-damage-payments.htm

Leaflet HB3 – 'Payment for People Severely Disabled by a Vaccine' (also available from above address or social security offices).

Wheelchairs, Provision of
(See Disabled Living Foundation; Remploy Orthitics in Aids and Equipment Section)

Wills for People with Learning Disability
(Contact Mencap Legal Department)

5

Holidays, Travel, Mobility

AA Disabled Traveller Guide
Automobile Association, Carr Ellison House, William Armstrong Road, Newcastle-upon-Tyne NE4 7YA
Disability Helpline 0800 262050 ▤ 0191 235 5111
email: customerservices@theaa.com
website: www.theaa.co.uk
Produces a comprehensive guide for people with disabilities, which lists hotel services and facilities, advisory bodies, motorway services, restaurants etc.

Access Travel (Lancs) Ltd
6 The Hillock, Astley, Lancs M29 7GW
☎ 01942 888844 ▤ 01942 891811
email: info@access-travel.co.uk
website: access-travel.co.uk
Travel and holidays for people in wheelchairs abroad. Details on request. ATOL protected.

Accessible Environments, Centre for
Nutmeg House, 60 Gainsford Street, London SE1 2NY
☎ 020 7357 8182 ▤ 020 7357 8183
email: info@cae.org.uk
website: www.cae.org.uk
Provides advice and information on making buildings and places accessible to all users, including people with disabilities, and in enhancing quality and design. Access consultancy, training, publications and videos, information services, quarterly journal.

Across Trust
Bridge House, 70-72 Bridge Road, East Molesey, Surrey KT8 9HF
☎ 020 8783 1355 ▤ 020 8783 1622
email: acrosst@across.org
website: www.across.org.uk
Takes parties of severely disabled people on pilgrimage to Lourdes, or across Europe, using specially adapted ambulances. (See also HCTP – The Pilgrimage Trust)

Adventure Education
(Now Institute for Outdoor Learning)

Aeromedical Services (AA Alert)
St John Ambulance, 27 St Johns Lane, London EC1M 4BU
☎ 0870 235 5321 ▤ 0870 235 0796
website: www.sja.org.uk
Escorts sick and disabled people nationally and internationally.

Air Transport Users Council
CAA House, 45-59 Kingsway, London WC2B 6TE
☎ 020 7240 6061 (9am-12pm, 2-5pm, Mon-Fri) ▤ 020 7240 7071
website: www.avc.org.uk
Advisory body for all airline passengers. Free booklet: 'Flight Plan- a passenger's guide to planning and using air travel' and a leaflet 'Travel Happy'.

Ashwellthorpe Hall Hotel
Ashwellthorpe, Norwich, Norfolk NR16 1EX
☎ 01508 489324 ▤ 01508 488409
email: ashwellthorpe@btclick.com
website: www.ashwellthorpehall.org.uk
Hotel with facilities for disabled people, their children and/or carers. Group holidays.

ATS Travel
Assistance Travel Services Ltd, 1 Tank Lane, Purfleet, Essex RM19 1TA
☎ 01708 863198 ▤ 01708 860514
email: atstravel@aol.com
website: www.assistedholidays.com
Worldwide tailor-made holidays for people with any type or any degree of disability, equipment hire, holiday insurance, tail-lift coaches, group touring holidays, specially designed caravans. Carers can be provided. Details on request. (See also Insurance for Travel)

Automobile Association
(See AA Disabled Traveller Guide)

Avon Tyrrell Activity Centre
Avon Tyrrell Centre, Bransgore, Hants BH23 8EE
☎ 01425 672347
email: info@avontyrrell.org.uk
Provides educational and holiday visits to groups of all kinds. Brochure on request.

Badaguish Outdoor Centre
Speyside Trust, Aviemore, Invernesshire PH22 1QU
☎ 01479 861285 ▤ 01479 861758
email: info@badaguish.org
website: www.badaguish.org
Activity holidays for individuals or small groups. All types and degrees of disability accepted.

Barrows Green Holiday Centre
Barrows Green House, Barrows Green, Kendal, Cumbria LA8 0JQ
☎ 01539 560307 ▤ 01539 561508

Activity and adventure holidays for people with learning disability, with or without additional disabilities, age 8-21 years. Run by Barnardo's.

Bendrigg Lodge
Old Hutton, Kendal, Cumbria LA8 ONR
☎ 01539 723766 📠 01539 722446
email: bendrigg@msn.com
website: www.bendrigg.org.uk
Residential outdoor activity centre offering courses for disabled and disadvantaged people.

Blue Badge Scheme (Parking Concessions for Disabled People)
DTLR Enquiry Line 020 7944 3000
email: blue.badge@dtlr.gov.uk
Information leaflet available from Social Services Departments or Department of Transport.

Break
1 Montague Road, Sheringham, Norfolk NR26 8LN
☎ 01263 822161 📠 01263 822181
email: office@break-charity.org.uk
website: www.break-charity.org
Holidays and respite care for children and adults with learning disabilities and families in which there is a member with special needs.

Bridget's Trust
Tennis Court Road, Cambridge CB2 1QF
☎ 01223 354312 📠 01223 461324
email: bridgets-administration@lists.cam.ac.uk
A hostel which provides care to disabled students during college and university terms. Now open to offer holidays to people with disabilities wishing to visit Cambridge outside term-time.

Calvert Trust, Exmoor
Wistlandpound, Kentisbury, Barnstable, Devon EX31 4SJ
☎ 01598 763221 Minicom 01598 763221
📠 01598 763063
website: www.calvert-trust.org.uk
Centre in north Devon offering residential activity holidays for disabled people in fully catered and self-catering accommodation. Inclusive activities include sailing, canoeing, climbing, riding and swimming. Brochure on request.

Calvert Trust, Cumbria
Little Crosthwaite, Underskiddaw, Keswick, Cumbria CA12 4QD
☎ 01768 772254 Minicom 01768 772254
📠 01768 771920
email: calvert.keswick@dial.pipex.com
website: www.calvert-trust.org.uk

Residential centre providing outdoor activities, holidays and courses for people with disabilities, groups, schools, families and friends. Activities include sailing, canoeing, horse riding, trap riding, orienteering, hill-walking, climbing, abseiling, paragliding.

Calvert Trust, Northumberland
Kielder Water, Hexham, Northumberland NE48 1BS
☎ 01434 250232 📠 01434 250015
email: enquiries@calvert-kielder.com
website: www.calvert-trust.org.uk
Activity and study holidays for people with a disability.

Camping and Caravanning for the Disabled
Mobility Information Service, Unit B1, Greenwood Court, Cartmel Drive, Shrewsbury SY1 3TB
☎ 01743 463072
Information and advice on camping for people with physical disabilities and their families.

Can Be Done Ltd
7-11 Kensington High Street, London W8 5NP
☎ 020 8907 2400 📠 020 8909 1854
email: cbdtravel@aol.com
website: www.canbedone.co.uk
Specialists in travel for people with disabilities. City breaks, self-drive holidays, coach tours, abroad and in the UK. Brochure on request.

Catholic Handicapped Fellowship, National Council of the
Mr J Mair, 15 Woodlands Park Drive, Blaydon, Tyne & Wear NE21 5PQ
☎ 0191 414 3221
Clubs, outings, parties, religious instruction for children and young adults with physical and/or learning disabilities.

Christian Lewis Children's Cancer Care
Barbara Thomas, Childcare Centre, 62 Walter Road, Swansea SA1 4PT
☎ 01792 480500 📠 01792 480700
email: enquiries@childrens-cancer-care.org.uk
website: www.christian-lewis-trust.org.uk
Three mobile home sites in Wales, Disneyland Paris and Disney World Florida for children with cancer and their families. Holiday insurance service.

Churchtown Activity Centre
Lanlivery, Bodmin, Cornwall PL30 5BT
☎ 01208 872148 📠 01208 873377
Adventure and recreational holidays, development courses, some respite care for people with special needs of any kind. Wide range of indoor and outdoor activities.

5

Coldwell Activity Centre

Back Lane, Southfield, Burnley, Lancs BB10 3RD
☎ 01282 601819 📠 01282 449525
email: admin@coldwellbiz.fsnet.co.uk-bookings
website: www.coldwell.org.uk
Holiday and respite accommodation, leisure and sport activities, for people with any type of disability or disadvantage.

Community Transport Association

Highbank, Halton Street, Hyde, Cheshire SK14 2NY
☎ 0161 366 6685 📠 0161 351 7221
email: ctuk@communitytransport.com
website: www.communitytransport.com
Support for groups or individuals requiring transport of children with special needs. Information on local community transport services for people with disabilities. Supplies minibuses to groups, collects and supplies used furniture to people on benefit.

Department of Transport Mobility Unit

(Now Disabled Persons Transport Advisory Committee)

Disability, Northern Ireland Council on

Disability Action, 2 Annadale Avenue, Belfast BT7 3JH
☎ 028 9029 7880 Text phone 028 9064 5779
📠 028 9049 1627
email: hq@disabilityaction.org
website: www.disabilityaction.org
Information on all aspects of disability, holidays, mobility, transport and travel.

Disabled Holiday Directory

6 Seaview Crescent, Goodwick, Pembrokeshire SA64 0AZ
☎ 01348 875592
email: sian@disabledholidaydirectory.co.uk
website: www.disabledholidaydirectory.co.uk
Comprehensive directory of holiday facilities for disabled people. (No brochures are printed.)

Disabled Persons Transport Advisory Committee

DPTAC Secretariat, Zone 1/14, Great Minster House, 76 Marsham Street, London SW1P 4DR
☎ 020 7947 8011 📠 020 7944 6998
email: dptac@dtlr.gov.uk
website: www.dptac.gov.uk
Deals with the implementation of the Disability Discrimination Act, access to the pedestrian environment and hosts the Disabled Persons Transport Advisory Committee. Advises the Government on transport as it affects people with disabilities.

Disaway Trust

Mrs L Simpkins, 55 Tolworth Park Road, Surbiton, Surrey KT6 7RJ
☎ 020 878 2054 📠 020 8543 3431
email: lynnesimpkins@hotmail.com
Group holidays for physically disabled people over 16 years.

Dockland Canal Boat Trust

Mick Boys, St John's Centre, Albert Road, North Woolwich, London E16 2JY
☎ 020 8511 2911 📠 020 8511 2911
email: mickboys@compuserve.com
website: ourworld.compuserve.com/homepages/MickBoys
Specially adapted canal boat for day or weekly hire, with special needs in mind. (See also Peter Le Marchant Trust)

Dogs for the Disabled

The Francis Hay Centre, Blacklocks Hill, Banbury, Oxon OX17 2BS
☎ 08700 776600 📠 0870 776602
email: info@dogsforthedisabled.org
website: www.dogsforthedisabled.org
Trains specially selected dogs to carry out tasks that assist disabled people.

Duke of Edinburgh Award Scheme

Gulliver House, Madeira Walk, Windsor, Berks SL4 1EU
☎ 01753 810753 📠 01753 810666
email: info@theaward.org
website: www.theaward.org
Camping courses and schemes, with places for disabled children and young people. Publishes several booklets and guides.

Elim Christian Centre

Gladstone Road, Northampton NN5 7EG
☎ 01604 757878 / 582027 📠 01604 753234
email: elimnorthampton@hotmail.com
website: elimcc.org.uk
Sunday services: 9am, 10:30am and 9pm. Weekly Cell Groups (meeting in homes), Youth Club and Sunday School, Milk and Honey Bookshop, Senior Citizen Lunch Club.

Elizabeth Fitzroy Homes

David Emmerson, Caxton House, Lower Street, Haslemere, Surrey GU27 2PE
☎ 01428 656766 📠 01428 643262
email: info@efitzroy.org.uk
website: www.efitzroy.org.uk
Holidays for people with physical disabilities or learning disability, over 19 years, including those with profound disabilities.

English Country Cottages

Stoney Bank, Farby, Barnoldswick, Lancs BB94 0EF

☎ 0870 781 1100 📠 0890 585 1150

email: ecc.enquiry@holidaycottagesgroup.com

website: www.english-country-cottages.co.uk

Wheelchair accessible properties in the UK.

Family Fund Trust, The

P.O. Box 50, York YO1 9ZX

☎ 01904 621115 📠 01904 652625

textphone 01904 658085

email: info@familyfundtrust.org.uk

website: www.familyfundtrust.org.uk

Grants may be given to help with the cost of a holiday for a family in which there is a severely disabled child under sixteen. Applications should be made in writing, giving the child's full name and date of birth, brief details of the child's disability and kind of help requested. (See also Financial Help for Holidays)

Family Holiday Association

16 Mortimer Street, London W1T 3JL

☎ 020 7436 3304 📠 020 7436 3302

email: info@fhaonline.org.uk

website: www.fhaonline.org.uk

Will provide a grant for a holiday to families who have not had a break together for at least four years. The family must be referred to them by a social worker, doctor or similar professional. Funds are limited so a selection procedure is necessary. (See also Financial Help for Holidays)

Farm Holidays

(See Gorslwyd Farm Holidays)

Field Studies Council

Blencathra Centre, Threlkeld, Keswick, Cumbria CA12 4SG

☎ 01768 779601 📠 01768 79264

email: fsc.blencathra@ukonline.co.uk

Runs a network of field study centres, including some centres offering accommodation for disabled people.

Financial Help for Holidays

(See Family Fund Trust; Family Holiday Association; Holiday Care; Pearson's Holiday Fund)

Girlguiding UK

17-19 Buckingham Palace Road, London SW1W 0PT

☎ 020 7834 6242 📠 020 7828 8317

email: chq@girlguiding.org.uk

website: www.girlguiding.org.uk

Facilities at some camps for girls with disabilities. (See also Scout Holiday Homes Trust)

Gorslwyd Farm Holidays

Bob & Jennie Donaldson, Gorslwyd Farm, Tan-y-Groes, Cardigan SA43 2HZ

☎ 01239 810 593 📠 01239 811 569

email: stevroni@talk21.com

Accessible holiday accommodation situated in a farm environment. Access for independent wheelchair users to accommodation, gardens, adventure play, nature trail, games room and farm animals.

Guide Dogs Adventure Group

Guide Dogs for the Blind Association, Hillfields, Burghfield Common, Reading, Berks RG7 3YG

☎ 0118 983 5555 📠 0118 983 5433

email: enquiries@dogsworldwide.com

website: www.dogsworldwide.com

Holidays and activities in the UK and abroad.

Gymnastics & Activity Holidays

(See Special Gymnastics Association in Useful addresses: Leisure)

Halcyon Care Holidays

27 River Street, Rhyl, Clwyd LL18 1PY

☎ 01745 342220

Escorted holidays in North Wales, Spain and Florida for people with a learning disability, with emphasis on freedom of choice for guests about the activities they take part in. Dietary and medical needs are met, transport and qualified staff are provided.

Handihols

(See Special Families Homeswap Register)

HCTP – The Pilgrimage Trust

Oakfield Park, 32 Bilton Road, Rugby, Warwickshire CV22 7HQ

☎ 01788 564646 📠 01788 564640

email: hcpt@hctp.org.uk

website: www.hcpt.org.uk

Takes children and adults with disabilities and from all backgrounds and religions, to Lourdes.

HELP (Holiday Endeavour for Lone Parents)

57 Owston Road, Carcroft, Doncaster, S. Yorks DN6 8DA

☎ 01302 728791 📠 01302 726959

email: francescamorris@bt.net

website: www.helpholidays.org

Low cost holidays for any lone parent (with custody or single access parent) with at least one child under 18 years. Information on holiday camps which have special needs facilities, help with cost of holiday if the criteria are met and the parent is referred by a professional third party in writing. (See also One Parent Family Holidays)

5

Hindleap Warren Outdoor Education Centre

Bernard Sunley Outdoor Education Centre, Hindleap Warren, Wych Cross, Forest Row, E. Sussex RH18 5JS

☎ 01342 822625 🖹 01342 822913

email: david.nottidge@hindlead.co.uk

website: www.hindleap.co.uk

A fully equipped residential centre offering a range of adventure activities, including archery, abseiling, canoeing and expeditions. Specialist provision for young people with special needs.

Holiday Care

2nd Floor, Imperial Buildings, Victoria Road, Horley, Surrey RH6 9DY

☎ 01293 774535 Minicom 01293 776943

🖹 01293 784647

email: holiday.care@virgin.net

website: www.care@virgin.net

An information service on suitable holiday accommodation for people with disabilities. Guides on all aspects of travel and holidays. Information on request. (See also Financial Help for Holidays)

Holidays for Disabled People Ltd

P.O. Box 164, Totton, Southampton SO40 9WZ

☎ 01252 332452

email: H4dp1@aol.com

Organises one week's holiday per year at a holiday centre in the UK for families, groups and individuals who have a physical disability. Smaller holidays are arranged, usually abroad, for groups of about 40 people and usually aimed at age groups 18-35 and 30-60 years. Send SAE for details.

Home Swapping

(See Special Families Homeswap Register)

Institute for Outdoor Learning

12 St Andrew's Churchyard, Penrith, Cumbria CA11 7YE

☎ 01768 891065 🖹 01768 891914

email: institute@outdoor-learning.org

website: www.outdoor-learning.org

Publishes books on working with people with disabilities in the outdoors ands sell the 'Kite' harness for enabling disabled people to climb. Publishes 'The Outdoor Source Book' – directory of outdoor providers, including specialists in disabilities.

Insurance for Travel

(See ATS Travel; Leisurecare Insurance Services; Travel Freedom; Travelcare Ltd)

Jane Hodge Hotel

Trerhyngyll, Cowbridge, Vale of Glamorgan CF7 7TN

☎ 01446 772608 🖹 01446 775831

A hotel equipped with a wide range of specially adapted facilities, sporting and leisure activities and personal care staff for children and their families and adults with special needs.

John Grooms Association

50 Scrutton Street, London EC2A 4XQ

☎ 020 7452 2000 🖹 020 7452 2001

email: info@johngrooms.org.uk

website: www.johngrooms.org.uk

Offers a variety of holidays for people of any age and with any disability, accompanied by helpers. Bungalows, holiday homes and chalets.

Jubilee Sailing Trust

Jubilee Yard, Hazel Road, Woolston, Southampton, Hants SO19 7GB

☎ 023 8044 9106 🖹 023 8044 9145

email: info@jst.org.uk

website: www.jst.org.uk

Sailing holidays for children and adults with special needs.

Kingfisher Barn

Rye Farm, Abingdon, Oxfordshire OX14 3NN

☎ 01235 537538 🖹 01235 537538

email: info@kingfisherbarn.com

website: www.kingfisherbarn.com

A range of self-catering holiday cottages, most fully accessible to wheelchair users. Also include ceiling hoist, wide doors, cot sides, comodes, indoor pool with hoists – lovely countryside with much to visit – office open 9am- 8pm, Monday-Friday, 9am-4pm, Saturday.

Leisurecare Insurance Services

Century House, 100 High Street, Cricklade, Wiltshire SN6 6AA

☎ 01793 750150 🖹 01793 750661

Travel insurance for people with medical problems and disabilities, their families and carers. Travel must be to countries within the European Union. Registered insurance brokers. (See also ATS Travel; Travel Freedom; Travelcare Ltd)

Low Mill

Askrigg, Leyburn, N. Yorks DL8 3HZ

☎ 01969 650432 🖹 01969 650729

email: lowmill@gofree.co.uk

Range of holidays, outdoor courses and activities for people with any kind of disability.

MAVIS (Mobility Advice and Vehicle Information Service)

O Wing, Macadam Avenue, Old Wokingham Road, Crowthorne, Berks RG45 6XD

☎ 01344 661000 Minicom 01344 661000

🖹 01344 661066

email: mavis@dft.gsi.gov.uk

website: www.mobilityunit.dft.gov.uk/mavis.htm

MAVIS was set up by the Department of Transport to help people with disabilities to make informed decisions about their own mobility needs. Practical advice on vehicle adaptation and suitable vehicle types for both drivers and passengers is given.

Medina Valley Centre for Outdoor Education

Dodnor Lane, Newport, Isle of Wight PO30 5TE

☎ 01983 522195 🖹 01983 825962

email: info@medinavalleycentre.org.uk

website: www.medinavalleycentre.org.uk

Outdoor and activity centre offering holidays and courses to schools and individuals. Activities include field studies in biology, geography and environmental studies (to A level), sailing courses. Welcomes people with physical or learning difficulties on any course as individuals or groups, with carers if necessary.

Mencap

Holiday Fund Administrator, Mencap, 123 Golden Lane, London EC1Y 0RT

☎ 020 7454 0454 🖹 020 7696 5548

email: holidayfund@mencap.org.uk

website: www.mencap.org.uk

Publishes a fact sheet containing information on holidays for children and adults with a learning disability and sources of funding for holidays.

Mobility Aids Service

88d South Street, Stanground, Peterborough PE2 8EZ

☎ 01733 344930

Information and guidance on mobility aids for children and adults with a disability.

Mobility Information Service

Unit B1, Greenwood Court, Cartmel Drive, Shrewsbury, Shropshire SY1 3TB

☎ 01743 761889 🖹 01743 463072

email: mis@kcuk.freeserve.co.uk

website: www.mis.org.uk

Lists of suitable cars for families with a disabled member and other advice on travel.

Mobility Matters

Independent Living Centre, Robert Jones and Agnes Hunt Orthopaedic, Gobowen, Oswestry, Shropshire SY10 7AG

☎ 01691 680180

Offers advice on all aspects of mobility.

Mobility Trust

Andrew Mackintosh, 50 High Street, Hungerford, Berks RG17 0NE

☎ 01488 686335 🖹 01488 686336

email: mobility@mobilitytrust.org.uk

Mobility Trust provides powered wheelchairs and scooters for severely disabled children and adults who cannot obtain them through statutory sources or purchase such equipment themselves. Does not give grants.

Motability

Goodman House, Station Approach, Harlow, Essex CM20 2ET

☎ 01279 635666

Helpline 01279 635666 🖹 01279 632000

website: www.motability.co.uk

A charity that helps disabled people and their families become more mobile. It does this by helping them to use the Higher Rate Mobility Component of their Disability Living Allowance (HRMC or DLA) to lease or buy a car or powered wheelchair or scooter. Anyone who is in receipt of the Higher Rate Mobility Component of DLA can apply. This includes children from three years old who can apply for cars as passengers provided they receive the correct allowance. Motability's charitable fund can help if you are unable to afford the advance payment on some lease vehicles or necessary adaptations to the vehicle. Grants are available for the least expensive option to meet your basic mobility needs.

MOVE International (Europe)

University of Wolverhampton, Gorwy Road, Walsall, W. Midlands WS1 3BD

☎ 01902 323066 🖹 01902 322858

email: move-europe@compuserve.com

website: www.wlv.ac.uk/sed/move/

The MOVE programme aims to provide mobility for people who have difficulty with sitting, standing and walking for use in schools, centres and at home. Runs training courses for teachers, conferences, newsletter.

One Parent Family Holidays

Kildonan Courtyard, Barrhill, Girvan, Ayrshire KA26 0PS

☎ 01465 821288 🖹 01465 821288

email: opfholiday@aol.com

website: www.opfh.org.uk

Holidays overseas for single parents and their children. See also HELP – (Holiday Endeavour for Lone Parents)

5

Orange Badge Scheme
(Now the Blue Badge Scheme)

Outward Bound Trust, The
207 Waterloo Road, London SE1 8XD
☎ 0870 513 4227 📠 017684 86983
email: enquiries@outwardbound-uk.org
website: www.outwardbound-uk.org
Will provide details of courses suitable for people with special needs.

Parking Concessions for Disabled People
(See Blue Badge Scheme)

Pearson's Holiday Fund
P.O. Box 123, Bishop's Waltham, Hampshire SO32 1ZE
☎ 01489 893260 📠 01489 893260
Partly funds holidays for needy and disadvantaged children. It cannot deal directly with individuals or families and all contact must be made through social services, clubs, schools, churches, doctors etc. Holidays are not arranged by the Fund. (See also Financial Help for Holidays)

Peter Le Marchant Trust
Canalside Moorings, Beeches Road, Loughborough, Leics LE11 2NS
☎ 01509 265590 📠 01509 265590
Holidays and day trips on inland waterways. All disabilities catered for. (See also Dockland Canal Boat Trust)

PHAB England
Summit House, Wandle, Croydon, Surrey CR0 1DF
☎ 020 8667 9443 📠 020 8681 1399
email: info@phabengland.org.uk
website: www.phabengland.org.uk
Organises clubs, holiday trips and exchanges for teenagers and adults with physical disabilities.

Pines Trust, The
Mrs Maureen Jones, The Pines, Bishop's Castle, Shropshire SY9 5JY
☎ 01588 638234
A large modern house, with its own garden and grounds, which has been converted into a self-catering holiday location for people with special needs of all ages. Up to 24 people can stay at one time. Open all year.

Queen Elizabeth's Foundation for Disabled People
Leatherhead Court, Leatherhead, Surrey KT22 0BN
☎ 01372 842204 📠 01372 884072

email: malcolm.clark@qefd.org
Holidays for people with severe physical disabilities, over the age of 16 years.

Queen Elizabeth's Foundation Mobility Centre
Damson Way, Fountain Drive, Carshalton, Surrey SM5 4NR
☎ 020 8770 1151
email: info@mobility-qe.org
Information and advice on outdoor mobility for people with a physical disability. Assessments for wheelchair users, car drivers and passengers.

RADAR
12 City Forum, 250 City Road, London EC1V 8AF
☎ 020 7250 3222 📠 020 7250 0212
email: radar@radar.org.uk
website: www.radar.org.uk
Provides regularly updated holiday guides and fact sheets on holidays in the UK and abroad, sport and activity holidays, holiday insurance and holiday finance. Publications: Getting There – a guide to long-distance travel for disabled people (£5.00), Holidays in Britain & Ireland 2003. Information packs about holidays in the UK and abroad. Also online version of Holiday Guide.

Red Cross Society, British
9 Grosvenor Crescent, London SW1X 7EJ
☎ 020 7234 5454 📠 020 7245 6315
website: www.redcross.org.uk
Transport and escort services, loan of equipment, e.g. wheelchairs.

RNIB Holiday Service
(See RNIB in Organisations Section)

Salvation Army
101 Newington Causeway, London SE1 6BN
☎ 020 7367 4706 📠 020 7367 4711
email: schools@salvationarmy.org.uk
website: www.salvationarmy.org.uk/schools
Provides a variety of services, including day centres, homes and holidays. Provides information to students and teachers about the Salvation Army.

Scope Holiday Service
(See Scope in Organisations Section)

Scout Holiday Homes Trust
Baden-Powell House, Queen's Gate, London SW7 5JS
☎ 020 7584 7030 📠 020 7590 5103
email: baden.powell.house@scout.org.uk
website: www.scoutbase.org.uk
Inexpensive self-catering holidays for families with a disabled member. Visitors need not be Scout members.

Sense, Scotland

5th Floor, Clydeway Centre, 45 Finneston Place, Glasgow G3 8JU

☎ 0141 564 2444 Minicom 0141 564 2442

▤ 0141 564 2443

email: info@sensescotland.org.uk

website: www.sensescotland.org.uk

Holidays and respite care for deaf/blind children, summer holiday programmes.

Shopmobility Schemes, National Federation of

12 City Forum, 250 City Road, London EC1V 8AF

☎ 020 7689 1040 ▤ 020 7689 1041

email: nfsuk@lineone.net

website: justmobility.co.uk/shop

Lends manual and powered wheelchairs and powered scooters to people with limited mobility, to enable them to shop and use leisure and commercial facilities in their locality.

Skiing Holidays

(See Leisure Section)

Southeast Hampshire YMCA

Fairthorne Manor, Curdridge, Southampton, Hants SO3 2GH

☎ 01489 785228 ▤ 01489 798936

email: info@fairthorne.co.uk

website: www.fairthorne.co.uk

Centre providing a wide range of activities: outdoor activities during summer holidays, holidays, respite, young carer's projects, special needs support unit to help individuals with special needs to integrate into summer and mainstream play schemes and holidays.

Special Families Homeswap Register

Erme House, Station Road, Plympton, Plymouth, Devon PL7 3AU

☎ 01752 347577 ▤ 01752 344611

email: med-serve@globalnet.co.uk

website: www.mywebpage.net/special-families/home

A register of families in which there is a disabled member, to provide opportunities for swapping homes for a holiday or break. Details on request.

St John's Ambulance Aeromedical Service

(See Aeromedical Service)

Stackpole Centre

Old Home Farm, Stackpole, Pembroke SA71 5DQ

☎ 01646 661425 ▤ 01646 661639

Wholly accessible holiday centre for groups and families.

TfL Access and Mobility

Transport for London, Windsor House, 42/50 Victoria Street, London SW1H 0TL

☎ 020 79414600 ▤ 020 79414605

email: accessandmobility@tfl.gov.uk

website: www.transportforlondon.gov.uk

Working with engineers and designers to make buses and Underground trains easier to use, with architects to improve facilities at bus and Underground stations as they are modernised, and with operators to ensure that their staff are aware of the needs of disabled and elderly passengers.

Toilet Key Scheme for Disabled People (National Key Scheme)

Provides a key to toilets for disabled people and list of special toilets throughout the country. Contact RADAR for details.

Travel Agents, Specialist

A list of travel agents specialising in holidays for disabled people is available from Disabled Living Foundation. (See Aids and Equipment Section)

Travel Freedom

Unit 2b, St David's Industrial Estate, Pengham NP2 1SW

☎ 01443 831000 Minicom 01443 831000

▤ 01443 839800

email: allan@travelfreedom.freeserve.co.uk

Free travel information and advice service for people with disabilities. Advises on route plans, accommodation and access and insurance. (See also Insurance for Travel)

Travelability

Accessible Travel & Leisure, Avionics House, Naas Lane, Gloucester GL2 4SN

☎ 08702 416127

email: info@atlholidays.com

website: www.travelability.co.uk

Information for users of wheelchairs, and those with difficulty in walking, on all aspects of planning a holiday. (See also Insurance for Travel)

Travelcare Ltd

68 High Street, Chislehurst, Kent BR7 5AQ

☎ 0800 181532 (freephone) ▤ 0208 295 13455

email: info@travelcare.co.uk

website: www.travelcare.co.uk

Offers travel insurance with no premium loading for people with disabilities.

5

Trefoil House Holiday Centre

Gogarbank, Edinburgh EH12 9DA
☎ 0131 339 3148 🖹 0131 317 7271
email: info@trefoil.org.uk
website: www.trefoil.org.uk
Individual, family and group holidays and special interest breaks for disabled people of all ages. All degrees of disability catered for.

Treloar Disability Assessment Centre

Holybourne, Alton, Hants GU34 4EN
☎ 01420 547403 🖹 01420 547434
email: hendersp@treloar.org.uk
website: www.treloar.org.uk
Provides assessment for choosing a suitable wheelchair and training in the use of wheelchairs.

Trevanion House

Trevanion Road, Wadebridge, Cornwall PL27 7PA
☎ 01208 814903 🖹 01208 816268
email: trevanion@trevanion.co.uk
website: www.trevanion.co.uk
Holidays and short-stay respite care for adults with learning disabilities, individuals or groups. Education and training, residential or day basis.

Tripscope

The Vassall Centre, Gill Avenue, Bristol BS16 2QQ
☎ 0845 758 5641 🖹 0117 939 7736
email: enquiries@tripscope.org.uk
website: www.tripscope.org.uk
Information on all aspects of travel for people with disabilities. Will assist with planning journeys. Telephone helpline on travel and transport.

Wheelchair provision

(See Mobility Trust)

Wingate Special Children's Trust, The

The Wingate Centre, Wrenbury Hall Drive, Wrenbury, Nantwich, Cheshire CW5 8ES
☎ 01270 780456 🖹 01270 781179
email: gym@wingate-sga.org.uk
website: www.wingate-sga.org.uk
A sports and holiday centre with accommodation and facilities adapted for people with disabilities. Caters for groups of 10 to 40. Information pack, listing activities and sports provided, on request.

Winged Fellowship Trust

Angel House, 20-32 Pentonville Road, London N1 9XD
☎ 020 7833 2594 🖹 020 7278 0370
email: admin@wft.org.uk
website: www.wft.org.uk
Holidays for people with disabilities and respite care for their carers. Helps to fund mobility equipment for children up to 18 years, for whom other funding is not available.

YMCA England

640 Forest Road, London E17 3DZ
☎ 020 8520 5599 🖹 020 8509 3190
email: enquiries@ymca.org.uk
website: www.ymca.org.uk
Wide variety of activity holidays. Details on request.

Youth Hostel Association, Northern Ireland

Hostelling International, 22-32 Donegal Road, Belfast BT12 5JN
☎ 01232 324733 🖹 01232 439699
email: info@hini.org.uk
website: www.hini.org.uk

Youth Hostels Association, England and Wales

Trevelyan House, Dimple Road, Matlock, Derbyshire DE4 3YH
☎ 0870 870 8808 🖹 01629 592702
email: customerservices@yha.org.uk
website: www.yha.org.uk
Welcomes people with disabilities. Several hostels with access for wheelchairs.

Youth Hostels Association, Scottish

7 Glebe Crescent, Stirling FK8 2JA
☎ 01786 891400 🖹 01786 891333
email: info@syha.org.uk
website: www.syha.org.uk

Section 6

Education Authorities in the UK

Education Authorities in the UK

Recent government legislation has stressed the importance of inclusive education. While there are many children for whom the best provision may still be within a special school environment, pupils with special educational needs should be able to attend their local mainstream school if this is the parents' wish. Contacting the Local Education Authority is the first step in locating a mainstream school in the area. In most cases the LEA will support this placement, and be able to give advice as to which school may best suit the needs of the child.

United Kingdom Education Department Headquarters

Department for Education and Skills (DfES)
Sanctuary Buildings
Great Smith Street
London
SW1P 3BT
☎ 020 7925 5000
🖹 020 7925 6000
Website: www.dfes.gov.uk

Scottish Executive Education Department
Victoria Quay
Edinburgh
EH6 6QQ
☎ 0131 556 8400
🖹 0131 244 8240
Website: www.scotland.gov.uk

Department of Education for Northern Ireland (DENI)
Rathgael House
43 Balloo Road
Bangor
County Down
BT19 7PR
☎ 028 9127 9279
🖹 028 9127 9100
Website: www.deni.gov.uk

National Assembly for Wales Education Department
Government Buildings
New Crown Buildings
Cathays Park
Cardiff
CF1 3NQ
☎ 029 2082 5111
🖹 029 2086 2111
Website: www.wales.gov.uk

England

Avon
See Bath & North East Somerset; Bristol, City of; North Somerset; and South Gloucestershire

Barking & Dagenham
Department of Education, Arts and Libraries
London Borough of Barking & Dagenham
Town Hall
Barking
Essex
IG11 7LU
☎ 020 8592 4500
🖹 020 8594 9837
Website: www.barking-dagenham.gov.uk

Barnet
Education Services
London Borough of Barnet
The Old Town Hall, 1 Friern Barnet Lane
London
N11 3DL
☎ 020 8359 2000
🖹 020 8359 3057
Website: www.barnet.gov.uk

Barnsley

Education Offices
Barnsley Metropolitan Borough Council
Berneslai Close
Barnsley
South Yorkshire
S70 2HS
☎ 01226 770770
🖹 01226 773099
Website: www.barnsley.gov.uk

Bath & North East Somerset

Cultural and Community Services
Bath & North East Somerset Council
PO Box 25
Riverside
Temple Street
Keynsham
Bristol
BS31 1DN
☎ 01225 395155
🖹 01225 394481
Website: www.bathnes.gov.uk

Bedfordshire

(See also Luton)
Bedfordshire County Council
County Hall
Cauldwell Street
Bedford
MK42 9AP
☎ 01234 363222
🖹 01234 228619
Website: www.bedfordshire.gov.uk

Berkshire

See Bracknell Forest; West Berkshire (Newbury);
Reading; Slough; Windsor & Maidenhead; and
Wokingham

Bexley

Education and Leisure Services
London Borough of Bexley Council
Hill View
Hill View Drive
Welling
Kent
DA16 3RY
☎ 020 8303 7777

🖹 020 8319 4302
Website: www.bexley.gov.uk

Birmingham

Education Service
Birmingham City Council
Education Offices
Margaret Street
Birmingham
B3 3BU
☎ 0121 303 2590
🖹 0121 303 1318
Website: www.birmingham.gov.uk

Blackburn with Darwen

(formerly Lancashire)
Blackburn with Darwen Borough Council
Town Hall
King William Street
Blackburn
Lancashire
BB1 7DY
☎ 01254 585585
🖹 01254 698388
Website: www.blackburn.gov.uk

Blackpool

(formerly Lancashire)
Blackpool Borough Council
Progress House
Clifton Road
Blackpool FY4 4US
☎ 01253 476518
🖹 01253 476504
Website: www.blackpool.gov.uk

Bolton

Bolton Metropolitan Borough Council
PO Box 53
Paderborn House
Civic Centre
Bolton
Lancashire
BL1 1JW
☎ 01204 332137
🖹 01204 332145
Website: www.bolton.gov.uk

Bournemouth

Bournemouth Borough Council
Dorset House
20-22 Christchurch Road
Bournemouth
BH1 3NL
☎ 01202 456223
🖷 01202 456191
Website: www.bournemouth.gov.uk

Bracknell Forest

(formerly Berkshire)
Bracknell Forest Council
Seymour House
38 Broadway
Bracknell
RG12 1AU
☎ 01344 424642
🖷 01344 354001
Website: www.bracknell-forest.gov.uk

Bradford

City of Bradford Metropolitan District
Council
Future House
Bolling Road
Bradford
West Yorkshire
BD4 7EB
☎ 01274 751840
🖷 01274 740612
Website: www.bradford.gov.uk

Brent

Education Offices
London Borough of Brent
Chesterfield House
9 Park Lane
Wembley
HA9 7RW
☎ 020 8937 3000
🖷 020 8937 3040
Website: www2.brent.gov.uk

Brighton & Hove

Brighton & Hove City Council
King's House, Grand Avenue
Hove
BN3 2LS
☎ 01273 290000
🖷 01273 293456
Website: www.brighton-hove.gov.uk

Bristol, City of

Education and Lifelong Learning
Bristol City Council
PO Box 57
The Council House
College Green
Bristol
BS99 7EB
☎ 0117 903 7961
🖷 0117 903 7963
Website: www.bristol-city.gov.uk

Bromley

Education Services
London Borough of Bromley
Civic Centre
Stockwell Close
Bromley
BR1 3UH
☎ 020 8464 3333
🖷 020 8313 4049
Website: www.bromley.gov.uk

Buckinghamshire

(See also Milton Keynes)
Buckinghamshire County Council
County Hall
Aylesbury
Buckinghamshire
HP20 1UZ
☎ 01296 395000
🖷 01296 383367
Website: www.buckscc.gov.uk

Bury

Education Department
Bury Metropolitan Borough Council
Athenaeum House
Market Street
Bury
Lancashire
BL9 0BN
☎ 0161 253 5000
🖷 0161 253 5653
Website: www.bury.gov.uk

6

Calderdale

Education Department
Calderdale Metropolitan Borough Council
PO Box 33
Northgate House
Northgate
Halifax
West Yorkshire
HX1 1UN
☎ 01422 357257
🖹 01422 392515
Website: www.calderdale.gov.uk

Cambridgeshire

(See also Peterborough, City of)
Cambridgeshire County Council
Castle Court
Shire Hall
Castle Hill
Cambridge
CB3 0AP
☎ 01223 717111
🖹 01223 717971
Website: www.cambridgeshire.gov.uk

Camden

Education Department
London Borough of Camden
Crowndale Centre
218-220 Eversholt Street
London
NW1 1BD
☎ 020 7911 1525
🖹 020 7911 1536
Website: www.camden.gov.uk

Cheshire

(See also Halton and Warrington)
Cheshire County Council
County Hall
Chester
CH1 1SQ
☎ 01244 602301
🖹 01244 603821
Website: www.cheshire.gov.uk

Cleveland

*See Hartlepool; Middlesbrough; Redcar &
Cleveland; and Stockton-on-Tees*

Cornwall

Education Offices
Cornwall County Council County Hall
Treyew Road
Truro
Cornwall
TR1 3AY
☎ 01872 322000
🖹 01872 323818
Website: www.cornwall.gov.uk

Corporation of London

Education Department
Corporation of London
PO Box 270
Guildhall
London
EC2P 2EJ
☎ 020 7332 1750
🖹 020 7332 1621
Website: www.cityoflondon.gov.uk

Coventry

Coventry City Council
Civic Centre
Earl Street
Coventry CV1 5RR
☎ 024 7683 1511
🖹 024 7683 1620
Website: www.coventry.gov.uk

Croydon

London Borough of Croydon
Taberner House
Park Lane
Croydon CR9 1TP
☎ 020 8760 5452
🖹 020 8760 5603
Website: www.croydon.gov.uk

Cumbria

Education Department
Cumbria County Council
5 Portland Square
Carlisle
CA1 1PU
☎ 01228 606060
🖹 01228 606896
Website: www.cumbria.gov.uk

Darlington
Education Services
Darlington Borough Council
Town Hall
Darlington
DL1 5QT
☎ 01325 380651
▤ 01325 382032
Website: www.darlington.gov.uk

Derby, City of
Derby City Council
Middleton House
27 St Mary's Gate
Derby
DE1 3NN
☎ 01332 293111
▤ 01332 716870
Website: www.derby.gov.uk

Derbyshire
(See also Derby, City of)
Derbyshire County Council
County Hall
Matlock
Derbyshire
DE4 3AG
☎ 01629 580000
▤ 01629 772213
Website: www.derbyshire.gov.uk

Devon
(See also Plymouth, City of; Torbay)
Devon County Council
County Hall
Exeter
EX2 4QG
☎ 01392 382059
▤ 01392 382203
Website: www.devon.gov.uk

Doncaster
Doncaster Metropolitan Borough Council
PO Box 266, The Council House
Doncaster
South Yorkshire
DN1 3AD
☎ 01302 737102
▤ 01302 737223
Website: www.doncaster.gov.uk

Dorset
(See also Bournemouth; Poole)
Education Department
Dorset County Council
County Hall
Colliton Park
Dorchester
Dorset
DT1 1XJ
☎ 01305 224166
▤ 01305 225057
Website: www.dorset-cc.gov.uk

Dudley
Dudley Metropolitan Borough Council
Westox House
1 Trinity Road
Dudley
West Midlands
DY1 1JQ
☎ 01384 814200
▤ 01384 814216
Website: www.dudley.gov.uk

Durham
(See also Darlington)
Education Department
Durham County Council
County Hall
Durham
DH1 5UJ
☎ 0191 383 4574
▤ 0191 386 0487
Website: www.durham.gov.uk

Ealing
London Borough of Ealing
5th Floor
Perceval House
14-16 Uxbridge Road
Ealing
London
W5 2HL
☎ 020 8579 2424
▤ 020 8280 1291
Website: www.ealing.gov.uk

6

East Riding of Yorkshire

East Riding of Yorkshire Council
County Hall
Beverley
East Riding of Yorkshire
HU17 9BA
☎ 01482 887700
🖹 01482 884920
Website: www.eastriding.gov.uk

East Sussex

(See also Brighton & Hove)
East Sussex County Council
PO Box 4
County Hall
St Anne's Crescent
Lewes
East Sussex
BN7 1SG
☎ 01273 481000
🖹 01273 481261
Website: www.eastsussexcc.gov.uk

Enfield

Education Department
London Borough of Enfield
PO Box 56
Civic Centre
Silver Street
Enfield
Middlesex
EN1 3XQ
☎ 020 8366 6565
🖹 020 8982 7375
Website: www.enfield.gov.uk

Essex

(See also Southend-on-Sea; Thurrock)
Learning Services
Essex County Council
PO Box 47
Chelmsford
CM2 6WN
☎ 01245 436231
🖹 01245 492759
Website: www.essexcc.gov.uk

Gateshead

Education Offices
Gateshead Council
Gateshead Civic Centre
Regent Street
Gateshead
Tyne and Wear
NE8 1HH
☎ 0191 477 1011
🖹 0191 490 1168
Website: www.gateshead.gov.uk

Gloucestershire

Gloucestershire County Council
Shire Hall
Gloucester
GL1 2TP
☎ 01452 425302
🖹 01452 426420
Website: www.gloscc.gov.uk

Greenwich

London Borough of Greenwich
9th Floor, Riverside House
Beresford Street
London
SE18 6DF
☎ 020 8854 8888
🖹 020 8855 2427
Website: www.greenwich.gov.uk

Hackney

London Borough of Hackney
Hackney Technology and Learning Centre
1 Reading Lane
London
E8 1GQ
☎ 020 8356 5000
🖹 020 8356 7295
Website: www.hackney.gov.uk

Halton (formerly Cheshire)

Education and Social Inclusion Directorate
Halton Borough Council
Grosvenor House
Halton Lea
Runcorn, Cheshire
WA7 2ED
☎ 0151 424 2061
🖹 0151 471 7321
Website: www.halton.gov.uk

Hammersmith and Fulham

London Borough of Hammersmith and
Fulham
Town Hall
King Street
London
W6 9JU
(Visitors to Cambridge House, Cambridge
Grove, London, W6 0LE)
☎ 020 8748 3020/3621
▤ 020 8576 5686
Website: www.lbhf.gov.uk

Hampshire

(See also Portsmouth; Southampton)
Hampshire County Council
The Castle
Winchester
Hampshire
SO23 8UG
☎ 01962 846452
▤ 01962 842355
Website: www.hants.gov.uk

Haringey

Education Services
London Borough of Haringey
48 Station Road
Wood Green
London
N22 7TY
☎ 020 8489 0000
▤ 020 8862 2906
Website: www.haringey.gov.uk

Harrow

London Borough of Harrow
PO Box 22
Civic Centre
Harrow
Middlesex
HA1 2UW
☎ 020 8424 1307
▤ 020 8427 0810
Website: www.harrow.gov.uk

Hartlepool

Hartlepool Borough Council
Civic Centre
Victoria Road
Hartlepool
Cleveland
TS24 8AY
☎ 01429 266522
▤ 01429 523777
Website: www.hartlepool.gov.uk

Havering

London Borough of Havering
The Broxhill Centre
Broxhill Road
Harold Hill
Romford
RM4 1XN
☎ 01708 433891
▤ 01708 433850
Website: www.havering.gov.uk

Hereford and Worcester

See Herefordshire; Worcestershire

Herefordshire (formerly Hereford &
Worcester)

Hereford Education and Conference Centre
Herefordshire Council
PO Box 185
Blackfriars Street
Hereford
HR4 9ZR
☎ 01432 260900
▤ 01432 260957
Website: www.herefordshire.gov.uk

Hertfordshire

Hertfordshire County Council
County Hall
Hertford
SG13 8DF
☎ 01992 555555
▤ 01992 588674
Website: www.hertscc.gov.uk

6

Hillingdon
London Borough of Hillingdon
Civic Centre
Uxbridge
Middlesex
UB8 1UW
☎ 01895 250111
🖹 01895 273636
Website: www.hillingdon.gov.uk

Hounslow
London Borough of Hounslow
Civic Centre
Lampton Road
Hounslow
Middlesex
TW3 4DN
☎ 020 8583 2600
🖹 020 8862 5249
Website: www.hounslow.gov.uk

Humberside
See East Riding of Yorkshire; Kingston upon Hull, City of; North Lincolnshire; North East Lincolnshire

Isle of Wight
Isle of Wight Council
County Hall
Newport
Isle of Wight
PO30 1UD
☎ 01983 821000
🖹 01983 826099
Website: www.iwight.gov.uk

Isles of Scilly
Council of the Isles of Scilly
Town Hall
St Mary's
Isles of Scilly
TR21 0LW
☎ 01720 422537
🖹 01720 422202
Website: www.scilly.gov.uk

Islington
London Borough of Islington
Laycock Street
London
N1 1TH
☎ 020 7527 5566
🖹 020 7457 5555
Website: www.islington.gov.uk

Kensington and Chelsea
Royal Borough of Kensington and Chelsea
Town Hall
Hornton Street
London
W8 7NX
☎ 020 7361 3334
🖹 020 7361 2078
Website: www.rbkc.gov.uk

Kent
(See also Medway)
Kent County Council
Sessions House
County Hall
Maidstone
Kent
ME14 1XQ
☎ 01622 671411
🖹 01622 694091
Website: www.kent.gov.uk

Kingston upon Hull, City of
Kingston upon Hull City Council
Essex House
Manor Street
Kingston upon Hull
HU1 1YD
☎ 01482 300300
🖹 01482 613407
Website: www.hullcc.gov.uk

Kingston upon Thames
Royal Borough of Kingston
Guildhall
High Street
Kingston upon Thames
Surrey
KT1 1EU
☎ 020 8546 2121
🖹 020 8547 5296
Website: www.kingston.gov.uk

Kirklees
Kirklees Metropolitan Council
Oldgate House
2 Oldgate
Huddersfield
HD1 6QW
☎ 01484 225000
🖹 01484 225264
Website: www.kirkleesmc.gov.uk

Knowsley
Education Offices
Knowsley Metropolitan Borough Council
Huyton Hey Road
Huyton
Merseyside
L36 5YH
☎ 0151 443 3231
🖹 0151 449 3852
Website: www.knowsley.gov.uk

Lambeth
London Borough of Lambeth
International House
Canterbury Crescent
London
SW9 7QE
☎ 020 7926 9896
🖹 020 7926 2296
Website: www.lambeth.gov.uk

Lancashire
(See also Blackburn with Darwen; Blackpool)
Lancashire County Council
PO Box 61
County Hall
Preston
PR1 8RJ
☎ 01772 254868
🖹 01772 261630
Website: www.lancashire.gov.uk

Leeds
Leeds Education Department
Selectapost 17
Merrion House
Merrion Centre
Leeds
LS2 8DT

☎ 0113 247 5590
🖹 0113 395 0219
Website: www.leeds.gov.uk

Leicester City
Leicester City Council
New Walk Centre
Welford Place
Leicester
LE1 6ZG
☎ 0116 254 9922
🖹 0116 233 9922
Website: www.leicester.gov.uk

Leicestershire
(See also Leicester City; Rutland)
Education Department
Leicestershire County Council
County Hall
Glenfield
Leicester
LE3 8RF
☎ 0116 265 6631
🖹 0116 265 6634
Website: www.leics.gov.uk

Lewisham
London Borough of Lewisham
Laurence House
Catford
London SE6 4SW
☎ 020 8314 6200
🖹 020 8314 3039
Website: www.lewisham.gov.uk

Lincolnshire
Lincolnshire County Council
County Offices
Newland
Lincoln
LN1 1YQ
☎ 01522 552222
🖹 01522 553257
Website: www.lincolnshire.gov.uk

6

Liverpool
Education Offices
Liverpool City Council
4th Floor
4 Renshaw Street
Liverpool
L1 4AD
☎ 0151 233 2822
🖷 0151 233 3029
Website: www.liverpool.gov.uk

London

Inner London See separate entries for
the former Inner London Education
Authority (ILEA) London Boroughs;
Camden, Corporation of London [covering
the one square mile of the City of London],
Greenwich, Hackney, Hammersmith &
Fulham, Islington, Kensington & Chelsea,
Lambeth, Lewisham, Southwark, Tower
Hamlets, Wandsworth, Westminster

Outer London See separate entries for
the following London Boroughs; Barking &
Dagenham, Barnet, Bexley, Brent, Bromley,
Croydon, Ealing, Enfield, Haringey, Harrow,
Havering, Hillingdon, Hounslow, Kingston
upon Thames, Merton, Newham, Redbridge,
Richmond upon Thames, Sutton, Waltham
Forest

Luton
Luton Borough Council
Unity House
111 Stuart Street
Luton
Bedfordshire
LU1 5NP
☎ 01582 548001
🖷 01582 548454
Website: www.luton.gov.uk

Manchester
Manchester City Council
Overseas House
Quay Street
Manchester
M3 3BB
☎ 0161 234 5000

🖷 0161 234 7147
Website: www.manchester.gov.uk

Medway (formerly Kent)
[former name Rochester and Gillingham]
Medway Council
Civic Centre
Strood
Rochester
Kent
ME2 4AU
☎ 01634 306000
🖷 01634 332756
Website: www.medway.gov.uk

Merton
London Borough of Merton
Merton Civic Centre
London Road
Morden
Surrey
SM4 5DX
☎ 020 8545 3118
🖷 020 8545 3443
Website: www.merton.gov.uk

Middlesbrough
Middlesbrough Council
PO Box 69
1st Floor
Vancouver House
Gurney Street
Middlesbrough
TS1 1EL
☎ 01642 245432
🖷 01642 264175
Website: www.middlesbrough.gov.uk

Milton Keynes
Milton Keynes Council
Saxon Court
502 Avebury Boulevard
Milton Keynes
MK9 3HS
☎ 01908 691691
🖷 01908 253289
Website: www.mkweb.co.uk

Newcastle upon Tyne
Education and Libraries Directorate
Newcastle City Council
Civic Centre
Barras Bridge
Newcastle upon Tyne
NE1 8PU
☎ 0191 232 8520
🖷 0191 211 4983
Website: www.newcastle.gov.uk

Newham
Education Offices
London Borough of Newham
Broadway House
322 High Street
Stratford
London
E15 1AJ
☎ 020 8555 5552
🖷 020 8503 0014
Website: www.newham.gov.uk

Norfolk
Norfolk County Council
County Hall
Martineau Lane
Norwich
NR1 2DL
☎ 01603 222146
🖷 01603 222119
Website: www.norfolk.gov.uk

North East Lincolnshire
North East Lincolnshire Council
7 Eleanor Street
Grimsby
DN32 9DU
☎ 01472 313131
🖷 01472 323020
Website: www.nelincs.gov.uk

North Lincolnshire
North Lincolnshire Council
PO Box 35
Hewson House
Station Road
Brigg
DN20 8XJ

☎ 01724 296296
🖷 01724 297242
Website: www.northlincs.gov.uk

North Somerset
North Somerset Council
PO Box 51
Town Hall
Weston-Super-Mare
BS23 1ZZ
☎ 01934 888888
🖷 01934 888834
Website: www.n-somerset.gov.uk

North Tyneside
Education Service
North Tyneside Council
Stephenson House
Stephenson Street
North Shields
Tyne & Wear
NE30 1QA
☎ 0191 200 5122
🖷 0191 200 6090
Website: www.northtyneside.gov.uk

North Yorkshire
(See also York, City of)
North Yorkshire County Council
County Hall
Northallerton
North Yorkshire
DL7 8AE
☎ 01609 780780
🖷 01609 778611
Website: www.northyorks.gov.uk

Northamptonshire
Northamptonshire County Council
PO Box 216
John Dryden House
8-10 The Lakes
Northampton
NN4 7DD
☎ 01604 236236
🖷 01604 236188
Website: www.northants-ecl.gov.uk

6

Northumberland
Education Department
Northumberland County Council
County Hall
Morpeth
Northumberland
NE61 2EF
☎ 01670 533000
🖷 01670 533750
Website: www.northumberland.gov.uk

Nottingham, City of (formerly
Nottinghamshire)
Nottingham City Council
Sandfield Centre
Sandfield Road
Lenton
Nottingham
NG7 1QH
☎ 0115 915 0706
🖷 0115 915 0658
Website: www.nottinghamcity.gov.uk

Nottinghamshire
Nottinghamshire County Council
County Hall
West Bridgford
Nottingham
NG2 7QP
☎ 0115 982 3823
🖷 0115 981 2824
Website: www.nottscc.gov.uk

Oldham
Oldham Metropolitan Borough Council
PO Box 40
Civic Centre
West Street
Oldham
OL1 1XJ
☎ 0161 911 4260
🖷 0161 911 3221
Website: www.oldham.gov.uk

Oxfordshire
Education Department
Oxfordshire County Council
Macclesfield House

New Road
Oxford
OX1 1NA
☎ 01865 815449
🖷 01865 791637
Website: education.oxfordshire.gov.uk/support

Peterborough, City of (formerly
Cambridgeshire)
Peterborough City Council
Bayard Place
Broadway
Peterborough
PE1 1FB
☎ 01733 748444
🖷 01733 748111
Website: www.peterborough.gov.uk

Plymouth, City of (formerly Devon)
City of Plymouth Council
Civic Centre
Plymouth
PL1 2AA
☎ 01752 307400
🖷 01752 307403
Website: www.plymouth.gov.uk

Poole
Borough of Poole
Civic Centre
Poole
Dorset
BH15 2RU
☎ 01202 633633
🖷 01202 633706
Website: www.poole.gov.uk

Portsmouth
Portsmouth City Council
Civic Offices
Guildhall Square
Portsmouth
PO1 2EA
☎ 023 9282 2251
🖷 023 9283 4159
Website: www.portsmouthcc.gov.uk

Reading (formerly Berkshire)
Reading Borough Council
Civic Offices
Civic Centre
Reading
RG1 7TD
☎ 0118 939 0900
🖷 0118 958 9770
Website: www.reading.gov.uk

Redbridge
Education Office
London Borough of Redbridge
Lynton House
255-259 High Road
Ilford
Essex
IG1 1NY
☎ 020 8478 3020
🖷 020 8478 9044
Website: www.redbridge.gov.uk

Redcar and Cleveland
Redcar and Cleveland Borough Council
PO Box 83
Council Offices
Kirkleatham Street
Redcar
TS10 1YA
☎ 01642 444344
🖷 01642 444122
Website: www.redcar-cleveland.gov.uk

Richmond upon Thames
London Borough of Richmond upon Thames
Education, Arts and Leisure Department
Regal House
London Road
Twickenham
TW1 3QB
☎ 020 8891 1411
🖷 020 8891 7714
Website: www.richmond.gov.uk

Rochdale
Education Department
PO Box 70
Municipal Offices
Smith Street

Rochdale
OL16 1YD
☎ 01706 647474
🖷 01706 658560
Website: www.rochdale.gov.uk

Rotherham
Rotherham Metropolitan Borough Council
Norfolk House
Walker Place
Rotherham
S65 1AS
☎ 01709 382121
🖷 01709 372056
Website: www.rotherham.gov.uk

Rutland
Rutland County Council
Catmose
Oakham
Rutland
LE15 6HP
Tel; 01572 722577
🖷 01572 757713
Website: www.rutnet.co.uk

Salford
Salford City Council
Minerva House
Pendlebury Road
Salford
M27 4AX
☎ 0161 778 0123
🖷 0161 728 6068
Website: www.salford.gov.uk

Sandwell
Sandwell Metropolitan Borough Council
PO Box 41
Shaftesbury House
402 High Street
West Bromwich
B70 9LT
☎ 0121 569 2200
🖷 0121 553 1528
Website: www.lea.sandwell.gov.uk

6

Sefton

Education Department
Sefton Metropolitan Borough Council
Town Hall
Bootle
Merseyside
L20 7AE
☎ 0151 922 4040
🖹 0151 934 3239
Website: www.sefton.gov.uk

Sheffield

Sheffield City Council
Education Department
Town Hall
Sheffield
S1 2HH
☎ 0114 273 5722
🖹 0114 273 6279
Website: www.sheffield.gov.uk

Shropshire

(See also Telford & Wrekin)
Shropshire County Council
The Shirehall
Abbey Foregate
Shrewsbury
SY2 6ND
☎ 01743 254307
🖹 01743 254415
Website: www.shropshire-cc.gov.uk

Slough (formerly Berkshire)

Slough Borough Council
Town Hall
Bath Road
Slough
SL1 3UQ
☎ 01753 875700
🖹 01753 692499
Website: www.slough.gov.uk

Solihull

Solihull Metropolitan Borough Council
PO Box 20
Council House
Solihull
West Midlands
B91 3QU
☎ 0121 704 6000
🖹 0121 704 6669
Website: www.solihull.gov.uk

Somerset

Somerset County Council
County Hall
Taunton
Somerset
TA1 4DY
☎ 01823 355455
🖹 01823 355332
Website: www.somerset.gov.uk

South Gloucestershire

South Gloucestershire Offices
Bowling Hill
Chipping Sodbury
BS37 6JX
☎ 01454 868686
🖹 01454 863263
Website: www.southglos.gov.uk

South Tyneside

Education Department
South Tyneside Council
Town Hall and Civic Offices
Westoe Road
South Shields
Tyne & Wear
NE33 2RL
☎ 0191 424 7733
🖹 0191 427 0584
Website: www.s-tyneside-mbc.gov.uk

Southampton

Southampton City Council
Frobisher House
5th Floor
Nelson Gate
Commercial Road
Southampton
SO15 1BZ
☎ 023 8083 3466
🖹 023 8083 3324
Website: www.southampton.gov.uk

Southend-on-Sea (formerly Essex)

Southend-on-Sea Borough Council
PO Box 6
Civic Centre
Victoria Avenue
Southend-on Sea SS2 6ER
☎ 01702 215000
🖹 01702 534939
Website: www.southend.gov.uk

Southwark

London Borough of Southwark
John Smith House
144-152 Walworth Road
London
SE17 1JL
☎ 020 7525 5050
🖹 020 7525 5025
Website: www.southwark.gov.uk

St Helens

Community Education & Leisure Services
St Helens Metropolitan Borough Council
The Rivington Centre
Rivington Road
St Helens
Merseyside
WA10 4ND
☎ 01744 455328
🖹 01744 455350
Website: www.sthelens.gov.uk

Staffordshire

(See also Stoke-on-Trent)
Staffordshire County Council
County Education Offices
Tipping Street
Stafford
ST16 2DH
☎ 01785 278653
🖹 01785 278639
Website: www.staffordshire.gov.uk

Stockport

Education Division
Stockport Metropolitan Borough Council
Stopford House
Piccadilly
Stockport

SK1 3XE
☎ 0161 480 4949
🖹 0161 953 0012
Website: www.stockportmbc.gov.uk

Stockton-on-Tees

Stockton-on-Tees Borough Council
PO Box 228
Municipal Buildings
Church Road
Stockton-on-Tees
TS18 1XE
☎ 01642 393939
🖹 01642 393479
Website: www.stockton-bc.gov.uk

Stoke-on-Trent

Stoke-on-Trent City Council
Education Department
Civic Centre
2nd Floor
Globe Street
Stoke-on-Trent
ST4 1HH
☎ 01782 232014
🖹 01782 236102
Website: www.stoke.gov.uk

Suffolk

Education Service
Suffolk County Council
St Andrew House
County Hall
Ipswich
IP4 1LJ
☎ 01473 584800
🖹 01473 584624
Website: www.suffolkcc.gov.uk

Sunderland

Sunderland City Council
PO Box No 101
Civic Centre
Sunderland
SR2 7DN
☎ 0191 553 1000
🖹 0191 553 1410
Website: www.sunderland.gov.uk

6

Surrey
County Hall
Penrhyn Road
Kingston upon Thames
KT1 2DJ
☎ 08456 009 009
🖹 020 8541 9503
Website: www.surreycc.gov.uk

Sutton
London Borough of Sutton
The Grove
Carshalton
SM5 3AL
☎ 020 8770 5000
🖹 020 8770 6545
Website: www.sutton.gov.uk

Swindon
Swindon Borough Council
Sanford House
Sanford Street
Swindon
SN1 1QH
☎ 01793 463000
🖹 01793 488597
Website: www.swindon.gov.uk

Tameside
Education Department
Tameside Metropolitan Borough Council
Council Offices
Wellington Road
Ashton-under-Lyne
OL6 6DL
☎ 0161 342 8355
🖹 0161 342 3260
Website: www.tameside.gov.uk

Telford & Wrekin (formerly
Shropshire)
Borough of Telford & Wrekin
PO Box 440
Civic Offices
Telford
TF3 4LD
☎ 01952 202100
🖹 01952 293946
Website: www.telford.gov.uk

Thurrock (formerly Essex)
Thurrock Council
Civic Offices
New Road
Grays
Essex
RM17 6GF
☎ 01375 652652
🖹 01375 652792
Website: www.thurrock.gov.uk/education

Torbay (formerly Devon)
Torbay Borough Council
Oldway Mansion
Paignton
Devon
TQ3 2TE
☎ 01803 208208
🖹 01803 208225
Website: www.torbay.gov.uk

Tower Hamlets
Education Department
Tower Hamlets Borough Council
Mulberry Place
5 Clove Crescent
London
E14 2BG
☎ 020 7364 5000
🖹 020 7364 4296
Website: www.towerhamlets.gov.uk

Trafford
Trafford Metropolitan Borough Council
PO Box 40
Trafford Town Hall
Talbot Road
Stretford
M32 0EL
☎ 0161 912 3251
🖹 0161 912 3075
Website: www.trafford.gov.uk

Wakefield
Education Department
Wakefield Metropolitan District Council
County Hall
Wakefield WF1 2QL
☎ 01924 306090
🖹 01924 305632
Website: www.wakefield.gov.uk

Walsall

Walsall Metropolitan Borough Council
The Civic Centre
Darwall Street
Walsall
West Midlands
WS1 1DQ
☎ 01922 650000
🖹 01922 722322
Website: www.walsall.gov.uk

Waltham Forest

London Borough of Waltham Forest
Lifelong Learning
Town Hall
Forest Road
Walthamstow
E17 4JF
☎ 020 8527 5544
🖹 020 8496 4558
Website: www.lbwf.gov.uk

Wandsworth

Wandsworth Borough Council
Town Hall
Wandsworth High Street
London
SW18 2PU
☎ 020 8871 8013
🖹 020 8871 8011
Website: www.wandsworth.gov.uk

Warrington (formerly Cheshire)

Education and Lifelong Learning
Warrington Borough Council
New Town House
Buttermarket Street
Warrington
WA1 2NH
☎ 01925 444400
🖹 01925 442929
Website: www.warrington.gov.uk

Warwickshire

Warwickshire County Council
PO Box 24
22 Northgate Street
Warwick
CV34 4SR
☎ 01926 410410
🖹 01926 412746
Website: www.warwickshire.gov.uk

West Berkshire (formerly Berkshire and Newbury)

West Berkshire Council
Avonbank House
West Street
Newbury
RG14 1BZ
☎ 01635 519726
🖹 01635 519725
Website: www.westberks.gov.uk

West Sussex

West Sussex County Council
County Hall
West Street
Chichester
West Sussex
PO19 1RF
☎ 01243 777100
🖹 01243 777229
Website: www.westsussex.gov.uk

Westminster

Westminster City Council
PO Box 240
Westminster City Hall
64 Victoria Street
London
SW1E 6QP
☎ 020 7641 6000
🖹 020 7641 3406
Website: www.westminster.gov.uk

Wigan

Education Department
Wigan Borough Council
Gateway House
Standishgate
Wigan
WN1 1AE
☎ 01942 244991
🖹 01942 828811
Website: www.wiganmbc.gov.uk

6

Wiltshire

(See also Swindon)
Wiltshire County Council
County Hall
Bythesea Road
Trowbridge
Wiltshire
BA14 8JB
☎ 01225 713000
▤ 01225 713982
Website: www.wiltshire.gov.uk

Windsor & Maidenhead, Royal Borough of (formerly Berkshire)

Royal Borough of Windsor & Maidenhead
Town Hall
St Ives Road
Maidenhead
SL6 1RF
☎ 01628 798888
▤ 01628 796256
Website: www.rbwm.gov.uk

Wirral

Metropolitan Borough of Wirral
Hamilton Building
Conway Street
Birkenhead
CH41 4FD
☎ 0151 666 2121
▤ 0151 666 4207
Website: www.wirral.gov.uk

Wokingham (formerly Berkshire)

Wokingham District Council
PO Box 156
Shute End
Wokingham
RG40 1WN
☎ 0118 974 6000
▤ 0118 974 6103
Website: www.wokingham.gov.uk

Wolverhampton

Education Department
Wolverhampton Metropolitan Borough
Council
Civic Centre
St Peter's Square
Wolverhampton
WV1 1RR
☎ 01902 556556
▤ 01902 554218
Website: www.wolverhampton.gov.uk

Worcestershire

Worcestershire County Council
County Education Department
PO Box 73
Spetchley Road
Worcester
WR5 2YA
☎ 01905 766859
▤ 01905 766156
Website: www.worcestershire.gov.uk

York, City of

City of York Council
10-12 George Hudson Street
York
YO1 6ZG
☎ 01904 613161
▤ 01904 554249
Website: www.york.gov.uk

Northern Ireland

Belfast
Education and Library Board
40 Academy Street
Belfast
BT1 2NQ
☎ 028 9056 4000
Website: www.belb.org.uk/

Western
Education and Library Board
Campsie House
1 Hospital Road
Omagh
Co Tyrone
BT79 0AW
☎ 028 8241 1411
Website: www.welbni.org/

North Eastern
Education and Library Board
County Hall
182 Galgorm Road
Ballymena
Co Antrim
BT42 1HN
☎ 028 2565 3333
Website: www.neelb.org.uk/

South Eastern
Education and Library Board
Grahamsbridge Road
Dundonald
Belfast
BT16 2HS
☎ 028 9056 6200
Website: www.seelb.org.uk/

Southern
Education and Library Board
3 Charlemont Place
The Mall
Armagh
BT61 9AX
☎ 028 3751 2200
Website: www.selb.org/

Council for Catholic Maintained Schools
160 High Street
Holywood
Co Down
BT18 9HT
☎ 028 9042 6972

6

Scotland

Aberdeen City Council
Summerhill Education Centre
Stronsay Drive
Aberdeen
AB15 6JA
☎ 01224 346 060
Website: www.aberdeencity.gov.uk

Aberdeenshire Council
Woodhill House
Westburn Road
Aberdeen
AB16 5GB
☎ 01224 664 630
Website: www.aberdeenshire.gov.uk/

Angus Council
County Buildings
Market Street
Forfar
DD8 3WE
☎ 01307 461 460
Website: www.angus.gov.uk/

Argyll and Bute Council
Argyll House
Alexandra Parade
Dunoon
Argyll
PA23 8AJ
☎ 01369 704 000
Website: www.argyll-bute.gov.uk/

Clackmannanshire Council
Lime Tree House
Alloa
FK10 1EX
☎ 01259 452 446
Website: www.clacks.gov.uk/

Dumfries and Galloway Council
30 Edinburgh Road
Dumfries
DG1 1NW
☎ 01387 260 000
Website: www.dumgal.gov.uk/

Dundee City Council
Tayside House
Crichton Street
Dundee
DD1 3RZ
☎ 01382 433 111
Website: www.dundeecity.gov.uk/

East Ayrshire Council
Council Headquarters
London Road
Kilmarnock
KA3 7BU
☎ 01563 576 000
Website: www.east-ayrshire.gov.uk/

East Dunbartonshire Council
Boclair House
100 Milngavie Road
Bearsden
Glasgow
G61 2TQ
☎ 0141 578 8742
Website: www.e-dunbarton.org.uk/

East Lothian Council
John Muir House
Haddington
EH41 3HA
☎ 01620 827 827
Website: www.eastlothian.gov.uk

East Renfrewshire Council
Eastwood Park
Rouken Glen Road
Giffnock
G46 6UG
☎ 0141 577 3430
Website: www.eastrenfrewshire.gov.uk/

City of Edinburgh Council
Wellington Court
10 Waterloo Place
Edinburgh
EH1 3EG
☎ 0131 469 3000
Website: www.edinburgh.gov.uk/

Falkirk Council
McLaren House
Marchmont Avenue
Polmont
FK2 0NZ
☎ 01324 506 600
Website: www.falkirk.gov.uk/

Fife Council
Fife House
North Street
Glenrothes
Fife
KY7 5LT
☎ 01592 414 141
Website: www.fife.gov.uk/

Glasgow City Council
Nye Bevan House
20 India Street
Glasgow
G2 4PF
☎ 0141 287 2000
Website: www.glasgow.gov.uk/

Highland Council
Glenurquhart Road
Inverness
IV3 5NX
☎ 01463 702 000
Website: www.highland.gov.uk/

Inverclyde Council
Department of Education Services
105 Dalrymple Street
Greenock
PA15 1HT
☎ 01475 712 824
Website: www.inverclyde.gov.uk/

Midlothian Council
Fairfield House
8 Lothian Road
Dalkeith
Midlothian
EH22 3ZG
☎ 0131 271 3718
Website: www.midlothian.gov.uk/

Moray Council
High Street
Elgin
IV30 1BX
☎ 01343 543 451
Website: www.moray.gov.uk/

North Ayrshire Council
Cunninghame House
Friars Croft
Irvine
KA12 8EE
☎ 01294 324 100
Website: www.north-ayrshire.gov.uk/

North Lanarkshire Council
Municipal Building
Kildonan Street
Coatbridge
ML5 3BT
☎ 01236 812 239
Website: www.northlan.gov.uk/

Orkney Islands Council
Schoolplace
Kirkwall
Orkney
KW15 1NY
☎ 01856 873 535
Website: www.orkney.gov.uk

Perth and Kinross Council
Blackfriars
Perth
PH1 5LT
☎ 01738 476 211
Website: www.pkc.gov.uk/

Renfrewshire Council
Cotton Street
Paisley
PA1 1LE
☎ 0141 842 5663
Website: www.renfrewshire.gov.uk/

Scottish Borders Council
Council Headquarters
Newtown St Boswells
Melrose
TD6 0SA
☎ 01835 824 000
Website: www.scotborders.gov.uk/

6

Shetlands Islands Council
Hayfield House
Hayfield Lane
Lerwick
Shetland
ZE1 0QD
☎ 01595 744 000
Website: www.shetland.gov.uk/

South Ayrshire Council
Wellington Square
Ayr
KA7 1DR
☎ 01292 612 000
Website: www.south-ayrshire.gov.uk/

South Lanarkshire Council
Floor 5
Council Offices
Almada Street
Hamilton
ML3 0AA
☎ 01698 454 444
Website: www.southlanarkshire.gov.uk/

Stirling Council
Viewforth
Stirling
FK8 2ET
☎ 01786 442 666
Website: www.stirling.gov.uk/

West Dunbartonshire Council
Council Offices
Garshake Road
Dumbarton
G82 1HG
☎ 01389 737 309
Website: www.west-dunbarton.gov.uk/

West Lothian Council
Lindsay House
South Bridge Street
Bathgate
EH48 1TS
☎ 01506 776 000
Website: www.westlothian.gov.uk

Comhairle nan Eilean Siar
Sandwick Road
Stornoway
Isle of Lewis
HS1 2BW
☎ 01851 709 530
Website: www.cne-siar.gov.uk/

Wales

Blaenau Gwent County
Borough Council
Municipal Offices
Civic Centre
Ebbw Vale
NP23 6XB
☎ 01495 355 434
Website: www.blaenau-gwent.gov.uk/

Bridgend County Borough Council
Civic Offices
Angel Street
Bridgend
CF31 1LX
☎ 01656 643 643
Website: www.bridgend.gov.uk/

Caerphilly County Borough Council
Nelson Road
Tredomen
Ystrad Mynach
Hengoed
CF82 7WF
☎ 01443 864 956
Website: www.caerphilly.gov.uk/

City and County of Cardiff
County Hall
Atlantic Wharf
Cardiff
CF10 4UW
☎ 029 2087 2000
Website: www.cardiff.gov.uk/

Carmarthenshire County Council
County Hall
Carmarthen
Carmarthenshire
SA31 1JP
☎ 01267 234 567
Website: www.carmarthenshire.gov.uk/

Ceredigion County Council
Penmorfa
Aberaeron
Ceredigion
SA46 0PA
☎ 01970 633 610
Website: www.ceredigion.gov.uk/

Conwy County Borough Council
Bodlondeb
Conwy
LL32 8DU
☎ 01492 574 000
Website: www.conwy.gov.uk/

Denbighshire County Council
Department of Lifelong Learning
Caledfryn
Smithfield Road
Denbigh
LL16 3RJ
☎ 01824 706 777
Website: www.denbighshire.gov.uk/

Flintshire County Council
County Hall
Mold
CH7 6NB
☎ 01352 704 023
Website: www.flintshire.gov.uk/

Gwynedd County Council
Council Offices
Shire Hall Street
Caernarfon
Gwynedd
LL55 1SH
☎ 01286 679 162
Website: www.gwynedd.gov.uk/

Isle of Anglesey County Council
Department of Education and Leisure
Park Mount
Glanhwfa
Llangefni
LL77 7EY
☎ 01248 752 900
Website: www.anglesey.gov.uk/

6

Merthyr Tydfil County Borough Council

Civic Centre
Castle Street
Merthyr Tydfil
☎ 01685 725 000
Website: www.merthyr.gov.uk/

Monmouthshire County Council

County Hall
Cwmbran
NP44 2XH
☎ 01633 644 644
Website: www.monmouthshire.gov.uk/

Neath Port Talbot

County Borough Council
Civic Centre
Port Talbot
SA13 1PJ
☎ 01639 763 333
Website: www.neath-porttalbot.gov.uk/

Newport City Council

Civic Centre
Newport
NP20 4UR
☎ 01633 244 491
Website: www.newport.gov.uk/

Pembrokeshire County Council

County Hall
Haverfordwest
Pembrokeshire
SA61 1TP
☎ 01437 764 551
Website: www.pembrokeshire.gov.uk/

Powys County Council

County Hall
Llandrindod Wells
Powys
LD1 5LG
☎ 01597 826 000
Website: www.powys.gov.uk/

Rhondda Cynon Taff County Borough Council

Education and Lifelong Learning
Ty Trevithick
Abercynon
Mountain Ash
CF45 4UQ
☎ 01443 744 000
Website: www.rhondda-cynon-taff.gov.uk/

City and County of Swansea

County Hall
Oystermouth Road
Swansea
SA1 3SN
☎ 01792 636 000
Website: www.swansea.gov.uk/

Torfaen County Borough Council

Civic Centre
Pontypool
Torfaen
NP4 6YB
☎ 01495 762 200
Website: www.torfaen.gov.uk/

The Vale of Glamorgan Council

Civic Offices
Holton Road
Barry
CF63 4RU
☎ 01446 700 111
Website: www.valeofglamorgan.gov.uk/

Wrexham County Borough Council

Education and Leisure Services
Ty Henblas
Queens Square
Wrexham
LL13 8AZ
☎ 01978 297 401
Website: www.wrexham.gov.uk/

Section 7

Special Schools in the UK

England

Barnet

Oakleigh School
Oakleigh Road North
Whetstone
London
N20 0DH
☎ 020 8368 5336
🖷 020 8361 6922
email: info@oakleigh.
barnet.sch.uk
Head: Jenny Gridley
No. of pupils: 67
Age range: 2-11
Funding: LEA
Type of School: Day
Special Needs: Profound,
Severe & Multiple
Learning Difficulties and
Autistic Spectrum
Disorder

Bath & NE Somerset

Farleigh College
Farleigh Castle
Farleigh Hungerford
Bath
BA3 6RW
☎ 01225 753 130
🖷 01225 756 921
No. of pupils: 90
Age range: 10-18

Fosse Way School
Longfellow Road
Radstock
BA3 3AL
☎ 01761 412 198
🖷 01761 411 751
email: fosseway-spe@
bathness.gov.uk
Head: Mr David Gregory
No. of pupils: 120
Age range: 3-19
Funding: LEA
Type of School: Residential
& Day
Special Needs: Severe &
Complex Learning
Difficulties and Autism

Hilltop School
Radstock
Bath
BA3 3LL
☎ 01761 432 179
Age range: 3-18

Lime Grove School
Lime Grove Gardens
Bath
BA2 4HE
☎ 01225 424 732
🖷 01225 466 305
Head: Mrs J D Pulham
No. of pupils: 45
Age range: 3-19
Funding: LEA
Type of School: Day
Special Needs: Profound &
Multiple Learning
Difficulties

Royal United Hospital School
Cynthia Mossman House
Combe Park
Bath
BA1 3NJ
☎ 01225 428 331
No. of pupils: 32
Age range: 4-11

Summerfield School
Weston Park East
Bath
BA1 2VY
☎ 01225 423 607
🖷 01225 461 637
Head: Mr Gwyn Williams
No. of pupils: 100
Age range: 7-16
Funding: LEA
Type of School: Day
Special Needs: Moderate
Learning Difficulties

Wansdyke School
Frome Road
Odd Down
Bath
BA2 5RF
No. of pupils: 78
Age range: 9-16
Funding: LEA
Type of School: Hostel

Special Needs: Emotional
& behavioural difficulties

Bedfordshire

Glenwood School
Beech Road
Dunstable
LU6 3LY
☎ 01582 667 106
🖷 01582 699 538
email: glenwood@
bedfordshire.gov.uk
web: www.dial.pipex.com
Head: Mrs S A Crosbie
No. of pupils: 130
Age range: 2-11
Funding: LEA
Type of School: Day
Special Needs: Wide range

Grange School
Halsey Road
Bedford
MK42 8AU
☎ 01234 407 100
🖷 01234 407 110
Head: Mrs C H Woodroffe
No. of pupils: 156
Age range: 5-16
Funding: LEA
Type of School: Day
Special Needs: Moderate
Learning Difficulties

Hillcrest School
Ridgeway Avenue
Dunstable
LU5 4QL
☎ 01582 661 983
🖷 01582 472 455
No. of pupils: 92
Age range: 11-19

Hitchmead School
Hitchmead Road
Biggleswade
SG16 0NL
☎ 01767 601 010
🖷 01767 601 010
No. of pupils: 107
Age range: 7-16

Lady Zia Wernher School
Ashcroft Road

Stopsley
Luton
LU2 9AY
☎ 01582 728 705
🖷 01582 722 384
email: ladyziawadmin@
luton.gov.uk
web: www.luton.gov.uk/
learning/schools/
schools_list
Head: Mrs Judith Jackson
No. of pupils: 76
Age range: 2-11
Funding: LEA
Type of School: Day
Special Needs: Wide range

McIntyre School
Westoning Manor
Church Road
Westoning
Bedford
MK45 5JW
Age range: 13-19

Montague House
78 Shakespeare Road
Bedford
MK40 2DN
☎ 01234 344025
No. of pupils: 12
Age range: 11-16
Funding: Independent
Type of School: Residential
Special Needs: Hearing
Impaired

Rainbow School
Chestnut Avenue
Bromham
Bedford
MK43 8HP
☎ 01234 822 596
🖷 01234 826 093
email: rainbow@deal.
bedfordshire.gov.uk
web: www.deal.
bedfordshire.gov.uk
Head: Mrs June R Mason
No. of pupils: 244
Age range: 3-19
Funding: LEA
Type of School: Day
Special Needs: Severe
Learning Difficulties

Ridgeway School
Hill Rise
Kempston
Bedford
MK42 7EB
☎ 01234 853 602
No. of pupils: 69
Age range: 3-19

St John's School
Austin Canons
Bedford Road
Kempston
Bedford
MK42 8AA
☎ 01234 345 565
🖷 01234 327 734
email: ronbabbage@
st-johns.ndo.co.uk
Head: Mr Ron Babbage
No. of pupils: 130
Age range: 2-19
Funding: LEA
Type of School: Day
Special Needs: Severe
Learning Difficulties &
Multi-sensory Impairment

Sunnyside School
The Baulk
Biggleswade
SG18 0PT
☎ 01767 222 662
🖷 01767 222 663
web: www.cableol.co.uk
Education Manager: Mrs
V G White
Age range: 3-19

Weatherfield School
Brewers Hill Road
Dunstable
LU6 1AF
☎ 01582 605 632
🖷 01582 605 632
Age range: 7-16

Berkshire

Addington School
Loddon Bridge Road
Woodley
Reading
RG5 4BS
☎ 0118 954 0444
🖷 0118 927 2480
email: office@addington.
wokingham.sch.uk
Head: Nick Burnett
No. of pupils: 210
Age range: 2-19
Funding: LEA

Type of School: Day
Special Needs: Moderate
& Severe Learning
Difficulties and Profound
& Multiple Learning
Difficulties and Autism

Annie Lawson School
Ravenswood Village
Nine Mile Ride
Crowthorne
RG45 6BQ
☎ 01344 755 508
🖷 01344 762 317
email: info@annielawson.
datanet.co.uk
web: www.annielawson.
datanet.co.uk
Head: Mr Mark Hughes
No. of pupils: 23
Age range: 11-19
Funding: Independent
Type of School: Residential
Special Needs: Profound &
Multiple Learning
Difficulties

Arbour Vale School
Stoke Road
Slough
SL2 5AY
☎ 01753 525 291
🖷 01753 691 415
email: office@arbourvale.
slough.sch.uk
web: www.avs.
datanet.co.uk/arbourvale
Head: Mrs Alison Beane
No. of pupils: 280
Age range: 2-19
Funding: LEA
Type of School: Day
Special Needs: Severe &
Complex Needs, Autism
and Moderate Learning
Difficulties

**Bridge House Home
School**
Padworth
Reading
RG7 0EN
☎ 0118 971 3176
Age range: 7-16

Brookfields School
Sage Road
Tilehurst
Reading
RG31 6SW
☎ 0118 942 1882
🖷 0118 945 5176

email: brkflds1@
rmplc.co.uk
web: www.rmplc.co.uk
Head: Mr J Byrne
No. of pupils: 250
Age range: 2-19
Funding: LEA
Type of School: Day
Special Needs: Profound &
Multiple Learning
Difficulties

**High Close School
(Barnardo's)**
Wiltshire Road
Wokingham
RG11 1TT
☎ 0118 978 5767
No. of pupils: 48
Age range: 10-16

Holyport Manor School
Ascot Road
Holyport
SL6 3LE
☎ 01628 623 196
🖷 01628 623 608
email: holyport@
manor_school_edu
Head: Mr Paul
Donkerslodt
No. of pupils: 200
Age range: 2-16
Funding: LEA
Type of School: Day
Special Needs: Multi-
sensory Impairments

Littledown School
Queens Road
Slough
SL1 3QW
☎ 01753 521 734
🖷 01753 575338
email: lesleyr@littledown.
slough.sch.uk
Head: Mrs L Redfern
No. of pupils: 2
Age range: 5-11
Funding: LEA
Type of School: Special
EBD Day
Special Needs: All

**Mary Hare Grammar
School**
Arlington Manor
Snelsmore Common
Newbury
RG14 3BQ
☎ 01635 244200 (voice/
minicom)

Textphone 01635 244260
🖷 01635 248019
email: office@
maryhare.org.uk
web: www.maryhare.org.uk
No. of pupils: 212
Age range: 11-18
Type of School:
Residential/Day
Special Needs: Severe or
Profound Hearing Loss

**Mary Hare Primary
School**
Mill Hall
Pigeons Farm Road
Thatcham
RG19 8XA
☎ 01635 573800 (voice/
minicom)
🖷 01635 524999
email: maryhareprimary@
mill.fsnet.co.uk
Contact: Tricia Weaver
(Secretary)
No. of pupils: 19
Funding: Non-maintained
Special School
Type of School: Residential
(weekly)/Day
Special Needs: Severe and
Profound Hearing Loss

**Reading Alternative
School**
40 Christchurch Road
Reading
RG2 7AY
☎ 0118 975 2095
Age range: 11-16

Southfield School
Gypsy Lane
Wokingham
RG11 2BN
Age range: 11-16

**Teaching & Support
Service (EOTAS)**
Schoolroom
Paediatric Dept
Wexham Park Hospital
Slough
SL2 4HL
☎ 01753 634610
🖷 01753 634610
email: staff@
wexhamparkteaching.
slough.sch.uk
web:
www.wexhamparkteaching.
slough.sch.uk

Teacher in charge: Mrs C
Parker
No. of pupils: 12
Age range: 4-16
Funding: LEA
Type of School: Hospital/
Out patients day

The Avenue School
Basingstoke Road
Reading
RG2 0EN
☎ 0118 901 5554
🖷 0118 901 5558
Acting Head: Mr P Sparks
No. of pupils: 163
Age range: 2-19
Funding: LEA
Type of School: Day
Special Needs: Moderate
Learning Difficulties

The Castle School
Love Lane
Donnington
Newbury
RG14 2JG
☎ 01635 42976
🖷 01635 551 725
Head: Mrs K Gray
No. of pupils: 149
Age range: 3-19
Funding: LEA
Type of School: Day
Special Needs: Moderate
Learning Difficulties,
Severe Learning
Difficulties, Autism and
Profound Multiple
Learning Difficulties

The Holy Brook School
145 Ashampstead Road
Southcote
Reading
RG30 2LT
☎ 0118 901 5489
🖷 0118 901 5488
email: admin.holybrook@
reading.gov.uk
Acting Head: Lyn Rowles
No. of pupils: 24
Age range: 5-11
Funding: LEA
Type of School: Day
Primary Special
Special Needs: Emotional
& Behavioural Difficulties

Bexley

Westbrooke School
South Gipsy Road

Welling
DA16 1JB
☎ 020 8304 1320
🖷 020 8304 6525
email: info@westbrooke.
bexley.sch.uk
Head: Mrs C A Hance
No. of pupils: 40
Age range: 5-11
Funding: LEA
Type of School: Day
Special Needs: Emotional
& behavioural difficulties

**Bolton
Metropolitan
Borough**

Rumworth
Armadale Road
Ladybridge
Bolton
BL3 4TP
☎ 01204 333 600
🖷 01204 333 602
email: head@rumworth.
bolton.sch.uk
Head: Mr Bill Bradbury
No. of pupils: 140
Age range: 12-19
Funding: LEA
Type of School: Day
Special Needs: Complex
and moderate learning
difficulties

Green Fold School
Highfield Road
Farnworth
Bolton
BL4 0RA
☎ 01204 333750
🖷 01204 333751
email: office@greenfold.
bolton.sch.uk
Head: Mrs C E Chapman
No. of pupils: 70
Age range: 3-11
Funding: LEA
Type of School: Day
Special Needs: Wide range

**Borough of
Poole**

Children's Education Unit
Schoolroom Ward A1
Poole General Hospital
Longfleet Road
Poole
BH15 2JB

☎ 01202 448 082
🖷 01202 448 082
email: janettewilliams@
poole.gov.uk
Hospital Teacher: Janette
Williams
Age range: 4-16
Funding: LEA
Type of School: Hospital
Special Needs: All school
age children

Bournemouth

The Bicknell School
Petersfield Road
Boscombe
Bournemouth
BH7 6QP
☎ 01202 424 361
🖷 01202 430 592
email: bicknell.school@
bournmouth.gov.uk
Head: Mr Brian Hooper
No. of pupils: 65
Age range: 11-16
Funding: Foundation
Type of School: Residential
Special Needs: Emotional
& behavioural difficulties

Bradford

Bolling Special School
Bowling Hall Road
Bradford
BD4 7SY
☎ 01274 721 962
🖷 01274 721 962
email: office@
bolling.ngfl.ac.uk
Head: Mrs Susan M Gill
No. of pupils: 95
Age range: 11-19
Funding: LEA
Type of School: Day
Special Needs: Profound &
Multiple Learning
Difficulties

Thorn Park School
Thorn Lane
Bingley Road
Bradford
BD9 6RY
☎ 01274 773 770
🖷 01274 770 387
email: davemuir@
thornpark.ngfl
web: www.aol.com
Head: Mr D Muir
No. of pupils: 90

Age range: 2-19
Funding: LEA
Type of School: Day
Special Needs: Profound &
Multiple Learning
Difficulties and Deafness

Brent

Grove Park Special School
Grove Park
Kingsbury
London
NW9 0JY
☎ 020 8204 3293
No. of pupils: 86
Age range: 2-19
Funding: LEA
Type of School: Day
Special Needs: Delicate
health/Physical Disability

Manor School
Chamberlayne Road
Kensal Rise
London
NW10 3NT
☎ 020 8968 3160
🖷 020 8968 3075
Head: Ms Jenny Drake
No. of pupils: 120
Age range: 4-11
Funding: LEA
Type of School: Day
Special Needs: Speech and
Language Difficulties,
Autism and Severe
Learning Difficulties

Brighton & Hove

Downs Park Special School
Foredown Road
Portslade
Brighton
BN41 2FU
☎ 01273 417 448
🖷 01273 439 619
Acting Head: Ms A Fulton
No. of pupils: 115
Age range: 4-16
Funding: LEA
Type of School: Day
Special Needs: Moderate
Learning Difficulties/
Emotional & Behavioural
Difficulties/ASD

Downs View School
Warren Road
Woodingdean
Brighton

7

BN2 6BB
☎ 01273 601 680
🖩 01273 699 240
Head: Ms Jane Reed
No. of pupils: 117
Age range: 4-19
Funding: LEA
Type of School: Day
Special Needs: Profound &
Multiple Learning
Difficulties, Multiple
Learning Difficulties,
Severe Learning
Difficulties and ASD

Hillside School
104 Lyndhurst Road
Cherry Trees
Further Education Centre
Hove
BN3 6FD
☎ 01273 821 579
🖩 01273 821 579
email: cherrytrees@
rmplc.co.uk
Senior Teacher: Len Parkyn
No. of pupils: 12
Age range: 18-19
Funding: LEA
Type of School: Day, FE
Special Needs: Severe and
Profound & Multiple
Learning Difficulties

**Patcham House Special
School**
7 Old London Road
Patcham
Brighton
BN1 8XR
☎ 01273 551028
🖩 01273 550465
email:
office@patchamhosue.
brighton-hove.sch.uk
web: www.patchamhouse.
brighton-have.sch.uk
Secretary: Angela Webb
No. of pupils: 70
Age range: 3-16
Funding: LEA
Type of School: Day
Special Needs: Physical &
Neurological impairment.
Medical conditions
emotionally withdrawn.

**St John's Residential
College**
Walpole Road
Brighton
BN2 2AF

☎ 01273 244000
🖩 01273 244038
web: www.st-johns.co.uk
Head: Mr Don Kent
No. of pupils: 93
Age range: 14-19
Type of School: Day
Special Needs: Variety

Uplands School
Lynchet Close
Hollingdean
Brighton
BN1 7FP
☎ 01273 558622
🖩 01273 558622
Head: Mr Paul Atkins
No. of pupils: 109
Age range: 11-16
Type of School: Day
Special Needs: Moderate
Learning Difficulties

Bristol

Briarwood School
Briar Way
Fishponds
Bristol
BS16 4EA
☎ 0117 965 7536
🖩 0117 9650599
Head: Mr David Hussey
No. of pupils: 86
Age range: 2-19
Funding: LEA
Type of School: Day
Special Needs: Severe
Learning Difficulties

**Bristol Hospital
Education Service**
Embleton Primary School
Gosforth Road
Southmead
Bristol
BS10 6DS
☎ 0117 3772377
🖩 0117 3772380
email: peter-wright@
bristol-city.gov.uk
Head: Peter Wright
Age range: 2-18
Funding: LEA
Type of School: Hospital
and home tuition

Claremont School
Henleaze Park
Westbury-on-Trym
Bristol
BS9 4LR

☎ 0117 924 7527
🖩 0117 942 6942
email: claremont@
bristol-city.gov.uk
web:
www.claremontspecial.ik.org
Head: Mr Bob Coburn
No. of pupils: 69
Age range: 2-11
Funding: LEA
Type of School: Day
Special Needs: Physical
Disabilities/Profound &
Multiple Learning
Difficulties

**Elmfield School for the
Deaf**
Greystoke Avenue
Westbury-on-Trym
Bristol
BS10 6AY
☎ 0117 950 1962
Textphone 0117 950 1741
🖩 0117 950 1962
Head: Ms Ros Way
No. of pupils: 62
Age range: 3-16
Funding: LEA
Type of School: Day
Special Needs: Hearing
Impaired

Filton Park
Charborough Road
Filton
Bristol
BS9 7RB
☎ 0117 969 4224
🖩 0117 931 5256
Funding: LEA

Florence Brown School
Leinster Avenue
Knowle
Bristol
BS4 1NN
☎ 0117 966 8152
🖩 0117 966 6537
Head: Mr Peter Evans
No. of pupils: 220
Age range: 5-16
Funding: LEA
Type of School: Day
Special Needs: Severe &
Complex Needs

Fulford School
Fulford Road
Hartcliffe
Bristol
BS13 9BP

☎ 0117 964 9806
No. of pupils: 66
Age range: 11-16

Henbury Manor School
Rectory Gardens
Henbury
Bristol
BS10 2AH
☎ 0117 950 2868
No. of pupils: 44
Age range: 3-19

Kingsweston School
Napier Miles Road
Kingsweston
Bristol
BS11 0UT
☎ 0117 987 3636
🖩 0117 987 2915
email: kingsweston.edu@
msn.com
web: www.msn.com
Head: Mr David Capel
No. of pupils: 190
Age range: 3-19
Funding: LEA
Type of School: Day
Special Needs: Moderate
Learning Difficulties

New Fosseway School
New Fosseway Road
Hengrove
Bristol
BS14 9LN
☎ 01275 839 411
No. of pupils: 87
Age range: 2-19

Springfield School
128 Richmond Road
Montpelier
Bristol
BS6 5ER
Age range: 7-16

St Christopher's School
Carisbrooke Lodge
Westbury Park
Bristol
BS6 7JE
☎ 0117 973 3301
🖩 0117 974 3665
Head: Ms Orna Matz
No. of pupils: 45
Age range: 6-19
Funding: Independent
Type of School: Residential
Special Needs: Wide
range

Bromley

Phoenix Pre-School Centre (SEN)
40 Masons Hill
Bromley
BR2 9JG
☎ 020 8466 8811
📄 020 8466 8855
email: phoenix.general@
phoenixsch.org.uk
Head: Mrs Helen Norris
No. of pupils: 38
Age range: 2-5
Funding: LEA
Type of School: Day
Special Needs: Profound &
Multiple Learning
Difficulties

Buckinghamshire

Alfriston School for Girls
Penn Road
Knolty Green
Beaconsfield
HP9 2TS
☎ 01494 673740
📄 01494 670177
email: office@
alfriston.bucks.sch.uk
Head: Mrs V Gordon
No. of pupils: 125
Age range: 11-18
Funding: LEA
Type of School:
Day/Weekly Residential
Special Needs: Multiple
Learning Difficulties –
Social/Emotional and
Physical Difficulties

Chiltern Gate School
Verney Avenue
High Wycombe
HP12 3NE
☎ 014945 326 221
Head: Mr W M Marshall
No. of pupils: 125
Age range: 4-11
Funding: LEA
Type of School: Day
Special Needs: Moderate
Learning Difficulties and
Emotional and behavioural
difficulties & Autism

Furze Down School
Verney Road
Winslow
MK18 3BL
☎ 01296 713 385
📄 01296 714 420

Heads: Mrs S Collins /
P J Dichler
No. of pupils: 110
Age range: 4-19
Funding: LEA
Type of School: Day
Special Needs: Moderate
Learning Difficulties/
Complex Needs

Heritage House School
Cameron Road
Chesham
HP5 3BP
No. of pupils: 85
Age range: 2-19
Funding: LEA
Type of School: Day
Special Needs: Severe
Learning Difficulties

Kynaston School
Kynaston Avenue
Aylesbury
HP22 5XE
Age range: 5-16

MacIntyre School
Old Manor House
Leighton Road
Wingrave
HP22 4PD
☎ 01296 681 274
📄 01296 681091
Head: Mrs Elizabeth
Haworth
No. of pupils: 36
Age range: 10-19
Funding: Independent
Type of School: Residential
Special Needs: Severe
Learning Difficulties,
Autism and additional
complex behaviours

Park Crescent School
Cressex Road
High Wycombe
HP12 4PR
☎ 01494 438 018
📄 01494 539 139
Head: Ms Suzanne
Pennington
No. of pupils: 27
Age range: 2-7
Funding: LEA
Type of School: Day
Special Needs: Profound &
Multiple Learning
Difficulties

Park School
Stocklake

Aylesbury
HP20 1DP
☎ 01296 423 507
📄 01296 433 353
email: admin@
park.bucks.sch.uk
Head: Mrs Ruth Cutler
No. of pupils: 85
Age range: 2-19
Funding: LEA
Type of School: Day
Special Needs: Severe
Learning Difficulties/
Complex SENs

Pebble Brook School
Churchill Avenue
Aylesbury
HP21 8LZ
☎ 01296 415 761
📄 01296 434 442
Head: Mrs J C Lloyd
No. of pupils: 70
Age range: 11-16
Funding: LEA
Type of School: Day
Special Needs: Profound &
Multiple Learning
Difficulties

Penn School
Church Road
Penn
High Wycombe
HP10 8LZ
☎ 01494 812 139
No. of pupils: 42
Age range: 5-16

Prestwood Lodge School
Nairdwood Lane
Prestwood
HP16 0QQ
☎ 01494 863 514
📄 01494 866 154
Head: Mr M Rosner
No. of pupils: 46
Age range: 11-16
Funding: LEA
Type of School: Boarding
Special Needs: Emotional
& behavioural difficulties

**Prestwood Lodge School
for Boys**
Nairdwood Lane
Prestwood
Great Missenden
HP16 0OQ
No. of pupils: 46
Age range: 11-16

Romans Field School
Shenley Road
Bletchley
Milton Keynes
MK3 7AW
☎ 01908 376 011
Age range: 5-12

Slated Row Special School
Old Wolverton Road
Wolverton
Milton Keynes
MK12 5NJ
☎ 01908 316 017
📄 01908 315 082
Head: Mr John O'Donnell
No. of pupils: 158
Age range: 4-19
Funding: LEA
Type of School: Day
Special Needs: Severe
Learning Difficulties

Stoke Leys School
Claydon Path
Kynaston Avenue
Aylesbury
HP21 9EF
Age range: 5-12

Stony Dean School
Orchard End Avenue
Off Pineapple Road
Amersham
HP7 9JW
☎ 01494 762 538
📄 01494 765 631
email: office@
stonydean.bucks.sch.uk
web: www.stonydean.co.uk
Head: Mr P G Newsholme
No. of pupils: 126
Age range: 11-18
Funding: LEA
Type of School:
Day/Residential
Special Needs: Wide range

The Gatehouse School
Crosslands
Stantonbury
Milton Keynes
MK14 6AX
☎ 01908 313 903
📄 01908 221 195
Head: Mrs Jan Park
No. of pupils: 40
Age range: 12-16
Funding: LEA
Type of School: Day/
Weekly Boarding
Special Needs: Emotional
& behavioural difficulties

7

The Redway School
Farmborough
Netherfield
Milton Keynes
MK6 4HG
☎ 01908 200 000
🖷 01908 206 420
email: the_redway@
milton-keynes.gov.uk
web: www.the.redway.
school.mcmail.com
Head: Mr Richard Fraser
No. of pupils: 120
Age range: 2-19
Funding: LEA
Type of School: Day
Special Needs: Profound &
Multiple Learning
Difficulties

The Walnuts School
Simpson
Milton Keynes
MK6 3AF
☎ 01908 670 032
🖷 01908 232 774
email: admin@walnuts.
milton-keynes.sch.uk
Head: Mr Nick Jackman
No. of pupils: 51
Age range: 4-12
Funding: LEA
Type of School: Day
Special Needs: Autism,
Speech & Language &
Communication
difficulties

Verney Avenue School
High Wycombe
HP12 3NE
No. of pupils: 73
Age range: 12-17

Vinio House School
Cressex Road
High Wycombe
HP12 4PR
No. of pupils: 77
Age range: 6-19

Wendover House School
Church Lane
Wendover
HP22 6NL
☎ 01296 622157
🖷 01296 622628
email: office@
wendoverhouse.bucks.ach.uk
No. of pupils: 71
Age range: 11-18
Type of School:

Residential/Day
Special Needs: Emotional
& Behavioural Difficulties

White Spire School
Rickley Lane
Bletchley
Milton Keynes
MK3 6EW
☎ 01908 373 266
No. of pupils: 163
Age range: 5-18

Calderdale

Highbury School
Lower Edge Road
Rastrick
Brighouse
HD6 3LD
☎ 01484 716 319
🖷 01484 721 893
email: admin@
highbury.calderdale.sch.uk
Head: Miss P J Sellers
No. of pupils: 40
Age range: 2-11
Funding: LEA
Type of School: Day
Special Needs: Wide range

**The William Henry Smith
School**
Boothroyd
Brighouse
HD6 3JW
☎ 01484 710 123
🖷 01484 721 658
email: general@
whsschool.org.uk
web: www.whsschool.org.uk
Head: Mr B J Heneghan
No. of pupils: 64
Age range: 8-16
Funding: Non-maintained
Type of School: Residential
Special Needs: Emotional
& behavioural difficulties

Cambridgeshire

Clayton School
Clayton Orton
Goldhay
Peterborough
PE2 5SD
☎ 01733 232 346
🖷 01733 230 879
Head: Mr Ron Telfer
No. of pupils: 45
Age range: 2-19
Funding: LEA

Type of School: Residential
Special Needs: Profound &
Multiple Learning
Difficulties

Ellindon School
Ellindon
Bretton
Peterborough
PE3 8RQ
☎ 01733 265 121
Age range: 9-16

Green Hedges School
Bar Lane
Stapleford
Cambridge
CB2 5BJ
☎ 01223 508 608
🖷 01223 508 678
Head: Mrs G B Newell
No. of pupils: 70
Age range: 2-19
Funding: LEA
Type of School: Day
Special Needs: Profound
and Multiple Learning
Difficulties

Heltwate School
Heltwate
North Bretton
Peterborough
PE3 8RL
☎ 01733 262 878
🖷 01733 331 192
Head: Mr D R Smith
No. of pupils: 101
Age range: 4-16
Funding: LEA
Type of School: Day
Special Needs: Severe
Learning Difficulties

Highfield School
Cambridge Road
Ely
CB7 4HW
No. of pupils: 66
Age range: 2-19

Littleton House School
High Street
Girton
Cambridge
CB3 0QL
☎ 01223 714217/714216
🖷 01223 568 884
email: office@littletonhouse.
cambs-schools.net
Head: Mr A Pyle
No. of pupils: 80

Age range: 11-16
Funding: LEA
Type of School: Residential
Special Needs: Emotional
& behavioural difficulties

Marshfields School
Eastern Close
Dogsthorpe
Peterborough
PE1 4PP
☎ 01733 568 058
No. of pupils: 154
Age range: 5-18

Meadowgate School
Meadowgate Lane
Wisbech
PE13 2JH
☎ 01945 461 836
🖷 01945 589 967
email: office@meadowgate.
cambs.schools.net
web: www.meadowgate.
cambs.sch.uk
Head: Mrs Rosa M Blunt
No. of pupils: 120
Age range: 2-19
Funding: LEA
Type of School: Day
Special Needs: Moderate
Learning Difficulties and
Severe & Profound &
Multiple Learning
Difficulties

Meldreth Manor School
Fenny Lane
Meldreth
Royston
SG8 6LG
☎ 01763 268000
🖷 01763 268099
web: www.members.
tripod.com/mmschool2
Head: Mr Eric Nash
No. of pupils: 72
Age range: 8-19
Funding: LEA/LSC/Social
Services
Type of School: Residential
& Day
Special Needs: Profound &
Multiple Learning
Difficulties and Cerebral
Palsy

Rees Thomas School
Downhams Road
Cambridge
CB4 1YB
☎ 01223 712100

email: office@reesthomas.
cambs-schools.net
web:
www.a7010.camcnty.gov.uk
Head: Mr Peter Smith
No. of pupils: 57
Age range: 2-19
Funding: LEA
Type of School: Day
Special Needs: Severe
Learning Difficulties/
Profound & Multiple
Learning Dificulties

Samuel Pepys School
Cromwell Road
St Neots
Cambs
PE19 2EZ
☎ 01480 375012
🖷 01480375014
email: office@pepysroad.
cambs-schools.net
Head: D Baldry
No. of pupils: 95
Age range: 3-19
Funding: LEA
Type of School: Special
Special Needs: MLD/SLD/
PMLD/Autism

Spring Common School
American Lane
Huntingdon
PE18 7TY
☎ 01480 377 403
🖷 01480 377 405
email:
SpringCommonSchool@
btinternet.com
web: www.btinternet.com
Head: Mrs Marie
Rawlings
No. of pupils: 136
Age range: 3-19
Funding: LEA
Type of School: Day
Special Needs: Profound &
Multiple Learning
Difficulties

Springfields School
Thames Road
Huntingdon
PE18 7QW
☎ 01480 375 106
🖷 01480 375 107
Head: Mr R S Keen
No. of pupils: 31
Age range: 3-10
Funding: LEA

Type of School: Day
Special Needs: Wide range

St George's School
Lane Avenue
Dogsthorpe
Peterborough
PE1 3RB
☎ 01733 562 058
🖷 01733 312 737
email: aab079@
peterborough.gov.uk
Head: Mr B A Rudgley
No. of pupils: 40
Age range: 2-19
Funding: LEA
Type of School: Day
Special Needs: Profound &
Multiple Learning
Difficulties

The Lady Adrian School
Courtney Way
Cambridge
CB4 2EE
☎ 01223 357 038
No. of pupils: 135
Age range: 7-16

The Manor School
Station Road
Wilburton
Ely
CB6 3RR
☎ 01353 740 229
🖷 01353 740 632
email: office@monorely.
cambs-schools.net
Head: Mr T Muran
No. of pupils: 62
Age range: 6-11
Funding: LEA
Type of School:
Day/Residential
Special Needs: Emotional
& Behavioural Difficulties

The Windmill School
Hinton Road
Fulbourn
Cambridge
CB1 5DZ
☎ 01223 712 210
🖷 01223 712 212
email: lyn@
windmillschool.co.uk
web:
www.windmillschool.co.uk
Head: Mrs Kate Kemp
No. of pupils: 64
Age range: 2-19

Funding: LEA
Type of School: Day
Special Needs: Severe
Learning Difficulties

Camden, London

**Royal Free Hospital
Children's School**
6th Floor – Riddell Ward
Pond Street
London
NW3 2QG
☎ 020 7794 0500 X 3553
🖷 020 7830 2302
Head: Manuela Beste
No. of pupils: 40
Age range: 5-16
Funding: LEA
Type of School: Hospital
Special Needs: Medical

Cheshire

Adelaide School
Adelaide Street
Crewe
CW1 3DT
☎ 01270 255661
🖷 01270 584577
email: head@adelaidestreet.
school.cheshire.org.uk
Head: L B Willday
No. of pupils: 35
Age range: 11-16
Type of School: Day
Special Needs: Emotional
& behavioural difficulties

Adelaide Street School
Adelaide Street
Crewe
CW1 3DT
☎ 01270 255 661
🖷 01270 584 577
Head: L B Willday
No. of pupils: 35
Age range: 11-16
Funding: LEA
Type of School: Day
Special Needs: Emotional
& behavioural difficulties

Ashley School (Mld)
Cawfield Avenue
Widnes
WA8 7HG
No. of pupils: 109
Age range: 8-16
Special Needs: Moderate
Learning Difficulties

Bethesda School
Schools Hill
Cheadle
SK8 1JE
No. of pupils: 25
Age range: 11-16

Brentwood School
Brentwood Avenue
Timperley
Altrincham
WA14 1SR
☎ 0161 928 8109
🖷 0161 928 4548
Head: Mrs Bernice Kostick
No. of pupils: 75
Age range: 11-19
Funding: LEA
Type of School: Day
Special Needs: Profound &
Multiple Learning
Difficulties

Brook Farm School
Brook Road
Tarporley
CW6 9HH
☎ 01829 732 201
🖷 01829 732 824
Head: N R Haslam
No. of pupils: 49
Age range: 9-16
Funding: LEA
Type of School: Day
Special Needs: Emotional
& behavioural difficulties

Brookfields School
Moorfield Road
Widnes
WA8 3JA
☎ 0151 424 4329
🖷 0151 495 3460
Head: Mr Chryssafi
No. of pupils: 73
Age range: 2-19
Funding: LEA
Type of School: Day
Special Needs: Severe
Learning Difficulties

Buglawton Hall School
Buxton Road
Congleton
CW12 3PQ
☎ 01260 274 492
No. of pupils: 43
Age range: 7-16

Castle Hill School
Lapwing Lane
Brinnington

7

Stockport
SK5 8LF
☎ 0161 494 6439
🖷 0161 406 6592
Head: Mr M E Marra
No. of pupils: 155
Age range: 11-16
Funding: LEA
Type of School: Day
Special Needs: Moderate
Learning Difficulties

Cavendish School
Lincoln Close
Runcorn
WA7 4YX
☎ 01928 561 706
🖷 01928 566 088
Head: Mrs B E Fowler
No. of pupils: 66
Age range: 2-19
Funding: LEA
Type of School: Day
Special Needs: Profound &
Multiple Learning
Difficulties

Chaigeley School
Lymm Road
Thelwall
Warrington
WA4 2TE
☎ 01925 752 357
🖷 01925 757 983
email: asg@
chaig.u-net.comm
web: www.u-net.comm/
chaig
Head: Dr Keith Gutteridge
No. of pupils: 75
Age range: 8-16
Funding: Non-maintained
Type of School: Day
Special Needs: Emotional
& behavioural difficulties

Chesnut Lodge School
Green Lane
Ditton
Widnes
WA8 7HF
☎ 0151 424 0679
🖷 0151 495 2141
email: head@chesnutlodge.
halton.sch.uk
Head: Mrs S Lancaster
No. of pupils: 80
Age range: 2-16
Funding: LEA
Type of School: Day
Special Needs: Physically
Handicapped

Cloughwood School
Stones Manor Lane
Hartford
Northwich
CW8 1NU
☎ 01606 76671
🖷 01606 783 486
Head: Mr D H Smith
No. of pupils: 68
Age range: 8-16
Funding: LEA
Type of School: Residential
Special Needs: Emotional
& behavioural difficulties

**Countess of Chester
Hospital Unit**
Children's Medical Ward
30 Liverpool Road
Chester
CH2 1BQ
☎ 01244 365 095
Age range: 5-16

Cromwell High School
Yewtree Lane
Dukinfield
Cheshire
SK16 5BJ
☎ 0161 338 9730
🖷 0161 338 9731
email: admin@
cromwell.tameside.sch.uk
Acting Head: Mrs Sarah
Cooper
No. of pupils: 70
Age range: 11-16
Funding: LEA
Type of School: Day
Special Needs: Profound &
Multiple Learning
Difficulties

**Dale Grove School
Secondary Centre**
Wilshaw Lane
Tameside
OL7 9RF
☎ 0161 330 7595
🖷 0161 330 7895
No. of pupils: 70
Age range: 5-16
Funding: LEA
Type of School: Day
Special Needs: Emotional
& Behavioural Difficulties

Dee Banks School
Dee Banks
Sandy Lane
Chester
CH3 5UX

☎ 01244 324 012
🖷 01244 346 723
No. of pupils: 75
Age range: 2-19

Delamere School
Irlam Road
Flixton
Urmston
Manchester
M41 6AP
☎ 0161 747 5893
🖷 0161 747 2960
email: delamereschool.
freeserve.co.uk
Head: Mrs Susan M
Huddart
No. of pupils: 76
Age range: 2-11
Funding: LEA
Type of School: Day
Special Needs: Severe
Learning Difficulties and
ASD

Delamere Forest School
Blakemere Lane
Norley
Frodsham
WA6 6NP
☎ 01928 788 263
🖷 01928 788 263
Head: Mrs J Vegoda
No. of pupils: 55
Age range: 6-17
Funding: Independent
Type of School: Residential
Special Needs: Wide range

Dorin Park School
Wealstone Lane
Upton-by-Chester
Chester
CH2 1HP
☎ 01244 381 951
🖷 01244 390 422
No. of pupils: 83
Age range: 2-16

Grappenhall Hall School
Church Lane
Grappenhall
Warrington
WA4 3EU
☎ 01925 263 895
🖷 01925 860 487
Head: Ms Angela Findlay
No. of pupils: 121
Age range: 5-19
Funding: LEA
Type of School:
Residential/Day

Special Needs: Complex
Emotional & behavioural
difficulties

Green Lane School
Green Lane
Padgate
Warrington
WA1 4JL
☎ 01925 480 128
🖷 01925 480 127
email: grnlane@
ccc.u-net.com
web: www.ccc.u-net.com
Head: Mr Paul King
No. of pupils: 117
Age range: 4-16
Funding: LEA
Type of School: Day
Special Needs: Autism,
Severe and Multiple
Learning Difficulties

Greenbank School
Off Greenbank Lane
Hartford
Northwich
CW8 1JW
☎ 01606 76521
🖷 01606 783 736
No. of pupils: 92
Age range: 6-19

Heaton School
St James Road
Heaton Moor
Stockport
SK4 4RE
☎ 0161 432 1931
🖷 0161 432 1931
Head: Ms Elizabeth A Seers
No. of pupils: 64
Age range: 11-19
Funding: LEA
Type of School: Day
Special Needs: Profound,
Severe & Multiple
Learning Difficulties

Hebden Green School
Woodford Lane West
Winsford
CW7 4EJ
☎ 01606 594 221
🖷 01606 861 549
email: kids@
hebden.net.com
web: www.hebden.net.com
Head: Mr Andrew Farren
No. of pupils: 120
Age range: 2-19
Funding: LEA

Type of School: Residential
Special Needs: Physical
disabilities

Hinderton School
Capenhurst Lane
Ellesmere Port
CH65 7AQ
☎ 0151 355 2177
📠 0151 3568765
email: head@hinderton.
school.cheshire.org.uk
Head: Mr Liam McCallion
No. of pupils: 21
Age range: 3-7
Funding: LEA
Type of School: Day
Special Needs: Autism

Leighton Hospital School
c/o Ward 16
Leighton Hospital
Crewe
CW1 4QJ
☎ 01270 580 444
📠 01270 580 444

Lisburne School
Half Moon Lane
Offerton
Stockport
SK2 5LB
☎ 0161 483 5045
📠 0161 456 4220
email: headteacher@
lisburnespecialschool.
stockport.sch.uk
web: www.portables
Head: Mrs D Woods
No. of pupils: 50
Age range: 4-11
Funding: LEA
Type of School: Day
Special Needs: Moderate
Learning Difficulties

Loushers Lane School
Loushers Lane
Warrington
WA4 2RF
☎ 01925 632 618
📠 01925 573 763
Head: Mrs C J Fleming
Age range: 2-19
Funding: LEA
Type of School: Day
Special Needs: Profound &
Multiple Learning
Difficulties

Oakdale School
Cheetham Hill Road

Dukinfield
SK16 5LD
☎ 0161 367 9299
📠 0161 367 9685
Head: Ms Irene Howard
No. of pupils: 103
Age range: 2-11
Funding: LEA
Type of School: Day
Special Needs: Profound &
Multiple Learning
Difficulties

Oaklands School
Montgomery Way
Winsford
CW7 1NU
☎ 01606 551 048
📠 01606 861 291
Head: Mr K D Boyle
No. of pupils: 110
Age range: 11-16
Funding: LEA
Type of School: Day
Special Needs: Multiple
Learning Difficulties

Overdale School
Powicke Drive
Romiley
Stockport
SK6 3DG
Age range: 2-11

Park Lane School
Park Lane
Macclesfield
SK11 8JR
☎ 01625 423 407
📠 01625 511 191
email: head@parklane.
school.cheshire.org.uk
web: www.parklane.
school.cheshire.org.uk
Head: Mr Dave Calvert
No. of pupils: 67
Age range: 2-19
Funding: LEA
Type of School: Day
Special Needs: Profound,
Severe, Complex &
Multiple Learning
Difficulties

Pictor School
30 Harboro Road
Sale
M33 5AH
☎ 0161 962 5432
📠 0161 905 2051
Head: Mrs J Spruce
No. of pupils: 65

Age range: 2-7
Funding: LEA
Type of School: Day
Special Needs: Wide range

Priory School
Urban Road
Sale
M33 1TU
No. of pupils: 42
Age range: 5-16

**Redsands Childrens
Centre**
Crewe Road
Willaston
Nantwich
CW5 6NQ

Rosebank School
Townfield Lane
Barnton
Northwich
CW8 4QP
☎ 01606 74975
📠 01606 783 564
Head: Mrs H K Johnson
No. of pupils: 50
Age range: 2-11
Funding: LEA
Type of School: Day
Special Needs: Autism
Assessment/Diagnostic

**Royal School for the Deaf
Manchester**
Stanley Road
Cheadle Hulme
SK8 6RQ
☎ 0161 610 0100
📠 0161 610 0101
email: info@
rsdmanchester.org
web:
www.rsdmanchester.org
Head: Mrs H Ward
No. of pupils: 70
Age range: 5-21
Funding: NMSS
Type of School: Residential
& Day
Special Needs:
Deaf/Complex Needs/
Severe communication
difficulties & SLD

Samuel Laycock School
Mereside
Stalybridge
SK15 1JF
☎ 0161 303 1321
📠 0161 338 4638

email: 357.7006@
connect.bt.com
web: www.connect.bt.com
Head: Mr Stan Andrew
No. of pupils: 129
Age range: 11-16
Funding: LEA
Type of School: Day
Special Needs: Moderate
Learning Difficulties

Springfield School
Crewe Green Road
Crewe
CW1 5HS
☎ 01270 582 446
📠 01270 258 281
email: head@
springfield.cheshire.sch.uk
web: www.springfieldce.
cheshire.sch.uk
Head: Mr Mark Swaine
No. of pupils: 106
Age range: 3-19
Funding: LEA
Type of School: Day
Special Needs: Severe &
Complex Learning Needs

St Andrew's Special Unit
Overleigh Road
Handbridge
Chester
CH4 7HL
☎ 01244 683 215
📠 01244 682 280
Age range: 5-16

St John Vianney RC School
Didsbury Road
Heaton Mersey
Stockport
SK4 3JH
Head: Mr M J Lochery
Age range: 5-16

St John Vianney School
Didsbury Road
Heaton Mersey
Stockport
SK4 2AA
☎ 0161 432 0510
📠 0161 442 2095
Head: Mr Michael
O'Donoghue
No. of pupils: 72
Age range: 4-11
Funding: Non-maintained
Type of School: Day
Special Needs: Moderate
Learning Difficulties

St John's Wood School
Longridge
Knutsford
WA16 8PA
☎ 01565 634 578
🖷 01565 750 187
Head: Mr A P Evans
No. of pupils: 35
Age range: 11-16
Funding: LEA
Type of School: Day
Special Needs: Emotional
& behavioural difficulties

The David Lewis School
Mill Lane
Warford
Alderley Edge
SK9 7UD
☎ 01565 640066
🖷 01565 640166
email: school@
davidlewis.org.uk
web: www.davidlewis.org.uk
Head of Education: D L
Good
No. of pupils: 64
Age range: 7-19
Funding: Non-maintained
Type of School:
Residential/Day
Special Needs: Profound &
Multiple Learning
Difficulties

The Harrison Centre
Boulting Avenue
Dallam
Warrington
WA5 5HG
☎ 01925 444 275
🖷 01925 444 267

The Russett School
Cheshire M S I Unit
Middlehurst Avenue
Weaverham
Northwich
CW8 3BW
☎ 01606 853 005
🖷 01606 854 669
Head: Mrs H M Watts
No. of pupils: 92
Age range: 4-16
Funding: LEA
Type of School: Day
Special Needs: Multi-
sensory impairments

Thornfield School
Mauldeth Road
Heaton Mersey

Stockport
SK4 3NB
No. of pupils: 61
Age range: 7-16

Wargrave House School
449 Wargrave Road
Newton-le-Willows
WA12 8RS
☎ 01925 224 899
🖷 01925 291 368
email: wargravehouse@
wargravehouse.com
Principal: Mrs P M
Maddock
No. of pupils: 68
Age range: 5-19
Funding: Independent
Type of School:
Day/Weekly Residential
Special Needs: ASD

Valley School
Whitehaven Road
Bramhall
Stockport
SK7 1EN
☎ 0161 439 7343
🖷 0161 439 0664
Head: Catherine Goodlet
No. of pupils: 65
Age range: 2-11
Funding: LEA
Type of School: Day
Special Needs: Profound &
Multiple Learning
Difficulties and Autism

Warrington Hospital Unit
Ward B10 School Room
Lovely Lane
Warrington
WA5 1QG
☎ 01925 662 057
🖷 01925 662 057
Head: Mrs H Aylin
Age range: 4-16
Funding: LEA
Type of School: Hospital
Special Needs: Medical

**Young People's Education
Unit**
Victoria Road
Macclesfield
SK10 3JF
Age range: 12-16

City of
Nottingham

Rosehill School
St Matthias' Road

Nottingham
NG3 2FE
☎ 0115 9155815
🖷 0115 9155816
email: headteacher@
rosehill.nottingham.sch.uk
web: www.rosehill.
nottingham.sch.uk
Head: Mr J K Pearson
No. of pupils: 70
Age range: 4-19
Funding: LEA
Type of School: Day
Special Needs: Autism

City of York
Council

**The Field School
(Limetrees Unit)**
31 Shipton Road
York
YO30 5RF
☎ 01904 652 908
Age range: 10-18

Cleveland

Abbey Hill School
Ketton Road
Hardwick
Stockton-on-Tees
TS19 8BU
☎ 01642 677 113
🖷 01642 679 198
email: mike.vening@
abbeyhill.stockton.sch.uk
web: www.abbeyhill.
stockton.sch.uk
Head: Mr Mike Vening
No. of pupils: 210
Age range: 11-19
Funding: LEA
Type of School: Day
Special Needs: Wide range

Ash Trees School
Bowes Road
Billingham
TS23 2BV
☎ 01642 563 712
🖷 01642 563 712
Head: Mr Iain O Bowran
Age range: 2-11
Funding: LEA
Type of School: Primary
Special Needs
Special Needs: Autism and
Emotional & Behavioural
Difficulties

Beverley School
Beverley Road

Saltersgill
Middlesbrough
TS4 3LQ
☎ 01642 277444
🖷 01642 277453
email: beverley.middlesbor.
se@ campus.bt.com
web: www.campus.bt.com
Head: Mrs Elaine McBean
No. of pupils: 95
Age range: 3-19
Funding: LEA
Type of School: Day
Special Needs: Hearing
Impaired

Bishopsmill School
Mill Lane
Norton
Stockton-on-Tees
TS20 1LG
☎ 01642 873 200
🖷 01642 873 202
No. of pupils: 64
Age range: 6-16

**Burn Valley Pupil Referral
Unit**
Elwick Road
Hartlepool
TS26 9NP
☎ 01429 265 637
🖷 01429 261 356
Head: Mr George Harris
No. of pupils: 24
Age range: 11-16
Funding: LEA
Type of School: Day
Special Needs: Emotional
& behavioural difficulties

Carisbrooke School
College Road
Middlesbrough
TS3 9JB
☎ 01642 240 595
🖷 01642 250 263

Catcote School
Catcote Road
Hartlepool
TS25 4EZ
☎ 01429 264 036
🖷 01429 234 452
Head: Mr Nigel Carden
No. of pupils: 120
Age range: 11-19
Funding: LEA
Type of School: Day
Special Needs: Profound &
Multiple Learning
Difficulties

Holmwood School
Saltersgill Avenue
Middlesbrough
TS4 3JS
☎ 01642 819 152
No. of pupils: 100
Age range: 6-11

Hospital & Home Tuition Service (Stockton)
Paediatric Unit
Ward 15
University Hospital of
North Tees
Stockton-on-Tees
TS19 8PE
☎ 01642 617617 Ext 4544
Coordinator: Mrs J A Newsome
Age range: 5-16
Funding: LEA
Type of School: Day
Special Needs: Wide range

Hospital Teaching
St Luke's Hospital
Marton Road
Marton
Middlesbrough
TS4 3AF
☎ 01642 850 850

Kirkleatham Hall School
Kirkleatham Village
Redcar
TS10 4QR
☎ 01642 483 009
🖷 01642 480 054
Head: Ms Gill Naylor
No. of pupils: 130
Age range: 3-19
Funding: LEA
Type of School: Day
Special Needs: Profound & Multiple Learning Difficulties

Priory Woods School
Tothill Avenue
Middlesbrough
TS3 0RH
☎ 01642 321 212
🖷 01642 326 800
Head: Mrs Bernadette Knill
No. of pupils: 132
Age range: 4-19
Funding: LEA
Type of School: Day
Special Needs: Profound & Multiple Learning Difficulties

Saltergill School
Worsall Road
Kirklevington
Yarm
TS15 9QD
☎ 01642 782 081
🖷 01642 783606
Head: Mr Andrew Riley
No. of pupils: 64
Age range: 6-16
Funding: LEA
Type of School: Residential
Special Needs: Emotional & behavioural difficulties

Springwell School (Primary)
Wiltshire Way
Hartlepool
TS26 0TB
☎ 01429 260 493
No. of pupils: 70
Age range: 5-11

Sunningdale School
Saltersgill Avenue
Middlesbrough
TS4 3PT
☎ 01642 317 744
No. of pupils: 68
Age range: 7-16

Thornhill School
Elwick Road
Hartlepool
TS26 0LQ
☎ 01429 276 906
🖷 01429 864 809
Head: Mr R T Watson
No. of pupils: 70
Age range: 2-19
Funding: LEA
Type of School: Day
Special Needs: Moderate Learning Difficulties

Tollesby School
Saltersgill Avenue
Middlesbrough
TS4 3JS
☎ 01642 815 965
🖷 01642 823 628
Head: Mr John Whittingham
No. of pupils: 127
Age range: 11-16
Funding: LEA
Type of School: Day
Special Needs: Moderate Learning Difficulties

Westlands School
Eltham Crescent

Thornaby
Stockton-on-Tees
TS17 9RA
☎ 01642 883 030
🖷 01642 883 070
email: westlands@
stockton.gov.uk
Head: Mr J E Jefferson
No. of pupils: 116
Age range: 5-16
Funding: LEA
Type of School: Boarding
Special Needs: Moderate Learning Difficulties/autism/EBD

Co Durham

Beaumont Hill Primary School & Technology College
Glebe Road
Darlington
DL1 3EB
☎ 01325 254 000
🖷 01325 254 222
Head: Dame Dela Smith
No. of pupils: 225
Age range: 2-19
Funding: LEA
Type of School: Day
Special Needs: Wide range

Beaumont Hill School
Glebe Road
Darlington
DL1 3EB
☎ 01325 254000
🖷 01325 254222
No. of pupils: 220
Age range: 3-19
Type of School: Day
Special Needs: Multiple, Severe and Profound Learning Difficulties, Autism and Emotional & behavioural difficulties

Durham Trinity School
(Kirkham Premises)
Aykley Heads
Durham
DH1 5TS
☎ 0191 384 7658
No. of pupils: 170
Age range: 2-19
Funding: LEA
Type of School: Day
Special Needs: Moderate Learning Difficulties and Profound & Multiple Learning Difficulties

Easington Glen Hill School
Crawlaw Road
Easington Colliery
Peterlee
SR8 3BQ
No. of pupils: 45
Age range: 2-19

Elemore Hall School
Littletown
Sherburn
Durham
DH6 1QD
☎ 0191 372 0275
No. of pupils: 63
Age range: 11-16

Hare Law School
Catchpole
Annfield Plain
Stanley
DH9 8DT
☎ 01207 234 547
No. of pupils: 90
Age range: 5-16

Horden Dene View School
Cotsford Park
Horden
Peterlee
SR8 4SZ
No. of pupils: 69
Age range: 4-16

Murphy Crescent School
Bishop Barrington
Campus
Woodhouse Lane
Bishop Auckland
DL14 6LA
☎ 01388 451 199
🖷 01388 451 594
email: murphy.crescent@
durhamlea.org.uk
web: www.rmplc.co.uk
Head: Mrs M Wilson
No. of pupils: 27
Age range: 2-19
Funding: LEA
Type of School: Day
Special Needs: Profound & Multiple Learning Difficulties

Rosebank School
Rutherford Terrace
Broom Road
Ferryhill
DL17 8AN
☎ 01740 651 555
🖷 01740 655590

7

Head: Mrs S Stubbs
No. of pupils: 35
Age range: 3-19
Funding: Independent
Type of School: Day
Special Needs: Moderate
Learning Difficulties and
Profound & Multiple
Learning Difficulties

Trouts Lane School
Hartside
Durham
DH1 5RH
Age range: 2-19

Villa Real School
Villa Real Road
Consett
DH8 6BH
☎ 01207 503 651
🖩 01207 500 755
email: villareal@
derwentside.org.uk
web:
www.derwentside.org.uk
Head: Mrs Fiona Wood
No. of pupils: 81
Age range: 2-19
Funding: LEA
Type of School: Day
Special Needs: Profound &
Multiple Learning
Difficulties, Severe Learning
Difficulties, Autism

Walworth School
Bluebell Way
Newton Aycliffe
Darlington
DL5 7LP
☎ 01325 300 194
No. of pupils: 93
Age range: 4-16

Warwick Road School
Bishop Auckland
DL14 6LS
☎ 01388 602 683
🖩 01388 662 840
Head: Mr G Price
No. of pupils: 93
Age range: 4-16
Funding: LEA
Type of School: Day
Special Needs: Moderate
Learning Difficulties

Whitworth House School
Whitworth Lane
Spennymoor
DL16 7QW

☎ 01388 816 061
No. of pupils: 133
Age range: 4-16

Windlestone Hall School
Rushyford
Chilton
Ferryhill
DL17 0LX
☎ 01388 720 337
No. of pupils: 100
Age range: 11-16

Cornwall

Curnow School
Drump Road
Redruth
TR15 1LU
No. of pupils: 122
Age range: 2-19

Doubletrees School
St Blazey
Par
PL24 2DS
☎ 01726 812 757
🖩 01726 812 896
email: enquiries@
doubletrees.cornwall.sch.uk
Head: Dr Mick Megee
No. of pupils: 100
Age range: 2-19
Funding: LEA
Type of School: Day
Special Needs: Profound &
Multiple Learning
Difficulties

Nancealverne School
Madron Road
Penzance
TR20 8TP
☎ 01736 365 039
🖩 01736 331 941
email: enquiries@
nancealverne.cornwall.sch.uk
Head: Mrs Fiona Cock
No. of pupils: 81
Age range: 2-19
Funding: LEA
Type of School: Day
Special Needs: Severe
Learning Difficulties

Pencalenick School
St Clement
Truro
TR1 1TE
☎ 01872 520 385
🖩 01872 520 729
email: mejakeman@
portables2.ngfl.gov.uk

web: www.portables2.
ngfl.gov.uk
Head: Mr Andy Barnett
No. of pupils: 133
Age range: 11-16
Funding: LEA
Type of School:
Residential/Day
Special Needs: Complex
Learning Difficulties

Wetherfield School
c/o Porthpean
Lanteglos
Fowey
PL23 1NQ
Age range: 6-13

Whitstone Head School
Whitstone
Holsworthy
EX22 6TJ
☎ 01288 341251
🖩 01288 341207
email: sethgent@
whitstonehead.sagehost.co.uk
School Administrator: Mr
S Gent
No. of pupils: 37
Age range: 11-16
Funding: Charitable Trust
Type of School:
Residential/Day
Special Needs: Emotional
& behavioural difficulties

Cumbria

Appletree School
Narland
Kendal
Cumbria
LA9 7QS
☎ 015395 60253
🖩 015395 61301
email: clair@
appletreeschool.co.uk
web:
www.appletreeschool.co.uk
Principal: Clair Davies
No. of pupils: 14
Age range: 7-12
Funding: Independent
Type of School: Residential
Special Needs: Emotional
& behavioural difficulties

Baliol School
Cautley Road
Sedbergh
LA10 5LQ
No. of pupils: 22
Age range: 11-16

Eden Grove School
Bolton
Appleby
CA16 6AJ
☎ 017683 61346
🖩 017683 61356
email: edengroveschool@
prioryhealthcare.com
web:
www.prioryhealthcare.com
Admissions Officer: Miss S
Mullen
No. of pupils: 78
Age range: 8-19
Funding: LEA/Social
Services/Health
Type of School: Residential
Special Needs: Emotional
& behavioural difficulties,
Multiple Learning
Difficulties, Autism and
Aspergers

Fell House Special School
Grangefell Road
Grange-over-Sands
LA11 6AS
☎ 015395 35926
🖩 015395 35926
email: fellhouse@
conectfree.co.uk
web:
www.appletreeschool.co.uk
Principal: Clair Davies
No. of pupils: 8
Age range: 7-12
Funding: Independent
Type of School: Residential
Special Needs: Emotional
& behavioural difficulties

George Hastwell School
Moor Tarn Lane
Walney Island
Barrow-in-Furness
LA14 3LW
☎ 01229 475253
🖩 01229 471418
email: admin@
ghastwell.cumbria.sch.uk
Head: Mr B Gummett
No. of pupils: 81
Age range: 2-19
Funding: LEA
Type of School: Day
Special Needs: Profound &
Multiple Learning
Difficulties

James Rennie School
Kingstown
Carlisle
CA3 0BX

☎ 01228 607 559
🖷 01228 607 563
email: adminoffice@
jamesrennie.sch.uk
Head: Mr Steven
Bowditch
No. of pupils: 145
Age range: 2-19
Funding: LEA
Type of School: Day
Special Needs: Severe
Learning Difficulties

Lowgate House School
Levens
Kendal
LA8 8NJ
☎ 015395 60124
🖷 015395 60648
email: lowgate.house@
virgin.net
No. of pupils: 16
Age range: 7-12
Funding: Independent
Type of School: Residential
Special Needs: Emotional
& Behavioural Difficulties

Mayfield School
Moresby Road
Hensingham
Whitehaven
CA28 8TU
No. of pupils: 80
Age range: 2-19

Riverside School
Whassett
Milnthorpe
LA7 7DN
☎ 01539 562 006
🖷 01539 562 667
Head: Mr G Waterhouse
No. of pupils: 72
Age range: 11-16
Funding: Independent
Type of School: Residential
Special Needs: Emotional
& behavioural difficulties

Sandgate School
Sandylands Road
Kendal
LA9 6JG
☎ 01539 773 636
🖷 01539 792 101
English coordinator: Mrs J
Wightman
No. of pupils: 49
Age range: 3-19
Funding: LEA
Type of School: Day
Special Needs: Wide range

Sandside Lodge School
Sandside Road
South Ulverston
LA12 9EF
☎ 01229 894 180
🖷 01229 894 180
email: sandsidelodge.
cumbria.sch.uk
web: www.sandsidelodge.
cumbria.sch.uk
Head: Mrs Jennifer
Billingham
No. of pupils: 62
Age range: 2-19
Funding: LEA
Type of School: Day
Special Needs: Severe
Learning Difficulties

Witherslack Hall School
Witherslack
Grange-over-Sands
LA11 6SD
☎ 01539 552 397
🖷 01539 552 419
Head: Mr F W Grist
No. of pupils: 66
Age range: 11-16
Funding: Independent
Type of School: Day
Special Needs: Emotional
& behavioural difficulties

York School
Upperby Road
Carlisle
CA2 4JE
Age range: 4-19

Derbyshire

Alderbrook School
Buxton Road
Chinley
SK12 6DR
Age range: 2-19

Ashgate Croft School
Ashgate Road
Ashgate
Chesterfield
S40 4BN
☎ 01246 275 111
🖷 01246 556 440
Head: Mr M Meaton
No. of pupils: 191
Age range: 2-19
Funding: LEA
Type of School: Day
Special Needs: Speech and
Language Difficulties,
EBD, PMLD, SLD,
MLD, Autism

Bennerley Fields School
Stratford Street
Ilkeston
DE7 8QZ
☎ 0115 932 6374
🖷 0115 932 6374
Head: Mrs Margaret C
Wadsley
No. of pupils: 75
Age range: 3-16
Funding: LEA
Type of School: Day
Special Needs: Profound &
Multiple Learning
Difficulties

Bladon House
Newton Road
Newton Solney
Burton-upon-Trent
DE15 0TA
☎ 01283 563 787
🖷 01283 510 980
email: bladonhouseschool@
honormead.btinternet.com
web: www.bladon-house-
school.co.uk
Head: Mrs Barbara Murfin
No. of pupils: 147
Age range: 5-19
Type of School:
Independent Special
Resedential School
Special Needs:
Communication
Disorders; Multiple &
Severe Learning
Difficulties; Autism

Brookside School
Breadsall
Derby
DE7 6AF
Age range: 11-16

Eastwood Grange School
Milken Lane
Ashover
Chesterfield
S41 0BA
☎ 01246 590255
🖷 01246 590 215
Head: Mr S R Salt
No. of pupils: 33
Age range: 11-16
Funding: LEA/SSD
Type of School: Residential
Special Needs: Emotional
& Behavioural Difficulties

**Holbrook Centre for
Autism**
Portway

Holbrook
Derby
DE56 0TE
☎ 01332 880 208
🖷 01332 781 916
email: dheald@
holbrookautism.
derbyshire.sch.uk
Head of centre: Mr David
Heald
No. of pupils: 31
Age range: 0-16
Funding: LEA
Type of School: Day/
Residential
Special Needs: Autism

Holly House School
Church Street North
Old Whittington
Chesterfield
S41 9QR
☎ 01246 450 530
🖷 01246 456 407
Head: Mr P V Briggs
No. of pupils: 40
Age range: 7-19
Funding: LEA
Type of School: Day
Special Needs: Moderate
Learning Difficulties

Honormead Ltd
Alderwasley Hall
Whatstandwell
Wirksworth
Derby
DE4 5SF

Ivy House School
249 Osmaston Road
Derby
DE23 8LG
☎ 01332 344 694
🖷 01332 344 658
email: admin@
ivyhouse.derby.sch.uk
Head: Mrs P A Sillitoe
No. of pupils: 72
Age range: 2-19
Funding: LEA
Type of School: Day
Special Needs: Profound &
Multiple Learning
Difficulties

John Duncan School
Corbar Road
Buxton
SK17 6RL
No. of pupils: 46
Age range: 7-17

7

North Lees Pupil Referral Centre
63a Duffield Road
Derby
DE22 1AA
☎ 01332 292 912

Parkwood School
Alfreton Park
Alfreton
DE55 7AL
☎ 01773 832 019
🖷 01773 833 227
email: info@
parkwood.derbys.sch.uk
web: www.yell.co.uk/sites/
parkwood-school/
Head: Mrs V Annis
No. of pupils: 44
Age range: 2-19
Funding: LEA
Type of School: Day
Special Needs: Profound &
Multiple Learning
Difficulties

Peak School
Buxton Road
Chinley
High Peak
SK23 6ES
☎ 01663 750 324
🖷 01663 751 359
Head: Mrs L C Scowcroft
No. of pupils: 42
Age range: 2-19
Funding: LEA
Type of School:
Residential
Special Needs: Severe
Learning Difficulties

Pegasus School
Caldwell Hall
Main Street
Derbyshire
DE12 6RS
☎ 01283 761 352
🖷 01283 761312
email: pegasus.school@
honormead.btinternet.com
Head: Mr Hugh Rodger
No. of pupils: 23
Age range: 8-19
Funding: Independent
Type of School:
Residential
Special Needs: Severe &
Complex Communication
and Learning Difficulties
with Challenging
Behaviour

**Royal School for the Deaf
Derby**
Ashbourne Road
Derby
DE22 3BH
☎ 01332 362512
Textphone 01332 362512
🖷 01332 299708
email: admin.rsdd@
virgin.net
web: www.rsd-derby.org
Head: Mr Timothy
Silvester
No. of pupils: 94
Age range: 3-16
Funding: Non-maintained
Type of School: Residential
Special Needs: Hearing
Impaired

St Andrews School
St Andrew's View
Breadsall Hilltop
Derby
DE21 4EW
☎ 01332 832 746
🖷 01332 830115
email: admin@
standrews.derby.sch.uk
Head: Mr M J Dawes
No. of pupils: 114
Age range: 11-19
Funding: LEA
Type of School:
Residential/Day
Special Needs: Severe
Learning Difficulties

St Clares School
Rough Heanor Road
Mickleover
Derby
DE35 5AZ
☎ 01332 511 757
Head: Mrs M Carmel
McKenna
No. of pupils: 108
Age range: 11-16
Funding: LEA
Type of School: Day
Special Needs: Sensory/
Communication
Difficulties

St Giles School
Hampshire Road
Derby
DE21 6BT
☎ 01332 343 039
🖷 01332 207 321
email: admin@
stgiles.derby.sch.uk

Head: Mr P J Walsh
No. of pupils: 80
Age range: 5-11
Funding: LEA
Type of School: Day
Special Needs: Moderate
Learning Difficulties,
Autism and Severe
Learning Difficulties

St Martin's School
Wisgreaves Road
Alvaston
Derby
DE24 8RQ
No. of pupils: 92
Age range: 11-16

Stanton Vale School
Lower Stanton Road
Ilkeston
DE7 4LR
☎ 0115 932 4783
🖷 0115 944 4053
Head: Mr M R Emly
No. of pupils: 65
Age range: 2-19
Funding: LEA
Type of School: Day
Special Needs: Multi-
sensory impairments

Stretton House
High Stairs Lane
Stretton
Derby
DE5 6FD
Age range: 7-16

Stubbin Wood School
Burlington Avenue
Langwith Junction
Mansfield
NG20 9AD
☎ 01623 742795
🖷 01623 742122
Head: Mr J M Youdan
No. of pupils: 160
Age range: 2-16
Funding: LEA
Type of School: Day
Special Needs: Multiple &
Severe Learning
Difficulties

Talbot House School
Talbot Road
Glossop
SK13 9DP
Age range: 7-16

Taxal Lodge School
Linglongs Road

Whaley Bridge
Derbyshire
SK12 7DS
No. of pupils: 30
Age range: 11-16

The Devles School
Hayes Lane
Swanwick
Derby
DE55 1AT
Age range: 5-16

Devon

Barley Lane School
Barley Lane
St Thomas
Exeter
EX4 1TA
No. of pupils: 48
Age range: 11-16
Funding: LEA
Type of School: Residential
Special Needs: Emotional
& behavioural difficulties

Bidwell Brook School
Shinners Bridge
Dartington
Totnes
TQ9 6JU
☎ 01803 864120
🖷 01803 860025
Head: Mrs S M Love
No. of pupils: 80
Age range: 3-16
Funding: LEA
Type of School: Day
Special Needs: Severe &
Profound and Multiple
Learning Difficulties

Chelfham Mill School
Chelfham
Barnstaple
EX32 7LA
☎ 01271 850448
🖷 01271 850235
email: Kchelfham@aol.com
web:
www.chelfhammillschool.com
Head: Mrs Katy Roberts
No. of pupils: 56
Age range: 7-13
Funding: Independent
Type of School: Residential
& Day
Special Needs: Emotional
& behavioural difficulties,
Aspergers and Gilles La
Tourette

Chelfham Senior School
Bere Alston
Yelverton
PL20 7EX
No. of pupils: 36
Age range: 11-17

Combe Pafford School
Steps Lane
Watcombe
Torquay
TQ2 8NL
No. of pupils: 155
Age range: 5-16
Funding: LEA
Type of School: Day
Special Needs: Moderate
Learning Difficulties

Courtlands School
Widey Lane
Crownhill
Plymouth
PL6 5JS
☎ 01752 776 848
🖷 01752 769 102
email: courtlands.school@
plymouth.gov.uk
web: www.courtlands.
school.plymouth.gov.uk
Head: Mr G H J
Dunkerley
No. of pupils: 93
Age range: 5-11
Funding: LEA
Type of School: Day
Special Needs: Moderate
Learning Difficulties

**Dame Hannah Rogers
School**
Woodland Road
Ivybridge
PL21 9HQ
☎ 01752 892 461
🖷 01752 898101
email: email@
damehannah.com
Head: Mr W R Evans
No. of pupils: 52
Age range: 8-19
Funding: Non-maintained
Type of School: Residential
& Day
Special Needs: Physical
Difficulties & Complex
Needs

Downham School
Horn Lane
Plymstock
Plymouth

PL9 9BR
☎ 01752 403 214
email: 7063@downham.
school.plymouth.gov.uk
web: www.downham.
school.plymouth.gov.uk
Head: Mr M E Maleham
No. of pupils: 84
Age range: 5-16
Funding: LEA
Special Needs: Severe
Learning Difficulties

Ellen Tinkham School
Hollow Lane
Exeter
EX1 3RW
☎ 01392 467 168
🖷 01392 464 011
Head: Dr Mick Megee
No. of pupils: 74
Age range: 4-19
Funding: LEA
Type of School: Day
Special Needs: Profound &
Multiple Learning
Difficulties

Hill Crest School
St John's Road
Exmouth
EX8 4ED
No. of pupils: 31
Age range: 11-16

**Hospital Education
Centre**
Wonford House Site
Dryden Road
Exeter
EX2 5AF
☎ 01392 403 472
🖷 01392 403 472
Head: Ms S L Morrison
No. of pupils: 69
Age range: 3-16
Funding: LEA
Type of School: Hospital
Special Needs: Psychiatric
Difficulties

Hospital School Rooms
Bramble Ward
R D & E Hospital
Barrack Road
Exeter
EX2 5DW
☎ 01392 402675
🖷 01392 402675
email: rdehossc@
devon.gov.uk

Age range: 4-16
Special Needs: Part of
Hospital – Education
Centre

Longcause School
St Maurice
Plympton
Plymouth
PL7 3JB
☎ 01752 336 881
🖷 01752 341 151
No. of pupils: 90
Age range: 5-17

Marland School
Peters Marland
Torrington
EX38 8QQ
☎ 01805 601 324
🖷 01805 601 298
email: admin@
marland.devon.sch.uk
Principal: Mr A J M Bates
No. of pupils: 38
Age range: 11-16
Funding: LEA
Type of School: Boarding
Special Needs: Emotional
& behavioural difficulties

Mayfield School
Moor Lane
Watcombe
Torquay
Devon
TQ2 8NU
☎ 01803 328375
email: admin@mayfield-
special.tarbay.sch.uk
Head: Mrs J M Palmer
No. of pupils: 94
Age range: 2-19
Funding: LEA
Type of School: Day
Special Needs: Profound &
Multiple Learning
Difficulties

Mill Water School
Littletown
Honiton
EX14 8ER
No. of pupils: 78
Age range: 5-16

Mount Tamar School
Row Lane
Higher Street
Budeaux
Plymouth
PL5 2EF

☎ 01752 365 128
🖷 01752 351 227
email: 7067@
mount-tamar.school.
plymouth.gov.uk
web: www.mount-tamar.
school.plymouth.gov.uk
Head: Mr Ian Weston
No. of pupils: 85
Age range: 5-16
Funding: LEA
Type of School: Day
Special Needs: Emotional
& behavioural difficulties

Oaklands Park School
John Nash Drive
Dawlish
EX7 9SF
☎ 01626 862 363
🖷 01626 888 566
Head: Mr Robert Pugh
No. of pupils: 52
Age range: 3-19
Funding: LEA
Type of School: Residential
Special Needs: Wide range

Pathfield Special School
Abbey Road
Barnstaple
EX31 1JU
☎ 01271 342 423
🖷 01271 232 252
email: admin@
pathfield.devon.sch.uk
web: www.911-7021.
devon-cc.gov.uk
Head: Sue Williams
No. of pupils: 110
Age range: 3-19
Funding: LEA
Type of School: Day
Special Needs: Profound
and Multiple Learning
Difficulties, SLD, ASD

Plymouth Hospital School
Level 12
Derriford Hospital
Derriford
Plymouth
PL6 8DH
☎ 01752 792 476
🖷 01752 792 476
email: hospital.school@
plymouth.gov.uk
web: www.hospital-school.
school.plymouth.gov.uk
Head: Mrs Ruth Bill
No. of pupils: 50
Age range: 5-16
Funding: LEA

7

Type of School: Day
Special Needs: Medical

Ratcliffe School
John Nash School
Oaklands Park
Dawlish
EX7 9RZ
☎ 01626 862939
🖷 01626 888101
email: admin@dawlish-
ratcliffe.devon.sch.uk
web: www.dawlish-
ratcliffe.devon.sch.uk
Principal: C Hackett
No. of pupils: 65
Age range: 8-16
Funding: LEA
Type of School: Residential
Special Needs: Emotional
& behavioural difficulties

**Royal West of England
Residential School for the
Deaf**
50 Topsham Road
Exeter
EX2 4NF
☎ 01392 272692
Textphone 01392 272692
🖷 01392 431146
email: info@
rsd-exeter.ac.uk
web: www.rsd-exeter.ac.uk
Principal: Mr J F Shaw
No. of pupils: 100
Age range: 3-19
Funding: Non-maintained
Type of School: Day/
Residential
Special Needs: Deaf

Southbrook School
Bishop Westell Road
Exeter
EX2 6JB
☎ 01392 258 373
🖷 01392 494 036
email: 7005@911-7005-
devon-cc.gov.uk
web: www.911-7005-
devon-cc.gov.uk
Head: Mrs H Green
No. of pupils: 112
Age range: 7-16
Funding: LEA
Type of School: Day
Special Needs: Complex &
General Learning
Difficulties

St Luke's School
Exeter Road

Teignmouth
TQ14 9JG

The Gables
Willand
Cullompton
EX15
Age range: 5-16

**The Lampard-Vachell
School**
St Johns Lane
Barnstaple
EX32 9DD
No. of pupils: 65
Age range: 5-16
Special Needs: Multiple
Learning Difficulties

Torhill Education Unit
Torhill Day Centre
Torhill Road
Torquay
TQ2 5RN
☎ 01803 298 254
🖷 01803 298 254
Head: Ms Jackie Sharpe
No. of pupils: 15
Age range: 14-16
Funding: LEA
Type of School: Pupil
Referral Unit
Special Needs: Emotional
& behavioural difficulties

Trengweath School
Hartley Road
Plymouth
PL3 5LP
No. of pupils: 20
Age range: 2-12

Vranch House School
Pinhoe Road
Exeter
EX4 8AD
☎ 01392 468 333
🖷 01392 463 818
email: education@
vranchhouse.org
Head: Ms M R C Boon
No. of pupils: 25
Age range: 2-12
Funding: Independent
Type of School: Day
Special Needs: Cerebral
Palsy

**West of England School
and College**
Countess Wear
Exeter
EX2 6HA

☎ 01392 454 200
🖷 01392 428 048
email: info@
westengland.devon.sch.uk
Head: Mr Paul Holland
No. of pupils: 200
Age range: 5-19
Funding: Registered
charity
Type of School: Day
Special Needs: Visually
Impaired

Woodlands School
Bodmin Road
Whitleigh
Plymouth
PL5 4DZ
☎ 01752 300101
🖷 01752 300102
email: woodlands.school@
plymouth.gov.uk
Head: Miss M Vatcher
No. of pupils: 83
Age range: 3-17
Funding: LEA
Type of School: Day
Special Needs: Physical
disabilities

Dorset

**Beaucroft Grant
Maintained School**
Wimborne Road
Colehill
Wimborne
BH23 8EZ
☎ 01202 886 083
🖷 01202 848 459
email: office@
beaucroft.dorset.sch.uk
web: www.beaucroft.ik.org
Head: Mr Andrew Mears
No. of pupils: 151
Age range: 4-17
Funding: LEA
Type of School: Day
Special Needs: Autism and
Multiple Learning
Difficulties

Castle Hill House
Bournemouth Road
Parkstone
Poole
BH14
Age range: 3-16

Langside School
Langside Avenue
Parkstone
Poole

BH12 5BN
☎ 01202 518 635
🖷 01202 531 513
email: jskinner@langside-
school.fsnet.co.uk
Head: Mr J Ashby
No. of pupils: 40
Age range: 3-19
Funding: Independent
Type of School: Day
Special Needs: Profound &
Multiple Learning
Difficulties

Linwood School
Alma Road
Bournemouth
BH9 1AJ
☎ 01202 525 107
🖷 01202 525 107
Head: Mr S Brown
No. of pupils: 175
Age range: 3-19
Funding: LEA
Type of School: Day
Special Needs: Moderate
Learning Difficulties and
Profound & Multiple
Learning Difficulties

Longspee School
Learoyd Road
Canford Heath
Poole
BH17 8PJ
☎ 01202 380 266
🖷 01202 380 270
Head: Mr E Bell
No. of pupils: 50
Age range: 4-11
Funding: LEA
Type of School: Day
Special Needs: Emotional
& behavioural difficulties

Montacute School
3 Canford Heath Road
Poole
BH17 9NG
☎ 01202 693 239
🖷 01202 657 363
email: montacute@
btinternet.com
Head: Mrs Marion
Sammons
No. of pupils: 75
Age range: 3-18
Funding: LEA
Type of School: Day
Special Needs: Profound &
Multiple Learning
Difficulties

Mountjoy School
Flood Lane
Bridport
DT6 3QG
☎ 01308 422 250
🖷 01308 458 664
Head: Mrs S G Hosking
No. of pupils: 44
Age range: 2-19
Funding: LEA
Type of School: Day
Special Needs: Profound &
Multiple Learning
Difficulties

Penwithen School
Winterborne Monkton
Dorchester
DT2 9PS
☎ 01305 266842
🖷 01305 262083
email: office@
penwithin.dorset.sch.uk
Head: Mrs S R Downes
No. of pupils: 50
Age range: 11-16
Type of School: Day &
Residential
Special Needs: Emotional
& Behavioural Difficulties

**Philip Green Memorial
School**
Boveridge Hosue
Cranborne
Wimborne
BH21 5RU
☎ 01725 517218
🖷 01725 517965
email: pgmschool@
hotmain.com
Head: Mrs L Walter
No. of pupils: 38
Age range: 11-19
Funding: Charity
Type of School: Residential
Special Needs: ASP, Speech
& language and Severe and
Multiple learning
Difficulties

Portfield School
4 Magdalen Lane
Christchurch
BH23 1PH
☎ 01202 486626
🖷 01202 483677
email: twas.portfield@
talk21.com
web: www.t-was.org.uk
No. of pupils: 42
Age range: 2-19

Funding: Charity
Type of School: Day and
Residential
Special Needs: Autism

Purbeck View School
Northbrook Road
Swanage
BH19 1PR
☎ 01929 422760
Head: Mrs Sue Goulding
No. of pupils: 44
Age range: 11-19
Type of School: Termly
boarding
Special Needs: Autism

Slades Farm School
Ensbury Avenue
Ensbury Park
Bournemouth
BH10 4HG
☎ 01202 518 189
No. of pupils: 57
Age range: 11-16

The Sheiling School
Horton Road
Ashley
Ringwood
BH24 2EB
☎ 01425 477488
🖷 01425 479536
email: enquiries@
sheilingschool.co.uk
web:
www.sheilingschool.co.uk
SENCO: Mrs Heide
Hoffman
No. of pupils: 48
Age range: 7-19
Funding: LEA/social
services/health
Type of School: Residential
Special Needs: Downs
syndrome/autistic
spectrum/fragile x/
Multiple & Severe
Learning difficulties/
williams syndrome/
microcapholy etc.

Victoria Education Centre
12 Lindsay Road
Branksome Park
Poole
BH13 6AS
☎ 01202 763 697
🖷 01202 768 078
email: principal@
victoriaschool.demon.co.uk
web: www.victoriaschool.
demon.co.uk

Head: Mr Paul Warner
No. of pupils: 115
Age range: 2-18
Funding: Non-maintained
Type of School: Day
Special Needs: Physical
disabilities & Specific
Learning Difficulties

Westfield School
Littlemoor Road
Preston
Weymouth
DT3 6AA
☎ 01305 833 518
🖷 01305 835 414
Head: Mr Phil Silvester
No. of pupils: 153
Age range: 3-16
Funding: Independent
Type of School: Day
Special Needs: Autism and
Moderate Learning
Difficulties

Winchelsea School
Guernsey Road
Parkstone
Poole
BH12 4LL
No. of pupils: 150
Age range: 3-16

Woodsford House School
Woodsford
Dorchester
DT2 8AT
☎ 01305 848 202
🖷 01305 848 891
No. of pupils: 6
Age range: 6-13
Funding: Independent
Type of School: Day
Special Needs: Dyslexia/
Dyspraxia

Wyvern School
307a Chickerell Road
Weymouth
DT4 0QU
☎ 01305 783 660
🖷 01305 770 965
email: bectal@04608
web: www.04608
Head: Ms Helen
Mackenzie
No. of pupils: 60
Age range: 2-19
Funding: LEA
Type of School: Day
Special Needs: Moderate
Learning Difficulties

Yewstock School
Honeymead Lane
Sturminster Newton
DT10 1EW
☎ 01258 472 796
🖷 01258 473 577
email: office@
yewstock.dorset.sch.uk
web:
www.yewstock.dorset.sch.uk
Head: Mr John Lineton
No. of pupils: 116
Age range: 2-19
Funding: LEA
Type of School: Day
Special Needs: Wide range

Dudley

Pens Meadow School
Ridge Hill
Brierley Hill Road
Wordsley
Stourbridge
DY8 5ST
☎ 01384 818 945
🖷 01384 818 946
email: info@pens-meadow.
dudley.gov.uk
web: www.pens.meadow.
dudley.gov.uk
Head: Mrs K Grew
No. of pupils: 70
Age range: 3-19
Funding: LEA
Type of School: Day
Special Needs: Severe
Learning Difficulties

Rosewood School
Overfield Road
Russells Hall Estate
Dudley
DY1 2NX
☎ 01384 816 800
🖷 01384 816 801
email: ejones@rosewood.
dudley.gov.uk
Acting Head: Mr C
Murphy
No. of pupils: 40
Age range: 11-16
Funding: LEA
Type of School: Day
Special Needs: Emotional,
Social & behavioural
difficulties

**The Mere Education
Centre**
Lawnswood Road
Wordsley

7

Stourbridge
DY8 5PQ
☎ 01384 818820
🖷 01384 818821
email: info@mere.
dudley.gov.uk
Centre Manager: Mrs B
Perks
Age range: 5-11
Funding: LEA
Type of School: Pupil
Referral Unit
Special Needs: Emotional,
Social & Behavioural
difficulties

East Riding of Yorkshire

Kings Mill School
Victoria Road
Driffield
YO25 6UG
☎ 01377 253 375
Head: Mr Peter Hall
No. of pupils: 57
Age range: 2-16
Funding: LEA
Type of School: Day
Special Needs: Severe
Learning Difficulties

East Sussex

Bowden House Special School
Firle Road
Seaford
BN25 2JB
No. of pupils: 47

Castledean School
Lynchet Close
Hollingdean
Brighton
BN1 7FP
☎ 01273 702 121
🖷 01273 702 112
Head: Mrs Valerie Ellis
No. of pupils: 64
Age range: 4-11
Funding: LEA
Type of School: Day
Special Needs: Moderate
Learning Difficulties

Chailey Heritage School
Haywards Heath Road
North Chailey
Lewes
BN8 4EF
☎ 01825 724 444

🖷 01825 723 773
email: chschool@
tiscali.co.uk
web: www.chs.org.uk
Head: Mr Alistair Bruce
No. of pupils: 95
Age range: 2-19
Funding: Non-maintained
Type of School: Residential
& Day
Special Needs: Wide range

Cuckmere House School
Eastbourne Road
Seaford
BN25 4BA
☎ 01323 893 319
🖷 01323 897 719
Head: Mr Frank A
Stanford
No. of pupils: 80
Age range: 9-16
Funding: LEA
Type of School: Day with
weekly boarding facility
Special Needs: Emotional,
Social & Behavioural
difficulties

Downs School
Beechy Avenue
Eastbourne
BN20 8NU
Age range: 2-9

Downs View Special School
Ash Cottage Annexe
Warren Road
Brighton
BN2 6DA
No. of pupils: 97
Age range: 3-19

Frewen College
Brickwall
Northiam
Rye
TN31 6NL
☎ 01797 252 494
🖷 01797 252 567
email: post@
frewcoll.demon.co.uk
web: www.frewcoll.
demon.co.uk
Head: Mr Simon Horsley
No. of pupils: 71
Age range: 9-17
Funding: Independent
Type of School: Day
Special Needs: Dyslexia

Glyne Gap School
Hastings Road
Bexhill
TN40 2PU
☎ 01424 217 720
🖷 01424 734962
web: www.glynegap.
e-sussex.sch.uk
Head: Mr John Hassell
No. of pupils: 98
Age range: 3-19
Funding: LEA
Type of School: Day
Special Needs: Profound &
Multiple Learning
Difficulties, SLD, ASD

Grove Park School
Church Road
Crowborough
TN6 1BN
☎ 01892 663 018
🖷 01892 653 170
Head: Ms Christine A
Moody
No. of pupils: 56
Age range: 3-19
Funding: LEA
Type of School: Day
Special Needs: Profound &
Multiple Learning
Difficulties

Hamilton Lodge School for Deaf Children
Walpole Road
Brighton
BN2 2ET
☎ 01273 682362
Textphone 01273 682362
🖷 01273 695742
email: hamiltonlodge@
ukonline.co.uk
web: www.ukonline.co.uk/
hamilton.lodge
Head: Mrs A K Duffy
No. of pupils: 86
Age range: 4-18
Funding: Independent
Type of School: Residential
Special Needs: Hearing
Impaired

Hazel Court School
Shinewater Lane
Eastbourne
BN23 8AT
☎ 01323 761061
Head: Peter Gordon
No. of pupils: 82
Age range: 2-19
Funding: LEA

Type of School: Day
Special Needs: Severe
Learning Difficulty –
Autism

Hazel Court Secondary School
Larkspur Drive
Eastbourne
BN23 8EJ
☎ 01323 465 720
No. of pupils: 141
Age range: 2-19
Funding: LEA
Type of School: Day
Special Needs: Severe
Learning Difficulties

Hillside School
Foredown Road
Portslade-by-Sea
BN41 2FU
☎ 01273 416 979
🖷 01273 417 512
email: office@hillside.
brighton-hove.sch.uk
web: www.hillside.
brighton-hove.sch.uk
Head: Mr Bob Wall
No. of pupils: 76
Age range: 3-19
Funding: LEA
Type of School: Day
Special Needs: Profound
and Multiple Learning
Difficulties, Severe
Learning Difficulties

Inglesea School
Fax Tile Barn Road
St Leonards-on-Sea
TN38 9QU
No. of pupils: 45
Age range: 7-16

Northease Manor School
Newhaven Road
Rodmell
Lewes
BN7 3EY
☎ 01273 472 915
🖷 01273 472 202
email: northease@msn.com
web: www.msn.com
Head: Mr P Stanley
No. of pupils: 86
Age range: 10-17
Funding: Independent
Type of School: Day and
weekly boarding
Special Needs: Dyslexia &
Specific Learning
Difficulties

Ovingdean Hall School
Greenways
Brighton
BN2 7BJ
☎ 01273 301929
Textphone 01273 301929
🖷 01273 305884
email: ovinhall@aol.com
Head: Mrs Pauline Hughes
No. of pupils: 150
Age range: 11-19
Funding: LEA
Type of School: Residential
(weekly)
Special Needs: Hearing
Impaired

Queensdown School
Queensdown School Road
Off Lewes Road
Brighton
BN1 7AL
No. of pupils: 47
Age range: 7-16

Saxon Mount School
Edinburgh Road
St Leonards-on-Sea
TN38 8DA
☎ 01424 426303
🖷 01424 444115
No. of pupils: 119
Age range: 11-16
Type of School: Special

St Anne's School
Rotten Row
Lewes
BN7 1LJ
☎ 01273 473 018
🖷 01273 480 435
Head: Ms Jennifer Arch
No. of pupils: 101
Age range: 4-16
Funding: LEA
Type of School: Day
Special Needs: Moderate
Learning Difficulties

St Mary's School
Horam
Heathfield
TN21 0BT
No. of pupils: 60
Age range: 11-19

St Mary's School
(Wrestwood)
Wrestwood Road
Bexhill-on-Sea
TN40 2LU
☎ 01424 730 740

🖷 01424 733 575
Head: Mr David Cassar
No. of pupils: 127
Age range: 7-19
Funding: Voluntary
Type of School:
Residential/Day
Special Needs: Moderate
Learning Difficulties,
Speech, Language and
Social Communication
disorder, Physical
difficulties & Complex
Medical Needs

The Lindfield School
(ESCC)
Lindfield Road
Hampden Park
Eastbourne
BN22 0BQ
☎ 01323 502 988
🖷 01323 500 433
email: thelindfieldschool@
hotmail.com
Head: Ms Jane Oatey
No. of pupils: 74
Age range: 10-16
Funding: LEA
Type of School: Day
Special Needs: Multiple
Learning Difficulties

The Mount Camphill
Community School
The Mount
Faircrouch Lane
Wadhurst
TN5 6PT
☎ 01892 782025
🖷 01892 782917
email: themount@
camphill.clava.net
No. of pupils: 38
Age range: 16-24
Funding: LEA, LSC, Social
Services
Type of School: Residential
College
Special Needs: Moderate
Learning Difficulties

Torfield School
Croft Road
Hastings
TN34 3JT
☎ 01424 428 228
🖷 01424 712322
email: admin@
torfieldsch.fsnet.co.uk
Head: Ms C McCarthy
No. of pupils: 102

Age range: 3-11
Funding: LEA
Type of School: Day
Special Needs: Autism,
Emotional & behavioural
difficulties, Complex
Needs, Speech &
Language Difficulties,
Severe Learning
Difficulties and Hearing
Impairment

Welands Ford School
Bodiam Manor
Bodiam
TN32 5UJ
Age range: 3-13

Essex

Oaktree School
Chase Side
Southgate
London
N14 4HN
☎ 020 8440 3100
🖷 020 8440 4891
Head: Mr J H Harrison
No. of pupils: 100
Age range: 5-17
Funding: LEA
Type of School: Day
Special Needs: Complex
needs

Brookfield House School
and Services
Alders Avenue
Woodford Green
IG8 9PY
☎ 020 8527 2464
🖷 020 8527 8328
Head: Ms Hefina Clasper
No. of pupils: 82
Age range: 3-16
Funding: LEA
Type of School: Day
Special Needs: Physical
disabilities

Cedar Hall School
Hart Road
Thundersley
Benfleet
SS7 3UQ
☎ 01268 774 723
🖷 01268 776 604
email: admin@
cedarhall.essex.sch.uk
Head: Mr Christopher Bent
No. of pupils: 117
Age range: 5-16

Funding: LEA
Type of School: Day
Special Needs: Moderate
Learning Difficulties

Corbets Tey School
Harwood Hall Lane
Corbets Tey
Upminster
RM14 2YQ
No. of pupils: 80
Age range: 4-16

Doucecroft School
163 High Street
Keluedon
Colchester
CO5 9JA
☎ 01376 570060
🖷 01376 570060
email: kc@
essexautistic.org.uk
web:
www.essexautistic.org.uk
Head: Kathy Cranmer
No. of pupils: 38
Age range: 2-19
Funding: LEA/Charity
Type of School:
Residential/Day
Special Needs: Autistic
Spectrum disorder and
Aspergers Syndrome

Dycorts School
Settle Road
Harold Hill
Romford
RM3 9YA
No. of pupils: 63
Age range: 4-16

Edwardstone House
School
Sherbourne Street
Edwardstone
Boxford
CO6 5PD
Age range: 9-13

Elmbrook School
Church Road
Basildon
SS14 2EX
☎ 01268 521 808
🖷 01268 271 872
Head: Mr S Horsted
No. of pupils: 72
Age range: 3-19
Funding: LEA
Type of School: Day
Special Needs: Wide range

7

Ethel Davis Special School
Barley Lane
Goodmayes
IG3 8XS
☎ 020 8599 1768
Head: Mr Peter
Bouldstridge
No. of pupils: 55
Age range: 3-19
Funding: LEA
Type of School: Day
Special Needs: Profound &
Multiple Learning
Difficulties

Fairview School
Fairview Road
Basildon
SS14 1PW
No. of pupils: 46
Age range: 8-16

Glenwood School
Rushbottom Lane
New Thundersley
Benfleet
SS7 4LW
☎ 01268 792 575
🖷 01268 750 907
email: admin@
glenwood.essex.sch.uk
Head: Mrs Judith Salter
No. of pupils: 82
Age range: 3-19
Funding: LEA
Type of School: Day
Special Needs: Complex
Learning Difficulties

Great Stony School
Ongar
CM5 0AD
Age range: 5-19

Hatton School
Roding Lane South
Woodford Green
IG8 8EU
☎ 0208 551 4131
🖷 0208 503 9066
email: hattonschool@
hotmail.com
SIP Coordinator: Sue
Layton
No. of pupils: 135
Age range: 4-11
Funding: LEA
Type of School: Day
Special Needs: Autism,
Specific Language
Impairment, General
Learning Difficulties

Havering Grange School
Havering Road North
Romford
RM1 4HR
Age range: 4-17

Homestead School
School Road
Langham
Colchester
CO4 5PA
☎ 01206 272303
🖷 01206 272927
No. of pupils: 50
Age range: 14-19
Special Needs: Emotional
& behavioural difficulties

Hyleford Leavers Unit
Starch House Lane
Fulwell Cross
Ilford
IG8 1PU
☎ 0208 500 9930
🖷 0208 501 4855
Head: Mrs Sue Hewitt
Age range: 16-19
Funding: LEA
Type of School: Day
Special Needs: Severe
Learning Difficulties and
Profound & Multiple
Learning Difficulties

Jacques Hall Foundation
Harwich Road
Bradfield
Manningtree
CO11 2XW
☎ 01255 870311
🖷 01255 870311
email:
admissionsjacqueshall@
prioryhealthcare.com
Admissions and
Assessment Officer: Mr
Chris Nicholson
No. of pupils: 23
Age range: 11-16
Funding: Social services/
Education & Health
Authority
Type of School: Residential
Special Needs: Emotional
& behavioural difficulties,
conduct disorder, ADHD,
PTS

Kingsdown School
Snakes Lane
Southend-on-Sea
SS2 6XT

☎ 01702 527 486
🖷 01702 526 762
Head: J F Hagyard
No. of pupils: 115
Age range: 2-19
Funding: LEA
Type of School: Day
Special Needs: Physically
and neurologically
impaired

Kingswode Hoe School
Sussex Road
Colchester
CO3 3QJ
☎ 01206 576408
🖷 01206 571477
email: admin@
kingswodehoe.essex.sch.uk
Head: Mrs Elizabeth
Drake
No. of pupils: 120
Age range: 5-16
Funding: LEA
Type of School: Day
Special Needs: Multiple
Learning Difficulties

Knightsmead School
Fortin Close
South Ockendon
RM15 5NH
☎ 01708 852956
🖷 01708 851741
email: headteacher@
knightsmead.thurrock.sch.uk
web: www.knightsmead.
thurrock.sch.uk
Head: Mr T D Miller
No. of pupils: 23
Age range: 3-19
Funding: LEA
Type of School: Day
Special Needs: Severe
Learning Difficulties

Lancaster School
Prittlewell Chase
Westcliff-on-Sea
SS0 0RT
☎ 01702 342 543
🖷 01701 352 630
email: office@
lancaster.southend.sch.uk
Head: Mrs Audrey Farrow
No. of pupils: 98
Age range: 2-19
Funding: LEA
Type of School: Day
Special Needs: Severe
Learning Difficulties

Lexden Springs School
Halstead Road
Lexden
Colchester
CO3 9AB
☎ 01206 563321
🖷 01206 570758
email: admin@
lexdensprings.essex.sch.uk
Head: Mr S H Goldsmith
No. of pupils: 62
Age range: 3-19
Funding: LEA
Type of School: Day
Special Needs: Severe
Learning Difficulties/
Profound & Multiple
Learning Difficulties

Market Field School
School Road
Elmstead Market
Colchester
CO7 7ET
☎ 01206 825 195
🖷 01206 825 234
Head: Mr Gary Smith
No. of pupils: 100
Age range: 5-16
Funding: LEA
Type of School: Day
Special Needs: Autism and
Moderate Learning
Difficulties

Moat House School
Church Road
Basildon
SS14 2NQ
No. of pupils: 51
Age range: 5-16

New Rush Hall School
Fencepiece Road
Hainault
Ilford
IG6 2LJ
No. of pupils: 40
Age range: 5-16

Oak View School
Whitehills Road
Loughton
IG10 1TS
☎ 020 8508 4293
🖷 020 8502 1864
email: admin@
oakview.essex.sch.uk
Headteacher: Mr S P
Armstrong
No. of pupils: 86
Age range: 3-19

Funding: LEA
Type of School: Day
Special Needs: Severe &
Multiple Learning
Difficulties

Peter Kirk School
Chapel Hill
Stansted Mountfitchet
Stansted
CM24 8AG
No. of pupils: 10
Age range: 4-16

Priory School
Burr Hill Chase
Southend-on-Sea
SS2 6PE
☎ 01702 347 490
No. of pupils: 46
Age range: 6-16
Funding: LEA
Type of School: Day
Special Needs: Emotional
& behavioural difficulties

Ravensbourne School
Neave Crescent
Faringdon Avenue
Harold Hill
Romford
RM3 8HN
☎ 01708 341 800
🖹 01708 371 848
Head: Mrs M Cameron
No. of pupils: 84
Age range: 2-19
Funding: LEA
Type of School: Day
Special Needs: Profound &
Multiple Learning
Difficulties

**Special Education
Resource Centre**
Hainault Road
Little Heath
Romford
RM6 5RX

St John's RC School
Turpins Lane
Woodford Bridge
Chigwell
IG8 8AX
Age range: 5-16

**St John's RC Special
School**
Turpins Lane
Woodford Bridge
IG8 0RQ

☎ 020 8504 1818
🖹 020 8559 2409
Head: Ms Marie Galvin
No. of pupils: 86
Age range: 5-19
Funding: Non-maintained
Type of School: Day
Special Needs: Speech and
Language Difficulties

St Nicholas' School
Philpott Avenue
Southend-on-Sea
SS2 4RL
☎ 01702 462 322
No. of pupils: 96
Age range: 5-16

The Castledon School
Bromfords Drive
Wickford
SS12 0PW
No. of pupils: 107
Age range: 5-16

The Commonside School
Commonside Road
Harlow
CM18 7EZ
No. of pupils: 69
Age range: 11-16

**The Edith Borthwick
School**
Fennes Road
Church Street
Bocking
Braintree
CO16 9AR
☎ 01376 326 436
🖹 01376 326 436
web: mail.edithborthwick-
spec.essex.sch.uk
Head: Mr Mike Jelly
No. of pupils: 153
Age range: 3-19
Funding: LEA
Type of School: Day
Special Needs: Wide range

**The Endeavour School
GM**
Hogarth Avenue
Brentwood
CM15 8BE
☎ 01277 217 330
🖹 01277 225 157
email: peter@
endeavour.essex.sch.uk
web:
www.endeavour.essex.sch.uk
Head: Mr P L Pryke

No. of pupils: 78
Age range: 4-16
Funding: Foundation
Special
Type of School: Day
Special Needs: Moderate
Learning Difficulties

The Green Wood School
25 Mill Chase
Halstead
CO9 2DQ
Age range: 7-17

The Hayward School
Maltease Road
Chelmsford
CM1 2PA
Head: Mr C L Reynolds
No. of pupils: 108
Age range: 4-16

The Heath School
Winstree Road
Stanway
Colchester
CO3 5QE
No. of pupils: 43
Age range: 11-16

The Leas School
Leas Road
Clacton-on-Sea
CO15 1DY
No. of pupils: 136
Age range: 3-16

The Mead School
Tendring Road
Harlow
CM18 6RN
No. of pupils: 49
Age range: 3-11

The Oxley Parker School
Mill Road
Colchester
CO4 5JF
Age range: 5-17

The Ramsden Hall School
Ramsden Heath
Billericay
CM11 1HN
No. of pupils: 44
Age range: 11-16

The St Christopher School
Mountdale Gardens
Leigh-on-Sea
SS9 4AW
☎ 01702 524 193
🖹 01702 526 761

email: thestchrisgmoff@
blueyonder.co.uk
Head: Mr Tom Wilson
No. of pupils: 110
Age range: 3-16
Funding: Foundation
Type of School: Day
Special Needs: Autism and
Complex Learning
Difficulties

Thriftwood School
Slades Lane
Galleywood
Chelmsford
CM2 8RW
☎ 01245 266 880
🖹 01245 490691
email: admin@
thriftwood.essex.co.uk
Head: Mrs Sally Davies
No. of pupils: 120
Age range: 5-16
Funding: LEA
Type of School: Day
Special Needs: Wide range

Treetops School
Dell Road
Grays
RM17 5LH
☎ 01375 372 723
🖹 01375 390 784
email: headteacher@
treetops.thurrock.sch.uk
Head: Mr Paul Smith
No. of pupils: 120
Age range: 5-16
Funding: LEA
Type of School: Day
Special Needs: Wide range

Trinity School
Heathway Site
Heathway
Dagenham
RM10 7SJ
☎ 020 8984 1449
🖹 020 8592 4312
Age range: 4-19

Tye Green School
Tendring Road
Harlow
CM18 6RN
No. of pupils: 44
Age range: 3-19

Woodcroft School
Whitakers Way
Loughton
IG10 1SQ

7

☎ 020 8508 1369
🖷 020 8502 4855
Head: Mr S W Booker
No. of pupils: 24
Age range: 2-11
Funding: Independent
Type of School: Day
Special Needs: Severe
Learning Difficulties

Woodlands School
Patching Hall Lane
Chelmsford
CM1 4BX
No. of pupils: 110
Age range: 3-19
Funding: LEA
Type of School: Day
Special Needs: Profound &
Multiple Learning
Difficulties

Gloucestershire

Amberley Ridge School
Rodborough Common
Stroud
GL5 5DB
email: mac@the-
bridge.demon.co.uk
web: www.the-bridge.
demon.co.uk
Head: Mr D MacDonald
No. of pupils: 86
Age range: 5-12
Funding: LEA
Type of School:
Day/Residential
Special Needs: Severe
Emotional & Behavioural
Difficulties

**Battledown Children's
Centre**
Harp Hill
Battledown
Cheltenham
GL52 6PZ
☎ 01242 525 472
🖷 01242 257 557
email: admin@battledown.
gloucs.sch.uk
Head: Mrs E M Rook
No. of pupils: 40
Age range: 2-7
Funding: LEA
Type of School: Day
Special Needs: Wide range

Belmont School
Warden Hill Road
Cheltenham
GL51 3AT

☎ 01242 216180
🖷 01242 227 827
email: admin@
belmont.gloucs.sch.uk
Acting Head: Mrs Helen
Dowell
No. of pupils: 60
Age range: 5-16
Funding: LEA
Type of School: Day
Special Needs: Moderate
Learning Difficulties

Bettridge School
Warden Hill Road
Cheltenham
GL52 5AT
☎ 01242 514 934
🖷 01242 514 934
Head: Mrs Mary Saunders
No. of pupils: 90
Age range: 2-16
Funding: LEA
Type of School: Day
Special Needs: Profound &
Multiple Learning
Difficulties

Bownham Park School
Rodborough Common
Stroud
GL5 5DA
☎ 01453 873 361
No. of pupils: 109
Age range: 11-16

Cam House School
Drake Lane
Dursley
GL11 5HD
☎ 01453 542 130
🖷 01453 547 067
email: admin@
camhouse.gloucs.sch.uk
web:
www.camhouseschool.ik.org
Head: Mrs B Turner
No. of pupils: 55
Age range: 10-16
Funding: LEA
Type of School: Residential
and Day
Special Needs: Emotional
& behavioural difficulties

Coln House School
Fairford
GL7 4DB
No. of pupils: 67
Age range: 9-16

**Cotswold Chine Horne
School**
Box

Stroud
GL6 9AG
☎ 01453 837550
🖷 01453 837555
email: mail@cotswold-
chine.org.uk
No. of pupils: 39
Age range: 9-16
Funding: Charitable
Educational Trust
Special Needs: EBD,
autism, MLD, epilepsy,
ADHD, etc.

Dean Hall School
Speech House Road
Coleford
GL16 7EJ
☎ 01594 822 175
🖷 01594 826 472
email: school@
deanhall.gloucs.sch.uk
web:
www.deanhallschool.ik.org
Head: Mr Neal Haddock
No. of pupils: 60
Age range: 5-16
Funding: LEA
Type of School: Day
Special Needs: Moderate
Learning Difficulties

New Barns School
Church Lane
Toddington
Cheltenham
GL54 5DH
No. of pupils: 32
Age range: 7-13

Oakdene School
Dockham Road
Cinderford
GL14 2AN
☎ 01594 822 693
🖷 01594 822 693
email: admin@
oakdene.gloucs.sch.uk
Head: Ms Eileen Oates
No. of pupils: 34
Age range: 3-16
Funding: LEA
Type of School: Day
Special Needs: Severe
Learning Difficulties

Paternoster School
Watermoor Road
Cirencester
GL7 1JS
☎ 01285 652480
🖷 01285 642490

email: admin@
paternoster.gloucs.sch.uk
Head: Mr P Barton
No. of pupils: 52
Age range: 2-19
Funding: LEA
Type of School: Day
Special Needs: Severe and
Profound & Multiple
Learning Difficulties

Sandford School
Seven Springs
Cheltenham
GL53 9NG
☎ 01242 870224
🖷 01242 870331
email: admin@
sandford.gloucs.sch.uk
Head: Mr S R Jones
No. of pupils: 90
Age range: 6-16
Funding: LEA
Type of School: Day
Special Needs: Emotional
& Behavioural Difficulties

St Rose's RC School
Stratford Lawn
Stroud
GL5 4AB
☎ 01453 763793
🖷 01453 752617
Head: Sister M Quentin
No. of pupils: 68
Age range: 2-18
Funding: LEA and charity
Type of School: Day/
Residential
Special Needs: PD,
Epilepsy, Speech and
Language

St Vincent's School
Central Cross Drive
Pittville
Cheltenham
GL50 4LA
Age range: 2-7

**The Alderman Knight
School**
Ashchurch Road
Tewkesbury
GL20 8JJ
No. of pupils: 114
Age range: 4-16

The Milestone School
Longford Lane
Gloucester

GL2 9EY
☎ 01452 522 637
No. of pupils: 109
Age range: 2-16

The Shrubberies School
Oldends Lane
Stonehouse
GL10 2DG
☎ 01453 822 155
🖩 01453 822 155
email: head@
shrubberies.gloucs.sch.uk
Head: Mr P J Morgan
No. of pupils: 91
Age range: 2-19
Funding: LEA
Type of School: Day
Special Needs: Profound &
Multiple Learning
Difficulties and Severe
Learning Difficulties

Greater London

Anerley School
Versailles Road
London
SE20 8AX
No. of pupils: 45
Age range: 11-18

Beatrice Tate School
St Judes Road
London
E2 9RW
☎ 020 7739 6249
🖩 020 7613 1507
email: admin@beatrice.
towerhamlets.sch.uk
Head: Mr Alan Black
No. of pupils: 50
Age range: 11-19
Funding: LEA
Type of School: Day
Special Needs: Severe
Learning Difficulties

Beechcroft School
Beechcroft Road
London
SW17 7DF
No. of pupils: 62
Age range: 11-18

Bredinghurst School
Stuart Road
London
SE15 3AZ
No. of pupils: 61
Age range: 11-16

Funding: LEA
Type of School: Day/
Residential
Special Needs: Emotional
& behavioural difficulties

Brent Knoll School
Mayow Road
London
SE23 2XH
No. of pupils: 134
Age range: 4-17

Bromley Hall School
Bromley Hall Road
London
E14 0LF
No. of pupils: 30
Age range: 3-16

Cambridge House School
159 Pepys Road
London
SW20 8NP
Age range: 5-11

Cambridge School
Cambridge Grove
London
W6 0LB
No. of pupils: 85
Age range: 11-16

Castlebar School
Hathaway Gardens
London
W13 0DH
☎ 0208 998 3135
🖩 0208 810 7597
email: dperkins@
castlebar.ealing.sch.uk
No. of pupils: 100
Age range: 3-11
Funding: LEA
Type of School: Day
Special Needs: Moderate
Learning Difficulties,
Severe Learning
Difficulties

Centre Academy
92 St John's Hill
Battersea
London
SW11 1SH
☎ 020 7738 0958
🖩 020 7738 9862
No. of pupils: 49
Age range: 8-18

Chalcot School
Harmood Street
Camden Town

London
NW1 8DP
☎ 020 7485 2147
🖩 020 7485 9297
email: chalcotschool@
btinternet.com
web: www.btinternet.com
Head: Ms Elizabeth Hales
No. of pupils: 45
Age range: 9-16
Funding: LEA
Type of School: Day
Special Needs: Emotional
& behavioural difficulties

Charlton School
Charlton Park Road
London
SE7 8HX
☎ 020 8854 6259
🖩 020 8855 1022
email: mailbox@
charlton.greenwich.sch.uk
web:
www.charltonschool.com
Head: Mr Mark Dale-
Emberton
No. of pupils: 70
Age range: 11-19
Funding: LEA
Special Needs: Wide range

Chartfield Delicate School
St Margarets Crescent
Putney
London
SW15 6HL
☎ 020 8788 7471
🖩 020 8788 8081
email: info@chartfield.
wandsworth.sch.uk
web: www.chartfield.
wandsworth.sch.uk
Head: Valerie Hand-
Armitage
No. of pupils: 102
Age range: 7-16
Funding: LEA
Type of School: Day
Special Needs: Wide range

**Chelsea Children's
Hospital School**
Chelsea & Westminster
Hospital
369 Fulham Road
London
SW10 9NH
☎ 020 8746 8672
🖩 020 8746 8683
email: chelseachild.school@
chelwest.org

web: www.chelwest.org
Head: Ms Janette Steel
Age range: 4-18
Funding: LEA
Type of School: Day
Special Needs: Psychiatric
Difficulties

Cherry Garden School
Macks Road
Bermondsey
London
SE16 3XU
☎ 020 7237 4050
🖩 020 7237 7513
email: admin@cherrygarden.
southwark.sch.uk
web: www.cherrygarden.
southwark.sch.uk
Head: Ms Teresa Neary
No. of pupils: 46
Age range: 2-11
Funding: LEA
Type of School: Day
Special Needs: Profound &
Multiple Learning
Difficulties

Churchfield School
Church Manorway
London
SE2 0HY
☎ 020 8854 3739
No. of pupils: 218
Age range: 11-16

**Clapham Park School and
Support Service**
127 Park Hill
London
SW4 9PA
☎ 020 8674 5639
🖩 020 8674 5639
email: cps/@rmplc.co.uk
web: www.rmplc.co.uk
Head: Ms Barbara
Raybould
No. of pupils: 121
Age range: 2-16
Funding: LEA
Type of School: Day
Special Needs: Visually
Impaired

Colebrooke School
Colebrooke Row
City Road
London
N1 8AF
No. of pupils: 30
Age range: 3-19

7

College Park School
Garway Road
London
W2 4PH
☎ 020 7641 4460
🖷 020 7641 5731
Head: Annie Anderson
Age range: 4-16
Funding: LEA
Type of School: Day
Special Needs: Moderate
Learning Difficulties

College Park School
Monmouth Road
London
W2 4UT
No. of pupils: 65
Age range: 5-16

Crusoe House School
Nile Street
London
N1 7RD
☎ 020 7251 3932
🖷 020 7250 0740
email: crusoeschool@
aol.com
web: www.Connect-2.co.uk
Head: Mr Graham Sacks
No. of pupils: 50
Age range: 11-16
Funding: LEA
Type of School: Day
Special Needs: Emotional
& behavioural difficulties

Downsview School
Tiger Way
Downs Road
Clapton
London
E5 8QP
☎ 020 8985 6833
🖷 020 8525 2449
web: www.downsview.
hackney.sch.uk
Head: Mr B Bulman
No. of pupils: 60
Age range: 4-11
Funding: LEA
Type of School: Day
Special Needs: Various

Eleanor Smith School
North Street
Plaistow
London
E13 9HN
Age range: 5-16

Elfrida Rathbone School
Haymerle Road

London
SE15 6SY
Age range: 5-16

Elm Court School
Elmcourt Road
London
SE27 9BZ
Age range: 5-16

F D Roosevelt School
Avenue Road
London
NW8 6HX
Age range: 2-18

Fairley House School
30 Causton Street
London
SW1P 4AU
No. of pupils: 90
Age range: 5-11
Funding: Independent
Type of School: Day
Special Needs: Delicate

Frank Barnes School
Harley Road
London
NW3 3BN
☎ 020 7586 4665
Textphone 020 7586 4665
Age range: 2-11

Garratt Park School
Waldron Road
Earlsfield
London
SW18 3TB
☎ 020 8946 5769
🖷 020 8947 5605
Head: Mrs Jennifer Price
No. of pupils: 130
Age range: 11-17
Funding: LEA
Type of School: Day
Special Needs: Moderate
Learning Difficulties

Greenfields School
Coppetts Road
Muswell Hill
London
N10 1JP
☎ 020 8444 5366
🖷 020 8883 5202
Head: Ms Sally Wood
No. of pupils: 27
Age range: 7-16
Funding: LEA
Type of School: Day
Special Needs: Emotional
& behavioural difficulties

Greenmead School
St Margarets Crescent
Putney
London
SW15 6HL
☎ 020 8789 1466
🖷 020 8788 5945
email: admin@greenmead.
wandsworth.sch.uk
Head: Angela Laxton
No. of pupils: 43
Age range: 3-11
Funding: LEA
Type of School: Day
Special Needs: Profound &
Multiple Learning
Difficulties and Severe
Physical Disabilities

Greenvale School
69 Perry Rise
Forest Hill
London
SE23 2QU
☎ 020 8699 6515
🖷 020 8291 3361
email: info@
greenvale.lewisham.sch.uk
web: www.greenvale.
lewisham.sch.uk
Head: Mr Peter Munro
No. of pupils: 63
Age range: 11-19
Funding: LEA
Type of School: Day
Special Needs: Profound &
Multiple Learning
Difficulties

Greenwood School
Welton Road
London
SE18 2JD
☎ 020 8854 5904
🖷 020 8316 2332
Age range: 5-11

Grenfell School
Myrdle Street
London
E1 1HL
No. of pupils: 26
Age range: 3-11
Funding: LEA
Type of School: Day
Special Needs: Moderate
Learning Difficulties

Griffen Manor School
Welton Road
Swingate Lane
London
SE18 2JD

☎ 020 8854 3905
🖷 020 8316 4905
Head: Mr Paul Sullivan
No. of pupils: 62
Age range: 5-18
Funding: LEA
Special Needs: Autism

Grove House School
Elmcourt Road
London
SE27 9BZ
Age range: 2-11

**Hampstead Dyslexia
Clinic & Centre for
Learning Disabilities**
690 Finchley Road
London
NW11 7NN
☎ 020 8455 5107
🖷 020 8455 5107
No. of pupils: 130
Age range: 5-30
Funding: Independent
Type of School: Day
Special Needs: Dyspraxia/
mild autistic spectrum
disorders/dyslexia

Harborough School
Elthorne Road
Holloway Road
London
N19 4AB
No. of pupils: 26
Age range: 3-19

Harpley School
Globe Road
London
E1 4DZ
No. of pupils: 114
Age range: 11-16

**Hawkswood School and
Centre**
Antlers Hill
Chingford
London
E4 7RT
☎ 020 8529 2561
Textphone 020 8529 2561
🖷 0208 524 8230
email: hawkswood@
ukonline.co.uk
Head: Ms K Khan
No. of pupils: 40
Age range: 2-16
Funding: LEA
Type of School: Day
Special Needs: Hearing

impaired; Social and
Communication difficulties;
Autistic Spectrum Disorder

Hay Lane School
Grove Park
Kingsbury
London
NW9 0JY
No. of pupils: 116
Age range: 2-19

Haymerle School
Haymerle Road
Peckham
London
SE15 6SY
☎ 020 7639 6080
🖷 020 7277 9906
Head: Sue Harte
No. of pupils: 84
Age range: 4-11
Funding: LEA
Type of School: Day
Special Needs: Wide range

Horizon School
Wordsworth Road
London
N16 8DA
☎ 020 7254 8096
No. of pupils: 85
Age range: 5-16

Hospital School
Vincent Square
London
SW1
Age range: 4-16

Hyde Farm School
Telferscot Road
London
SW12 0HW
☎ 020 8673 4758
Age range: 5-16

Ickburgh School
Ickburgh Road
Clapton
London
E5 8AD
☎ 020 8806 4638
🖷 020 8806 7189
Head: Mr Phil Goss
No. of pupils: 90
Age range: 2-19
Funding: LEA
Type of School: Day
Special Needs: Profound &
Multiple Learning
Difficulties

J F K Post 16 Provision
Tollgate Road
London
E16 3LQ
☎ 020 7474 6326
🖷 020 7476 8941
email: admin.jfkpost16@
pops.newham.gov.uk
web: www.campus.bt.com
Head: Gill Goldsmith
No. of pupils: 20
Age range: 16-19
Funding: LEA
Type of School: Day
Special Needs: Profound &
Multiple Learning
Difficulties

Jack Taylor School
Ainsworth Way
Boundary Road
London
NW8 0HY
☎ 020 7328 6731
🖷 02073281590
email: deputy@
jacktaylor.camden.sch.uk
Deputy Head: Ms J
Ashmore
No. of pupils: 60
Age range: 5-19
Funding: LEA
Type of School: Day
Special Needs: Severe
Learning Difficulties &
Profound and Multiple
Learning Difficulties

Jack Tizard School
Finlay Street
London
SW6 6HB
☎ 020 7736 7949
🖷 020 7384 2790
email: JackTizard@aol.com
web: members.aol.com/
jacktizard
Head: Mr T Baker
No. of pupils: 80
Age range: 2-19
Funding: LEA
Type of School: Day
Special Needs: Severe
Learning Difficulties

John F Kennedy School
Pitchford Street
Stratford
London
E15 2RZ
☎ 020 8534 8544
🖷 020 8555 3530

Head: Mrs G A
Goldsmith
No. of pupils: 60
Age range: 2-19
Funding: LEA
Type of School: Day
Special Needs: Autistic
Spectrum Disorders, Severe
Learning Difficulties &
Profound and Multiple
Learning Difficulties

**Joseph Clarke School and
Service**
Vincent Road
Highams Park
London
E4 9PP
☎ 020 8527 8818
🖷 020 8523 5003
Head: Mr Frank J Smith
No. of pupils: 118
Age range: 2-19
Funding: LEA
Type of School: Day
Special Needs: Visually
Impaired

Lansbury Unit
c/o 'S' Corridor
Langdon School
Sussex Road
London
E6 2PS
Age range: 4-16

Lansdowne School
Argyll Close
(Off Dalyell Road)
London
SW9 9QL
Age range: 4-16

**Lea Green School and
Centre**
Leyton Green Road
London
E10 6DB
No. of pupils: 36
Age range: 4-16

Linden Lodge
61 Princes Way
London
SW19 6JB
No. of pupils: 75
Age range: 4-18

Mapledown School
Claremont Road
Cricklewood
London

NW2 1TR
☎ 020 8455 4111
🖷 020 8455 4895
email: info@
mapledown.barnet.sch.uk
Head: Mr John Feltham
No. of pupils: 60
Age range: 11-19
Funding: LEA
Type of School: Day
Special Needs: Profound &
Multiple Learning
Difficulties and Severe
Learning Difficulties

**Maudsley & Bethlem
Royal Hospital School**
Children's Department
Denmark Hill
London
SE5 8AZ
Age range: 4-16

Maze Hill School
Royal Hill
Greenwich
London
SE10 8PY
☎ 020 8853 4547
Head: Ms Pip Hardaker
No. of pupils: 89
Age range: 11-19
Funding: LEA
Type of School: Day
Special Needs: Profound &
Multiple Learning
Difficulties

Meadowgate School
Revelon Road
London
SE4 2PR
Age range: 5-16

Moatbridge School
Eltham Palace Road
London
SE9 5LX
☎ 020 8850 8081
No. of pupils: 45
Age range: 8-16

Mortimer School
Dingley Lane
Woodfield Avenue
Streatham
London
SW16 1AY
☎ 020 8677 7521
Head: Mrs Marie Stern
No. of pupils: 80
Age range: 4-11

7

Funding: LEA
Type of School: Day
Special Needs: Moderate
Learning Difficulties

Moselle School
Adams Road
Tottenham
London
N17 6HW
☎ 020 8808 8869
🖹 020 8801 7074
Head: Mr A S Redpath
No. of pupils: 125
Age range: 5-19
Funding: LEA
Type of School: Day
Special Needs: Wide range

Newham School for The Deaf
(Junior Department)
Tunmarsh Lane
London
E13 9NB
Age range: 3-5

Nine Acres School
Robert Street
Plumstead
London
SE18 7NB
☎ 020 8317 7659
🖹 020 8317 2315
email: mark.dale-emberton@virgin.net
web: www.virgin.net
Head: Mr Mark Dale-Emberton
No. of pupils: 60
Age range: 5-19
Funding: LEA
Type of School: Day
Special Needs: Profound & Multiple Learning Difficulties

Northway School
The Fairway
Mill Hill
London
NW7 3HS
☎ 020 8959 4232
🖹 020 8959 6436
email: northway@rmplc.co.uk
web: www.rmplc.co.uk
Head: Mr Ed Runham
No. of pupils: 85
Age range: 5-11
Funding: LEA
Type of School: Day
Special Needs: Wide range

Oak Lodge School
Heath View
East Finchley
London
N2 0QY
☎ 020 8444 6711
🖹 020 8444 6468
Head: Ms Lynda Walker
No. of pupils: 140
Age range: 11-18
Funding: LEA
Type of School: Day
Special Needs: Wide range

Oak Lodge School
101 Nightingale Lane
London
SW12 8NA
☎ 020 8673 3453
🖹 020 8673 9397
email: info@oaklodge.wandsworth.sch.uk
web: www.oaklodge.wandsworth.sch.uj
Head: Mr Peter Merrifield
No. of pupils: 86
Age range: 11-19
Funding: LEA
Type of School: Day & Boarding
Special Needs: Hearing Impaired

Paddock School
Priory Lane
London
SW15 5RT
No. of pupils: 116
Age range: 3-19

Parayhouse School
New Kings School Annex
New Kings Road
Fulham
London
SW5 4LY
☎ 0207 751 0914
🖹 0207 751 0914
email: slj@parayhouse.demon.co.uk admin@phs-special. demon.co.uk
Head: Ms Sarah L Jackson
No. of pupils: 40
Age range: 8-16
Funding: Independent
Type of School: Day
Special Needs: Speech and Language Difficulties

Phoenix Primary & Secondary School
49 Bow Road

Bow
London
E3 2AD
☎ 020 8980 4740
🖹 020 8980 6342
email: phoenixschool@email.MSN.com
web: www.email.MSN.com
Head: Mr Stewart Harris
No. of pupils: 135
Age range: 5-16
Funding: LEA
Type of School: Day
Special Needs: Moderate Learning Difficulties, Autism and Language & Communication Difficulties

Primary Pupil Referral Unit
Kennington Children's Centre
20 Kennington Park Gardens
London
SE11 4AX
☎ 020 7926 8420
🖹 020 7926 8414
email: PrimaryPupilReferralUnit@hotmail.com
Acting Head: Anne Sturman
No. of pupils: 40
Age range: 5-11
Funding: LEA
Type of School: Day
Special Needs: Emotional & behavioural difficulties

Priory School
Tennison Road
South Norwood
London
SE25 5RR
☎ 020 8653 8222
🖹 020 8771 6761
Head: Mrs Margaret A Simpson
No. of pupils: 49
Age range: 12-19
Funding: LEA
Type of School: Day
Special Needs: Severe Learning Difficulties

Queen Elizabeth II Jubilee School
Kennet Road
London
W9 3LG
☎ 020 7641 5825

🖹 020 7641 5823
Head: Ms Mary Loughran
No. of pupils: 64
Age range: 5-19
Funding: LEA
Type of School: Day
Special Needs: Profound & Multiple Learning Difficulties

Queensmill School
Clancarty Road
Fulham
London
SW6 3AA
☎ 020 7384 2330
🖹 020 7384 2750
email: queensmill@hotmail.com
Head: Mrs Jennifer Page
No. of pupils: 62
Age range: 3-11
Funding: LEA
Type of School: Day
Special Needs: Autism and Speech & Language Difficulties

Richard Cloudesley School
Golden Lane
London
EC1Y 0TJ
☎ 020 7251 1161
🖹 020 7251 4911
No. of pupils: 55
Age range: 2-18
Funding: LEA
Type of School: Day
Special Needs: Wide range

Rosemary Primary School
75 Prebend Street
London
N1 8PW
☎ 020 7226 8223
🖹 020 7359 9842
Head: Mr J A Wolger
No. of pupils: 76
Age range: 2-11
Funding: LEA
Type of School: Day
Special Needs: Profound & Multiple Learning Difficulties, Autism, Severe Learning Difficulties

Rosemary Secondary School
15 Woodbridge Street
London
EC1R 0LL

☎ 020 7253 6893
🖷 020 7336 6046
email: rossec@
gpo.sonnet.co.uk
web: www.gpo.sonnet.co.uk
Head: Mr Jim Wolger
No. of pupils: 38
Age range: 11-19
Funding: LEA
Type of School: Day
Special Needs: Severe
Learning Difficulties

Russet House School
11 Autumn Close
Enfield
EN1 4JA
☎ 020 8350 0650
🖷 020 8350 0651
email: russethouse.Office@
enfield.gov.uk
Head: Mrs Julie Foster
No. of pupils: 66
Age range: 3-11
Funding: LEA
Type of School: Day
Special Needs: Autism and
Assessment Nursery

Samuel Rhodes School
Dowrey Street
Richmond Avenue
Islington
London
N1 0LS
☎ 020 7837 9075
🖷 020 7837 4030
email:
admin@samuelrhodes.
islington.sch.uk
Head: Jackie Blount
No. of pupils: 104
Age range: 5-16
Funding: LEA
Type of School: Day
Special Needs: Moderate
Learning Difficulties

Shelley School
Oakden Street
London
SE11 4UG
☎ 020 7735 9081
🖷 020 7735 9082
email: admin@
shelley.lambeth.sch.uk
Head: Ms Maria Lozano-
Luoma
No. of pupils: 41
Age range: 11-19
Funding: LEA
Type of School: Day

Special Needs: Severe
Learning Difficulties

SILD
Whitefield Schools
MacDonald Road
London
E17 4AZ
☎ 020 8531 3426
🖷 020 8527 3613
email: whitefield_edu@
msn.com

Spa School
Monnow Road
London
SE1 5RN
No. of pupils: 75
Age range: 11-17

St Ann's School
Springfield Road
Hanwell
London
W7 3JP
☎ 020 8567 6291
🖷 020 8840 4664
email: adminmail@
stanns.ealing.sch.uk
Head: Ms Gillian Carver
No. of pupils: 61
Age range: 12-19
Funding: LEA
Type of School: Day
Special Needs: Severe
Learning Difficulties/
Profound & Multiple
Learning Difficulties

**St George's Hospital
School**
5th Floor
Lanesborough Wing
Blackshaw Road
London
SW17 0QT
Age range: 2-19

Stormont House School
Downs Park Road
London
E5 8NP
No. of pupils: 126
Age range: 5-16
Funding: LEA
Type of School: Day
Special Needs: Delicate
and Speech & Language
Difficulties

Susan Isaacs School
Forthbridge Road
London

SW11 5NX
Age range: 5-16

Swiss Cottage School
Avenue Road
London
NW8 6HX
☎ 020 7681 8080
🖷 020 7681 8082
Head: Ms Kay Bedford
No. of pupils: 125
Age range: 2-16
Funding: LEA
Type of School: Day
Special Needs: Moderate
Learning Difficulties

Sybil Elgar School
10 Florence Road
Ealing
London
W5 3TX
No. of pupils: 69
Age range: 11-19

**The Children's Hospital
School**
The GOS Hospital for
Children NHS Trust
Great Ormond Street
London
WC1N 3JH
☎ 020 7813 8269
🖷 020 7813 8269
email: yhgos@aol.com
web: www.schoolsite.
edex.net.uk/262/
Head: Mrs Yvonne Hill
No. of pupils: 123
Age range: 5-19
Funding: Foundation
Special
Type of School: Hospital
Special Needs: Wide
Range

The Dominie School
1 Mandeville Courtyard
142 Battersea Park Road
London
SW11 4NB
☎ 020 7720 8783
No. of pupils: 32
Age range: 6-13

The Highshore School
Bellenden Road
London
SE15 5BB
☎ 020 7639 7211
🖷 020 7252 9024/
0207 732 4207

email: jackathighshore@
tiscali.co.uk
Head: Mrs Y Conlon
No. of pupils: 128
Age range: 11-17
Funding: LEA
Type of School: Day
Special Needs: Wide range

**The Hornsby Dyslexia
Centre**
71 West Side
Wandsworth Common
London
SW18
Age range: 5-18

**The Hornsey Trust for
Children with Cerebral
Palsy**
Conductive Education
Centre
54 Muswell Hill
London
N10 3ST
☎ 020 8444 7242
🖷 020 8444 7241
email: info@
hornseytrust.org.uk
web:
www.hornseytrust.org.uk
Head of Administration:
Kathleen Hewson
No. of pupils: 20
Age range: 0-7
Funding: Charity
Type of School: Day
Special Needs: Children
with Cerebral Palsey and
associated difficulties

The Livity School
Mandrell Road
Brixton
London
SW2 5DW
☎ 020 7733 0681
🖷 020 7738 7154
email: admin@the livity-
special.lambeth.sch.uk
Head: Ms Geraldine Lee
No. of pupils: 65
Age range: 3-11
Funding: LEA
Type of School: Day
Special Needs: Profound &
Multiple Learning
Difficulties. Primary
school for complex needs

The Moat School
Bishop's Avenue

7

Fulham
London
SW6 6EG
☎ 020 7610 9018
🖷 020 7610 9098
email: office@
moatschool.org.uk
web:
www.moatschool.org.uk
Headmaster: Mr Robert
Carlysle
No. of pupils: 90
Age range: 11-16
Funding: Independent/
Fees paid by charity
Type of School: Day
Special Needs: Dyslexia
and other related specific
learning disorders

The Vale School
Vale Road
London
N4 1PG
No. of pupils: 66
Age range: 2-19

**The Whitefield School
and Centre**
MacDonald Road
Walthamstow
London
E17 4AZ
No. of pupils: 300
Age range: 2-19

Thurlow Park School
Elmcourt Road
London
SE27 9BZ
☎ 020 8670 3975
🖷 020 8761 8922
email: thurlowp@
globalnet.co.uk
web: www.globalnet.co.uk
Head: Mr John Barrow
No. of pupils: 50
Age range: 2-16
Funding: Independent
Type of School: Day
Special Needs: Wide range

Tuke School
Woods Road
London
SE15 2PX
☎ 020 7639 5584
🖷 020 7635 8937
Head: Heidi Tully
No. of pupils: 43
Age range: 11-19
Funding: LEA

Type of School: Day
Special Needs: Severe
Learning Difficulties

Vernon House School
Drury Way
London
NW10 0NQ
No. of pupils: 43
Age range: 5-11

Watergate School
12 Church Grove
Lewisham
London
SE13 7UU
☎ 020 8314 1751
🖷 020 8690 1681
Head: Ms Alison Youd
No. of pupils: 65
Age range: 2-11
Funding: LEA
Type of School: Day
Special Needs: Profound &
Multiple Learning
Difficulties

West Lea School
Haselbury Road
Edmonton
London
N9 9TU
☎ 020 8807 2656
🖷 020 8803 5203
email: westlea.office@
enfield.gov.uk
Head: Mrs A Fox
No. of pupils: 105
Age range: 3-17
Funding: LEA
Type of School: Day

William Morris School
Folly Lane
Walthamstow
London
E17 5NT
☎ 020 8503 2225
🖷 020 8503 2227
Head: Ms A Duncan
No. of pupils: 153
Age range: 11-19
Funding: LEA
Type of School: Day
Special Needs: Moderate
Learning Difficulties

Willowfield School
Heron Road
Milkwood Road
London
SE24 0HY

No. of pupils: 30
Age range: 9-17

Woodfield School
Glenwood Avenue
Kingsbury
London
NW9 7LY
☎ 020 8205 1977
🖷 020 8205 5877
Head: Mr Hywel Williams
Age range: 11-16
Funding: LEA
Type of School: Day
Special Needs: Moderate
Learning Difficulties

Woodlane High
Du Care Road
London
W12 0TN
☎ 020 8743 5668
🖷 020 8743 9138
Head: Mr Nicholas Holt
No. of pupils: 55
Age range: 11-16
Funding: LEA
Type of School: Day
Special Needs: Delicate

Wycliffe School
Wickersley Road
London
SW11 5QS
Age range: 5-16

Greater Manchester

Alderman Kay School
Tintern Road Hollin
Middleton
M24 6JG
☎ 0161 643 4917
Head: J M Clark
No. of pupils: 116
Age range: 5-16
Funding: LEA
Type of School: Day
Special Needs: Profound &
Multiple Learning
Difficulties

**Barlow Hall Primary
School**
Assessment Provision
Darley Avenue
Chorlton-cum-Hardy
Manchester
M21 7JG
☎ 0161 881 1934
🖷 0161 861 8367

email: head.barlowhall@
mecgrid.org.uk
Head: Mr J A Scally
No. of pupils: 320
Age range: 3-11
Funding: LEA
Type of School: Day

**Booth Hall Hospital
School & Home Teaching
Serivce**
Charlestown Road
Manchester
M9 7AA
☎ 0161 220 5118
🖷 0161 220 5600
Head: Ms Helen E Jones
Age range: 2-18
Funding: LEA
Type of School: Hospital

Children's Hospital School
Hospital Road
Pendlebury
Swinton
M27 4HA
No. of pupils: 66
Age range: 3-16

**Cloughside School c/o
The Gardener Unit**
Bury New Road
Prestwich
Manchester
M25 3BL
☎ 0161 773 9121
🖷 0161 772 3478
email: nc-cloughside@
hotmail.com
Head: Mr N M Cooke
No. of pupils: 30
Age range: 11-18
Funding: LEA
Type of School: Hospital
Special Needs: Psychiatric
Difficulties

Elms Bank High School
Ripon Avenue
Whitefield
Manchester
M45 8PJ
☎ 0161 766 1597
🖷 0161 796 5018
email:
elms.bank.manchester.sp.@
campus.bt.com
web: www.campus.bt.com
Head: Ms Lynn Lines
No. of pupils: 147
Age range: 11-19
Funding: LEA

Type of School: Day
Special Needs: Profound &
Multiple Learning
Difficulties

**Gorton Brook First
School**
Belle Vue Street
Manchester
M12 5PW
☎ 0161 223 1822
🖹 0161 223 2731
Age range: 2-13

Grange School
77 Dickenson Road
Rusholme
M14 5AZ
☎ 0161 248 4841
🖹 0161 248 6715
Head: Mrs Ann Fitzpatrick
No. of pupils: 48
Age range: 4-19
Funding: LEA
Type of School: Day
Special Needs: Autism &
Complex Learning
Difficulties

**Green Hall Primary
School**
Green Hall Close
Atherton
Manchester
M46 9HP
☎ 01942 883928
🖹 01942 870069
email: greenhall.
wigan.sch.uk
Head: Mr Triska
No. of pupils: 98
Age range: 4-11
Funding: LEA
Type of School: Day
Special Needs: Multiple
Learning Difficulties

**Greenwood Primary
School**
Stafford Road
Eccles
Salford
M30 9ED
No. of pupils: 78
Age range: 3-11

Hardman Fold School
Dean Street
Failsworth
M35 0DQ
No. of pupils: 75
Age range: 11-16

**Hawthorns Community
School**
Corporation Road
Audenshaw
M34 5LZ
☎ 0161 336 3389
Head: Mrs Moira
Thompson
No. of pupils: 50
Age range: 4-11
Funding: LEA
Type of School: Day
Special Needs: Complex &
Multiple Needs, ASD,
Speech & Language and
Emotional & behavioural
difficulties

Highfield School
St John's Road
Mosley Common
Worsley
M28 4AL
Age range: 6-16

Lancasterian School
Elizabeth Slinger Road
West Didsbury
Manchester
M20 2XA
☎ 0161 445 0123
🖹 0161 445 6826
email: Lancasterianschool@
yahoo.co.uk
Head: Mr Roger Billinge
No. of pupils: 100
Age range: 2-16
Funding: LEA
Type of School: Day
Special Needs: Physical
disabilities

Longford Park School
Longford Park
Off Cromwell Road
Stretford
Manchester
M32 8QE
☎ 0161 881 2341
🖹 0161 860 4121
Head: Mr Michael G Coxe
No. of pupils: 56
Age range: 4-11
Funding: LEA
Type of School: Day
Special Needs: Moderate
Learning Difficulties

**Medlock Valley High
School**
Palmerston Street
Ancoats

M12 6PT
☎ 0161 274 4667
No. of pupils: 166
Age range: 11-16

Melland High School
Holmcroft Road
Gorton
M18 7NG
☎ 0161 223 9915
🖹 0161 230 6919
Head: Mrs Judith O'Kane
No. of pupils: 110
Age range: 11-19
Funding: LEA
Type of School: Day
Special Needs: Profound &
Multiple Learning
Difficulties

**Millwood Primary Special
School**
Fletcher Fold Road
Bury
BL9 9RX
☎ 0161 253 6083
🖹 0161 253 6085
Head:
No. of pupils: 86
Age range: 2-11
Funding: LEA
Type of School: Day
Special Needs: Moderate
Learning Difficulties,
Severe Learning
Difficulties, Profound &
Multiple Learning
Difficulties and associated
disabilities

**Northumberland High
School**
Northumberland Street
Salford
M7 4RP
No. of pupils: 29
Age range: 11-16

Oakwood High School
Park Lane
Salford
M6 7RQ
No. of pupils: 153
Age range: 11-17

**Parkes Field Primary
School**
Barton Road
Swinton
M27 5LP
No. of pupils: 52
Age range: 3-11

**Peacock School (Central
District Support Services)**
Peacock Close
Gorton
M18 8AY
☎ 0161 223 0458
🖹 0161 223 1222
Head: Ms Joy Rose
No. of pupils: 290
Age range: 5-16
Funding: LEA
Type of School: Day
Special Needs: Emotional
& behavioural difficulties

Piper Hill School
200 Yew Tree Lane
Manchester
M23 0FF
☎ 0161 998 4068
🖹 0161 945 6625
No. of pupils: 82
Age range: 11-19

Richmond Park School
Cochrane Avenue
Longsight
M12 4FA
☎ 0161 273 4894
🖹 0161 273 8341
Head: Mrs Joan Holt
No. of pupils: 80
Age range: 5-11
Funding: LEA
Type of School: Day
Special Needs: Moderate
Learning Difficulties

Rodney House School
388 Slade Lane
Burnage
M19 2HT
☎ 0161 224 2774
🖹 0161 225 5186
Head: Ms Mary Isherwood
No. of pupils: 48
Age range: 0-7
Funding: LEA
Type of School: Day
Special Needs: Wide range

Roundwood School
Roundwood Road
Northenden
M22 4AB
☎ 0161 998 4138
🖹 0161 946 0495
Head: Mrs Sandra Hibbert
No. of pupils: 230
Age range: 11-16
Funding: LEA
Type of School: Day

7

Special Needs: Moderate
Learning Difficulties

Shawgrove School
Cavendish Road
West Didsbury
Manchester
M20 1QB
☎ 0161 445 9435
🖹 0161 445 0386
Head: Mr H S Taylor
No. of pupils: 20
Age range: 3-11
Funding: LEA
Type of School: Day
Special Needs: Visually
Impaired

Southern Cross School
Barlow Hall Road
Manchester
M21 2JJ
☎ 0161 881 2695
Age range: 5-16

**Springwood Primary
Special School**
Barton Road
Swinton
Manchester
M22 5LD
☎ 0161 778 0022
🖹 0161 727 5767
Head: Mrs Anthea
Darlington
No. of pupils: 165
Age range: 2-11
Funding: LEA
Type of School: Day
Special Needs: Profound &
Multiple Learning
Difficulties

The Grange School
Pilgrim Drive
Manchester
M11 3TD
☎ 0161 223 2744
🖹 0161 220 8711
No. of pupils: 48
Age range: 4-19

The Two Porches School
Gloucester Street
Atherton
M46 0HX
☎ 01942 882012
🖹 01942 889650
Head: Mrs L A Roberts
No. of pupils: 46
Age range: 2-19
Type of School: Day

**Whitworth Park First
School**
Monton Street
Moss Street
Manchester
M14 4GP
☎ 0161 226 2079
🖹 0161 226 9614
Age range: 2-12

Woodside First School
Crossacres Road
Manchester
M22 5DR
☎ 0161 437 5697
🖹 0161 498 0297
Age range: 5-12

Hampshire

Allington Manor School
Allington Lane
Fairoak
Eastleigh
SO50 7DE
☎ 023 8069 2621
🖹 023 8069 2621
Head: Dr L F Lowestein
No. of pupils: 15
Age range: 7-19
Type of School: Day
Special Needs: Speech and
Language Difficulties

**Aster House Pupil
Referral Unit**
Aster Road
Swaythling
Southampton
SO16 3BG
☎ 023 8055 7520
🖹 023 8067 8301

Baycroft School
Gosport Road
Stubbington
Fareham
PO14 2AE
☎ 01329 664 151
🖹 01329 668 601
Head: Mr R A Hendry
No. of pupils: 170
Age range: 11-16
Funding: LEA
Type of School: Day
Special Needs: Wide range

**Chestnut House Pupil
Referral Unit**
Warren Crescent
Shirley Warren
Southampton

SO16 6AY
☎ 023 8077 5632

Cliffdale Primary School
Battenburg Avenue
North End
Portsmouth
PO2 0ZN
☎ 023 9266 2601
🖹 023 9266 0506
Head: Mrs Jane Sansome
No. of pupils: 100
Age range: 4-11
Funding: LEA
Type of School: Day
Special Needs: Moderate
Learning Difficulties

Coxlease School
High Coxlease House
Clay Hill
Lyndhurst
SO43 7DE
☎ 023 8028 3633
🖹 023 8028 2515
web:
www.coxleaseschool.co.uk
Bursar: Mr J Colclough
No. of pupils: 49
Age range: 9-17
Funding: Independent
Type of School: Boarding
Special Needs: Emotional
& behavioural difficulties

Dove House School
Sutton Road
Basingstoke
RG21 2SU
☎ 01256 351555
🖹 01256 329749
No. of pupils: 91
Age range: 11-16
Funding: LEA
Type of School: Day
Special Needs: Multiple
Learning Difficulties and
Autism

Forest Edge School
Lydlynch Road
Totton
Southampton
SO40 3DW
☎ 023 8086 4949
🖹 023 8087 2294
Head: Miss R Wiles
No. of pupils: 58
Age range: 4-11
Funding: LEA
Type of School: Day
Special Needs: Wide range

Grateley House School
Grateley
Andover
SP11 8JR
☎ 01264 889 751
🖹 01264 889 212
Head: Mr S Browne
No. of pupils: 39
Age range: 11-16
Funding: Independent
Special Needs: Wide range

Greenacres School
Andover Road
Winchester
SO22 6AU
☎ 01962 862 450
🖹 01962 842093
email:
chris.gayler@greenacres.ha
nts.sch.uk
Head: Christine Gayler
No. of pupils: 40
Age range: 3-19
Funding: LEA
Type of School: Day
Special Needs: Profound &
Multiple and Severe
Learning Difficulties and
Autism

Heathfield School
Oldbury Way
Peak Lane
Fareham
PO14 3BN
☎ 01329 845150
🖹 01329 846548
email: stella.muirhead@
heathfield.hants.sch.uk
Head: Stella Muirhead
No. of pupils: 125
Age range: 3-11
Funding: LEA
Type of School: Day
Special Needs: MLD –
Autism, Physical
Disability, Sensory
Imapirments, EBD,
Language Delay/Disorder,
etc.

Henry Tyndale School
Ship Lane
Farnborough
GU14 8BX
☎ 01252 544 577
🖹 01252 377 411
email: 7000afao@
hants.gov.uk
web: www.hants.gov.uk
Head: Mr R Thompson

No. of pupils: 115
Age range: 4-19
Funding: LEA
Type of School: Day
Special Needs: Profound &
Multiple Learning
Difficulties

Henry Tyndale School
Ship Lane
Farnborough
GU14 8BX
☎ 01252 544577
🖹 01252 377411
email: admin@
henrytyndale.hants.sch.uk
Headmaster: Mr R
Thomson
No. of pupils: 117
Age range: 2-19
Funding: LEA
Type of School: Day
Special Needs: Autism and
Complex Learning
Difficulties, Profound,
Multiple and Severe
Learning Difficulties

Highlands Tutorial Centre
Reginald Road
Southsea
Portsmouth
PO4 9HN
☎ 023 9273 4824
No. of pupils: 15
Age range: 16-18

Hill House School
Rope Hill
Boldre
Lymington
SO41 8NE
No. of pupils: 18
Age range: 11-19

Hope Lodge School
22 Midanbury Lane
Bitterne Park
Southampton
SO18 4HP
☎ 023 8063 4346
🖹 023 8023 1789
Head: Mr Martin Carter
No. of pupils: 57
Age range: 4-19
Funding: Independent
Type of School:
Day/Weekly Residential
Special Needs: Autism

Icknield School
River Way

Andover
SP11 6LT
☎ 01264 365 297
🖹 01264 334 794
Head: Mr Stephen Steer-
Smith
No. of pupils: 58
Age range: 2-19
Funding: LEA
Type of School: Day
Special Needs: Severe
Learning Difficulties

Lakeside School
Winchester Road
Chandler's Ford
SO53 2DW
☎ 023 80266633
🖹 023 80267147
Head: Mr G Evans
No. of pupils: 62
Age range: 11-16
Funding: LEA
Type of School: Residential
& Day
Special Needs: Emotional
& Behavioural Difficulties

Lankhills School
Andover Road
Winchester
SO23 7BU
☎ 01962 854 537
🖹 01962 849 419
Head: Mr Rod Wakelam
No. of pupils: 136
Age range: 11-19
Funding: Independent
Type of School: Day
Special Needs: Moderate
Learning Difficulties

Limington House School
St Andrew's Road
Basingstoke
RG22 6PS
☎ 01256 322 148
🖹 01256 358 778
Head: Mr Mervyn J C
Balson
No. of pupils: 80
Age range: 2-19
Funding: LEA
Type of School: Day
Special Needs: Profound &
Multiple Learning
Difficulties

Lord Mayor Treloar School
Upper Froyle
Alton
GU34 4LA

☎ 01420 547 425
🖹 01420 542 708
email: admissions@
treloar.org.uk
web: www.treloar.org.uk
Head: Mr Neil Clark
No. of pupils: 125
Age range: 7-16
Funding: Registered
charity
Type of School: Day
Special Needs: Wide range

Maple Ridge School
Maple Crescent
Basingstoke
RG21 2SX
☎ 01256 323639
🖹 01256 841059
No. of pupils: 62
Age range: 4-11
Funding: LEA
Special Needs: Multiple
Learning Difficulties and
Autism

**Medecroft Opportunity
Centre**
Sparkford Road
Winchester
SO22 4NJ
☎ 01962 860 393
email: 7751with@
hantsnet.gov.uk
web: www.hantsnet.gov.uk
Head: Mrs Olivia Peak
No. of pupils: 60
Age range: 0-5
Funding: LEA
Type of School: Nursery
Special Needs: Speech and
Language Difficulties

Mordaunt School
Rose Road
Southampton
SO14 6TE
☎ 023 8022 9017
🖹 023 8033 6112
Head: Miss C Spiller
No. of pupils: 30
Age range: 3-19
Funding: Independent
Type of School: Day
Special Needs: Profound &
Multiple Learning
Difficulties

Netley Court School
Victoria Road
Netley Abbey
Southampton

SO31 5DR
☎ 023 8045 3259
🖹 023 8045 5438
email: info@netleycourt.
southampton.sch.uk
Head: Mrs J Partridge
No. of pupils: 43
Age range: 4-11
Funding: LEA
Type of School: Day
Special Needs: Wide range

Norman Gate School
Vigo Road
Andover
SP10 1JZ
☎ 01264 323 423
🖹 01264 354 891
Acting Head: Mr Rob Brain
No. of pupils: 61
Age range: 3-11
Funding: LEA
Type of School: Day
Special Needs: Mild Autism

North End Centre
Wymering Road
Portsmouth
PO2 7HX
☎ 023 9266 9964

Rachel Madocks School
Eagle Avenue
Cowplain
Waterlooville
Portsmouthy
PO8 9XP
☎ 023 9224 1818
🖹 023 9226 9521
email: admin@rachel-
madocks.hants.org.uk
Head: Mrs Chrys Browne
No. of pupils: 74
Age range: 2-19
Funding: LEA
Type of School: Day
Special Needs: Profound,
Severe & Multiple
Learning Difficulties and
Autism

Red Lodge School
Vermont Close
Off Winchester Road
Southampton
SO16 7LT
☎ 023 8076 7660
🖹 023 8076 7643
Head: Miss Susan Mackie
No. of pupils: 150
Age range: 11-16
Funding: LEA

7

Type of School: Day
Special Needs: Multiple
Learning Difficulties

Redwood Park School
Wembley Grove
Cosham
Portsmouth
PO6 2RY
☎ 023 9237 7500
🖷 023 9220 1104
Head: Mrs Elizabeth A Nye
No. of pupils: 130
Age range: 11-16
Funding: LEA
Type of School: Day
Special Needs: Wide range

Ridgeway House School
Peartree Avenue
Bitterne
Southampton
SO19 7JL
☎ 023 8044 8897
No. of pupils: 89
Age range: 11-19

Rosemary Portal School
Shepherds Lane
Winchester
SO21 1AJ
Age range: 7-12

Salterns School
6 Commercial Road
Southampton
SO4 3AF
No. of pupils: 57
Age range: 2-16

Saxon Wood School
Rooksdown
Barron Place
Basingstoke
RG24 9NH
☎ 01256 356 635
🖷 01256 323 713
email: headteacher@
saxonwood.hants.sch.uk
web: www.saxonwood.
hants.sch.uk
Head: Mr Paul Skinner
No. of pupils: 50
Age range: 2-11
Funding: LEA
Type of School: Day
Special Needs: Physical
Disabilities or complex
medical needs

Shepherds Down School
Shepherds Lane

Compton
Winchester
SO21 2AJ
☎ 01962 713 445
🖷 01962 713 453
email: general@
shepherdsdown.hants.gov.uk
Head: Mr T Gazzard
No. of pupils: 110
Age range: 4-11
Funding: LEA
Type of School: Day
Special Needs: Profound &
Multiple Learning
Difficulties

Southdown School
Shepherds Lane
Compton
Winchester
SO21 2AH
Age range: 3-7

Southlands School
Vicar's Hill
Boldre
Lymington
SO41 5QB
☎ 01590 675 350
🖷 01590 671 891
email: sgething@
hesleygroup.co.uk
web:
www.hesleygroup.co.uk
Head: Sue Gething
No. of pupils: 62
Age range: 8-19
Funding: Independent
Type of School: Residential
Special Needs: Aspergers
Syndrome

St Edward's School
Melchet Court
Sherfield English
Romsey
SO51 6ZR
Age range: 10-16

St Francis School
Patchway Drive
Oldbury Way
Fareham
PO14 3BN
☎ 01329 845 730
🖷 01329 847 217
Head: Mrs Sue Chalmers
No. of pupils: 98
Age range: 2-19
Funding: LEA
Special Needs: Severe
Learning Difficulties

Tankerville School
Romsey Road
Eastleigh
SO5 4AJ
No. of pupils: 54
Age range: 2-19

**The Compass Pupil
Referral Unit**
Warren Avenue
Shirley Warren
Southampton
SO16 6AH
☎ 023 8077 2572
Centre Manager: Mr Rob
Gilroy
No. of pupils: 32
Age range: 14-16

The Foxbury School
Perth Road
Bridgemary
Gosport
PO13 0XX
Age range: 5-11

The Futcher School
Drayton Lane
Drayton
Portsmouth
PO6 1HG
☎ 023 9237 5318
No. of pupils: 84
Age range: 2-17

The Glenwood School
Silvester Road
Cowplain
Portsmouth
PO8 8TR
No. of pupils: 94
Age range: 11-16

The Loddon School
Wildmoor Lane
Sherfield-on-Loddon
Hook
RG27 0JD
☎ 01256 882 394
🖷 01256 882 929
email: marion@
cornick.demon.co.uk
web: www.loddon-
school.demon.co.uk
Principal: Marion Cornick
No. of pupils: 27
Age range: 8-18
Funding: Charity
Type of School: Residential
Special Needs: Autism,
Severe Learning Difficulties
& Challenging Behaviour

The Mark Way School
Batchelors Barn Road
Andover
SP10 1HR
☎ 01264 351 835
🖷 01264 366 276
Head: Mr A Oakley
No. of pupils: 75
Age range: 11-16
Funding: LEA
Type of School: Day
Special Needs: Multiple
Learning Difficulties and
Autism

The Meadow School
Mill Chase Road
Bordon
GU35 0HA
☎ 01420 474 396
🖷 01420 488 329
Head: Mr P Greenwood
No. of pupils: 130
Age range: 4-16
Funding: LEA
Type of School: Day
Special Needs: Wide range

**The Polygon Special
School**
Handel Terrace
Southampton
SO15 2FH
☎ 023 8063 6776
No. of pupils: 47
Age range: 11-16

The Samuel Cody School
Lynchford Road
Farnborough
GU14 6BJ
☎ 01252 314 720
Head: Mr L Bevan
No. of pupils: 83
Age range: 11-16
Funding: LEA
Type of School: Day
Special Needs: Moderate
Learning Difficulties

The Sevenoaks Centre
Sundridge Close
Cosham
Portsmouth
PO6 3JL
☎ 023 9221 4492
🖷 023 9221 4509
Head: Ms Sally Garrett
No. of pupils: 55
Age range: 11-16
Funding: LEA
Type of School: Pupil

Referral Unit
Special Needs: Delicate
health

The Waterloo School
Warfield Avenue
Waterlooville
Portsmouth
PO7 7JJ
Age range: 6-16

Treloar College
Holybourne
Alton
GU34 4EN
☎ 01420 547400
🖷 01420 542708
email: principal@
treloar.org.uk
Principal: Dr G K Jowett
No. of pupils: 174
Age range: 16-25
Funding: L & SC
Type of School: Residential
Special Needs: Further
Education College for
physically disabled

Vermont School
Vermont Close
Off Winchester Road
Bassett
Southampton
SO16 7LT
☎ 023 8076 7988
🖷 023 8076 6902
Head: Mr Eric Bell
No. of pupils: 35
Age range: 4-11
Funding: LEA
Type of School: Day
Special Needs: Emotional
& behavioural difficulties

Waterside Unit
151 Locksway Road
Southsea
Portsmouth
PO4 8LD
☎ 023 9273 4823
Age range: 4-16

Whitedown School
Albert Road
Alton
GU34 1LP
☎ 01420 82201
🖷 01420 542 837
Head: Mrs Barbara Livings
No. of pupils: 41
Age range: 2-19
Funding: LEA

Type of School: Day
Special Needs: Wide range

Wolverdene Special School
22 Love Lane
Andover
SP10 2AF
☎ 01264 362 350
🖷 01264 396 600
email: 7067anao@
hants.gov.uk
web: www.hants.gov.uk
Head: Mr R A Ford
No. of pupils: 42
Age range: 5-11
Funding: LEA
Type of School: Day
Special Needs: Emotional
& behavioural difficulties

Herefordshire

Barrs Court School
Barrs Court Road
Hereford
HR1 1EQ
☎ 01432 265 035
🖷 01432 353 988
web:
www.barrscourtschool.ik.org
Head: Mr R Aird
No. of pupils: 40
Age range: 11-19
Funding: LEA
Type of School: Day
Special Needs: Severe
learning difficulties and
profound and multiple
learning difficulties

Blackmarston School
Hondon Close
Hereford
HR2 7NX
☎ 01432 272376
🖷 01432 272376
email: admin@
blackmarston.hereford.sch.uk
web:
www.blackmarston.sch.uk
Head: Mrs Sian Bailey
No. of pupils: 45
Age range: 2-11
Funding: LEA
Type of School: Day
Special Needs: Severe,
Profound & Multiple
Learning Difficulties

Rowden House School
Rowden
Bromyard
HR7 4LS

☎ 01885 488 096
🖷 01885 483 361
email: rowdenhouseschool@
msn.com
web: www.msn.com
Head: Ms Heather Hardy
No. of pupils: 30
Age range: 11-19
Funding: Independent
Special Needs: Severe
Learning Difficulties

**Westfield School and
Leominster Early Years
Centre**
Westfield Walk
Leominster
HR6 8HD
☎ 01568 613 147
🖷 01568 613 147
Head: Mrs Pat Chesters
No. of pupils: 65
Age range: 2-19
Funding: LEA
Type of School: Day
Special Needs: Assessment
Centre

Hertfordshire

Amwell View School
St Margaret's
Stanstead Abbotts
Ware
SG12 8EH
No. of pupils: 83
Age range: 2-19

Batchwood School
Townsend Drive
St Albans
AL3 5RP
☎ 01727 765 195
Head: Mr M E Hopkins
No. of pupils: 50
Age range: 11-16
Funding: LEA
Type of School: Day
Special Needs: Emotional
& behavioural difficulties

Boxmoor House School
Box Lane
Hemel Hempstead
HP3 0DF
No. of pupils: 64
Age range: 11-16
Funding: LEA
Type of School:
Day/Weekly Residential
Special Needs: Emotional
& behavioural difficulties

Brandles Close School
Weston Way
Baldock
SG7 6EY
No. of pupils: 28
Age range: 11-16

Breakspeare School
Gallows Hill Lane
Abbots Langley
Watford
WD5 0BU
No. of pupils: 64
Age range: 2-19
Special Needs: Severe
Learning Disabilities

Colnbrook School
Hayling Road South
Oxhey
Watford
WD19 7UY
☎ 020 8428 1281
🖷 020 8421 5359
email: admin.colnbrook@
thegrid.org.uk
web:
www.colnbrook.herts.sch.uk
Head: Mr Richard Hill
No. of pupils: 88
Age range: 4-11
Funding: LEA
Type of School: Day
Special Needs: Moderate
Learning Difficulties/
Autism

Falconer School
Falconer Road
Bushey
WD23 3AT
☎ 020 8950 2505
🖷 020 8421 8107
Head: Mr J Page
No. of pupils: 60
Age range: 11-16
Funding: LEA
Type of School: Day
Special Needs: Emotional
& behavioural difficulties

Garston Manor School
Horseshoe Lane
Garston
Watford
WD25 7HR
☎ 01923 673 757
🖷 01923 440 344
email: gmanorschl@aol.com
web: www.aol.com
Head: Mr D N Harrison
No. of pupils: 115

7

Age range: 11-16
Funding: LEA
Type of School: Day
Special Needs: Moderate
Learning Difficulties

Greenside School
Shephall Green
Stevenage
SG2 9XS
☎ 01438 315 356
🖹 01438 748 034
Head: Anne Biglands
No. of pupils: 96
Age range: 2-19
Funding: LEA
Type of School: Day
Special Needs: Profound &
Multiple Learning
Difficulties

Hailey Hall School
3 Hailey Lane
Hertford
SG13 7PB
☎ 01922 465 208
🖹 01922 460 851
email: haileyhs@
rmplc.co.uk
web: www.rmplc.co.uk
Head: Mr B Evans
No. of pupils: 60
Age range: 11-16
Funding: LEA
Type of School: Day
Special Needs: Emotional
& behavioural difficulties

Heathlands School
Heathlands Drive
St Albans
AL3 5AY
☎ 01727 868596
Textphone 01727 868596
🖹 01727 860015
Head: Ms M G Davis
No. of pupils: 99
Age range: 3-16
Funding: LEA
Type of School: Day
Special Needs: Hearing
Impaired

Hengrove School
Chivery
Tring
HP23 6LE
☎ 01296 622 136
No. of pupils: 18
Age range: 9-16

Knightsfield School
Knightsfield
Welwyn Garden City
AL8 7LW
☎ 01707 376874
Textphone 01707 376874
🖹 01707 321738
Head: Mrs L M Leith
No. of pupils: 50
Age range: 11-16
Funding: LEA
Type of School: Residential
Special Needs: Hearing
Impaired

Lakeside School
Lemsford Lane
Welwyn Garden City
AL8 6YW
☎ 01707 327 410
🖹 01707 393 352
email: admin.lakeside@
thegrid.org.uk
Head: Mrs J Chamberlain
No. of pupils: 60
Age range: 2-19
Funding: LEA
Type of School: Day
Special Needs: Severe
Learning Difficulties

Lonsdale School
Webb Rise
Stevenage
SG1 5QU
☎ 01438 357 631
🖹 01438 742 583
Head: Mrs Philippa Clark
No. of pupils: 84
Age range: 3-19
Funding: LEA
Type of School: Residential
Special Needs: Wide range

Pinewood School
Hoe Lane
Ware
SG12 9PB
☎ 01920 412211
🖹 01920 411100
No. of pupils: 145
Age range: 11-16
Funding: LEA
Type of School: Day
Special Needs: Multiple
Learning Difficulties

Radlett Lodge School
Herper Lane
Radlett
WD7 9HW

☎ 01923 854922
🖹 01923 859922
email: radlett.lodge@
nas.org.uk
web: www.nas.org.uk
Principal: Lynda Tucker
No. of pupils: 49
Age range: 3-11
Funding: Independent
Type of School: Special
Special Needs: Autism and
Asperger Syndrome

South Lodge School
High Street
Baldock
SG7 6BX
No. of pupils: 26
Age range: 13-16

Southfield School
Travellers Lane
Hatfield
AL10 8TJ

**St Elizabeth's RC Special
School**
Much Hadham
SG10 6EW
☎ 01279 844 270
🖹 01279 843 903
Head: Mr Gordon Phillips
No. of pupils: 70
Age range: 5-19
Funding: Non-maintained
Type of School: Day
Special Needs: Speech and
Language Difficulties

St Lukes School
Crough Hall Lane
Redbourn
AL3 7ET
No. of pupils: 167
Age range: 9-16

The Cedar School
Redbridge Lane
Nursling
Southampton
SO16 0XN
☎ 023 8073 4205
🖹 023 8073 8231
email: head@
cedar.southampton.sch.uk
web: www.cedar.
southampton.sch.uk
Head: Mr Brian Hart
No. of pupils: 90
Age range: 3-16
Funding: LEA
Type of School: Day

Special Needs: Physical
disabilities

The Collett School
Lockers Park Lane
Hemel Hempstead
HP1 1TQ
No. of pupils: 115
Age range: 4-16

The Valley School
Valley Way
Stevenage
SG2 9AB
No. of pupils: 188
Age range: 3-18

Watling View School
Watling View
St Albans
AL1 2NU
No. of pupils: 76
Age range: 2-19

Woodfield School
Malmes Croft
Leverstock Green
Hemel Hempstead
HP3 8RL
No. of pupils: 76
Age range: 3-19
Funding: LEA
Type of School: Day
Special Needs: Severe
Learning Difficulties

Woolgrove School
Pryor Way
Letchworth
SG6 2PT
☎ 01462 622 422
🖹 01462 622 022
email: admin.woolgrove@
thegrid.org.uk
web: www.woolgrove.org.uk
Head: Dr Rona V Tutt
No. of pupils: 108
Age range: 5-11
Funding: LEA
Type of School: Day
Special Needs: Autism and
Moderate Learning
Difficulties

Hillingdon

**RNIB Sunshine House
School**
33 Dene Road
Northwood
HA6 2DD
☎ 01923 822 538

📠 01923 826 227
Head: Mrs Loraine Stewart
No. of pupils: 50
Age range: 2-11
Funding: Voluntary
Type of School: Day non-maintained special school with some weekly boarding
Special Needs: Visually Impaired

Hounslow

Syon Park School
Twickenham Road
Isleworth
TW7 6AU
☎ 020 85604300
📠 020 85698104
Head: Mr R Nowobilski
No. of pupils: 50
Age range: 11-16
Funding: LEA
Type of School: Day special
Special Needs: Emotional & behavioural difficulties

Isle of Man

Glencrutchery School
Glencrutchery Road
Douglas
IM2 6EB
No. of pupils: 9
Age range: 4-16

Noble's Hospital (Unit)
Children's Ward
Noble's Hospital
Douglas
IM1 4QA
☎ 01624 642 399
Head: Mrs Mary Maylott
Age range: 4-18
Funding: LEA
Type of School: Hospital
Special Needs: Medical

Isle of Wight

Medina House School
School Lane
Newport
PO30 2HS
☎ 01983 522 917
No. of pupils: 96
Age range: 2-19

St Catherine's School and Grove Hill Further Education Centre
Grove Road

Ventnor
PO38 1TT
email: gs@
stcaths.demon.co.uk
web:
www.stcaths.demon.co.uk
No. of pupils: 78
Age range: 7-18
Funding: Non-maintained
Type of School: Residential
Special Needs: Speech and Language Difficulties

Watergate School
Watergate Road
Newport
PO30 1XW
☎ 01983 514 634
📠 01983 533 911
Head: Mrs Anne Hunt-Davies
No. of pupils: 230
Age range: 3-18
Funding: LEA
Type of School: Day
Special Needs: Moderate Learning Difficulties

Kent

Abbey Court School
Rede Court Road
Strood
ME2 3SP
☎ 01634 338 220
📠 01634 338 221
email: office@
abbeycourt.medway.sch.uk
web: www.abbeycourt.
medway.sch.uk
Head: Ms Karen Joy
No. of pupils: 125
Age range: 4-19
Funding: LEA
Type of School: Day
Special Needs: Severe Learning Difficulties

Barn End Centre
High Road
Dartford
DA2 7DP
☎ 01322 228 395
No. of pupils: 32
Age range: 11-14
Type of School: Pupil Referral Unit

Beaver Education Project
Beaver Centre
135 Beaver Lane
Ashford

TN23 2NX
☎ 01233 622 533
📠 01233 640 978
email: manager@beaver-ed-project.kent.sch.uk
Head: Mrs J Hurn
No. of pupils: 20
Age range: 11-16
Funding: LEA
Type of School: Pupil Referral Unit
Special Needs: Emotional & Behavioural Difficulties

Beckmead School
Monks Orchard Road
Beckenham
BR3 3BZ
☎ 020 8777 9311
📠 020 8777 6550
Age range: 5-16
Special Needs: Emotional & behavioural difficulties

Bethlem & Maudsley Hospital School
Monks Orchard Road
Beckenham
BR3 3BX
☎ 020 8777 1897
📠 020 8777 1239
Head: Wendy French
No. of pupils: 25
Age range: 5-18
Type of School: Residential
Special Needs: Psychiatric Difficulties

Bourne Place
Nizels Lane
Hildenborough
Tonbridge
TN11 8NS
☎ 01732 832 666
📠 01732 832 073
Age range: 11-19

Bower Grove
Fant Lane
Maidstone
ME16 8NL
☎ 01622 726 773
📠 01622 725 025
email: headteacher@
bower-grove.kent.sch.uk
Head: Mr T Phipps
No. of pupils: 200
Age range: 5-16
Funding: LEA
Type of School: Day
Special Needs: Complex Learning Needs including

speech, language, autism, communication, physical & sensory, Learning Difficulties and Emotional & behavioural difficulties

Bradfields School
Churchill Avenue
Chatham
ME5 0LB
☎ 01634 683 990
📠 01634 683 571
Head: Mr P J Harris
No. of pupils: 182
Age range: 11-19
Funding: LEA
Type of School: Day
Special Needs: Moderate Learning Difficulties

Bradstow School
34 Dumpton Park Drive
Broadstairs
CT10 1BY
☎ 01843 862123
📠 01843 866648
No. of pupils: 50
Age range: 6-19
Type of School: Residential
Special Needs: Autism

Brook Education Centre
Park Road
Folkestone
CT19 5BY
☎ 01303 221 350
📠 01303 221 372
No. of pupils: 60
Age range: 11-16

Broomhill Bank School
Broomhill Road
Rusthall
Tunbridge Wells
TN3 0TB
☎ 01892 522 666
📠 01892 522 666
Head: Mr P A Barnett
No. of pupils: 75
Age range: 8-19
Funding: LEA
Type of School: Day
Special Needs: Profound & Multiple Learning Difficulties

Burwood School
Avalon Road
Orpington
BR6 9BD
☎ 01689 821 205
📠 01689 820 593

7

email: admin@
burwood.bromley.sch.uk
Head: Mr Terry O'Leary
Quinn
No. of pupils: 40
Age range: 7-16
Funding: LEA
Type of School: Day
Special Needs: Emotional
& behavioural difficulties

Burwood School
Avalon Road
Orpington
BR6 9BD
☎ 01689 821205
▤ 01689 820593
No. of pupils: 42
Age range: 9-16
Funding: LEA
Type of School: Day
Special Needs: Emotional
& Behavioural Difficulties

Centre Class
Old Caretakers House
St Marys Road
Swanley
BR8 7TE
☎ 01322 665 209
▤ 01322 665 209
Acting Teacher in Charge:
Mrs Sue Brown
No. of pupils: 20
Age range: 5-11

Charles Street Unit
Charles Street
Tunbridge Wells
TN4 0DS
☎ 01892 534 589
No. of pupils: 42
Age range: 11-16

Charlton Court
East Sutton
Maidstone
ME17 3DQ
☎ 01622 842 424
▤ 01622 844 220
No. of pupils: 16
Age range: 11-16

Coney Hill School
Croydon Road
Hayes
BR2 7AG
☎ 020 8462 7419
▤ 020 84622019
email: coney.hull@
shaftesburysoc.org.uk
Head: Miss Margaret
Rimmer

No. of pupils: 25
Age range: 5-16
Funding: Non-maintained
Type of School:
Residential/Day
Special Needs: Profound &
Multiple Learning
Difficulties and Sensory
Impairment

Dartford Hospital School
Joyce Green Hospital
Dartford
DA1 5PL
Age range: 3-18

Dorton House School
Seal
Sevenoaks
TN15 0ED
☎ 01732 592 650
▤ 01732 592 670
email: dortonhouseschool@
rlsb.org.uk
web: www.rlsb.org.uk
Head: Mr Brian Cooney
No. of pupils: 82
Age range: 5-16
Funding: Non-maintained
Type of School: Day
Special Needs: Visually
Impaired

East Court School
Victoria Parade
Ramsgate
CT11 8ED
☎ 01843 592 077
▤ 01843 592 418
email: dyslexia@
eastcourtschool.co.uk
web:
www.eastcourtschool.co.uk
Head: Dr M E Thomson
No. of pupils: 75
Age range: 7-14
Funding: Independent
Type of School: Day &
Boarding
Special Needs: Dyslexia

Five Acre Wood School
Boughton Lane
Maidstone
ME15 9QL
☎ 01622 743 925
▤ 01622 744 828
Head: Ms Jill Kratochvil
No. of pupils: 62
Age range: 4-19
Funding: LEA
Type of School: Day

Special Needs: Profound &
Multiple Learning
Difficulties

Foxwood School
Seabrook Road
Hythe
CT21 5QJ
☎ 01303 261 155
▤ 01303 262 355
email: foxwood_edu@
msn.com
web:
www.foxwood.kent.sch.uk
Head: Mr Chris Soulsby
No. of pupils: 112
Age range: 2-19
Funding: LEA
Type of School: Residential
Special Needs: Multi-
sensory impairments

Furness School
Rowhill Road
Hextable
Swanley
BR8 7RP
☎ 01322 662 937
▤ 01322 615033
email: headteacher@
furness.kent.sch.uk
Acting Principal: Mr D
Dawson
No. of pupils: 67
Age range: 11-16
Funding: LEA
Type of School:
Residential/Day
Special Needs: Emotional
& behavioural difficulties

Gap House School
1 South Cliff Parade
Broadstairs
CT10 1TJ
☎ 01843 861 679
▤ 01843 868 828
No. of pupils: 48
Age range: 5-11

Glebe School
Hawes Lane
West Wickham
BR4 9AE
☎ 020 8777 4540
▤ 020 8777 5572
email: info@
glebe.bromley.sch.uk
web:
www.glebe.bromley.sch.uk
Head: Mr K Seed
No. of pupils: 181

Age range: 11-16
Funding: Foundation
Type of School: Day
Special Needs: Moderate
Learning Difficulties

Grange Park School
Birling Road
Leybourne
West Malling
ME19 5QA
☎ 01732 842 144
▤ 01732 848 004
email: grange-park@
kent.sch.uk
web: www.kent.sch.uk
Head: Mrs Jean Hanley
No. of pupils: 33
Age range: 11-19
Funding: LEA
Type of School: Day
Special Needs: Autism

Greystones School
Hythe Road
Ashford
TN24 0QF
☎ 01233 621 302
▤ 01233 630 467
No. of pupils: 122
Age range: 5-19

Grosvenor House
30 Victoria Park
Herne Bay
CT6 5BL
☎ 01227 375 397
No. of pupils: 32
Age range: 11-16

Halstead Place School
Church Road
Halstead
Sevenoaks
TN14 7HQ
☎ 01959 533 294
Head: Mr N Rees-Davies
No. of pupils: 56
Age range: 11-16
Funding: LEA
Type of School: Boarding
Special Needs: Emotional
& behavioural difficulties

Harbour School
Elms Vale Road
Dover
CT17 9PS
☎ 01304 201 964
▤ 01304 225 000
email: office@
harbour.kent.sch.uk

web:
www.harbour.kent.sch.uk
Head: Mr A Berresford
No. of pupils: 138
Age range: 5-16
Funding: LEA
Type of School: Day
Special
Special Needs: Multiple
Learning Difficulties

Helen Allison School
Longfield Road
Meophan
Gravesend
DA13 0EW
☎ 01474 814 878
🖷 01474 812 033
email: HelenAllison@
nas.org.uk
web: www.nas.org.uk
Head: Mrs Jacqui Ashton
Smith
No. of pupils: 70
Age range: 5-19
Funding: LEA
Type of School: Day
Special Needs: Autism

Highview School
Moat Farm Road
Folkestone
CT19 5DJ
☎ 01303 258 755
🖷 01303 251185
No. of pupils: 103
Age range: 5-16
Funding: LEA
Type of School: Day
Special Needs: Moderate
Learning Difficulties

Ifield School
Cedar Avenue
Gravesend
DA12 5JT
☎ 01474 365 485
🖷 01474 569 744
email: ifieldsch@aol.com
web: www.aol.com
Head: Mr Simon Harrison
No. of pupils: 170
Age range: 5-16
Funding: LEA
Type of School: Day
Special Needs: Profound &
Multiple Learning
Difficulties

Knotley School
Springfield Gardens
West Wickham

BR4 9PX
No. of pupils: 26
Age range: 11-18

Laleham School
Northdown Park Road
Margate
CT9 2TP
☎ 01843 221 946
No. of pupils: 135
Age range: 11-16
Funding: LEA
Special Needs: SPLD
(Dyslexia)

Marjorie McClure School
Hawkwood Lane
Chislehurst
BR7 5PS
☎ 020 8467 0174
🖷 020 8467 3275
Head: Dr Jeffrey Wardle
No. of pupils: 85
Age range: 3-19
Funding: LEA
Type of School: Day
Special Needs: Physical
disbilities or medical
conditions with associated
learning difficulties or
sensory impairments

Marlborough School
Marlborough Park Avenue
Sidcup
DA15 9DP
☎ 020 8300 6896
No. of pupils: 58
Age range: 2-19

Meadows School
London Road
Southborough
Tunbridge Wells
TN14 7EX
☎ 01892 529 144
🖷 01892 527 787
Head: Mr Robert Schaedel
No. of pupils: 56
Age range: 10-16
Funding: Non-maintained
Type of School: Day
Special Needs: Moderate
Learning Difficulties

Meeting House School
Pendragon Road
Downham
Bromley
BR1 5LD
Age range: 5-16

**Mid Kent Behaviour
Support Service**
(Primary Team) Education
& Libraries
Bishops Terrace
Bishops Way
Maidstone
ME14 1AF
☎ 01622 605116
🖷 01622 605113
Age range: 5-11

Milestone School
Ash Road
New Ash Green
DA3 8JZ
☎ 01474 709 420
🖷 01474 707 170
email: headteacher@
mileston.kent.sch.uk
Head: Eileen Flanagan
No. of pupils: 160
Age range: 2-19
Funding: LEA
Type of School: Day
Special Needs: Severe
Learning Difficulties &
Autism

Northwood Centre
Highfield Road
Ramsgate
CT12 6QB
No. of pupils: 27
Age range: 11-16

Oakley School
Pembury Road
Tunbridge Wells
TN2 4NF
☎ 01892 823096
🖷 01892 823836
No. of pupils: 130
Age range: 5-19
Type of School: Special
Needs

Parkfield School
Parkfield Road
Folkestone
CT19 5BY
Age range: 5-19

Parkwood Hall School
Beechenlea Lane
Swanley
BR8 8DR
☎ 01322 664441
🖷 01322 613163
email: info@parkwoodhall.
kensington-chelsea.sch.uk
Head: Mrs H Dando

No. of pupils: 68
Age range: 8-19
Funding: LEA
Type of School:
Residential/Day
Special Needs: Moderate/
Severe Learning
Difficulties

Pendragon School
Pendragon Road
Bromley
BR1 5LD
No. of pupils: 133
Age range: 11-17

Phoenix Centre
Main Road
Longfield
DA3 7PW
☎ 01474 705 377
No. of pupils: 67
Age range: 11-16

Portal House School
Sea Street
St Margaret's-at-Cliffe
Dover
CT15 6AR
☎ 01304 853 033
🖷 01304 853 526
email: headteacher@
portal-house.kent.sch.uk
Head: Mr L Sage
No. of pupils: 40
Age range: 5-11
Funding: LEA
Type of School:
Residential/Day
Special Needs: Emotional
& behavioural difficulties

Pupil Referral Service
Kingwood Hayes Lane
Bromley
BR2 9EA
☎ 020 8290 0274
🖷 020 8466 7061
PRU Coordinator: Mr Jon
Costley
No. of pupils: 84
Age range: 11-16
Funding: LEA
Type of School: Pupil
Referral Unit
Special Needs: All
excluded pupils

**Rectory Paddock School
and Research Unit**
Main Road
St Paul's Cray

7

Orpington
BR5 3HS
☎ 01689 870 519
🖷 01689 898 818
Head: Dr V I Hinchcliffe
No. of pupils: 75
Age range: 4-19
Funding: LEA
Type of School: Day
Special Needs: Profound &
Multiple Learning
Difficulties

Ridge View School
Cage Green Road
Tonbridge
TN10 4PT
☎ 01732 771 384
🖷 01732 770 344
email: headteacher@
ridge-view.kent.sch.uk
web: www.ridge-
view.kent.sch.uk
Head: Mr A Carver
No. of pupils: 102
Age range: 3-19
Funding: LEA
Type of School: Day
Special Needs: Profound,
Severe and Multiple
Learning Disabilities and
Autism

Ripplevale School
Chapel Lane
Ripple
Deal
CT14 8JG
☎ 01304 373 866
🖷 01304 381 011
No. of pupils: 36
Age range: 9-16

Riverside School
Clockhouse
Ashford
TN23 4YN
No. of pupils: 50
Age range: 3-19
Funding: LEA
Type of School: Day
Special Needs: Profound &
Multiple Learning
Difficulties

Rowhill School
Stock Lane
Wilmington
Dartford
DA2 7BZ
☎ 01322 225 490
🖷 01322 291 433

Head: Mr Steven
McGuinness
No. of pupils: 125
Age range: 5-17
Funding: LEA
Type of School: Day
Special Needs: Moderate
Learning Difficulties

**Royal Sea Bathing
Hospital School**
Canterbury Road
Margate
CT9 5BQ
Age range: 3-16

Shawcroft School
Crockenhill Road
St Mary Cray
Orpington
BR5 4ES
Age range: 5-17

Shenstone School
94 Old Road
Crayford
DA1 4DZ
☎ 01322 524 145
🖷 01322 523 551
Head: Mrs L Aldcroft
No. of pupils: 60
Age range: 2-11
Funding: LEA
Type of School: Day
Special Needs: Profound &
Multiple Learning
Difficulties

St Anthony's School
St Anthony's Way
Cliftonville
Margate
CT9 3RA
☎ 01843 292 015
🖷 01843 231 574
Head: Mr R O'Dell
No. of pupils: 165
Age range: 3-16
Funding: LEA
Type of School: Day
Special Needs: Moderate
Learning Difficulties

St Bartholomew's School
Attlee Way
North Street
Milton Regis
Sittingbourne
ME10 2HF
☎ 01795 477 888
🖷 01795 478 833
email: headteacher@st-
bartholomews.kent.sch.uk

Head: Ms Geraldine
Hurstfield
No. of pupils: 65
Age range: 5-16
Funding: LEA
Type of School: Day

St Nicholas School
Holme Oak Close
Nunnery Fields
Canterbury
CT1 3JJ
☎ 01227 464 316
No. of pupils: 100
Age range: 4-19
Funding: LEA
Type of School: Day
Special Needs: Profound &
Multiple Learning
Difficulties

St Thomas School
Swanstree Avenue
Sittingbourne
ME10 4NL
☎ 01795 477 788
🖷 01795 477 771
Head: Mr P J Rankin
No. of pupils: 140
Age range: 5-19
Funding: LEA
Type of School: Day
Special Needs: Moderate
Learning Difficulties

Stone Bay School
70 Stone Road
Broadstairs
CT10 1EB
☎ 01843 863 421
🖷 01843 866 652
email: headteacher@
stone.boy.kent.sch.uk
Head: Mr R Edey
No. of pupils: 63
Age range: 11-19
Funding: LEA
Type of School: Day/
Residential
Special Needs: Autism,
Challenging behaviour

Swale Centre
Ufton Lane
Sittingbourne
ME10 1JB
☎ 01795 478 643
No. of pupils: 16
Age range: 11-16

Swinford Manor School
Great Chart
Ashford

TN23 3BT
☎ 01233 622 958
🖷 01233 662 177
email: headteacher@
swinford.idps.co.uk
Acting Head: Mr R W Law
No. of pupils: 62
Age range: 11-16
Funding: LEA
Type of School: Day
Special Needs: Emotional
& behavioural difficulties

**The Caldecott
Community**
Mersham Le Hatch
Ashford
TN25 5NH
☎ 01233 503 954
🖷 01233 502 650
No. of pupils: 80
Age range: 5-19

The Cedars
Bower Mount Road
Maidstone
ME16 8AU
☎ 01622 753 772
🖷 01622 693 622
No. of pupils: 23
Age range: 11-16

The Foreland School
Lanthorne Road
Broadstairs
CT10 3NX
☎ 01843 863 891
🖷 01843 860 710
email: foreland@
foreland.kent.sch.uk
Head: Peter Hare
No. of pupils: 141
Age range: 3-19
Funding: LEA
Type of School: Day
Special Needs: Severe
Learning Difficulties

The Helen Allison School
29 The Overcliffe
Gravesend
DA11 0EH
No. of pupils: 46
Age range: 3-16

The Orchard School
Cambridge Road
Canterbury
CT1 3QQ
☎ 01227 769 220
🖷 01227 781 589

email: office@
orchard.kent.sch.uk
web: www.orchard.ik.org
Head: Mr B S Shelley
No. of pupils: 120
Age range: 11-16
Funding: LEA
Type of School: Special
Special Needs: Multiple
Learning Difficulties

**The Royal School for
Deaf Children Margate &
Westgate College for Deaf
People**
Victoria Road
Margate
CT9 1NB
☎ 01843 227561
Textphone 01843 227561
🖷 01843 227637
email: enquiries@
royalschoolfordeaf.
kent.sch.uk
web: www.royalschoolfor
deaf.kent.sch.uk
Head: Mr Christopher
Owen
No. of pupils: 170
Age range: 4-25
Funding: Registered
charity
Type of School:
Residential/Day
Special Needs: Profoundly
Deaf, Hearing Impaired,
Deaf/Blind & Autistic

Valence School
Westerham
TN16 1QN
☎ 01959 562 156
🖷 01959 565 046
No. of pupils: 115
Age range: 4-19

**West Kent Hospital
School Service**
Woodview Campus
Main Road
Longfield
DA3 7PW
☎ 01474 708 762
🖷 01474 708 767
Head: Mrs J M Locke
Funding: Registered
charity
Type of School: Hospital
Special Needs: Medical

Woodbrook School
2 Hayne Road

Beckenham
BR3 4HY
☎ 020 8650 7205
🖷 020 8289 5728
Head: Mr Steve Gillow
No. of pupils: 67
Age range: 4-19
Funding: LEA
Type of School: Day
Special Needs: Profound &
Multiple Learning
Difficulties

Woodside School
Halt Robin Road
Belvedere
DA17 6DW
☎ 01322 433 494
🖷 01322 433 442
Head: Ms Linda Crooks
No. of pupils: 205
Age range: 5-16
Funding: LEA
Type of School: Day
Special Needs: Wide range

Woodside School
Woodside Road
Bexleyheath
DA7 6LB
☎ 01322 529 240
No. of pupils: 179
Age range: 5-16

Kingston-upon-Hull

Frederick Holmes School
Inglemire Lane
Kingston upon Hull
HU6 8JJ
☎ 01482 804 766
🖷 01482 806 967
email: admin@
frederickholmes.hull.sch.uk
web: www.frederickholmes
school.co.uk
Head: Dominic Boyes
No. of pupils: 97
Age range: 2-19
Funding: LEA
Type of School: Day
community special school
Special Needs: Physical
disabilities

Tweendykes School
Tweendykes Road
Kingston upon Hull
HU7 4XJ
☎ 01482 826508
🖷 01482 839597

email: admin@
tweendykes.hull.sch.uk
Head: Mr Angus Ogilvie
No. of pupils: 80
Age range: 3-16
Funding: LEA
Type of School: Day
Special Needs: Severe
Learning Difficulties

Kingston-upon-Thames

Bedelsford School
Grange Road
Kingston-upon-Thames
KT1 2QZ
☎ 020 8546 9838
🖷 020 8296 9238
email: BDS@rbksch.uk
web: www.bedelsford.
kingston.sch.uk
Head: Mr John Murfitt
No. of pupils: 64
Age range: 2-16
Funding: LEA
Type of School: Day
Special Needs: Physical
Disabilities

St Philip's School
Harrow Close
Leatherhead Road
Chessington
KT9 2HP
☎ 020 8397 2672
🖷 020 8391 5431
email: phs@rbksch.org
Head: Mrs Helen Goodall
No. of pupils: 128
Age range: 5-16
Funding: LEA
Type of School: Day
Special Needs: Moderate
Learning Difficulties

Kirklees

Lydgate School
Kirkroyds Lane
New Mill
Huddersfield
HD9 1LS
☎ 01484 222 484
🖷 01484 222 485
Head: Mr Bill Goler
No. of pupils: 88
Age range: 5-16
Funding: LEA
Type of School: Day
Special Needs: Moderate
Learning Difficulties

Ravenshall School
Ravensthorpe Road
Thornhill Lees
Dewsbury
WF12 9EE
☎ 01924 325 234
🖷 01924 325 235
email: head.ravenshall@
kirklees-schools.org.uk
Head: Mr C E Newby
No. of pupils: 88
Age range: 11-16
Funding: LEA
Type of School: Day
Special Needs: Moderate
Learning Difficulties

Knowsley

**Northern Primary
Support Centre**
Bramcote Walk
Northwood
L33 9UR
☎ 0151 477 8140
🖷 0151 477 8141
email: knowsleynorthern.
de@knowsley.gov.uk
Head: Mrs Barbara Twiss
No. of pupils: 62
Age range: 3-11
Funding: LEA
Type of School: Day
Special Needs: Speech and
Language Difficulties and
Profound, Severe and
Multiple Learning
Difficulties

The Elms School
Whitethorn Drive
Stockbridge Village
Liverpool
L28 1RX
☎ 0151 47783507
🖷 0151 449 3584
email: theelms@
knowsley.gov.uk
Head: Mrs Linda Lowe
No. of pupils: 115
Age range: 2-19
Funding: LEA
Type of School: Day
Special Needs: Severe
Learning Difficulties,
Autism and Complex
Needs

Lancashire

Alf Kaufman School
Highwood

7

Norden
Rochdale
OL11 5XP
☎ 01706 359153
Head: Paul Geldeart
No. of pupils: 32
Age range: 3-11
Funding: LEA
Type of School: Day
Special Needs: Physical
Disabilities

Ashton Rose Hill School
Soughers Lane
Bryn
Wigan
WN4 0JS
No. of pupils: 97
Age range: 7-16

Astley Park School
Harrington Road
Chorley
PR7 1JZ
No. of pupils: 122
Age range: 4-17

Bank Hey School
Heys Lane
Blackburn
BB2 4NW
☎ 01254 261 655
🖷 01254 673 375
Head: Mr T Feeley
No. of pupils: 40
Age range: 11-16
Funding: LEA
Type of School: Day
Special Needs: Emotional
& behavioural difficulties

Beacon Special School
Tanhouse Road
Tanhouse
Skelmersdale
WN8 6BA
☎ 01695 721066
🖷 01695 732932
Head: Mr J H Taylor
No. of pupils: 72
Age range: 5-16
Funding: LEA
Special Needs: Emotional
& Behavioural Difficulties

Beech Tree School
Meadow Lane
Bamber Bridge
Preston
PR5 8LN
☎ 01772 323 131
🖷 01772 322 187

email: beechtreeschool@
easynet.co.uk
Head: Ms Lucy Bayliss
No. of pupils: 14
Age range: 7-16
Funding: Registered
charity
Type of School: Boarding
Special Needs: Severe
Learning Difficulties

Birtenshaw Hall School
Darwen Road
Bromley Cross
Bolton
BL7 9AB
☎ 01204 304 230
🖷 01204 597 995
Principal: Mr C D
Jamieson
No. of pupils: 46
Age range: 3-19
Funding: Non-maintained
Type of School:
Residential/Day
Special Needs: Wide range

Birtle View School
George Street
Heywood
Rochdale
OL10 4PW
☎ 01706 368 821
🖷 01706 620 760
Head: Mrs Anne
Richardson
No. of pupils: 50
Age range: 2-19
Funding: LEA
Type of School: Day
Special Needs: Profound &
Multiple Learning
Difficulties

Black Moss School
School Lane
Skelmersdale
WN8 8EH
☎ 01695 721 487
🖷 01695 559 078
email: headteacher@
blackmoss.lancsngfl.ac.uk
web:
www.blackmoss.fsnet.co.uk
Head: Mr P F Boycott
No. of pupils: 96
Age range: 4-18
Funding: LEA
Type of School: Day
Special Needs: Moderate
Learning Difficulties

**Blackamoor Special
School**
Roman Road
Blackburn
BB1 2LA
☎ 01254 52843
🖷 01254 677 479
email: blackamoor.band.
sp.@campus.bt.com
web: www.campus.bt.com/
campusworld/orgs/org
Head: Mrs A L Abram
No. of pupils: 80
Age range: 4-16
Funding: LEA
Type of School: Day
Special Needs: Wide range

**Bleasdale House,
Residential/Day Special
School**
27 Emesgate Lane
Silverdale
Carnforth
LA5 0RG
☎ 01524 701 217
🖷 01524 702 044
email: head@
bleasdale.lancsngfl.ac.uk
web: www.bleasdale.
lancsngfl.ac.uk
Head: Mrs Lesley Ormrod
No. of pupils: 45
Age range: 2-19
Funding: LEA
Type of School: Residential
& Day
Special Needs: Profound &
Multiple Learning
Difficulties

Bolton Dyslexia Institute
Kildonan House
Ramsbottom Road
Horwich
BL6 7DH

Borsdane Brook School
Princess Street
Hindley
Wigan
WN2 3HJ
Head: Mr D A Fox
No. of pupils: 187
Age range: 5-16

Broadfield School
Fielding Lane
Oswaldtwistle
BB5 3BE
☎ 01254 381 782
🖷 01254 396 805

Head: Mrs Jane White
No. of pupils: 101
Age range: 4-16
Funding: LEA
Type of School: Day
Special Needs: Moderate
Learning Difficulties

Broadlands Special School
Blackamoor Campus
Roman Road
Blackburn
BB1 2LA
☎ 01254 56044
🖷 01254 278 760
Head: Mrs D Mitchell
Age range: 3-5
Funding: LEA
Type of School: Day
Special Needs: Wide range

Brookfield School
Fouldrey Avenue
Poulton-le-Fylde
FY6 7HE
☎ 01253 886 895
🖷 01253 882 845
email: head@
brookfield56.lancsngfl.ac.uk
web: www.btinternet.com
Head: Mr I M Thomas
No. of pupils: 40
Age range: 11-16
Funding: LEA
Type of School: Day
Special Needs: Emotional
& behavioural difficulties

Brownhill School
Heights Lane
Rochdale
OL12 0PZ
☎ 01706 648990
🖷 01706 648537
email: office@
brownhill.rochdale.sch.uk
web: www.brownhill.
rochdale.sch.uk
Head: Lesley Persico
No. of pupils: 70
Age range: 7-16
Funding: LEA
Type of School: Day
Special Needs: SEBO

Calder View School
March Street
Burnley
BB12 0BU
No. of pupils: 144
Age range: 5-16

Cedar House School
Kirkby Lonsdale
Carnforth
LA6 2HW
☎ 01524 271181
Head: Mrs G Ridgway
No. of pupils: 70
Age range: 9-16
Type of School: Day/
Residential
Special Needs: Emotional
and behavioural difficulties
and learning difficulties

Cribden House School
Haslingden
Rawtenstall
Rossendale
BB4 6RX
No. of pupils: 27
Age range: 5-11

Crosshill School
Shadsworth Road
Blackburn
BB1 2HR
☎ 01254 667 713
No. of pupils: 142
Age range: 5-16

Crowthorn School
(NCH Action for
Children)
Broadhead Road
Edgworth
Bolton
BL7 0JS
☎ 01204 852 143
▤ 01204 853 682
Head: Mr Stan Forster
No. of pupils: 65
Age range: 7-16
Funding: Voluntary
Type of School: Day
Special Needs: Dyspraxia

Dame Evelyn Fox School
Roman Road
Blackburn
BB1 2LA
☎ 01254 56808
No. of pupils: 112
Age range: 2-19

Elms School
Moor Park
Blackpool Road
Preston
PR1 6AU
☎ 01772 792 681
▤ 01772 654 940
Head: Ms Carol Murphy
No. of pupils: 70

Age range: 2-19
Funding: LEA
Type of School: Day
Special Needs: Profound &
Multiple Learning
Difficulties

Ferney Field School
Hunt Lane
Chadderton
Oldham
OL9 0LS
No. of pupils: 120
Age range: 5-11

Firwood School
Crompton Way
Bolton
BL2 3AF
☎ 01204 333 044
▤ 01204 333 045
No. of pupils: 83
Age range: 11-19

Foxdenton School
Foxdenton Lane
Chadderton
Oldham
OL9 9QR
☎ 0161 284 5335
▤ 0161 284 5338
Head: Ms Mel R Farrar
No. of pupils: 107
Age range: 2-11
Funding: LEA
Type of School: Day
Special Needs: Moderate
Learning Difficulties

**Garth House Assessment
Centre**
25 Snadycroft
Farringdon Lane
Ribbleton
Preston
PR2 6LX

Gibfield School
Gibfield Road
Colne
BB8 8JT
No. of pupils: 134
Age range: 5-16

Gorse Bank School
Foxdenton Lane
Chadderton
Oldham
OL9 9QR
☎ 0161 284 5168
▤ 0161 284 5225
Head: Mrs A Greaves
No. of pupils: 55

Age range: 5-19
Funding: LEA
Type of School: Day
Special Needs: Profound &
Multiple Learning
Difficulties

Great Arley School
Holly Road
Thornton Cleveleys
FY5 4HH
No. of pupils: 96
Age range: 4-16

High Birch School
Bolton Road
Rochdale
OL11 4RA
☎ 01706 631752
▤ 01706 642663
email: the head@highbirch.
rochdale.school.uk.org
web: www.highbirch.
rochdale.school.uk.org
Deputy head/Acting head:
Mrs J Herring
No. of pupils: 142
Age range: 3-19
Funding: LEA
Type of School: Day
Special Needs: SLD/MLD

Highfurlong School
Blackpool Old Road
Blackpool
FY3 7LR
☎ 01253 392 188
Age range: 3-19

Hill Top School
Arncliffe Rise
Pennine Meadows
Oldham
OL4 2LZ
☎ 0161 620 6070
▤ 0161 624 3558
email: ELS.Hilltop@
oldham.gov.uk
web: www.oldham.gov.uk
Acting Head: Mr S
L'Estrange
No. of pupils: 57
Age range: 11-19
Funding: LEA
Type of School: Day
Special Needs: Specific
Learning Difficulties

Hillside School
Ribchester Road
Longridge
Preston
PR3 3XB

☎ 01772 782205
▤ 01772 782471
email: head@
hillside.lancsngfl.ac.uk
Head: Mr G T Fitzpatrick
No. of pupils: 60
Age range: 2-16
Funding: LEA
Type of School: Day
Special Needs: Autism

**Hindley Borsdane Brook
School**
Park Centre
Park Road
Hindley
Wigan
WN2 3RY
☎ 01942 259 378
▤ 01942 526 147
No. of pupils: 180
Age range: 5-16
Funding: LEA
Type of School: Day
Special Needs: Moderate
Learning Difficulties

Hope School
Kelvin Grove
Marks Bridge
Wigan
WN3 6SP
☎ 01942 824 150
▤ 01942 230 361
Head: Mr P Dahlstrom
No. of pupils: 120
Age range: 2-19
Funding: LEA
Type of School: Day
Special Needs: Profound &
Multiple Learning
Difficulties

Innes School
Ings Lane
Rochdale
OL12 7AL
☎ 01706 646 605
▤ 01706 648 783
email: office@
innes.rochdale.sch.uk
Head: Mrs Ann Wilson
No. of pupils: 65
Age range: 2-19
Funding: LEA
Type of School: Day
Special Needs: Profound &
Multiple Learning
Difficulties

Kingsbury School
School Lane

7

Skelmersdale
WN8 8EH
☎ 01695 722 991
🖷 01695 722 991
email:
kingsbry1st@aol.com
web: www.aol.com
Head: Mr John Hajnrych
No. of pupils: 60
Age range: 2-19
Funding: LEA
Type of School: Day
Special Needs: Profound &
Multiple Learning
Difficulties

Larches House School
Larches Lane
Preston
PR2 1QE
☎ 01772 728 567
🖷 01772 723 294
Age range: 11-15
Type of School: Pupil
Referral Unit

Lever Park School
Stocks Park Drive
Horwich
Bolton
BL6 6DE
☎ 01204 691 608
🖷 01204 698 858
Head: J H Young
No. of pupils: 49
Age range: 8-16
Funding: LEA
Type of School: Day
Special Needs: Emotional
& behavioural difficulties

Lostock Park School
Tempest Road
Bolton
BL6 4EL
Age range: 12-16

Marland Fold School
Rosary Road
Fitton Hill
Oldham
OL8 2RP
☎ 0161 911 3175
No. of pupils: 105
Age range: 11-19
Special Needs: Moderate
Learning Difficulties and
Severe & Profound &
Multiple Learning
Difficulties

Massey Hall School
Half Acre Lane

Thelwall
Warrington
WA4 3JQ
☎ 01925 752016
🖷 01925 756308
Head: Mr C Gleave
No. of pupils: 46
Age range: 10-16
Funding: LEA
Type of School: Residential
Special Needs: Emotional
& behavioural difficulties

Mayfield School
Gloucester Road
Chorley
PR7 3HN
☎ 01257 263 063
🖷 01257 263 072
Head: Mr Peter Monk
No. of pupils: 60
Age range: 2-19
Funding: LEA
Type of School: Day
Special Needs: Profound &
Multiple Learning
Difficulties

Mere Oaks School
Wigan Road
Boars Head
Standish
Wigan
WN1 2RF
☎ 01942 243 481
🖷 01942 231 121
email: enquiries@aimw.
mereoaks.wigan.scu.uk
web: mereoaks.co.uk
Head: Mrs J Leach
No. of pupils: 123
Age range: 2-19
Funding: LEA
Type of School: Day
Special Needs: Physical
disabilities

Montrose School
Montrose Avenue
Pemberton
Wigan
WN5 9XN
☎ 01942 223 431
Head: Mr Alan Farmer
No. of pupils: 126
Age range: 7-16
Funding: LEA
Type of School: Day
Special Needs: Moderate
Learning Difficulties

Moor Hey School
Far Croft

Lostock Hall
Preston
PR5 5SS
☎ 01772 336 976
🖷 01772 696 670
Head: Mr C W T Wilson
No. of pupils: 100
Age range: 5-16
Funding: LEA
Type of School: Day
Special Needs: Moderate
Learning Difficulties

Moorbrook School
Ainslie Road
Preston
PR2 3DB
☎ 01772 774752
🖷 01772 713256
Acting Head: Mrs W Fisher
No. of pupils: 40
Age range: 11-16
Funding: LEA
Type of School: Day
Special Needs: Emotional
& Behavioural Difficulties

Moorfield School
Moor Park
Preston
PR1 6AA
No. of pupils: 68
Age range: 2-19

Morecambe Road School
Morecambe Road
Morecambe
LA3 3AB
Age range: 3-16

North Cliffe School
Blackburn Old Road
Great Harwood
Blackburn
BB6 7UW
☎ 01254 885 245
🖷 01254 877 953
email: head@
north-cliffe.lancsngfl.ac.uk
Head: Mr R L Whitaker
No. of pupils: 65
Age range: 5-16
Funding: LEA
Type of School: Day
Special Needs: Moderate
Learning Difficulties

Nugent House School
Carr Mill Road
Billinge
Wigan
WN5 7TT

☎ 01744 892551
🖷 01744 895697
email: jane.bienias@
zen.co.uk
No. of pupils: 93
Age range: 7-19

Park Dean School
St Martin's Road
Fitton Hill
Oldham
OL8 2PZ
☎ 0161 620 0231
🖷 0161 633 9534
email: info@
parkdean.oldham.sch.uk
Head: Mr G Quinn
No. of pupils: 115
Age range: 2-19
Funding: LEA
Type of School: Day
Special Needs: Physical &
Sensory Impairments

Park School
158 Whitegate Drive
Blackpool
FY3 9HF
☎ 01253 764 130
🖷 01253 791 108
Head: Mr Keith Berry
No. of pupils: 145
Age range: 4-16
Funding: LEA
Type of School: Day
Special Needs: Moderate
Learning Difficulties

Parkside School
Aughton Street
Ormskirk
L39 3BS
Age range: 2-18

Pear Tree School
29 Station Road
Kirkham
Preston
PR4 2HA
No. of pupils: 58
Age range: 2-19

Pontville Special School
Blackmoss Lane
Ormskirk
L39 4TW
☎ 01695 578 734
🖷 01695 579 224
email: office@
pontville.co.uk
web: www.pontville.co.uk
Head: Mr Richard Farbon

No. of pupils: 62
Age range: 11-19
Funding: Independent
Type of School:
Residential/Day
Special Needs: Moderate
Learning Difficulties

Primrose Hill School
Harrogate Crescent
Burnley
BB10 2NX
☎ 01282 424 216
🖳 01282 831 415
email: school@
primrose23.lancsngfl.ac.uk
Head: Mr Gerard McCabe
No. of pupils: 45
Age range: 4-16
Funding: LEA
Type of School: Day
Special Needs: Physical
difficulties

Red Marsh School
Holly Road
Thornton Cleveleys
FY5 4HH
☎ 01253 868451
🖳 01253 868451
email: head@
red-marsh.lancsngfl.ac.uk
Head: Miss D Halpin
No. of pupils: 37
Age range: 2-19
Funding: LEA
Type of School: Day
Special Needs: Severe
Learning Difficulties

Rose Hill Senior School
Park Road
Hindley
Wigan
WN2 3RY
☎ 01942 258 975
🖳 01942 271 627
Head: Mr M Myerscough
No. of pupils: 76
Age range: 11-16
Funding: LEA
Type of School: Day
Special Needs: Emotional
& behavioural difficulties

Rossendale School
Bamford Road
Ramsbottom
BL0 0RT
☎ 01706 822779
🖳 01706 821457
email: peter.cheetham@
bosinternet.com

Head: Mr D G Duncan
No. of pupils: 56
Age range: 8-16
Funding: LEA
Type of School: Day &
Weekly term-time boarding
Special Needs: Emotional
& behavioural difficulties

**Royal Cross Primary
School**
Elswick Road
Ashton-on-Ribble
Preston
PR2 1NT
☎ 01772 729705
🖳 01772 729866
email: head@
lancsngfl.ac.uk
web: www.wemp.
freeserve.co.uk/rcps
Head: Ms Ruth
Nottingham
No. of pupils: 30
Age range: 4-11
Funding: LEA/
Community Special School
Type of School: Day
Special Needs: Hearing
Impaired and Speech/
Language Difficulties

**Secondary Pupil Referral
Service**
The Globe Centre
St. James Square
Accrington
BB5 0RE
☎ 01254 220794
email: caroline.potteroed.
lancscc.gov.uk
Head: Caroline Potter
No. of pupils: 86
Age range: 11-16
Funding: LEA
Special Needs: PRU
Excluded pupils

Sherburn School
Moor Park
Blackpool Road
Preston
PR1 6AA
☎ 01772 795 749
🖳 01772 652 096
email: head@
sherburn.lancsngfl.ac.uk
Head: Mr M R Moss
No. of pupils: 86
Age range: 4-16
Funding: LEA
Type of School: Day

Special Needs: Moderate
Learning Difficulties

Stocks Park School
Stocks Park Drive
Horwich
Bolton
BL6 4DE
No. of pupils: 36
Age range: 6-12

Summerseat School
Summerseat Lane
Holcombe Brook
Ramsbottom
Bury
BL0 9UD
Age range: 7-17

**Tameside Home and
Hospital Teaching Service**
Boiler House Cottage
Tameside General Hospital
Fountain Street
Ashton-under-Lyne
OL6 9RW
☎ 0161 331 6772
🖳 0161 331 6772
Head: Mr Malcolm Knight
Age range: 5-16
Funding: Hospital
Type of School: Day
Special Needs: Emotional
& behavioural difficulties

Tanfield School
Borsdane Avenue
Hindley
Wigan
WN2 3HJ
No. of pupils: 82
Age range: 2-19

The Coppice School
Ash Grove
Bamber Bridge
Preston
PR5 6GY
☎ 01772 336342
🖳 01772 620826
email: head@
coppice.lancsngfl.ac.uk
Head: Mrs A Jenkins
No. of pupils: 63
Age range: 2-19
Funding: LEA
Type of School: Day
Special Needs: Severe
Learning Difficulties

The Loyne School
Sefton Drive
Lancaster

LA1 2PZ
☎ 01524 64543
🖳 01524 845 118
Head: Dr Jonathan Steele
No. of pupils: 60
Age range: 2-19
Funding: LEA
Type of School: Day
Special Needs: Profound &
Multiple Learning
Difficulties

**Thomasson Memorial
School**
Devonshire Road
Bolton
BL1 4PJ
☎ 01204 843063
🖳 01204 495675
Age range: 3-17

Tor View School
Clod Lane
Haslingden
Rossendale
BB4 6LR
☎ 01706 214 640
🖳 01706 215 797
email: office@
torview.lancsngfl.ac.uk
web: www.torview.
lancsngfl.ac.uk
Head: Mr Andy Squire
No. of pupils: 106
Age range: 4-19
Funding: LEA
Type of School: Day
Special Needs: Wide range

Townhouse Special School
Townhouse Road
Nelson
BB9 8DG
☎ 01282 614 013
🖳 01282 691970
email: head@
townhouse.lancsngfl.ac.uk
Head: Mrs D Morris
No. of pupils: 42
Age range: 2-19
Funding: LEA
Type of School: Day
Special Needs: Profound &
Multiple Learning
Difficulties/Autism/HI/VI/
Severe learning difficulties/
PD

Tullyallan School
Salisbury Road
Darwen

7

BB3 1HZ
☎ 01254 702 317
🖷 01254 761 235
Head: Mrs Jill P Holman
No. of pupils: 50
Age range: 5-16
Funding: LEA
Type of School: Day
Special Needs: Emotional
& behavioural difficulties

Underley Hall School
Kirkby Lonsdale
Carnforth
LA6 2HE
☎ 015242 71206
🖷 015242 72581
email: underleyes@
hotmail.com
Head: Mr John Parkinson
No. of pupils: 70
Age range: 9-16
Funding: Independent
Type of School: Residential
Special Needs: Emotional
& Behavioural Difficulties

Wennington Hall School
Lodge Lane
Wennington
Lancaster
LA2 8NS
☎ 01524 221 333
🖷 01524 222 140
Head: Mr J W N
Prendergast
No. of pupils: 70
Age range: 11-16
Funding: LEA
Type of School: Residential
Special Needs: Emotional
& behavioural difficulties

Westway School
March Street
Burnley
BB12 0BU
☎ 01282 704499
🖷 01282 704500
email: head@
westway.lancsngfl.ac.uk
Associate Head: Mrs J
Greck
No. of pupils: 30
Age range: 3-19
Funding: LEA
Type of School: Day
Special Needs: Severe and
Profound & Multiple
Learning Difficulties

White Ash School
Thwaites Road

Oswaldtwistle
BB5 4QG
☎ 01254 235 772
🖷 01254 385 652
email: head@
whiteash.lancsngfl.ac.uk
web: www.whiteash.
lancsngfl.ac.uk
Head: Mr B D Frew
No. of pupils: 40
Age range: 3-19
Funding: LEA
Type of School: Day
Special Needs: Profound &
Multiple Learning
Difficulties/Severe Learning
Difficulties/Autism

**Willow Grove Primary
School**
Willow Grove
Ashton-in-Makerfield
Wigan
WN4 8XF
☎ 01942 727 717
🖷 01942 271 627
Head: Mrs V Pearson
No. of pupils: 56
Age range: 5-11
Funding: LEA
Type of School: Day
Special Needs: Emotional
& behavioural difficulties

Woodlands School
Whitegate Drive
Blackpool
FY3 9HF
☎ 01253 316 722
🖷 01253 316 723
email: admin@woodlands.
blackpool.sch.uk
web: www.woodlands.
blackpool.sch.uk
Head: Mr S J Forde
No. of pupils: 86
Age range: 2-19
Funding: LEA
Type of School: Day
Special Needs: Profound &
Multiple Learning
Difficulties

Woodside Junior School
425 Chorley New Road
Bolton
BL1 5DH
Age range: 5-12

**Wrightington Hospital
Education Unit**
Ward 1
Hall Lane

Wigan
WN6 9EP
Age range: 4-16

Wyredale School
Fuldrey Avenue
Poulton-le-Fylde
FY6 7HE
Age range: 11-16

Leicestershire

Emily Fortey School
Glenfield Road
Leicester
LE3 6DG
☎ 0116 285 7395
🖷 0116 254 6493
email: adminoffice@
emilyfortey.leicester.sch.uk
web: www.emilyfortey.
leicester.sch.uk
Head: Mr M W
Thompson
No. of pupils: 80
Age range: 4-19
Type of School: Day
Special Needs: Speech and
Language Disorder

Ash Field School
Broad Avenue
Leicester
LE5 4PY
☎ 0116 273 7151
🖷 0116 273 9962
Head: Mr David Bateson
No. of pupils: 120
Age range: 5-19
Funding: LEA
Type of School: Day
Special Needs: Physical
disabilities

Ashmount School
Beacon Road
Loughborough
LE11 2BG
No. of pupils: 58
Age range: 3-19

Birkett House School
Launceston Road
Wigston
Leicester
LE18 2FZ
☎ 0116 288 5802
🖷 0116 257 1932
Head: Mr S Welton
No. of pupils: 75
Age range: 5-19
Funding: LEA

Type of School: Residential
Special Needs: Profound &
Multiple Learning
Difficulties

Children's Hospital School
Leicester Royal Infirmary
(NHS Trust)
Leicester
LE1 5WW
☎ 0116 258 5330
🖷 0116 247 1060
email: office@
chslri.demon.co.uk
web: www.chslri.
demon.co.uk
Head: Mr A Osborne
No. of pupils: 116
Age range: 2-19
Funding: Independent
Type of School: Hospital
Special Needs: Medical

Craven Lodge School
Burton Road
Melton Mowbray
LE13 1DJ
Age range: 5-11

Dorothy Goodman School
Middlefield Lane
Hinckley
LE10 0RB
☎ 01455 634 582
🖷 01455 613 667
email: info@
dorothygoodman.leics.sch.uk
Head: Mr Tony Smith
No. of pupils: 66
Age range: 3-19
Funding: LEA
Type of School: Day
Special Needs: Autism and
Severe Learning
Difficulties, Profound &
Multiple Learning
Difficulties

Forest Way School
Cropston Drive
Coalville
LE67 4HS
☎ 01530 831 899
🖷 01530 814 069
email: forestway@
forestway.leics.sch.uk
Head: Ms Lynn Slinger
No. of pupils: 93
Age range: 3-19
Funding: LEA
Type of School: Day
Special Needs: Severe
Learning Difficulties

Greenacres School
Glenfield Road
Leicester
LE3 6DN
Age range: 5-19

Manorbrooke School
Carisbrooke Road
Leicester
LE2 3PB
Age range: 7-16

Maplewell Hall School
Maplewell Road
Woodhouse Eaves
Loughborough
LE12 8QY
Age range: 11-19

Nether Hall School
Netherhall Road
Leicester
LE5 1DT
☎ 0116 241 7258
🖷 0116 241 7259
Head: Mr P J Goodchild
No. of pupils: 85
Age range: 5-19
Funding: LEA
Type of School: Day
Special Needs: Profound &
Multiple Learning
Difficulties

The Grange School
Knossington
Oakham
LE15 8LY
☎ 01664 454 264
Age range: 8-16

The Millgate Centre
18A Scott Street
Leicester
LE2 6DW
☎ 0116 270 4922
🖷 0116 270 8753
Head: N J Shaw
No. of pupils: 46
Age range: 11-16
Funding: LEA
Type of School: Boarding
Special Needs: Emotional
& behavioural difficulties

The Mount School
The Mount
Leicester Road
Melton Mowbray
LE13 0DA
☎ 01664 562418
🖷 01664 410281

email: admin@
themount.leics.sch.uk
Head: Mr P Henshaw
No. of pupils: 25
Age range: 5-19
Funding: LEA
Type of School: Day
Special Needs: Severe
Learning Difficulties and
Profound & Multiple
Learning Difficulties

Western Park School
Western Park
Leicester
LE3 6HX
No. of pupils: 41
Age range: 5-19

Lewisham

New Woodlands School
49 Shroffold Road
Downham
Bromley
BR1 5PD
☎ 020 8314 9911
🖷 020 8314 3475
email: newwoodlands
school@hotmail.com
Head: Mr D Harper
No. of pupils: 40
Age range: 5-11
Funding: LEA
Type of School: Day
Special Needs: Emotional
& Behavioural Difficulties

Lincolnshire

Ambergate School
Dysart Road
Grantham
NG31 7LP
☎ 01476 564 957
🖷 01476 573 870
Head: Ms Cynthia Jones
No. of pupils: 64
Age range: 5-16
Funding: LEA
Type of School: Day
Special Needs: Profound &
Multiple Learning
Difficulties

Ash Villa School
Willoughby Road
South Rauceby
Sleaford
NG34 8PP
☎ 01529 416 046
🖷 01529 488 239

Head: Mr Dale Robinson
No. of pupils: 20
Age range: 8-16
Funding: LEA
Type of School: Day
Special Needs: Wide range

Broughton House College
Brant Broughton
Lincoln
LN5 0SL
☎ 01400 272 929
🖷 01400 273 438
Head: Mr Bob Noble
No. of pupils: 23
Age range: 16-25
Funding: Independent
Special Needs: Severe
Learning Difficulties &
Autism

Deighton Close School
Deighton Close
Louth
LN11 0RS
☎ 01507 605287
🖷 01507 610341
email: enquiries@
deighton-close.lincs.sch.uk
Head: Mr David Fuller
No. of pupils: 69
Age range: 6-16
Funding: LEA
Type of School: Day
Special Needs: Emotional
& behavioural difficulties

Eresby Special School
Eresby Avenue
Spilsby
PE23 5HU
☎ 01790 752 441
Head: Mr Dave
Middlehurst
No. of pupils: 41
Age range: 2-19
Funding: LEA
Type of School: Day
Special Needs: Wide range

Garth School
Pinchbeck Road
Spalding
PE11 1QF
☎ 01775 725566
🖷 01775 768829
email: enquiries@
garth.lines.sch.uk
web:
www.garthschool.co.uk
Head: Mrs L Dowson
No. of pupils: 30

Age range: 2-19
Funding: LEA
Type of School: Day
Special Needs: Severe
Learning Difficulties

Gosberton House School
11 Westhorpe Road
Gosberton
Spalding
PE11 4EW
☎ 01775 840 250
🖷 01775 841 017
Head: Ms L Stanton
Age range: 5-11
Funding: LEA
Type of School: Day
Special Needs: Moderate
Learning Difficulties/
Autistic Spectrum Disorder

John Fielding School
Ashlawn Drive
Boston
PE21 9PX
☎ 01205 363 395
🖷 01205 357 696
Head: Sandra Meakin
No. of pupils: 30
Age range: 2-19
Funding: LEA
Type of School: Day
Special Needs: Severe
Learning Difficulties

Kisimul School
The Old Vicarage
High Street
Swinderby
LN6 9LU
☎ 01522 868 279
🖷 01522 866 000
email: sueshaw@
kisimul.co.uk
web: www.kisimul.co.uk
Head: Mrs S J Shaw
No. of pupils: 28
Age range: 10-19
Funding: Independent
Type of School: Residential
Special Needs: Autism and
Severe Learning Difficulties

Pilgrim Hospital School
(School Office) 4th Floor
Sibsey Road
Fishtoft
Boston
PE21 9QS
☎ 01205 364801 Ext 2641
🖷 01205 368151
email: enquiries@
pilgrimhospital.lincs.sch.uk

7

Head: Mrs C M Seymour
Age range: 0-16
Funding: LEA
Type of School: Hospital

Queen's Park School
South Park
Lincoln
LN5 8EW
No. of pupils: 98
Age range: 3-19

Sandon School
Sandon Close
Grantham
NG31 9AX
☎ 01476 564 994
🖷 01476 592 195
Head: Mrs Janet M Roddis
No. of pupils: 55
Age range: 2-19
Funding: LEA
Type of School: Day
Special Needs: Severe
Learning Difficulties

St Bernards School
Wood Lane
Louth
LN11 8RS
☎ 01507 603 776
🖷 01507 603 914
email: stbersch@aol.com
web: www.aol.com
Head: Mr Mike Warren
No. of pupils: 50
Age range: 2-19
Funding: LEA
Type of School: Day
Special Needs: Wide range

St Christopher's School
Hykeham Road
Lincoln
LN6 8AR
☎ 01522 528 378
🖷 01522 521 110
Head: Miss M Evans
No. of pupils: 155
Age range: 4-16
Funding: LEA
Type of School: Day
Special Needs: Assessment
Centre

St Francis School
Wickenby Crescent
Lincoln
LN1 3TJ
No. of pupils: 83
Age range: 2-18

St Lawrence School
Bowl Alley Lane
Horncastle
LN9 5EJ
☎ 01507 522563
🖷 01507 522974
email: enquiries@st-
lawrence-special.lincs.sch.uk
Head: Mr D Smith
No. of pupils: 120
Age range: 5-16
Funding: LEA
Type of School: Day &
Boarding
Special Needs: Moderate
Learning Difficulties

The Beckett School
White's Wood Lane
Gainsborough
DN21 1TW
☎ 01427 612 139
🖷 01427 616 776
email: susan.hayter@
beckett.lincs.sch.uk
Head: Ms Susan Hayter
No. of pupils: 27
Age range: 2-19
Funding: LEA
Type of School: Day
Special Needs: Severe
Learning Difficulties

The Priory School
Neville Avenue
Spalding
PE11 2EH
☎ 01775 724 080
🖷 01775 713 860
email: priorysch@aol.com
web: www.aol.com
Head: Mr Brian Howes
No. of pupils: 90
Age range: 11-16
Funding: LEA
Type of School: Day
Special Needs: Moderate
Learning Difficulties

**The William Harrison
School**
Middlefield Lane
Gainsborough
DN21 1PU
☎ 01427 615498
🖷 01427 615498
email: sheenagh.swlt@
william-harrison.lincs.sch.uk
Head: Dr M J Blackband
No. of pupils: 103
Age range: 3-16
Funding: LEA

Type of School: Day
Special Needs: Moderate
Learning Difficulties,
Autism and Speech &
Language

The Willoughby School
South Road
Bourne
PE10 9JE
No. of pupils: 61
Age range: 2-19

Liverpool

Watergate School
Speke Road
Liverpool
L25 8QA
☎ 0151 428 5812
email: watergate-ao@
watergate.liverpool.sch.uk
Head: Mr P J Richardson
No. of pupils: 129
Age range: 4-16
Funding: LEA
Type of School: Day
Special Needs: Complex
Learning and language
Difficulties

Luton

Mill Hill County High
Oak Hill Campus
Church Hill Road
East Barnet
EN4 8XE
☎ 020 8361 4639
🖷 020 8361 4435
email: Mdingwall@
oakhillschool.org.uk
Head: Mr Michael
Dingwall
No. of pupils: 34
Age range: 11-16
Funding: LEA
Type of School: Day
Special Needs: Emotional
& Behavioural Difficulties

William C Harvey School
Adams Road
London
N17 6HW
☎ 020 8808 7120
🖷 020 8885 2719
email: office@
wch.haringey.sch.uk
web: portablesl.ngfl.gov.uk/
dwgodfrey/
Head: Ms M Sumner

No. of pupils: 70
Age range: 4-19
Funding: LEA
Type of School: Day
Special Needs: SLD, PMLD

Oaklands School
Woodlands Road
Isleworth
TW7 6JZ
☎ 0208 560 3569
🖷 0208 568 8805
Head: Mrs Elizabeth
Felstead
No. of pupils: 72
Age range: 11-19
Funding: LEA
Type of School: Day
Special Needs: Severe
learning difficulties

Richmond Hill School
Sunridge Avenue
Luton
LU2 7JL
☎ 01582 721 019
🖷 01582 453093
email: richmond.hill.
admin@luton.gov.uk
Head: Mrs J Jackson
No. of pupils: 70
Age range: 5-11
Special Needs: Complex
Learning Difficulties

**Woodlands Secondary
School**
Northwell Drive
Luton
LU3 3SP
☎ 01582 572 880
🖷 01582 565506
Head: Mrs S Read
No. of pupils: 132
Age range: 11-19
Funding: LEA
Type of School: Day
Special Needs: Severe,
Complex, Profound and
Multiple Learning
Difficulties and ASD

Manchester

Camberwell Park School
Bank House Road
Blackley
Manchester
M9 8LT
☎ 0161 740 1897
🖷 0161 740 3473
Head: Pam Stanier

Age range: 2-11
Funding: LEA
Type of School: Day
Special Needs: Severe
Learning Difficulties

Ewing School
Central Road
Didsbury
Manchester
M20 4ZA
☎ 0161 445 0745
🖹 0161 438 0510
Head: Pat Derbyshire
No. of pupils: 78
Age range: 5-16
Funding: LEA
Type of School: Day
Special Needs: Speech and
Language Disorder

Newbrook School
Newholme Road
West Didsbury
Manchester
M20 2XZ
☎ 0161 445 5172
🖹 0161 438 0058
Bursar: Mrs Gregson
Age range: 2-16
Funding: LEA
Type of School: Day
Special Needs: Hearing
Impaired

The Birches School
Newholme Road
West Didsbury
Manchester
M20 2XZ
☎ 0161 448 8894
🖹 0161 445 4970
email: head.thebirches@
mecgrid.org.uk
Head: Mrs Marie Morgan
No. of pupils: 95
Age range: 2-11
Funding: LEA
Type of School: Day
Special Needs: Severe
Learning Difficulties and
Profound & Multiple
Learning Difficulties

Medway Council

The Danecourt School
Hotel Road
Watling Street
Gillingham
ME8 6AA
☎ 01634 232 589

🖹 01634 263 822
email: PETEA002@
medway.org.uk
Head: Mrs Ann Peters
No. of pupils: 112
Age range: 4-11
Funding: LEA
Type of School: Day
Special Needs: Multiple
Learning Difficulties

Merseyside

Abbots Lea School
Beaconsfield Road
Liverpool
L25 6EE
No. of pupils: 55
Age range: 4-16

Alder Hey School
Eaton Road
Liverpool
L12 2AP
☎ 0151 228 4811
🖹 0151 225 5366
Head: Mr Paul Morrison
Funding: LEA
Type of School: Hospital
Special Needs: Medical

Alice Elliott School
Childwall Abbey Road
Liverpool
L16 5EY
Age range: 2-16

**Arrowe Park Hospital
School**
Arrowe Park Road
Upton
Wirral
L49 5PE
Age range: 2-19

Capenhurst Grange School
Chester Road
Great Sutton
South Wirral
L66 2NA
☎ 0151 339 5141
🖹 0151 348 0348
No. of pupils: 57
Age range: 11-16

**Central Primary Support
Centre**
Mossbrow Road
Huyton
L36 7SY
Age range: 5-16
Funding: LEA

Special Needs: Moderate
Learning Difficulties

Clare Mount School
Fender Lane
Moreton
Wirral
CH46 9PA
No. of pupils: 218
Age range: 11-19

Clarence House School
31 West Lane
Freshfield
Formby
L37 7AZ
☎ 01704 872 151
🖹 01704 831 001
Head: Ms Moria Bird
No. of pupils: 119
Age range: 8-16
Funding: Voluntary
Type of School: Residential
Special Needs: Emotional
& behavioural difficulties

Clatterbridge School
Bebington
Wirral
L63 4JY
Age range: 3-13

Elleray Park School
Elleray Park Road
Wallasey
Wirral
CH45 0LH
☎ 0151 639 3594
🖹 0151 638 8823
Head: Mr David Quaife
No. of pupils: 80
Age range: 2-11
Funding: LEA
Type of School: Day
Special Needs: Complex
learning difficulties

Ernest Cookson School
Mill Lane
West Derby
Liverpool
L12 7JA
☎ 0151 220 1874
🖹 0151 252 1238
Head: Mr S W Roberts
No. of pupils: 50
Age range: 5-16
Funding: LEA
Type of School: Day
Special Needs: Emotional
& behavioural difficulties

Finchlea School
Mill Lane
Old Swan
Liverpool
L13 5TF
☎ 0151 228 2578
No. of pupils: 30
Age range: 4-19

Foxfield School
Douglas Drive
Moreton
Wirral
L46 6BT
☎ 0151 677 8555
🖹 0151 678 5480
Head: Mr Andre Baird
No. of pupils: 100
Age range: 11-19
Funding: LEA
Type of School: Day
Special Needs: Profound &
Multiple Learning
Difficulties

Gilbrook School
Pilgrim Street
Birkenhead
L41 5EH
Age range: 4-11

Grantside School
Mill Road
Liverpool
L6 2AS
No. of pupils: 41
Age range: 8-16

Greenways School
Beechwood Road South
Grassendale
Liverpool
L19 0LD
☎ 0151 427 1175
🖹 0151 4275343
email: greenways-ht@
greenways.liverpool.sch.uk
Head: Mrs D Williams
No. of pupils: 25
Age range: 3-7
Funding: LEA
Type of School: Day
Special Needs: Assessment
Centre

Hamblett School
Rainford Road
St Helens
WA10 6BX
☎ 01744 678770
🖹 01744 678772
Head: Mr R Brownlow

7

No. of pupils: 60
Age range: 3-16
Funding: LEA
Type of School: Day
Special Needs: Medical,
Autism

Harold Magnay School
Woolton Hill Road
Liverpool
L25 6JA
☎ 0151 428 6305
🗎 0151 428 1103
Head: Mr Mark Little
No. of pupils: 75
Age range: 2-11
Funding: LEA
Type of School: Day
Special Needs: Physical
disabilities

Hayfield School
Manor Drive
Upton
Wirral
CH49 4LN
☎ 0151 677 9303
No. of pupils: 120
Age range: 4-11

Highfield School
Bailey Lane
Halewood
Liverpool
L26 0TY
No. of pupils: 47
Age range: 6-16

Hurst School
Hard Lane
St Helens
WA10 6PN
☎ 01744 25643
🗎 01744 616310
email: hurst@
sthelens.org.uk
Head: Mr M J Carolan
No. of pupils: 170
Age range: 4-16
Funding: LEA
Type of School: Day
Special Needs: Multiple
Learning Difficulties

Kilgarth School
Cavendish Street
Birkenhead
Wirral
CH41 8BA
☎ 0151 652 8071
🗎 0151 653 3427
email: Schooloffice@

kilgarth.wirral.sch.uk
Head: Ms J M Dawson
No. of pupils: 53
Age range: 11-16
Funding: LEA
Special Needs: Emotional
& behavioural difficulties

**Knowsley Southern
Primary Support Centre**
Arncliffe Road
Halewood
Liverpool
L25 9QE
No. of pupils: 39
Age range: 5-18

Longmoor School
Sherwoods Lane
Fazakerley
Liverpool
L10 1LW
☎ 0151 525 5733
No. of pupils: 100
Age range: 2-19

Lower Lee School
Beaconsfield Road
Woolton
Liverpool
L25 6EF
☎ 0151 428 4071
🗎 0151 428 4737
Head: Mr Paul Wright
No. of pupils: 45
Age range: 7-17
Funding: LEA
Type of School: Boarding
Special Needs: Emotional
& behavioural difficulties

Margaret Beavan School
Almonds Green
West Derby
L12 5HP
☎ 0151 226 1306
Acting Head: Mrs P Favour
No. of pupils: 139
Age range: 4-17
Funding: LEA
Type of School: Day
Special Needs: Multiple
Learning Difficulties

Meadow Bank School
Sherwoods Lane
Fazakerley
Liverpool
L10 1LW
☎ 0151 525 3451
🗎 0151 524 1284
Head: Mrs Carole Clancy

No. of pupils: 141
Age range: 5-17
Funding: LEA
Type of School: Day
Special Needs: Speech and
Language Difficulties

Meadowside School
Pool Lane
Woodchurch
Birkenhead
L49 5LR
☎ 0151 678 7711
🗎 0151 678 9155
Head: Ms L Kane
No. of pupils: 78
Age range: 11-19
Funding: LEA
Type of School: Day
Special Needs: Profound &
Multiple Learning
Difficulties

Merefield School
Westminster Drive
Southport
PR8 2QZ
☎ 01704 577 163
No. of pupils: 35
Age range: 2-19
Funding: LEA
Type of School: Day
Special Needs: Profound &
Multiple Learning
Difficulties

**Mersey View Special
School**
Minehead Road
Liverpool
L17 6AX
☎ 0151 427 1863
🗎 0151 494 3091
email: merseyview-ao@
merseyview.liverpool.sch.uk
No. of pupils: 95
Age range: 5-16
Funding: LEA
Type of School: Day
Special Needs: Complex
Learning Difficulties

Mill Green School
Mill Lane
Newton-le-Willows
WA12 8BG
☎ 01744 678760
🗎 01774678761
email: millgreen@
sthelens.org.uk
Head: Mr Paul Cronin
No. of pupils: 82

Age range: 2-19
Funding: LEA
Type of School: Day
Special Needs: Profound &
Multiple Learning
Difficulties

**Millstead Special Needs
Primary School**
Old Mill Lane
Wavertree
Liverpool
L15 8LW
☎ 0151 722 0974
Head: Ms Margaret Lucas
No. of pupils: 50
Age range: 2-11
Funding: LEA
Type of School: Day
Special Needs: Profound &
Multiple Learning
Difficulties

Orrets Meadow School
Chapelhill Road
Moreton
L46 9QQ
☎ 0151 678 8070
🗎 0151 677 4663
Head: Mrs S E Blythe
No. of pupils: 66
Age range: 7-11
Funding: LEA
Type of School: Day
Special Needs: Specific
Learning Difficulties

Palmerston School
Beaconsfield Road
Woolton
Liverpool
L25 6EE
☎ 0151 428 2128
🗎 0151 421 0985
Head: Mr J F Wright
No. of pupils: 63
Age range: 11-19
Funding: LEA
Type of School: Day
Special Needs: Severe
Learning Difficulties &
Profound and Multiple
Learning Difficulties

Parkfield School
Bracknell Avenue
Southdene
Kirkby
L32 9PW
☎ 0151 546 6355
🗎 0151 546 2806
Head: Mr A Taylor

No. of pupils: 72
Age range: 6-17
Funding: LEA
Type of School: Day
Special Needs: Emotional
& behavioural difficulties

**Penkford School &
Resource Centre**
Wharf Road
Newton-le-Willows
WA12 9XZ
Acting Head: Mr D
Hartley
No. of pupils: 98
Age range: 10-16
Funding: LEA
Type of School: Day
Special Needs: Emotional
& Behavioural Difficulties

Princes Primary School
Selborne Street
Toxteth
Liverpool
L8 1YQ
☎ 0151 709 2602
🖷 0151 709 2627
Head: Mrs V Healy
No. of pupils: 61
Age range: 2-11
Funding: LEA
Type of School: Day
Special Needs: Profound &
Multiple Learning
Difficulties, Autism and
Severe Learning
Difficulties

Redbridge High School
Sherwoods Lane
Fazakerley
Liverpool
L10 1LW
☎ 0151 525 5733
🖷 0151 524 0435
email: redbridge-ht@
redbridge.liverpool.sch.uk
Head: Mrs Shelagh Coates
No. of pupils: 90
Age range: 11-19
Funding: LEA
Type of School: Day
Special Needs: Autism,
Profound, Severe and
Multiple Learning
Difficulties

**Rivington County
Primary School**
Hearing Impairment Unit
Tennis Street North

St Helens
WA10 6LF
☎ 01744 27490
🖷 01744 615 015
email: ljtraves@
portables.ngfl.gov.uk
web:
www.portables.ngfl.gov.uk
Head: Mrs L J Traves
No. of pupils: 8
Age range: 3-11
Funding: LEA
Type of School: Day
Special Needs: Hearing
Impaired

**Robins Lane Language
Unit**
Robins Lane CP School
Kimmel Street
St Helens
WA9 3NF
Age range: 4-7

Ronald House School
De Villiers Avenue
Crosby
L23 2TH
☎ 0151 924 3671
🖷 0151 931 5083
Head: Mr S Dempsey
No. of pupils: 125
Age range: 11-16
Funding: LEA
Type of School: Day
Special Needs: Moderate
Learning Difficulties

Rowan Park
Sterrix Lane
Litherlang
Liverpool
L21
Head: Mrs Jane Kelly
No. of pupils: 110
Age range: 2-19
Funding: LEA
Type of School: Day
Special Needs: Severe
Learning Difficulties and
ASD

Rowan Park Lower School
St Lukes Road
Crosby
Liverpool
L23 5SZ
☎ 0151 330 0523
🖷 0151 330 0524
Head: Mrs Jane Kelly
No. of pupils: 38
Age range: 2-11

Funding: LEA
Type of School: Day
Special Needs: Severe
Learning Difficulties

Royal School for the Blind
Church Road North
Wavertree
Liverpool
L15 6TQ
☎ 0151 733 1012
🖷 0151 733 1703
email: rsblind@
globalnet.co.uk
web: www.rsblind.org.uk
Head: Mr J P Byrne
No. of pupils: 54
Age range: 2-19
Funding: Voluntary/charity
Type of School: Day/
Residential
Special Needs: Profound &
Multiple Learning
Difficulties and Hearing
Impaired and Visually
Impaired

Sandfield Park School
Sandfield Walk
Liverpool
L12 1LH
☎ 0151 228 0324
🖷 0151 252 1273
Head: Mr J Hudson
No. of pupils: 75
Age range: 11-19
Funding: LEA
Type of School: Day
Special Needs: Physical
disabilities

**School of The Good
Shepherd**
Sterrix Lane
Liverpool
L21 0DA
☎ 0151 928 6165
Head: Mr Alan Sullivan
No. of pupils: 40
Age range: 2-17
Funding: LEA
Type of School: Day
Special Needs: Medical

Springfield School
Cawthorne Close
Southdene
Kirkby
L32 3XQ
☎ 0151 549 1425
🖷 0151 546 8995
Head: Mr I Cordingley

No. of pupils: 80
Age range: 2-19
Funding: LEA
Type of School: Day
Special Needs: Profound &
Multiple Learning
Difficulties

St Vincent's School
Yew Tree Lane
Liverpool
L12 9HN
No. of pupils: 97
Age range: 4-17

Stanley School
Pensby Road
Thingwall
Wirral
CH61 7UG
☎ 0151 648 3171
🖷 0151 648 6887
Head: Mr A B Newman
No. of pupils: 90
Age range: 2-11
Type of School: Day
Special Needs: Autism and
Complex Learning
Difficulties

**The Phoenix Primary
School**
Lowerson Road
Liverpool
L11 8LW
☎ 0151 226 0309
🖷 0151 287 2200
Acting Head: Ms Brenda
Tonge
No. of pupils: 30
Age range: 2-5
Funding: LEA
Type of School: Day
Special Needs: Wide range

Thingwall House
Thomas Lane
Liverpool
L14 5NS
Age range: 4-16

**West Kirby Residential
School**
Meols Drive
West Kirby
Wirral
CH48 5DH
☎ 0151 632 3201
🖷 0151 632 0621
Head: Mr G W Williams
No. of pupils: 105

7

Age range: 5-16
Funding: Non-maintained
Type of School: Boarding/
Day
Special Needs: Wide range

Wheathill School
Naylorsfield Drive
Liverpool
L27 0YD
No. of pupils: 73
Age range: 4-16

White Thorn School
Ranworth Square
Norn's Green
Liverpool
L11 3DQ
☎ 0151 233 4094
🖹 0151 233 4096
No. of pupils: 30
Age range: 3-7
Funding: LEA
Type of School: Day
Special Needs: Severe &
Moderate Learning
Difficulties, SEBD

Wirral Hospitals' School
Solar Campus
235 Leasowe Road
Wallasey
CH45 8HS
☎ 0151 637 6310
🖹 0151 637 6287
email: solaridp@aol.com
Head: Mr I D Price
No. of pupils: 120
Age range: 3-18
Funding: LEA
Type of School: Day
Special Needs: Medical

Middlesex

Alexandra School
Alexandra Avenue
South Harrow
HA2 9DX
Age range: 5-16

Aylands School
Keswick Drive
Enfield
EN3 6NY
☎ 020 8761 229
🖹 020 8787 505
Head: Mr Daniel P Feeley
No. of pupils: 40
Age range: 7-16
Funding: LEA
Type of School: Day

Special Needs: Emotional
& behavioural difficulties

Belvue School
Rowdell Road
Northolt
UB5 6AG
No. of pupils: 132
Age range: 12-18

Chantry School
Falling Lane
Yiewsley
West Drayton
UB7 8AB
Age range: 11-16

Clarendon School
Hanworth Road
Hampton
TW12 3DH
☎ 020 8979 5102
🖹 020 8941 3069
Head: Mrs Ann Coward
No. of pupils: 100
Age range: 7-16
Funding: LEA
Type of School: Day
Special Needs: Multiple
Learning Difficulties

Durants School
4 Pitfield Way
Enfield
EN3 5BY
☎ 020 8804 1980
🖹 020 8804 0976
Head: Mr Keith Bovair
No. of pupils: 120
Age range: 5-19
Funding: LEA
Type of School: Day
Special Needs: Moderate
Learning Difficulties

Dyslexia Institute
133 Gresham Road
Staines
TW18 2AJ
☎ 01784 463 851
🖹 01784 460 747
email: info@
dyslexia-inst.org.uk
web: www.dyslexia-
inst.org.uk
Age range: 4-50
Funding: Registered charity
Type of School:
Educational Institute
Special Needs: Dyslexia/
Literacy & Numeracy
Difficulties

Grangewood School
Fore Street
Eastcote
Pinner
HA5 2JQ
No. of pupils: 70
Age range: 3-11

Hedgewood School
Weymouth Road
Hayes
UB4 8NF
No. of pupils: 70
Age range: 5-11

John Chilton School
Compton Crescent
Northolt
UB5 5LD
No. of pupils: 85
Age range: 2-17

Kingsley High School
Whittlesea Road
Harrow Weald
HP3 6ND
☎ 020 8421 3676
🖹 020 8421 7597
Head: Ms Kay Johnson
No. of pupils: 100
Age range: 12-19
Funding: LEA
Type of School: Day
Special Needs: Profound &
Multiple Learning
Difficulties

Mandeville School
Eastcote Lane North
Northolt
UB5 4HW
☎ 020 8864 4921
🖹 020 8423 1096
email: mandev@
ealing.gov.uk
web: www.ealing.gov.uk
Head: Mrs Christine Marks
No. of pupils: 80
Age range: 2-12
Funding: LEA
Type of School: Day
Special Needs: Severe
Learning Difficulties

Marjory Kinnon School
Hatton Road
Bedfont
TW14 9QZ
☎ 020 8890 8890
🖹 020 8890 2032
email: marjory.kinnon@
hounslow.gov.uk
Head: Mr David Harris

No. of pupils: 171
Age range: 4-18
Funding: LEA
Type of School: Day
Special Needs: Moderate
Learning Difficulties

Moorcroft School
Bramble Close
Hillingdon
Uxbridge
UB8 3BF
☎ 01895 437 799
🖹 01895 438 123
email: moorcroftsch@
freeserve.co.uk
Head: Mary Geddes
No. of pupils: 68
Age range: 11-19
Funding: LEA
Type of School: Day
Special Needs: Severe
Learning Difficulties

Oldfield House Unit
Oldfield Road
Hampton
TW12 2HP
☎ 020 8979 5102
🖹 020 8941 8605
Teacher in Charge: Mr
Alan Simons
Type of School: Day
Special Needs: Emotional
& behavioural difficulties

**Pield Heath House RC
School**
Pield Heath Road
Uxbridge
UB8 3NW
☎ 01895 258 507
🖹 01895 256 497
email: pieldheath@
btconnect.com
web: www.btconnect.com
Head: Sister Julie Rose
No. of pupils: 100
Age range: 7-19
Funding: Non-maintained
Type of School:
Day/Residential (weekly
boarding)
Special Needs: Moderate
Learning Difficulties

**Royal National
Orthopaedic Hospital
School**
Brockley Hill
Stanmore
HA7 4LP
Age range: 2-18

Shaftesbury High School
Headstone Lane
Harrow
HA3 6LE
☎ 020 8428 2482
🖨 020 8420 2361
email: shafbury@
rmplc.co.uk
web: www.rmplc.co.uk
Head: Mr Paul Williams
No. of pupils: 85
Age range: 11-17
Funding: LEA
Type of School: Day
Special Needs: Severe
Learning Difficulties

The Cedars School
High Street
Cranford
TW4 6LN
No. of pupils: 47
Age range: 5-11

The Lindon Bennett School
Main Street
Hanworth
TW13 6ST
No. of pupils: 68
Age range: 2-11

The Meadow School
Royal Lane
Hillingdon
UB8 3QU
☎ 01895 443 310
🖨 01895 420 925
Head: Mr Roger Payne
No. of pupils: 183
Age range: 11-18
Funding: LEA
Type of School: Day
Special Needs: Moderate
Learning Difficulties

The Parkway School
High Street
Cranford
Hounslow
TW5 9RU
Age range: 4-16

The Willows School
Stipularis Drive
Hayes
UB4 9QB
☎ 020 8841 7176
🖨 020 8842 4443
email: twillows@
lbhill.gov.uk
web: www.lbhill.gov.uk
Head: Mrs Frances King

No. of pupils: 30
Age range: 5-11
Funding: LEA
Type of School: Day
Special Needs: Emotional
& behavioural difficulties

Waverley School
105 The Ride
Enfield
EN3 7DL
☎ 020 8805 1858
🖨 020 8805 4397
email: info@
waverley.enfield.sch.uk
Head: Mrs Louise Gibbs
No. of pupils: 120
Age range: 3-19
Funding: LEA
Type of School: Day
Special Needs: Severe,
Profound & Multiple
Learning Difficulties

Woodlands First & Middle School
Whittlesea Road
Harrow Weald
HP3 6ND
☎ 020 8421 3637
🖨 020 8421 7597
Head: Ms Kay Johnson
No. of pupils: 100
Age range: 3-12
Funding: LEA
Type of School: Day
Special Needs: Profound &
Multiple Learning
Difficulties

Norfolk

Alderman Jackson School
Marsh Lane
Gaywood
King's Lynn
PE30 3AE
☎ 01553 672 779
🖨 01553 670 344
email: office@
aldermanjackson.
norfolk.sch.uk
Head: Debby Mc Carthy
No. of pupils: 67
Age range: 3-19
Funding: LEA
Type of School: Day
Special Needs: Severe
Learning Difficulties

Banham Marshalls College
Church Hill

Banham
NR16 2HN
Age range: 7-17

Chapel Road School
Chapel Road
Attleborough
NR17 2DS
☎ 01953 453 116
Head: Mrs K Heap
No. of pupils: 59
Age range: 4-19
Funding: LEA
Type of School: Day
Special Needs: Severe
Learnig Difficulties

Eaton Hall School
Pettus Road
Norwich
NR4 7BU
☎ 01603 457 480
Head: Mr J J Lees
No. of pupils: 40
Age range: 7-16
Funding: LEA
Type of School: Residential
Special Needs: Emotional
& Behavioural Difficulties

Edinburgh Road School
Norwich Road
Holt
NR25 6SL
☎ 01263 713 358
🖨 01263 711 281
email:
head@edinburghroad.
norfolk.sch.uk
Head: Ms Diane Whitham
No. of pupils: 34
Age range: 4-19
Funding: LEA
Type of School: Day
Special Needs: Profound &
Multiple Learning
Difficulties and Severe
Learning Difficulties

Ethel Tipple School
Winston Churchill Drive
Fairstead
Kings Lynn
PE30 4RP
☎ 01553 763 679
🖨 01553 770321
email: office@
etheltipple.norfolk.sch.uk
Head: Mr G L Wilkinson
No. of pupils: 89
Age range: 7-16
Funding: LEA

Type of School: Day
Special Needs: Multiple
Learning Difficulties

Fred Nicholson School
Westfield Road
Dereham
NR19 1JB
☎ 01362 693 915
🖨 01362 693 298
email: fred.nicholson@
argonet.co.uk
web: www.argonet.co.uk
Head: Mr M Clayton
No. of pupils: 95
Age range: 7-16
Funding: LEA
Type of School: Day
Special Needs: Moderate
Learning Difficulties

Hall School
St Faiths Road
Old Catton
Norwich
NR6 7AD
☎ 01603 466 467
🖨 01603 466 407
email: head@
hall,norfolk.sch.uk
web:
www.oldcattonhallspecial.
norfolk.sch.u
Head: Mrs Angela Ruthven
No. of pupils: 80
Age range: 3-19
Funding: LEA
Type of School: Day
Special Needs: Severe
Learning Difficulties

Harford Manor School
43 Ipswich Road
Norwich
NR2 2LN
☎ 01603 451 809
🖨 01603 453 508
Head: Mr Geoff Kitchen
No. of pupils: 70
Age range: 3-19
Funding: LEA
Type of School: Day
Special Needs: Profound &
Multiple Learning
Difficulties

John Grant School
St George's Drive
Caister-on-Sea
Great Yarmouth
NR31 0LJ
☎ 01493 720 158

7

No. of pupils: 74
Age range: 4-19

Parkside School
College Road
Norwich
NR2 3JA
☎ 01603 441 126
🖨 01603 441 128
email: office@
parkside.norfolk.sch.uk
Head: Mr B Payne
No. of pupils: 145
Age range: 8-16
Funding: LEA
Type of School: Day
Special Needs: Moderate
Learning Difficulties

Sheridan House School
Southburgh
Thetford
IP25 7TJ
No. of pupils: 106
Age range: 8-16

Sidestrand Hall School
Cromer Road
Sidestrand
Cromer
NR27 0NH
☎ 01263 578 144
No. of pupils: 106
Age range: 7-16

Social Education &
Training Project
191b Armes Street
Norwich
NR2 4EN
Age range: 6-18

St Andrew's School
Lower Common
East Runton
NR27 9PG
☎ 01263 511 727
🖨 01263 511 727
Head: Ms Gillian Baker
No. of pupils: 6
Age range: 6-12
Funding: Registered
charity
Type of School: Day
Special Needs: Dyspraxia,
dyslexia, autism,
communication difficulties

The Clare School
South Park Avenue
Norwich
NR4 7AU

☎ 01603 454 199
No. of pupils: 96
Age range: 4-19

North East Lincolnshire

Cambridge Park School
Cambridge Road
Grimsby
DN34 5EB
☎ 01472 230 110
🖨 01472 230 113
email: office@
cambridgepark.
ne-lincs.sch.uk
web: www.cambridgepark.
ne-lincs.sch.uk
Head: Mrs G Kendall
No. of pupils: 145
Age range: 3-16
Funding: LEA
Type of School: Day
Special Needs: Wide range

Humberston Park School
St Thomas Close
Humberston
Grimsby
DN36 4HS
☎ 01472 590645
Head: Mr A A Zielinski
No. of pupils: 88
Age range: 3-19
Funding: LEA
Type of School: Day
Special Needs: Profound &
Multiple Learning
Difficulties

Phoenix House PRU/Park
House Annexe
Harold Street
Grimsby
DN32 7NQ
☎ 01472 351 412
Age range: 7-16
Funding: LEA
Type of School: Day
Special Needs: Emotional
& Behavioural Difficulties

North Humberside

Bridgeview School
Ferriby Road
Hessle
HU13 0HR
No. of pupils: 81
Age range: 7-16

Driffield Kings Mill
School
Victoria Road
Driffield
YO25 7UG
No. of pupils: 68
Age range: 2-18

Dyslexia Institute
27 Prospect Street
Bridlington
YO15 2AE
Age range: 5-18

Ganton School
Springhead Avenue
Willerby Road
Anlaby
Hull
HU5 5YJ
No. of pupils: 108
Age range: 2-19

Northcott School
Dulverton Close
Bransholme
Hull
HU7 4EL
☎ 01482 825 311
No. of pupils: 96
Age range: 5-16

Riverside School
Ainsty Street
Goole
DN14 5JS
No. of pupils: 44
Age range: 3-16

South Wolds School
Dalton Holme
Beverley
HU17 7PB
No. of pupils: 76
Age range: 8-16

St Anne's School
St Helen's Drive
Welton
Brough
HU15 1NR
No. of pupils: 73
Age range: 2-19

Teskey King School
Inglemire Lane
Kingston upon Hull
HU6 8JH
No. of pupils: 118
Age range: 4-16

North Lincolnshire

St Hugh's School
Bushfield Road
Scunthorpe
DN16 1NB
☎ 01724 842 960
🖨 01724 282 311
web: www.st-hughes.
lincs.sch.uk
Head: Chris Darlington
No. of pupils: 120
Age range: 11-19
Funding: LEA
Type of School: Day
Special Needs: Profound,
Severe, Complex &
Multiple Learning
Difficulties, Sensory
difficulties and Autism

St Luke's School
Burghley Road
Scunthorpe
DN16 1JD
☎ 01724 844 560
🖨 01724 279 090
Head: Mr Robert Ashdown
No. of pupils: 80
Age range: 3-16
Funding: LEA
Type of School: Day
Special Needs: Profound &
Multiple Learning
Difficulties

North Somerset

Baytree School
Baytree Road
Weston-Super-Mare
BS22 8HG
☎ 01934 625 567
🖨 01934 643 405
email: baytree.special@
n-somerset.gov.uk
web: www.baytreespecial
school.ik.org
Head: Ms Carol Penney
No. of pupils: 67
Age range: 3-19
Funding: LEA
Type of School: Day
Special Needs: Profound &
Multiple Learning
Difficulties and Severe
Learning Difficulties

Ravenswood School
Pound Lane
Nailsea
BS48 2NN

☎ 01275 854 134
🖷 01275 810 876
Head: Mrs G A Sawyer
No. of pupils: 120
Age range: 3-19
Funding: LEA
Type of School: Day
Special Needs: Moderate
Learning difficulties &
Severe Learning
Difficulties & Autism

Westhaven School
Ellesmere Road
Uphill
Weston-Super-Mare
BS23 4UT
☎ 01934 632 171
🖷 01934 645 596
Head: Mrs J Moss
No. of pupils: 75
Age range: 7-16
Funding: LEA
Type of School: Day
Special Needs: Moderate
Learning Difficulties,
emotional needs, ASD,
SPLD and PH

North Yorkshire

Breckenbrough School
Sandhutton
Thirsk
YO7 4EN
☎ 01845 587238
🖷 01845 587385
email: office@
breckenbrough.org.uk
web: www.breckenbrough
school.co.uk
Headmaster: Mr Trevor
Bennett
No. of pupils: 31
Age range: 10-17
Funding: LEA
Type of School: Residential
Special Needs: Emotional
& behavioural difficulties,
ADHD and ADD

Brompton Hall School
Brompton by Sawdon
Scarborough
YO13 9DB
☎ 01723 859121
🖷 01723 850239
email: admin@
bromptonhall.
n-yorks.sch.uk
Head: Mr Mark Mihkelson
No. of pupils: 40

Age range: 8-16
Funding: LEA
Type of School: Residential
special
Special Needs: Emotional
& behavioural difficulties

Brooklands School
Burnside Avenue
Skipton
BD23 2LX
No. of pupils: 55
Age range: 2-19

Dyslexia Institute
14 Haywra Street
Harrogate
HG1 5BJ
☎ 01423 522111
🖷 01423 521393
Principal: Mrs D Wisdom
Age range: 5
Funding: Charity
Type of School: Children/
adults attend for sessions
of teaching and then
return to school/work/etc.
Special Needs: Dyslexia

Galtres School
Bad Bargain Lane
Burnholme
York
YO31 0LW
☎ 01904 415 924
🖷 01904 431 281
email: galtres.school@
york.gov.uk
web: www.york.gov.uk
Head: Mr George Gilmore
No. of pupils: 65
Age range: 11-19
Funding: LEA
Type of School: Day
Special Needs: Profound &
Multiple Learning
Difficulties

Henshaws College
Bogs Lane
Starbeck
Harrogate
HG1 4ED
☎ 01423 864 451
🖷 01423 885 095
email: lynne.gilland@
hsbp.co.uk
web: www.hsbp.co.uk
Principal: Mrs J Cole
No. of pupils: 65
Age range: 16

Funding: Non-maintained
Type of School: Residential
Special Needs: Visually
Impaired & Additional
Difficulties

Lidgett Grove School
Wheatland's Grove
Acomb
York
YO2 5NH
Age range: 2-12

Mowbray School
Masham Road
Bedale
DL8 2SD
☎ 01677 422 446
🖷 01677 426 056
Head: Mr Jonathan Tearle
No. of pupils: 148
Age range: 2-16
Funding: LEA
Type of School: Day
Special Needs: Speech and
Language Difficulties &
Autism

Netherside Hall School
Threshfield
Skipton
BD23 5PP
☎ 01756 752324
🖷 01756 753227
email: admin@
nethersidehall.
n-yorks.sch.uk
web:
www.nethersidehall.co.uk
School Administrator: Mrs
G H Foster
No. of pupils: 46
Age range: 10-16
Funding: LEA
Type of School: Special
Residential School with
some provision for day
pupils
Special Needs: Specific
Learning Difficulties
(Dyslexia)

Northfield School
Beckfield Lane
Acomb
York
YO2 5RQ
☎ 01904 791 315
No. of pupils: 118
Age range: 3-16

Spring Hill School
Palace Road
Ripon
HG4 3HN
☎ 01765 603 320
🖷 01765 607 549
Head: Mrs J Clarke
No. of pupils: 38
Age range: 10-19
Funding: Voluntary
Type of School: Residential
Special Needs: Severe
Learning Difficulties

Springhead School
Barry's Lane
Seamer Road
Scarborough
YO12 4HA
No. of pupils: 51
Age range: 2-19

Springwater School
High Street
Starbeck
Harrogate
HG2 7LW
☎ 01423 883 214
🖷 01423 881 465
email: admin@
springwater.n-yorks.sch.uk
Head: Ms Gabirelle M
Cook
No. of pupils: 50
Age range: 2-19
Funding: LEA
Type of School: Day
Special Needs: Multi-
sensory impairments,
Emotional & behavioural
difficulties, Autism and
Severe, Profound and
Multiple Learning
Difficulties

The Dales School
Morton-on-Swale
Northallerton
DL7 9QW
No. of pupils: 71
Age range: 2-19

The Forest School
Park Lane
Knaresborough
HG5 0DQ
☎ 01423 864 583
🖷 01423 861 145
Head: Mrs S M B Wootton
No. of pupils: 118
Age range: 3-16

7

Funding: LEA
Type of School: Day
Special Needs: Moderate
Learning Difficulties &
Speech and Langauge
Difficulties

The Woodlands School
Woodlands Drive
Scarborough
YO12 6QN
☎ 01723 373 260
Textphone 01723 371715
email: headteacher@
woodlands.n-yorks.sch.uk
Head: Mr P Edmondson
No. of pupils: 96
Age range: 2-16
Funding: LEA
Type of School: Residential
& Day
Special Needs: Multiple
Learning Difficulties and
Autism

Welburn Hall School
Welburn
Kirkbymoorside
YO62 7HQ
☎ 01751 431 218
🖷 01751 433 157
Head: Mr J V Hall
No. of pupils: 50
Age range: 8-18
Funding: LEA
Type of School: Day
Special Needs: Physical
disabilities & Moderate
Learning Difficulties &
Speech and Language
Difficulties

Northamptonshire

Billing Brook School
Penistone Road
Lumbertubs
Northampton
NN3 4EZ
☎ 01604 406 329
No. of pupils: 143
Age range: 3-16

Fairfields School
Trinity Avenue
Northampton
NN2 6JN
☎ 01604 714 777
🖷 01604 714 245
Head: Mrs Jill Wilson
No. of pupils: 67
Age range: 3-11

Funding: LEA
Type of School: Day
Special Needs: Medical

Friars School
Friars Close
Wellingborough
NN8 2LA
☎ 01933 304 950
🖷 01933 304 951
Head: Mrs P A Norton
No. of pupils: 145
Age range: 11-16
Funding: LEA
Type of School: Day
Special Needs: Moderate
Learning Difficulties

Greenfields School
Harborough Road
Northampton
NN2 8LR
☎ 01604 843 657
🖷 01604 843657
email: head@greenfields.
northants-ed.gov.uk
Head Teacher: Mrs J
Moralee
No. of pupils: 60
Age range: 11-19
Funding: LEA
Type of School: Day
Special Needs:
Autism/Profound &
Multiple Learning
difficulties

Highfield School
273 Welford Road
Northampton
NN2 8PW
☎ 01604 846 018
No. of pupils: 41
Age range: 5-11

Isebrook School
Eastleigh Road
Kettering
NN15 6PT
☎ 01536 500 030
🖷 01536 500 031
email: isebrook@
easymail.rmplc.co.uk
Acting Head: John
Parkinson
No. of pupils: 85
Age range: 11-16
Funding: LEA
Type of School: Day
Special Needs: Wide
range

Kingsley School
Churchill Way
Kettering
NN15 5DP
☎ 01536 316 880
🖷 01536 415 755
email: mailbox@
kingsleyschool.fsnet.co.uk
Head: Ms J C Thompson
No. of pupils: 132
Age range: 3-11
Funding: LEA
Type of School: Day
Special Needs: Generic

Northgate School
Queen's Park Parade
Northampton
NN2 6LR
☎ 01604 714 098
No. of pupils: 116
Age range: 7-16

Potterspury Lodge School
Towcester
NN12 7LL
☎ 01908 542 912
🖷 01908 543 399
email: potterspury.lodge@
btinternet.com
web: www.potterspury.
lodge.btinternet.co.uk
Principal: Miss G Lietz
No. of pupils: 52
Age range: 8-16
Funding: Independent,
Charitable Trust
Type of School: Day &
Residential
Special Needs: Emotional
& behavioural difficulties
and Asperger Syndrome

Raeburn School
Raeburn Road
Northampton
NN2 7EU
☎ 01604 460 017
🖷 01604 460 024
email: raeburn.school@
cableol.co.uk
web: www.cableol.co.uk
Head: Mr David Lloyd
No. of pupils: 50
Age range: 11-16
Funding: LEA
Type of School: Day
Special Needs: Emotional
& behavioural difficulties

**RNIB Rushton Hall
School**
Rushton

Kettering
NN14 1RR
☎ 01536 710506
🖷 01536 418 506
email: dhussey@
rnib.org.uk
web: www.rnib.org.uk
Head: Mr D Hussey
No. of pupils: 35
Age range: 5-12
Funding: Non-maintained
Type of School: Residential
Special Needs: Visually
Impaired

Rowan Gate School
Finedon Road
Wellingborough
NN8 4NS
☎ 01933 304 970
No. of pupils: 82
Age range: 3-11
Funding: LEA
Type of School: Day
Special Needs: Moderate,
Severe, Profound &
Multiple Learning
Difficulties and Autism

The Orchard School
Beatrice Road
Kettering
NN16 9QR
☎ 01536 513 726
No. of pupils: 39
Age range: 11-16

Wren Spinney School
Westover Road
Kettering
NN15 7LB
☎ 01536 481 939
🖷 01536 312 689
email: head.7010@
nemis.org.uk
web: www.nemis.org.uk
Head: Mr S Cullingford-
Agnew
Age range: 11-19
Funding: LEA
Type of School: Day
Special Needs: Wide range

Northumberland

**Barndale House Special
School**
Howling Lane
Alnwick
NE66 1DQ
☎ 01665 602 541
🖷 01665 606370

No. of pupils: 38
Age range: 3-19
Type of School: Part
Day/residential (weekdays)
Special Needs: Autism and
Severe Learning
Difficulties

**Child & Adolescent
Psychiatric Unit**
Prudhoe & Monkton
Hospital
Prudhoe
NE42 5NT
☎ 01661 514 589

Cleaswell Hill School
School Avenue
Guide Post
Choppington
NE62 5DJ
☎ 01670 823 182
🖥 01670 827044
email: kburdis@
portables1.ngfl.gov.uk
web: www.portables1.
ngfl.gov.uk
Head: Mr R J Hope
No. of pupils: 105
Age range: 5-16
Funding: LEA
Type of School: Day
Special Needs: Moderate
Learning Difficulties

Collingwood School
Stobhillgate
Morpeth
NE61 2HA
☎ 01670 516 374
🖥 01670 510 973
email: email@collingwood.
northumberland.sch.uk
Head: Ms Cynthia
Hetherington
No. of pupils: 120
Age range: 5-16
Funding: LEA
Type of School: Day
Special Needs: Moderate
Learning Difficulties

East Hartford School
Scott Street
East Hartford
Cramlington
NE23 9AR
☎ 01670 713 881
Head: Mr W K Telfer
No. of pupils: 52
Age range: 4-11
Funding: LEA

Special Needs: Moderate
Learning Difficulties

Gallowhill Hall School
Whalton
Morpeth
NE61 3TU
☎ 01661 881 662
🖥 01661 881 857
No. of pupils: 39
Age range: 11-16

Hackwood Park School
Gallows Bank
Hexham
NE46 1AU
☎ 01434 604 039
Head: Mr John Wells
No. of pupils: 60
Age range: 4-17
Funding: LEA
Type of School: Day
Special Needs: Moderate
Learning Difficulties

Hillcrest School
East View Avenue
East Farm
Cramlington
NE23 9DY
☎ 01670 713 632
🖥 01670 735 695
No. of pupils: 66
Age range: 11-16

Northgate Hospital
Morpeth
NE61 3BP
☎ 01670 394 177

**Nunnykirk Centre for
Dyslexia**
Netherwitton
Morpeth
NE61 4PB
☎ 01670 772 685
🖥 01670 772 434
email: secretary@
nkirk.freeserve.co.uk
Head: S Dalby-Ball
No. of pupils: 45
Age range: 7-16
Funding: Registered
charity
Type of School: Day/
Weekly Boarding
Special Needs: Dyslexia

Priory School
Dene Park
Hexham
NE46 1HN

☎ 01434 605 021
🖥 01434 609 022
email: admin@hexham.
northumberland.sch.uk
Head: Mr Michael
Thompson
No. of pupils: 36
Age range: 3-19
Funding: LEA
Type of School: Day
Special Needs: Severe
Learning Difficulties

**Talbot House Special
School**
North Terrace
Seghill
NE23 7EB
No. of pupils: 33
Age range: 11-16

The Grove School
Grove Gardens
Tweedmouth
Berwick-upon-Tweed
TD15 2EN
☎ 01289 306 390
🖥 01289 306 994
email: admin@thegrove.
northumberland.sch.uk
Head: Mrs E E Brown
No. of pupils: 26
Age range: 3-19
Funding: LEA
Type of School: Day
Special Needs: Autism,
Severe Learning
Difficulties, Challenging
Behaviour and Hearing
Impaired

Nottingham City

Aspley Wood School
Robins Wood Road
Aspley
Nottingham
NG8 3LD
☎ 0115 913 1400
🖥 0115 913 1404
web: www.aspleywood.
nottingham.sch.uk
Head: Mrs Barbara More
No. of pupils: 42
Age range: 3-16
Funding: LEA
Type of School: Day
Special Needs: Physical
Disabilities with associated
difficulties

Shepherd Special School
Harvey Road

Bilborough
Nottingham
NG8 3BB
☎ 0115 9153265
🖥 0115 9153264
email: shepherd_school@
hotmail.com
web:
www.shepherdschool.org.uk
Head: Mr David S Stewart
No. of pupils: 113
Age range: 3-19
Funding: LEA
Type of School: Day
Special Needs: Profound &
Multiple Learning
Difficulties

Nottinghamshire

**Arnold Derrymount
School**
Churchmoor Lane
Arnold
Nottingham
NG5 8HN
No. of pupils: 59
Age range: 5-16

Ash Lea School
Owthorpe Road
Cotgrave
Nottingham
NG12 3PA
No. of pupils: 70
Age range: 3-19
Type of School: Day
Special Needs: SLD,
MLD, Autism

Beech Hill School
Fairholme Drive
Mansfield
NG19 6DX
No. of pupils: 60
Age range: 11-16

Bracken Hill School
Chartwell Road
Kirkby-in-Ashfield
Nottingham
NG17 7HZ
☎ 01623 477268
🖥 01623 477298
email: office@
brackenhill.nottscc.gov.uk
Head: Mr Andrew
Kawalek
No. of pupils: 65
Age range: 5-19
Special Needs: Severe &
Multiple Learning
Difficulties and ASD

7

Brackenfield Special School
Bracken Road
Long Eaton
NG10 4DA
☎ 0115 973 3710
🖷 0115 972 1272
Head: Dr J M Chadha
No. of pupils: 78
Age range: 5-17
Funding: LEA
Type of School: Day
Special Needs: Wide range

Carlton Digby School
61 Digby Avenue
Mapperley
NG3 6DS
☎ 0115 956 8289
🖷 0115 956 8290
Head: Mrs Glenys Clifton
No. of pupils: 67
Age range: 3-19
Funding: LEA
Type of School: Day
Special Needs: Profound &
Multiple Learning
Difficulties

City Hospital
Education Base
Nottingham
NG5 1PB
☎ 0115 962 7600
email: rstephenson@
cityhospital.connet.org.uk
Head of Education: R
Stephenson
Age range: 5-16
Funding: LEA
Type of School: Hospital
Special Needs: Medical

Down House School
Helmsley Road
Rainworth
NG21 0DQ
☎ 01623 795 361
Head: Ms Monica Uden
No. of pupils: 95
Age range: 5-16
Funding: Non-maintained
Special Needs: Speech and
Language Difficulties

Fountaindale School
Nottingham Road
Mansfield
NG18 5BA
☎ 01623 792 671
🖷 01623 797 849
email: admin@
fountaindale.notts.sch.uk

m.dengel@
fountaindale.notts.sch.uk
No. of pupils: 74
Age range: 3-19
Funding: LEA

Kinder School
Bassetlaw District General
Hospital
Kilton Hill
Worksop
S81 0BD
Age range: 4-16

Martlet School
Newgate Street
Worksop
S80 2LW
No. of pupils: 7
Age range: 10-16

Nethergate School
Swansdowne Drive
Clifton
Nottingham
NG11 8HX
☎ 0115 9152959
🖷 0115 9152958
email: admin@
nethergate.nottingham
Head: Mrs S Johnson-
Marshall
No. of pupils: 66
Age range: 5-19
Funding: LEA
Type of School: Day
Special Needs: Moderate
Learning Difficulties

Newark Orchard School
Administration Centre
Appletongate
Newark
NG24 1JR
☎ 01636 682 255
🖷 01636 682 266
email: n-orchard.sch@
diamond.co.uk
web: www.diamond.co.uk
Head: Mrs Sharon Jefferies
No. of pupils: 79
Age range: 3-19
Funding: LEA
Type of School: Residential
Special Needs: Profound &
Multiple Learning
Difficulties

**Queen's Medical Centre
Education Base**
E Floor East Block
Queens Medical Centre

Nottingham
NG7 2UH
☎ 0115 970 9753
🖷 0115 924 4292
email: qmceducbase@
aol.com
web: www.nottscc.gov.uk
Head: Mrs Hazel
Coalwood
No. of pupils: 30
Age range: 5-16
Funding: LEA
Type of School: Hospital
Special Needs: Medical

Redgate School
Somersall Street
Mansfield
NG19 6EL
☎ 01623 455944
🖷 01623 455778
Age range: 3-11

Rutland House School
Elm Bank
Mapperley
Nottingham
NG3 5AJ
☎ 0115 962 1315
🖷 0115 962 2867
Head: Mrs Carole Oviatt-
Ham
No. of pupils: 35
Age range: 5-19
Funding: Independent
Type of School: Day
Special Needs: Profound &
Multiple Learning
Difficulties

St Anne's Hospital School
Fairmead Close
Off Wells Road
Nottingham
NG3 3AL
Age range: 5-16

St Giles School
North Road
Retford
DN22 7XN
☎ 01777 703 683
🖷 01777 705 324
email: head@st-giles.
nottscc.gov.uk
web: www.st-giles.
nottscc.gov.uk
Head: Ms Catherine Kirk
No. of pupils: 93
Age range: 3-19
Funding: LEA
Type of School: Day

Special Needs: Profound &
Multiple Learning
Difficulties

Stubton Hall School
Stubton
Newark
NG23 5DD
☎ 01636 626 607
No. of pupils: 52
Age range: 7-16

**Sutherland House School
(Primary Department)**
Sutherland Road
Nottingham
NG3 7AP
Head: Mrs M Allen
No. of pupils: 28
Age range: 6-12
Funding: Independent
Type of School: Day
Special Needs: Autism

The Orchard School
Town Site
Appletongate
Newark
NG24 1JP
No. of pupils: 71
Age range: 2-16

Westbrook School
Thoresby Road
Long Eaton
Nottingham
NG10 3NP
☎ 0115 972 9769
🖷 0115 946 3566
Head: Mr David J Ingham
No. of pupils: 92
Age range: 3-16
Funding: LEA
Type of School: Day
Special Needs: Physical
disabilities

Woodlands School
Beechdale Road
Nottingham
NG8 3EZ
☎ 0115 9155734
🖷 0115 9155736
Acting Head: Anne Davies
No. of pupils: 100
Age range: 4-16
Funding: LEA
Type of School: Day
Special Needs: Moderate
Learning Difficulties,
Autism, Emotional &
behavioural difficulties and
Complex Needs (ASD)

Yeoman Park School
Park Hall Road
Mansfield Woodhouse
Mansfield
NG19 8PS
☎ 01623 459540
Textphone 01623 459526
Head: Mr P Betts
No. of pupils: 73
Age range: 3-19
Funding: LEA
Type of School: Day
Special Needs: SLD,
PMLD

Oxfordshire

Bardwell School
Hendon Place
Sunderland Drive
Bicester
OX26 4RZ
☎ 01869 242 182
🖷 01869 243 211
email: office@
bardwell.oxon.sch.uk
Head: Mrs Chris Hughes
No. of pupils: 55
Age range: 2-16
Funding: LEA
Type of School: Day
Special Needs: Profound &
Multiple Learning
Difficulties, Severe
Learning Difficulties,
Autism and Language
Impairment

Bessels Leigh School
Bessels Leigh
Abingdon
OX13 5QB
☎ 01865 390 436
🖷 01865 390 688
Principal: Mr John Boulton
No. of pupils: 38
Age range: 11-17
Funding: Non-maintained
Type of School: Boarding
Special Needs: Emotional
& behavioural difficulties

Bishopswood School
Grove Road
Sponning Common
Reading
RG4 9JT
☎ 0118 972 4311
🖷 0118 972 1019
email: headteacher@
bishopswood.oxon.sch.uk
web: www.bishopswood.

oxon.sch.uk
Head: Mrs J Wager
No. of pupils: 57
Age range: 2-16
Funding: LEA
Type of School: Day
Special Needs: Profound,
Severe and Multiple
Learning Difficulties

Bruern Abbey School
Bruern
OX7 6PZ
☎ 01993 831 831
🖷 01993 831 666
No. of pupils: 18
Age range: 7-13

Fitzwaryn School
Denchworth Road
Wantage
OX12 9ET
☎ 01235 764 504
🖷 01235 768 728
email: fitzwaryn@
oxon.sch.uk
web:
www.fitzwaryn.oxon.sch.uk
Head: Marion Tighe
No. of pupils: 75
Age range: 3-16
Funding: LEA
Type of School: Day
Special Needs: Moderate
Learning Difficulties and
Profound & Multiple
Learning Difficulties

Frank Wise School
Hornbeam Close
Banbury
OX16 9RL
☎ 01295 263 520
🖷 01295 273 141
email: info@
frankwise.oxon.sch.uk
web: www.frankwise.
oxon.sch.uk
Head: Mr Kevin Griffiths
No. of pupils: 78
Age range: 2-16
Funding: LEA
Type of School: Day
Special Needs: Profound &
Multiple Learning
Difficulties

Iffley Mead School
Iffley Turn
Oxford
OX4 4DU
☎ 01865 747 606

🖷 01865 711 134
No. of pupils: 107
Age range: 5-16

John Watson School
Littleworth Road
Wheatley
Oxford
OX33 1NN
☎ 01865 452725
🖷 01865 452724
email: office@
johnwatson.oxon.sch.uk
Head: Mrs S A Withey
No. of pupils: 66
Age range: 2-16
Funding: LEA
Type of School: Day
Special Needs: Severe
Learning Difficulties

Mabel Prichard School
St Nicholas Road
Littlemore
Oxford
OX4 4PN
☎ 01865 777 878
🖷 01865 775 218
No. of pupils: 68
Age range: 2-16
Funding: LEA
Type of School: Day
Special Needs: Wide range

Mulberry Bush School
Standlake
Witney
OX8 7RW
☎ 01865 300202
🖷 01865 300084
email: john.diamond@
mulberrybush.oxon.sch.uk
Director: Mr John
Diamond
No. of pupils: 36
Age range: 5-12
Funding: Registered charity
Type of School: Residential
Special Needs: Emotional
& behavioural difficulties

Northern House School
South Parade
Summertown
Oxford
OX2 7JN
☎ 01865 557 004
🖷 01865 511 210
email: headteacher@
northern-house.oxon.sch.uk
Age range: 5-13
Funding: LEA

Type of School: Day
Special Needs: Emotional
& behavioural difficulties

Northfield School
Knights Road
Blackbird Leys
Oxford
OX4 5DQ
☎ 01865 771 703
🖷 01865 773 873
email: office@
northfield.oxon.sch.uk
Head: Mr Mark Blencowe
No. of pupils: 78
Age range: 11-16
Funding: LEA
Type of School: Day
Special Needs: Emotional
& behavioural difficulties

Ormerod School
Waynflete Road
Headington
Oxford
OX3 8DD
☎ 01865 744 173
🖷 01865 741 489
email: office@
ormerod.oxon.sch.uk
No. of pupils: 44
Age range: 2-16
Funding: LEA
Type of School: Day
Special Needs: Wide range

**Oxford Hospitals
Education Service**
Nuffield Orthopeadic
Centre
Park Hospital for Children
Headington
OX3 7LQ
☎ 01865 227 554
🖷 01865 742 348
Age range: 5-16

Penhurst School
New Street
Chipping Norton
OX7 5HU
☎ 01608 642 559
🖷 01608 647 029
Head: Mr Richard Aird
No. of pupils: 28
Age range: 5-19
Funding: Voluntary
Type of School: Residential
Special Needs: Profound &
Multiple Learning
Difficulties

7

Springfield School
9 Moorland Close
Witney
OX8 5LN
☎ 01993 703 963
🖹 01993 708 796
Head: Ms Christina Niner
No. of pupils: 90
Age range: 2-16
Funding: LEA
Type of School: Day
Special Needs: Profound &
Multiple Learning
Difficulties

**St Nicholas School
Autistic Unit**
Raymund Road
Marston
Oxford
OX3 0PJ
☎ 01865 762071
Deputy Head of Autistic
Unit: Mr Richard Brooks
No. of pupils: 14
Age range: 5-11
Funding: LEA
Type of School: Day
Special Needs: Autism

**Swalcliffe Park School
Trust**
Swalcliffe
Banbury
OX15 5EP
No. of pupils: 50
Age range: 11-18

Tesdale School
Blacknall Road
Abingdon
OX14 5HE
Age range: 11-16

The Kingfisher School
Radley Road
Abingdon
OX14 3RR
☎ 01235 523 843
🖹 01235 554 051
No. of pupils: 118
Age range: 2-16

**The Ormerod School at
the Marlborough School**
Marlborough School
Shipton Road
Woodstock
OX20 1L
No. of pupils: 30
Age range: 11-16

Funding: LEA
Type of School: Day
Special Needs: Physical
disability and associated
learning and
communication problems

Woodeaton Manor School
Woodeaton
Oxford
OX3 9TS
☎ 01865 558 722
🖹 01865 311 561
Age range: 8-16

Plymouth

Hillside School
Bodmin Road
Whitleigh
Plymouth
PL5 4DZ
☎ 01752 773 875
🖹 01752 775 761
Head: Mr D Whitton
No. of pupils: 140
Age range: 11-16
Special Needs: Emotional
& Behavioural Difficulties
and Multiple Learning
Difficulties

Mill Ford School
Rochford Crescent
Ernesettle
Plymouth
PL5 2PY
☎ 01752 300 270
🖹 01752 300 109
email: millford.school@
plymouth.gov.uk
web: www.millford.school.
plymouth.gov.uk
Head: Mr John Hill
No. of pupils: 115
Age range: 3-19
Funding: LEA
Type of School: Day
Special Needs: Profound
and Multiple Learning
Difficulties, Severe
Learning Difficulties,
Autism

**Plymouth Tuition Service:
Young mothers' centre**
Lancaster Gardens
Whitleigh
Plymouth
PL5 4AA
☎ 01752 786 696
🖹 01752 786 696

email: plymouth.
youngmotherscentre@
plymouth.gov.uk
Head: Mrs Jackie Moir
No. of pupils: 18
Age range: 14-16
Funding: LEA
Type of School: Pupil
Referral Unit
Special Needs: Pregnant/
parenting

**Plymouth Tuition Servive
PRU**
Bretonside
Plymouth
PL4 0AT
☎ 01752 229 351
🖹 01752 229 351
email: bretonside.tuition@
plymouth.gov.uk
Head: Mr Norman Cooke
No. of pupils: 140
Age range: 14-16
Funding: LEA
Type of School: Pupil
Referral Unit
Special Needs: Emotional
& behavioural difficulties

Portsmouth

East Shore School
Eastern Road
Portsmouth
PO3 6EP
☎ 023 9283 9331
🖹 023 9287 2504
Head: Mr Paul Clarke
No. of pupils: 80
Age range: 2-19
Funding: LEA
Type of School: Day
Special Needs: Severe
Learning Difficulties

**Waterside School &
Hostel**
Tipner Lane
Tipner
Portsmouth
PO2 8RA
☎ 023 9266 5664
🖹 023 9265 3333
email: tstokes@waterside.
portsmouth.sch.uk
Head: Mr T S Stokes
No. of pupils: 70
Age range: 11-16
Funding: LEA
Type of School: Day with
hostel provision

Special Needs: Emotional
& behavioural difficulties

**Willows Nursery School
& Early Excellence Centre**
Battenburg Avenue
North End
Portsmouth
PO2 0SN
☎ 023 9266 6918
🖹 023 9265 2247
email: anneswann@
willows.portsmouth.sch.uk
Head: Anne Swann
No. of pupils: 36
Age range: 2-5
Funding: LEA
Type of School: Day
Special Needs: Any

Redbridge

Hyleford School
Loxford Lane
Ilford
IG3 9AR
☎ 020 8590 7272
🖹 020 8503 8028
Head: Mrs G D Morgan
No. of pupils: 77
Age range: 3-19
Funding: LEA
Type of School: Day
Special Needs: Profound &
Multiple Learning
Difficulties

Little Heath School
Hainault Road
Little Heath
Romford
RM6 5RX
☎ 020 8599 4864
🖹 020 8590 8953
email: dware@
littleheath.essex.sch.uk
web: www.littleheath.
essex.sch.uk
Head: Mr P B Johnson
No. of pupils: 138
Age range: 11-18
Funding: LEA
Type of School: Day
Special Needs: Moderate
Learning Difficulties

Richmond

**Cassel Hospital Inpatient
& Day Unit**
Ham Common
Richmond
TW10 7JF

☎ 020 8940 8181
🖷 020 8237 2996
Teacher in charge: Lee Marsden
Age range: 5-18
Funding: LEA
Type of School: Unit in psychotherapy hospital
Special Needs: Emotional & behavioural difficulties

Rochdale

Rydings School
Great Howarth
Wardle Road
Rochdale
OL12 9HJ
☎ 01706 657993
🖷 01706 647112
email: jaz@rydings.
rochdale.sch.uk
web: www.rydings@
rochdale.sch.uk
Head: Mr R A Jazwinski
No. of pupils: 89
Age range: 4-16
Funding: LEA
Type of School: Day
Special Needs: Multiple, Complex and Severe Learning Difficulties and Emotional & behavioural difficulties

Salford

New Croft High School
Seedley Road
Salford
M6 5NQ
☎ 0161 736 6415
🖷 0161 736 9957
Acting Head: Mrs June Redhead
No. of pupils: 75
Age range: 11-19
Funding: LEA
Type of School: Day
Special Needs: Severe, Profound, Multiple and Complex Learning Difficulties

Royal Manchester Children's Hospital School
Hospital Road
Pendlebury
Swinton
Manchester
M27 4HA
☎ 0161 7941151

🖷 0161 7272534
email: royalmanchester.
childrenshospital@
salford.gov.uk
Head: Mrs B I Purdy
No. of pupils: 140
Age range: 2-19
Funding: LEA
Type of School: Day Hospital
Special Needs: All types

Sandwell MBC

The Orchard School
Holly Lane
Smethwick
West Midlands
B66 1QN
☎ 0121 558 2560
🖷 0121 555 6034
Deputy Head: Mrs Diane Ellingham
No. of pupils: 45
Age range: 9-11
Funding: LEA
Type of School: Day
Special Needs: Profound & Multiple Learning Difficulties

Sefton

Birkdale School for Hearing Impaired Children
40 Lancaster Road
Birkdale
Southport
PR8 2JY
☎ 01704 567220
Textphone 01704 567220
🖷 01704 568342
email: admin@birkdale-school.merseyside.org
web: www.bshic.co.uk
Head: Mrs Anne Wood
No. of pupils: 35
Age range: 5-19
Funding: Non-maintained
Type of School: Day & Weekly/termly Boarding
Special Needs: Hearing Impaired

Newfield School
Edge Lane
Crosby
Liverpool
L23 4TG
☎ 0151 924 9620
🖷 0151 932 9025

Bursar: Helen Jones
No. of pupils: 74
Age range: 4-16
Funding: LEA
Type of School: Day
Special Needs: Emotional & Behavioural Difficulties

Peterhouse School
Preston New Road
Southport
PR9 8PA
☎ 01704 506 682
🖷 01704 506683
email: peterhouse.admin@autisminitiatives.org
web: www.autisminitiatives.org/peterhouse
Head of Education: Mrs B Matthews
No. of pupils: 48
Age range: 5-19
Funding: LEA
Type of School: Day/Weekly Boarding
Special Needs: Autism & Aspergers syndrome

Presfield School
Preston New Road
Southport
PR9 8PA
☎ 01704 227 831
🖷 01704 232 306
Head: Mr E T Powell
No. of pupils: 80
Age range: 4-16
Funding: LEA
Type of School: Day
Special Needs: Moderate Learning Difficulties

Shropshire

Ashley Residential School
Top Rock Road
Ashley
Market Drayton
TF9 4LX
Age range: 11-16

Charles Darwin School
North Road
Wellington
Telford
TF1 3ET
No. of pupils: 23
Age range: 13-16

Cotsbrook School
Higford

Shifnal
TF11 9ET
☎ 01952 750 237
No. of pupils: 11
Age range: 11-16

Cruckton Hall School
Cruckton
Shrewsbury
SY5 8PR
☎ 01743 860 206
🖷 01743 860 206
email: pdm@cruckton.demon.co.uk
web: www.cruckton.demon.co.uk
Head: Mr P D Mayhew
No. of pupils: 42
Age range: 9-16
Funding: Independent
Type of School: Residential
Special Needs: Moderate Learning Difficulties

Haughton School
Queen Street
Madeley
Telford
TF7 4BW
☎ 01952 684 995
🖷 01952 583 616
Acting Head: Mrs J B Logan
No. of pupils: 140
Age range: 4-16
Funding: LEA
Type of School: Day
Special Needs: Multiple Learning Difficulties, Autism

Hilltop School
Fishmore Road
Ludlow
SY8 3DP
Age range: 11-16

Mount Gilbert School
Hinkshay Road
Dawley
Telford
TF3 1DG
☎ 01952 272 473
🖷 01952 272 474
Head: Mrs A Valentini
No. of pupils: 43
Age range: 11-16
Type of School: Special school
Special Needs: Emotional & behavioural difficulties

7

Orthopaedic Hospital School
Oswestry
SY10 7AG
Age range: 4-16

Overley Hall School
Wellington
Telford
TF6 5HE
☎ 01952 740 262
🖷 01952 740262
email: info@
overleyhall.com
web: www.overleyhall.com
Principal: Mr W O'Hagan
No. of pupils: 17
Age range: 9-19
Funding: LEA/SSD/Dio H
Type of School: Residential
Special Needs: Epilepsy,
ASD, Complex & Severe
Learning Difficulties

Queen's Park School
Queens Road
Oswestry
SY11 2HZ
☎ 01691 652 416
No. of pupils: 50
Age range: 7-16

RNIB Condover Hall School
Condover
Shrewsbury
SY5 7AH
☎ 01743 872 320
🖷 01743 873 310
email: condover.office@
rnib.org.uk
web:
www.condoverhallschool.com
Principle: Mr Harry Dicks
No. of pupils: 56
Age range: 8-25
Funding: Non-maintained
Type of School: Residential
Special Needs: Visually
Impaired and additional
disabilities

Severndale School
Hearne Way
Monkmoor
Shrewsbury
SY3 8PA
☎ 01743 351 091
🖷 01743 352 482
email: post@
severndale.enta.net
web:
www.severndale.enta.net

Head: Mr Chris Davies
No. of pupils: 174
Age range: 3-19
Funding: LEA
Type of School: Day
Special Needs: Severe
Learning Difficulties

Shotton Hall School
Harmer Hill
Shrewsbury
SY4 3DW
No. of pupils: 25
Age range: 10-18

Southall School
Off Rowan Avenue
Dawley
Telford
TF4 3PN
☎ 01952 592485
Head: Mr A J Day
No. of pupils: 155
Age range: 4-16
Funding: LEA
Type of School: Day
Special Needs: Multiple
Learning Difficulties and
Autism

The Bridge School
Grange Avenue
Stirchley
Telford
TF3 1UP
☎ 01952 417 020
🖷 01952 417 022
Head: Mrs U Van-Den-
Berg
No. of pupils: 155
Age range: 3-19
Funding: LEA
Type of School: Day
Special Needs: Profound &
Multiple Learning
Difficulties

Thomas Parker School
Brookside
Telford
TF3 3AS
Age range: 4-16

Trench Hall Centre
Tilley Green
Wem
SY4 5PY
☎ 01939 232 372
Head of centre: Mr Robin
wilson
No. of pupils: 56
Age range: 11-16

Funding: LEA
Type of School: Day
Special Needs: Emotional
& behavioural difficulties

Somerset

Avalon School
Brooks Road
Street
BA16 0PS
☎ 01458 448 031
🖷 01458 447 380
Head: Mrs Jean King
No. of pupils: 88
Age range: 4-16
Funding: LEA
Type of School: Day
Special Needs: Speech and
Language Difficulties

Childscourt Boarding School
Lattiford House
Wincanton
BA9 8AH
☎ 01963 32213
No. of pupils: 45
Age range: 9-19

Critchill Special School
Nunney Road
Frome
BA11 4LB
☎ 01373 464 148
🖷 01373 453 481
email: office@
critchill.somerset.sch.uk
Head: Mr Leslie J Rowsell
No. of pupils: 65
Age range: 4-16
Funding: LEA
Type of School: Day
Special Needs: Moderate,
Severe and Profound &
Multiple Learning
Difficulties

Croydon Hall School
Felon's Oak
Minehead
TA24 6QT
☎ 01984 40249
Age range: 5-11

Edington & Shapwick School
Mark Road
Burtle
Bridgwater
TA7 8NJ

☎ 01278 722 012
🖷 01278 723 812
email: edington@
edingtonshapwick.co.uk
web:
www.edingtonshapwick.co.uk
Joint headmaster: Mr D C
Walker
No. of pupils: 165
Age range: 8-18
Funding: Independent
Type of School: Day
Special Needs: Specific
Learning Difficulties

Elmwood School
Hamp Avenue
Bridgwater
TA6 6AP
☎ 01278 422 866
🖷 01278 445 157
email: office@
elmwood.somerset.sch.uk
Head: Mrs Jaqui Tobin
No. of pupils: 81
Age range: 4-16
Funding: LEA
Type of School: Day
Special Needs: Moderate,
Complex & Severe
Learning Difficulties and
Autism

Fairmead School
Mudford Road
Yeovil
BA21 4NZ
☎ 01935 421 295
🖷 01935 410 552
email: sch.617@
educ.somerset.gov.uk
Head: Mrs V Brookham
No. of pupils: 96
Age range: 4-16
Funding: LEA
Type of School: Day
Special Needs: Complex
and Multiple Learning
Difficulties

Fiveways School
Victoria Road
Yeovil
BA21 5AZ
☎ 01935 476 227
🖷 01935 411 287
Head: Mr Collis
No. of pupils: 67
Age range: 4-19
Funding: LEA
Type of School: Day
Special Needs: Wide range

Glevum School
Kelston Close
Yate
BS17 4SZ
☎ 01454 318 219
No. of pupils: 90
Age range: 5-16

Kingsdon Manor School
Kingsdon
Somerton
TA11 7JZ
☎ 01935 840 323
No. of pupils: 40
Age range: 11-16

Mark College
Blackford Road
Mark
Highbridge
TA9 4NP
☎ 01278 641 632
🖷 01278 641 426
email: post@
markcollege.somerset.sch.uk
web: www.markcollege.
somerset.sch.uk
Head: Mrs J Kay
No. of pupils: 80
Age range: 10-17
Funding: Independent
Type of School: Residential
& Day
Special Needs: Dyslexia

Monkton Priors School
Pickeridge Close
Taunton
TA2 7HW
☎ 01823 275 569
🖷 01823 330 277
Head: Mr Glyn Toller
No. of pupils: 72
Age range: 5-16
Funding: LEA
Type of School: Day
Special Needs: Moderate
Learning Difficulties

Penrose School
Albert Street
Bridgwater
TA6 7ET
☎ 01278 423 660
🖷 01278 431 075
email: office@
penrose.somerset.sch.uk
Head: Susan Neale
No. of pupils: 42
Age range: 2-19
Funding: LEA

Type of School: Day
Special Needs: Severe
Learning Difficulties

Periton Mead School
Periton Road
Minehead
TA24 8DS
☎ 01643 702 013
No. of pupils: 40
Age range: 11-16

Sedgemoor
Ashwell Park
Ilminster
Somerset
TA19 9DX
☎ 01460 258000
🖷 01460 258006
Head: Liz Sharple
No. of pupils: 100
Age range: 11-16
Funding: Independent
Type of School: Residential
Special Needs: Hearing
Impaired, Emotional
Behavioural Difficulties &
Aspergers

Selworthy School
Selworthy Road
Taunton
TA2 8HD
☎ 01823 284 970
🖷 01823 336 519
Head: Mr David Machell
No. of pupils: 65
Age range: 2-19
Funding: LEA
Type of School: Day
Special Needs: Wide
range

The Marchant-Holliday School
North Cheriton
Templecombe
BA8 0AH
☎ 01963 33234
🖷 01963 33432
email: marcholsch.office@
talk21.com
Head: Mr J M Robertson
No. of pupils: 40
Age range: 7-12
Funding: Registered
charity
Type of School: Residential
Special Needs: Emotional
& Behavioural Difficulties,
Dyslexia & Autism

South Gloucestershire

Filton Park School
Charborough Road
Filton
BS12 7RB
☎ 0117 969 4224
Age range: 11-16

Grimsbury Park School
Tower Road
North Warmley
BS30 2XL
☎ 0117 967 3422
🖷 0117 935 2768
Head: Mr Stephen Morris
No. of pupils: 86
Age range: 3-19
Funding: LEA
Type of School: Day
Special Needs: Wide range

New Siblands School
Easton Hill Road
Thornbury
BS35 2JU
☎ 01454 866754
No. of pupils: 64
Age range: 2-19

Warmley Tower School
Tower Road North
Warmley
BS15 2XL
☎ 0117 967 6572
No. of pupils: 103
Age range: 5-16

South Yorkshire

Abbey School
Little Common Lane
Kimberworth
Rotherham
S61 2RA
No. of pupils: 132
Age range: 5-16

Anchorage School (Lower)
Cusworth Lane
York Road
Doncaster
DN5 8JL
☎ 01302 788 484
🖷 01302 390 135
No. of pupils: 152
Age range: 4-11

Anchorage Upper School
Barnsley Road
Scawsby
Doncaster

DN5 7UB
☎ 01302 391006
🖷 01302 390 135
email: admin@
anchorage.doncaster.sch.uk
No. of pupils: 162
Age range: 5-16
Funding: LEA
Type of School: Day
Special Needs: Autism and
Emotional and
Behavioural Difficulties

Athelstane School
Old Road
Conisbrough
Doncaster
DN12 3LR
☎ 01709 864 978
🖷 01709 770 172
Head: Mrs S Atkinson
No. of pupils: 120
Age range: 4-16
Funding: LEA
Type of School: Day
Special Needs: Moderate
Learning Difficulties

Bents Green Secondary School
Ringinglow Road
Sheffield
S11 7TB
☎ 0114 2363545
🖷 0114 2621904
email: enquiries@
bentsgreen.sheffield.sch.uk
No. of pupils: 103
Age range: 11-16
Type of School:
Residential/Day
Special Needs: Autism &
Communication
Difficulties

Broad Elms School
Broad Elms Lane
Sheffield
S11 9RQ
No. of pupils: 36
Age range: 4-12

Cedar School
Cedar Road
Balby
Doncaster
DN4 9HT
☎ 01302 853 361
🖷 01302 853 922
No. of pupils: 79
Age range: 3-19

7

Chase School
Ash Hill
Hatfield
Doncaster
DN7 6JH
☎ 01302 844 883
🖷 01302 841 052
Head: Mr W John Evans
No. of pupils: 95
Age range: 3-19
Funding: LEA
Type of School: Day
Special Needs: Autism and
Severe Learning
Difficulties

Crevesford School
St Helens Boulevard
Carlton Road
Barnsley
S71 2AY
No. of pupils: 64
Age range: 2-19
Funding: LEA
Type of School: Day
Special Needs: Profound &
Multiple Learning
Difficulties

Deerlands School
Lindsay Road
Sheffield
S5 7WE
☎ 0114 2400271
🖷 0114 2571237
Head: Miss K M Stallard
No. of pupils: 40
Age range: 11-16
Type of School: Day
Special Needs: Emotional
& behavioural difficulties

Dr John Worrall School
Maltby Street
Attercliffe
Sheffield
S9 2QA
No. of pupils: 56
Age range: 5-16

East Hill Primary School
East Bank Road
Sheffield
S2 3PX
☎ 0114 272 9897
Head: Mr Terry Johnson
No. of pupils: 56
Age range: 5-11
Funding: LEA
Type of School: Day
Special Needs: Moderate
Learning Difficulties

**East Hill Secondary
School**
41 East Bank Road
Sheffield
S2 3PX
☎ 0114 276 0245
🖷 0114 272 8829
email: enquiries@easthill-
sec.sheffield.sch.uk
Head: Mr Keith Jenkins
No. of pupils: 110
Age range: 11-16
Funding: LEA
Type of School: Day
Special Needs: Moderate
Learning Difficulties

Fernbank School
Village Street
Adwick-le-Street
Doncaster
DN6 7AA
☎ 01302 723 571
🖷 01302 724 196
Head: Mr Wright
No. of pupils: 74
Age range: 3-19
Funding: LEA
Type of School: Day
Special Needs: Profound &
Multiple Learning
Difficulties and Severe
Learning Difficulties

**Folkwood Secondary
School**
Ringinglow Road
Sheffield
S11 7TB
No. of pupils: 42
Age range: 10-16

Fullerton House School
Off Tickhill Square
Denaby
Doncaster
DN12 4AR
☎ 01709 861 663
🖷 01709 869 635
email: doconner@
fullerton.fq.co.uk
web: www.hesleygroup.com
Head: Mr David
O'Conner
No. of pupils: 36
Age range: 8-19
Funding: Independent
Type of School: Residential
Special Needs: Severe
Learning Difficulties,
Autism and Challenging
Behaviour

Green Arbour School
Locksley Drive
Thurcroft
Rotherham
S66 9NT
☎ 01709 542 539
🖷 01709 703 198
email: green-
arbour.special@
rotherham.gov.uk
web:
www.greenarbour.co.uk
Head: Mr Philip
Gawthorpe
No. of pupils: 140
Age range: 5-16
Funding: LEA
Type of School: Day
Special Needs: Wide
range

Greenacre School
Keresforth Hill Road
Barnsley
S70 6RG
☎ 01226 287 165
🖷 01226 295 328
Head: Mr John Short
No. of pupils: 169
Age range: 3-19
Funding: LEA
Type of School: Day
Special Needs: Moderate
Learning Difficulties,
Autism, Profound &
Multiple Learning
Difficulties and Severe
Learning Difficulties

Hallam Lodge
96 Tapton Crescent Road
Sheffield
S10 5DD

Hesley Village College
Tickhill
Doncaster
DN11 9HH
☎ 01308 868313
email: sekins@
hesleygroup.co.uk
Head: Mrs S P Ekins
No. of pupils: 72
Age range: 16
Funding: LEA/Health/
Social Services
Type of School: Residential
College
Special Needs: Autism/
Social Challenging
Behaviour

Hilltop School
Larch Road
Maltby
Rotherham
S66 8AZ
☎ 01709 813 386
🖷 01709 798 383
Head: Mr Peter Leach
No. of pupils: 82
Age range: 2-19
Funding: LEA
Type of School: Day
Special Needs: Profound &
Multiple Learning
Difficulties

**Hospital Education
(Sheffield HHES)**
Sheffield Childrens
Hospital
Western Bank
Sheffield
S10 2TJ
☎ 0114 271 7146
email: icook@sheffch-
tr.treat.nhs.uk
web: www.sheffch-
tr.treat.nhs.uk
Head: Dr Irene Cook
No. of pupils: 2000
Age range: 5-18
Funding: LEA
Type of School: Hospital
Special Needs: Medical

**Hospital & Home
Education Service**
Clarkhouse Centre
24 Clarkhouse Road
Sheffield
S10 2LB
☎ 0114 2683853
🖷 0114 2683853
Head: Mrs Avril Bramhall
Age range: 4-16
Funding: LEA
Type of School: Hospital

Kelford School
Oakdale Road
Rotherham
S61 2NU
☎ 01709 512 088
🖷 01709 512 091
email: susang@kelford-
school.co.uk/kelford.special
@rotheram.gov.uk
Head: Mrs Susan
Greenhough
No. of pupils: 110
Age range: 2-19
Funding: LEA

Type of School: Day
Special Needs: Profound &
Multiple Learning
Difficulties

**Leger Way Pupil Referral
Unit**
Leger Way
Doncaster
DN2 5RW
☎ 01302 340 287
🖷 01302 340 287
Head: Mr M R
Hammerton
No. of pupils: 30
Age range: 1-6
Funding: LEA
Type of School: Pupil
Referral Unit
Special Needs: Emotional
& behavioural difficulties

**Mossbrook Infant and
Junior School**
Bochum Parkway
Norton
Sheffield
S8 8JR
☎ 0114 237 2768
🖷 0114 283 9253
email: enquiries@
mossbrook.sheffield.sch,uk
web: www.mossbrook.
sheffield.sch.uk
Head: Ms Maggie Brough
No. of pupils: 76
Age range: 4-11
Funding: LEA
Type of School: Residential
Special Needs: Wide range,
including autism and SLD

Milton School
Storey Street
Swinton
Mexborough
S64 8QG
☎ 01709 570246
🖷 01709 572009
email: office@
milton.rotherham.sch.uk
Head: Mr C D Garford
No. of pupils: 115
Age range: 4-16
Funding: LEA
Type of School: Day
Special Needs: Multiple
Learning Difficulties and
Autism

Newman School
East Bawtry Road

Whiston
Rotherham
S60 3LX
☎ 01709 828 262
🖷 01709 821 162
email: office@newman.
rotherham.sch.uk
Head: Mrs S Garland-
Grimes
No. of pupils: 96
Age range: 2-19
Funding: LEA
Type of School: Day
Special Needs: Medical/
Physical Disabilities

**Norfolk Park Primary
School**
Park Grange Road
Sheffield
S2 3QF
No. of pupils: 50
Age range: 3-11

Oakes Park School
Matthews Lane
Norton
Sheffield
S8 8JS
No. of pupils: 57
Age range: 2-19

Oakes Park School
Hemsworth Road
Norton
Sheffield
S8 8LN
☎ 0114 255 6754
🖷 0114 255 4533
Head: Mrs P Johnson
No. of pupils: 55
Age range: 2-19
Funding: LEA
Type of School: Day
Special Needs: Sensory/
Communication
Difficulties

Oakwood School
Oakwood Young People's
Centre
Northern General Hospital
Herries Road
Sheffield
S5 7AU
☎ 0114 226 1691
🖷 0114 226 1962
email: enquiries@
oakwood.sheffield.sch.uk
Head: Mrs W Dudley
No. of pupils: 25
Age range: 11-18
Funding: LEA

Type of School:
Residential/Day
Special Needs: Emotional
& behavioural difficulties

Rossington Hall School
Bawtry Road
Rossington
Doncaster
DN11 0HS
☎ 01302 868 365
🖷 01302 865 620
No. of pupils: 123
Age range: 5-16

Rowan Special School
Durvale Court
Furniss Avenue
Sheffield
S17 3PT
☎ 0114 2350479
🖷 0114 2350478
email: enquiries@
rowan.sheffield.sch.uk
Head: Ms S A Chantler
No. of pupils: 64
Age range: 4-11
Funding: LEA
Type of School: Day
Special Needs: Severe
Communication
Difficulties

Sandall Wood School
Leger Way
Doncaster
DN2 6HQ
☎ 01302 322 044
🖷 01302 739 927
Head: Mrs Carol M Ray
No. of pupils: 65
Age range: 3-19
Funding: LEA
Type of School: Day
Special Needs: Medical

**Shirle Hill Hospital
School**
Cherry Tree Road
Sheffield
S11 9AA
No. of pupils: 14
Age range: 3-13
Special Needs: Emotional
& Behavioural Difficulties

Tapton Mount School
20 Manchester Road
Sheffield
S10 5DG
No. of pupils: 20
Age range: 4-12

The Gables School
Bondfield Crescent
Wombwell
Barnsley
S73 8TL
No. of pupils: 57
Age range: 2-19

The Robert Ogden School
Clayton Lane
Thurnscoe
Rotherham
S63 0BE
☎ 01709 874443
Training Co-ordinator:
Mrs J Symonds
No. of pupils: 136
Age range: 3-19
Special Needs: Autism

**The Rowan Primary
School**
4 Durvale Court
Sheffield
S11 8RB
☎ 0114 235 0479
🖷 0114 235 0478
Head: Mr Rob Quayle
No. of pupils: 64
Age range: 4-10
Funding: LEA
Type of School: Day
Special Needs: Speech and
Language Difficulties

Whiston Grange School
East Bawtry Road
Whiston
Rotherham
S60 3LX
☎ 01709 828 838
🖷 01709 828 838
Head: Mrs P Storey
No. of pupils: 43
Age range: 11-16
Funding: LEA
Type of School: Day
Special Needs: Emotional,
behavioural and social
difficulties

Wilsic Hall School
Wadworth
Doncaster
DN11 9AG
Textphone 01302 856382
email: mhenderson@
hesleygroup.co.uk
web: www.hesleygroup.co.uk
No. of pupils: 33
Age range: 11-19
Funding: Independent

7

Type of School: Residential
Special Needs: Severe
Learning Difficulties,
Autism, Severe
Challenging Behaviour

Woolley Wood School
Oaks Fold Road
Sheffield
S5 0TG
☎ 0114 245 6885
▤ 0114 257 0269
Head: Ms M J Holly
No. of pupils: 56
Age range: 3-11
Funding: LEA
Type of School: Day
Special Needs: Profound &
Multiple Learning
Difficulties

**Yorkshire Residential
School for Deaf Children**
Leger Way
Doncaster
DN2 6AY
☎ 01302 322822
Textphone 01302 344524
▤ 01302 342166
email: enquiries@
yrsd-dcd.org.uk
web: www.yrsd-dcd.org.uk
No. of pupils: 211
Age range: 3-19

Southwark

Beormund Primary School
Crosby Row
Long Lane
London
SE1 3PS
☎ 020 7525 9027
▤ 020 7525 9026
Head: Sharon Gray
No. of pupils: 35
Age range: 5-11
Funding: LEA
Type of School: Day
Special Needs: Emotional
& behavioural difficulties

**Guys Evelina Hospital
School**
Guys Hospital Tower
St Thomas Street
London
SE1 9RT
☎ 020 79554841
▤ 020 79554197
email: school@
guys-evelina.demon.co.uk
Head: Ms Christine Wood

No. of pupils: 35
Age range: 2-19
Funding: LEA
Type of School: Hospital
Special Needs: Various

Staffordshire

Abbey Hill School
Greasley Road
Bucknall
Stoke-on-Trent
ST2 8LG
☎ 01782 234 727
▤ 01782 234 729
Head: Mrs Merrilyn
Coutonidis
No. of pupils: 222
Age range: 3-18
Funding: LEA
Type of School: Day
Special Needs: Autism &
Moderate Learning
Difficulties & Severe
Learning Difficulties

Ace Centre
Milton Street
Shelton
Stoke-on-Trent
ST14LE
☎ 01782 235646
▤ 01782 595 509
Head of centre: Mrs R
Chambers
No. of pupils: 12
Funding: LEA
Type of School: Day
Special Needs: SEBD

Aynsley School
Aynsley's Drive
Blythe Bridge
Stoke-on-Trent
ST11 9HJ
☎ 01782 392 071
▤ 01782 388 911
Head: Mr I T Jeffery
No. of pupils: 120
Age range: 4-18
Funding: LEA
Type of School: Day
Special Needs: Moderate
Learning Difficulties

Beecroft Hill School
Brunswick Road
Cannock
WS11 2SF
☎ 01543 510 216
▤ 01543 510 222
No. of pupils: 86
Age range: 2-19

Blackfriars School
Priory Road
Newcastle-under-Lyme
ST5 2TF
☎ 01782 297 780
▤ 01782 297 784
email: admin@
blackfriars.staffs.sch.uk
web: www.sln.org.uk/
blackfriars
Head: Mr Clive Lilley
No. of pupils: 180
Age range: 2-19
Funding: LEA
Type of School: Day
Special Needs: Physical &
Medical difficulties with
associated learning and
sensory difficulties

Cicely Haughton School
Westwood Manor
Wetley Rocks
Stoke-on-Trent
ST9 0BX
☎ 01782 550 202
▤ 01782 550202
Head: Mr N Phillips
No. of pupils: 54
Age range: 5-11
Funding: LEA
Type of School:
Residential/Day
Special Needs: Emotional
& Behavioural Difficulties

Coppice Special School
Abbots Way
Westlands
Newcastle-under-Lyme
ST5 2EY
☎ 01782 297490
▤ 01782 297496
email: office@
coppice.staff.sch.uk
Head: Mr Andrew Black
No. of pupils: 135
Age range: 4-16
Funding: LEA
Type of School: Day
Special Needs: Moderate
Learning Difficulties and
Emotional & behavioural
difficulties

Crown School
Bitham Lane Stretton
Burton-upon-Trent
DE13 9BP
☎ 01283 239 700
▤ 01283 239701
email: headteacher@
crown.staffs.sch.uk

Head: Mrs J Harris
No. of pupils: 94
Age range: 3-18
Funding: LEA
Type of School: Day
Special Needs: Profound &
Multiple Learning
Difficulties

**Greenhall Community
Special School**
Second Avenue
Holmcroft
Stafford
ST16 1PS
☎ 01785 246 159
▤ 01785 215 490
Age range: 2-5

Heathfield School
Chell Heath Road
Chell Heath
Stoke-on-Trent
ST6 6PD
☎ 01782 234 494
No. of pupils: 54
Age range: 2-19

Horton Lodge School
Rudyard
Leek
ST13 8RB
☎ 01538 306 214
▤ 001538 306 006
email: headteacher@
hortonlodgestaffs.sch.uk
web:
www.hortonlodgestaffs.sch.uk
Head: Ms C J Coles
No. of pupils: 61
Age range: 2-11
Type of School: Residential
Special Needs: Physical
Disabilities

Kemball School
Duke Street
Fenton
Stoke-on-Trent
ST4 3NR
☎ 01782 234 879
▤ 01782 234 880
email: liz.spooner@
dial.pipex.com
web: www.dial.pipex.com
Head: Mrs E Spooner
No. of pupils: 77
Age range: 2-19
Funding: LEA
Type of School: Day
Special Needs: Severe
Learning Difficulties

Longdon Hall School
Longdon Green
Rugeley
WS15 4PT
☎ 01543 490 634
🖹 01543 492 140
email: longdonhallschool@
honormead.btinternet.com
web: www.honormead.
btinternet.com
Head: Mrs C A Georgeson
No. of pupils: 96
Age range: 5-19
Funding: Independent
Type of School: Residential
Special Needs: Autism

Loxley Hall School
Stafford Road
Uttoxeter
ST14 8RS
☎ 01889 256390
No. of pupils: 60
Age range: 11-16
Funding: LEA
Type of School: Residential
Special
Special Needs: Emotional
& behavioural difficulties

Maple Hayes Hall School
Abnalls Lane
Lichfield
WS13 8BL
☎ 01543 264 387
🖹 01543 262 022
email: office@
dyslexia.gb.com
web: www.dyslexia.gb.com
Head: Dr D J Brown
No. of pupils: 100
Age range: 7-17
Funding: LEA
Type of School: Day
Special Needs: Dyslexia
and Specific Learning
Difficulties

Marshlands School
Lansdowne Way
Wildwood
Stafford
ST17 4RD
☎ 01785 664 475
No. of pupils: 44
Age range: 2-19

Meadows Special School
Tunstall Road
Biddulph
Stoke-on-Trent
ST8 7AB

☎ 01782 297 920
No. of pupils: 121
Age range: 3-19

Merryfields School
Hoon Avenue
Newcastle-under-Lyme
ST5 9NY
☎ 01782 296 076
🖹 01782 715 332
Head: Mrs Anne Bird
No. of pupils: 84
Age range: 2-19
Funding: LEA
Type of School: Day
Special Needs: Profound &
Multiple Learning
Difficulties

Middlehurst School
Turnhurst Road
Chell
Stoke-on-Trent
ST6 6NQ
☎ 01782 234 612
🖹 01782 236 407
No. of pupils: 100
Age range: 3-16
Funding: LEA
Type of School: Day
Special Needs: Moderate
Learning Difficulties

Newhouse School
Newhouse Road
Bucknall
Stoke-on-Trent
ST2 8BH
☎ 01782 264 163
Age range: 10-16

**Queen's Croft
Community School**
Birmingham Road
Lichfield
WS13 6PJ
☎ 01543 510 669
🖹 01543 510 673
email: office@
queenscroft.staffs.sch.uk
Head: Mr J Edwards
No. of pupils: 150
Age range: 5-16

Quince Tree School
Quince
Tamworth
B77 4EN
☎ 01827 475 740
🖹 01827 475 740
email: headteacher@
quincetree.staffs.sch.uk

web:
www.quincetree.staffs.sch.uk
Head: V A Vernon
No. of pupils: 80
Age range: 2-19
Funding: LEA
Special Needs: Severe
Learning Difficulties

Rocklands School
Wissage Road
Lichfield
WS13 6SW
☎ 01543 510 760
🖹 01543 510 762
Head: Mr A J Dooley
No. of pupils: 84
Age range: 2-19
Funding: LEA
Type of School: Day
Special Needs: Wide range

Saxon Hill School
Kings Hill Road
Lichfield
WS14 9DE
☎ 01543 510 615
🖹 01543 510 626
email: headteacher@
saxonhill.staffs.sch.uk
web:
www.saxonhill.staffs.sch.uk
Head: Mr D J Butcher
No. of pupils: 112
Age range: 2-19
Funding: LEA
Type of School:
Day/Residential
Special Needs: Physical
disabilities

Springfield Special School
Springfield Road
Leek
ST13 6LQ
☎ 01538 383 558
🖹 01538 383 558
email: headteacher@
springfield.staffs.sch.uk
Head: Mrs Irene Corden
No. of pupils: 45
Age range: 2-19
Funding: LEA
Type of School: Day
Special Needs: Wide range

Stretton Brook School
Bitham Lane Stretton
Burton-upon-Trent
DE13 0HB
☎ 01283 239 161
🖹 01283 239 168

email: headteacher@
strettonbrook.staffs.sch.uk
web: www.strettonbrook.
staffs.sch.uk
Head: Mr ST Gair
No. of pupils: 124
Age range: 4-18
Funding: LEA
Type of School: Day

**The Mount School for the
Deaf**
Penkhull
Stoke-on-Trent
ST4 7JU
☎ 01782 236140
Textphone 01782 236140
🖹 01782 236140
Age range: 2-16

The Park School
Solway Close
Leyfields
Tamworth
B79 8EB
☎ 01827 475 690
🖹 01827 475 697
email: office@
park.staffs.sch.uk
web: www.park.staffs.sch.uk
Head: Mr Frank Bartlett
No. of pupils: 130
Age range: 4-16
Funding: LEA
Type of School: Day
Special Needs: Moderate
Learning Difficulties

**Walton Hall Special
School**
Stafford Road
Eccleshall
ST21 6JR
☎ 01785 850 420
🖹 01785 850 225
No. of pupils: 126
Age range: 5-18

Westwood School
Blithbury
Rugeley
WS15 3JQ
☎ 01889 504 353
🖹 01889 504 361
No. of pupils: 48

**Whittington Grange
School**
Burton Road
Whittington
Lichfield

7

WS14 9NU
☎ 01543 432 296
🖷 01543 433 254
Head: Mr David J Winzor
No. of pupils: 30
Age range: 11-16
Funding: LEA
Type of School: Residential
Special Needs: Emotional
& behavioural difficulties

William Baxter School
Stanley Road
Hednesford
WS12 4JS
☎ 01543 423 714
🖷 01543 423 714
email: headteacher@
williambaxter.staffs.sch.uk
web: www.williambaxter.
staffs.sch.uk
Head: Mrs C M Allsop
No. of pupils: 120
Age range: 4-16
Funding: LEA

Suffolk

Ashley School
Ashley Downs
Lowestoft
NR32 4EU
☎ 01502 574 847
🖷 01502 531 920
Head: Mr David Field
No. of pupils: 120
Age range: 7-16
Funding: LEA
Type of School: Residential
& Day
Special Needs: Moderate
Learning Difficulties

Beacon Hill School
Stone Lodge Lane West
Ipswich
IP2 9HW
No. of pupils: 137
Age range: 5-16

Belstead School
Sprites Lane
Ipswich
IP8 3ND
☎ 01473 556 200
🖷 01473 556 209
Head: Sue Chesworth
No. of pupils: 76
Age range: 11-19
Funding: LEA
Type of School: Day
Special Needs: Profound &

Multiple Learning
Difficulties

Bramfield House School
Walpole Road
Bramfield
Halesworth
IP19 9AB
No. of pupils: 33
Age range: 10-16

Hampden House
Cats Lane
Great Cornard
Sudbury
CO10 6SF
☎ 01787 333583
email: mcharlton2@
compuserve.com
Head: Mr M W Charlton
No. of pupils: 22
Age range: 7-16
Funding: LEA
Type of School: Day &
Residential
Special Needs: Emotional
& Behavioural Difficulties

Heathside School
Heath Road
Ipswich
IP4 5SN
☎ 01473 725 508
🖷 01473 724 419
Head: Mr O Doran
No. of pupils: 61
Age range: 3-11
Funding: LEA
Type of School: Day
Special Needs: Profound &
Multiple Learning
Difficulties, Autism and
Severe Learning
Difficulties

**Hillcroft Preparatory
School**
The Dyslexia Unit
Walnutree Manor
Haughley Green
Stowmarket
IP14 3RQ
☎ 01449 673 003
🖷 01449 613 072
Head: Mr Fred Rapsey
No. of pupils: 90
Age range: 2-13
Funding: Independent
Type of School: Day
Special Needs: Dyslexia,
Dyspraxia, Asperger
Syndrome, etc.

Hillside Special School
Hitchcock Place
Sudbury
CO10 1NN
☎ 01787 372 808
🖷 01787 375 249
email: ad.hillside.s@
talk21.com
Head: Miss June Freeman
No. of pupils: 71
Age range: 3-19
Funding: LEA
Type of School: Day
Special Needs: Severe
Learning Difficulties/
Profound & Multiple
Learning Difficulties/
Autism

Old Warren House School
Warren Road
Lowestoft
NR32 4QD
☎ 01502 511 794
🖷 01502 511 794
Head: Mr Ian Johnson
No. of pupils: 35
Age range: 14-16
Funding: LEA
Type of School: Pupil
Referral Unit
Special Needs: Emotional
& behavioural difficulties

Priory School
Mount Road
Bury St Edmunds
IP32 7BH
No. of pupils: 101
Age range: 7-16

Riverwalk School
South Close
Bury St Edmunds
IP33 3QE
☎ 01284 764 280
🖷 01284 705 943
Head: Mr Barry Ellis
No. of pupils: 103
Age range: 3-19
Funding: LEA
Type of School: Day
Special Needs: Severe
Learning Difficulties

The Kingsford Centre
Chilton Way
Stowmarket
IP14 1SZ
☎ 01449 613931
🖷 01449 775421
No. of pupils: 24

Age range: 7-11
Funding: LEA
Type of School: Pupil
Referral Unit
Special Needs: Emotional
& behavioural Difficulties

The Old Rectory School
Church Road
Brettenham
Ipswich
IP7 7QR
☎ 01449 736 404
🖷 01449 737 881
email: oldrectoryschool@
aol.com
web:
www.theoldrectorschool.com
Head: Miss Furlong
No. of pupils: 50
Age range: 7-13
Funding: Independent
Type of School: Day
Special Needs: Wide range

The Ryes School
Little Henny
Sudbury
CO10 7EA
☎ 01787 374 998
🖷 01787 371 995
email: office@
ryes-school.demon.co.uk
Head: Mr Torsten Friedag
No. of pupils: 30
Age range: 7-16
Funding: Independent
Type of School: Residential
Special Needs: Wide range

Thomas Wolsey School
642 Old Norwich Road
Ipswich
IP1 6LU
☎ 01473 467 600
🖷 01473 465 225
email: office@
thomaswolsey.com
web:
www.thomaswolsey.com
Head: Mrs Nancy McArdle
No. of pupils: 82
Age range: 3-19
Funding: LEA
Type of School: Day
Special Needs: Medical

Warren School
Clarkes Lane
Oulton Broad
Lowestoft
NR33 8HT

☎ 01502 561 893
🖨 01502 561 893
email: ad.warren.s@
talk21.com
Head: Mr Chris Moore
No. of pupils: 107
Age range: 3-19
Funding: LEA
Type of School: Day
Special Needs: Profound,
Severe & Multiple
Learning Difficulties

Surrey

Bensham Manor
Ecclesbourne Road
Thornton Heath
CR7 7BR
☎ 020 8684 0116
Head: Mrs E J Green
No. of pupils: 170
Age range: 11-16
Funding: LEA
Type of School: Day
Special Needs: Moderate
Learning Difficulties

Brooklands School
27 Wray Park Road
Reigate
RH2 0DF
☎ 01737 249 941
🖨 01737 242 017
email: office@
brooklands.surrey.sch.uk
Head: Mrs Susan Wakenell
No. of pupils: 82
Age range: 2-10
Funding: LEA
Type of School: Day
Special Needs: Profound &
Multiple Learning
Difficulties/Severe
Learning Difficulties

Carew Manor School
Church Road
Wallington
SM6 7NH
☎ 020 8647 8349
🖨 020 8647 1739
Head: M Midgley
No. of pupils: 128
Age range: 7-16
Funding: LEA
Type of School: Day
Special Needs: Moderate
Learning Difficulties

Carwarden House School
118 Upper Chobham Road

Camberley
GU15 1EJ
No. of pupils: 138
Age range: 7-16

Clifton Hill School
Chaldon Road
Caterham
CR3 5PH
☎ 01883 347 740
🖨 01883 349 617
email: info@
clifton-hill.surrey.sch.uk
Head: Mrs Marion
Unsworth
No. of pupils: 80
Age range: 8-19
Funding: LEA
Type of School: Day
Special Needs: Profound &
Multiple Learning
Difficulties

Cricket Green School
Lower Green West
Mitcham
CR4 3AF
☎ 020 8640 1177
🖨 020 8640 4539
email: schcgss@
merton.gov.uk
Head: Mrs Celia Dawson
No. of pupils: 120
Age range: 5-16
Funding: LEA
Special Needs: Diverse
Learning Needs

Dysart School
Dukes Avenue
Kingston-upon-Thames
KT2 5QY
No. of pupils: 65
Age range: 2-19
Funding: LEA
Type of School: Day
Special Needs: Wide range

Fordway Centre
Stanwell Road
Ashford
TW15 3DX
☎ 01784 243365
🖨 01784 423664
No. of pupils: 24
Age range: 5-11
Funding: LEA
Type of School: Day
Special Needs: Emotional
& behavioural difficulties

Gosden House School
Bramley

Guildford
GU5 0AH
☎ 01483 892 008
email: Info@GosdenHouse.
Surrey.SCH.UK**
web: www.gosdenhouse.
surrey.SCH.UK**
Head: Mr Jon David
No. of pupils: 120
Age range: 5-16
Funding: LEA
Type of School: Residential
Special Needs: Moderate
Learning Difficulties and
Speech and Language
Difficulties

Grafham Grange School
Bramley
Guildford
GU5 0LH
No. of pupils: 32
Age range: 10-16

Heathermount School
Devenish Road
Ascot
SL5 9PG
☎ 01344 875 101
🖨 01344 875 102
email: heathermount@
compuserve.com
web: www.compuserve.com
Principal of Children's
Services: Ms Stephanie Lord
No. of pupils: 62
Age range: 3-19
Funding: NMS
Type of School: Residential
& Day
Special Needs: Aspergers

**Helen Arkell Dyslexia
Centre**
Frensham
Farnham
GU10 3BW
☎ 01252 792 400
Academic Director: Mrs
Bernadette McLean
Age range: 6-16
Funding: Registered charity

**Hospital & Individual
Tuition Service**
Draper's Building
The Drive
Orchard Hill
Carshalton
SM5 4NR
☎ 020 8770 8146
Head of Serive: Mrs M
Csillag

No. of pupils: 220
Age range: 5-19
Funding: LEA

John Nightingale School
Hurst Road
West Molesey
KT8 9QS
☎ 020 8224 9119
🖨 020 8224 9118
Head: Mr A Withers
No. of pupils: 47
Age range: 11-16
Funding: LEA
Type of School: Day
Special Needs: Emotional
& behavioural difficulties

Limpsfield Grange School
89 Bluehouse Lane
Oxted
RH8 0RZ
☎ 01883 713 928
🖨 01883 730 578
email: secretary@
limpsfield-grange.
surrey.sch.uk
Head: Mrs J A Humphreys
No. of pupils: 56
Age range: 11-16
Funding: LEA
Type of School: Girls
Special Needs: Wide range

**Linden Bridge School &
Spring Centre**
Grafton Road
Worcester Park
KT4 7JW
☎ 020 8330 3009
🖨 020 8330 6811
email: info@
linden-bridge.surrey.sch.uk
No. of pupils: 120
Age range: 4-19
Funding: LEA
Type of School:
Residential/Day
Special Needs: Autism

Link Day Primary School
138 Croydon Road
Beddington
Croydon
CR0 4PG
☎ 020 8688 5239
No. of pupils: 36
Age range: 6-12

Manor Mead School
Laleham Road
Shepperton

7

TW17 8EL
☎ 01932 241 834
🖷 01932 248 927
email: office@
manor-mead.surrey.sch.uk
Head: Mrs Fiona Neal
No. of pupils: 55
Age range: 2-11
Funding: LEA
Type of School: Day
Special Needs: Severe
Learning Difficulties

Meath School, ICAN
Brox Road
Ottershaw
KT16 0LF
☎ 01932 872302
🖷 01932 875180
email: meath@ican.org.uk
web: www.ican.org.uk
Head: Mr J Parrott
No. of pupils: 75
Age range: 5-11
Funding: LEA
Type of School: Residential
& Day
Special Needs: Speech &
Language Difficulties

Melrose School
Church Road
Mitcham
CR4 3BE
No. of pupils: 43
Age range: 9-16

Mill Lane Hurst Green
Oxted
RH8 9AQ
☎ 01883 712 271
🖷 01883 716 722
No. of pupils: 84
Age range: 7-16
Funding: Non-maintained
Special Needs: Speech and
Language Difficulties

**Moon Hall School for
Dyslexic Children**
Pasturewood Lane
Holmbury St Mary
Dorking
RH5 6LO
☎ 01306 731 464
🖷 01306 731 504
email: moonhall@
rmplc.co.uk
web: www.rmplc.co.uk/
eduweb/sites/moonhall/
Head: Mrs Jill Lovett
No. of pupils: 104

Age range: 7-13
Funding: Registered charity
Type of School: Day
Special Needs: Dyslexia

More House School
Frensham
Farnham
GU10 3AP
☎ 01252 792303
🖷 01252 797601
email: schooloffice@
morehouse.surrey.sch.uk
No. of pupils: 192
Age range: 9-18
Type of School: Day &
Boarding

**National Centre for Young
People with Epilepsy**
St Piers Lane
Lingfield
RH7 6PW
☎ 01342 832 243
🖷 01342 834 639
email: info@ncype.org.uk
web: www.ncype.org.uk
No. of pupils: 200
Age range: 5-19
Funding: Registered charity
Type of School: Residential
& Day
Special Needs: Epilepsy
and other neurological &
behavioural disorders

Philip Southcote School
Addlestonemoor
Addlestone
Surrey
KT15 2QH
☎ 01932 652326
🖷 01932 567092
email: info@philip-
southcote.surrey.sch.uk
Head: Mr G L Rogers
No. of pupils: 110
Age range: 7-16
Funding: LEA
Type of School: Day
Special Needs: Multiple
Learning Difficulties

Phoenix Centre
Alpine Road
Redhill
RH1 2HY
☎ 01737 767521
🖷 01737 767521
email: head@phoenix-
centre.surrey.sch.uk
Head of Centre: Thelma
Bartlett

No. of pupils: 6
Age range: 5-11
Funding: LEA
Type of School: Pupil
Referral Unit
Special Needs: Emotional
& Behavioural Difficulties

Pond Meadow School
Pond Meadow
Park Barn
Guildford
GU2 8YG
☎ 01483 532239
🖷 01483 537049
email: office@pond-
meadow.surrey.sch.uk
Head: David Monk
No. of pupils: 62
Age range: 2-19
Funding: LEA
Type of School: Day
Special Needs: Autism and
Severe Learning
Difficulties

Portesbery School
Portesbery Road
Camberley
GU15 3SZ
☎ 01276 63078
🖷 01276 29234
Head: Anne Davies
No. of pupils: 62
Age range: 2-19
Funding: LEA
Type of School: Day
Special Needs: Severe
Learning Difficulties

Pyrford Centre
Engliff Lane
Pyrford
Woking
GU22 8SU
☎ 01932 342 451
🖷 01932 336 517
Acting Head: Mrs M
Reddick
No. of pupils: 24
Age range: 11-16
Funding: LEA
Type of School: Day
Special Needs: Emotional
& behavioural difficulties

Red Gates School
489 Purley Way
Croydon
CR0 4RG
☎ 020 8688 1761
🖷 020 8680 2167
Age range: 3-14

Red House School
Brighton Road
Tadworth
KT20 6AY
Age range: 8-16

Rutherford School
1a Melville Avenue
South Croydon
CR2 7HZ
☎ 020 8688 7560
🖷 020 8406 8220
email: rutherford@
garwoodfoundation.org.uk
web: www.garwood
foundation.org.uk
Head: Mrs Ruth Hills
No. of pupils: 24
Age range: 2-12
Funding: Independent
Type of School: Day
Special Needs: Medical

Sherwood Park School
Streeters Lane
Wallington
SM6 7NP
☎ 020 8773 9930
🖷 020 8770 6788
No. of pupils: 77
Age range: 2-19
Funding: LEA
Type of School: Day
Special Needs: Severe
Learning
Difficulties/Profound &
Multiple Learning
Difficulties

Sidlow Bridge Centre
Irons Bottom Lane
Sidlow
Reigate
RH2 8PP
Age range: 11-16

St Ann's School
Bordesley Road
Morden
SM4 5LT
☎ 020 8648 9737
🖷 020 8640 5185
Head: Ms Tina Harvey
No. of pupils: 90
Age range: 2-19
Funding: LEA
Type of School: Day
Special Needs: Profound &
Multiple Learning
Difficulties

St Dominic's School
Hambledon

Godalming
GU8 4DX
☎ 01428 684 693
🖹 01428 685 018
email: office@
stdominicsschool.org.uk
Head: Mr Gerry Chapman
No. of pupils: 95
Age range: 8-16
Funding: Non-maintained
Type of School: Day &
Weekly Boarding
Special Needs: Specific
Learning Difficulties and
Speech & Language &
Social Communication
Difficulties

St Giles School
Pampisford Road
Croydon
CR2 6DF
☎ 020 8680 2141
🖹 020 8681 6359
email: admin@
st-giles.croydon.sch.uk
Head: Mrs J Thomas
No. of pupils: 113
Age range: 2-16
Funding: LEA
Type of School: Day
Special Needs: PD

St Joseph's School
Amlets Lane
Cranleigh
GU6 7NQ
No. of pupils: 66
Age range: 8-19
Funding: Independent
Type of School: Day
Special Needs: Moderate
Learning Difficulties &
Speech and Language
Difficulties

**St Margaret's School at
Tadworth Court**
Tadworth Court
Tadworth
KT20 5RU
☎ 01737 357 171
🖹 01737 359 189
Head: Mrs J E
Cunningham
No. of pupils: 40
Age range: 8-19
Funding: Registered charity
Type of School: Boarding
Special Needs: Medical

St Nicholas School
Taynton Drive

Merstham
Redhill
RH1 3PU
No. of pupils: 65
Age range: 10-16

St Nicholas School
Reedham Drive
Old Lodge Lane
Purley
CR8 4DN
☎ 020 8660 4861
🖹 020 8660 8119
email: headteacher@
st-nicholas.croydon.sch.uk
Head: Mrs J Melton
No. of pupils: 103
Age range: 4-11
Funding: LEA
Type of School: Day
Special Needs: Mild,
Speech & Communication
Disorders and Autism

Starhurst School
Chart Lane South
Dorking
RH5 4DB
No. of pupils: 65
Age range: 11-16

Strathmore School
Meadlands Drive,
Petersham
Richmond
TW10 7ED
No. of pupils: 45
Age range: 3-19

Sunnydown School
Portley House
152 Whyteleafe Road
Caterham
CR3 5ED
No. of pupils: 74
Age range: 10-16

Sycamore Centre
14 West Hill
Epsom
KT19 8HR
Age range: 4-16

The Abbey School
Menin Way
Farnham
GU9 8DY
☎ 01252 725059
🖹 01252 737300
email: info@
abbey.surrey.sch.uk
Head: Ms A Scott

No. of pupils: 85
Age range: 7-16
Type of School: Day
Special Needs: Learning
Difficulties and
Communication Disorders

The Knowl Hill School
School Lane
Pirbright
GU24 0JN
☎ 01483 797 032
🖹 01483 797 641
web: www.knowlhill.org.uk
Head: Mrs A J Bareford
No. of pupils: 45
Age range: 7-16
Funding: Independent
Type of School: Day
Special Needs: Dyslexia

**The Link Secondary
School**
82/86 Croydon Road
Beddington
CR0 4PD
☎ 020 8688 7691
🖹 020 8688 5522
email: admin@link-
sec.sutton.sch.uk
Head: Mr W E Fuller
No. of pupils: 38
Age range: 11-16
Funding: Non-maintained
Type of School: Day
Special Needs: Language
and Communication

The Park School
Onslow Crescent
Woking
GU22 7BX
No. of pupils: 97
Age range: 8-16

The Ridgeway School
14 Frensham Road
Farnham
GU9 8HB
No. of pupils: 88
Age range: 2-19

Thornchace
Grove Road
Merrow
Guildford
Age range: 11-16

**Victoria House Pupil
Referral Unit**
Southbridge Place
Croydon

CR04HA
☎ 0208 6860393
🖹 0208 6800890
Head: Helen Logan
No. of pupils: 50
Age range: 4-11
Funding: LEA
Type of School: Day
Special Needs: EBD

Walton Leigh School
Queens Road
Walton-on-Thames
KT12 5AB
☎ 01932 223 243
🖹 01932 254 320
email: admin@
walton-leigh.surrey.sch.uk
Head: Ms Linda Curtis
No. of pupils: 63
Age range: 12-19
Funding: LEA
Type of School: Day
Special Needs: Profound,
Severe & Multiple
Learning Difficulties

Wandle Valley School
Welbeck Road
Carshalton
SM5 1LP
No. of pupils: 79
Age range: 5-16

West Hill School
Kingston Road
Leatherhead
KT22 7PW
No. of pupils: 137
Age range: 7-16

Wey House School
Horsham Road
Bramley
Guildford
GU5 0BJ
☎ 01483 898130
🖹 01483 894642
email: info@
weyhouse.surrey.sch.uk
No. of pupils: 35
Age range: 7-11
Type of School: Residential
& Day
Special Needs: Emotional
& behavioural difficulties

Wishmore Cross School
Alpha Road
Chobham
GU24 8NS
No. of pupils: 58
Age range: 10-17

7

Woodfield School
Sunstone Grove
Merstham
RH1 3PR
☎ 01737 642 623
🖷 01737 642 775
email: info@
woodfield.surrey.sch.uk
Head: Mrs S Lawrence
No. of pupils: 140
Age range: 8-16
Funding: LEA
Type of School: Day
Special Needs: Learning
Difficulties

Woodlands School
Fortyfoot Road
Leatherhead
KT22 8RY
☎ 01327 377 922
🖷 01327 376 434
web: info@
woodlands.surrey.sch.uk
Head: Mrs H Taylor
No. of pupils: 80
Age range: 2-19
Funding: LEA
Type of School: Day
Special Needs: Severe
Learning Difficulties

Tyne & Wear

Ashleigh School
Charlotte Street
North Shields
NE30 1BP
No. of pupils: 78
Age range: 2-19
Funding: LEA
Special Needs: Severe
Learning Difficulties

Bamburgh School
Norham Avenue
South Shields
NE34 7TD
☎ 0191 4540671
🖷 0191 4271931
email: bamschool@
balk21.com
Head: Mrs J M Fawcett
No. of pupils: 140
Age range: 2-19

Barbara Priestman School
Meadowside
Sunderland
SR2 7QN
No. of pupils: 134
Age range: 3-19

Bleach Green PRU
The Millway Centre
Sheriff Hill
Gateshead
NE9 5PQ
☎ 0191 420 0606
Age range: 10-14
Type of School: Day

Brunswick Beech School
Brunswick Village
Newcastle upon Tyne
NE13 7DR
No. of pupils: 75
Age range: 2-11

Castle Dene School
Freeman Road
Newcastle upon Tyne
NE3 1SZ
No. of pupils: 42
Age range: 6-16

Condercum House Special School
Condercum Road
Newcastle upon Tyne
NE4

Davenport School
Durham Road
Houghton-le-Spring
DH5 8NF
☎ 0191 553 6572
🖷 0191 553 6575
email: davenport@
schools.sunderland.gov.uk
Head: Mrs Katherine
Elliott
No. of pupils: 81
Age range: 3-11
Funding: LEA
Type of School: Day
Special Needs: Autism and
Severe Learning Difficulties

Dryden School
Shotley Gardens
Gateshead
NE9 5UR
☎ 0191 4203811/2
🖷 0191 4203701
email: drydenschool@
gateshead.gov.uk
Senior Clerk: Mrs
Elizabeth Hutchison
No. of pupils: 50
Age range: 11-19
Funding: LEA
Type of School: Day
Special Needs: Severe
Learning Difficulties

Epinay School
Clervaux Terrace
Jarrow
NE32 5UP
No. of pupils: 104
Age range: 4-16

Eslington School
Leafield House
Birtley Lane
Birtley
DH3 2LR
Age range: 7-11
Special Needs: Emotional
& Behavioural Difficulties

Felstead School
Fordfield Road (North
Side)
Sunderland
SR4 0DA
No. of pupils: 155
Age range: 13-19

Furrowfield School
Whitehill Drive
Felling
Gateshead
NE10 9RZ
No. of pupils: 79
Age range: 7-16
Funding: LEA
Type of School: Residential
Special Needs: Emotional
& behavioural difficulties

Glebe School
Woodburn Drive
Whitley Bay
NE26 3HW
☎ 0191 200 8776
🖷 0191 200 8774
Head: Mrs Linda Turner
No. of pupils: 100
Age range: 4-11
Funding: LEA
Type of School: Day
Special Needs: Moderate
Learning Difficulties

Greenfields School
Victoria Road East
Hebburn
NE31 1YQ
No. of pupils: 45
Age range: 2-19

Hewburn School
Wealcroft
Leam Lane
Felling
Gateshead

NE10 8LT
Age range: 3-16

Hospital Teaching Unit
Wards 19-23
Queen Elizabeth Hospital
Sheriff Hill
Gateshead
NE9 6SX
Age range: 4-16

Jesmond Dene House
Jesmond Dene Road
Newcastle upon Tyne
NE2 2EY
No. of pupils: 32
Age range: 7-19

Kenton Lodge School
Kenton Road
Newcastle upon Tyne
NE3 4PD
Age range: 9-13

Maplewood School
Redcar Road
Sunderland
SR5 5PA
☎ 0191 553 5587
🖷 0191 553 5585
Head: Mrs Jo Wilson
No. of pupils: 90
Age range: 5-13.5
Funding: LEA
Type of School: Day
Special Needs: Emotional
& behavioural difficulties

Margaret Sutton
Ashley Road
South Shields
NE34 0PF
☎ 0191 455 3309
🖷 0191 422 0702
No. of pupils: 120
Age range: 4-17
Funding: LEA
Type of School: Day
Special Needs: Moderate
Learning Difficulties

**Newcastle Upon Tyne
Hospital Teaching Service**
Level 7
Freeman Hospital
Freeman Road
Newcastle upon Tyne
NE7 7DN
Age range: 4-16

**Northern Counties School
for the Deaf**
Great North Road

Newcastle upon Tyne
NE2 3BB
☎ 0191 281 5821
Textphone 0191 281 5821
🖷 0191 281 5060
email: k.j.c.lewis@
schools.ncl.ac.uk
web: www.schools.ncl.ac.uk
Head: Mr K J C Lewis
No. of pupils: 100
Age range: 3-19
Funding: Non-maintained
Type of School: Day
Special Needs: Multi-
sensory impairments

Oakfield College
Condercum Road
Newcastle upon Tyne
NE4 8XJ
No. of pupils: 74
Age range: 14-18

Oakleigh Gardens School
Oakleigh Gardens
Cleadon
Sunderland
SR6 7PT
☎ 0191 536 2590
🖷 0191 519 0213
No. of pupils: 51
Age range: 2-19
Funding: LEA
Type of School: Day
Special Needs: Profound &
Multiple Learning
Difficulties, Severe learning
difficulties

Parkside School
Mullen Road
Wallsend
NE28 9HA
☎ 0191 200 7254
🖷 0191 200 7255
Head: Ms Helen M Jones
No. of pupils: 93
Age range: 2-19
Funding: LEA
Type of School: Day
Special Needs: Profound &
Multiple Learning
Difficulties

Parkway School
Hillhead Parkway
West Denton
Newcastle upon Tyne
NE5 1DP
No. of pupils: 135
Age range: 11-19

Pendower Hall School
Bertram Crescent
Newcastle upon Tyne
NE15 6PY
No. of pupils: 140
Age range: 2-19

Portland School
Portland Road
Sunderland
SR3 1SS
No. of pupils: 83
Age range: 13-19

Southlands School
Beach Road
Tynemouth
North Shields
NE30 2QR
☎ 0191 200 6348
🖷 0191 200 5674
Head: Mr D J Erskine
No. of pupils: 122
Age range: 11-16
Funding: LEA
Type of School: Day
Special Needs: Moderate
Learning Difficulties

Springwell Dene School
Swindon Road
Sunderland
SR3 4EE
☎ 0191 553 6067
🖷 0191 528 2295
email: springwelldene@
enterprise.net
web: homepages.enterprise.
net/springwelldene
Head: Mr J F McKnight
No. of pupils: 65
Age range: 13-16
Funding: LEA
Type of School: Day
Special Needs: Emotional
& behavioural difficulties

St Peter's School
Freeman Road
South Gosforth
Newcastle upon Tyne
NE3 1SZ
No. of pupils: 90
Age range: 2-11

Sunningdale School
Shaftoe Road
Sunderland
SR3 4HA
Age range: 3-13

**Talbot House Special
School**
Hexham Road
Walbottle
Newcastle upon Tyne
NE15 8HW
☎ 0191 229 0111
Head: Mr Andre James
No. of pupils: 50
Age range: 11-16
Funding: Registered charity
Type of School: Day
Special Needs: Emotional
& behavioural difficulties

The Cedars School
Ivy Lane
Low Fell
Gateshead
NE9 6QD
☎ 0191 4877591
🖷 0191 4820926
Head: Mr E Bartley
No. of pupils: 84
Age range: 3-16
Funding: LEA
Type of School: Special
Special Needs: Autism and
Emotional & Behavioural
Difficulties

The School
Station Road
Forest Hall
Newcastle upon Tyne
NE12 8YY
☎ 0191 266 5451
🖷 0191 266 8435
No. of pupils: 145
Age range: 3-16
Funding: Independent
Type of School: Day
Special Needs: Cerebral
Palsy & Speech and
Language Difficulties

Thornhill Park School
21 Thornhill Park
Sunderland
SR2 7LA
☎ 0191 514 0659
🖷 0191 510 8642
Head: Mrs Pat Watson
No. of pupils: 85
Age range: 4-19
Funding: Registered
charity
Type of School: Day
Special Needs: Autism

Walkerdene School
Westbourne Avenue
Walkerdene
Newcastle upon Tyne
NE6 4HQ
No. of pupils: 155
Age range: 11-19

Wellbank School
Well Bank Road
Donwell
Washington
NE37 1NL
☎ 0191 219 3860
Head: Mrs Jane MacLeod
No. of pupils: 70
Age range: 3-13
Funding: LEA
Type of School: Day
Special Needs: Profound &
Multiple Learning
Difficulties

Westlands School
Hillhead Parkway
West Denton
Newcastle upon Tyne
NE5 1DS
☎ 0191 267 5435
🖷 0191 267 9857
Head: Mr Chris Liddell
No. of pupils: 52
Age range: 5-11
Funding: LEA
Type of School: Day
Special Needs: Wide range

Woodlawn School
Langley Avenue
Monkseaton
Whitley Bay
NE25 9DF
☎ 0191 251 2516
No. of pupils: 95
Age range: 2-16

Warwickshire

Blythe School
Packington Lane
Coleshill
Birmingham
B46 3JE
☎ 01675 463 590
🖷 01675 463 584
Head: Ms Gill Simpson
No. of pupils: 79
Age range: 2-19
Funding: LEA
Type of School: Day
Special Needs: Severe
Learning Difficulties

7

Brooke Primary School
Overslade Lane
Rugby
CV22 6DY
☎ 01788 812324
Head: Mrs Sheila Cowen
No. of pupils: 100
Age range: 2-11
Funding: LEA
Type of School: Day
Special Needs: Profound &
Multiple Learning
Difficulties

Brooke School
Overslade Lane
Rugby
CV22 6DY
☎ 01788 812 324
📠 01788 522 866
email: admin@
7023.wgfl.net
web: www.brooke.wgfl.net
Head: Mrs Sheila Cowen
No. of pupils: 100
Age range: 2-19
Funding: LEA
Type of School: Day
Special Needs: Profound &
Multiple Learning
Difficulties

Exhall Grange School
Wheelwright Lane
Ash Green
Coventry
CV7 9HP
☎ 024 7636 4200
📠 024 7664 5055
email: admin@
exhallgrangeschool.org.uk
web: www.exhallgrange.
warwickshire.sch.uk
Head: Mr Richard G
Bignell
No. of pupils: 180
Age range: 2-19
Funding: LEA
Type of School: Residential
Special Needs: Visually
Impaired & Physical
disabilities

Leyland School
Leyland Road
Nuneaton
CV11 4RP
☎ 024 7638 5313
No. of pupils: 100
Age range: 2-19

**Marie Corelli Special
School**
Drayton Avenue

Stratford-upon-Avon
CV37 9PT
☎ 01789 205 992
No. of pupils: 73
Age range: 4-16

Ridgeway School
Montague Road
Warwick
CV34 5LW
☎ 01926 491 987
📠 01926 407 317
Head: Mrs Patricia Flynn
No. of pupils: 96
Age range: 2-19
Funding: LEA
Type of School: Day
Special Needs: Profound &
Multiple Learning
Difficulties

River House School
Stratford Road
Henley-in-Arden
B95 6AD
☎ 01564 792 514
📠 01564 792 179
Head: Mr M Turner
No. of pupils: 40
Age range: 11-16
Funding: LEA
Type of School: Day
Special Needs: Emotional
& behavioural difficulties

Sparrowdale School
Spon Lane
Grendon
CV9 2PD
☎ 01827 713 436
📠 01827 720 472
web: ankerpartners.org.uk/
sparrowdale
Head: Margaret Pomfrett
No. of pupils: 117
Age range: 4-16
Funding: LEA
Type of School: Day
Special Needs: Moderate
Learning Difficulties

The Griff School
Coventry Road
Nuneaton
CV10 7AX
☎ 024 7638 3315
📠 024 7637 1768
Head: Ms Ruth Worrall
No. of pupils: 154
Age range: 4-16
Funding: LEA
Type of School: Day

Special Needs: Moderate
Learning Difficulties

**The Lambert Special
School**
Blue Cap Road
Stratford-upon-Avon
CV37 6TQ
Acting Head:
No. of pupils: 83
Age range: 2-19
Funding: LEA
Type of School: Day
Special Needs: Profound &
Multiple Learning
Difficulties

**The Round Oak School &
Support Service**
Pound Lane
Lillington
Leamington Spa
CV32 7RT
☎ 01926 335 566
📠 01926 886163
Head: Miss Puffin Pocock
No. of pupils: 80
Age range: 4-16
Funding: LEA
Type of School: Day
Special Needs: Moderate
Learning Difficulties,
Behaviour, Autism and
ADHD

West Midlands

Alice Stevens School
Ashington Grove
Coventry
CV3 4DE
☎ 024 763 03776
📠 024 7630 6173
email: admin@
alicestevens.coventry.sch.uk
Head: R I McAllister
No. of pupils: 190
Age range: 11-19
Funding: LEA
Type of School: Day
Special Needs: Multiple
Learning Difficulties

Arden School
Arden Road
Smethwick
Sandwell
B67 6AL
☎ 0121 558 0275
📠 0121 555 6036
Head: Mrs Barbara Miller
No. of pupils: 95

Age range: 5-16
Funding: LEA
Type of School: Day
Special Needs: Moderate
Learning Difficulties

Baginton Fields School
Sedgmoor Road
Coventry
CV3 4EA
☎ 024 76 303854
📠 024 763 04247
email: sigrant@
bagintonfields.
coventry.sch.uk
Head: Mr S Grant
No. of pupils: 95
Age range: 11-19
Funding: LEA
Type of School: Day
Special Needs: Wide range

**Baskerville Residential
School**
Fellows Lane
Birmingham
B17 9TS
Age range: 11-19

Beaufort School
16 Coleshill Road
Birmingham
B36 8AA
☎ 0121 783 3886
📠 0121 783 6994
email: enquiry@beaufort.
bham.sch.uk
Acting Head: Mr Nick
Rigby
No. of pupils: 40
Age range: 3-11
Funding: LEA
Type of School: Primary
Special Day
Special Needs: Profound &
Multiple Learning
Difficulties and Severe
Learning Difficulties

Blakeley School
Dudley Road East
Oldbury
Warley
B69 3BU
No. of pupils: 100
Age range: 5-16

Braidwood School
Perry Common Road
Erdington
Birmingham
B23 7AT

☎ 0121 373 5558
Textphone 0121 373 5558
▤ 0121 382 5844
email: braidwood@
rmplc.co.uk
web: www.rmplc.co.uk
Head: Mrs Fiona Ison-Jacques
No. of pupils: 62
Age range: 11-18
Funding: LEA
Type of School: Day
Special Needs: Hearing Impaired

Brays School
Brays Road
Sheldon
Birmingham
B26 1NS
Age range: 2-16

Bridge Special School
Reservoir Road
Erdington
Birmingham
B23 6DE
☎ 0121 373 8265
▤ 0121 377 7619
Head: Mr Steve White
Age range: 3-13
Funding: LEA
Type of School: Day
Special Needs: Severe Learning Difficulties

Calthorpe School
Darwin Street
Highgate
Birmingham
B12 0TJ
☎ 0121 773 4637
▤ 0121 773 0708
Head: Mr G Hardy
No. of pupils: 249
Age range: 2-19
Funding: LEA
Type of School: Day
Special Needs: Wide range

Castle School
Odell Road
Leamore
Walsall
WS3 2ED
☎ 01922 710129
▤ 01922 710835
Head: Mrs White
No. of pupils: 108
Age range: 4-19
Funding: LEA
Type of School: Day

Special Needs: Moderate Learning Difficulties and Complex Needs

Cherry Oak School
60 Frederick Road
Selly Oak
Birmingham
B29 6PB
☎ 0121 472 1263
Head: Mrs L Fowler
No. of pupils: 54
Age range: 3-11
Funding: LEA
Type of School: Day
Special Needs: Severe Learning Difficulties

Cherry Trees School
Giggetty Lane
Wombourne
Wolverhampton
WV5 0AX
☎ 01902 894 484
▤ 01902 894 484
email: headteacher@
cherrytrees.staffs.sch.uk
Head: Mrs L J Allman
No. of pupils: 38
Age range: 3-19
Funding: LEA
Type of School: Day
Special Needs: Severe Learning Difficulties/Profound and Multiple Learning Difficulties/Challenging Behaviours

Children's Hospital School
Ladywood Middleway
Birmingham
B16 8ET
Age range: 2-16

Corley Residential School
Corley
Coventry
CV7 8AZ
No. of pupils: 68
Age range: 11-16

Coventry Hospital School
Coventry & Warwickshire Hospital
Stoney Stanton Road
Coventry
CV1 4FH
Age range: 4-16

Dame Ellen Pinscut School
Ardencote Road

Kings Heath
Birmingham
B13 0RW
☎ 0121 444 2487
▤ 0121 444 7295
email: sylvia.rodgers@
dameellenpinscut.
bham.sch.uk
web:
www.dameellenpinscut.
bham.sch.uk
Head: Sylvia Rodgers
No. of pupils: 145
Age range: 4-11
Funding: LEA
Type of School: Day
Special Needs: Moderate Learning Difficulties

Dartmouth School
Tiverton Road
Wyken
Coventry
CV2 3DN
☎ 024 7644 4141
▤ 024 7645 3838
email: dartmouth.cov@
rmplc.co.uk
web: www.rmplc.co.uk
Head: Mr P S Davies
No. of pupils: 65
Age range: 11-16
Funding: LEA
Type of School: Day
Special Needs: Emotional & behavioural difficulties

Daw End School
Floyds Lane
Rushall
Walsall
WS4 1LF
☎ 01922 721 081
▤ 01922 636 187
email: postbox@
daw-end.walsall.sch.uk
Head: Mr A C S Fairfull
No. of pupils: 61
Age range: 5-16
Funding: LEA
Type of School: Day & Residential
Special Needs: Emotional & behavioural difficulties

Deedmore Primary Special School
Petitor Crescent
Coventry
CV2 1EW
☎ 024 7661 2271
▤ 024 7660 3986

Head: Mr G L Wilkinson
No. of pupils: 65
Age range: 3-11
Funding: LEA
Type of School: Day
Special Needs: Moderate Learning Difficulties

Dyslexia Institute
Provincial House
69 South Parade
Sutton Coldfield
B72 1QU
☎ 0121 354 6855
▤ 0121 355 3662
email: sutton@
dyslexia-inst.org.uk
Principal: Mrs Jayne James
Age range: 5-16
Funding: Charity
Special Needs: Dyslexia

Fairhaven Children's Centre
Stream Road
Wordsley
Stourbridge
DY8 5QU
Age range: 13-17

Fitzwarren School
Upper Church Lane
Tipton
DY4 9PF
No. of pupils: 80
Age range: 4-16

Forest Oak School
Lanchester Way
Castle Bromwich
Birmingham
B36 9LF
☎ 0121 748 3411
▤ 0121 749 7534
email: office@forest-oak.solihull.sch.uk
Head: Mrs P Sankey
No. of pupils: 100
Age range: 4-16
Funding: LEA
Type of School: Day
Special Needs: Moderate Learning Difficulties

Fox Hollies School
419 Fox Hollies Road
Birmingham
B27 7QA
☎ 0121 777 6566
▤ 0121 778 4148
email: pbaker@
foxholli.bham.sch.uk

7

web:
www.foxholli.bham.sch.uk
Administrator: Mrs
Kathryn O'Leary
No. of pupils: 67
Age range: 11-19
Funding: LEA
Type of School: Day
Special Needs: Severe
Learning Difficulties

George Auden School
Bell Hill
Northfield
Birmingham
B31 1LD
☎ 0121 475 3826
🖹 0121 475 1167
email: admin@
georgea.bham.sch.uk
web:
www.georgea.bham.sch.uk
Head: Mr B Jackson
No. of pupils: 50
Age range: 2-11
Funding: LEA
Type of School: Day
Special Needs: Visually
Impaired

Glenvale School
Jervoise Street
West Bromwich
B70 9LZ
☎ 0121 525 2873
🖹 0121 553 6133
Head: Mrs Helen Atkins
No. of pupils: 83
Age range: 3-19
Funding: LEA
Type of School: Day
Special Needs: Severe
Learning Difficulties

**Good Hope Hospital
Teaching Unit**
Harvey Ward
Rectory Road
Sutton Coldfield
B75 7RR
Age range: 4-16

Green Park School
Green Park Avenue
Stowlawn Bilston
Wolverhampton
WV11 6EH
No. of pupils: 66
Age range: 5-19
Funding: LEA
Type of School: Day
Special Needs: Profound &

Multiple Learning
Difficulties

Halesbury School
Feldon Lane
Halesowen
B62 9DR
☎ 01384 818 630
🖹 01384 818 631
Head: Mr Malcolm
Leighton
No. of pupils: 120
Age range: 4-16
Funding: LEA
Type of School: Day
Special Needs: Moderate
Learning Difficulties &
Autism & Speech and
Language Difficulties

Hallmoor School
Hallmoor Road
Kitts Green
Birmingham
B33 9QY
☎ 0121 783 3972
🖹 0121783 3481
email: enquiry@
hallmoor.bham.sch.uk
web:
www.hallmoor.bham.sch.uk
Head: Ms Sue Charvis
No. of pupils: 240
Age range: 4-19
Funding: LEA
Type of School: Day
Special Needs: Moderate
Learning Difficulties plus
additional needs

Hamilton School
Hamilton Road
Handsworth
Birmingham
B21 8AH
☎ 0121 554 1676
🖹 0121 554 4808
email: srogers@
edmail.birmingham.gov.uk
web: www.edmail.
birmingham.gov.uk
Head: Mr Nigel Carter
No. of pupils: 75
Age range: 3-11
Funding: LEA
Type of School: Day
Special Needs: Moderate
Learning Difficulties

Hawkesbury Fields School
Aldermans Green Road
Coventry

CV2 1PL
☎ 024 7636 7075
🖹 024 7664 5388
email: hawkes1@
rmplc.co.uk
web: www.rmplc.co.uk
Head: Ms Janet Thompson
No. of pupils: 58
Age range: 2-11
Funding: LEA
Type of School: Day
Special Needs: Profound &
Multiple Learning
Difficulties

Hazel Oak School
Hazeloak Road
Shirley
Solihull
B90 2AZ
No. of pupils: 100
Age range: 5-16
Funding: LEA
Type of School: Day
Special Needs: Autistic
Spectrum Disorders

**Heartlands Hospital
School**
Yardley Green Road
Birmingham
B9 5PX
☎ 0121 753 3831
🖹 0121 772 3184
email: dhoban.herathos@
jamesbrindley.bham.sch.uk
Head: Diane Hoban
No. of pupils: 30
Age range: 2-16
Type of School: Hospital

**Hunters Hill Residential
School**
Spirehouse Lane
Blackwell
Bromsgrove
B60 1QD
☎ 0121 445 1320
🖹 0121 445 2496
email: enquiry@
huntshill.bham.sch.uk
web:
www.huntershill.org.uk
No. of pupils: 76
Age range: 11-16
Funding: LEA/'RAZERS'/
Charity
Type of School:
Redidential 5 day/4 night
(term time only)
Special Needs: Emotional
& behavioural difficulties

**James Brindley Hospital
School**
Willows Centre
Queensbridge Road
Birmingham
B13 8QB
☎ 0121 449 3322
🖹 0121 442 2274
email: clive.hartwell@
jamesbrindley.bham.sch.uk
Head of Education: Mr C
Hartwell
No. of pupils: 40
Age range: 11-18
Funding: LEA
Type of School: Hospital
Special Needs: Medical
referrals only

Jane Lane School
Churchill Road
Bentley
Walsall
WS2 0JH
No. of pupils: 133
Age range: 5-16

Kingstanding School
Old Oscott Hill
Kingstanding
Birmingham
B44 9SP
☎ 0121 360 8222
🖹 0121 366 6394
email: enquiry@
kingstnd.bham.sch.uk
web:
www.kingstnd.bham.sch.uk
Head: Michele C Pipe
No. of pupils: 81
Age range: 11-19
Funding: LEA
Type of School: Day
Special Needs: Profound,
Severe & Multiple
Learning Difficulties

Knowle School
Dudley Road
Rowley Regis
B65 8JY
☎ 0121 559 1868
Head: Mrs C J Willetts
No. of pupils: 80
Age range: 4-16
Funding: LEA
Type of School: Day
Special Needs: Moderate
Learning Difficulties

Langley School
Lindridge Road

Sutton Coldfield
B75 7HU
Head: Mr Alan Reid
No. of pupils: 120
Age range: 3-11
Funding: LEA
Type of School: Day
Special Needs: Moderate
Learning Difficulties

Lindsworth School
Monyhull Hall Road
Birmingham
B30 3QA
No. of pupils: 93
Age range: 10-17

Longmoor School and Residential Unit
Coppice View Road
Sutton Coldfield
B73 6UE
☎ 0121 353 7833
🖹 0121 353 9228
Head: Mrs Veronica Jenkins
Age range: 2-13
Funding: LEA
Type of School: Residential
Special Needs: Severe
Learning Difficulties

Longwill School
Bell Hill
Birmingham
B31 1LD
☎ 0121 475 3923
🖹 0121 476 6362
email: bday@rmplc.co.uk
web: www.rmplc.co.uk/sites/bday
Age range: 5-16

Mary Elliot School
Brewer Street
Walsall
WS2 8BA
☎ 01922 720706
🖹 01922 612298
email: postbox@mary-elliot.walsall.sch.uk
web: www.mary-elliot.walsall.sch.uk
Head: Mrs E A Jordan
No. of pupils: 51
Age range: 14-19
Type of School: Special

Mayfield Special School
Finch Road
Birmingham
B20 1HP
☎ 0121 554 3354

🖹 0121 554 5358
email: finchmay@aol.com
web: www.aol.com
Head: Mr Paul Jenkins
No. of pupils: 106
Age range: 5-16
Funding: LEA
Type of School: Day
Special Needs: Moderate
Learning Difficulties

Merstone School
Exeter Drive
Marston Green
Birmingham
B37 5NX
☎ 0121 788 8122
🖹 0121 779 2800
email: office@merstone.solihull.sch.uk
web: www.solihull.gov.uk
Head: Mrs Amanda R Mordey
No. of pupils: 69
Age range: 2-19
Funding: LEA
Type of School: Day
Special Needs: Severe
Learning Difficulties

Oakwood School
Druids Walk
Walsall Wood
Walsall
WS9 9JS
☎ 01543 452 040
🖹 01543 453 982
Head: Mrs Kay E Mills
No. of pupils: 58
Age range: 2-14
Funding: LEA
Type of School: Day
Special Needs: Profound & Multiple Learning Difficulties

Old Hall School
Bentley Lane
Walsall
WS2 7LU
☎ 01902 368 045
🖹 01902 634 144
Head: Mr Phil Nickless
No. of pupils: 84
Age range: 2-14
Funding: LEA
Type of School: Day
Special Needs: Severe
Learning Difficulties

Old Park School
Corbyn Road

Russells Hall Estate
Dudley
DY1 2JZ
☎ 01384 818 905
🖹 01384 818 906
Acting Head: Mrs G Cartwright
No. of pupils: 140
Age range: 3-19
Funding: LEA
Type of School: Day
Special Needs: Severe
Learning Difficulties

Orchard School
Coopers Lane
Smethwick
Warley
B67 7DW
☎ 0121 558 1069
🖹 0121 565 0940
No. of pupils: 94
Age range: 2-11
Funding: LEA
Type of School: Day
Special Needs: Complex & Profound Learning Difficulties

Penn Fields School
Birches Barn Road
Penn Fields
Wolverhampton
WV3 7BJ
No. of pupils: 150
Age range: 4-16

Penn Hall School
Vicarage Road
Penn
Wolverhampton
WV4 5HP
☎ 01902 558 355
🖹 01902 558 363
email: admin@pennhall.wolverhants.sch.uk
web: www.pennhall.wolverhants.sch.uk
Head: Mr Alun Stoll
No. of pupils: 80
Age range: 3-19
Funding: LEA
Type of School: Day
Special Needs: Physical disabilities

Priestley Smith School
Perry Common Road
Erdington
Birmingham
B23 7AT
☎ 0121 373 5493

email: vbendall@priestley.bham.sch.uk
Head: Mr C G Lewis
No. of pupils: 70
Age range: 2-17
Funding: LEA
Type of School: Day
Special Needs: Visually Impaired

Regent School
Red Lion Close
Tividale
Warley
B69 1TP
No. of pupils: 55
Age range: 2-19

Reynalds Cross School
Kineton Green Road
Olton
Solihull
B92 7ER
No. of pupils: 52
Age range: 2-19

Saltwells House
Pedmore Road
Brierley Hill
Dudley
DY5 1TF
Age range: 10-16

Selly Oak School
Oak Tree Lane
Birmingham
B29 6HZ
☎ 0121 472 0876
🖹 0121 415 5379
email: School@sellyoak.bham.sch.uk
Acting Deputy Head: Mr Graham Ridley
No. of pupils: 379
Age range: 11-19
Funding: LEA
Type of School: Day
Special Needs: Profound & Multiple Learning Difficulties

Shenstone Lodge School
Birmingham Road
Lichfield
WS14 0LB
☎ 01543 480 369
🖹 01543 481 104
Head: Mr S P Butt
No. of pupils: 25
Age range: 5-11
Funding: LEA
Type of School: Residential

7

Special Needs: Emotional
& behavioural difficulties
& Autism

Sherbourne Fields School
Rowington Close
Coventry
CV6 1PS
☎ 024 7659 1501
🖹 024 7659 0517
Head: Ms Elaine Hancox
No. of pupils: 125
Age range: 3-19
Funding: LEA
Type of School: Day
Special Needs: Medical

Springfield House School
Kenilworth Road
Knowle
Solihull
B93 0AJ
☎ 01564 772 772
🖹 01564 771 767
Head: Pat Jacques
No. of pupils: 50
Age range: 4-11
Funding: LEA
Special Needs: Emotional
& behavioural difficulties

Stowlawn Nursery
Green Park Avenue
Bilston
WV14 6EH
Age range: 2-7

Sunfield School
Clent Grove
Clent
Stourbridge
DY9 9PB
☎ 01562 882253
🖹 01562 883856
email: sunfield@
sunfield.worcs.sch.uk
Head of Education: Mrs
Francine Griffith
No. of pupils: 72
Age range: 6-19
Funding: Registered charity
Type of School:
Residential/Day for 6
pupils
Special Needs: Severe and
complex learning needs
and Profound Autistic
Spectrum Disorder

Sutton School
Scotts Green Close
Dudley

DY1 2DU
email: info@sutton.
dudley.gov.uk
web: www.eduldudley.
gov.uk/schools/sutton/m
No. of pupils: 120
Age range: 12-16
Funding: LEA
Type of School: Day
Special Needs: Moderate
Learning Difficulties

Tettenhall Wood School
School Road
Tettenhall Wood
Wolverhampton
WV6 8EJ
☎ 01902 556 519
🖹 01902 556 520
email: tettenhallwood
specialschool@
wolverhampton.gov.uk
web: www.tettenwood.
biblio.net/
Head: Mr M Mahoney
No. of pupils: 56
Age range: 5-19
Funding: LEA
Type of School: Day
Special Needs: Severe
Learning Difficulties

The Birchley School
Throne Road
Rowley Regis
Warley
B65 9JP
Age range: 5-16

The Brier School
Cottage Street
Brierley Hill
Dudley
DY5 1RE
No. of pupils: 125
Age range: 4-16

The Meadows School
Hawthorne Lane
Coventry
CV4 9PB
No. of pupils: 32
Age range: 11-16

The Pines School
Dreghorn Road
Castle Bromwich
Birmingham
B36 8LL
☎ 0121 747 6136
🖹 0121 747 6136
email: admin@
pinessp.bham.sch.uk

web:
www.pinessp.bham.sch.uk
Head: Mr S G Tuft
Age range: 5-11
Funding: LEA
Type of School: Day
Special Needs: Severe
Learning Difficulties

The Queensbury School
Wood End Road
Birmingham
B24 8BL
No. of pupils: 231
Age range: 11-19

The Underwood School
Rowden Drive
Birmingham
B23 5UL
No. of pupils: 53
Age range: 11-17

**The Woodlands Hospital
Teaching Centre**
The Royal Orthopaedic
Hospital
Bristol Road South
Northfield
Birmingham
B31 2AP
Age range: 4-16

The Woodsetton School
Tipton Road
Woodsetton
Dudley
DY3 1BY
No. of pupils: 120
Age range: 4-16

**Three Crowns Special
School**
Skip Lane
Walsall
WS5 3NB
☎ 01922 721 119
🖹 01922 648 624
email: ddeemong@three-
crowns.walsall.sch.uk
Acting Head: Mrs Rita
McRobert
No. of pupils: 58
Age range: 3-19
Funding: LEA
Type of School:
Community Day
Special Needs: Physical
disabilities

Three Spires School
Kingsbury Road
Coventry

CV6 1PJ
Age range: 3-11

Tiverton School
Rowington Close
Off Kingsbury Road
Coventry
CV6 1PR
Age range: 2-11

Uffculme School
Queensbridge Road
Moseley
Birmingham
B13 8QB
☎ 0121 449 1081
🖹 0121 442 2207
Head: Mr A MacDonald
No. of pupils: 116
Age range: 3-11
Type of School: Day
Special Needs: Autism

Victoria School
Bell Hill
Northfield
Birmingham
B31 1LD
☎ 0121 476 0478
🖹 0121 411 2357
email: admin@
victoria.bham.sch.uk
web: www.rmplc.co.uk.\
educweb\sites\victoria
Head: Mr Ian Glen
No. of pupils: 216
Age range: 2-19
Funding: LEA
Type of School: Day
Special Needs: Deaf/blind

Wainbody Wood School
Stoneleigh Road
Coventry
CV4 7AB
Age range: 5-16

**Westcroft School and
Sports College**
Greenacres Avenue
Underhill
Wolverhampton
WV10 8NZ
☎ 01902 558 350
🖹 01902 558 342
email: scockhill@
westcroft.biblio.net
Head: Mr A M Chilvers
No. of pupils: 180
Age range: 4-16
Funding: LEA
Type of School: Day

Special Needs: Moderate
Learning Difficulties

Westminster School
Westminster Road
West Bromwich
B71 2JN
☎ 0121 5882421/5434
🖷 01215885451
Head: Mrs D Williams
No. of pupils: 230
Age range: 10-18
Funding: LEA
Type of School: Day
Special
Special Needs: MLD

Wightwick Hall School
Tinacre Hill
Wolverhampton
WV6 8DA
☎ 01902 761 889
🖷 01902 765 080
Head: P H W Archer
No. of pupils: 108
Age range: 3-16
Funding: LEA
Special Needs: Wide range

Wilson Stuart School
Perry Common Road
Erdington
Birmingham
B23 7AT
☎ 0121 373 4475
🖷 0121 373 9842
email: enquiry@
wilsonst.bha.sch.uk
Head: Mrs Anne
Tomkinson
No. of pupils: 144
Age range: 2½-19
Type of School: Special
Special Needs: Physically
Disabled

West Sussex

Abbotsford School
Cuckfield Road
Burgess Hill
RH15 8RE
No. of pupils: 69
Age range: 7-16

Brantridge School
Staplefield Place
Staplefield
Haywards Heath
RH17 6EQ
☎ 01444 400 228
🖷 01444 401 083

Head: Mr N White
No. of pupils: 36
Age range: 6-13
Funding: LEA
Type of School: Residential
Special Needs: Emotional
& behavioural difficulties,
Specific Learning
Difficulties

Catherington School
Martyrs Avenue
Langley Green
Crawley
RH11 7SF
No. of pupils: 89
Age range: 2-19

Cornfield School
Cornfield Close
Littlehampton
BN17 6HY
☎ 01903 731 277
🖷 01903 731 288
email: head@cornfield.
w-sussex.sch.uk
Head: Mrs S M Roberts
No. of pupils: 50
Age range: 11-16
Funding: LEA
Type of School: Day
Special Needs: Emotional,
Social & behavioural
difficulties

Court Meadow School
Hanlye Lane
Cuckfield
Haywards Heath
RH17 5HN
☎ 01444 454 535
🖷 01444 412 289
email: office@
courtmeadow.
w-sussex.sch.uk
Head: Mrs J Hedges
No. of pupils: 93
Age range: 2-19
Funding: LEA
Type of School: Day
Special Needs: Severe
Learning Difficulties

Deerswood School
Ifield Green
Crawley
RH11 0HG
☎ 01293 520351
🖷 01293 510559
email: office@
deerswood.w-sussex.sch.uk
Head: Mr M R Turney

No. of pupils: 163
Age range: 4-16
Funding: LEA
Type of School: Day
Special Needs: Autism and
Multiple Learning
Difficulties

Farney Close School
Bolney Court
Crossways
Bolney
Haywards Heath
RH17 5RD
☎ 01444 881811
🖷 01444 881957
email: head@
farneyclose.co.uk
web: www.farneyclose.co.uk
Head: Mr Barry Robinson
No. of pupils: 63
Age range: 11-16
Funding: Charity
Type of School: Residential
Special Needs: Emotional
& behavioural difficulties

Fordwater School
Summersdale Road
Chichester
PO19 6PP
Head: Mr R Rendall
No. of pupils: 106
Age range: 2-19

Herons Dale School
Hawkins Crescent
Shoreham
BN43 6TN
No. of pupils: 109
Age range: 5-16

Highdown School
Durrington Lane
Worthing
BN13 2QQ
☎ 01903 249611
email: office@
highdown.w-sussex.sch.uk
Head: Mr G R Elliker
No. of pupils: 128
Age range: 3-19
Funding: LEA
Special Needs: SLD,
PMD, ASD

Ingfield Manor School
Five Oaks
Billingshurst
RH14 9AX
☎ 01403 782 294
Head: Mrs Cherryl

Donovan
No. of pupils: 48
Age range: 4-11
Funding: Independent
Type of School: Day
Special Needs: Cerebral
Palsy

John Horniman School
Fax Park Road
Worthing
BN11 2AS
☎ 01903 200 317
🖷 01903 214 151
Head: Ms Janet Dunn
No. of pupils: 31
Age range: 4-11
Funding: Non-maintained
Type of School: Residential
Special Needs: Speech and
Language Difficulties

Littlegreen School
Compton
Chichester
PO18 9NW
☎ 023 9263 1259
🖷 023 9263 1740
Head: Mr A Bicknell
No. of pupils: 37
Age range: 7-14
Funding: LEA
Type of School: Negotiated
Residential Provision
Special Needs: Emotional
& behavioural difficulties

Mid-Sussex Area PRU
Marie Place
Leylands Road
Burgess Hill
RH15 8JD

Muntham House School
Barns Green
Horsham
RH13 7NJ
☎ 01403 730 302
🖷 01403 730 510
email: office@
munthamhouse.
w-sussex.sch.uk
web: www.munthamhouse.
w-sussex.sch.uk
Principal: Mr Richard
Boyle
No. of pupils: 50
Age range: 8-18
Funding: Non-maintained
Type of School: Boarding
Special Needs: Emotional
& behavioural difficulties

7

Newick House School
Birchwood Grove Road
Burgess Hill
RH15 0DP
No. of pupils: 134
Age range: 4-16

**North Eastern Area
(Crawley) PRU**
Worth Annexe
Turners Hill Road
Worth
Crawley
RH10 7RN
☎ 01293 883209
🖷 01293 886833
Teacher in Charge: Miss A
Jackson
No. of pupils: 20
Funding: LEA
Type of School: Day
Special Needs: Emotional
& Behavioural Difficulties

Palatine School
Palatine Road
Worthing
BN12 6JP
☎ 01903 242 835
🖷 01903 700 264
Head: Mr Duncan Clough
No. of pupils: 157
Age range: 5-16
Funding: LEA
Type of School: Day
Special Needs: Moderate
Learning Difficulties

Philpots Manor School
West Hoathly
East Grinstead
RH19 4PR
☎ 01342 810 268/
01342 811 382
Administrator: Mr Simon
Blaxland-de Lange
No. of pupils: 70
Age range: 6-19
Funding: Independent
Type of School: Day/
Residential
Special Needs: Moderate
Learning Difficulties,
EBD, Autism, ADHD

PRU South (Chichester)
Fletcher Place Building
North Mundham
Chichester
PO20 1JR
☎ 01243 788044
🖷 01243 788990

email: prusouth@
pavilion.co.uk
Head of Unit: Mr R
Stepien
No. of pupils: 22
Age range: 13-16
Funding: LEA
Type of School: Pupil
Referral Unit

**Queen Elizabeth II Silver
Jubilee School**
Comptons Lane
Horsham
RH13 5NW
☎ 01403 266 215
🖷 01403 270 109
email: office@
queenelizabeth2.
w-success.sch.uk
Head: Mrs Lesley Dyer
No. of pupils: 45
Age range: 2-19
Funding: LEA
Type of School: Day
Special Needs: Profound &
Multiple Learning
Difficulties

St Anthony's School
Woodlands Lane
Chichester
PO19 3PA
☎ 01243 785965
🖷 01243 530206
email: st-anthonys@
pavilion.co.uk
web: www.pavilion.co.uk/
st-anthonys/
Head: Mr Toby Salt
No. of pupils: 150
Age range: 5-16
Funding: LEA
Type of School: Day
Special Needs: Moderate
Learning Difficulties

St Cuthman's School
Stedham
Midhurst
GU29 0QL
☎ 01730 812 331
🖷 01730 812 335
email: office@admin.st-
cuthmans.w-sussex.sch.uk
Head: Mr Howard Rooks
No. of pupils: 95
Age range: 7-16
Funding: LEA
Type of School: Day
Special Needs: Moderate
Learning Difficulties

West Yorkshire

Beaconsfield Centre
Bennett Street
Halifax
HX3 9JG
Age range: 5-11

Braithwaite School
Braithwaite Road
Keighley
BD22 6PR
☎ 01535 603 041
🖷 01535 691 227
email: office@braithwaite.
ngfk.ac.uk
Head: Mrs P A Pearson
No. of pupils: 90
Age range: 2-19
Funding: LEA
Type of School: Day
Special Needs: Moderate
Learning Difficulties

Branshaw School
Oxford Street
Oakworth Road
Keighley
BD21 1QX
☎ 01535 662 739
🖷 01535 676 021
Head: Mrs J E Graveson
Age range: 2-19
Funding: LEA
Type of School: Day
Special Needs: Profound &
Multiple Learning
Difficulties

Broomfield School
Broom Place
Leeds
LS10 5JP
☎ 0113 277 1603
🖷 0113 277 1622
email: dd@
broomfieldschool.
demon.co.uk
web:
www.broomfieldschool.
demon.co.uk
Head: Mr David M W
Dewhirst
No. of pupils: 80
Age range: 2-19
Funding: LEA
Type of School: Day
Special Needs: Visually
Impaired

Chapel Grange School
Rhodesway
Bradford

BD8 0DQ
No. of pupils: 100
Age range: 11-19
Funding: LEA
Special Needs: Wide range

Elmete Wood School
Elmete Lane
Leeds
LS8 2LJ
☎ 0113 265 5457
No. of pupils: 113
Age range: 11-19

Fairfield School
Dale Lane
Heckmondwike
WF16 9PA
No. of pupils: 90
Age range: 3-19
Type of School: Special
Special Needs: Severe &
Profound Learning
Difficulties

Fearnville School
Oakwood Lane
Leeds
LS8 3LF
☎ 0113 240 1693
Age range: 3-11

Grafton School
Craven Road
Off Woodhouse Street
Leeds
LS6 2SN
☎ 0113 293 0323
🖷 0113 293 0331
Head: Mr Michael K
Purches
No. of pupils: 76
Age range: 3-11
Funding: LEA
Type of School: Day
Special Needs: Moderate
Learning Difficulties

Green Leas School
Green Lane
Carleton
Pontefract
WF8 3NW
☎ 01977 722 815
🖷 01977 722 815
Head: Mr S R Mulligan
No. of pupils: 140
Age range: 11-16
Funding: LEA
Type of School: Day
Special Needs: Moderate
Learning Difficulties

Greenfield School
Boothroyd Drive
Idle
Bradford
BD10 8LU
☎ 01274 614 092
🖪 01274 613840
email: office@
greenfield.ngfl.ac.uk
Head: Ms Janet G Taylor
No. of pupils: 60
Age range: 2-11
Funding: LEA
Type of School: Day
Special Needs:
Severe/Complex Learning
Difficulties and Autism

Green Meadows School
Bradford Road
Leeds
LS20 8PP
☎ 01943 878536
🖪 01943 878443
Head: Mrs D E Seed
No. of pupils: 134
Age range: 2-19
Funding: LEA
Type of School: Special
School
Special Needs: All Generic

Hartshead Moor School
Halifax Road
Cleckheaton
BD19 6LP
No. of pupils: 85
Age range: 5-16

Hawksworth Hall School
Hawksworth
Guiseley
Leeds
LS20 8NU
No. of pupils: 19
Age range: 4-12

Haycliffe School
Haycliffe Lane
Little Horton
Bradford
BD5 9ET
☎ 01274 576 123
🖪 01274 770 555
email: haycliffe@
haycliffe.ngfl.ac.uk
web: www.camput.bt.com
Head: Mr Keith Fair
No. of pupils: 125
Age range: 11-19
Funding: LEA
Special Needs: Learning
Difficulties

Heaton Royds School
Redburn Drive
Shipley
BD18 3AZ
☎ 01274 583 759
🖪 01274 589 397
Head: Ms Mary Fowler
No. of pupils: 45
Age range: 2-11
Funding: LEA
Type of School: Day
Special Needs: Severe
Learning Difficulties

Highfields School
Cemetery Road
Edgerton
Huddersfield
HD1 5NF
☎ 01484 226 659
🖪 01484 226 660
email: Highfields@
geo2.poptel.org.uk
web:
www.geo2.poptel.org.uk
Head: Mr Richard Ware
No. of pupils: 70
Age range: 3-19
Funding: LEA
Type of School: Day
Special Needs: Profound &
Multiple Learning
Difficulties

Holly Bank School
Roe Head
Far Common Road
Mirfield
WF14 0DQ
☎ 01924 490 833
🖪 01924 491 464
email: holly.bank@
ukonline.co.uk
web: www.ukonline.co.uk
Head: Ms Sue Garland-
Grimes
No. of pupils: 55
Age range: 5-19
Funding: Non-maintained
Type of School: Residential
Special Needs: Medical,
Physical Disability and
Severe and Profound
Learning Difficulties

John Jamieson School
Hollin Hill Drive
Leeds
LS8 2PW
☎ 0113 293 0236
🖪 0113 293 0237
Acting Head: Ms Sally Joy

No. of pupils: 97
Age range: 2-19
Type of School: Special
Special Needs: Physical
Disability and Medical
Needs

Kingsland
Aberford Road
Stanley
Wakefield
WF3 4BA
☎ 01924 303100
No. of pupils: 70
Age range: 2-11
Type of School: Day
Special Needs: Severe,
Profound & Multiple
Learning Difficulties and
Autism

Lister Lane School
Lister Lane
Bradford
BD2 4LL
Age range: 3-13

Longley School
Smithy Lane
Huddersfield
HD5 8JE
☎ 01484 223 937
🖪 01484 511 520
Head: Mr Mike Hogarth
No. of pupils: 140
Age range: 4-17
Funding: LEA
Type of School: Day
Special Needs: Wide
range

Milestone School
4 Town Street
Stanningley
Leeds
LS28 6HL
☎ 0113 214 6107
🖪 0113 255 9162
Head: Mr J C Tearle
No. of pupils: 57
Age range: 2-19
Funding: LEA
Type of School: Day
Special Needs: Profound &
Multiple Learning
Difficulties

Moor Top School
Barnsley Road
Ackworth
Pontefract
WF7 7DT

No. of pupils: 51
Age range: 7-16

**Netherlands Avenue
School and Community
Nursery**
Netherlands Avenue
Odsal
Bradford
BD6 1EA
☎ 01274 677 711
🖪 01274 673108
email: office@
netherlands.ngfl.ac.uk
Head: Mr Gary Bowden
No. of pupils: 100
Age range: 2-11
Funding: LEA
Type of School: Day
Special Needs: Wide range

Newcliff House School
Fawcett Lane
Leeds
LS12 4PF
☎ 0113 263 7273
Age range: 5-11

Nortonthorpe Hall School
Busker Lane
Scissett
Huddersfield
HD8 9JU
☎ 01484 222921
🖪 01484 222966
Head: Mr M P
Ironmonger
No. of pupils: 72
Age range: 7-16
Funding: LEA
Type of School: Residential
& Day
Special Needs: Emotional
& Behavioural difficulties

Pathways School
Poplar Avenue
Townville
Castleford
WF10 3QJ
☎ 01977 723085
🖪 01997 723088
email: headteacher@
pathways.wakefield.sch.uk
Head: Miss Yvonne Limb
No. of pupils: 60
Age range: 5-11
Funding: LEA
Type of School: Day
Special Needs: Multiple
Learning Difficulties and
ASD

7

Penny Field School
Tongue Lane
Leeds
LS6 4QD
☎ 0113 278 3577
🖷 0113 278 3577
Head: Mrs Hilary Barrett
No. of pupils: 78
Age range: 2-19
Funding: LEA
Type of School: Day
Special Needs: Multi-
sensory impairments

**Pinderfields Hospital
School**
Aberford Road
Wakefield
WF1 4DG
No. of pupils: 50
Age range: 2-18

Ravenscliffe School
Skircoat Green
Halifax
HX3 0RZ
No. of pupils: 97
Age range: 11-19

Richard Oastler School
Cardigan Lane
Leeds
LS4 2LE
☎ 0113 278 2261
Age range: 4-11

Roundwood Hill School
St George's Road
Lupset
Wakefield
WF2 8BB
☎ 01924 364 195
🖷 01924 375 395
Head: Mrs M E Smith
No. of pupils: 120
Age range: 11-16
Funding: LEA
Type of School: Day
Special Needs: Moderate
Learning Difficulties

**St John's Catholic School
for the Deaf**
Church Street
Boston Spa
LS23 6DF
☎ 01937 842144
🖷 01937 541471
Head: Mr T M Wrynne
No. of pupils: 90
Age range: 3-19
Funding: Non-maintained

Type of School: Residential
Special Needs: Hearing
Impaired

Stonegate School
Stonegate Road
Leeds
LS6 4QJ
☎ 0113 278 6464
🖷 0113 274 5277
Head: Mr P Bailey
No. of pupils: 75
Age range: 11-16
Funding: LEA
Type of School: Day
Special Needs: Emotional
& behavioural difficulties

**Temple Bank School and
Support Service for the
Visually Impaired**
Daisy Hill Lane
Bradford
BD9 6BN
☎ 01274 776 566
🖷 01274 776 599
email: enquiries@
templebank.bradford.sch.uk
Head: Mr R C Neal
No. of pupils: 50
Age range: 2-19
Funding: LEA
Type of School: Day
Special Needs: Visually
Impaired

The Park School
Lawefield Lane
Wakefield
WF2 8SX
No. of pupils: 58
Age range: 2-19

The Priory School
Pontefract Road
Crofton
Wakefield
WF4 1LL
No. of pupils: 87
Age range: 7-16

Turnshaws School
Turnshaw Avenue
Kirkburton
Huddersfield
HD8 0TJ
☎ 01484 222 760
🖷 01484 222 761
email: tss@
turnshaws.kirklees.sch.uk
web: www.cabletel-
schools.org.uk/turnshaw.s

Head: Ms Gill Taylor
No. of pupils: 50
Age range: 3-19
Funding: LEA
Type of School: Day
Special Needs: Profound &
Multiple Learning
Difficulties

Victoria Park School
Victoria Park Grove
Bramley
Leeds
LS13 2RD
☎ 0113 278 3957
🖷 0113 278 6143
email: victoria.leeds.se@
campus.bt.com
web: www.campus.bt.com
Head: Mr P J Miller
No. of pupils: 125
Age range: 11-19
Funding: LEA
Type of School: Day
Special Needs: Moderate
Learning Difficulties

**Wedgwood School and
Community Nursery**
Landscove Avenue
Bradford
BO4 0NQ
☎ 01274 687 236
🖷 01274 686 735
email: wedgew@
legend.co.uk
Head: Mrs J Godward
No. of pupils: 68
Age range: 2-11
Funding: LEA
Type of School: Day
Special Needs: Profound &
Multiple Learning
Difficulties

West Oaks School
Westwood Way
Boston Spa
Wetherby
LS23 6DX
☎ 01937 844 772
No. of pupils: 114
Age range: 2-19

Wood Bank School
Dene View
Luddenden
Halifax
HX2 6PB
☎ 01422 884 170
🖷 01422 884671
email: admin@
woodbank.calderdale.sch.uk

Head: Jane Ingham
No. of pupils: 40
Age range: 2-11
Funding: LEA
Type of School: Day
Special Needs: Profound
and Multiple Learning
Difficulties, Severe
Learning Difficulties, ASD

Wiltshire

Appleford School
Shrewton
Salisbury
SP3 4HL
No. of pupils: 90
Age range: 7-13

Burton Hill School
Malmesbury
SN16 0EG
☎ 01666 822 685
🖷 01666 826 022
email: principal@
shaftesbury-bh.
presel.co.uk
web:
www.shaftesburysch.org
Head: Mr Philip Drake
No. of pupils: 41
Age range: 8-19
Funding: Non-maintained
Type of School: Residential
Special Needs: Physical
and learning disability

Calder House School
Thickwood Lane
Colerne
Chippenham
SN14 8BN
☎ 01225 742 329
🖷 01225 742 329
No. of pupils: 23
Age range: 5-13

Chalet School
Liden Drive
Liden
Swindon
SN3 6EX
☎ 01793 534537
Head: Mrs M Topping
No. of pupils: 42
Age range: 3-11
Funding: LEA
Type of School: Day
Special Needs: Complex
Learning Difficulties

Crowdys Hill School
Jefferies Avenue

Swindon
SN2 7HJ
☎ 01793 332400
🖷 01793 331860
email: head/admin@
crowdyshill.swindon.sch.uk
Head: Mr Keith Smith
No. of pupils: 160
Age range: 11-16
Funding: LEA
Type of School: Day
Special Needs: Multiple &
Complex Learning
Difficulties

Downland School
Downlands
Devizes
SN10 5EF
No. of pupils: 56
Age range: 11-16

Exeter House School
Friary Lane
Salisbury
SP1 2HA
No. of pupils: 54
Age range: 2-19

**Exeter House Special
School**
Somerset Road
Salisbury
SP1 3BL
☎ 01722 334 168
🖷 01722 334 168
Head: Mrs G Heather
No. of pupils: 65
Age range: 3-19
Funding: LEA
Type of School: Day
Special Needs: Profound &
Multiple Learning
Difficulties

Larkrise School
Ashton Street
Trowbridge
BA14 7EB
☎ 01225 761434
🖷 01225 774585
email: head@
larkrise.wilts.sch.uk
Head: Mrs C F Goodwin
No. of pupils: 63
Age range: 2-19
Funding: LEA
Type of School: Day
Special Needs: Severe
LearningDifficulties &
Profound & Multiple
Learning Difficulties

Notton House School
28 Notton
Lacock
Chippenham
SN15 2NF
☎ 01249 730 407
No. of pupils: 43
Age range: 10-16

Nyland School
Nyland Road
Nythe
Swindon
SN3 3RD
☎ 01793 535023
🖷 01793 332068
Age range: 4-11
Funding: LEA
Type of School: Day
Special Needs: Emotional
and Behavioural
Difficulties

**Pembroke Park First
School**
Penruddock Close
Salisbury
SP2 9HH
Head: Mrs S Wagstaff
Age range: 2-9
Funding: LEA
Type of School: Day
Special Needs: Physical
disabilities

Rowdeford School
Rowde
Devizes
SN10 2QQ
☎ 01380 850309
🖷 01380 859708
Head: Mr G Darnell
No. of pupils: 91
Age range: 11-16
Funding: LEA

Springfields School
Curzon Street
Calne
SN11 0DR
No. of pupils: 57
Age range: 10-16

St Luke's School
Cricklade Road
Swindon
SN2 5AH
☎ 01793 705 566
No. of pupils: 54
Age range: 11-16

St Nicholas School
Malmesbury Road

Chippenham
SN15 1QF
☎ 01249 650 435
No. of pupils: 61
Age range: 2-19

Uplands School
Leigh Road
Penhill
Swindon
SN2 5DE
☎ 01793 724 751
🖷 01793 703 396
Head: Miss Mary Bishop
No. of pupils: 72
Age range: 11-19
Funding: LEA
Type of School: Day
Special Needs: Profound &
Multiple Learning
Difficulties

Worcestershire

**Alexander Patterson
School**
Park Gate Road
Wolverley
Kidderminster
DY10 3PU
☎ 01562 851 396
🖷 01562 851 192
email: head@
alexpatt.worcs.sch.uk
Head: Mrs Marilyn Calvert
No. of pupils: 80
Age range: 2-19
Funding: LEA
Type of School: Day
Special Needs: Wide range

Blakebrook School
Bewdley Road
Kidderminster
DY11 6RL
☎ 01562 753 066
🖷 01562 824 533
Head: Mr M D G Russell
No. of pupils: 53
Age range: 3-19
Funding: LEA
Type of School: Day
Special Needs: Profound &
Multiple Learning
Difficulties

Chadsgrove School
Meadow Road
Catshill
Bromsgrove
B61 0JL
☎ 01527 871 511

🖷 01527 579 341
Head: Mr Richard Aust
No. of pupils: 112
Age range: 2-19
Funding: LEA
Type of School: Day
Special Needs: Physical
Disabilities, Profound and
Multiple Learning
Difficulties and Visual
Impairment

Cliffey House School
Hanley Castle
Worcester
WR8 0AD
☎ 01684 310 336
🖷 01684 310076
Head: Mr A Dickens
No. of pupils: 90
Age range: 11-16
Funding: LEA
Type of School: Day
Special Needs: Moderate
Learning Difficulties &
Autism

Kinloss Special School
Martley
Worcester
WR6 6QB
No. of pupils: 63
Age range: 10-17

Manor Park School
Turnpike Close St John's
Worcester
WR2 6AB
☎ 01905 423 403
🖷 01905 748 338
web:
www.manorparkschool.com
Head: Mr David Palmer
No. of pupils: 78
Age range: 4-19
Funding: LEA
Type of School: Day
Special Needs: Profound &
Multiple Learning
Difficulties & SLD

Pitcheroak School
Willow Way
Batchley
Redditch
B97 6PQ
No. of pupils: 189
Age range: 3-19

Rigby Hall School
Rigby Lane
Bromsgrove

7

B60 2EP
☎ 01527 875 475
🖷 01527 870 211
Head: Mrs P A Griffiths
No. of pupils: 110
Age range: 3-18
Funding: LEA
Type of School: Day
Special Needs: Moderate
Learning Difficulties &
Severe Learning
Difficulties

Riversides School
Thorneloe Road
Worcester
WR1 3HZ
☎ 01905 21261
🖷 01905 22247
email: head@riverside.
worcs.sch.uk
Head: Mrs Barbara L Scott
No. of pupils: 55
Age range: 7-16
Funding: LEA
Type of School: Day
Special Needs: Emotional
& behavioural difficulties

RNIB New College
Whittington Road

Worcester
WR5 2JX
☎ 01905 763933
🖷 01905 763277
email: hodgetts@
rnibnew.demon.co.uk
Liason Teacher: Irene
Hodgetts
No. of pupils: 95
Age range: 11-19
Funding: LEA
Type of School: Residential
Special Needs: Visually
Impaired

Rose Hill School
Windermere Drive
Warndon
Worcester
WR4 9JL
☎ 01905 454 828
🖷 01905 453 695
email: admin@
rosehill.worcs.sch.uk
web: www.rosehill.
worcs.sch.uk
Head: Mr F W Steel
No. of pupils: 80
Age range: 3-19
Funding: LEA
Type of School: Day

Special Needs: Physical
Disabilities/Profound &
Multiple Learning
Difficulties

Skilts Residential School
Gorcott Hill
Redditch
B98 9ET
Age range: 3-11

Stourminster School
Comberton Road
Kidderminster
DY10 3DX
Head: Mr G E James
No. of pupils: 93
Age range: 8-19

**The Alexander Patterston
School**
Lea Castle Hospital
Cookley
Kidderminster
DY10 3PP
No. of pupils: 115
Age range: 2-19
Special Needs: Moderate
Learning Difficulties and
Profound & Multiple
Learning Difficulties and
Autism

**The Vale of Evesham
School**
Four Pools Lane
Evesham
WR11 1BN
☎ 01386 443367
🖷 01386 765787
Head: Mr E P Matthews
No. of pupils: 150
Age range: 4-19
Type of School: Residential
Special Needs: All

**Thornton House School
& Nursery Assessment
Unit**
Wylds Lane
Worcester
WR5 1DR
☎ 01905 355 525
🖷 01905 358 867
email: Head@thschool.
freeserve.co.uk
Head: Mr H B Thomas
No. of pupils: 156
Age range: 2-11
Funding: LEA
Type of School: Day
Special Needs: Moderate
Learning Difficulties &
Autism

Northern Ireland

Belfast

Belfast Hospital School
Royal Belfast Hospital for
Sick Children
Falls Road
Belfast
BT12 6BE

Cedar Lodge School
Gray's Lane
Newtownabbey
BT36 7EB
☎ 028 9077 7292
🖷 028 9037 1535
Head: G Bunting
No. of pupils: 150
Age range: 4-16
Funding: LEA
Type of School: Day
Special Needs: Delicate
health

**Dufferin & Ava Hospital
School**
Wakehurst House
Belfast City Hospital
Lisburn Road
Belfast
BT9 7AB
Age range: 4-16

Fleming Fulton School
35 Upper Malone Road
Belfast
BT9 6TY
☎ 028 9061 3877
🖷 028 9062 7975
email: flemingfulton@
school.ntl.com
web: www.websites.
ntl.com/~flemfltn/
Acting Principal: Mr J W
Taylor
No. of pupils: 163
Age range: 2-19
Funding: LEA
Type of School: Day
Special Needs: Physical
disabilities

**Greenwood House
Assessment Centre**
Greenwood Avenue
Belfast
BT4 3JJ
No. of pupils: 60
Age range: 4-8

Harberton Special School
Harberton Park
Belfast
BT9 6TX
☎ 028 9038 1525
Head: Mr Martin
McGlade
No. of pupils: 200
Age range: 4-11
Funding: LEA
Special Needs: Moderate
Learning Difficulties

Longstone Special School
Millars Lane
Dundonald
Belfast
BT16 0DA
☎ 028 9048 0071
🖷 028 9048 1927
email: staff.Longstone@
dnet.co.uk
web: www.dnet.co.uk
Head: Mr T Howard
No. of pupils: 200
Age range: 4-16
Funding: LEA
Type of School: Day
Special Needs: Moderate
Learning Difficulties

**Mitchell House Special
School**
Marmont
Holywood Road
Belfast
BT4 2GU
Age range: 2-19

**Mosgrave Park Hospital
School**
Stockman's Lane
Balmoral
Belfast
BT9 7JB
Age range: 4-16

**Park Education Resource
Centre**
Ravenhill Road
Belfast
BT6 8GH
Age range: 11-16

**St Francis De Sales School
for Children with
Hearing, Speech and
Language Difficulties**
Beechmount Drive

Belfast
BT12 7LU
☎ 028 9024 5599
Age range: 3-11

**St Gerard's Educational
Resource Centre**
Upper Springfield Road
Belfast
BT12 7QP
☎ 028 9032 5249
🖷 028 9023 5484
Head: Mr Robert O
Rooney
No. of pupils: 240
Age range: 4-16
Funding: Independent
Type of School: Day
Special Needs: Moderate
Learning Difficulties

St Joseph's College
St Vincent's Centre
6 Willowfield Drive
Belfast
BT6 8HN
☎ 028 90 461 444
🖷 028 90 454 565
Teacher-in-charge: Mr B
Davey
No. of pupils: 30
Age range: 11-18
Funding: LEA
Type of School: Day
Special Needs: Emotional
& behavioural difficulties

St Paul's Primary School
Cavendish Square
Belfast
BT12 7AA
No. of pupils: 180
Age range: 4-16

The Lindsay School
Forster Green Hospital
110 Saintfield Road
Belfast
BT8 4HD
☎ 028 9079 3681
🖷 028 9079 9683
Head: Mr Phillip W
Doherty
No. of pupils: 25
Age range: 4-14
Funding: LEA
Type of School: Day

Special Needs: Emotional
& behavioural difficulties

Tor Bank Special School
7-8 Upper Newtownards
Road
Dundonald
Belfast
BT16 1RG
☎ 02890 484147
🖷 02890 489654
Principal: Mr Colin Davis
No. of pupils: 140
Age range: 3-19
Funding: LEA (SEELB)
Type of School: Special 'S'
Special Needs: Severe
learning difficulties

Co Antrim

Beechgrove Special School
91 Fry's Road
Ballymena
BT43 7EN
☎ 01266 48264
🖷 01266 48264
Head: Mrs Alison Pinches
No. of pupils: 24
Age range: 3-11
Funding: LEA
Type of School: Day
Special Needs: Physical
disabilities

Dunfane School
91 Frys Road
Ballymena
BT43 7EN
☎ 01266 48263
🖷 01266 41434
Head: Mrs Oonagh
McCann
No. of pupils: 152
Age range: 4-16
Funding: Independent
Type of School: Day
Special Needs: Moderate
Learning Difficulties

Hill Croft School
Abbots Road
Newtownabbey
BT37 9RA
☎ 028 90 863262
🖷 028 90 868159
Principal: Mrs B McAvley
No. of pupils: 78
Age range: 3-19

7

Jordanstown Schools for Children with Auditory or Visual Impairments
85 Jordanstown Road
Newtownabbey
BT37 0QE
☎ 028 9086 3541
Textphone 028 9086 3541
🖹 028 9086 4356
Head: Mr S L Clarke
No. of pupils: 106
Age range: 4-19
Funding: Voluntary
Special Needs: Visually Impaired/Hearing Impaired

Loughan School
22 Old Ballymoney Road
Ballymena
BT43 6LX
☎ 01266 652 944
🖹 01266 652 944
Head:
No. of pupils: 70
Age range: 4-19
Funding: LEA
Type of School: Day
Special Needs: Severe Learning Difficulties

Muckamore House School
29 Oldstone Road
Antrim
BT41 4PY
☎ 01849 428 946
Head: Mrs D Miskelly
No. of pupils: 34
Age range: 3-19
Funding: LEA
Type of School: Day
Special Needs: Wide range

Roddensvale School
The Roddens
Larne
BT40 1PU
Age range: 4-19

Rosstulla Special School
Jordanstown
Newtownabbey
BT37 0QF
Age range: 5-16

Co Armagh

Brookfield Special School
6 Halfpenney Gate Road
Moira
Craigavon
BT67 0HN

No. of pupils: 84
Age range: 5-11

Ceara School
Lough Road
Lurgan
Craigavon
BT66 6JJ
☎ 01762 323 312
🖹 01762 349 670
No. of pupils: 48
Age range: 4-19

Fallowfield School
Lough Road
Lurgan
Craigavon
BT66 6LX
No. of pupils: 29
Age range: 10-16

Hospital and Home Teaching Service
Room 15
Sacred Heart Primary School
Edward Street
Lurgan
BT66 6DG
No. of pupils: 7
Age range: 5-16

Lisanally Special School
Lisanally Lane
Armagh
BT61 7HF
☎ 01861 523 563
🖹 01861 527 544
Head: Mrs M Williams
No. of pupils: 102
Age range: 4-19
Funding: LEA
Type of School: Day
Special Needs: Wide range

Co Down

Ardmore House Special School
95a Saul Street
Downpatrick
BT30 6NJ
☎ 01396 614 881
🖹 01396 614 919
Head: Mr W Dale
No. of pupils: 24
Age range: 11-16
Funding: LEA
Type of School: Day
Special Needs: Emotional & behavioural difficulties

Beechlawn School
3 Dromore Road
Hillsborough
BT26 6PA
☎ 01846 682 302
🖹 01846 689 329
Age range: 8-16

Clifton Special School
15 Ballyholme Road
Bangor
BT20 5JH
☎ 01247 270 210
Head: Mrs J H Crowther
No. of pupils: 105
Age range: 3-19
Funding: LEA
Type of School: Day
Special Needs: Profound & Multiple Learning Difficulties, Severe Learning Difficulties, Autism, EBD

Daisy Hill Hospital School
5 Hospital Road
Newry
BT35 8DR
No. of pupils: 6
Age range: 5-16

Donard School
22A Castlewellan Road
Banbridge
BT32 3XY
☎ 028 406 62357
No. of pupils: 40
Age range: 4-19
Funding: LEA
Type of School: Day
Special Needs: SLD

Killard House School
North Road
Newtownards
BT23 3AN
Age range: 5-16

Knockevin Special School
29 Racecourse Hill
Killough Road
Downpatrick
BT30 6PU
Age range: 3-19

Rathfriland Hill School
Rathfriland Hill
Newry
BT34 1HU
No. of pupils: 91
Age range: 4-19

Co Fermanagh

Killadeas Special School
Killadeas
Irvinestown
Enniskillen
BT7 4AY
No. of pupils: 53
Age range: 4-16

Co Londonderry

Altnagelvin Hospital School Tuition Service
Ground Floor
Altnagelvin Area Hospital
Altnagelvin
Londonderry
BT47 6SB
☎ 02871 611 453/
02871 611 454
🖹 02871 611 292
Head: Mrs Dorothy Campbell
No. of pupils: 213
Age range: 5-16
Funding: Hospital
Type of School: Hospital
Special Needs: Medical, Emotional, Behavioural

Belmont House Special School
Racecourse Road
Londonderry
BT48 7RE
☎ 02871 351266
🖹 02871 351125
Head: Mr Tommy McCully
No. of pupils: 186
Age range: 3-17
Funding: LEA
Type of School: Day
Special Needs: Moderate Learning Difficulties

Foyle View Special School
15 Racecourse Road
Londonderry
BT48 7RB
☎ 01504 263 270
🖹 01504 264 017
Head: Gillian Boyd
No. of pupils: 109
Age range: 3-19
Funding: LEA
Type of School: Day
Special Needs: Severe Learning Difficulties

Glasvey Special School
15 Loughermore Road
Ballykelly
BT49 9PB
☎ 01504 762 462
🖷 01504 767 772
Head: Mrs Lynn Wilson
No. of pupils: 37
Age range: 3-19
Funding: LEA
Type of School: Day
Special Needs: Profound &
Multiple Learning
Difficulties & Autism

**Greystone Hall Special
School**
Fax Ballyquin Road
Limavady
BT49 9ET
No. of pupils: 87
Age range: 8-16

Sandelford School
4 Rugby Avenue
Coleraine
BT52 1JL
☎ 01270 343062
🖷 01270 328448
Acting Principal: Mr J
Gribbon

No. of pupils: 120
Age range: 3-19
Funding: LEA
Type of School: Day
Special Needs: Severe
Learning Difficulties

Townparks School
55 Hospital Road
Magherafelt
BT45 5EG
Age range: 4-19

Co Tyrone

Cranny Special School
4a Deverney Road
Omagh
BT79 0JJ
☎ 01662 242 939
Head: Mrs K McGerty
No. of pupils: 38
Age range: 3-19
Funding: LEA
Type of School: Day
Special Needs: Severe
Learning Difficulties

Glenside Special School
45a Derry Road
Strabane

BT82 8DY
No. of pupils: 47
Age range: 4-16

Heatherbank School
17 Deverney Road
Omagh
BT79 0ND
No. of pupils: 147
Age range: 4-16

**South Tyrone Hospital
School**
Carland Road
Dungannon
BT70 1HT
Age range: 5-16

Southern
Education and
Library Board

Sperrinview School
8 Coalisland Road
Dungannon
BT71 6FA
☎ 028 8772 2467
🖷 028 8772 3604
email: asherry@sperrinview.
dungannon.isi.sch.uk

Head: Mr Olvier Sherry
No. of pupils: 70
Age range: 3-19
Funding: LEA
Type of School: Day
Special Needs: Severe
Learning Difficulties

Western
Education and
Library Board

Erne School
Derrygonnelly Road
Enniskillen
BT74 7EY
☎ 028 66323942
🖷 028 66323942
email:
info@ernesp.enniskillen.ni.
sch.uk
Head: Mrs K Turnbull
No. of pupils: 136
Age range: 4-16
Funding: LEA
Type of School: Day
Special Needs: Moderate
Learning Difficulties

7

Scotland

Aberdeen City

Aberdeen School for The Deaf
Regent Walk
Aberdeen
AB24 1SX
☎ 01224 480303
Textphone 01224 480303
🖷 01224 276675
email: enquiries@schoolfor
deaf.aberdeen.sch.uk
Head: Mrs Alison Martin
No. of pupils: 17
Age range: 2-11
Funding: LEA
Type of School: Day
Special Needs: Hearing
Impaired

Beechwood School
Raeden Park Road
Aberdeen
AB15 5PD
☎ 01224 323 405
🖷 01224 311 192
Head: Mr Andrew C Young
No. of pupils: 72
Age range: 5-18
Funding: LEA
Type of School: Day
Special Needs: All

**Carden House School
(Orange Unit)**
Dyce Primary School
Gordon Terrace
Dyce
Aberdeen
AB21 7BD
☎ 01224 770 362
Age range: 5-12

**Cordyce Residential
School**
Riverview Drive
Dyce
Aberdeen
AB21 7NF
☎ 01224 724 215
🖷 01224 772 738
Age range: 7-16

Hazlewood School
Fernielea Road
Aberdeen
AB15 6GU
☎ 01224 321 363

🖷 01224 311 162
email: enquiries@
hazlewood.aberdeen.sch.uk
Head: Mrs Rhona Jarvis
No. of pupils: 80
Age range: 4-18
Funding: LEA
Type of School: Day
Special Needs: Moderate
Learning Difficulties and
Severe and Profound
Learning Difficulties

**Linksfield Academy
Partially Hearing Unit**
520 King Street
Aberdeen
AB2 1SS
☎ 01224 481 343
Age range: 11-16

Marlpool School
Cloverfield Gardens
Bucksburn
Aberdeen
AB21 9QN
☎ 01224 712 735
🖷 01224 712 524
email: enquiries@
marlpool.aberdeen.sch.uk
web: www.class6.ik.org
Head: Mrs Hilary Gordon
No. of pupils: 70
Age range: 5-19
Type of School: Day
Special Needs: Generic
with many pupils on
Autistic Spectrum

Oakbank School
Midstocket Road
Aberdeen
AB15 5XP
☎ 01224 313 347
🖷 01224 312 017
email: oakbankschool@
hotmail.com
Principal: Mrs Jane C
Arrowsmith
No. of pupils: 42
Age range: 12-17
Funding: Independent/
Charity
Type of School: Residential
Special Needs: Social,
Emotional and
Behavioural Difficulties

Pitfodels School
North Deeside Road
Cults
Aberdeen
AB15 9PN
☎ 01224 868 480
🖷 01224 861 512
Age range: 4-18

Raeden Centre
Mid-Stocket Road
Aberdeen
AB15 5PD
☎ 01224 321 381
🖷 01224 311 109
Head: Mrs K Threadgold
No. of pupils: 45
Age range: 3-6

Redcraigs
Craighill School
Hetherwick Road
Aberdeen
AB12 5ST
☎ 01224 897 641

**Royal Aberdeen Hospital
for Sick Children**
Education Unit
Wards 2 & 4 Lowit Unit
Cornhill Road
Aberdeen
AB25 2ZG
☎ 01224 681 818

**The Camphill Rudolf
Steiner Schools**
Central Office
Murtle Estate
Bieldside
Aberdeen
AB1 9EP
☎ 01224 867 935
email: office@crss.org.uk
web: www.crss.org.uk
Administrator: Mr H
Hansmann
No. of pupils: 98
Age range: 4-19
Funding: Independent
Type of School: Residential
Special Needs: Moderate
Learning Difficulties and
Profound & Multiple
Learning Difficulties

Tullos Primary School
Girdleness Road

Aberdeen
AB11 8FJ
☎ 01224 876 621
🖷 01224 899415
email:
enquiries@tullosprimary.
aberdeen.sch.uk
Head: Ellen Smith
No. of pupils: 340
Age range: 3-11
Funding: LEA
Type of School: Day
Special Needs: Special
Educational Needs Base

Aberdeenshire

**Banff Academy
Curriculum Support Unit**
Bellevue Road
Banff
AB45 1BY
☎ 01261 812591
🖷 01261 815491
Principal Teacher SEN: Ms
Maureen Forsyth
No. of pupils: 50
Age range: 12-18
Funding: LEA
Type of School: Day
Special Needs: All

Carronhill School
Mill of Forest Road
Stonehaven
AB39 2GZ
☎ 01569 763 886
🖷 01569 762332
No. of pupils: 30
Age range: 3-18
Funding: LEA
Type of School: Day
Special Needs: All

Ellon Academy
School Hill
Ellon
AB41 9AX
☎ 01358 720 715
🖷 01358 723 758
email: Ellon.ac@
RMPLC.co.uk
web: www.rmplc.co.uk/
eduweb/site/ellon.ac
Head: Dr B Wilkins
No. of pupils: 1700
Age range: 12-18

Funding: LEA
Special Needs: Wide range

Gordon Schools Special Unit
Castle Street
Huntly
AB54 4SE
☎ 01466 792 181 X 15
🖷 01466 794 715
email: gordonschools.aca@
aberdeenshire.gov.uk
Rector: Mr John Swan
No. of pupils: 850
Age range: 3-18
Funding: LEA
Type of School: Day
Special Needs: All

Linn Moor Residential School
Peterculter
Aberdeen
AB14 0PJ
☎ 01224 732246
🖷 01224 735261
email: info@
linnmoorschool.co.uk
web:
www.linnmoorschool.co.uk
Type of School: Residential
Special Needs: Severe &
Complex Learning
Difficulties and Emotional
& Behavioural Difficulties

St Andrew's School
St Andrew's Gardens
Inverurie
AB51 3XT
☎ 01467 621 215
🖷 01467 621 215
Age range: 4-18

The Anna Ritchie School
Grange Gardens
Peterhead
AB42 2AP
☎ 01779 473 293
🖷 01779 479 963
Age range: 2-16

The Ogilvie School
School Road
Keith
AB55 3ES
☎ 01542 882 000
Age range: 5-16

The Stevenson Education Centre
Victoria Street

Fraserburgh
AB43 9PJ
☎ 01346 510 187
🖷 01346 512 523
email: the_stevenson_
centre_edu@msn.com
web: www.msn.com
Head: Ms Jenny Kinnon
No. of pupils: 18
Age range: 11-16
Funding: LEA
Type of School: Day
Special Needs: Emotional
& behavioural difficulties

Westfield School
Argyll Road
Fraserburgh
AB43 9BL
☎ 01346 518 699
🖷 01346 510 231
Head: Mr Gordon
Davidson
No. of pupils: 62
Age range: 3-18
Funding: LEA
Type of School: Day
Special Needs: Profound &
Multiple Learning
Difficulties

Woodlands School
Craigton Road
Cults
AB15 9PR
☎ 01224 868 814
Head: Mr Malcolm
Johnston
No. of pupils: 54
Age range: 5-18
Funding: LEA
Type of School: Day
Special Needs: Profound &
Multiple Learning
Difficulties

Argyll & Bute

Drummore Learning Centre
Soroba Road
Oban
PA34 3SB
☎ 01631 564 811
Age range: 4-16

Parklands School
27 Charlotte Street
Helensburgh
G84 7EZ
☎ 01436 673 714
🖷 01436 677 864

Head: Mrs Louise Downie
No. of pupils: 27
Age range: 5-19
Funding: LEA
Type of School: Day
Special Needs: Profound &
Multiple Learning
Difficulties

Whitegates Learning Centre
Lochgilphead
Argyll
PA31 8SY
☎ 01546 602 583
🖷 01546 606 026
Head of Centre: Mrs E
Mackenzie
No. of pupils: 53
Age range: 3-18
Type of School: Day
Special Needs: Autism and
Various Learning
Difficulties

Ayrshire

Invergarven School
15 Henrietta Street
Girvan
KA26 9AL
No. of pupils: 12
Age range: 5-18
Funding: LEA
Type of School: Day
Special Needs: Wide range

James McFarlane School
Dalry Road
Ardrossan
KA22 7DQ
No. of pupils: 32
Age range: 4-19
Funding: LEA
Type of School: Day
Special Needs: Profound &
Multiple Learning
Difficulties

City of Edinburgh

Cairnpark School
17 Redhall House Drive
Edinburgh
EH14 1JA
☎ 0131 443 0903
Age range: 12-16

Canonmills School
Rodney Street
Edinburgh
EH7 4EL

☎ 0131 556 6000
🖷 0131 557 5709
Head: Mrs Margaret I
Wilson
No. of pupils: 54
Age range: 12-16
Funding: LEA
Type of School: Day
Special Needs: Emotional
& behavioural difficulties

Donaldson's College
West Coates
Edinburgh
EH12 5JJ
☎ 0131 337 9911
Textphone 0131 337 9911
🖷 0131 337 1654
email: admin@donaldsons-
coll.edin.sch.uk
web:
www.donaldsons.org.uk
Principal: Mrs Janet L Allan
No. of pupils: 80
Age range: 3-18
Funding: LEA
Type of School: Day/
Residential

Drylaw School
Easter Drylaw Drive
Edinburgh
EH4 2RY
☎ 0131 343 6116
Age range: 5-12

Graysmill School
1 Redhall House Drive
Edinburgh
EH14 1JE
☎ 0131 443 8096
Age range: 3-18

Howdenhall Education Service
39 Howdenhall Road
Edinburgh
EH16 6PG
☎ 0131 664 8488
🖷 0131 664 3549
Head: Mrs Fiona Dickens
No. of pupils: 21
Age range: 9-16
Funding: LEA
Type of School: Residential
Special Needs: Emotional
and behavioural difficulties

Kaimes School
140 Lasswade Road
Edinburgh
EH16 6RT

7

☎ 0131 664 8241
No. of pupils: 76
Age range: 5-18
Funding: LEA
Type of School: Day

Kingsinch School
233 Gilmerton Road
Edinburgh
EH16 5UD
☎ 0131 664 1911
🖷 0131 672 3035
Head: Ms J Eales
No. of pupils: 83
Age range: 5-17
Funding: LEA
Type of School: Day
Special Needs: Moderate
Learning Difficulties in
complex range, Autism,
EBD, Speech and language
difficulties

Oaklands School
40 Broomhouse Crescent
Edinburgh
EH11 3UB
☎ 0131 467 7867
🖷 0131 443 5100
Head: Ms Sue Harland
No. of pupils: 30
Age range: 5-18
Funding: LEA
Type of School: Day
Special Needs: Profound &
Multiple Learning
Difficulties

Piershill School
70 Willowbrae Road
Edinburgh
EH8 7HA
☎ 0131 661 1488
🖷 0131 661 1488
Head: Mrs E A Simpson
No. of pupils: 24
Age range: 9-12
Funding: LEA
Type of School: Day
Special Needs: Emotional
& behavioural difficulties

Pilrig Park School
Balfour Place
Edinburgh
EH6 5DW
☎ 0131 554 7024
Age range: 12-16

Prospect Bank School
81 Restalrig Road
Edinburgh

EH6 8BQ
☎ 0131 553 2239
Age range: 5-12

**St Giles Services for The
Hearing Impaired**
Broomhouse Crescent
Edinburgh
EH11 4UB
☎ 0131 443 0304
Age range: 5-18

St Katharine's Unit
29 Balmwell Terrace
Edinburgh
EH16 6PS
☎ 0131 672 1109

St Nicholas School
Gorgie Road
Edinburgh
EH11 2RG
☎ 0131 337 6077
🖷 01313132322
email: headteacher@
stnicholas.edin.sch.uk
Head: Mrs C McLaren
No. of pupils: 70
Age range: 5-16
Funding: LEA
Type of School: Day
Special Needs: Moderate
Learning Difficulties

The Royal Blind School
Craigmillar Park
Edinburgh
EH16 5NA
☎ 0131 667 1100
🖷 0131 662 9700
email: royblisc@
globalnet.co.uk
web: schoolsite.edex.net.uk/
index.htm
Head: Mr Kevin Tansley
No. of pupils: 119
Age range: 3-19
Funding: Independent
Type of School: Residential
Special Needs: Visually
Impaired

Willowpark School
347 Gorgie Road
Edinburgh
EH11 2RG
☎ 0131 337 1622
🖷 0131 337 1709
Head: Mrs A Mooney
No. of pupils: 70
Age range: 5-18
Funding: LEA

Type of School: Day
Special Needs: Wide range

Clackmannanshire

**Clackmannanshire
Primary Schools' Support
Service**
c/o Park Primary School
East Castle Street
Alloa
FK10 1AN
☎ 01259 212 151
Head: Mrs Janice
Robertson
No. of pupils: 85
Age range: 4-11
Funding: LEA
Type of School: Day
Special Needs: Emotional
& behavioural difficulties

Fairfield School
Pompee Road
Sauchie
FK10 3BX
No. of pupils: 23
Age range: 11-18
Funding: LEA
Type of School: Day
Special Needs: Severe
Learning Difficulties

Dumfries and
Galloway

Langlands School
Loreburn Park
Dumfries
DG1 1LS
☎ 01387 267 834
email: langlands@
amw.dungal.net
Head: Mrs M Rinaldi
No. of pupils: 18
Age range: 5-18
Funding: LEA
Type of School: Day
Special Needs: Profound &
Multiple Learning
Difficulties

Merton Hall
Newton Stewart
DG8 6QL
☎ 0167 12447
Age range: 5-16

Woodlands School
Corsbie Road
Newton Stewart
DG8 6JB

☎ 0167 12480
Age range: 7-18

Dundee City

Children's Unit School
Dudhope House
15 Dudhope Terrace
Dundee
DD3 6HH
☎ 01382 346554
Acting Principal Teacher:
Mrs M J Munro
No. of pupils: 6
Age range: 5-12
Funding: Education/
Health
Type of School: Hospital
Special Needs: Mental
Health

Kingspark School
Gillburn Road
Dundee
DD3 0AB
☎ 01382 436 284
No. of pupils: 175
Age range: 5-16

Parkview School
309 Blackness Road
Dundee
DD2 1SH
☎ 01382 67903
Age range: 4-16

East Ayrshire

Hillside School
Dalgleish Avenue
Cumnock
KA18 1QQ
☎ 01290 423 239
🖷 01290 425 870

**Hospital Education
Service**
Crosshouse Hospital
Ward 1a
Room 54
Kilmarnock
KA2 0BE
☎ 01563 521 133

Park School
Grassyards Road
Kilmarnock
KA3 7BB
☎ 01563 525 316
🖷 01563 525 465
Age range: 5-16

Witchhill School
Witch Road
Kilmarnock
KA3 1JF
☎ 01563 533 863
Age range: 3-16

Woodstock School
30 North Hamilton Street
Kilmarnock
KA1 2QJ
☎ 01563 533 550
🖷 01563 573 808
Head: Mrs Norah Craig
Age range: 5-16
Funding: LEA
Special Needs: Severe
Learning Difficulties

East
Renfrewshire

Campsie View School
Boghead Road
Lenzie
Glasgow
G66 4DR
☎ 0141 777 6269
🖷 0141 775 3551
Head: Ms Carol P Bowie
No. of pupils: 60
Age range: 2-19
Funding: LEA
Type of School: Day
Special Needs: Complex

The Isobel Mair School
1A Drumby Crescent
Clarkston
G76 7HN
☎ 0141 5774546
🖷 0141 5717737
Head: Mrs E A Horne
Age range: 5-18

Glasgow City

Glenrothes Education Centre
Rimbleton Avenue
Glenrothes
KY6 2BZ
☎ 01592 415608
🖷 01592 415609
No. of pupils: 30
Age range: 12-16
Type of School: Day
Special Needs: Social, emotional and behavioural

Headwell School
Headwell Avenue
Dunfermline
KY12 0JU
☎ 01383 721 589
Head: Mrs Jane Lopez
No. of pupils: 34
Age range: 5-18
Funding: LEA
Type of School: Day
Special Needs: Severe & complex needs

Hyndhead School
Barncraig Street
Buckhaven
Leven
KY8 1JE
☎ 01592 414 499
No. of pupils: 21
Age range: 3-16

John Fergus School
Erskine Place
Glenrothes
KY7 4JB
☎ 01592 415 335
Head: Mrs M A Sankey
No. of pupils: 22
Age range: 3-19
Funding: LEA
Type of School: Day
Special Needs: Severe
Learning Difficulties

Kilmaron School
Balgarvie Road
Cupar
KY15 4PE
☎ 01334 653 125
Age range: 3-16

Linwood Hall School
Linwood Drive
Leven
KY8 5RB
☎ 01333 592 525
🖷 01333 592 525
No. of pupils: 31
Age range: 11-16

Lochgelly North School
6 Mcgregor Avenue
Lochgelly
KY5 9PE
☎ 01592 418 110
No. of pupils: 18
Age range: 3-18

Robert Henryson School
Linburn Road
Dunfermline

KY11 4LD
☎ 01383 728 004
No. of pupils: 51
Age range: 3-19

Rosslyn School
Viewforth Terrace
Kirkcaldy
KY1 3BP
☎ 01592 415 930
🖷 01592 415909
Head: Mrs G Macfarlane
No. of pupils: 20
Age range: 3-19
Funding: LEA
Type of School: Day
Special Needs: Profound &
Complex Learning
Difficulties

Starley Hall School
Aberdour Road
Burntisland
KY3 0AG
☎ 01383 860 314
🖷 01383 860 956
email: info@
starleyhallschool.co.uk
web:
www.starleyhallschool.co.uk
Director: Mr Philip Barton
No. of pupils: 30
Age range: 10-17
Funding: Independent
Type of School: Residential
Special Needs: Emotional
& behavioural difficulties

Abercorn Secondary School
195 Garscube Road
Glasgow
G4 9QH
☎ 0141 332 6212
🖷 0141 353 2180
Head: Ms Patricia Smith
No. of pupils: 140
Age range: 11-18
Funding: LEA
Type of School: Day
Special Needs: Moderate
Learning Difficulties

Ashcraig School
100 Avenue End Road
Craigend
Glasgow
G33 3SW
☎ 0141 774 3428
🖷 0141 774 5571
email: library@ashcraig.
glas.cabletel-schools.org.uk

web: www.ashcraig.glas.
cabletel-schools.org
Head: Mr John Doran
No. of pupils: 142
Age range: 12-18
Funding: LEA
Type of School: Day
Special Needs: Visually
Impaired

Broomlea School
168 Broomhill Drive
Glasgow
G11 7NH
☎ 0141 339 6494
No. of pupils: 37
Age range: 2-12
Type of School: Complex
learning

Carnbooth School
Carnbooth House
Carmunnock
Glasgow
G76 9EG
☎ 0141 644 2773
🖷 0141 644 3136
email: carnbooth@aol.com
Head: Ms Catherine Clark
No. of pupils: 13
Age range: 4-16
Funding: LEA
Type of School: Day/
Residential
Special Needs: Deafblind

Cartvale School
Carmichael Place
Glasgow
G42 9SY
☎ 0141 649 4811
No. of pupils: 18
Age range: 12-16

Croftcroighn School
180 Findochty Street
Garthamlock
Glasgow
G33 5EP
☎ 0141 774 7777
Head: Mrs Wilma Craig
No. of pupils: 63
Age range: 2-11
Funding: LEA
Type of School: Day
Special Needs: Profound &
Multiple Learning
Difficulties

Douglas Inch Centre
Woodside Terrace
Glasgow

7

G3 7UY
☎ 0141 2118000
🖳 0141 2118005
Senior teachers: Mary
Storrie and Fiona Booth
No. of pupils: 24
Age range: 14-16
Funding: LEA
Type of School: Day
Special Needs: Chronic
truancy

Drummore School
129 Drummore Road
Glasgow
G15 7NH
☎ 0141 944 1323
No. of pupils: 67
Age range: 5-12

Drumpark School
Coatbridge Road
Bargeddie
Glasgow
G69 7TW
☎ 01236 423 955
🖳 01236 423 879
Head: Mr Sutherland
No. of pupils: 200
Age range: 3-18
Funding: LEA
Type of School: Day
Special Needs: Range of
special needs

East Park School
1092 Marghill Road
Glasgow
G20 9TD
☎ 0141 946 8315
🖳 0141 946 2838
Head: Mrs L Gray
No. of pupils: 30
Age range: 5-19
Funding: Independent
Type of School: Day
Special Needs: Profound &
Multiple Learning
Difficulties

Eastmuir School
211 Hallhill Road
Glasgow
G33 4QL
☎ 0141 771 3464
No. of pupils: 70
Age range: 5-12

Fallside School
Sanderson Avenue
Viewpark
Uddingston

G71 6JZ
☎ 01698 747 721
🖳 01698 747 166
Head: Mr C McGarvey
No. of pupils: 26
Age range: 12-16
Funding: LEA
Type of School: Day
Special Needs: Emotional
& behavioural difficulties

Gadburn School
70 Rockfield Road
Glasgow
G21 3DZ
☎ 0141 558 5373
No. of pupils: 66
Age range: 5-12

**Gartnavel Royal Hospital
School**
Adolescent Psychiatric
Unit, Ward 1
1055 Great Western Road
Glasgow
G12 0XH
☎ 0141 2113552
🖳 0141 2113551
Assistant coordinator: Miss
L Brown
No. of pupils: 24
Age range: 11-18
Funding: LEA
Type of School: Hospital
Special Needs: Psychiatric

Glencryan School
Greenfaulds Ring Road
Cumbernauld
G67 2XJ
☎ 01236 724 125
🖳 01236 732 625
Head: Ms Annabel Irvine
No. of pupils: 146
Age range: 2-18
Funding: LEA
Type of School: Day
Special Needs: Moderate
Learning Difficulties

**Greenburn Primary
School**
Maxwellton Avenue
Calderwood
East Kilbride
G74 3DU
☎ 01355 237 278
🖳 01355 237 278
Head: Ms Adelaide J
Duffy
No. of pupils: 70
Age range: 2-12

Funding: LEA
Type of School: Day
Special Needs: Wide range

Greenview School
47 Greenhead Street
Glasgow
G40 1DG
☎ 0141 554 2818
No. of pupils: 36
Age range: 5-13

**Hairmyres Hospital
School**
East Kilbride
G75 8RG
☎ 01355 220 292
Age range: 4-16

Hampden School
80 Ardnahoe Avenue
Glasgow
G42 0DL
☎ 0141 647 7720
No. of pupils: 29
Age range: 2-12

Hollybrook School
135 Hollybrook Street
Govanhill
Glasgow
G42 7HU
☎ 0141 423 5937
Head: Mrs Mary P Horn
No. of pupils: 120
Age range: 12-18
Funding: LEA
Type of School: Day
Special Needs: Moderate
Learning Difficulties

Howford School
487 Crookston Road
Glasgow
G53 7TX
☎ 0141 882 2605
No. of pupils: 70
Age range: 5-12

Kelbourne School
109 Hotspur Street
Glasgow
G20 8LH
☎ 0141 946 1405
🖳 0141 945 0044
email: kelbourne@
kschool.fsnet.co.uk
Head: Mrs M McIntosh
No. of pupils: 50
Age range: 2-12
Funding: LEA
Type of School: Day

Special Needs: Physical
disability, range of
additional needs; provision
of 5-14 and pre-5
mainstream curriculum

**Kelvin Bank Day Care
Centre**
Kilsyth Road
Kirkintilloch
G66 1RP
☎ 0141 776 7107
Age range: 2-16

Kelvin School
69 Nairn Street
Glasgow
G3 8SE
☎ 0141 339 5835
No. of pupils: 37
Age range: 5-16

Kennyhill School
375 Cumbernauld Ruad
Glasgow
G31 3LP
☎ 0141 554 2765
🖳 0141 554 0846
Head: Ms Isabel Orr
No. of pupils: 120
Age range: 11-19
Funding: LEA
Type of School: Day
Special Needs: Moderate
Learning Difficulties

Kirkriggs School
500 Croftfoot Road
Glasgow
G45 0NJ
☎ 0141 634 7158
No. of pupils: 65
Age range: 5-12

Ladywell School
12a Victoria Park Drive
South
Glasgow
G14 9RN
☎ 0141 959 6665
No. of pupils: 32
Age range: 12-16
Type of School: Day
Special Needs: Emotional
& behavioural difficulties

Langlands School
100 Mallaig Road
Glasgow
G51 4PE
☎ 0141 445 1132
No. of pupils: 57
Age range: 4-12

Linburn School
77 Linburn Road
Glasgow
G52 4EX
☎ 0141 883 2082
Head: Ms Margaret Hardie
No. of pupils: 40
Age range: 12-18
Funding: LEA
Special Needs: Profound &
Multiple Learning
Difficulties

Merkland School
Langmuir Road
Kirkintilloch
G66 2QF
☎ 0141 578 0177
🖷 0141 777 8139
email: office@merkland.
e-dunbarton.sch.uk
web: www.aol.com
Head: Mrs I E McLure
No. of pupils: 80
Age range: 5-18
Funding: LEA
Type of School: Day
Special Needs: Moderate
Learning Difficulties

**Middlefield Residential
School**
26 Partickhill Road
Glasgow
G11 5BP
☎ 0141 334 0159
🖷 0141 3398832
email: middlefieldschool@
hotmail.com
Acting Head: Mrs
Elizabeth McKenna
No. of pupils: 24
Age range: 5-16
Funding: LEA
Type of School: Residential
Special Needs: Autism

Milton School
6 Liddesdale Terrace
Glasgow
G22 5HL
☎ 0141 762 2102
Age range: 12-16

Mossknowe School
Kildrum Road
Cumbernauld
G67 2EL
☎ 01236 720 405
Age range: 4-16

**Nerston Residential
School**
Nerston

East Kilbride
G74 4PD
☎ 01355 279 242
No. of pupils: 16
Age range: 5-13

Newhills School
Newhills Road
Glasgow
G33 4HJ
☎ 0141 773 1296
No. of pupils: 41
Age range: 12-16

Parkhead Hospital School
Ward 1
81 Salamanca Street
Glasgow
G31 5PN
☎ 0141 554 7951
Age range: 4-16

Parkhouse School
Buckley Street
Glasgow
G22 6DJ
☎ 0141 336 8391
Age range: 5-16

Pentland School
Pentland Road
Chryston
Glasgow
G69 9DL
Age range: 5-12

Redburn School
Kildrum Rina Road
Kildrum
Cumbernauld
G67 2EL
☎ 01236 736 743
🖷 01236 736 904
Head: Ms Mary H O'Brien
No. of pupils: 64
Age range: 2-19
Funding: LEA
Special Needs: Profound &
Multiple Learning
Difficulties

Richmond Park School
30 Logan Street
Glasgow
G5 0HP
☎ 0141 429 6095
No. of pupils: 89
Age range: 5-12

Rosevale School
48 Scalpay Street
Glasgow

G22 7DD
☎ 0141 772 1756
No. of pupils: 40
Age range: 5-13

**Royal Hospital for Sick
Children**
7th Floor,
QM Tower
Royal Hospital For Sick
Children
Yorkhill
Glasgow
G3 8SJ
☎ 0141 201 0014
🖷 0141 201 0876
Head: Mr Peter Feeley
Age range: 5-18
Funding: LEA
Type of School: Hospital
Special Needs: Psychiatric
Difficulties

Sanderson High School
High Common Road
St Leonards
East Kilbride
G74 2LX
☎ 01355 249 073

**Springboig St John's Boys
School/St Francis Day
Unit**
1190 Edinburgh Road
Glasgow
G33 4EH
☎ 0141 774 9791
🖷 0141 774 4613
Principal: Mr W Fitzgerald
No. of pupils: 72
Age range: 14-17
Type of School:
Residential/Day
Special Needs: Emotional
and Behavioural
Difficulties

Springhill School
Livingstone Drive
East Kilbride
G75 0AB
☎ 01355 229 657
Age range: 5-18

St Aidan's School
255 Rigby Street
Glasgow
G32 6DJ
☎ 0141 556 6276
No. of pupils: 115
Age range: 12-16

St Joan of Arc School
722 Balmore Road
Glasgow
G22 6QS
☎ 0141 336 6885
🖷 0141 336 6375
Head: Ms Marie M
McCusker
No. of pupils: 90
Age range: 11-19
Funding: LEA
Type of School: Day
Special Needs: Severe
Learning Difficulties

St Kevin's Primary School
25 Fountainwell Road
Glasgow
G21 1TN
No. of pupils: 70
Age range: 5-12
Funding: LEA
Type of School: Day
Special Needs: Moderate
Learning Difficulties

St Oswald's School
83 Brunton Street
Glasgow
G44 3NF
☎ 0141 637 3952
🖷 0141 633 0669
Head: Mr G McDonnell
No. of pupils: 129
Age range: 11-18
Funding: LEA
Type of School: Day
Special Needs: Moderate
Learning Difficulties

St Raymond's School
384 Drakemire Drive
Glasgow
G45 9SR
☎ 0141 634 1551
Age range: 5-12

**St Vincent's School for the
Deafblind**
30 Fullarton Avenue
Tollcross
Glasgow
G32 8NJ
☎ 0141 778 2254
No. of pupils: 37
Age range: 2-16

Highland

Drummond School
Drummond Road
Inverness
IV2 4NZ

7

☎ 01463 233 091
🖷 01463 713106
Head: Mr D MacLeod
No. of pupils: 114
Age range: 3-19
Funding: LEA
Type of School: Day
Special Needs: Wide range

Mount Pleasant Special Education Unit
Mount Pleasant School
Castletown Road
Thurso
KW14 8HL
☎ 01847 893 419
🖷 01847 892601
email: mountpleasant.
primary@highland.gov.uk
Teacher SEU: Mrs C Gunn
No. of pupils: 5
Age range: 3-12
Type of School: Day

Pulteneytown Academy Special Education Unit
Seaforth Avenue
Wick
KW1 5ND
☎ 01955 602 649

Raddery School
Fortrose
IV10 8SN
☎ 01381 20271
Age range: 9-16

Raig Phandrig Hospital School
Inverness
IV3 8PJ
Age range: 4-16

St Clements School
Tulloch Street
Dingwall
IV15 9JZ
☎ 01349 863 284
Head: Joan Livingstone
No. of pupils: 40
Age range: 3-19
Funding: LEA
Type of School: Day
Special Needs: Profound & Multiple Learning Difficulties

St Duthus School
Academy Street
Tain
IV19 1ED

☎ 01862 894 407
Head: Mrs M Mackenzie
No. of pupils: 10
Age range: 3-19
Funding: LEA
Type of School: Day
Special Needs: Profound & Multiple Learning Difficulties

Tordale School
Brora
KW9 6LN
☎ 01408 21351
Age range: 5-16

Midlothian

Garvel School for the Deaf
Chester Road
Larkfield
Greenock
PA16 0TT
☎ 01475 635477
Textphone 01475 791612
🖷 01475 637230
Acting Head: Ms Catherine B Tulloch
No. of pupils: 18
Age range: 2-18
Funding: LEA
Type of School: Day
Special Needs: Hearing Impaired

Lugton School
Lugton Brae
Dalkeith
EH22 1JX
Acting Head:
No. of pupils: 137
Age range: 5-17
Funding: LEA
Type of School: Day
Special Needs: Moderate Learning Difficulties

St Joseph's Hospital School
32 Carnethie Street
Rosewell
EH24 9EG
☎ 0131 440 2022
Age range: 4-16

Westfield School
Lugton Brae
Dalkeith
EH22 1JX
☎ 0131 663 7145
Age range: 5-16

Moray

Cranloch School
Llanbryde
IV30 3LB
☎ 01343 842 428
🖷 01343 843 953
Age range: 7-16

North Ayrshire

Haysholm School
Bank Street
Irvine
KA12 0NE
☎ 01294 272 481
Age range: 5-16

James Reid School
Primrose Place
Saltcoats
KA21 6LH
☎ 01294 467 105
Age range: 5-16
Type of School: Day

Stanecastle School
Burns Crescent
Girdle Toll
Irvine
KA11 1AQ
☎ 01294 211 914
Age range: 4-16

North Lanarkshire

Alexander Anderson Home
Thornlea Park
Wishaw
ML2
☎ 01698 372 003
Age range: 5-16

Avon School
Carlisle Road
Hamilton
ML3 7EW
☎ 01698 285 444
Age range: 5-16

Bothwellpark School
Annan Street
Motherwell
ML1 2DL
☎ 01698 230 700

Clydeview School
Magna Street
Motherwell
ML1 3QZ
☎ 01698 264 843
🖷 01698 276 038

Head: Mrs A D Donaldson
No. of pupils: 28
Age range: 3-12
Funding: LEA
Type of School: Day
Special Needs: Severe Learning Difficulties

Craighead School
Whistleberry Road
Hamilton
ML3 0EG
☎ 01698 285 678
Age range: 2-16

Devonview School
Devonview Street
Airdrie
ML6 9DH
Age range: 5-16

Firpark School
Firpark Street
Motherwell
ML1 2PR
☎ 01698 251 313
Age range: 5-16

Hamilton School for the Deaf
Wellhall Road
Hamilton
ML3 9JE
☎ 01698 286618
Textphone 01698 286618
🖷 01698 425172

Law Hospital School
Carluke
ML8 5ER
☎ 01698 361 100
Age range: 4-16

Mavisbank School
Mitchell Street
Airdrie
ML6 0EB
Age range: 5-18

Monklands Hospital School
Peadiatric Ward
Monkscourt Avenue
Airdrie
ML6 0JS
Age range: 4-16

Pentland School
Tay Street
Coatbridge
ML5 2NA
☎ 01236 420 471
🖷 01236 434844
Head: Mr Iain S Porteous

No. of pupils: 26
Funding: LEA
Type of School: Day
Special Needs: Emotional
& Behavioural Difficulties

**Ridgepark Residential
School**
Mousebank Road
Lanark
ML11 7RA
☎ 01555 662 151
🖷 01555 662 859
Age range: 5-16

Stanmore House School
Lanark
ML11 7RR
☎ 01555 665 041
🖷 01555 665 480
Head: Miss Hazel Aitken
No. of pupils: 66
Age range: 2-18
Funding: Independent
Type of School: Residential
Special Needs: Profound &
Multiple Learning
Difficulties

**Stonehouse Hospital
School**
Stonehouse
Larkhall
ML9 3NT
☎ 01698 793 521
Age range: 4-16

Victoria Park School
Market Road
Carluke
ML8 4BE
☎ 01555 750 591
🖷 01555 750 591
Age range: 5-18

Willowbank School
229 Bank Street
Coatbridge
ML5 1EG
☎ 01236 421 911

Orkney Islands

Glaitness Aurrida School
Pickaquoy Road
Kirkwall
KW15 1RP
☎ 01856 850 487
Head: Mr Terry Delaney
No. of pupils: 20
Age range: 2-19
Funding: LEA

Type of School: Day
Special Needs: Profound &
Multiple Learning
Difficulties

Perth and Kinross

Cherrybank School
Viewlands Terrace
Perth
PH2 0LZ
☎ 01738 622 147
email: headteacher@
cherrybank.pkc.sch.org
No. of pupils: 19
Age range: 2-12
Funding: LEA
Type of School: Day
Special Needs: Profound –
Complex SEN

**Ochil Tower (Rudolf
Steiner) School**
140 High Street
Auchterarder
PH3 1AD
☎ 01764 62416
No. of pupils: 35
Age range: 6-18

The Glebe School
Abbey Road
Scone
Perth
PH2 6LW
☎ 01738 551 493
No. of pupils: 22
Age range: 5-16

Renfrewshire

Clippens School
Brediland Road
Linwood
Paisley
PA3 3JP
☎ 01505 325 333
Age range: 5-18

Corseford School
Howwood Road
Kilbarchan
PA10 2NT
☎ 01505 702 141
🖷 01505 702 445
Head: Mrs Marbeth Boyle
No. of pupils: 70
Age range: 0-19
Funding: Independent
Special Needs: Physical
disabilities

Gateside School
Craigielinn Avenue
Glenburn
Paisley
PA2 8RH
☎ 0141 884 2090
🖷 0141 884 6844
Head: Ms Elizabeth Quinn
No. of pupils: 140
Age range: 3-18
Funding: LEA
Special Needs: Visually
Impaired

Glenburn School
Inverkip Road
Greenock
PA16 0QG
☎ 01475 634 611
🖷 01475 638 872
Head: Mrs Eileen McGeer
No. of pupils: 92
Age range: 5-18
Funding: LEA
Type of School: Day
Special Needs: Speech and
Language Difficulties

**Hunterhill Tutorial
Centre**
Cartha Crescent
Paisley
PA2 7EL
☎ 0141 889 6876
🖷 0141 849 1896
Head: Mrs Jillian MacLean
Age range: 5-16
Funding: LEA
Type of School: Day
Special Needs: Emotional
& behavioural difficulties

Kersland School
Ben Nevis Road
Paisley
PA2 7BU
Age range: 5-18
Funding: LEA
Type of School: Day
Special Needs: Profound &
Multiple Learning
Difficulties

Lilybank School
Birkmyre Avenue
Port Glasgow
PA14 5AN
☎ 01475 745 121
No. of pupils: 60
Age range: 5-16

**The Good Shepherd
Centre**
Greenock Road

Bishopton
PA7 5PF
☎ 01505 862 814
email: goodshepc@aol.com
web: www.aol.com
Head: Mr Fergus McCann
No. of pupils: 54
Age range: 13-16

The Mary Russell School
Hawkhead Road
Paisley
PA2 7BE
☎ 0141 889 7628
Age range: 5-18

Scottish Borders

**Chirnside Primary School
Special Class**
Duns
TD11 3XH
☎ 01890 818 274
Age range: 5-16

Elmbank Centre
Lover's Walk
Dumfries
DG1 1LR
☎ 01387 254 438
🖷 01387 254 438
email: behsup@aol.com
web: www.aol.com
Head: Mr William
Maxwell
Funding: LEA
Type of School: Day
Special Needs: Moderate
Learning Difficulties

**Galashiels Academy
Senior Special Class**
Galashiels
TD1 3HU
☎ 01896 754 788
Age range: 12-16

**Hawick High School
Senior Special Class**
Hawick
TD9 0EG
☎ 01450 372 429
Age range: 12-16

Kelso High School
Bowmont Street
Kelso
TD5 7EG
☎ 01573 224 444
🖷 01573 227340
Head: Mr C Robertson

7

No. of pupils: 690
Age range: 12-16
Funding: LEA
Type of School: Day
Special Needs: Moderate
Learning Difficulties

Lanark Lodge Day Care Unit
Bridgend
Duns
TD11 3EX
Age range: 5-16

Langlee Primary School Special Unit
Langlee Drive
Galashiels
TD1 2EB
☎ 01896 757 892
Age range: 3-16

Peebles High School Special Class
Springwood Road
Peebles
EH45 9HB
☎ 01721 720 291
Age range: 12-18

Wilton Education & Social Work Centre
36 Princes Street
Hawick
TD9 7AY
☎ 01450 378 644
🖳 01450 370 538
Head: Mrs Moira Buckle
No. of pupils: 18
Age range: 11-16
Funding: LEA
Type of School: Day
Special Needs: Emotional & behavioural difficulties

South Ayrshire

Craigpark School
Belmont Avenue
Ayr
KA7 2ND
☎ 01292 288 982
🖳 01292 618 764
Head: Ms Lorraine Stoddart
No. of pupils: 24
Age range: 2-19
Funding: LEA
Type of School: Day
Special Needs: Profound & Multiple Learning Difficulties

Red Brae Residential School
24 Alloway Road
Maybole
KA19 8AA
☎ 01655 83104
🖳 01655 889500
General Manager: Miss L Galbraith
No. of pupils: 32
Age range: 10-16
Funding: Independent
Type of School: Day
Special Needs: EBD, ADHD, Asperger's

Seafield Hospital School
Doonfoot Road
Ayr
KA7 4DW
Age range: 4-16

South Park School
38 Belmont Avenue
Ayr
KA7 2MB
☎ 01292 282 259
Age range: 5-16

Stirlingshire

West Mains School
Logie Park
East Mains
East Kilbride
G74 4BU
☎ 01355 249 938
🖳 01355 225 814
email: mht@eo14.ecsu.org
web: www.eo14.ecsu.org
Head: Mrs May Campbell
No. of pupils: 26
Age range: 5-9
Funding: LEA
Type of School: Day
Special Needs: Speech and Language Difficulties

Charles M Brown Unit
c/o Fallin Primary School
Lamont Crescent
Fallin
Stirling
FK7 7EJ
☎ 01786 816 756
🖳 01786 812 803
No. of pupils: 11

Dawson Park School
Haugh Street
Bainsford

Falkirk
FK2 7QY
☎ 01324 621 072
No. of pupils: 231
Age range: 5-18

Falkirk Day Unit
Abercrombie Street
Camelon
Falkirk
FK1 4HA
☎ 01324 622 483
🖳 0134 503719
email: Falkirkdayunit@falkirk.gov.uk
Head: Mr Gordon Bell
No. of pupils: 34
Age range: 11-16
Funding: LEA

Kildean School
Drip Road
Stirling
FK8 1RW
☎ 01786 473 985
No. of pupils: 17
Age range: 3-12

Rossvail School
108 Glasgow Road
Camelon
Falkirk
FK1 4JS
☎ 01324 632 237
No. of pupils: 22
Age range: 4-16

Royal Infirmary Hospital School
Stirling
FK1 5QE
Age range: 4-16

Torwood School
Stirling Road
Torwood
Larbert
FK5 4SR
☎ 01324 503 470
🖳 01324 503 471
Head: Ms Jinty Stewart
No. of pupils: 21
Age range: 4-11
Funding: LEA
Type of School: Day
Special Needs: Profound & Multiple Learning Difficulties

Whins of Milton School
Fairhill Road
Whins of Milton

Stirling
FK7 0LL
☎ 01786 812 667
🖳 01786 812 873
Head: Miss S Boyd
No. of pupils: 36
Age range: 6-12
Funding: LEA
Type of School: Day
Special Needs: Wide range

Windsor Park School for the Deaf
Bantaskine Road
Falkirk
FK1 5HT
☎ 01324 508640
Textphone 01324 508640
🖳 01324 508647
Head: Mrs Catherine Finestone
No. of pupils: 16
Age range: 4-16
Funding: LEA
Type of School: Day
Special Needs: Hearing Impairment, outreach service for hearing and visual impairment

West Dunbartonshire

Cunard Unit
Cochno Street
Clydebank
G81 1RQ
☎ 0141 952 6614
Age range: 5-12

Elmwood School
Meadow Road
Dumbarton
G82 2DS
☎ 01389 762 166
Age range: 3-12

Kilpatrick School
Mountblow Road
Dalmuir
Clydebank
G81 4SW
☎ 01389 872 171
Head: Ms Radcliffe
No. of pupils: 142
Age range: 3-19
Funding: LEA
Type of School: Day
Special Needs: Profound & Multiple Learning Difficulties

West Lothian

Beatlie School
Main Street
Winchburgh
EH52 6RB
☎ 01506 890 350
No. of pupils: 36
Age range: 3-16

Cedarbank School
Ladywell East
Livingston
EH54 6DR
☎ 01506 442 172
Age range: 3-16

Pinewood School
Elm Grove
Blackburn
Bathgate
EH47 7QX
☎ 01506 656 374
🖹 01506 650716
No. of pupils: 64
Age range: 5-16

Willowgrove House
Willowgrove
Craigshill
EH54 6DD
☎ 01506 434 274
Age range: 4-16

Western Isles

**Stornoway Primary
School Special Unit**
Jamieson Drive
Stornoway
HS1 2LF
☎ 01851 704 700
Age range: 4-16

7

Wales

Blaenau Gwent

Pen-Y-Cwm School
Beaufort Hill
Ebbw Vale
NP23 5QD
☎ 01495 304 031
🖷 01495 302 448
email: penycwm@
hotmail.com
Head: Mr Robert
Dickenson
No. of pupils: 55
Age range: 3-19
Funding: LEA
Type of School: Day
Special Needs: Profound &
Multiple Learning
Difficulties

Bridgend

Heronsbridge School
Ewenny Road
Bridgend
CF31 3HT
Age range: 5-16

Ysgol Bryn Castell
Llangewydd Road
Bridgend
CF31 4JP
☎ 01656 767 517
Head: Mr G Le Page
No. of pupils: 172
Age range: 3-19
Funding: LEA
Type of School: Day
Special Needs: Emotional
& behavioural difficulties,
Autistic Spectrum,
Multiple and Severe
Learning Dificulties and
Complex Disorders

Ysgol Cefn-Glas
Llangewydd Road
Bridgend
CF31 4JP
☎ 01656 646 969
🖷 01656 649 379
No. of pupils: 162
Age range: 7-16

Caerphilly

**Rhymney Valley Pupil
Referral Unit**
Old Gelligaer Village School

Gelligaer
Hengoed
CF82 8EF

Trinity Fields School
Caerphilly Road
Yshrad Mynach
Hengoed
CF82 7XW
☎ 01443 866000
🖷 01443 866045
email: tflsa@
caerphilly.org.uk
web: www.schoolsite.
edex.net/1114
No. of pupils: 136
Age range: 3-19
Funding: LEA
Type of School: Day

**Trinity Fields School &
Resource Centre**
Caerphilly Road
Ystrad Mynach
Hencoed
CF82 7DT
☎ 01443 866 000
🖷 01443 866 045
Head: Mr Mark Hughes
No. of pupils: 104
Age range: 3-19
Funding: LEA
Type of School: Day
Special Needs: Profound &
Multiple Learning
Difficulties

Cardiff

Craig-y-Parc School
Heol-Y-Parc
Pentyrch
Cardiff
CF4 8NB
☎ 029 2089 0397
No. of pupils: 56
Age range: 3-16

Greenhill School
Heol Brynglas
Rhiwbina
Cardiff
CF4 6UJ
☎ 029 2069 3786
🖷 029 2062 1991
email: AnLewis@
cardiff.gov.uk
Head: A R Lewis

No. of pupils: 56
Age range: 11-16
Funding: LEA
Type of School: Day
Special Needs: Emotional
& behavioural difficulties

**Meadowbank Special
School**
Colwill Road
Gabalfa
Cardiff
CF14 2QQ
☎ 0292 0616 018
🖷 02920 610 118
email: Schooladmin@
meadowbanksp.cardiff.sch.uk
Head: Mrs Carolyn Arthurs
No. of pupils: 38
Age range: 4-11
Funding: LEA
Type of School: Day
Special Needs: Speech and
Language Difficulties

**Preswylfa Nursery
Assessment Unit**
Clive Road
Cardiff
CF5 1GN
Age range: 2-5

Riverbank Special School
Vincent Road
Ely
Cardiff
CF5 5AQ
No. of pupils: 70
Age range: 4-11
Funding: LEA
Type of School: Day
Special Needs: Moderate
Learning Difficulties &
Severe Learning Difficulties

The Court Special School
96 Station Road
Llanishen
Cardiff
CF4 5UX
☎ 029 2075 2713
🖷 029 2076 3895
Head: Mr W G Rees
No. of pupils: 35
Age range: 5-11
Funding: LEA
Type of School: Day
Special Needs: Emotional
& behavioural difficulties

The Hollies School
Brynheulog
Pentwyn
Cardiff
CF2 7XG
☎ 029 2073 4411
🖷 029 2054 0239
Head: Mrs Christine
Matthews
No. of pupils: 92
Age range: 3-11
Funding: LEA
Type of School: Day
Special Needs: Assessment

Ty Gwyn Special School
Ty Gwyn Road
Penylan
Cardiff
CF2 5JG
☎ 029 2048 5570
🖷 029 2045 3922
Head: Mr D W Dwyer
No. of pupils: 82
Age range: 3-19
Funding: LEA
Type of School: Day
Special Needs: Profound &
Multiple Learning
Difficulties

Woodlands High School
Vincent Road
Ely
Cardiff
CF5 5AQ
☎ 029 2056 1279
🖷 029 20576185
email: headteacher@
cardiff.gov.uk
Head: Mrs E A Dunne
No. of pupils: 125
Age range: 13-16
Funding: LEA
Type of School: Day
Special Needs: Learning
Difficulties

Carmarthenshire

**Aalton House Pupil
Referral Unit**
Aalton House Farm
Johnstown
Carmarthen
SA31
☎ 01267 235 923

Ammanford Special Unit
Ammanford CP School
Ammanford
SA18 2NS
Age range: 2-16

Cartref-y-Gelli PRU
Limegrove Avenue
Carmarthen
SA31 1SN
☎ 0126 73619
email: gellipru@
satproj.org.uk
web: www.satproj.org.uk
Head: Mrs P Williams
No. of pupils: 10
Age range: 11-16
Funding: LEA
Type of School: Pupil
Referral Unit
Special Needs: Emotional
& behavioural difficulties

Heol Goffa Special School
Heol Goffa
Llanelli
SA15 3LS
☎ 01554 759 465
Head: Mr R A Davies
No. of pupils: 74
Age range: 3-19
Funding: LEA
Type of School: Day
Special Needs: Severe
Learning Disabilities

**Llwynhendy Pupil
Referral Unit**
Trallwm Road
Llanelli
SA14 9ED
☎ 01554 778 136

Pwll Pupil Referral Unit
Pwll Road
Llanelli
SA15 4BG
☎ 01554 777 727

Whitemill Special Unit
Whitemill
Carmarthen
SA32 7EN
☎ 01267 235 655
Age range: 11-19

Ysgol Rhydygors
Llanstephan Road
Johnstown
Carmarthen
SA31 3QU
☎ 01267 231 171

No. of pupils: 47
Age range: 5-16

Conwy

Cedar Court School
65 Victoria Park
Colwyn Bay
LL29 7AJ
☎ 01492 533 199
🖷 01492 535 030
Head: Mrs Pamela Stanley
No. of pupils: 18
Age range: 11-18
Funding: LEA
Type of School: Residential
Special Needs: Emotional
& behavioural difficulties

Ysgol Gogarth
Nant y Gamar Road
Craig y Don
Llandudno
LL30 1YF
☎ 01492 860 077
🖷 01492 870 109
email: gogarth@conwy.
u-net.com
web: www.conwy.
u-net.com
Head: Mr I G Jones
No. of pupils: 120
Age range: 3-19
Funding: LEA
Type of School: Residential
Special Needs: Multi-
sensory impairments

Ysgol-y-Graig
Penrhos Avenue
Old Colwyn
Colwyn Bay
LL29 9HW
☎ 01492 516 838
No. of pupils: 47
Age range: 2-19

Denbighshire

**Dewi Sant Education
Centre**
Dewi Sant
Rhuddlan Road
Denbighshire
Rhyl
LL18 2RE
☎ 01745 344 390
🖷 01745 344390
Teacher in charge: Mr L
Townson
Funding: LEA
Type of School: Day

Rhuallt Support Unit
Rhuallt
St Asaph
LL17 0TO
☎ 01745 583 375
Age range: 3-5

Ysgol Plas Brondyffryn
Ystrad Road
Denbigh
LL16 4RH
☎ 01745 813 841
Head: Dr M J Toman
No. of pupils: 95
Age range: 3-19
Funding: LEA
Type of School: Day
Special Needs: Wide range

Ysgol Tir Morfa
Ffordd Derwen
Rhyl
LL18 2RN
☎ 01745 350 388
🖷 01745 343 193
email: stephen.murphy@
denbighshire.gov.uk
web:
www.denbighshire.gov.uk
Head: Mr Stephen Murphy
No. of pupils: 182
Age range: 3-19
Funding: LEA
Type of School: Day
Special Needs: Moderate
Learning Difficulties

Flintshire

Bryn Glas School
Clayton Road
Mold
CH7 1SU
Age range: 4-16

Ysgol Belmont
Windmill Road
Buckley
CH7 3HA
☎ 01244 543 971
🖷 01244 546 358
Head: Mr D G Jones
No. of pupils: 155
Age range: 3-19
Funding: LEA
Type of School: Day
Special Needs: Moderate
Learning Difficulties

Ysgol Delyn
Alexandra Road
Mold
CH7 1HJ

☎ 01352 755 701
🖷 01352 755 701
Head: Mrs Val Newman
No. of pupils: 50
Age range: 2-19
Funding: LEA
Type of School: Day
Special Needs: Severe
Learning Difficulties

Ysgol Talfryn
Brynford
Holywell
CH8 8AD
☎ 01352 710 698
Age range: 6-16

Ysgol Y Bryn
King George Street
Shotton
CH5 1EA
☎ 01244 830 281
🖷 01244 815 009
email: ysgo-y-bryn@
clara.net
web: www.clara.net
Head: Mrs S A Taylor
No. of pupils: 59
Age range: 2-19
Funding: LEA
Type of School: Day
Special Needs: Severe
Learning Difficulties

Gwynedd

Ysgol Hafod Lon
Y Ffor
Pwllheli
LL53 6US
☎ 01766 810 626
🖷 01766 810 002
Head: Mrs D Rhian Davies
No. of pupils: 22
Age range: 4-19
Funding: LEA
Type of School: Day
Special Needs: Profound &
Multiple Learning
Difficulties

Ysgol Pendalar
Ffordd Victoria
Caernarfon
Gwynedd
LL55 2RN
☎ 01286 672 141
🖷 01286 678 186
email: pennaeth@
pendalar.gwynedd.sch.uk
web: www.pendalar.
gwynedd.sch.uk

7

Head: Mr Evan Jones
No. of pupils: 74
Age range: 3-19
Funding: LEA
Type of School: Day
Special Needs: Wide range

Ysgol Treborth
Bangor
LL57 2RX
☎ 01248 353 527
Age range: 5-18

Ysgol Wern Yr Wylan
Cwn Road
Llandudno
LL30 1EG
Age range: 5-16

Isle of Anglesey

Ysgol Y Bont
Industrial Estate
Llangefni
LL77 7JA
☎ 01248 750 151
🖷 01248 724 056
email: prifathro@
ybont.gwead.cymru.org
web: www.ybont.gwead.
cymru.org
Head: Mr D Hughes
No. of pupils: 120
Age range: 3-19
Funding: LEA
Type of School: Day
Special Needs: Moderate
Learning Difficulties and
Profound & Multiple
Learning Difficulties

Merthyr Tydfil

Greenfield Special School
Duffryn Road
Pentrebach
Merthyr Tydfil
CF48 4BJ
☎ 01443 690 468
🖷 01443 692 010
email: GSchool134@
aol.com
web: www.aol.com
Head: Mrs C M Arthur
No. of pupils: 147
Age range: 2-19
Funding: LEA
Type of School: Day
Special Needs: Wide range

Pupil Referral Unit
Merthyr Psychological
Centre

Alexandra Avenue
Penydarren
Merthyr Tydfil
CF47 9AF
☎ 01685 721 733
🖷 01685 388 477

Monmouthshire

Mounton House School
Pwllmeyric
Chepstow
NP6 6LA
☎ 01291 630871
🖷 01291 635055
Head: M L Munting
No. of pupils: 65
Age range: 7-16
Funding: LEA
Type of School: Residential
Special Needs: Emotional
& behavioural difficulties

Neath Port Talbot

Briton Ferry (Special) School
Ynysmaerdy Road
Briton Ferry
Neath
SA11 2TL
☎ 01639 813 100
🖷 01639 814 707
email: britonferry.special@
neath-porttalbot.gov.uk
Head: Ms Marian Scales
No. of pupils: 32
Age range: 2-19
Funding: LEA
Type of School: Day
Special Needs: Profound &
Multiple Learning
Difficulties

Ysgol Hendre School
Main Road
Bryncoch
Neath
SA10 7TY
☎ 01639 642 786
🖷 01639 644 294
Head: Mr Paul Smith
No. of pupils: 75
Age range: 11-16
Funding: LEA
Type of School: Residential
Special Needs: Deaf/blind

Newport

Newport Special School
Maesglas Road

Newport
NP20 3DG
☎ 01633 815 480
🖷 01633 817 956
Head: Mrs M L Meynick
No. of pupils: 86
Age range: 3-19
Funding: LEA
Type of School: Day
Special Needs: Severe
Learning Difficulties

Westfield Lower School
Westfield Way
Malpas
Newport
NP9 6EW
☎ 01633 855 170
No. of pupils: 55
Age range: 2-13

Pembrokeshire

Pembrokeshire Pupil Referral Service
Pembroke Centre
East End Square
Pembroke
SA71 4DG
☎ 01646 682 213
🖷 01646 682 213
Head: Mrs J A Jones
No. of pupils: 100
Age range: 4-16
Funding: LEA
Type of School: Pupil
Referral Unit
Special Needs: Emotional
& behavioural difficulties

Portfield School
Portfield
Haverfordwest
SA16 1BS
☎ 01437 762 701
🖷 01437 769 158
Head: Mrs Sue Painter
No. of pupils: 68
Age range: 2-19
Funding: LEA
Type of School: Day
Special Needs: Profound &
Multiple Learning
Difficulties/Severe
Learning Difficulties

Powys

Brynllywarch Hall School
Kerry
Newtown
SY16 4PB
☎ 01686 670276

🖷 01686 670894
email: head@
brynllywarch.powys.sch.uk
Head: Mr D C Williams
No. of pupils: 54
Age range: 9-16
Funding: LEA
Type of School:
Residential/Day
Special Needs: Emotional
& behavioural difficulties
and Multiple Learning
Difficulties

Tregynon Hall Therapeutic Community
Cefngwyddfod
Trelynon
Newtown
SY16 3BG
No. of pupils: 22
Age range: 9-16

Womaston School
Walton
Presteigne
LD8 2PT
☎ 01544 230 308
🖷 01544 231 317
email: womaston@
macintyre-care.org
Head: Mr Martin Bertulis
No. of pupils: 16
Age range: 11-19
Funding: Voluntary
Type of School: Boarding
Special Needs: Autism and
Severe Learning
Difficulties

Ysgol Cedewain
Maes Yrhandir
Newtown
SY16 1LH
☎ 01686 627 454
🖷 01686 621 867
Head: Mr Peter A Tudor
No. of pupils: 40
Age range: 3-19
Funding: LEA
Type of School: Day
Special Needs: Severe
Learning Difficulties

Ysgol Penmaes
Canal Road
Brecon
LD3 7HL
☎ 01874 623 508
🖷 01874 625 197
email: admin@
penmaes.powys.sch.uk

web: www.penmaes.
powys.sch.uk
Head: Mr Ian Elliot
No. of pupils: 63
Age range: 2-19
Funding: LEA
Type of School: Day
Special Needs: Severe,
Profound & Multiple
Learning Difficulties and
ASD

Rhondda, Cynon, Taff

**Cynon Valley Referral
Unit Psychological Centre**
Old Boy's Grammar
School
Hirwaun Road
Trecynon
Aberdare
CF44 8DY
☎ 01685 876 062

Maesgwyn Special School
Cwmdare Road
Aberdare
CF44 8RE
☎ 01685 873 933
🖷 01685 873 933
Head: Mrs Valerie Jones
No. of pupils: 100
Age range: 11-18
Funding: LEA
Type of School: Day
Special Needs: Moderate
Learning Difficulties

Park Lane Special School
Park Lane Trecynon
Aberdare
CF44 8HN
Acting Head:
No. of pupils: 51
Age range: 3-20
Funding: LEA
Type of School: Day
Special Needs: Profound &
Multiple Learning
Difficulties & Autism

Rhondda Special School
Brithweunydd Road
Trealaw
Tonypandy
CF40 2UH
☎ 01443 433046
🖷 01443 440034
email: rhondda.special@
rhonddaspe.rctednet.net
Head: Andy Henderson

No. of pupils: 80
Age range: 3-19
Funding: LEA
Type of School: Day
Special Needs: Profound,
Severe & Multiple
Learning Difficulties

**Taff Ely Referral Unit
Psychological Centre**
Pwll-Gwaun Infant School
Seaton Street
Pwll-Gwaun
Pontypridd
CF37 1JA

**Tai Centre Cinas:
Tylorstown Site PRU**
Edmund Street
Tylorstown
CF43 3HH
☎ 01443 730 956

**Tai Centre Dinas:
Natgwyn Site PRU**
Hendrecafn Road
Penygraig
Tonypandy
CF40 1LJ
☎ 01443 432 067

Ysgol Ty Coch
Lansdale Drive
Tonteg
Pontypridd
CF38 1PG
☎ 01443 203 471
Age range: 4-19

Swansea

**Penybryn Senior Special
School**
Maytree Autistic Unit
Glasbury Road Morriston
Swansea
SA6 7PA
☎ 01792 799 064
Head: Mr Adrian G
Williams
No. of pupils: 115
Age range: 11-19
Funding: LEA
Type of School: Day
Special Needs: Autism

Ysgol Crug Glas
Croft Street
Swansea
SA1 1QA
☎ 01792 652 388
🖷 01792 457 774

Head: Elizabeth Jones
No. of pupils: 50
Age range: 2-19
Funding: LEA
Type of School: Day
Special Needs: Profound &
Multiple Learning
Difficulties

Torfaen

Ashgrove School
Sully Road
Penarth
CF64 2TP
☎ 029 2070 4212
Textphone 029 2070 4212/
4841
🖷 029 2070 1945
email: ashgrove@
rmplc.co.uk
web: www.ashgroveschool.
demon.co.uk
Head: B M Brayford
No. of pupils: 71
Age range: 4-19
Funding: LEA
Type of School: Day
Special Needs: Hearing
Impaired

Headlands School
Paget Place
Penarth
CF64 1YY
☎ 029 2070 9771
No. of pupils: 40
Age range: 11-16

Ysgol Erw'r Delyn
St Cyres Road
Penarth
CF64 2WR
No. of pupils: 57
Age range: 3-19
Funding: LEA
Type of School: Day
Special Needs: Profound &
Multiple Learning
Difficulties

Ysgol Maes Dyfan
Gibbonsdown Rise
Barry
CF63 1DT
☎ 01446 732 112
🖷 01446 742 316
email: emmaesdyf@
rmplc.co.uk
web: www.rmplc.co.uk
Head: Mr M J Righton
No. of pupils: 95

Age range: 3-19
Funding: LEA
Type of School: Day
Special Needs: Moderate
Learning Difficulties &
Severe Learning
Difficulties

Crownbridge School
Greenhill Road
Sebastopol
Pontypool
NP4 5YW
☎ 01495 758 739
🖷 01495 750 177
Head: Mr Rob Phillips
No. of pupils: 75
Age range: 3-19
Funding: LEA
Type of School: Day
Special Needs: Profound &
Multiple Learning
Difficulties

Wrexham

Borras Park Junior School
Hearing Impaired Unit
Borras Park Road
Borras Park
LL12 7TH
☎ 01978 359 694
🖷 01978 266 429
Head: Mr G O Jones
No. of pupils: 13
Age range: 7-11
Funding: LEA
Type of School:
Mainstream School and
Hearing Impaired Unit
Special Needs: Hearing
Impaired

Park Avenue
Wrexham
LL12 7AH
☎ 01978 290 101
Age range: 2-7

St Christopher's School
Holt Road
Wrexham
LL13 8NE
☎ 01978 265 237
🖷 01978 262 370
Head: Ms Maxine P Grant
No. of pupils: 240
Age range: 7-19
Funding: LEA
Type of School: Day
Special Needs: Wide
range

7

Worthenbury School
Mulsford Lane
Worthenbury
Wrexham
LL13 0AP
☎ 01948 770 673
No. of pupils: 6

Wrexham Support Centre
Park Avenue
Wrexham
LL12 7AH
☎ 01978 359 831
No. of pupils: 45
Age range: 11-16

Ysgol Powys
Dodds Lane
Gwersyllt
LL11 4PA
☎ 01978 755 921
Age range: 3-19

Channel Islands

Mont Varouf School
Le Neuf Chemin
St Saviour
Guernsey
GY7 9FG
☎ 01481 263135
🖷 01481 266635
Head: Mrs Jane Stephens
No. of pupils: 40
Age range: 4-19
Funding: LEA
Type of School: Day
Special Needs: Wide range

Oakvale School
Collings Road
St Peter Port
Guernsey
GY1 1FW
☎ 01481 723046
🖷 01481 701071
email:
office@oakvale.sch.gg
Head: Mr A Brown
No. of pupils: 108
Age range: 7-17
Funding: Staks of
Guernsey
Type of School: Day
Special Needs: Multiple
Learning Difficulties

The Longfield Centre
Maurepas Road
St Peter Port
Guernsey
GY1 2DS
☎ 01481 722 339
🖷 01481 728 941
Head: Mr R W Battye
No. of pupils: 25
Age range: 3-7
Funding: LEA
Type of School: Day
Special Needs: Moderate
Learning Difficulties

7

Section 8

Useful Websites, Discussion Lists and Conferences on the World-Wide Web

Useful Websites, Discussion Lists and Conferences on the World-Wide Web

8

The World-Wide Web is a vast collection of websites with a wide range of provenance. Since the first edition of the digest, the range and quality of information have increased dramatically. There are still nuggets of information to be found produced by individuals in their own time. At the same time there are sites that promote an approach with little reference to the validity, alternative viewpoints or a wider conception of needs. More promising are the sites produced by national organisations whose sites now contain a wealth of information and advice based upon extensive expertise. The following is an eclectic mix of the best of the sites.

You can also search the web yourself by using a search engine such as:

www.google.com

Entering two phrases enclosed in quotes such as 'Educational Implications' 'Fragile X' would produce a range of sites with hopefully relevant information. It is worth reading the guidance on making searches so you make efficient use of your time on the web.

Special Needs Information, Legislation, Guidance and Context

ACE (Advisory Centre for Education) provide guidance and interpretation of the law in relation to special educational needs.

www.ace-ed.org.uk

The Department for Education and Skills (DfES) provides a site devoted to special needs issues including downloadable documents including the Code of Practice on Special Education Needs.

http://www.dfes.gov.uk/sen/

The Disability Rights Commission (DRC) is an independent body set up by the Government to help secure civil rights for disabled people. It contains a large collection of briefings and guidance.

www.drc.org.uk

National Association for Special Educational Needs (NASEN): Provides a list of their publications, policy documents, responses to consultations and a research archive that can be searched by members.

www.nasen.org.uk

The Office of Standards in Education (OFSTED) provides reports and evaluations on schools and educational services in England.

www.ofsted.gov.uk

The National Disability Team (NDT) is funded by the Higher Education Funding Council. It manages and coordinates projects to enhance disability provision in 50 higher education institutions in England and Northern Ireland.

www.natdisteam.ac.uk

The Qualifications and Curriculum Authority (QCA) provide guidance on inclusion and equal opportunities in relation to the national curriculum. These include the inclusion statement and the 'P' levels for pupils with learning difficulties.

www.qca.org.uk/ca/inclusion/
www.nc.uk.net/ld/

Skill: The National Bureau for Students with Disabilities. Skill promotes opportunities for young people and adults with any kind of disability in post-16 education, training and employment across the UK.

www.skill.org.uk

The Teacher Training Agency (TTA) provides downloads of its publications including its standards for special educational needs coordinators and specialist special educational needs teaching.

www.tta.gov.uk

Inclusion

The British Education Communications Technology Agency's (BECTA) inclusion site has a searchable database of resources including documents.

http://inclusion.ngfl.gov.uk/

The Centre for Studies in Inclusive Education (CSIE) provides a range of resources in support of inclusion including a comprehensive guide to inclusion issues.

www.csie.org.uk

The Enabling Education Network (EENET) provides access to a broad-based body of expertise and experience in the practice of inclusive education world-wide.

www.eenet.org.uk

Inclusion Philosophy and Practice: An American site from the Education Department of the University of Northern Iowa which has briefings on teaching strategies, decision making and approaches.

www.uni.edu/coe/inclusion

Individual Education Plans

Success for All: The Scottish Office for Education project on Individual Education Plans contains a range of guidance and case studies.

www.success.norcol.ac.uk/success/

Parental Partnership

ACE (Advisory Centre for Education) supplies online documents on obtaining extra help and dealing with schools and LEAs.

www.ace-ed.org.uk/advice.html

The Independent Panel for Special Education Advice (IPSEA) is a volunteer organisation providing support for parents of children with special educational needs and/or disabilities in obtaining provision particularly in relation to tribunals.

www.ipsea.org.uk

The DfES standards site section on parental involvement.

www.standards.dfee.gov.uk/parentalinvolvement

ASCD, the Association for Supervision and Curriculum Development based in Canada has a tutorial on the importance of parent teacher partnership.

www.ascd.org/pdi/demo/parent/parent1.htm

The DfES South Eastern Regional partnership for Special Educational Needs have a downloadable book on working constructively with parents.

www.sersen.uk.net/parents.htm

The Nottingham and Nottinghamshire Parent Partnership Project which has useful documents for parents including visiting schools, making your views matter and the role of the learning support assistants.

www.pppnotts.org.uk

8

Pupil Participation

The National Childrens' Bureau (NCB) promotes the interests and well-being of all children and young people across every aspect of their lives. Advocating for the participation of children and young people in all matters affecting them and challenging disadvantage in childhood.

www.ncb.org.uk

The Education and Social Research Council have funded a project on 'Consulting pupils about teaching and Learning' based at Homerton College, Cambridge. It contains a wide range of reports and briefings mainly focused on mainstream practice.

www.consultingpupils.co.uk

Research

Name	Department for Education and Skills Best Practice Research Scholarships
Link	www.dfes.gov.uk/bprs/pinfo.cfm
Comments	Best Practice Research Scholarships
Name	UK Office of National Statistics: Neighbourhood
Link	http://www.statistics.gov.uk/neighbourhood/home.asp
Comments	Postcode-based data
Name	Scottish Council for Educational Research Spotlights
Link	www.scre.ac.uk/tpr/trspotlightmenu.html
Comments	Very useful case studies and guides on educational research

Individual Needs

Attention Deficit Hyperactivity Disorder

Name	One Add Place
Link	www.oneaddplace.com/
Comments	US-based comprehensive links and news on the subject
Name	Thanet Adders
Link	www.adders.org
Comments	Originally a parents' ADHD group in North East Kent. This site contains a great deal of information on the topic

Autistic Spectrum

Name	All Lewisham Autism Support
Link	http://www.lewisham.gov.uk/volorgs/alas/
Comments	Very wide range of links and resources

Name	Asperger Syndrome Resources
Link	**http://www.udel.edu/bkirby/asperger/**
Comments	A US-wide range of useful articles

Name	Autismconnect
Link	**www.autismconnect.org**
Comments	A world-wide central information point for this topic

Name	Autism On-Line Discussion Group (UK)
Link	**http://www.autism-uk.ed.ac.uk/**
Comments	Provides details of how to join

Name	Autism Society of America
Link	**http://www.autism-society.org/**
Comments	A wide range of US related on-line resources

Name	Centre for the Study of Autism
Link	**http://www.autism.org/dan.html**
Comments	Stephen Edelman's site with a range of summary informnation

Name	Do2Learn
Link	**www.do2learn.com**
Comments	Commercial site with many free resources

Name	Environmental and Preventive Health Center of Atlanta
Link	**http://www.envprevhealthctratl.com/**
Comments	Examples of medical and dietary approaches

Name	National Autistic Society
Link	**www.nas.org.uk**
Comments	Well designed, comprehensive and up to date

Name	Scottish Society for Autism
Link	**www.autism-in-scotland**
Comments	The Scottish Society for Autism

Name	Shoe Box Tasks
Link	**www.shoeboxtasks.com**
Comments	Commercial site showing and selling innovative learning materials designed for children and adults with special needs

Name	Temple Grandin's Web Page
Link	**http://www.grandin.com/**
Comments	An able person with autism who has published two books

Name	The Asperger Syndrome Society (US)
Link	**www.aspen.org**
Comments	US society with useful articles on-line

Name	The Autism Research Unit
Link	**http://osiris.sunderland.ac.uk/autism/index.html**
Comments	Sunderland University's The Autism Research Unit

8

Name	The Options Institute
Link	**http://www.option.org/**
Comments	Site of the Options intervention

Name	The UK National Autistic Society
Link	**http://www.oneworld.org/autism_uk/**
Comments	A wide range of on-line resources

Name	Tony Attwood's Home Pages
Link	**www.TonyAttwood.com**
Comments	Useful pages by the best-selling author of *Asperger Syndrome*

Name	Treatment and Education of Autistic and Related Communication Handicapped Children
Link	**http://www.unc.edu/depts/teacch/**
Comments	The site of the TEACCH programme at the University of North Carolina

Name	Visual Supports
Link	**http://neurosci.health.ufl.edu/visual.html**
Comments	A briefing by Florida's CARD centre

Dyslexia

Name	British Dyslexia Association
Link	**www.bda-dyslexia.org.uk**
Comments	A very comprehensive site

Name	Iansyst
Link	**www.dyslexic.com**
Comments	A commercial vendor specialising in technology to support learners with dyslexia

Dyspraxia

Name	The Dyspraxia Foundation
Link	**www.dyspraxiafoundation.org.uk**
Comments	Useful resources and strategies that includes an explanation for children

Emotional Behavioural Difficulty

Name	Association of Workers with Children with Emotional Behavioural Difficulties
Link	**www.awcebd.co.uk**
Comments	A growing site for teachers and workers in this area

Name	Jenny Moseley's Quality Circle Time Site
Link	**www.circle-time.co.uk**
Comments	Includes resources to be freely downloaded or ordered

Name   Disruptive and Disaffected Pupils In Mainstream Schools
Link   **http://www.users.globalnet.co.uk/~ebdstudy/index.htm**
Comments   Metropolitan Borough of Stockport's useful site, if a bit too medical

Name   How to Manage Disruptive Behavior in Inclusive Classrooms
Link   **http://www.cec.sped.org/bk/focus/daniels.htm**
Comments   A Council for Exceptional Children (US) Resource

Name   The Discipline Problem and Ways to Deal With It
Link   **http://www.cec.sped.org/bk/focus/.htm**
Comments   A Council for Exceptional Children (US) Resource

Name   University of Dundee: Promoting Social Competence
Link   **http://www.dundee.ac.uk/psychology/prosoc.htm**
Comments   The University of Dundee's Project website

Hearing Impairment and Deafness

Name   Deaf club
Link   **www.deafclub.co.uk**
Comments   Comprehensive and well maintained site supporting the deaf community. Includes deaf search engine and mailing list

Name   Deafsign
Link   **http://www.deafsign.com/**
Comments   The site has a number of interesting features including: an interactive discussion forum, email subscription list, BSL sample section, myth buster resources for schools

Name   Royal National Institute for the Deaf (RNID)
Link   **www.rnid.org.uk**
Comments   As well as interactive finger spelling translation from text, it includes an illustrative video library of words and phrases in British Sign Language

Language and Communication

Name   Association for all speech impaired children (AFASIC)
Link   **www.afasic.org.uk**
Comments   An organisation run for parents and professionals

Name   British Stammering Association
Link   **www.stammering.org**
Comments   Contains extensive advice across all age ranges

Name   Closing the Gap
Link   **http://www.closingthegap.com/**
Comments   US Extensive website and journal on Assistive Technology

8

Name	Communication Disorders Treatment and Research Clinic
Link	**http://www.cchs.usyd.edu.au/csd/clinic/index.html**
Comments	Briefings from the University of Sydney

Name	Communications Forum
Link	**www.communicationsforum.org.uk**
Comments	A coalition of organisations dealing with all kinds of communication difficulties

Name	ICAN
Link	**www.ican.org.uk**
Comments	Website of an organisation dealing with language and communication difficulties

Name	Makaton Vocabulary Development Project
Link	**www.makaton.org**
Comments	Resources for the Makaton™ signing and symbols

Name	NAPLIC
Link	**www.naplic.org.uk**
Comments	The National Association for professionals concerned with children who have difficulties with speech, language and communication

Name	NICeST (National Information Centre for speech-language therapy
Link	**http://library.hcs.ucl.ac.uk**
Comments	Provides a free enquiry service to clinicians and anyone seeking literature on speech-language issues

Name	Royal College of Speech and Language Therapists
Link	**http://www.rcslt.org.uk/**
Comments	The professional body for speech and language therapists

Name	Speakability
Link	**www.ada-uk.org**
Comments	Formerly Action for Dysphasic Adults

Name	The Hanen Society
Link	**www.hanen.org**
Comments	Canadian language development approach

Learning Difficulty

Name	Down's Syndrome Organisation
Link	**www.downs-syndrome.org.uk**
Comments	Over 200 pages of information dealing with educational provision and the inclusion of people with Down's Syndrome

Name	Down Syndrome Educational Trust
Link	**www.downsed.org.uk**
Comments	A centre of expertise in this area

Name	The Foundation for People with Learning Difficulties
Link	**www.learningdisabilities.org.uk**
Comments	Very useful site with high quality resources

Name	Learning Difficulties On-line
Link	**http://www.ldonline.org/**
Comments	A large American site on the topic

Name	Mencap
Link	**www.mencap.org.uk/**
Comments	A range of resources supporting people with learning difficulties

Name	People First
Link	**www.peoplefirst.org.uk**
Comments	An organisation of people with learning difficulties speaking up for themselves

Medical Conditions

Name	Contact A Family
Link	**www.cafamily.org.uk**
Comments	A site with an authorative guide to low incidence medical conditions and disabilities

Mental Health

Name	The Mental Health Foundation
Link	**www.mentalhealth.org.uk**
Comments	Very good website with a wealth of resources

Name	Mental Health Matters
Link	**www.mental-health-matters.com/**
Comments	A very slick US site on mental health matters

Physical Disabilities

Name	The Advisory Centre for Communication Devices and Access (ACE)
Link	**www.acecentre.org.uk**
Comments	Provides information on communication and access devices for pupils with disabilities

Name	Communication Aids for Language and Learning (CALL)
Link	**http://callcentre.education.ed.ac.uk/**
Comments	A Scottish site dealing with communication aids technology and disabilities

8

Name	Techdis
Link	**www.techdis.ac.uk**
Comments	A comprehensive site for Higher Education including an extensive database of enabling technology

Name	SCOPE
Link	**www.scope.org.uk**
Comments	Has a range of information for people with disability and carers and educators with responsibilities in this area

Name	The TRACE centre
Link	**www.rnib.org.uk**
Comments	The US authoritative site dealing with most aspects of access for people with disability

Visual Impairment and Blindness

Name	The Royal National Institute for the Blind
Link	**www.rnib.org.uk**
Comments	A comprehensive site

Name	The Webring on Blindness
Link	**www.webring.org/cgi-bin/webring?ring=bvi;list**
Comments	This loose collection of websites is dedicated to sites that are by and/or for people who are blind or visually impaired

Other Organisations and Suppliers

Publishers

Name	Amazon UK
Link	**www.amazon.co.uk**
Comments	The well-known UK version of the American on-line book store has a search facility which often throws up useful book suggestion which you can then order from your local book shop

Name	David Fulton Publishers
Link	**www.fultonpublishers.co.uk**
Comments	The publisher of this book has a vast range of SEN books which can be searched and bought on-line

Name	Jessica Kingsley Publishers
Link	**www.jkp.com/specneds.html**
Comments	Publish a wide range of books especially on the Autistic Spectrum

Name	Lucky Duck Publications
Link:	**www.luckyduck.co.uk**
Comments	Publish a range of useful books and videos related to social and emotional development

Name	RoutledgeFalmer
Link	**www.routledgefalmer.co.uk**
Comments	A useful selection of books on inclusion

Schools

Name	Chris Abbott's List of Special School Sites
Link	**www.kcl.ac.uk/depsta/education/research/internetsen.html**
Comments	A collection of links to sites of Special Schools and Pupil Referral units

Technology

Name	Crick Software
Link	**www.cricksoft.com**
Comments	Produce useful software including the widely acclaimed on-screen keyboard software 'clicker'

Name	Higher Education National Software Archive (HENSA)
Link	**http://micros.hensa.ac.uk/access/**
Comments	A collection of free or shareware software for access

Name	Inclusive Technology
Link:	**www.inclusive.co.uk**
Comments	Publish a large range of software and technology to support access and inclusion

Name	Widgit Software
Link	**www.widgit.co.uk**
Comments	Publish a range of software to address learning difficulties specialising in symbol software

8

Discussion Lists

These are email discussion lists related to different areas of special educational need and/or inclusion. Discussion lists frequently archive their messages so that threads of discussion can still be read. BECTA provide links to the following at

http://www.becta.org.uk/inclusion/discussion/bectalists.html

community-languages	for those interested in what's going on in the world of Community Languages and ICT, from fonts for Urdu to sharing ideas for authentic language websites
distance-learning	for those wishing to share good practice and information in developing distance learning for pupils not in school
Dyslexia-wales	for teachers, support staff, educational professionals and others with an interest in dyslexia issues in Wales
eal-bilingual	for teachers of English as an additional language, specialist classroom assistants, and others involved in teaching pupils from ethnic and linguistic minorities
easyspeak	for exchanging ideas about the education of children and young people with language and communication difficulties
EBD-Forum	a forum for discussing issues relating to the education of pupils with emotional and behavioural difficulties
esol-group	for those involved in teaching English as a second language
fforwm-aaa	a discussion group relating to SEN issues in Wales which welcomes contributions in the Welsh language
High-Ability	a forum for discussing issues relating to the education of able children
index-inclusion	a forum for users of Index for Inclusion materials – including schools, education authorities and researchers – to make comments about the Index and to ask questions about its use in schools, to provide answers and share information
pd-net	for professionals involved in the education of children with physical and neurological disabilities and complex medical needs
PRU-talk	a mailing list for managers of pupil referral units (PRU)
Respect4all	a UK-based discussion forum aimed at teachers, support staff and other educational professionals, and it supports the development of practice and resources reflecting cultural diversity within our society and engendering respect for all through the National Curriculum

SCENT	for professionals involved in the delivery of education to learners with medical conditions
senco-forum	for discussing issues relating to SENCOs' work
Senco-forum-digest	for special needs coordinators, those in local authority services, and others involved in supporting pupils with special educational needs
SENIT	for those with a particular interest in finding out about IT solutions to support pupils
SLD-forum	for professionals involved in the education of learners with severe, profound and multiple learning difficulties
Speech recognition	for those who wish to share practical advice about the use and potential for speech recognition in educational settings
ToD	for Teachers of the Deaf and associated professionals involved in teaching deaf learners in schools
trav-ed	for practitioners with an interest in Traveller education
VI-Forum	for those with an interest in teaching students with visual impairments

Mike Blamires
Principal Lecturer
Faculty of Education
Canterbury Christ Church University College
Canterbury
Kent

8

Section

9

Recommended Reading

Recommended Reading

9

This section was initially compiled by Barbara Sakarya and a team from the Turner Library, Whitefield School. It has been updated for the second edition by Gillian Goodchild and her colleagues

The Turner Library serves local and long distance members with a range of services: book loan, journal and reference, *Current Awareness Bulletin*, article delivery, database searches and book sales. The library collection reflects the needs of teachers, parents, learning support staff, educational psychologists, therapists and anyone with an interest in Special Educational Needs.

Local members can take advantage of all services in the library. Long distance members may opt for the bi-monthly *Current Awareness Bulletin*, offering article delivery and ease of keeping up to date with the latest SEN developments in nearly 100 international journals. All membership is by annual subscription at reasonable rates.

To find out more, write, call, fax or email: The Turner Library – Special Educational Needs Information Service, Whitefield Schools and Centre, Macdonald Road, Walthamstow, London, E17 4AZ ☎ 020 8531 8703 📄 020 8527 0907 Email: whitefield_edu@msn.com

Able/Gifted/Talented Children

Bearne E. (1996) *Differentiation and Diversity in the Primary School.* London: Routledge.
Clark C. and Callow R. (2002) *Educating the Gifted and Talented: Resource Issues and Processes for Teachers.* London: David Fulton Publishers.
Eyre D. (1997) *Able Children in Ordinary Schools.* London: David Fulton Publishers.
George D. (1995) *Gifted Education: Identification and Provision.* London: David Fulton Publishers.
Gross M. (1993) *Exceptionally Gifted Children.* London: Routledge.
Koshy V. and Casey R. (1997) *Effective Provision for Able and Exceptionally Able Children: Practical Help for Schools.* London: Hodder & Stoughton.
Lee-Corbin H. and Denicolo P. (1998) *Recognising and Supporting Able Children in Primary Schools.* London: David Fulton Publishers.
Leyden S. (1998) *Supporting the Child of Exceptional Ability: At Home and School,* 2nd edn. London: David Fulton Publishers.
Porter L. (1999) *Gifted Young Children: A Guide for Teachers and Parents.* Buckingham: Open University Press.
Webster C. (1999) *Able and Gifted Children.* Dunstable: Folens.

Asperger Syndrome

Attwood T. (1998) *Asperger's Syndrome: A Guide for Parents and Professionals.* London: Jessica Kingsley.

Cumine V., Leach J. and Stevenson G. (1998) *Asperger Syndrome: A Practical Guide for Teachers.* London: David Fulton Publishers.

Davies J. (1999) *Able Autistic Children with Asperger's Syndrome: A Booklet for Brothers and Sisters.* Nottingham: University of Nottingham/Mental Health Foundation.

Frith U. (1991) *Autism and Asperger Syndrome.* Cambridge: Cambridge University Press.

Howlin P. (1998) *Children with Autism and Asperger Syndrome: A Guide for Practitioners and Carers.* Chichester: John Wiley & Sons.

Jackson N. (2002) *Standing Down, Falling Up: Asperger's Syndrome from the Inside Out.* Bristol: Lucky Duck Publishing.

Jordan R. and Jones G. (1999) *Meeting the Needs of Children with Autistic Spectrum Disorders.* London: David Fulton Publishers.

Leicester City Council (1998) *Asperger Syndrome – Practical Strategies for the Classroom: A Teacher's Guide.* London: National Autistic Society.

Sainsbury C. (2000) *Martian in the Playground: Understanding the Schoolchild with Aspeger's Syndrome.* Bristol: Lucky Duck Publishing.

Schopler E., Mesibov G. and Kunce L. J. (eds) (1998) *Asperger Syndrome or High-Functioning Autism.* London: Plenum Press.

Attention Deficit Hyperactivity Disorder

Barkley R. A. (1998) *Attention-deficit Hyperactivity Disorder: A Handbook for Diagnosis and Treatment,* 2nd edn. New York: Guilford Press.

Cooper P. and Bilton K. (eds) (1999) *Attention Deficit Hyperactivity Disorder (ADHD): Research, Practice and Opinion.* London: Whurr Publishers.

Dengate S. (1998) *Fed Up: Understanding how Food Affects your Child and What You Can Do about It.* New South Wales: Random House.

Green C. and Chee K. (1995) *Understanding ADHD: A Parents' Guide to Attention Deficit Hyperactivity Disorder in Children.* London: Vermilion.

Kewley G. D. (2001) *Attention Deficit Hyperactivity Disorder: Recognition, Reality and Resolution.* London: David Fulton Publishers.

Lynn G. T. (2000) *Survival Structures for Parenting Children with Bipolar Disorder: Innovative Parenting and Counselling Techniques for Helping Children with Bipolar Disorder and the Conditions that may Occur with it.* London: Jessica Kingsley.

Munden A. and Arcelus J. (1999) *The AD/HD Handbook: A Guide for Parents and Professionals on Attention Deficit/Hyperactivity Disorder.* London: Jessica Kingsley.

Pentecost D. (2000) *Parenting the ADD Child: Can't do? Won't do?* London: Jessica Kingsley.

Robb J. and Letts H. (1997) *Creating Kids Who Can Concentrate: Proven Strategies for Beating ADD Without Drugs.* London: Hodder & Stoughton.

Spilsbury L. (2001) *What Does It Mean to Have Attention Deficit Hyperactivity Disorder?* Oxford: Heinemann.

Autism

Aarons M. and Gittens T. (1999) *The Handbook of Autism: A Guide for Parents and Professionals,* 2nd edn. London: Routledge.

Baron-Cohen S. and Bolton P. (1993) *Autism: The Facts.* Oxford: Oxford University Press.

Clements J. and Zarkowska E. (2000) *Behavioural Concerns and Autistic Spectrum Disorders: Explanations and Strategies for Change.* London: Jessica Kingsley.

Cumine V., Leach J. and Stevenson G. (2000) *Autism in the Early Years.* London: David Fulton Publishers.

Howlin P. (1997) *Autism: Preparing for Adulthood.* London: Routledge.

Jordan R. (2001) *Autism with Severe Learning Difficulties: A Guide for Parents and Professionals.* London: Souvenir Press.

Legge B. (2002) *Can't Eat. Won't Eat: Dietary Difficulties and Autistic Spectrum Disorders.* London: Jessica Kingsley.

Potter C. and Whittaker C. (2001) *Enabling Communication in Children with Autism.* London: Jessica Kingsley.

Powell S. (ed.) (2000) *Helping Children with Autism to Learn.* London: David Fulton Publishers.

Schopler E. (ed.) (1995) *Parent Survival Manual: A Guide to Crisis Resolution in Autism and Related Developmental Disorders.* London: Plenum Press.

Wheeler M. (1998) *Toilet Training for Individuals with Autism and Related Disorders: A Comprehensive Guide for Parents and Teachers.* Arlington, TX: Future Horizons.

Williams D. (1996) *Autism: An Inside-out Approach.* London: Jessica Kingsley.

Wing L. (1996) *The Autistic Spectrum: A Guide for Parents and Professionals.* London: Constable & Co.

Bullying

Broadwood J. *et al.* (1997) *Promoting Positive Behaviour: Activities for Preventing Bullying in Primary Schools.* London: Learning by Design.

Department for Education (1994) *Bullying: Don't Suffer in Silence: An Anti-bullying Pack for Schools* (includes video). London: HMSO.

Herbert C. (1996) *A Guide for Parents: STOP BULLYING.* Cambridge: Carrie Herbert Publishing.

Rigby K. (1996) *Bullying in Schools and What to Do about it.* London: Jessica Kingsley.

Sharp S. and Cowie H. (1998) *Counselling and Supporting Children in Distress.* London: Sage.

Sharp S. and Smith K. (1994) *Tackling Bullying in your School: A Practical Handbook for Teachers.* London: Routledge.

Challenging Behaviour/Behaviour Management

Ayers H., Clarke D. and Murray A. (2000) *Perspectives on Behaviour: A Practical Guide to Effective Interventions for Teachers,* 2nd edn. London: David Fulton Publishers.

Bliss T. (1998) *Label with Care: A Behaviour Management Book for Parents.* Bristol: Lucky Duck Publishing.

9

Corrie L. (2002) *Investigating Troublesome Classroom Behaviour: Practical Tools for Teachers.* London: Routledge.

Faupel A., Herrick E. and Sharp P. (1999) *Anger Management: A Practical Guide.* London: David Fulton Publishers.

Harris J. *et al.* (2001) *Positive approaches to Challenging Behaviour: Workbooks 1–6,* 2nd edn. Kidderminster: BILD.

Hewett D. (ed.) (1998) *Challenging Behaviour: Principles and Practice.* London: David Fulton Publishers.

MacGrath M. (1998) *The Art of Teaching Peacefully: Improving Behaviour and Reducing Conflict in the Classroom.* London: David Fulton Publishers.

Mathieson K. and Price M. (2002) *Better Behaviour in Classrooms: A Framework for Inclusive Behaviour Management.* London: Routledge Falmer.

Rogers W. A. (1995) *Behaviour Management: A Whole School Approach.* Cheltenham: Scholastic Publications.

Visser J. (2000) *Managing Behaviour in Classrooms.* London: David Fulton Publishers.

Down's Syndrome

Cicchetti D. and Beeghly M. (1990) *Children with Down Syndrome: A Developmental Perspective.* Cambridge: Cambridge University Press.

Down's Syndrome Association (2001) *Including Pupils with Down's Syndrome: Information for Teachers and Learning Support Assistants – Secondary.* London: Down's Syndrome Association.

Dykens E. M., Hodapp R. M. and Finucane B. M. (2000) *Genetics and Mental Retardation Syndromes: A New Look at Behavior and Interventions.* Baltimore, MD: Paul H. Brookes.

Lorenz S. (1998) *Children with Down's Syndrome: A Guide for Teachers and Learning Support Assistants in Mainstream Primary and Secondary Schools.* London: David Fulton Publishers.

Oelwein P. L. (1995) *Teaching Reading to Children with Down Syndrome: A Guide for Parents and Teachers.* Maryland, MD: Woodbine House.

Pueschel S. M. (1990) *A parent's guide to Down Syndrome: Towards a Brighter Future.* Baltimore, MD: Paul H. Brookes.

Pueschel S. M. and Sustrova M. (1997) *Adolescents with Down Syndrome: Towards a More Fulfilling Life.* Baltimore, MD: Paul H. Brookes

Ramcharan P., Roberts G., Grant G. and Borland J. (eds.) (1997) *Empowerment in Everyday Life: Learning Disability.* London: Jessica Kingsley.

Van Dyke M. D. (ed.) (1995) *Medical and Surgical Care for Children with Down Syndrome: A Guide for Parents.* Maryland, MD: Woodbine House.

Dyslexia

Broomfield H. and Combley M. (1997) *Overcoming Dyslexia: A Practical Guide for the Classroom.* London: Whurr Publishers.

Henderson A. (1998) *Maths for the Dyslexic: A Practical Guide.* London: David Fulton Publishers.

Holloway J. (2000) *Dyslexia in Focus at Sixteen Plus: An Inclusive Teaching Approach.* Tamworth: NASEN.

Hulme C. and Snowling M. (1994) *Reading Development and Dyslexia.* London: Whurr Publishers.

McGuiness D. (1998) *Why Children Can't Read and What We Can Do about it.* London: Penguin.

Raymond S. (2001) *Supporting Dyslexic Pupils 7–14 across the Curriculum.* London: David Fulton Publishers.

Riddick B. (1996) *Living with Dyslexia: The Social and Emotional Consequences of Specific Learning Difficulties.* London: Routledge.

SENSS (1999) *Specific Learning Difficulties/Dyslexia: Literacy Games.* Croydon: SENSS.

Snowling M. and Stackhouse J. (eds) (1996) *Dyslexia, Speech and Language: A Practitioner's Handbook.* London: Whurr Publishers.

Tod J. (2000) *Dyslexia.* London: David Fulton Publishers.

Dyspraxia

Boon M. (2001) *Helping Children with Dyspraxia.* London: Jessica Kingsley.

Donaldson M. L. (1995) *Children with Language Impairments.* London: Jessica Kingsley.

Kirby A. (1999) *Dyspraxia: The Hidden Handicap.* London: Souvenir Press.

MacIntyre C. (2000) *Dyspraxia in the Early Years.* London: David Fulton Publishers.

Portwood M. (1999) *Developmental Dyspraxia: Identification and Intervention. A Manual for Parents and Professionals,* 2nd edn. London: David Fulton Publishers.

Portwood M. (2000) *Understanding Developmental Dyspraxia: A Textbook for Students and Professionals.* London: David Fulton Publishers.

Ripley K. *et al.* (1997) *Dyspraxia: A Guide for Teachers and Parents.* London: David Fulton Publishers.

Ripley K. (2001) *Inclusion for Children with Dyspraxia/DCD: A Handbook for Teachers.* London: David Fulton Publishers.

Emotional and Behavioural Difficulties

Cole T., Visser J. and Upton G. (1998) *Effective Schooling for Pupils with Emotional and Behavioural Difficulties.* London: David Fulton Publishers.

Cooper P. (ed.) (1999) *Understanding and Supporting Children with Emotional and Behavioural Difficulties.* London: Jessica Kingsley.

Cornwall J. and Tod J. (1998) *Emotional and Behavioural Difficulties.* London: David Fulton Publishers.

Fogell J. and Long R. (1997) *Spotlight on Special Educational Needs: Emotional and Behavioural Difficulties.* Tamworth: NASEN.

Hill F. and Parsons L. (2000) *Teamwork in the Management of Emotional and Behavioural Difficulties: Developing Peer Support Systems for Teachers in Mainstream and Special Schools.* London: David Fulton Publishers.

Long R. (2000) *Making Sense of Behaviour: Supporting Pupils with Emotional and Behavioural Difficulties through Consistency.* Tamworth: NASEN.

9

Long R. and Fogell J. (1999) *Supporting Pupils with Emotional Difficulties.* London: David Fulton Publishers.

McNamara S. and Moreton G. (2001) *Changing Behaviour: Teaching Children with Emotional and Behavioural Difficulties in Primary and Secondary Classrooms,* 2nd edn. London: David Fulton Publishers.

Thacker J., Strudwick D. and Babbedge E. (2002) *Educating Children with Emotional and Behavioural Difficulties: Inclusive Practice in Mainstream Schools.* London: Routledge.

Zionts P. *et al.* (2002) *Emotional and Behavioral Problems: A Handbook for Understanding and Handling Students.* California: Corwin Press and London: Sage.

Epilepsy

Appleton R. E. *et al.* (1997) *Your Child's Epilepsy: A Parent's Guide.* London: Class Publishing.

Freeman J. M., Vining E. P. G. and Pillas D. J. (1990) *Seizures and Epilepsy in Childhood: A Guide for Parents.* Baltimore, MD: Johns Hopkins University Press.

Homan J. (1997) *Spotlight on Special Educational Needs: Medical Conditions.* Tamworth: NASEN.

Johnson M. and Parkinson G. (2002) *Epilepsy: A Practical Guide.* London: David Fulton Publishers.

Schachter S. C. and Schomer D. (eds) (1997) *The Comprehensive Evaluation and Treatment of Epilepsy: A Practical Guide.* London: Academic Press.

Varma V. (1993) *Coping with Unhappy Children.* London: Cassell.

Exclusion/Truancy/Disaffection

Blandford S. (1998) *IEPs: Managing Discipline in Schools.* London: Routledge.

Booth T. and Ainscow M. (1998) *From Them to Us: An International Study of Inclusion in Education.* London: Routledge.

Hornby G., Atkinson M. and Howard J. (1997) *Controversial Issues in Special Education.* London: David Fulton Publishing.

Klein R. (1999) *Defying Disaffection: How Schools are Winning the Hearts and Minds of Reluctant Students.* Staffordshire: Trentham Books.

Lovey J., Dorking J. and Evans R. (1993) *Exclusion from School: Provision for Disaffection at Key Stage 4.* London: David Fulton Publishers.

Sanders D. and Handry L. B. (1997) *New Perspectives on Disaffection.* London: Cassell.

Hearing Impairments

Brown N. and Murdoch H. (eds) (1994) *Unit 1: Sight, Hearing and Sensory Impairment.* Birmingham: University of Birmingham.

Fraser B. (1996) *Supporting Children with Hearing Impairment in Mainstream Schools.* Birmingham: Questions Publishing.

Freeland A. (1989) *Deafness: The Facts.* Oxford: Oxford University Press.

Jordan E. (1995) *A Curriculum for All? 5–14 and Special Needs.* Edinburgh: Moray House Publications.

McCracken W. and Sutherland H. (1991) *Deaf-ability not Disability: A Guide for Parents of Hearing Impaired Children.* Clevedon: Multilingual Matters.

Morgan-Jones R. A. (2001) *Hearing Differently: The Impact of Hearing Impairment on Family Life.* London: Whurr Publishers.

Stokes J. (ed.) (1999) *Hearing Impaired Infants: Support in the First Eighteen Months.* London: Whurr Publishers.

Watson L. (1996) *Spotlight on Special Educational Needs: Hearing Impairment.* Tamworth: NASEN.

Watson L. *et al.* (1999) *Deaf and Hearing Impaired Pupils in Mainstream Schools.* London: David Fulton Publishers.

ICT and SEN

Banes D. and Coles C. (1995) *IT for All: Developing an IT Curriculum for Pupils with Severe or Profound and Multiple Learning Difficulties.* London: David Fulton Publishers.

BECTA (2000) *Dyslexia and ICT: Building on Success.* London: BECTA.

Blamires M. (ed.) (1999) *Enabling Technology for Inclusion.* London: Paul Chapman Publishing.

Farmer M. and Farmer G. (2000) *Supporting Information and Communications Technology: A Handbook for Those who Assist in Early Years Settings.* London: David Fulton Publishers.

Hardy C. *et al.* (2002) *Autism and ICT: A Guide for Teachers and Parents.* London: David Fulton Publishers.

Keates A. (2002) *Dyslexia and Information and Communications Technology: A Guide for Teachers and Parents,* 2nd edn. London: David Fulton Publishers.

McKeown S. (2000) *Unlocking Potential: How ICT Can Support Children with Special Needs.* Birmingham: Questions Publishing.

Rose R., Ferguson A., Coles C. and Banes D. (eds) (1994, revised 1996) *Implementing the Whole Curriculum for Pupils with Learning Difficulties.* London: David Fulton Publishers.

Inclusion

Ainscow M. (1999) *Understanding the Development of Inclusive Schools.* London: Falmer Press.

Cheminais R. (2001) *Developing Inclusive School Practice: A Practical Guide.* London: David Fulton Publishers.

Clark C., Dyson A. and Millward A. (1995) *Towards Inclusive Schools?* London: David Fulton Publishers.

Cornwall J. (1997) *Access to Learning for Pupils with Disabilities.* London: David Fulton Publishers.

Dorchester Curriculum Group (2002) *Towards a Curriculum for All: A Practical Guide for Developing an Inclusive Curriculum for Pupils Attaining Significantly Below Age-related Expectations.* London: David Fulton Publishers.

Drifte C. (2001) *Special needs in Early Years Settings: A Guide for Practitioners.* London: David Fulton Publishers.

9

Hall J.T. (1997) *Social Devaluation and Special Education: The Right to Full Mainstream Inclusion and an Honest Statement.* London: Jessica Kingsley.

Lorenz S. (2002) *First Steps in Inclusion: A Handbook for Parents, Teachers and Governors and LEAs.* London: David Fulton Publishers.

Mittler P. (2000) *Working Towards Inclusive Education.* London: David Fulton Publishers.

Sebba J. and Sachdev D. (1997) *What Works in Inclusive Education?* London: Barnardos.

Tilstone C. *et al.* (1998) *Promoting Inclusive Practice.* London: Routledge.

Learning Difficulties – Moderate/Severe

Babbage R., Byers R. and Redding H. (1999) *Approaches to Teaching and Learning: Including Children with Learning Difficulties.* London: David Fulton Publishers.

Berger A. and Gross J. (eds) (1999) *Teaching the Literacy Hour in an Inclusive Classroom: Supporting Pupils with Learning Difficulties in a Mainstream Environment.* London: David Fulton Publishers.

Beveridge S. (1996) *Spotlight on Special Educational Needs: Learning Difficulties.* Tamworth: NASEN.

Carpenter B., Ashdown R. and Bovair K. (eds) (2001) *Enabling Access: Effective Teaching and Learning for Pupils with Learning Difficulties,* 2nd edn. London: David Fulton Publishers.

Fawcus M. (ed.) (1997) *Children with Learning Difficulties: A Collaborative Approach to their Education and Management.* London: Whurr Publishers.

Hewett D. and Nind M. (eds) (1998) *Interaction in Action: Reflections on the Use of Intensive Interaction.* London: David Fulton Publishers.

Latham C. and Miles A. (2001) *Communication, Curriculum and Classroom Practice.* London: David Fulton Publishers.

Mansfield M. (2000) *A Parent's Guide for Special Needs: What to Do if Your Child has Learning Difficulties.* Northampton: Home and School Council.

Mat D. *et al.* (2001) *Transition and Change in the Lives of People with Intellectual Disabilities.* London: Jessica Kingsley.

Nind M. and Hewett D. (1994) *Access to Communication: Developing the Basics of Communication with People with Severe Learning Difficulties through Intensive Interaction.* London: David Fulton Publishers.

Sebba J., Byers R, and Rose R. (1995) *Redefining the Whole Curriculum for Pupils with Learning Difficulties,* revised edn. London: David Fulton Publishers.

Smith D. (2000) *From Key Stage 2 to Key Stage 3: Smoothing the Transfer for Pupils with Learning Difficulties.* Tamworth: NASEN.

Learning Difficulties – Profound and Multiple/Compex Needs

Clark S. (1991) *Children with Profound/Complex Physical and Learning Difficulties.* Tamworth: NASEN.

Coupe O'Kane J. and Goldbart J. (1998) *Communication before Speech: Development and Assessment,* 2nd edn. London: David Fulton Publishers.

Coupe-O'Kane J. and Smith B. (1994) *Taking Control: Enabling People with Learning Difficulties.* London: David Fulton Publishers.

Davis J. (2001) *A Sensory Approach to the Curriculum for Pupils with Profound and Multiple Learning Difficulties.* London: David Fulton Publishers.

Hogg J., Sebba J. and Lambe L. (1990) *Profound Retardation and Multiple Impairment. Vol 3. Medical and Physical Care and Management.* London: Chapman Hall.

Lacey P. and Ouvry C. (1998) *People with Profound and Multiple Learning Difficulties: A Collaborative Approach to Meeting Complex Needs.* London: David Fulton Publishers.

Longhorn F. (1988) *A Sensory Curriculum for Very Special People: A Practical Approach to Curriculum Planning.* London: Souvenir Press.

Maskell S. *et al.* (2001) *Baseline Assessment, Curriculum and Target Setting for Pupils with Profound and Multiple Learning Difficulties.* London: David Fulton Publishers.

Nind M. and Hewett D. (2001) *A Practical Guide to Intensive Interaction.* Kidderminster: BILD.

Pagliano P. (1999) *Multisensory Environments.* London: David Fulton Publishers.

Sherborne V. (1990) *Developmental Movement for Children: Mainstream, Special Needs and Pre-school.* Cambridge: Cambridge University Press.

Siegel-Causey E. and Guess D. (1989) *Enhancing Non-symbolic Communications among Learners with Severe Disabilities.* Baltimore, MD: Paul H. Brookes.

Ware J. (1994) *Educating Children with Profound and Multiple Learning Difficulties.* London: David Fulton Publishers.

Ware J. (1996) *Creating a Responsive Environment for People with Profound and Multiple Learning Difficulties.* London: David Fulton Publishers.

Learning Support Assistants

Balshaw M. (1999) *Help in the Classroom,* 2nd edn. London: David Fulton Publishers.

Birkett V. (2001) *How to . . . Survive and Succeed as a Teaching Assistant.* Wisbech, Cambs: LDA.

Fox G. (1998) *A Handbook for Learning Support Assistants: Teachers and Assistants Working Together.* London: David Fulton Publishers.

Fox G. (2001) *Supporting Children with Behaviour Difficulties: A Guide for Assistants in Schools.* London: David Fulton Publishers.

Fox G. and Halliwell M. (2000) *Supporting Literacy and Numeracy: A Guide for Teaching Assistants.* London: David Fulton Publishers.

Lorenz S. (1998) *Effective In-class Support: The Management of Support Staff in Mainstream and Special Schools.* London: David Fulton Publishers.

O'Brien T. and Garner P. (eds) (2001) *Untold Stories: Learning Support Assistants and their Work.* Stoke on Trent: Trentham Books.

Watkinson A. (2002) *Assisting Learning and Supporting Teaching: A Practical Guide for the Teaching Assistant.* London: David Fulton Publishers.

Multisensory Impairment/Deafblind

Aitken S. and Buultjens M. (1992) *Vision for Doing: Assessing Functional Vision of Learners who are Multiply Disabled.* Edinburgh: Moray House Publications.

Aitken S., Buultjens M., Clark C., Eyre J. T. and Pease L. (eds) (2000*) Teaching Children who are Deafblind: Contact, Communication and Learning.* London: David Fulton Publishers.

9

Etheridge D. (1995) *The Education of Dual Sensory Impaired Children: Recognizing and Developing Ability.* London: David Fulton Publishers.

McInnes J. M. (ed.) *A Guide to Planning and Support for Individuals who are Deafblind.* Toronto: University of Toronto Press.

McInnes J. M. and Treffrey J. A. (1982) *Deaf-blind Infants and Children: A Developmental Guide.* Toronto: University of Toronto Press.

Nielsen L. (1993) *Early Learning Step by Step: Children with Visual Impairments and Multiple Disabilities.* Birmingham: Sikon.

Ockelford A. (1993) *Objects of Reference.* London: RNIB.

Pagliano P. (1999) *Multisensory Environments.* London: David Fulton Publishers.

Porter J. *et al.* (1997) *Curriculum Access for Deafblind Children.* London: DfEE.

RNIB (1998) *Approaches…to Working with Children with Multiple Disabilities and a Visual Impairment.* London: RNIB.

Wyman R. (2000) *Making Sense Together: Practical Approaches to Supporting Children who Have Multisensory Impairments,* 2nd edn. London: Souvenir Press.

Parents and SEN

Dale M. (1996) *Working with Families with Special Needs: Partnerships and Practice.* London: Routledge.

Farrell M. (2002) *The Special Education Handbook* (2nd edn). London: David Fulton Publishers.

Mansfield M. (2000) *A Parent's Guide for Special Needs: What to Do if Your Child Has Learning Difficulties.* Northampton: Home and School Council.

Naseef R. A. (2001) *Special Children, Challenged Parents: The Struggles and Rewards of Raising a Child with a Disability.* 2nd edn. London: Jessica Kingsley.

Schwartz S. and Heller Miller J. E. (1996) *The New Language of Toys: Teaching Communication Skills to Children with Special Needs. A Guide for Parents and Teachers.* Maryland, MD: Woodbine House.

Vernon J. (1999) *Parent Partnership and Special Educational Needs: Perspectives on Developing Good Practice.* (Research report # RR162) London: DfEE.

Whalley M. (1997) *Working with Parents.* London: Hodder & Stoughton.

Wolfendale S. (ed.) (1997) *Working with Parents of SEN Children after the Code of Practice.* London: David Fulton Publishers.

Wolfendale S. (ed.) (2002) *Parent Partnership Services for Special Educational Needs: Celebrations and Challenges.* London: David Fulton Publishers.

Wright J. and Poynter R. (1996) *Taking Action! Your Child's Right to Special Education: The Definitive Guide for Parents, Teachers, Advocates and Advice Workers.* Birmingham: Questions Publishing.

Physical Disabilities

Cornwall J. (1996) *Choice, Opportunity and Learning: Educating Children and Young People who are Physically Disabled.* London: David Fulton Publishers.

Cornwall J. and Robertson C. (1999) *Individual Education Plans: Physical Disabilities and Medical Conditions.* London: David Fulton Publishers.

Haskell S. H. and Narrett E. K (1993) *The Education of Children with Physical and Neurological Disabilities,* 3rd edn. London: Chapman Hall.

Jowsey S. E. (1988) *Can I Play Too? Physical Education for Physically Disabled Children in Mainstream Schools.* London: David Fulton Publishers.

Kenward H. (1996) *Spotlight on Special Educational Needs: Physical Disabilities.* Tamworth: NASEN.

SENCOs

Birkett V. (2000) *How to…Survive and Succeed as a SENCO in the Primary School.* Wisbech, Cambs: LDA.

Cowne E. (2000) *The SENCO Handbook: Working within a Whole School Approach,* 3rd edn. London: David Fulton Publishers.

Dwyfor Davies J., Garner P. and Lee J. (eds) (1998) *Managing Special Needs in Mainstream Schools: The Role of the SENCO.* London: David Fulton Publishers.

Jones F., Jones K. and Szwed C. (2001) *The SENCO as Teacher and Manager: A Guide for Practitioners and Trainers.* London: David Fulton Publishers.

Lorenz S. (1998) *Supporting Support Assistants: A Practical Handbook for SENCOs in Mainstream Primary and Secondary Schools.* London: David Fulton Publishers.

Moss G. (ed.) *Effective Management of Special Needs.* Birmingham: Questions Publishing.

Phillips S., Goodwin J. and Heron R. (1999) *Management Skills for SEN Coordinators in the Primary School.* London: Falmer Press.

Shuttleworth V. (2000) *The Special Educational Needs Coordinator: Maximizing your Potential.* London: Pearson Education.

Sex Education and Social Skills

Adcock K. and Stanley G. (1996) *Sexual Health Education and Children and Young People with Learning Disabilities: A Practical Way of Working for Professional, Parents and Carers.* Kidderminster: BILD.

Barratt P. *et al.* (2000) *Developing Children's Social Communication Skills: Practical Resources.* London: David Fulton Publishers.

Collins M. (2001) *Because We're Worth It: Enhancing Self-esteem in Young Children.* Bristol: Lucky Duck Publishing.

Craft A. (1994) *Sexuality and Learning Disabilities.* London: Routledge.

Craft A. and Stewart D. (1993) *What About Us? Sex Education for Children with Disabilities.* Northampton: Home and School Council.

Gray C. (2002) *My Social Stories Book.* London: Jessica Kingsley.

Lees J. and Plant S. (2000) *Passport: A Framework for Personal and Social Development.* London: Calouste Gulbenkian Foundation.

Longhorn F. (1996) *Sex Education and Sexuality for Very Special People: A Sensory Approach.* Wootton, Bedfordshire: Catalyst Education Resources Ltd.

McLaughlin C. and Byers R. (2001) *Personal and Social Development for All.* London: David Fulton Publishers.

RNIB (1996) *Sex Education for Visually Impaired Children with Additional Disabilities: Developing School Policies and Programmes.* London: RNIB.

9

Schwier K. M. and Hingsburger D. (2000) *Sexuality: Your Sons and Daughters with Intellectual Disabilities*. London: Jessica Kingsley.

SENJIT (1991) *Guidelines for Sex Education for Governors, Teachers and Others Working with Pupils with Special Educational Needs in Specialist Provision*, 3rd edn. London: SENJIT.

Sher B. (1998) *Self-esteem Games: 300 Fun Activities that Make Children Feel Good about Themselves*. London: John Wiley & Sons.

Warden D. and Christie D. (1997) *Teaching Social Behaviour: Classroom Activities to Foster Children's Interpersonal Awareness*. London: David Fulton Publishers.

Speech and Language Disorders

AFASIC (n.d.) *Glossary Sheets on Speech and Language Impairments*. London: AFASIC.

Bishop D. V. M. and Leonard L. B. (eds) (2000) *Speech and Language Impairments in Children: Causes, Characteristics, Interventions and Outcomes*. Hove: Psychology Press.

Chiat S. (2000) *Understanding Children with Language Problems*. Cambridge: Cambridge University Press.

Daines B., Fleming P. and Miller C. (1996) *Spotlight on Special Educational Needs: Speech and Language Difficulties*. Tamworth: NASEN.

Grunwell P. (1990) *Developmental Speech Disorders*. Edinburgh: Churchill Livingstone.

Law J. and Elias J. (1996) *Trouble Talking: A Guide for the Parents of Children with Speech and Language Difficulties*. London: Jessica Kingsley.

Locke A. and Beech M. (1991) *Teaching Talking: Teaching Procedures Handbook*. Windsor: NFER-Nelson.

Martin D. (2000) *Teaching Children with Speech and Language Difficulties*. London: David Fulton Publishers.

Ripley K., Barrett J. and Fleming P. (2001) *Inclusion for Children with Speech and Language Impairments: Accessing the Curriculum and Promoting Personal and Social Development*. London: David Fulton Publishers.

Visual Impairments

Arter C. et al. (1999) *Children with a Visual Impairment in a Mainstream Setting: A Guide for Teachers*. London: David Fulton Publishers.

Best A. (1992) *Teaching Children with Visual Impairments*. Milton Keynes: Open University Press.

Bowman R. et al. (2001) *Disorders of Vision in Children: A Guide for Teachers and Carers*. London: RNIB.

Condon J. (1998) *When It's Hard to See*. London: Franklin Watts.

Lear R. (1998) *Look at it This Way: Toys and Activities for Children with a Visual Impairment*. Oxford: Butterworth-Heinemann.

Mason H. (1995) *Spotlight on Special Educational Needs: Visual Impairment*. Tamworth: NASEN.

Mason H. et al. (eds) (1997) *Visual Impairment: Access to Education for Children and Young People*. London: David Fulton Publishers.

Van der Poel J. H. (1997) *Visual Impairment: Understanding the Needs of Young Children*. Birmingham: Sikon.

Webster A. and Roe J. (1998) *Children with Visual Impairments: Social Interaction, Language and Learning.* London: Routledge.

Wolffe K. E. (ed.) (1999) *Skills for Success: A Career Education Handbook for Children and Adolescents with Visual Impairments.* New York: American Foundation for the Blind.

Additional RNIB and AFB Resources

Mangold S. S. (1982) *A Teacher's Guide to the Special Educational Needs of Blind and Visually Handicapped Children.* New York: American Foundation for the Blind.

RNIB (1995) *Play it My Way.* London: RNIB.

Huebner K. M. *et al.* (1995) *Hand in Hand.* Vol 2. New York: American Foundation for the Blind.

Ellis A. and Frankenberg A. (1991) *What Shall We Do To Help? A Guide for Mainstream Nursery and Playgroup Leaders Caring for Visually Impaired Children.* London: RNIB.

RNIB Videos (1993) *The World in Our Hands: Part 1; My Baby is Blind. The World in Our Hands: Part 2; Moving On. The World In Our Hands: Part 3; Sounds Important. The World In Our Hands: Part 4; Clap Your Hands and Stamp Your Feet. The World In Our Hands: Part 5; It's Me.* London: RNIB.

RNIB Videos (1995) *One of the Family: Making Contact; One of the Family: That's What It's All About!; One of the Family: Going My Way; One of the Family: First Sight.* London: RNIB.

Ockelford A. (1993) *Objects of Reference.* London: RNIB.

Ockleford A. (1996) *Music Matters: Factors in the Music Education of Children and Young People who are Visually Impaired.* London: RNIB.

9

For Product Safety Concerns and Information please contact our EU representative GPSR@taylorandfrancis.com Taylor & Francis Verlag GmbH, Kaufingerstraße 24, 80331 München, Germany

Batch number: 08159097

Printed by Printforce, the Netherlands